P9-BTN-238

CLARENCE DARROW

ALSO BY JOHN A. FARRELL

Tip O'Neill and the Democratic Century

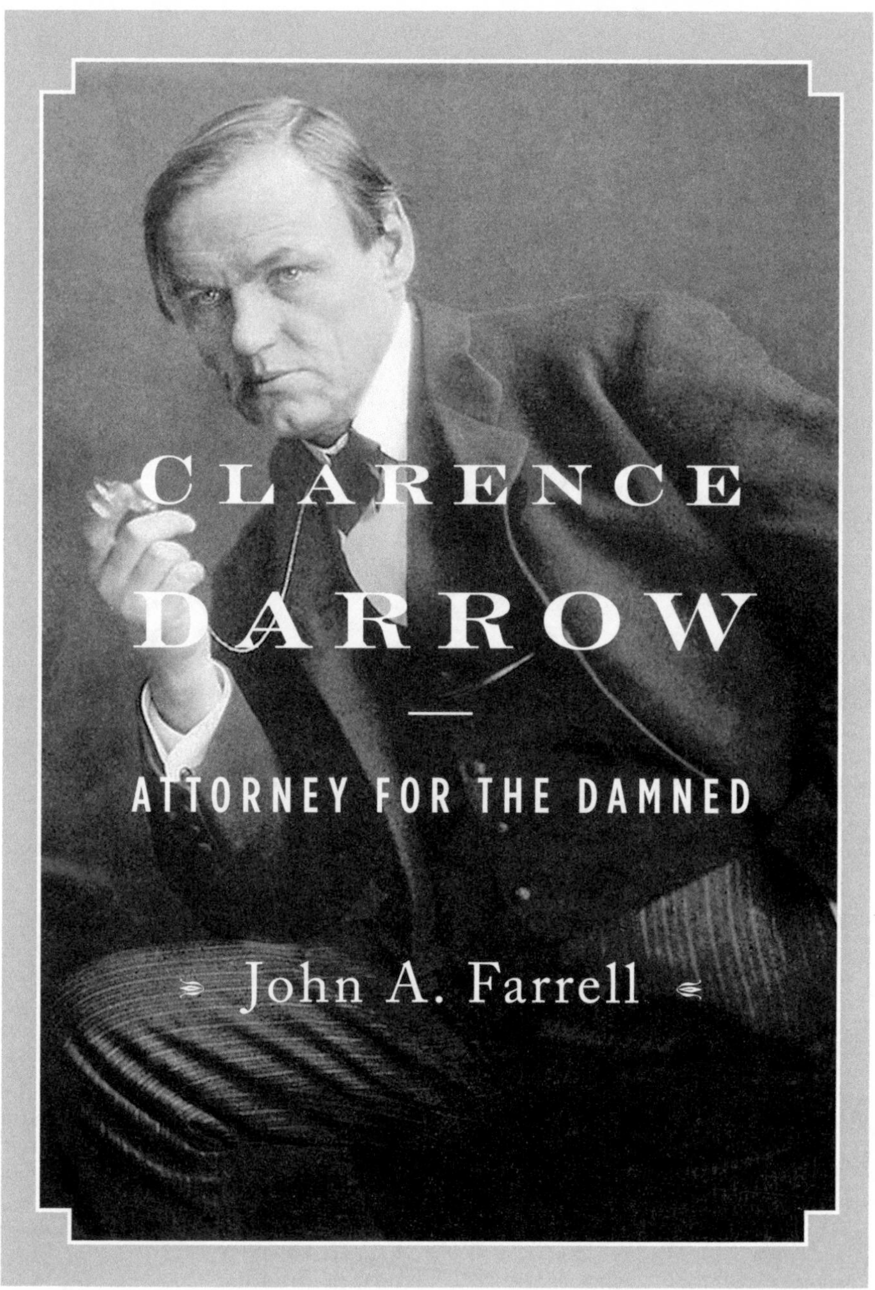

DOUBLEDAY New York London Toronto Sydney Auckland

B
DARROW
FAR

Copyright © 2011 by John A. Farrell

All rights reserved. Published in the United States by Doubleday,
a division of Random House, Inc., New York,
and in Canada by Random House of Canada Limited, Toronto.

www.doubleday.com

DOUBLEDAY and the portrayal of an anchor with a dolphin
are registered trademarks of Random House, Inc.

Page 563 constitutes an extension of this copyright page.

Portions of this work were previously published in *American History*.

Excerpts from *The Story of My Life* by Clarence Darrow reprinted
by permission of the Darrow family, all rights reserved.

Book design by Maria Carella
Title page photograph courtesy of
Library of Congress Prints & Photographs Division
Jacket illustration © Chicago History Museum/Getty Images

Library of Congress Cataloging-in-Publication Data
Farrell, John A. (John Aloysius)
Clarence Darrow : attorney for the damned / John A. Farrell.
p. cm.
Includes bibliographical references and index.
1. Darrow, Clarence, 1857-1938. 2. Lawyers—United States—Biography. [1. Lawyers.]
I. Title.
KF373.D35F37 2011
340.092—dc22
[B] 2010046273

ISBN 978-0-385-52258-8

PRINTED IN THE UNITED STATES OF AMERICA

1 3 5 7 9 10 8 6 4 2

First Edition

To Caitlin and John

CONTENTS

CLARENCE DARROW

Introduction

JEFFERSON'S HEIR

Some rude awakening must come.

Clarence Darrow, sitting at his desk in the law offices of the Chicago & North Western Railway Company on an April morning in 1893, had much to be pleased about. In the six years since he arrived in Chicago, he had carved a fine niche. The mayor and governor asked his advice. The newspapers covered his speeches. He had taken a real estate dispute to the Illinois Supreme Court and won his client a $500,000 award that, so large for its time, got front-page attention. He had a pleasant house, a proper wife, influential friends, and a son he loved. As first assistant counsel to a mighty railroad, he had a salary and social standing to be envied by the city's glut of aspiring lawyers: dire, sepulchral figures, languishing in the courts, longing for the stroke of fortune that would land them such a choice position.[1]

Darrow had just turned thirty-six. He was a tall man for his time, with high cheekbones and a formidable brow that could give him the look of a young Lincoln: no disadvantage in Illinois. His eyes were a soft blue and his smile, a law partner would recall, was "wreathed in good nature and irresistible charm." He had a kind of rough charisma that, he was discovering, charmed the pretty girls who attended his talks and lectures.[2]

Small-town Ohio could not hold him and so he had come to Chicago, to the flickering gaslight, the smoke and cinder, the clamor and hoot and honk of that most American city. He had applied himself, in the courts by day and by making the rounds of political clubs and debating societies in the evenings. And he had sought as mentors rich and famous men, and had prospered from their interest. If Darrow sought a template for success, he needed look no further than his boss and patron, the railroad's general counsel, whose office was next to his in the law department at Fifth Avenue and Lake Street, in downtown Chicago.

William C. Goudy was a trailblazer in a new specialty of the industrial age: the "corporation lawyer." With his bearded chin and stern demeanor, Goudy looked like an Amish elder, and though friends insisted that he had a warm heart, he was cold and direct in his professional affairs. He was said to be a millionaire, and Darrow knew him as "ultra conservative."[3] As a chieftain of the Illinois "silk-stocking" Democrats, Goudy served as an adviser to President Grover Cleveland, who had just been elected to a second term, and who shared his corporate sympathies. "No harm shall come to any business interest as the result of administrative policy so long as I am President," Cleveland boasted. Goudy was a close friend, as well, of Chief Justice Melville Fuller, a Chicagoan who led the era's notoriously conservative Supreme Court, known for decisions shielding monopolies and trusts, outlawing the income tax, and, in the infamous *Plessy v. Ferguson*, authorizing racial segregation.[4]

In the Gilded Age, when the interests of politicians and industrialists ran in tandem—or could be made to do so with a timely payoff—Goudy's political ties enhanced his appeal to the clients who secured his services. He represented the Vanderbilt railroad empire, the great Armour meatpacking firm, and other powerful interests in their wars against government regulation. It was said that Congress passed the Interstate Commerce Act in part to counteract Goudy, who so ably promoted the rights of corporations and monopolists to run their affairs as they saw fit, without regard to the public interest.[5]

Goudy and the railroad were, this day, engaged in one such battle with the people of Chicago. That great midway between the crops and natural resources of the West and the markets and capital of the East was a wicker of railroad tracks. Five million engines and freight cars passed through Chicago each year, on 1,400 miles of rails. As the city's population leaped, so did the number of those killed and injured by trains traversing its roads and alleys at the thousands of street-level crossings. It was Darrow's duty to represent the railroad in court, fighting to limit the compensation sought by the victims or their families.

The carnage was ghastly. "A stranger's first impression of Chicago is that of the barbarous gridironed streets," a British visitor wrote, "his second is that of the multitude of mutilated people . . . the mangled remnant of the massacre." In a single month that spring, there were forty-five deaths. One story suffices, that of the mother driving home, who froze at the roar of an approaching train. A passerby pulled her from the driver's bench, but her two young daughters were left behind to be shattered and tossed in the shards of the carriage as their wounded horse bellowed in pain.

But the railroads were tough, and abetted by public officials who collected "lavish bribery . . . year after year," the *Chicago Times* reported. When, finally, the city council voted to compel the railroads to raise their tracks, the companies went to court. "There is no power on earth which can compel us to elevate our tracks," said a confident Marvin Hughitt, the president of the Chicago & North Western. "The opinions of the best lawyers in the country have been obtained." A test case was pending at the Supreme Court, and earlier that month Goudy had traveled to Washington to speak to the chief justice and visit with his allies at the White House. He returned to Chicago cheered about his company's prospects.[6]

HERE, THEN, WAS a blueprint for Darrow's aspirations. He was no scion of a wealthy family like his liberal friends, the muckraker Henry Demarest Lloyd or the philanthropist Jane Addams, who used her inheritance to found the Hull House settlement for immigrants in Chicago's West Side ghetto. Darrow's parents, though educated, were moneyless. He tasted want and shame as a child, and "I never have been able to get over the dread of being poor, and the fear of it," he would confide to a friend. Nor were there government programs in this laissez-faire era for a man to fall back on in hard times, illness, or old age. The only social safety net was the free lunch offered in workingmen's saloons, and a bit of floor space on which to sleep in municipal hallways during Chicago's bitter winters. Darrow had a deep interest in learning, and in literature, "but he has been under the awful compulsion of the age, to make money," his friend Brand Whitlock would tell a confidant. "Have you ever reflected that we of this time are kept so busy making a living that we never find time to live?"[7]

Yet Darrow chafed in corporate harness. There was something missing in the Goudy model. If Darrow's cunning was a defining attribute, more so was his empathy. He was "sensitiveness and egotism all twisted as the strands of a rope . . . a great character of wonderful sweetness, of profound intelligence, of Godlike patience and tenderness—shot through with queer pettiness—about money, about criticism," one of his lovers, Mary Field Parton, would confide to her diary. What saved him was his "extraordinarily" acute compassion, she concluded, "the edges of his emotions sensitive as the antennae of insects."

Darrow felt guilty working for a corporation, where his legal skills and his boss's clout were employed at union busting, or to limit the relief sought by the pitiful victims of the railway crossings. He longed for peace of mind. "It seems to me, and *for me*, that I have no right to save myself when the injustice is so great," he would tell Addams.[8]

Around him was injustice in abundance. The slaughter at Chicago's railway crossings was emblematic of conditions in the Gilded Age, when the United States grappled with economic and social transformations that many Americans feared, with some justification, might trigger revolution. Immigrants packed the tenements of the cities, where women took piecework in squalid, ill-lit flats, while men and children labored in the factories, mills, mines, and collieries for twelve hours a day, six or seven days a week, for cents. Unions were assailed; a political and corporate aristocracy employed the police, the state militia, and private armies of detectives to disperse—or gun down—striking workers. Blacks were condemned to lynch law. Congress, the judiciary, and the state legislatures were corrupted, and the criminal justice system was no such thing. "The rich and powerful are seldom indicted and never tried," one of the city's leading lawyers, W. S. Forrest, told an audience in 1892. "Manslaughter is committed by corporations with impunity. Men are convicted who are innocent. Even in ordinary trials, the forms of law are frequently set aside and the rules of evidence ignored."[9]

Chicago witnessed all the era's ills. Drenched in blood, bone-weary workers slaughtered the illimitable herds of hogs and cattle that clanked by them on the assembly lines of the stockyards. At McCormick Reaper and other storied industrial works, union organizers fighting for higher wages or an eight-hour day were locked out, harassed, and beaten by police. The houses of prostitution never closed in Little Cheyenne and the Levee, nor the predatory gambling and drinking dens. The city was divided along class lines and still seething that spring from the 1886 bombing that killed seven policemen at a workers' rally in the Haymarket, and the subsequent public delirium that sent four guiltless anarchists to the gallows. The city's smokestacks cast a famous pall, to rival that of London, across the prairie sky, and the polluted water spurred outbreaks of cholera. A visitor from England, well versed in the miseries of the industrial age, was stunned. "Chicago is a pocket edition of hell," he wrote, "and if it is not, then hell is a pocket edition of Chicago."[10]

Darrow had delved into politics, joining the movement to assist the Haymarket defendants and employing his talents and political connections to persuade the Illinois legislature to pass a bill regulating sweatshops and child labor. More than a year before, he had written to Lloyd, confessing his shame at working for the railroad and praising a protest that his friend had led after a police raid on a union meeting. "You dare to say what is true," Darrow told him. "Your speech . . . made me feel that I am a hypocrite and a slave, and added to my resolution to make my term of servitude short." But he could not summon the will to act. The months passed, and his time of "servitude" dragged on.[11]

Darrow's conscience was still struggling with his comfort on the morning of Thursday, April 27, when, shortly after eleven a.m., Goudy finished dictating a letter, dismissed his secretary, and summoned his first visitor—a retired Civil War hero, General John McArthur—into his office. Darrow prepared to join them.

"Good morning, Judge," McArthur said, greeting his friend Goudy. Then: "You don't look very well . . . are you ill?"

Goudy seemed stricken, and gasped. McArthur cried out in alarm, and Darrow rushed in, as Goudy collapsed at his desk.

Darrow and McArthur carried the lawyer to a couch. Goudy stared up at Darrow with pleading eyes, said nothing, and died.

The great man's heart attack was front-page news in Chicago. "He lived only a few minutes," Darrow told the reporters. "It all happened so suddenly that we can scarcely appreciate that Mr. Goudy is really dead." Darrow was a pallbearer at the funeral. He had lost his patron, and his paradigm.

Goudy's death changed Darrow's life. That weekend, the newspapers carried the story: C. S. Darrow was leaving his position as lawyer for the railroad to go to work for Mayor Carter Harrison. No one then perceived that this was the birth of the grandest legal career in American history. In 1893, of Darrow's future clients, Eugene Debs was still an obscure labor leader with dreams of forming a national railway union. Patrick Prendergast was a mumbling paperboy, lost in delusions. Bill Haywood was a frontier ruffian. Nathan Leopold, Richard Loeb, Ossian Sweet, and John Scopes were not yet born.

And yet, in little more than a year, Darrow would be battling to keep Debs and the other ringleaders of a turbulent workers' uprising out of prison, and to save the demented Prendergast, by then an infamous assassin, from the hangman. He would be on his way to becoming an American icon, his name synonymous with a passionate, eloquent, and miraculous defense of the underdog. Journalist Lincoln Steffens would cite Darrow's departure from the railroad as the "turning point" in his friend's life. "Darrow counted the cost; he seems always to have counted the cost," Steffens wrote, but "he found himself off-side, and had to cross over to where he belonged."

And so was born, said Steffens, "the attorney for the damned."[12]

He had magnificent presence. He would walk into a courtroom, the conversation would stop, and people would murmur, "There's Darrow." He was over six feet tall, and handsome in a roughcast way, with eyes set deep and the bold cheekbones that evoked, as George Bernard Shaw once said, a Mohican brave. His hair was brown, and straight and fine, with a famously unruly lock that was apt to drift down to his forehead. His face, in middle age, was deeply lined; his skin charitably described as leatherlike, or bronzed. His ears lacked lobes, a puckish touch; his chin was cleft. His voice was a melodious grumble of a baritone, flowing from a deep chest. "He had what the French call in a woman—the beauty of the Devil; the charm of the imperfect," one female admirer recalled. His eyes roamed restlessly until those times when, with intent fury, they bore into a witness or a foe.[13]

What most impressed those who witnessed Darrow in court were his big, evocative shoulders, which he hunched or tossed this way and that, like a bull in the corrida. His wife Ruby ordered special shirts and had his hats custom made, wider at the brim and higher in the crown, to offset the bulk of that upper body. "The powerful orator hulking his way slowly, thoughtfully, extemporizing," wrote Steffens. "Hands in pocket, head down and eyes up, wondering what it is all about, to the inevitable conclusion, which he throws off with a toss of his shrugging shoulders."[14]

"His clothes were a mess, wrinkled, untidy," noted jounalist William Allen White. "He slouched when he walked and he walked like a cat. I always thought of him as Kipling's cat, who walked alone."[15] He would slouch, as well, in his seat at the defense table, sinking indolently toward the horizontal, a signal to the jurors that nothing they were hearing from the prosecutor was important. It was all, of course, performance. "The picture of Darrow drawling in front of a jury box was a notable scene," wrote the Chicago newsman and author Ben Hecht, whom Darrow defended from the censors. "The great barrister artfully gotten up in baggy pants, frayed linen, and string tie, and 'playing dumb' for a jury as if he were no lawyer at all, but a cracker-barrel philosopher groping for a bit of human truth."[16]

Darrow crafted an American archetype: advocate for the common folk, hooking his thumbs in his vest or suspenders, regarding the jury from beneath that cascading shock of hair, speaking with plain but emotional conviction of the nobility of man, the frailty of mankind, and the threat to liberty posed by narrow-minded men of wealth—"the good people," he called them, with no shortage of sarcasm—and their legal guns-for-hire.

"With the land and possessions of America rapidly passing into the hands of a favored few," he would roar, "with thousands of men and women in idleness and want; with wages constantly tending to a lower level . . . with the knowledge that the servants of the people elected to correct abuses are bought and sold in legislative halls at the bidding of corporations and individuals: with all these notorious evils sapping the foundations of popular government and destroying personal liberty, some rude awakening must come.

"And if it shall come," he warned, "when you then look abroad over the ruin and desolation, remember the long years in which the storm was rising, and do not blame the thunderbolt."[17]

It was quite a show. In the days before radio and motion pictures, the era's courthouse clashes and public debates played the role of mass entertainment. It was not unusual for the gallery to be packed with prominent lawyers, off-duty judges, newspapermen, and politicians, and the hallways outside jammed with spectators trying to get in, all to see Darrow close for the defense. At times a mob of thousands would spill through the corridors, down the stairs, and out into the yard, to surround a courthouse and listen at the windows.

Darrow savored the attention. "In corporation law practice he was but an invisible cog in a great machine. And he disliked being invisible," said the writer Louis Adamic. "His superior powers and wit, of which he was more and more conscious, demanded function and expression. The actor-egoist in him sought opportunities to play great parts. Hero parts."[18] It wasn't only ego. Darrow employed his celebrity to shape public opinion, knowing that jurors reflect communities. "Cases are not won in the courtroom alone, and no one on earth knows this better than Darrow," said his friend Erskine Wood. "His first move is to get the outside atmosphere right for his case and he sticks at nothing to do this."

In lectures and public speaking, Darrow affected a humble awkwardness; in court, simplicity, to endear him to his audience. He might start with his arms folded, tapping his gold spectacles on his shoulder, his brow contracted in thought. Often, he would lean on the rail, as if to take the jurors into his confidence, talking so softly that those in the back row would lean toward him to listen. Then, suddenly, his demeanor would change. His voice would turn harsh; his jaw muscles would tighten. Soaring in a crescendo, he would swing his arms, shake clenched fists at heaven, or point a finger in the face of his opponent. And then the storm would pass, the sun would return, the jurors would relax, and Darrow would be genial and engaging, lightening the mood with a wisecrack. He never addressed juries, he said. He talked to them.

He often used laughter as a weapon. "We will never get a conviction unless we can make this case more serious," one frustrated prosecutor told his associates, as he watched Darrow captivate the courtroom. His galluses were a favorite prop, and he wore them long after belts became the fashion. "The old man used to crack his suspenders like the explosion of a .45," a Chicago newspaperman recalled. "I used to think he'd break a rib."[19]

Darrow's appeals to juries were all about context. The haughty judges and the lean and hungry prosecutors of Victorian America knew their duty; they were there to exact vengeance, and to safeguard property and propriety. But Darrow believed that jurors, if given the opportunity and a skillful enough invitation, could be persuaded to look past the legal particulars, to judge a defendant in the context of the times, and consider the situational factors that prompt behavior. He sought to make even the most hideous of crimes comprehensible.

A juror "begins by assuming that a man charged with a crime is guilty. He sees before him, not an ordinary human being like himself, but a creature of whom he thinks as a criminal," Darrow said. "The first task of a lawyer . . . is to put forward the human side of his client, to show that jury that the defendant is merely a man like themselves."[20]

Darrow would "stand up, slouch his shoulders, talk quietly and . . . hardly mention the facts," said Arthur Garfield Hays, his co-counsel in several celebrated cases. "In homely language and with a great wealth of illustrations he would talk about human beings, the difficulties of life, the futility of human plans, the misfortunes of the defendant, the strange workings of fate and chance that had landed him in his trouble. Darrow would try to make the jury understand, not so much the case, as the defendant."

It was not unusual, in the late nineteenth and early twentieth centuries, for lawyers to take many hours—spread over two or three days—to give a closing argument in a significant case. Darrow did so without notes, in marvelous displays of intellect and concentration. Taking his time, Darrow worked like a weaver, ranging back and forth across the crime, laying down threads, reviving assertions in different form, showing the facts from different angles. To a modern ear, his rhetoric seems to sprawl. But when he was done he had reshaped the case. "He will travel far beyond the immediate issue of guilt or innocence," said Hays. "The whole background of the case takes on a different coloring."[21]

It was more than a tactic. It was his creed. Darrow was a determinist. He did not believe in free will, nor good and evil, nor choice. There were no moral absolutes, no truth, and no justice. There was only mercy. "We are all poor, blind creatures bound hand and foot by the invisible chains of heredity and environment, doing pretty much what we have to do in a barbarous and cruel world. That's about all there is to any court case," he said.

He had no faith in God or churches, and won notoriety in the Jazz Age as the country's most prominent and outspoken atheist. He built his moral code upon life's very pointlessness, and the comfort and tolerance that human beings can offer to their doomed fellow travelers on what he called this "graveyard planet." His infidel status gave Darrow the distinctive fortune of being among the most beloved and the most hated men in America.

"Mr. Darrow is the greatest criminal lawyer in America today. His courtesy is noticeable, his ability is known," said one prosecutor who was pitted against him. "Great God! The good that a man of his ability could have done if he had aligned himself with the forces of right, instead of aligning himself with that which strikes its poisonous fangs at the bosom of Christianity."[22]

Which of his clients won Darrow the public's greatest disapprobation? Was it Prendergast? The homosexual thrill killers Nathan Leopold and Richard Loeb, who murdered fourteen-year-old Bobby Franks? Or James McNamara and his brother John, responsible for the bombing of the *Los Angeles Times* and the fiery death of twenty employees? Big Bill Haywood, the leftist union rabble-rouser accused of deploying union executioners and assassins? The socialist Debs? The anarchists arrested for the Haymarket bombing? The American communists in the days of the Red Scare after World War I? Or perhaps, in that era of prejudice and bigotry, it was the black men whom Darrow volunteered to defend—Isaac Bond; the Scottsboro boys; Ossian and Henry Sweet and others—charged with the rape of white women, or the murder of white men.

These were only the more notable misfits. He was a practicing defense lawyer, and in his time he represented gangsters, psychopaths, gamblers, bank robbers, drunk drivers, rum runners, yellow journalists, union goons, crooked politicians and greedy corporations, bunko men, and many a scorned woman like Emma Simpson, the socialite who smuggled a handgun into court and shot her philandering husband in the midst of their divorce proceeding. "You've killed him!" said a shocked clerk. "I hope so," said Emma. Meeting the classic definition of chutzpah, Darrow convinced the jury to have mercy on the widow.

"His instantaneous reaction toward people—especially people in trouble—was the welling forth of that tremendous, instinctive kindliness and sympathy," Nathan Leopold recalled. "It was so genuine, so immediate, so unforced. And it embraced the whole world. Or, at least, nearly the whole world. The only things Mr. Darrow hated were what he considered cruelty, narrow-mindedness, or obstinate stupidity. Against these he fought with every weapon he could lay a hand to."[23]

IN HIS PERSONAL life, Darrow was a notorious rake—a professed sensualist who took much pleasure from the chase, seduction, and act of love. He relied on "physical nearness" to escape the "emptiness" and the "spiritual isolation" of his life, said Mary Field Parton, for he was often lonely, haunted by death, and prey to melancholy. "Sex," he told her, was "the only feeling in the world that can make you forget for a little while."[24]

Work was an anodyne as well. "Even as I have fought for freedom," he said, "I have always had a consciousness that I was doing it to keep myself occupied so I might forget myself." Every man had his "dope," said Darrow, whether it was "religions, philosophies, creeds, whisky, cocaine, morphine . . . anything to take away the reality."

Darrow's practice was nondiscriminatory, and the rich were as welcome as the poor, if not more so. As with many things in Darrow's life, his attitude toward money was marked by contradictions. "He is a strange mixture of craft and courage, generosity and penuriousness, consideration and despotism, honesty and deviousness," one longtime friend told another. "And yet he has a big brain and a kind heart." Darrow was a foolish and impulsive investor, ever scheming to recover, who could be alternately tight and free with the balled-up wads of bills and the silver in his pockets.

But the fat fees from monopolists and elegant divorcées helped offset the costs of defending folks like poor Tommy Crosby, a thirteen-year-old charged with shooting a sheriff who had been sent to evict the boy and his widowed mother from their home three days before Christmas. Darrow told the whole sad story to the jury and dared them to send Tommy to the hangman. Of course they did not. And when no one else would defend a crazed killer like Russell Pethick, the grocery boy who slashed Ella Coppersmith to death with a butcher knife, cut the throat of her two-year-old son, and sexually abused her corpse, Chicagoans were not surprised to learn that Darrow had taken the case. He saved Pethick—and Crosby and Simpson and two or three score like them—from the noose and the electric chair. "I have known him a lifetime," Wood wrote. "His almost insane desire is to *save life*."

"Well what can a fellow do," Darrow asked, "when some poor devil comes to him, without a cent or a friend in the world, trembling in his shoes and begging for a chance before the law?"[25]

HE WAS A Byronic hero—intelligent, captivating, jaded, moody; a renegade, with small regard for rank or privilege. He scorned society and its norms, and this seeped into his practice of the law. He would employ any trick to save a client. "To him the world was equally unmoral above as well as below," said the Progressive Era reformer Frederic Howe. "So why be squeamish about it in criminal cases?"

"Do not the rich and powerful bribe juries, intimidate and coerce judges as well as juries?" Darrow asked. "Do they shrink from any weapon?"

"A great many people in this world believe the end justifies the means. I don't know but I do myself," he told the court in his closing argument in the Leopold and Loeb trial.

The first time that Steffens called on him, Darrow laughed the muckraker out of his office. "Oh, I know," Darrow said scornfully. "You are the man that believes in honesty!"

"I never knew," said Howe, "whether I admired or disliked him most. His realism hurt my illusions when it encountered them, and I hated having my illusions hurt."

And yet. Darrow had ineffable compassion for those who faced loss or despair or persecution. His "strongly emotional nature" was nourished by his upbringing. His father was the book-loving owner of a rural furniture shop, an abolitionist who steeped his family in the values of liberty and equality and taught his son to suspect and challenge authority. "He was always in rebellion against religious and political creeds of the narrow and smug community in which he dwelt," Darrow recalled. His parents were "friends of all oppressed people, and every new and humane and despised cause."[26]

With such a childhood, and a "vivid imagination," Darrow recalled, "not only could I put myself in the other person's place, but I could not avoid doing so."

Compassion was the unifying theory in Darrow's chaotic universe.

The bench in Darrow's outer office was invariably filled by "men in overalls, their arms in slings; by women huddled in shawls and threadbare clothes, wan-faced, waiting for Darrow," a friend recalled. A less charitable pal described them as "the types one would expect in a fortune teller's parlor . . . including half wits, whom even God could not teach anything."

Darrow would emerge at the end of the day, see the long line, sigh, and offer an understanding smile. Sunday dinners would grow cold as he sat with a supplicant for an hour or more, patiently hearing the facts of the case and offering advice. Depending on how he was fixed at the time, a third or more of Darrow's cases earned him nothing.

"The Gilded Age go-getter . . . was strong in Darrow," wrote Adamic. "Had he remained a corporation lawyer, he would probably be a multi-millionaire . . . But he did not. And is not. He could not. Always it seemed there was a conflict in Darrow. The idealist in him, with his inbred sensitive imagination which made him see and understand the plight of unfortunates, was never suppressed. That phase of him rebelled against the ambitious go-getter and politician."

"Everything about Darrow suggests a cynic," said the publisher E. W. Scripps, in as perceptive an analysis as was ever made about the man. "Everything but one thing, and that is—an entire lack of real cynicism."[27]

HE WAS JEFFERSON'S heir—his time's foremost champion of personal liberty. When he was a boy, Darrow liked to say, the hired man had dignity; he dined with the family of his employer, shared their pew on Sunday, and could court the boss's daughter. "There were no . . . banks, no big stores, very little money and nobody had a monopoly of either riches or poverty," Darrow recalled. "The community was truly democratic."

But the nation's founding principles were stretched beyond recognition in the roar of the industrial age. At Darrow's birth, in 1857, America had one hundred public high schools and thirty thousand miles of railroads, and produced ten thousand tons of steel a year. By the time he turned forty the United States was a commercial titan, with six thousand high schools and 200,000 miles of railroad, and had surpassed Great Britain as the world's leading steel producer, with 6 million tons a year. The population doubled as millions of immigrants poured through the Atlantic seaports, filling the mining towns of Appalachia, the tenements of New York, and the factories, docks, and stockyards of Chicago with cheap manpower and desperately poor families.

The Constitution, with its fierce defense of individual rights, had been written in times when each man was his own agent, free to claim land on the endless frontier and trade labor or goods on fair terms. But the coming of steam power, railroads, oil, and factory production lines yielded huge economies of scale. The fierce new economy demanded, not a yeoman's sense of inquiry and initiative, but rote labor at minimal cost. By the turn of the century there were no more "harness shops, wagon shops, blacksmith shops or furniture shops," he noted. "All these things are made in the centers of industry and made by machines. The workman merely feeds them."[28]

A shrewd and lucky few made great fortunes—Carnegie in steel, Morgan in finance, Rockefeller in oil—and attributed their success to God, hard work, and pluck. They found in the writings of Charles Darwin and Herbert Spencer the comforting assurance that the poor deserved their lot; it was nature's way of furthering the race, by weeding out the weak. They ordered their managers to lower costs and, when workers organized guilds or unions, brought in immigrants to take away jobs. If the union men fought back, then private armies and local militias were summoned to break up the strikes and demonstrations, often with volleys of rifle fire. According to the courts, a worker's only right was to negotiate, man to man, with an employer, and to take himself elsewhere if the terms were not to his liking. And none married the boss's daughter. Atop the social order, the robber barons flaunted their aristocratic aspirations by dressing up like eighteenth-century European royalty at spectacular parties, hiring semi-naked chorus girls to jump out of cakes, and hanging diamond collars on their dogs.

The industrial plutocracy squeezed huge subsidies from the federal government (the railroads alone got $350 million and 242,000 square miles of land) and controlled the legal establishment, right up to the Supreme Court, where the justices worked diligently at redefining the Bill of Rights as a guarantee of property, above all else. "From the time in earliest records when Eve took loving possession of even the forbidden apple, the idea of property and sacredness of the right of its possession has never departed from the race," Justice David Brewer told the graduates at

Yale. "The love of acquirement, mingled with the joy of possession, is the real stimulus to human activity."

The jurists who resisted—Brandeis, Holmes, Darrow—would be honored by history as great dissenters and mediocrities like Brewer forgotten, but that was no consolation to the working men and women of the time. And by the 1890s the great economic relief valve—the frontier—was gone. Its absence heightened "the sharp contrast between the traditional idea of America—as the land of opportunity, the land of the self-made man, free from class distinctions, and from the power of wealth," wrote historian Frederick Turner, "and the existing America, so unlike the earlier ideal."[29]

With the growth of the state came new, intrusive police powers and prescriptions for social remedy. Though Darrow spent decades in radical and populist politics, he had no illusions about the ability of liberalism, or socialism, or any other man-made "ism" to cure social ills. Well ahead of most of his contemporaries, Darrow foresaw the dangers posed by totalitarian creeds and regimes. He was an early foe of Italian and German fascism. But his commitment to individual freedom left him wary of all government, and ultimately led him into clashes, as well, with the liberal presidents Woodrow Wilson and Franklin Roosevelt.

"It is the mediocre, the thimble-riggers, the cheap players to the crowd, the men who take the customs and thoughts of the common people, who weave them into song and oratory and feed them back to the crowd, who get their votes," he said. "And from them nothing ever did come and I fear nothing can."

"Many of his most passionate interests were rooted not merely in his moral idealism and his human pity, but . . . in his distrust of government," wrote his friend the theologian John Haynes Holmes. "He hated and denounced Prohibition because it was an invasion by the State of the liberties of the individual. He fought capital punishment because it was the State laying its bloody hand upon some poor forlorn individual who it had earlier betrayed by neglect or oppression."

THE GREAT THEME of Darrow's life, the long war he fought in his march through courtrooms and cases, was the defense of individual liberty from modernity's relentless, crushing, impersonal forces. "No era of the world has ever witnessed such a rapid concentration of wealth and power as this one in which we live," Darrow warned. "History furnishes . . . abundant lessons of the inevitable result."

"All the greatness of America, all her marvelous wealth, all the wonders . . . are a monument to the wisdom of liberty," Darrow said. But "our liberty produced prosperity, and this prosperity looks with doubting eye upon the mother who gave it breath, and threatens to strangle her to death."

Americans needed a new sustaining myth. In his defense of the underdog Darrow helped create one. He gave it a narrative voice, kept it supplied with sympathetic characters, and forged his own place in folklore. "If the underdog got on top he would probably be just as rotten as the upper dog, but in the meantime I am for him," Darrow said. "He needs friends a damn sight more than the other fellow."[30]

Americans drew strength watching Darrow rage against the machine. They can again today. There is something grand and epic in his fierce resistance to those inexorable oppressive forces that, in varying guises, inspired the rebels in his ancestry and the abolitionists of his boyhood, imperiled freedom in his lifetime, and pose a threat to liberty today.

"The marks of battle are all over his face," wrote the journalist H. L. Mencken. "He has been through more wars than a whole regiment of Pershings. And most of them have been struggles to the death, without codes or quarter.

"Has he always won?" Mencken asked. "Actually, no. His cause seems lost among us."

"Imbecilities, you say, live on? They do," wrote Mencken. "But they are not as safe as they used to be."[31]

Chapter 1

REBELLIONS

I had little respect for the opinion of the crowd.

Samuel Eddy, the son of an English vicar, was in his early twenties in August of 1630, when he went aboard the good ship *Handmaid* and embarked from London for the New World. The young tailor was headed for Plymouth, where the *Mayflower* had landed ten years before. The journey was marked by savage storms and the ship lost all its masts, and ten of the twenty-eight cows it carried, before limping into port in late October. Samuel and his brother John intended to join a family friend, John Winthrop, who had left four months earlier with the first settlers of the Massachusetts Bay Colony, intent on building their city on a hill. But only John joined Winthrop in Boston. Samuel found a wife in Plymouth, a peppery lass named Elizabeth Savery, and stayed with the Pilgrims.

The descendants of John and Samuel spread throughout New England, where they were known for sturdy physiques, long lives, and many sons. "This extraordinary multiplication accounts for the fact that, while the Eddys as a family are not poor, not many of them are very rich," said the Reverend Zachary Eddy at a family reunion in 1880. "Estates . . . have been divided among many heirs."

"We are a large-brained family, but . . . there have been but few manifestations of remarkable intellectual power," Eddy said, with a candor seldom exhibited on such occasions. "Our family has produced no great statesman, or philosopher, or orator, or poet, or historian, or man of science." Somewhat wistfully, he said: "We have been at a dead level of respectability for three hundred years."[1]

That was soon to change. A line of the family had rooted in what is now northeast Ohio when Moore Eddy arrived from Connecticut in 1830. There, he married Elizabeth Whittaker, whose parents had made the six-week trip from New England in a wagon drawn by oxen. Moore and his wife lived in a log cabin, cleared land in the virgin forest, and raised five children. At school, their daughter Emily met a dreamy young man named Amirus Darrow. They were married and on April 18, 1857, welcomed their fifth child, Clarence, to the world.[2]

He would be everything but respectable.

THE FIRST DARROW to arrive in America, according to the family genealogists, was George Darrow, who came to Connecticut in the late seventeenth century. It's said he was snatched by a press gang and forced into service in the Royal Navy, but jumped ship in the Americas and made his way to New London, a port with a reputation for unruly behavior. "It was easy to raise a mob here; easy to get up a feast, a frolick or a fracas," an early town historian wrote. "Men who had long been rovers, and unaccustomed to restraint, gathered here . . . Violations of modesty and purity before marriage, were but too frequent."

There was sufficient sport and opportunity, and enough Indians in the forests, to keep the family in New London for two more generations. But by the middle of the next century the Darrow clan, like the Eddys, was generating too many children. A number of Darrows left Connecticut and made their way up the Hudson River valley in New York. Their wandering was interrupted, and then accelerated, by the great events of the American Revolution.[3]

Clarence Darrow took pride in his rebel ancestors. Several fought in the Revolution, at storied places like Lexington and Saratoga. His great-grandfather Ammirus joined George Washington's army in 1778, at the age of seventeen, as an aide-de-camp for a cousin, Captain Christopher Darrow, who had served at Bunker Hill. Ammirus and his brother Jedediah were at the battle of Monmouth that summer, but their service with Washington ended when Christopher was court-martialed after challenging the actions of an incompetent superior. Christopher was ultimately vindicated, but Ammirus and his brother returned to New York, where they joined in one of the Revolution's grislier chapters.[4]

The Loyalists and their Iroquois allies in upstate New York had taken to raiding—murdering settlers, scalping, and hauling women and children off as slaves. The death of one of Ammirus's comrades, Lieutenant Thomas Boyd, illustrates the savagery of the frontier war. The Iroquois nailed an end of his intestines to a tree, and forced their captive to trudge around its trunk until he was eviscerated. Then they cut off his head and mounted it on a pole. The Americans responded in kind. One patriot who served with Ammirus, a marksman named Tim Murphy, was known for his collection of scalps. In the fall of 1780, the Darrow brothers were stationed with Murphy in the Schoharie River valley when the army of Loyalist colonel Sir John Johnson invaded the region. Ammirus's term of service was up, but he volunteered to remain—a decision that looked dubious when the patriots were cornered in a fort at Middleburgh. Their commander panicked and tried to surrender, but Murphy pushed him aside and fired on the British officers who approached under a white flag to parlay. Johnson's Indian allies had no patience for a siege, and he led them to plunder elsewhere.

The war took Ammirus west and north of Albany, deep into the woods and mountains, where the Mohawk Valley patriots fought a series of battles against Loyalist forces led by Captain Walter Butler, hated by the settlers for his role in earlier massacres. Ammirus was there when Butler, defying his enemies from across a creek, was shot from his horse in the Black River country. Word of Butler's death thrilled the American settlers in New York, perhaps as much as the news then arriving from Virginia, where General Cornwallis had surrendered at Yorktown.[5]

Ammirus returned to New London after the war, where he wooed his wife-to-be, Sarah Malona.[6] Within a few years he and his family were making their way to the Black River region he had visited during the war. Sarah bore twelve children. Jedediah, the oldest boy, was Clarence Darrow's grandfather. He was a furniture maker, known for his skill as a craftsman and his happy disposition. Clarence's aunt Sarah recalled a strict Methodist upbringing, the frightful cold of the north woods, and the warm maple syrup of her grandfather's sugar house. The countryside was covered with hemlock, pine, and balsam, and the streams were alive with fish. She liked to gather wildflowers, and spruce gum to chew, and to feed the tamed bears at Graves Tavern. In winter, she and her brother Amirus would go sledding on snow so deep it covered the fences, "making the country look like one vast field."[7]

Ammirus passed away in 1824, with Jedediah and young Amirus at his bedside. Then Jedediah and his family moved on and settled in the Western Reserve.

THE WESTERN RESERVE, where Clarence Darrow was born and lived until the age of thirty, was a rectangular block of land west of the Pennsylvania border, stretching along the shore of Lake Erie. It was granted to Connecticut after the Revolution to resolve a violent border dispute with Pennsylvania. Coming from Connecticut, the most radical of the Puritan colonies, the Western Reserve's inhabitants shared a fierce commitment to liberty. Their relatives in New England, dispatching fishing fleets and clipper ships around the globe, grew more cosmopolitan in the nineteenth century, but the inhabitants of the Reserve were, politically, frozen in time. If anything, their radical vision grew stronger, fueled by a Puritan sense of duty. Many were abolitionists, risking life and property to smuggle fugitive slaves to Canada via the Underground Railroad.

Amirus Darrow was the oldest of Jedediah's sons. He learned carpentry from his father, then set out to become a preacher, studying first with the Methodists at Allegheny College and then at the new Unitarian seminary in Meadville, Pennsylvania. "This ambition was born of [his] intense love of books," his son Clarence would recall. "The trade of a parson was thought to be an intellectual calling." The Eddy clan, sound farming folk who valued shrewdness and hard labor, thought Emily's new husband was impractical. For although he displayed some characteristic Darrow traits—restlessness, rebelliousness, fertility—Amirus stood out mostly for his inefficacious thirst for learning. He had wide-ranging interests in literature, theology, and political theory, and Clarence and his brothers and sisters were raised in a home crammed with books and ideas. "How my father managed to buy the books I cannot tell," Darrow wrote. "Neither by nature nor by training had he any business ability or any faculty for getting money."

Amirus would study at four colleges and acquire two postsecondary degrees, but he never became more than a shopkeeper.

"Nature had some grudge against my father," Darrow recalled. "Day after day and year after year he was compelled to walk the short and narrow path . . . while his mind was roving over scenes of great battles, decayed empires, dead languages and the starry heavens above . . . To his dying day, he lived in a walking trance."

Amirus was a disciple of Thomas Jefferson and savored the works of the atheist pamphleteer Tom Paine, the heretical David Hume, the infidel Volney's ruminations on natural law, and the writings of the French libertarian and skewer of religious orthodoxy, Voltaire. He read, as well, from the evolutionists Charles Darwin and Herbert Spencer. His love for scholarship and disputatious nature appear to have cost Amirus his faith, for he never did practice as a minister of the Lord. He became a freethinker, one of a class of American rationalists who put no faith in organized religion, or in a Supreme Being who ordered the lives of men. "He began to doubt. He doubted Hell, and he even questioned Heaven and God," Darrow remembered. Amirus forsook the pulpit, acquired a degree from Cleveland University, then chose to practice his father's craft, making furniture in tiny Farmdale, Ohio.

Amirus and the wide-eyed Emily, who was five or six years younger than her husband, labored as well at the happy business of procreation. After Everett and Channing came Mary, and a baby boy who died in infancy; then Clarence and Hubert and Herman and Jennie.[8] When Clarence Seward Darrow arrived in the world on that spring morning in 1857, Amirus was still naming sons after his heroes. Everett and Channing had been christened after prominent Unitarian leaders; William Seward was a militant abolitionist, a lawyer, a U.S. senator, and former governor of New York.

Seward was an "agitator," known for his defense of immigrants and fugitive blacks and for his pioneering use of the insanity defense. In 1846, he showed moral—even physical—courage when he defied the local mobs and agreed to represent William Freeman, a deranged black man who had invaded the home of a prosperous farmer and murdered the man and his pregnant wife, infant daughter, and mother-in-law. The case was political strychnine, but "a higher law and a louder voice called him to the defense of the demented, forsaken wretch," wrote Seward's biographer in 1853, in a volume that no doubt had a place in Amirus Darrow's library. Seward hired medical experts and carried the defense through the courts. "And all this for whom? For a *Negro!*—the poorest and lowest of his degraded caste," one commentator wrote.

"I am not the prisoner's lawyer—I am the lawyer for society, for mankind," Seward told the jurors, in a closing argument whose format and fire would be matched by his namesake in years ahead. "The color of the prisoner's skin, and the form of his features, are not impressed upon the spiritual immortal mind which works beneath . . . He is still your brother, and mine."

Such was the hero whom Amirus honored, and hoped his son would emulate.[9]

Everett recalled that Amirus "took a prominent part in the antislavery agitation." And in Darrow's accounts of his boyhood, he recalls his father speaking admiringly of men like John Brown, Frederick Douglass, and Wendell Phillips, and writes of how members of the abolitionist "army," when passing through town, would "make my father's home their stopping place." In his later years, Darrow told people that his father had helped shelter runaway slaves.[10]

Three of Clarence's uncles served in the Union Army in the Civil War—one was wounded, another survived captivity—but Amirus did not join them. He was well past forty, and had that growing brood to support. In 1864, Amirus enrolled at the University of Michigan to study law, but he failed to complete his studies and returned to Ohio. He moved his family a few miles to Kinsman where, on the main road leading north from town, Amirus invested in a furniture store, set up a barnlike "machine shop" to make cabinets, chairs, coffins, and cupboards, and installed his wife and children in a strange, octagonal home that sang of nonconformity.[11]

KINSMAN WAS ONE of the thousands of such midwestern towns: a homogeneous community of several hundred souls, a dusty village square, and some tall shade trees on the banks of a shallow river—the Pymatuning, in this case—that supplied its boys with the requisite fishing holes and a sandy bend for swimming. It had woods and fields to roam and hills to coast, a graveyard with an iron gate, and a Presbyterian church with a tall white steeple that commanded the skyline like the spires of New England.

"It would be hard to make a town better fitted for boys," Darrow remembered. He and his brothers and their friends ran barefoot in all but the coldest months, playing games like fox and geese, or skin the cat. They clapped gunpowder between the blacksmith's anvils for the required salutes on Independence Day, went skating when the ponds and creeks froze, and plucked tiny gifts from Christmas trees lit by wax candles at church. They walked to the local schoolhouse with dinner pails of lunch and pie, and were generally tardy because, as Darrow recalled, "there were always birds in the trees and stones in the road and no child ever knew any pain except his own."

Clarence had a sloppy demeanor, with a lock of lanky hair that invariably fell upon his forehead, and a lazy, easygoing personality. One prissy classmate remembered turning in her seat and gasping at his arithmetic: barely legible and blotted with ink. "I never seemed able to finish any work that I began; some more alluring prospect ever beckoned me," Darrow would confess. He was a dedicated whittler, aimlessly shaving sticks until "it became as mechanical as breathing." A favorite book was *The Story of a Bad Boy*, a tale of mischievous youth. As he grew older, he became devoted to the adventure novels of Thomas Mayne Reid and Frederick Marryat. One of Kinsman's most "alluring prospects" was baseball, a sport that acquired its modern rules and format at midcentury, caught the popular imagination, and swept across the land. "I once thought that when the time should come that I could no longer play ball there would be nothing left in life," Darrow said. Skills and equipment were rudimentary; scores of forty runs were not uncommon. Darrow was sturdy and broad-shouldered as he reached adolescence: a good-enough first baseman, and good-enough-looking, his sister Jennie recalled, to acquire the attention of Kinsman's girls.

The Darrows' eight-sided home, a relic of an eighteenth-century architectural fad, was made of chestnut beams and concrete, with large rooms and closets and a wraparound veranda. Clarence and three brothers shared two beds in one of the upstairs bedrooms. Downstairs was a kitchen, a parlor, and his father's study, lit at night by kerosene lamps. The yard was sheltered by a towering elm, and across the street was a tin shop whose proprietor, Cliff Fitch, doubled as a justice of the peace. Nearby was Lorenzo Roberts, the blacksmith who knew some law, and Collin's grocery, where, as a boy, Darrow took a nickel he'd received for Christmas, mumbled a request for almonds—a treat he'd heard of but never tasted—and was sold a small bag of alum. He went home with puckered lips and told his mother that he could not understand why people liked the stuff.[12]

Its Puritan roots made Kinsman a "narrow and smug community," Darrow remembered. Material success was seen as proof of character and not—as was often the case—of avarice, or luck, or intrigue. Conformity was a smothering virtue. Clarence preferred the approach of some Darrow relatives who never amounted to much of anything, but seemed to have a good time doing so. "I had an uncle or two—not very prominent," he would recall. "They were engaged largely in fiddling and drinking whiskey, which is not a bad way to kill time while we are here." To their children, Amirus and Emily were distant and demanding. "They were New England people, raised in the Puritan school of life . . . demonstrations of affection were signs of weakness rather than of love," Darrow remembered.[13]

THE YEARS OF Darrow's upbringing were a volatile era in American government, and Amirus's interests ensured that the household was immersed in the turmoil. Jefferson and other members of the Revolutionary generation were still living when Amirus was born, but the nation had already begun its transformation from Arcadian domain to commercial giant. The pace of change, wrought by wondrous inventions, cheap labor, and new sources of energy, accelerated after the Civil War. The status of the individual was diminished in this increasingly mechanistic world, as Americans struggled to apply the principles of liberty in the industrial age.

The Republicans of the Gilded Age had a concise theory: government was a guarantor of property rights. If but one man in a thousand took the liberty conferred by the Constitution, clawed his way up from the factory floor, and built a business empire, the others did not have a right to deprive him of his gains. If the Morgan family were better bankers, or the Vanderbilts more adept at running railroads, so be it. And if a mill worker or a railway switchman didn't like the wages offered, well, they had the right to quit.

Liberals like Amirus thought it preposterous that an Ohio farm boy or a seamstress from eastern Europe could negotiate with a corporation. Workers penned up in company towns, by industries whose ownership was clustered in trusts, had no leverage. Nor did farmers, who were forced to ship crops on monopolistic railroads. The American economy was producing huge extremes of poverty and wealth, and quaked with recurring "panics" and depressions. But the government's power to regulate and tax, and the workers' right to take collective action, were curbed by the courts.

Amirus subscribed to the *New York Weekly Tribune*, whose exuberant editor, Horace Greeley, championed westward expansion, abolitionism, and the interests of the workingman. The paper, with its eclectic mix of correspondents and coverage of political fads, became the Darrow household's "political and social Bible," Clarence recalled. Amirus was a supporter—one of the few in Trumbull County—when Greeley made his unsuccessful run for president as a Republican liberal aligned with the Democrats in 1872. The household's hopes were doused again in 1876 when Democrat Samuel Tilden won the popular vote for the presidency, but lost the White House to skullduggery.

Amirus was an admirer, as well, of Peter Cooper, a Unitarian philosopher who ran for president as the candidate of the Greenback Party. It was just the sort of hopeless cause to attract Amirus, and he joined the movement, an insurrection of farmers and laborers united in their opposition to Republican tight-money policies. "He had moved his soiled and tattered tent to a new battlefield and was fighting the same stubborn sullen threatening public opinion for a new and yet more doubtful cause," Clarence recalled. The "determined band of agitators" that visited during the abolitionist days now returned to the Darrow home. "They were always poor, often ragged, and a far-off look seemed to haunt their eyes, as if gazing into space at something beyond the stars," he recalled. "They would sit with my father for hours in his little study, where they told each other of their vision and their hopes."

In 1883, Amirus ran for the state senate. He finished fourth in a field of five candidates, with 146 votes.[14]

Clarence Darrow loved his father, and admired the courage and the wit that Amirus displayed when besting his neighbors in arguments about politics or religion. "My father had directed my thought and reading. He had taught me to question rather than accept," he remembered. "I had little respect for the opinion of the crowd. My instinct was to doubt the majority."

Darrow had, as well, a particularly keen sense of compassion. As a boy, he was known for sticking up for the weaker children of the town, his sister Mary recalled, and her family was astonished when, after their mother slaughtered and cooked a chicken that Clarence had favored, he fled the house and refused to eat fowl ever again. He had nursed the frail thing as a chick, carried it around on his shoulder, and named it "David." Later in life, he would add veal and lamb to his list of forsaken foods. Not surprisingly, this empathetic soul was moved by his father's talk about injustice. "I listened so rapturously and believed so strongly," he recalled, and "looked with the same unflagging hope for the promised star . . . the brilliant rainbow."

Yet it was not easy, in that small town, to be the son of the local apostate. The good people in the Kinsman congregations shunned the Darrow furniture shop, and their children eyed the family warily. For their father's strange ways, Darrow and his siblings faced "the social boycott that the Godly . . . enforced" against the "children of darkness," he recalled. As Darrow made his way through adolescence, he began to view his father as harebrained and weak—a man who had "pathetically" come to "glory in his reputation as the village infidel." Amirus had raised his children to be skeptics, and Clarence turned that skepticism toward his father. He was angry, and ashamed of being angry, as he watched Amirus consign himself to failure. "A simple child he always was": this was Darrow's ultimate, dismissive verdict. He would be different. He would show them. He would show them all.[15]

In the summer of 1872, Emily Darrow died.

Everett had gone to Europe to study and that spring he received a letter from Clarence, alerting him that their mother was ill. Before Everett could leave for home, Amirus wrote him with the awful news. "The doctors have finally pronounced it a cancer," he told his son. "There is no chance for her recovery."

"Try to bear up and be reconciled," Amirus wrote. "She does not suffer so much as she did."

As the tumor grew, blocking her small intestine, Emily was confined to bed. "I feel so ready to go," she told Mary. "Death is nothing for sure but rest, and if I might get well now it would only be a few years longer that I could live, for life is so short."

"It is just a dream, and you will all find it so when your time comes," she told her frightened children.

Emily's death came during hard times for the family, when Amirus had been forced to take a second job teaching school. The days of Clarence's childhood were over, as he picked up the slack in the furniture shop. "Clarence is almost a man and does a man's work," Mary reported to Everett, and she postponed her own plans to attend the University of Michigan. Clarence described the "blank despair" that settled over the house, and Mary told Everett how "everything that made it bright and pleasant is gone."

Clarence was fifteen when his mother died. But he described himself in memoirs as a "little child" and "very young" and "quite little" when he lost her. Her death fed his hunger for affection. He was the fifth of eight children in that Puritan home, and had "no feeling of a time when either my father or my mother took me, or any other member of our family, in their arms," he wrote. "I cannot recall that my mother ever gave me a kiss or a caress." Years later, Darrow would joke that he never could master the verb *love*. He would rush into an early marriage, cheat, divorce, marry again, and never stop reaching for women's hands, or waists, for comfort. "That verb has never grown easier," he wrote.

Emily's rites were agony for Clarence. She was laid out in the parlor of their home. As was customary in small towns, Amirus's line of hardwood furniture also included coffins, which led him to double as the local undertaker. Between funerals, the Darrow chickens roosted on the hearse, which now needed to be cleaned and its black flowers attached, and Black Hawk, the mare, hitched to take it to the graveyard. Clarence was overwhelmed by "shudder and horror" and an "endless regret that I did not tell her that I loved her." In the years after, he visited her grave but once.[16]

Amirus did no draining or embalming; in those years the relatives would simply wash and clothe a corpse for burial. But there were recurring funerals, and the coffins stored in a corner of the shop that Clarence refused to visit after dark. Intellectually, he confronted the questions of existence, always declining the easy solace of religion. Emotionally, he was scared. Friends knew not to raise the subject with him. He visited seers and mediums, and at one point near the end of life Darrow asked his wife to kill herself on his deathbed, because he could not face the crossing alone. As with many other essential matters—politics, money, and his relationships with women, to cite just a few—Darrow's feelings toward death were rife with contradiction. As a lawyer, his greatest fear was to lose a client to the gallows. And yet he did not shy away. Darrow repeatedly took on capital cases, many seemingly hopeless, where his private terrors inspired some of his greatest performances.[17]

THE LAW GAVE Darrow his ticket out of Kinsman. He was a student in secondary school when Emily died, studying at the local public "academy." A year later, his family scraped together enough money to send him to a preparatory course at Allegheny College. He did not last long. The "Panic of 1873" plunged the nation into depression, and ended Darrow's college days. Like Everett and Mary and Amirus before him, Clarence took a job as a schoolteacher, in his case at the District No. 3 school, a few miles away in the town of Vernon. He received $100 for the three-month autumn term. He was a colorful sight in those days of the "Long Depression," wearing a bowler and driving through town in a shabby contraption: an old sleigh that his father had converted into a buggy. He was a lax instructor who refused to employ corporal discipline and let the boys stretch their hour of recess. The choicest part of the job, he'd say, was the good meals and pie he got when invited to supper by the families of his students.

Oratory was part of the curriculum, and as a student Clarence had excelled at memorizing his "pieces" and presenting them with dramatic flourish. His own classmates would long remember his recitation of "Darius Green and His Flying Machine" ("Darius was clearly of the opinion / That the air is also man's dominion / And that, with paddle or fin or pinion / We soon or late / Shall navigate"). The Darrows had a custom of reading aloud for one another at the dining room table or while gathered in the sitting room on winter nights. He attended, and soon was entering, the speaking contests held at town picnics and the evening declamation series in the local schoolhouse. He liked to sit in, as well, on the arguments held before "Justice" Fitch. "Every time there was a lawsuit I used to go to the tinsmith's law shop and listen to those country pettifoggers abuse each other," he recalled. "They talked so much and abused each other and the witnesses so violently that I thought I would rather be a lawyer than anything else in the world." The blacksmith, Lorenzo Roberts, let Darrow read his law books.

He taught for three years, but the legal profession seemed a better way to make money, and he nurtured a conceit that "I was made for better things." His father had studied law and so, Darrow decided, should he.[18]

* *

The Darrows placed great faith in education. As each child graduated from college, he or she devoted a share of their earnings to help the next pay tuition. As times got better, it was Clarence's turn for higher learning. Amirus, Mary, and Everett contributed, and he set off for the University of Michigan school of law in the fall of 1877, at the age of twenty. He made no significant impression in his year in Ann Arbor, did not graduate, and never acquired a law degree. His only notoriety was not the best kind. He got in a spat with his landlady. Darrow "could not or would not pay for his rooms, and accordingly left them one day last week, telling Mrs. Foley that he had left his trunk and its contents and those he said would pay his indebtedness to her. She was, of course, glad to get even this from him. But on opening the trunk it was found to be filled with "wood, burnt boots and other things of equal value," the local paper reported. "This should warn all others from trusting him."

Darrow replied with a letter to the editor, calling Mrs. Foley's account "nearly all an entire fabrication." He had paid his rent, and was moving out, when they bickered over alleged damage to his room. She had seized his trunk, said Darrow, and half of the wood heating fuel he left behind. "Although poor, I value my reputation too highly to dispose of it for the small sum in controversy," Darrow said. "I will prove by witnesses the above facts, as stated by me, to be true, to any one who will call at my present boarding place."[19]

The costs of law school were not terribly high—$50 covered tuition and fees—but still an obstacle for Darrow. And for American lawyers in that era, a law degree was an exception. Most took jobs as clerks in a local attorney's office and "read law" to prepare for the bar exam. So

Darrow found work in a Youngstown, Ohio, firm and studied there. He remembered sitting through one libel case with his mentor, and being puzzled when that learned man pronounced the newspaper's action as "libeelious."

"Libelous, correctly pronounced, has a dry technical, colorless sound, but when pronounced libeelious it sounds frightfully evil," the attorney told him. "I know the men on the jury. I have grown up with some of them. I know how they feel about evil wicked things and I knew just what response that evil-sounding word would evoke." In later years, Darrow told fanciful stories about the bar examination (most of them involving alcohol), which took place at a room in the Tod House, a local tavern. The general theme of his tales, that his examination was a casual ceremony given by genial members of the local legal fraternity, is credible. "They were all good fellows and wanted to help us through," he recalled.

Darrow returned to Kinsman, which had, in the blacksmith, all the lawyers it needed. So he heeded Greeley's famous advice. The twenty-one-year-old lawyer had gone west, the local press reported, to make a start in "the territories." Custer had but recently died at Little Big Horn, and the cattle drives and wagon trains were still toting cowboys, sodbusters, and gunslingers to the Wild West when Darrow passed through a scenic part of central Kansas, along the Chisholm Trail. In the town of McPherson a group of two dozen Ohio families had founded a settlement called the "Ashtabula Colony." Darrow visited, liked what he saw, and rented an office, intent on making his fortune on the rolling Kansas plains. But something changed his mind, and he moved on. Maybe the risk and the isolation were daunting. Or maybe the something was a woman.

In the spring of 1880, Darrow married Jessie Ohl. She was a little younger than he, a rural lass he had known in Kinsman and courted for years. He made her laugh and took her to dances in the town hall, and she went to see him lecture and debate. She came from a prosperous farming family that owned land in Ohio and Minnesota. Her money helped pay for Darrow's law books, and they settled in Andover, a tiny community a dozen miles from Kinsman.

Andover was a hick burg, with a square of buildings, wood sidewalks, and hitching racks surrounded by fields. Darrow and Jessie roomed above a store, in a second-floor apartment that doubled as an office and a home.

He took, as a helper, James Roberts, the son of Lorenzo the blacksmith. Roberts read law with Darrow and went on to become a judge. In time the town acquired a pool hall and a tavern, where the blind barmaid ascertained what mugs were full by sticking her thumb in the beer. Darrow found a kindred spirit in Wat Morley, the freethinking owner of a clothing store, whose feud with the barmaid and her husband—Morley had suggested that they lacked a marriage license—bloomed into a slander suit that provided the town with invaluable diversion.

A lawsuit, in those days, was like a medieval tournament, Darrow recalled. "Every one, for miles around, had heard of the case and taken sides . . . Neighborhoods, churches, lodges and entire communities were divided as if in war . . . Audiences assembled from far and near." It was Morley who, in one of Darrow's first showdowns, gave him some memorable advice. Get to the justice of the peace's home early on the morning of the trial, Morley said, and introduce yourself with a jug of whiskey. Darrow did so, only to find that the opposing attorney had gotten there the evening before, and caroused with the jurist all night.[20]

The law gave Darrow a glimpse at the sins of his neighbors, which they labored so hard to hide. The experience confirmed what his father had taught him about "the right sort" of people. "The only way I got any money was defending farmers who sold hard cider, because we had a prohibition law in those days in northern Ohio," said Darrow. "Then I used to defend deacons for watering the milk before they sent it to the factory."

"Membership in a church in no way affected these cases of dilution," he noted.

Darrow's talents as an orator made him a popular guest at patriotic events and other celebrations, and the speech-making was good advertising for his law practice. In 1881, the farmers in Wayne celebrated the end-of-summer harvest with a September picnic. Rigs stirred the dust on the county roads and families gathered for backslaps and hugs, home-cooked suppers, music from a brass band, songs, and Darrow's speech. He gave them what they wanted to hear, with an ode to Manifest Destiny.

"Friends and Neighbors . . . Your presence and appearance here today, on this occasion, means that you are all contented with your lot," he said. "It means happiness, prosperity and peace; it means that you exist under the protecting arm of a Government which guarantees to you the legitimate product of your industry and your toil.

"One hundred years ago, nay, eighty years ago, naught but the giant oak and other forest trees stood where the bright and yellow grain in golden wreath was harvested but yesterday; the untutored savage of the wood had pitched his tent upon the spot where you are living now; the tomahawk and scalping knife did their barbarous deeds of cruelty and blood.

"But destiny, whose laws we all obey, had decreed that another and a better race should find these treasures . . . And so today we meet to celebrate this golden harvest time."

In 1883, Darrow became a father when Jessie gave birth to a son, whom they named Paul. Darrow felt that he was ready for a bigger stage and was urged to seek one by an admiring judge who had heard him try cases. They moved to Ashtabula.[21]

IT WAS DURING his stay in Ashtabula that Darrow launched a career in politics, which he would pursue for the next twenty years. He fell in with the Democrats, who were glad to have him, for he was a handsome, well-spoken young man. He served as secretary of the county party and was a delegate to the state convention. He worked on the victorious presidential campaign of Grover Cleveland in 1884, then ran for the state senate and lost. He entered the race for Ashtabula County prosecutor and lost. He finally found a race he could win when, with the help of a friendly judge, Darrow was elected Ashtabula's city solicitor, with a salary of $75 a month.

Darrow now added a partisan edge to his rhetoric. After an 1884 trip to Washington, D.C., he filed a report in the local Democratic newspaper in which, with mock consternation, he told how in "the sacred marble halls" of Congress he had found "a real, living, terrible saloon."

"I sat down at one of the tables and wept in silence," Darrow wrote. "To make sure of the character of the place, I ordered drinks." The Republicans, he told audiences, were a "party that talks temperance in Ohio and runs a gin mill in Washington."

A Memorial Day address in 1886 contained the expected patriotic flourishes—and a radical proposal, as well. "Once more we bring the tender tokens of our love, the Spring's bright flowers and garlands green, and strew them o'er our soldiers' graves," he began. "We hear the fife's shrill notes, the drum's loud beat and the bugle's clarion call, we hear the roar and din of strife, the cannon's deadly peal, the war horse neigh and see the wounded and the slain. Once more we watch the daily tidings from the South and with quickly beating hearts we scan the list to know whose loved one has fallen in the fray. We see the pall; the bier; the hearse and view again the brave boys, cold in death."

But the dreams of the Founding Fathers, and the sacrifice of those who died in the Civil War, would not be fulfilled until women could vote, Darrow said. In denying women the ballot, "we defame the principles for which our fathers fought," he told the crowd. "Strange that men . . . without a blush of shame . . . take from woman, the class who needs it most, and as a class the most fitted for its use, the only weapon which a self-governing people have the right to use—the ballot box."

Darrow shared cases with a lawyer named Charles Lawyer and worked as a public defender. And throughout his years in Ashtabula, Darrow kept up a running fight on behalf of James Brockway. In March 1885, Brockway had cared for a wealthy but sick "inebriate" and, in return for his help, been promised a gilt-trimmed horse harness. But then the drunkard was assigned a guardian, Cornelius Jewell, who refused to honor the deal. Darrow tried the case—*Brockway v. Jewell*—before a justice of the peace and lost. Unwilling to give up, he fought the case through retrials and appeals until finally he prevailed, nine years after it was first contested, in the Ohio Supreme Court. It was a battle over principle, not money. The harness was worth $30.

Ohio was beginning to take notice. In August 1886 he went to the state Democratic convention in Toledo. One newspaper called Darrow "a young man of brilliant attainments" who "already enjoys an enviable reputation as a lawyer and an orator." Another noted how Darrow "brought his candidate before the convention in a masterful manner. He has a scholarly look, a perfectly beardless face and a deep rich voice."

But life was tame in what Darrow took to calling "benighted Ashtabula." There was little chance as a Democrat to win higher office. The poker games with pals were fun, but it was still a place where life and commerce came to a halt and everyone gathered to see the spectacle when the movers hoisted a safe through an upstairs window. He had lots of time to read, and to the books he had discovered in his father's library, he added a small volume on crime, recommended by a local judge: *Our*

Penal Machinery and Its Victims, written and self-published by a Chicagoan named John Peter Altgeld. It argued that biological and social conditions, and not willful deviltry, were the source of criminal behavior. Darrow became an acolyte, as well, of Robert Ingersoll, an elegant orator and famous agnostic, whose willingness to champion freethinking philosophy in the face of popular disapproval made him, in Darrow's eyes, a "soul of matchless courage."

And Darrow was moved by *Progress and Poverty*, a bestselling political tract written by Henry George. An Ashtabula banker brought it to his attention, and it made a marked impression. "In factories where labor-saving machinery has reached its most wonderful development, little children are at work . . . Amid the greatest accumulations of wealth, men die of starvation . . . Everywhere the greed of gain, the worship of wealth, shows the fear of want," George wrote. He advocated a heavy "single tax" on property, to ensure equality.[22]

Darrow's radical soul was stirring. Jessie might be comfortable in Ohio, but he desired more. "I had accumulated $500 in cash and wanted to buy a home. Of course, I don't suppose I did, but the family wanted it," Darrow recalled. "Wives always want homes, something to bring a man to at night . . . it stabilizes things. Wives are great stabilizers."

"I made a bargain with a fellow for that home, which I was to pay $3,500 for—$500 down and the rest as long as I lived," said Darrow. "He came up the next morning to bring the deed, and he said he could not bring it because his wife would not sign it." In some versions of the tale Darrow, provoked, tells the seller, "I don't want your fool house anyhow, I am moving to Chicago." In others, he tells off the wife. What really matters is, he told it to himself. Great men were doing great things, and he wanted to be among them.

The March 5, 1887, edition of the *Ashtabula Standard* carried the news. "City Solicitor CS Darrow has decided to locate in Chicago," it said, "and early next month will shake the dust of Ashtabula from his feet and take up his abode in the wickedest city in the United States."[23]

Chapter 2

CHICAGO

Chicago was a mining camp, five stories high.

Clarence Darrow arrived in Chicago in the spring of 1887, knowing no one of any consequence, lost in the flocks of other young pilgrims seeking their fortunes in the great boomtown in the middle of the continent. Chicago's unbridled growth, corsair creed, and mesmerizing license gave the city its magnetic pull. The Great Lakes port had ninety thousand inhabitants in the year Darrow was born. By the time he arrived at the age of thirty, there were a million people living there, and it had become the nation's second-largest city. Everyone came from somewhere else; most were foreign born. "First in violence, deepest in dirt," wrote journalist Lincoln Steffens. "Loud, lawless, unlovely, ill-smelling, irreverent, new; an overgrown gawk of a village, the 'tough' among cities, a spectacle for the nations."[1]

The Chicagoans were a truly intrepid lot. When their effluence despoiled Lake Michigan and threatened to slay them all with cholera, they reversed the flow of the Chicago River and sent the sewage down the Mississippi. When the lake sand gave way beneath their buildings, they lifted the city, block by block. In 1871 the famous Chicago fire razed the downtown, destroying eighteen thousand buildings. From tent cities out on the prairie, emissaries were dispatched to assure Wall Street and Capitol Hill that Chicago would rebuild; that wall and shingle could be consumed, but not the great kinetic spirit of the town.

The fields and pastures of the Republic shipped grain and hogs and cattle to Chicago to be butchered, processed, and sent east. In return came fine goods and imports, and a tide of immigrants from Ireland, Germany, the Baltics, Poland, Scandinavia, and Italy. The city was known as the "Rome of Railroads," for its immense depots and switchyards. The McCormick Reaper Works and the Pullman Palace Car Company topped the manufacturing sector. Gustavus Swift and Philip Armour built mighty packinghouses, feeding on the herds of livestock slaughtered at the Union Stockyards. The docks were crowded with stevedores, unloading lumber and iron ore from the Great Lakes fleet. Towering grain elevators competed with that new architectural phenomenon, the skyscraper, to define the city skyline.

With splendor came sin and corruption. The bucket-shop bars, faro games, and bordellos ran all night. "City Hall . . . is filled with brothel-keepers, saloon-keepers and prize-fighters, ready to barter the rights of citizens for a song," wrote John Burns, a visiting British socialist.[2] From 1875 to 1890, the homicide rate soared by 413 percent, driven by brawls in the saloons and gunfire in the alleys. The legal domain that Darrow entered was worthy of the town. "Chicago was a mining camp, five stories high," the journalist George Ade recalled. "It was owned by the gamblers" and "the minor courts were controlled by agents of crime." Attorneys worked in rundown buildings, with the invariable leather chair, rolltop desk, and bust of Lincoln. A few hundred dollars was, for a few years yet, a significant fee. Fistfights broke out in court. Verdicts could be purchased. "I could cite many cases of organized attempts to bilk my companies on absolutely fictitious testimony," the streetcar baron Charles Yerkes recalled. And so, said Yerkes, "I bribed juries."

Darrow rented a desk in an office downtown on LaSalle Street. Among the first to engage his services was Dr. Charles Arnold, who had been sued for slander by Richard McDonough, a rival for an office in the "Grand Lodge of the Knights and Ladies of Honor." Darrow presented witnesses who testified that, as Arnold had claimed, McDonough did indeed run "a bawdy house" on Madison Street. A clerk who manned the front desk told how the male guests, to disguise their identities, signed the register as Grover Cleveland. Arnold described the hotel as a den of sin where "Negroes with white women, white men with Negro women, young girls with old men and old women with young men" came and went, staying but an hour, with no luggage, "in a manner that demonstrated their abandoned purpose."

"What kind of women go there?" Darrow asked a German barber who worked nearby.

"Shippies."

"How do you know they're chippies?"

"Vell, they got their hair cut, and I know 'em."

Darrow earned little that first year. He was homesick and awed, but not alone: the whole Darrow clan was moving to the city. Darrow's older brother Everett and sister Mary worked as public school teachers and lived on the West Side at 907 Sawyer Avenue, where Amirus and Darrow's youngest sister, Jennie, another teacher, soon joined them. After renting a house in Englewood, Darrow and Jessie moved to 905 Sawyer Avenue. Within months, his brothers Hubert, a musician, and Herman, a teacher and a printer, had arrived.

And Darrow had an uncle in Chicago—his mother's brother, William "Horse" Eddy, a trader and breeder who ran a stable and carriage shop on Dearborn Street. Profane, loquacious, and opinionated, Eddy was "quite a character," the *Tribune* noted, a "man of shrewd discernment and radical politics." He had arrived in Chicago from Ohio in the 1840s and made his fortune in livestock and real estate. He was an abolitionist who, during the Civil War, had gained fame for horsewhipping Wilbur Storey, the Lincoln-hating editor of the *Chicago Times*. Eddy became wealthy, civic-minded, and almost respectable, and helped found the city's Republican Party. But he lost almost everything in the great fire, and took to drinking, brawling, and waging hopeless campaigns for office. In the face of various religious revivals, he remained an infidel. "Tain't natural to think a man is going to be roasted after death because some people say so," he explained.

Darrow took to Eddy and agreed to represent him in a seemingly hopeless lawsuit he had filed to recover a disputed thirty-acre tract of land near Auburn Park. It took six years, and Darrow had to carry the case to the Illinois Supreme Court, but he won his uncle title to the now-valuable property. W. H. EDDY RECOVERS HALF A MILLION, read the front-page headline in the *Tribune*. It was Darrow's first big legal triumph.[3]

VICTORIAN AMERICA LOVED its clubs, and Darrow became a stalwart at the Land and Labor Club, the Andrew Jackson League, the Secular Union, the Equal Suffrage Club, the Women's Physiological Institute, the Personal Rights League, and other organizations. Getting known was good for business. So were letters to the editor. Just days after arriving in Chicago, Darrow wrote the *Inter Ocean,* decrying the widespread practice by which wealthy landowners lied about the assessed value of their properties. "About the only class . . . that pays taxes on the full value of their personal property are those of widows, orphans and imbeciles."

Many in the community were struck by Darrow's speaking skills, his wry sense of humor, and his restless, inquiring mind. George Schilling was a prominent trade unionist when he encountered Darrow at a gathering of freethinkers. The other speakers had gone too far in mocking the ministry of Jesus Christ, and Darrow "jumped in, and with a ten-minute speech defended the carpenter's son of Judea with such a sympathetic, persuasive voice that I fell in love with him," Schilling recalled. "We became fast friends."

Though Darrow admired Christ's teachings, he doubted his divinity, and was a regular with Schilling at the Secular Union. It had been organized to oppose the "infliction" of religion on secular society, and met, appropriately, in an abandoned church. "The religion for which we are struggling and which must prevail in the future is not based upon . . . a Supreme Being," Darrow told a standing-room-only crowd of nonbelievers at Easter in 1888. "But . . . a foundation deep in human reason."

Here, Darrow expressed the deterministic philosophy that would guide him all his life. "The worst of all cruel creeds and of all the bloody wrongs inflicted by the past can be found in the barbarous belief that man is a free moral agent," he said.

"The political and religious rulers of the world have ever taught that each individual possessed the power to choose the right or wrong . . . and if he chose the bad it was because he . . . preferred the sin," said Darrow. That was ignorance, and folly. Man was but a leaf, tossed and bashed in the "great moving restless universe of which he forms so small a part."

Darrow enlisted in the local Democracy, as the party was called, and was dispatched to Rock Island, Warren, Dixon, and other small towns on behalf of President Cleveland in the 1888 election. After an appearance at a YMCA hall in Moline, he was described as a "Chicago orator and reformer" and hailed for his "brilliant and forcible exposition." He was not so well received when debating in Belvidere. "Poor Darrow," the *Tribune* reported, was "completely demolished." So, in that Republican year, was Cleveland.

Darrow sought out influential men in the community to cultivate their friendship. To the wealthy reformer Henry Demarest Lloyd, Darrow sent an ingratiating note asking to "allow me to thank you for your brave and able letter in yesterday's *Herald*. It will do much good. The cause of organized labor is fortunate in having such a champion." Lloyd was a scholar and a journalist related through marriage to an owner of the conservative *Tribune*. With long white hair and a drooping mustache, he looked a bit like Mark Twain. As early as 1881, he had started writing about the pernicious influence of trusts and monopolies, and his 1894 book *Wealth Against Commonwealth* was a model for muckrakers to come. His home in Winnetka became a salon for radicals. It wasn't long before Darrow was attending. "He is one of our best young lawyers," Lloyd told a friend, "and a zealous friend of the working men."[4]

LLOYD AND DARROW would join many crusades in the coming years, but none so eruptive as that which brought them together during Darrow's first months in Chicago—the execution of the Haymarket defendants. It was "not the first unholy verdict rendered by a jury and sustained by a court, but it is perhaps the most unrighteous," Darrow declared.

In the fall of 1897, as three hundred policemen armed with rifles and shotguns guarded the approaches to the Cook County jail, four men cloaked in spectral shrouds dropped through the gallows and, kicking and writhing, slowly strangled to death. The hangman had erred, their necks did not break, and it took them time to die. Albert Parsons, August Spies, George Engel, and Adolph Fischer were anarchists, a word which came to evoke nihilism, but which then described a utopian philosophy.

The anarchists saw the one-sided nature of the transaction between capital and labor, witnessed the great disparity in wealth that resulted, and recognized the awful toll that the industrial age took on workers. They believed that men would rise, seize power from the ruling class, and live without government or laws. The most aggressive formed paramilitary groups like the Irish Labor Guards or the Bohemian Sharpshooters, who, before the authorities banned such activities, drilled in the parks and paraded with rifles and uniforms.

The movement's short-term goals were modest, however, and shared by mainstream labor groups. American wage earners, using strikes and boycotts, were demanding an end to ten- or twelve-hour shifts and agitating for an eight-hour day that spring. On May 3, 1886, in a clash at the McCormick works, the police opened fired, killing several men. A protest was called for the next night at an intersection called the Haymarket.

The rally was small and orderly, but as it drew to an end, an officious police captain ordered his men to clear the street. Someone threw a bomb at the advancing police column, and in the explosion and resultant gunfire, dozens of officers were wounded, eight fatally. "Goaded to madness, the police were . . . as dangerous as any mob, for they were blinded by passion and unable to distinguish between the peaceable citizen and the Nihilist assassin," the *Tribune* reported.

"Excitement was at fever heat," Darrow recalled. The public hysteria was not limited to Chicago. In an "acute outbreak of anarchy a Gatling gun . . . is the sovereign remedy," the *New York Times* advised. "Later on hemp, in judicious doses, has an admirable effect."

None of the anarchists was conclusively tied to the furtive bomber. Six of the defendants were not at the scene that night, and the two others were on the speakers' platform, not down on the sidewalk from where the bomb was thrown. Their crime was incitement: they were alleged to have inspired the assassin with their ideas. "There is no evidence," Albert Parsons wrote, "that I or any of us killed, or had anything to do with the killing . . . But it was proven clearly that we were, all of us, anarchists, socialists, communists . . . unionists. It was proven that three of us were editors of labor papers; that five of us were labor organizers and speakers at workingmen's mass meetings . . . Of these crimes against the capitalist class they found us guilty."

Judge Joseph Gary, conducting the trial as a public spectacle (he saved seats behind his bench for stylish young ladies who giggled and ate candy), gave wide latitude to the prosecution and, with his closing instructions to the jury, ushered the anarchists to their deaths. If the defendants "by print or speech" had encouraged a murderous act, Gary told the jurors, "then all such conspirators are guilty of such murder, whether the person who perpetrated such murder can be identified or not."[5]

Darrow was outraged. He had arrived in Chicago in the period between the trial and the executions, and joined a group of prominent citizens urging clemency for the defendants. Those who did so paid a price. Lloyd, a leader in the movement, was disinherited by his wife's wealthy family. William Black, the anarchists' attorney, had earned the Medal of Honor in the Civil War but now was shunned. The trial "left me in debt, without a business and without a clientage, and in a community all of whose wealthy citizens were in active hostility to me," he wrote.[6] Nevertheless, Darrow enlisted. In August 1887, he wrote a letter to his friends at the *Democratic Standard* in Ashtabula, recounting a visit with the anarchists in jail.

"They are a good looking intelligent lot of men. At first they were not inclined to talk, but after assuring them that I was something of a crank myself . . . they entered freely into conversation," Darrow reported. "They imagine that wealth is so strong that it controls legislation and elections and that we can only abolish present evils by wiping out capital and starting over new.

"It is very hard for one who, like me, believes that the injustice of the world can only be remedied through law, and order and system, to understand how intelligent men can believe that the repeal of all laws can better the world; but this is their doctrine."

The real issue at stake in the Haymarket case, Darrow told the folks back in Ohio, was free speech: "Whether one who advocates doctrines that the world believes to be wild and revolutionary, who wildly and generally advises killing and destroying, without however counseling the doing of a particular act against any particular person, can be held guilty of murder.

"I believe the establishment of such a doctrine would be a vital blow at freedom of speech and of the press," Darrow wrote.

He added, as an afterthought: "You will see by this that I still retain my unfortunate habit of looking at main questions in a different light from the majority."

"I hope you will not conclude that I am an Anarchist," he wrote. "I think their doctrines are wild if their eyes are not."[7]

At the time, Darrow was a member of a single-tax group inspired by author Henry George, who had initially supported the Haymarket defendants but now was running for political office in New York, and modulating his beliefs. He infuriated Darrow and the others by declining to publish the club's resolution asking for clemency in his organization's newspaper.[8] Darrow wrote a stinging letter to *The Solidarity,* a labor publication in New York, accusing George of cowardice.

"Think what dangers hang around free speech if a thoughtless word, a foolish sentence or an unguarded utterance may, after months or years, be said to cause another's death," Darrow said. He dissected the case, criticized Gary's conduct of the trial, and finished with a flourish.

"I have my dreams of a future time when injustice and oppression will be banished from the earth; when hunger, cold and want with tattered rags, and hollow eyes, shall keep pace no more with luxury and wealth," Darrow said. He compared the anarchists to the abolitionists, and especially John Brown: "The image of a brave heroic man, standing calmly on the scaffold waiting for the cause he loved so well."

"It has been ever thus," Darrow wrote. "Sometime, when the bitter feelings of the hour are gone, justice touched with pity and regret will look down on Chicago's barbarous feast of blood . . . and deal fairly by the memory of the death."[9]

The clash with George soured Darrow to the single-tax cause. When George came to Chicago in 1889 to speak at a gathering of the American Tariff Reform League, Darrow joined those who foiled his efforts to dominate the proceedings. In his turn at the rostrum, Darrow assailed his former hero. The solution to the country's economic inequities was not the single tax but free trade, Darrow said, and his ringing denunciation of Republican economic policy won him wide notice, even if the next day's *Tribune* did refer to him as "Charles" Darrow.

He was, he later conceded, "oratorical" in those days. "Commerce has been the greatest civilizer of the earth; it has called into existence the ship with her white wings and throbbing heart, and sent her laden with her freight of human souls to penetrate the mists and darkness hanging over unknown lands; it has made a chart of the trackless seas and over them its pioneers have traveled to the darkest corners of the globe with the first glad tiding of the coming morn," he said. "It has carried the civilization, literature, art and religion of one land and showered these like the dews of heaven to coax forth the flowers of light and life from the moldy and decaying superstitions of the past."

The Republican Party's support for a protectionist tariff was blocking that white-winged ship of throbbing heart, Darrow said. And it enriched the master at the expense of the workingman. "What force during these years of plenty has been tearing the wife from the workman's home and his children from school? It is the greed of those whom your unjust laws have made rich and great that is sending fathers, husbands and brothers to the street and filling up the factories with the mother and the tender child," he said. "In the name of humanity, has not property been protected quite enough? Shall we not do something for the poor and the weak?"

Years later, Darrow acknowledged that he had drowned "such ideas as I had" in "a cloud of sounding metrical phrases." But to his immense satisfaction, the reaction to his speech equaled that given George. The *Herald* was among the papers that praised him. "Darrow has a strong, clear voice, a good presence, and will take front rank among the orators of Chicago," it declared. The speech marked him as a comer, and journalists started paying attention to the "scholarly young lawyer."

"Never again have I felt that exquisite thrill of triumph," Darrow recalled. But he was not content; he yearned to convert ideas to action. He and Lloyd explored a scheme to buy the *Chicago Times* and provide the city with a radical labor voice. And he had been in Chicago for but a short while when he told his socialist friend Schilling: "What ought to be done now is to take a man like Judge Altgeld; first elect him mayor of Chicago, then governor of Illinois."[10]

Of Darrow's mentors, John Peter Altgeld had the most vivid personality and the most lasting impact. "He was the first man to know there was a Clarence Darrow," Darrow said.

Altgeld was the son of German immigrants who had settled in Ohio. At the age of sixteen he enlisted in the Union Army and after the war worked as a laborer and schoolteacher while studying law at night. He came to Chicago in 1875, made his fortune in real estate, and was elected judge. Altgeld was shy and diffident, but well read, ambitious, and intense. "His character was that of the philosopher, of the seer, of the dreamer, of the idealist" yet "there was mixed with that . . . the practical touch of the politician," said Darrow. "He knew how to play to those cheap feelings which the politician uses to inspire the vulgar mob."

Altgeld's political success was all the more notable for his alien disposition. He had a German accent, short-cropped nappy hair, and a bit of a harelip hidden beneath his beard. He was a congenital outsider, attuned to the difficulties faced by the workingmen hauled into his court. He developed a following in the immigrant wards and trade unions and, after publishing his judicial philosophy in the book that had caught Darrow's attention in Ashtabula, was embraced by liberals too. But Altgeld was no dreamy socialist; in practice he could be ruthless. "I want power, to get hold of the handle that controls things," he told Schilling. "When I do, I will give it a twist." On the mantel in his library was a bust of Minerva, the Roman goddess of wisdom. But there was also a bust of Augustus Caesar.

Darrow had called on Altgeld soon after arriving in Chicago. They were compatible politically and shared a contempt for political leaders who, as Altgeld put it, were "moral cowards, following the music wagon of their times." Here was an Amirus, but with courage, steel, and the knack of making money. "It will always be a source of pride to me that I knew him . . . that there never was a time that I did not love and follow him," Darrow recalled. He adopted Altgeld's blend of passion and calculation. The judge was "absolutely honest in his ends and equally as unscrupulous in the means he used to attain them," Darrow said, admiringly. "He would do whatever would serve his purpose when he was right. He'd use all the tools of the other side—stop at nothing."

One of Altgeld's enemies was Judge Gary, the man who hanged the Haymarket anarchists, and their feud had long-lasting consequences for Darrow. The hard feelings stemmed from their political differences, but also from Altgeld's investments in real estate. He had purchased a building along the Chicago River, only to have its value damaged by the city's construction of a bridge. After consulting with the city attorney, Altgeld agreed to have experts testify and abide by a jury's verdict.

Mayor John Roche, however, was a political foe of the city attorney. Two mischievous members of the mayor's staff—John Green and Clarence Knight—arrived at the courtroom, where they suggested that Judge Altgeld was using improper influence. Altgeld lost his temper, jumped to his feet, and, in a confrontation that made headlines as far away as New York, waved his fist and called Green "a damned liar!" Altgeld won the case, but was fined $100 and publicly humiliated for his outburst. And when an appellate panel reversed his victory he sent a seething letter to the judges, one of whom was Gary.

Altgeld first took revenge on Roche, a Republican who ran for reelection against Democrat DeWitt Cregier in 1889. Altgeld spent some

$5,000 to distribute a campaign leaflet, topped by Cregier's name, that listed Democratic and Republican candidates and identified them as an "anti-machine" ticket. Enough Republicans were fooled into voting for the slate to cost Roche his job.[11]

Knight was Altgeld's next victim. In June, Cregier fired the ten-year veteran of the city legal staff. "Judge Altgeld was after my scalp," Knight told reporters. The new assistant counsel was the unknown C. S. Darrow, who had campaigned for Cregier and been rewarded with an obscure position—special assessment attorney—at City Hall. His promotion to a $5,000-a-year job caught the press by surprise. "Mr. Darrow is of too recent establishment in Chicago to be widely known, but in so far as he has made a record here it all seems to be creditable," the *Daily News* reported. "Almost from the time of his arrival he has signalized himself . . . in the sessions of all societies and bodies convened for the discussion of social and political doctrine . . . He sealed his great serviceability to the Democratic Party by some excellent work on the stump."[12]

Darrow profited from his time at City Hall, learning municipal law, advising Mayor Cregier, and obtaining a first-rate education in the wild and blighted habitudes of the city's politics. "A rare conglomeration of city fathers ruled Chicago in the Nineties," Carter Harrison Jr., a five-term mayor, would recall. They were "a low-browed, dull-witted, base-minded gang of plug-uglies, with no outstanding characteristic beyond an unquenchable lust for money."[13]

Altgeld and Darrow were joined in Cregier's camp—at least for a time, since things were always shifting as the boys chased the better deal—by the city's gambling kingpin, Michael Cassius "King Mike" McDonald, corrupter of cops and public officials, and the boss of the city's vice district, Joseph "Chesterfield Joe" Mackin, fresh from Joliet Prison. With them were aspiring scoundrels like Michael "Hinky Dink" Kenna and John "Bathhouse" Coughlin, a Laurel-and-Hardy pair destined for fame as the "lords of the Levee," the downtown sin sector. Kenna, a spry, poker-faced little wizard, ran the Workingman's Exchange, a saloon and gambling den that became the headquarters of the First Ward political organization. In return for a cut of the action, he arranged police protection for the pimps and barkeeps, and in return for votes on Election Day found tramps a place to flop. Coughlin was "a rubber"—a masseur at the Turkish baths—who graduated to the exalted status of alderman.

He was known for his elocution and unique dishabille—he wore Prince Albert coats of billiard-cloth green, plaid and mauve vests, lavender trousers, pink kid gloves, and gleaming yellow pumps. Kenna and Coughlin were a team, and they followed the advice of Senator Billy Mason, who told Bathhouse, "You and Mike stick to th' small stuff. There's little risk and in the long run it pays a damned sight more." For many years they hosted the annual First Ward balls, garish events at which gamblers, pols, saloon-keepers, cops, and prostitutes joined in a nightlong carousal of dance, drink, and rapine.

Making his way in this Gomorrah, Darrow steered clear of the worst offenses. He drew up ordinances, crafted legal opinions that upheld the city's power to regulate guns and public utilities, and advanced Chicago's right to condemn private property and annex land for civic improvements, such as the Columbian Exposition, the upcoming world's fair. He prevailed in a weeklong trial defending the city in a $200,000 lawsuit filed by Warren Springer, a landowner whose property was devalued by municipal street work. He helped settle a carpenters' strike. And when a politically connected German American police captain named Herman Schluetter gunned down an organizer of the secret Celtic society Clan Na Gael in early 1890, raising ethnic tensions to dangerous levels, the mayor and the officer turned to Darrow for advice. Darrow counseled Cregier, as well, when the mayor was charged with selling police protection to downtown bookies. And the public was appreciative when Darrow hauled the venal streetcar baron Yerkes into court for failing to keep his conveyances heated in Chicago's frigid winter.

Amid the general mediocrity of the Cregier administration, Darrow won good reviews. "The appointment of CS Darrow to his present position by Mayor Cregier covers a multitude of sins of other appointments," one journalist reported. "Darrow is able, fearless, independent with a fine sense of political honor and integrity, and with all his merit possesses a modesty that overshadows the whole."

Darrow was lucky, as well. His boss, the corporation counsel, became ill and took an extended leave, and Darrow was placed in charge of all the city's legal affairs. By the spring of 1890—three years after his arrival in Chicago—he was a star, mentioned as a candidate for high office, and hosting strategy meetings of Cregier's political organization. His rise, said the *Inter Ocean*, was "almost phenomenal." In the summer of 1890, his friends launched a "boom" for Darrow in the Second District race for Congress. It was snuffed by the need to name an Irishman and give ethnic balance to the ticket. The *Tribune* got his name wrong again ("Charles Sumner Darrow"), but mourned his defeat.[14]

Darrow earned his first unfavorable bout of publicity after undertaking a clandestine assignment on Altgeld's behalf in 1891. U.S. senators were elected by state legislatures in that era, and the voters had sent 101 Democrats, 100 Republicans, and three independent populists to Springfield. Most expected that the populists would ultimately give Democrat John Palmer the required absolute majority. But the balloting dragged on for weeks, with Democratic newspapers exhorting the "Immortal 101" to stand by Palmer "until the last ballot."

In February, Darrow took the train to Springfield, where he quietly urged Palmer to withdraw and tried to persuade the populists to anoint Altgeld. "C. S. Darrow . . . has made himself famous," the *Chicago Post* announced, after news of the mission leaked. His attempt "to break the solid Democratic front and to defeat Palmer" was seen as "treachery" and "despicable conduct." In an editorial, the *Herald* called on Cregier to fire the upstart.

The storm passed and, on the 154th ballot, Palmer was elected. But the episode did not dim Altgeld's resolve, and he set out to be governor. He barnstormed the state and impressed the Democracy with his willingness to spend his own money to get elected, while Darrow, Schilling, and other lieutenants assembled a coalition of immigrant laborers, silk-stocking liberals, bucket-house gamblers, and socialist dreamers. Speaking for the good people, the *Tribune* publisher Joseph Medill labeled Altgeld a "jesuitical little socialistic demagogue," but in 1892 he defeated a Republican incumbent and became the state's first Democratic governor since before the Civil War.[15]

As Darrow rocketed through Chicago's legal and political ranks, his social and intellectual appetites soared. He settled Jessie and Paul in a new home on Vincennes Avenue but roamed the city without her. "When he became a big figure in a big city, their interests became different," his son Paul recalled. Jessie was loyal; she skimped on her own clothes and jewelry so that Darrow could dress well. While she stayed home, Darrow doffed his coat and danced to "Annie Rooney" at the annual picnic of the Cook County Democracy; partied with the University of Michigan alumni society; led the city law department's baseball team in a contest against the county clerks; and judged the sailing races at the Fox Lake Yacht Club regatta. He began, as well, a dangerous flirtation with a young stenographer in the city law office, Katherine Leckie.

When Mayor Cregier lost his bid for reelection, Altgeld called on William Goudy, an old friend and business associate, and got Darrow his position in the legal office of the Chicago & North Western Railway Company. As a member of the Iroquois Club, an organization of upscale Democrats, Darrow joined Goudy, Altgeld, and others at swank dinners and receptions, making friends with fellow strivers like lawyer Stephen Gregory, Judge Edward Dunne, a young banker named W. W. Catlin, and Judge William Barnum, whose daughter Gertrude would become a lifelong adorer. The "Iroquois club never does anything by halves," the *Tribune* reported. For its tenth-anniversary dinner, in 1891, the club imported thousands of American Beauty and La France roses, filled two stupendous punch bowls with liquor, ice, and fruit, and decorated its dining room with relics from the Custer massacre. The club's leaders, dressed in buckskin and feather headdresses, welcomed guests to a dinner of oysters, caviar, lobster salad, "pate of prairie chicken aux truffles," partridge, salmon, and boar. Many of the "Iroquois braves" were also members of the Sunset Club, an organization of "genial and tolerant fellows" that met each fortnight for debates on social and political issues. Catlin drew up a "declaration of principles" that included "No By-Laws . . . No Bores . . . No Preaching . . . No Dead Beats."

Darrow had found success. Like many in his generation in those days of periodic panics, when banks and businesses failed, he feared the snares of poverty and recognized the benefit of working for a wealthy corporation. His avidity disturbed some of his compatriots in progressive politics. Jane Addams had opened the Hull House social settlement in the West Side slums of Chicago in 1889. She and the other refined young ladies who came to do good works in the ghetto joined Darrow on many liberal causes—most notably the landmark bill that limited child labor, established an eight-hour day for women working in factories, and banned the harmful sweatshops that exploited immigrants. Darrow was the bill's advocate in Springfield, and his lobbying helped get it passed over the opposition of the state's manufacturing interests. He was also the lawyer whom the settlements turned to when a young man from the ghetto got in trouble with the law. But Addams recalled that Darrow was also "interested very much in advancing his own career in his profession—and in the financial side" during their early years in Chicago. She remembered "having to go among my friends and acquaintances, with my hand out, helping to raise funds to pay some of the big fees that Mr. Darrow demanded."[16]

That was Chicago. The dollar ruled. The wealthiest citizens set the city's standards from quiet offices high above the factory floor, or in their splendid drawing rooms. The great newspapers, and their editors, were fiercely conservative. The "good people" sang psalms on Sundays, equipped the local militia with ten-barreled Gatling guns to mow down striking workers, and launched crusades to close down the saloons. "These were church people who had grown rich on running grist mills, plumbing factories, piano factories; they were managers of dry-goods stores, and proprietors of elevators and wholesale candy houses," said Edgar Lee Masters, another young lawyer drawn to the city. "These were the specimens of odious respectability and . . . hypocrisy."

But if avarice ranked among Darrow's attributes, it did not supplant compassion. When he was confronted by a hard-luck case, it tortured him to think he might help and had not. It took nerve to cross the social divide, yet Darrow did. There was little to be gained by striving to ease the dreary lives of the working class, yet Darrow did. Respectable folks frowned at those who spoke on behalf of anarchists, Irish and Russian revolutionaries, and foreign-born workers, yet Darrow did. Trouble found the man who pleaded for trade unions and women's suffrage, yet Darrow did. He seemed to go out of his way to vex the people and institutions that bestowed wealth. While employed at the railroad he joined the crusade to regulate the sweatshops, and another to give the public control of gas and electric utilities. He electrified a crowd of radicals at the Central Music Hall with his call for a revolution in Russia. And at the Sunset Club, Darrow spoke out against capital punishment, scolding his wealthy colleagues for their indifference when a young African American lad was executed.

"The State of Illinois erected a scaffold in the City of Chicago, and they led up its steps a poor, weak, ignorant boy, a child of African descent; of that race which has in all ages received persecution and cruelty . . . a young boy who . . . had never known the pressure of a kindly hand, or the tones of a gentle voice," Darrow said. "The State of Illinois laid its hands upon this boy but once, and then it strangled him to death."[17]

Darrow spoke out for reform of marriage laws and shocked respectable Chicago by taking the case of Sarah Higgins, who was sued for infidelity by her wealthy husband. Walter Higgins had hired detectives to trail his wife, and they collected irrefutable evidence. But Darrow mounted a dogged defense of her right to happiness, charging Walter with adultery and cruelty.

"What wonder if this woman's feet had gone astray, if she had wandered into the broad road leading to destruction! What wonder if she, heart sore and weary, had fallen by the wayside! She, a loving little woman . . . neglected by her husband and left alone when her baby was born while he was drinking wine with an actress," Darrow said. "Can the court blame her, can any one condemn her if she sought for sympathy or yearned for the glance of affection her husband denied her? Who shall say that her act of sin, her first fall, was totally without excuse?"

Tears streamed down Darrow's cheeks. Sarah sobbed. Every woman in the courtroom wept. "The male portion of the audience could not but be affected and even Judge Tuley turned his head away and shaded his face with his hand," the *Times* reported. Walter Higgins's attorney saw where things were going and took his client aside. They stopped the trial and negotiated a settlement. Walter admitted to desertion and promised to pay alimony. And Sarah Higgins was granted the divorce.[18]

GOUDY'S SUDDEN DEATH, in the spring of 1893, propelled Darrow in even more radical directions. That week he wrote his friends, urging them to attend the upcoming meeting of the Chicago Law Club. Before the assembled lawyers and judges of Chicago, he was going to confront Judge Gary.

When Altgeld was elected, hopes had soared in liberal circles that the governor would pardon the three remaining imprisoned anarchists. Many of those who had argued for clemency—Lloyd and Darrow and Schilling among them—were Altgeld's allies. Darrow pushed Altgeld and was surprised by the cool response. "I am going over the record carefully and if I conclude these Anarchists ought to be freed I will free them," the governor told his protégé. "But make no mistake—if I do it I will be a dead man politically."[19]

"I expected that Altgeld would do something about the Anarchists right away," Darrow recalled. "But six months went by and he had not done a thing. I was pretty much disgusted."

Then fortune gave the anarchists a gift: Gary chose to publish a long defense of his conduct in the *Century* magazine. He had grown prickly over the years, as critics skewered his performance. The anarchists had been "rightly punished, not for opinions, but for horrid deeds," Gary wrote. The dead men were motivated by base "envy" of "people whose condition in life was better than their own."

Darrow knew that Gary's brief would fan Altgeld's anger. With all his other striking qualities, Altgeld was a hater, and "the truth was, he hated Gary," Darrow said. And so Darrow drafted a counterargument that would serve as a prospectus for a pardon and got himself on an upcoming Law Club program. "My Dear Lloyd . . . I am to read a paper to the law club on Judge Gary's article," Darrow wrote his friend. "Judge Gary (high executioner) will be there and the debate will perhaps be lively."[20]

Lively, yes. "The venerable judge himself sat upon Mr. Darrow's left and listened to . . . the outspoken criticisms," the *Tribune* reported.

"One day, when the fierce heat is dead and the public mind regains its poise, we will calmly look back upon the tragedy and wish it might be blotted out," Darrow said. "Sometime, while we will deplore the methods of these men, we will recognize that not one of them would have inflicted pain on any one who lives, except they thought that they were lessening the sum of human sorrow by their act."

"One day, let us hope ere long, we will call back to liberty" the three imprisoned anarchists, he said, "and wish that we might call the dead back from their graves as well."

Gary was unrelenting. Darrow was "a young man of generous feeling," but obviously "the victim of a dangerous sentimentalism," the *Journal* reported. The "venerable judge . . . stood firm as a rock against the enemies of social order."[21]

Darrow now returned to work at City Hall for Mayor Carter Harrison, who had just won another term (his fifth) as mayor and needed a skilled litigant in the counsel's office. Harrison had been lured from retirement by the opportunity to serve as the "World's Fair Mayor" and preside over the Columbian Exposition and the lovely White City that had been built on the lakeshore. President Cleveland came to the May 1 dedication, among the first of the 27 million visitors who would walk the Court of Honor; visit the mammoth, electrically lit exhibition halls; ride the stunning new amusement—the Ferris wheel—on the Midway Plaisance; and enjoy performers like Harry Houdini, Buffalo Bill, and Scott Joplin. One of Darrow's first assignments was to open the fair on Sundays. Darrow was a foe of Sabbath closing laws, and there were political considerations as well: laborers and factory hands worked a six-day week and would miss the fun if the fair were closed on their day off.

Darrow took part in the celebration, strolled the grounds, and spoke at a lakefront park during the "Labor Congress"—one of many thematic gatherings held at the exposition. He especially loved the circuslike atmosphere of the Midway. The Vincennes Avenue house was close by, and the Darrows often opened their home to out-of-town guests. He was busy that summer, finishing up some legal work for the railroad and working on the Sunday closings issue when Altgeld, without warning, pardoned the anarchists, igniting a volcanic reaction.[22]

On the evening of June 26, Samuel Fielden, Oscar Neebe, and Michael Schwab emerged from the stone portal of the penitentiary at Joliet, free men. Altgeld's pardon message was no lofty treatise on justice: it was a scathing, eighteen-thousand-word attack on Judge Gary. "If he had done it differently, he might have gotten away with it better," Darrow would recall. "But that bitter hatred of his got mixed up in it . . . He played right into their hands."[23]

Gary, said Altgeld, had appointed a biased bailiff—a man determined that the anarchists should hang—to supervise the selection of a jury. Gary had approved the seating of tainted jurors, including a relative of one of the dead policemen. Gary had frustrated the defense with unfair rulings. Gary had condemned the defendants without evidence of ties to the bomb thrower. "There was no case against them," Altgeld wrote. The men had been convicted, imprisoned, and executed by "a jury prejudiced to start with [and] a judge pressing for conviction . . . amid the almost irresistible fury."[24]

It was a profile in rancor, but also in courage. In pardoning the three defendants, "Governor Altgeld has committed political suicide," said the *New York Times.* "It reveals him either as an enemy to the safeguards of society, or as a reckless demagogue."[25] So it went, and went for weeks, in Chicago, Philadelphia, Washington, and other cities. "I was . . . bred to fear him," Henry L. Mencken, twelve years old that summer, would recall. "What I gathered from my elders . . . was that Altgeld was a shameless advocate of rapine and assassination, an enemy alike to the Constitution and the Ten Commandments—a bloody and insatiable Anarchist."[26]

Darrow, Lloyd, and Schilling tried to battle back. They published a pamphlet on Altgeld's behalf, and Darrow scolded his colleagues at the Sunset Club.

"When you gentlemen want something, it is liberty," he told an audience of two hundred lawyers, ministers, and businessmen. "When some man tells you you're wrong, that some other way is better, that is license. And you immediately apply a dose of hemp."[27]

Mayor Harrison was in a bind, for Gary was his friend. In September, Altgeld met with the mayor in an attempt to resolve their differences. But Harrison was immovable and before the day was out Darrow had announced his resignation, effective immediately. He joined three former judges—Lorin Collins, Adams Goodrich, and William Vincent—in a new law firm, with offices in the splendid Rookery building, one of the new "skyscrapers" made possible by the development of the elevator.

Altgeld didn't flinch. He set out to defeat Gary in the fall election, with Darrow as his instrument. "Altgeld has picked out his candidate to oppose Judge Gary; his nominee is C. S. Darrow," the *Tribune* reported. "It was he who prepared the brief on which Gov. Altgeld's attack on the courts and on Judge Gary was based. He entertains strong socialistic views and is altogether a man after Altgeld's own heart."

The *Journal* portrayed Darrow as "an able and a dangerous young man" and noted the alacrity with which Darrow had accepted work for the Chicago & North Western, "one of the monopolies he had inveighed against when younger." Chicago was familiar with that kind of opportunism; what puzzled the *Journal* editors was why Darrow, having landed a cushy position with the railroad, had not stayed there. Most men who "pose as Socialists" abandon such views when "they work their way into a lucrative connection with the established order," the paper noted. Darrow had not.

Hard times were at hand that fall. Railroads failed, the stock market crashed, and the Panic of 1893 gripped the country; in Chicago, it busted banks and trading firms and threw 100,000 men out of work. The corridors of City Hall were filled with the homeless, who sought warmth and a dry floor on which to sleep. Darrow served on a civic committee to find jobs and food for the armies of unemployed and represented Austin W. Wright, whose commodity trading firm was one of those that went bust. He worked as Altgeld's lieutenant and helped craft a Democratic "unity" slate for that fall's elections. But Gary coasted to reelection in a year when security was a top concern. When asked why they lost, Democratic leaders replied, "Altgeld and Gary."

It was a bad year in which to defend anarchists; especially after Patrick Prendergast rang the mayor's doorbell, and shot Carter Harrison dead.[28]

Chapter 3

PRENDERGAST

The hand of Him who made him shook.

Carter Harrison was murdered on the final weekend of the great Exposition. More than 100,000 citizens filed by the glass-topped coffin at City Hall, and a half million lined the mayor's funeral route on All Saints' Day. Dirge-playing bands, militia units, and tens of thousands of official mourners—Darrow among them—conveyed the dead chieftain to his resting place. On the back of the hearse was a wreath from Annie Howard, the twenty-five-year-old fiancée of the sixty-eight-year-old mayor; they had planned to marry that month.

Harrison had spoken at a closing ceremony for the fair that Saturday. He was home in his Italianate mansion, dozing in a chair, when Prendergast came to the door. A maid summoned the mayor, and as he entered the foyer his assassin raised a revolver and opened fire. Harrison staggered back, his hand over his heart, and fell to the floor. "This is death," he murmured. Prendergast exchanged gunshots with a coachman, then took the streetcar to the Des Plaines Street police station, and surrendered to the astonished desk sergeant.

The economic hard times, the furor over the anarchists, and the mayor's assassination seemed to join together in one awful, portentous hour, spoiling the glow of the fair. The newspapers insisted that Prendergast be hanged. So, even, did the prisoners in the Cook County jail, who shouted "Lynch the killer!" as the mayor's cortege passed by.[1] But on November 18, the *Herald* published a letter from Darrow, resisting the rush to judgment.

"If any further evidence were needed to show that man had his origin in the brute creation, the conduct and utterances of the public in reference to the shooting of our mayor has furnished that proof," Darrow wrote. "It seems as if the whole community has gone mad at the sign of blood.

"Most men admit that the prisoner was insane and yet lawyers, doctors, merchants and men of all classes are almost unanimous in saying that, whether sane or insane, the wretched being ought to hang," said Darrow.

"It may not matter much to the unfortunate prisoner or even to his mother and brother whether he shall live or die; but the spectacle of a civilized community pitilessly killing a crazy man will furnish an example of cruelty and fury that in some way must bear evil fruit," he warned. "We cannot sow the wind without reaping the whirlwind."[2]

William Seward could not have said it better. Prendergast was a slight twenty-five-year-old newspaper deliveryman with red hair, crossed eyes, and many delusions. He told the police that he shot the mayor because Harrison had reneged on a promise to name him his counsel. He was known to Darrow and others as a crank who showed up at single-tax-club meetings and sent incoherent postcards to public officials. He had been spotted banging his head against the trees in Humboldt Park, roaming Wisconsin in a blanket, telling farmers about his correspondence with the pope, and sitting in church, mouth agape, head lolling back and eyes rolling. "Insanity was written all over the man," the Harrison family's newspaper, the *Chicago Times*, reported. It cited a police superintendent, who said the killer was "mad as a March hare."[3]

Nevertheless, the state moved swiftly to trial, seeking the death penalty. The prosecution was led by A. S. Trude, one of the city's foremost criminal lawyers, who was appointed as a special counsel in a deal quietly brokered by the *Tribune* company. Darrow closely followed the proceedings, seeking out and talking to the medical witnesses, and tracking the testimony. Two expert doctors who had been hired by the state to declare that Prendergast was competent to stand trial instead declared him insane. "That poor devil is crazy," said Dr. Archibald Church, a specialist in mental illness at the Illinois State Hospital. But Trude earned his pay. The jury took but an hour to reach a verdict. Prendergast was condemned to death.[4]

Darrow took Jessie and Paul to southern California during the holidays, where they visited friends and took in the Tournament of Roses.

And he continued to act as Altgeld's man in the Democratic Party's labyrinthine councils. The well-loved Mayor Harrison had imposed a kind of order on the city's politics, and the process of replacing him commenced, one week after his death, with a riot in the crepe-draped council chambers. The police were called to break up the "demonical" clerks and aldermen, who wrestled one another to the floor and swung chairs, canes, and spittoons.[5]

Then, in February, Chicago was startled by news that two of the city's rising legal stars—Darrow and Stephen S. Gregory—had taken command of the Prendergast case and would ask the courts for a new trial. Gregory was a brilliant lawyer who would one day be elected president of the American Bar Association. He was prematurely balding, hailed from Wisconsin, and called himself a reformer. Had Darrow more respect for convention, his career may well have mirrored Gregory's. "He was emotional and sympathetic, he was devoted to the principles of liberty and always fought for the poor and oppressed," Darrow recalled. "In spite of all this, he had a fine practice."[6]

They meshed well: the solemn, precise Gregory an expert in case work and tactics, and Darrow the master of stirring arguments. They began by alleging that Trude had used unqualified witnesses during the first trial. Meanwhile, Prendergast roamed the courtroom, interrupted his lawyers, and mumbled and muttered and growled. At one point he sat down beside Trude and asked, "You have no personal feeling against me, have you?" When the man who sought to have him hanged said no, Prendergast looked pleased and said, "Well, I have no enmity against you, either." In his closing remarks, Trude accused Prendergast of feigning mental illness. "What we need here is less mercy and more justice," the prosecutor told the judge.

On the afternoon of February 19, Darrow began the final argument. He spoke for three hours that day, and two hours the next morning. "Human life is cheap in Cook County, but the price has not been set by the criminals. It has been set by men in high places. From doctors, from lawyers, from preachers goes up the cry 'Hang him! Hang him!' " Darrow said.

It was Darrow's first summation in a major criminal case. As he would throughout his career, he mixed doses of philosophy and poetry with the law. Not for the last time, he argued that men's actions are determined not by choice, but by the unshakable influences of heredity and environment.

"The only reason why we have a right to punish any individual is because that individual has willfully and conscientiously done wrong," he said. "Unless this boy is sane he did not do this act. It was done by Him who made the boy."

Darrow cherished the fatalistic sentiments of *The Rubáiyát of Omar Khayyám,* a collection of archaic verse translated by Edward FitzGerald that was popular in the Gilded Age. From it he took the analogy with which he closed his remarks.

The killer was only God's flawed crockery, Darrow told the judge. "The hand of Him who made him shook."[7]

It was a plea, said the *Post*, "so masterful, so feelingly made and so pathetic that during the delivery the courtroom did not echo a sound save that of the pleader's voice." Masterful, maybe, but not persuasive. On February 23, Judge Theodore Brentano rejected the motion for a new trial and set March 23 as the day for the hanging.[8]

Darrow and Gregory asked the state supreme court for a stay of execution. Two days before Prendergast was scheduled to die, the Supreme Court turned them down. Darrow gathered signatures on a petition from a half dozen liberal judges, and took a train to Springfield. Altgeld was out of the state and not likely to invite another roasting by pardoning Prendergast, but Darrow hoped to persuade Lieutenant Governor John Gill to grant a reprieve. Stretching the truth, Darrow told Gill that "Mr. Trude, the prosecutor, has told me repeatedly that this man ought not to be hanged and that he, himself, would interfere before the execution could take place." Now Trude was traveling, Darrow told Gill, and could not be reached.

Later, Trude complained that "Darrow has perverted, to my injury, private talks we had in the judge's room." It was an early demonstration of Darrow's willingness to dispose of the customary ethical standards—like accuracy or confidentiality—when a client was facing unjust punishment, especially in a capital case. This time, it was counterproductive. Even if Darrow had not misrepresented Trude's remarks, he had cast the prosecutor in an embarrassing light and snuffed out any hope that the state might accept a deal. When he returned from his travels, Trude worked with renewed vigor to ensure that Prendergast was executed.

Gill declined to grant the reprieve. Brand Whitlock, an aide to Altgeld who had taken Prendergast's side, remembered meeting Darrow that day. The lawyer's face showed fatigue and "world-weariness," Whitlock said. But on learning that Whitlock was an ally, "there suddenly appeared a smile as winning as a woman's" and a greeting with "the timber of human sympathy and the humor of a peculiar drawl."

"Well, you're all right then," Darrow said. As he waited for the train back to Chicago, they discovered a mutual passion for literature, and Whitlock gave Darrow one of his unpublished short stories to read.

Gregory was more successful. He went to the North Side criminal court of his college classmate and former partner Judge Arthur Chetlain and argued that Prendergast had become insane *since* his trial and so, under a little-noted Illinois statute, was entitled to have his sentence reviewed, yet again, by a jury. Just before midnight on Good Friday, less than twelve hours before Prendergast was to hang, Chetlain granted a reprieve.[9]

Harrison's sons—Preston and Carter Jr.—had taken over their father's newspaper. Mindful of the family's feelings, Darrow had made a courtesy call on young Carter before entering the case. The *Times* had given extensive coverage to the trial, much of it fair, as long as Prendergast was making a steady march toward the gallows. Now the brothers erupted. The *Times* slighted Gregory as a common bankruptcy lawyer who used methods "unworthy of a shyster." And Darrow was a hypocrite, "a regular Don Quixote, always chasing windmills and ever ready to remove imaginary wrongs, without being able to remove the beam out of his own eye." He was a "yellow bilious-looking man with a rugged homely face and hair as straight as an Indian," the *Times* reported, "sanguine, fond of notoriety, having about as much regard for the conventionalities as a heathen." Not for the last time, a reporter noted Darrow's sartorial defects. "He wears his clothes as if they had been thrown on him, and they always look as if they had known him a long time."

The Harrisons saved the worst for Judge Chetlain. They began publishing "toothsome . . . news morsels" alleging that the judge, who lived downtown in a bachelor apartment, had fathered two children with a young Swedish servant girl, whom he had married in secret and stashed in an immigrant neighborhood on the outskirts of the city. "It was an out-of-town wedding," the paper said dryly, after doing the math in a front-page story and suggesting that "blonde . . . pretty buxom Lottie" was pregnant on her nuptial day. The rest of the city's newspapers picked up the story, and Chetlain had to be restrained from assaulting an editor. It no doubt came as a relief to the judge when Trude asked the courts to postpone the matter until Chetlain's term on the criminal branch of the county courts was over.[10]

Judge John B. Payne took over in June and put the "insanity trial" on a fast track. On June 20, they began. Prendergast sent a note up to the judge, claiming to be the Democratic Party's candidate for president. Payne put it aside and told the lawyers, "Daylight is burning, gentlemen."

Trude urged the jurors to rein in their sympathy. The assassin had a fine team of defense attorneys, blessed with "intelligence and cunning" and motivated by a thirst for notoriety, he said. "The more guilty of murder, the more foul and cruel that the murder is in its nature, the more green would be the laurels which would entwine themselves around the brows of these gentlemen who appear here."[11]

The defense called its doctors, who offered their opinions and read excerpts from the defendant's mad scribbling. On the trial's second day, Prendergast took the stand and, at the invitation of the defense, was examined by Judge Payne. At times the defendant was cheerful and helpful, at other times petulant.

"Where did you get the pistol?" the judge asked him.

"I can't answer that question. I do not consider it my duty," Prendergast replied.

"You killed Harrison. What more right have you to live than Mr. Harrison had?" the judge asked.

"I have a certain divine right," said Prendergast. It had been granted him, he told the judge, by St. Peter.[12]

The two sides ended a parade of forty-two witnesses and began final arguments on July 2. Darrow, again, closed for the defense. Spectators took every seat, jammed the aisles, and surrounded the judge's bench.

"I was one of those . . . following him to his last resting place," Darrow said of Mayor Harrison. "Could he speak to you today from his great heart and his charitable mind he would ask you to save the city that he loved . . . from the infamous disgrace of sending a lunatic to the scaffold."

Darrow's tribute to the mayor was received in "profound silence," the

Times reported. "Tears stood in the eyes of many as he paused at its close, overcome by deep feeling."

At the end of the allotted hour, Darrow brought his remarks to an end. "To lead this poor lunatic to the scaffold . . . would wreak infinite injury," he said. "There is no power on earth to tell how many hearts would be calloused, how many souls would be wrecked, how many blood stains would come upon the conscience of men."

Now, as in March, he blamed the Maker, not the vessel. "Here is Prendergast, the product of the infinite God, not of his own making," Darrow said. "He comes here for some inscrutable reason, the same as you and I, without his will, without his knowledge, because the infinite God of the infinite universe saw fit to make him as He willed. His fault is not the fault of Prendergast. It is the fault of the infinite power that made him the object you find today.

"I beseech of you, gentlemen, do not visit upon this poor boy the afflictions which God Almighty placed upon him for some inscrutable reason unknown to us.

"This poor, weak, misshapen vessel, I place in your protection and your hands," Darrow said. "I beg of you gentlemen take it gently, tenderly, carefully. Do not, I beseech you, do not break the clay, for though weak and cracked and useless it is the handiwork of the infinite God."[13]

The following morning, Judge Payne read his instructions to the jury. In less than two hours, it reached a verdict. Prendergast would die.

"Mr. Darrow's closing argument would have swept us all off our feet," said juror William Steinke, who admitted that some of his colleagues had been moved to tears. But the jury felt a duty to avenge the murdered mayor. "We felt that we could not be honest and still allow such an appeal to influence our decision."

Now began the grim last dance of lawyers in a capital case. Darrow and Gregory offered a motion for a new trial; it was denied. On July 11, Darrow took the train to Springfield, accompanied by attorney James Harlan, to see Altgeld. All three men knew the visit was useless, but the governor welcomed the two lawyers, joined them at dinner, and rode with them in a carriage around town. There was no changing his mind.

Darrow and Gregory tried federal court, but the judge declined to intervene. "Yes, it is all over," Darrow told the reporters as the courthouse emptied. "The country seems determined to hang an insane man and I guess we will have to allow it to do so." Prendergast went meekly to his death on Friday, July 13. Gregory was there to offer what comfort he could to the condemned man, but Darrow was not. It was all too horrid, and disheartening, and sad.[14]

The editors at the *Tribune* should have been pleased. Yet something marred their joy. The Harrisons had taken the side of striking workers in that year's industrial unrest and scored great circulation gains. The *Tribune*'s editor, Joseph Medill, viewed the mayor's sons as ingrates.

"It was the *Tribune* that prevented the insanity inquiry from being tried before a judge selected by the murderer's lawyers, and resulted in having the trial before a sterner and less sympathetic jurist. And it was the *Tribune*'s powerful special attorney who successfully prosecuted your father's murderer to the gallows," Medill wrote Carter Harrison Jr. "The assassin would never have been hung but for his work, supplemented by that of the *Tribune*."[15]

It was a revealing glimpse of how things were, and the powers that Darrow defied, in Chicago. Yet the truth was as stark as fresh dirt on a grave. The defense of Patrick Prendergast had been Darrow's first big criminal case. And he had lost the mad newsboy to the hangman's rope.

Chapter 4

POPULIST

Ghosts of the wicked city, the gold-crushed hungry hell.

As Darrow toiled to rescue crazy Patrick Prendergast, events outside the courthouse supplied an apt backdrop. Chicago was rocked by rage and anarchy, as federal troops and marshals battled mobs of unemployed and striking laborers in the violent climax of a nationwide workers' uprising. It was called the "Debs Rebellion," after Eugene Debs, whose American Railway Union was crushed by President Cleveland for its audacity and its leaders seized and jailed after bringing commerce to a standstill throughout most of the country.

Darrow had been shaken by the state's relentless insistence on killing Prendergast. Now he watched its army and its judges, deployed at the behest of corporations, quell the collective action of American workingmen. The experience left him angry and alienated. The idealist who had said, when he arrived in Chicago, that the "injustice of the world can only be remedied through law, and order and system" began to reconsider.

The Panic of 1893 had set events in motion by exposing the gap between the gilded lifestyles of the robber barons and the grinding, depersonalizing existence of the industrial workforce. The usually restrained labor leader, Sam Gompers, captured the militant mood in January 1894 at a rally in New York when he chanted: "Oh angels shut thine eyes / Let conflagration illumine the outraged skies! / Let red Nemesis burn the hellish clan / And chaos end the slavery of man!" There were strikes across the country, and spontaneous "armies of the Commonweal" comprised of out-of-work men, bankrupt farmers, and tramps marched on state capitals and Washington. On April 24, the *Times* broke away from its coverage of the Prendergast case to report that Kelly's Army was camping in Iowa, that Coxey's Army was heading toward Washington, and that the financial markets were quaking: "A wave of panic swept over the exchange . . . Stocks tumbled . . . Moneybags shuddered and resolved to swell their contributions to the support of the militia on the morrow. The Vanderbilts, the Goulds, the Huntingtons, the Pullmans and all the other plutocrats got home before dark, nor breathed they comfortably until they had double barred their doors and found refuge behind the solid masonry of their castles."[1]

Debs was a native of Terre Haute, Indiana, where he met early success as a local politician and railway union officer. He was tall, thin, and balding, indefatigable and brave. "There may have lived some time, some where, a kindlier . . . more generous man . . . but I have never known him," Darrow said. "He never felt fear. He had the courage of the babe who has no conception of the word." The labor movement was fragmented at the time, which allowed the railroads to pit rival occupations—engineers, firemen, switchmen, and the like—against one another. To resolve the problem, Debs launched the ARU in Chicago in 1893. It grew rapidly, especially after a successful strike against the Great Northern Railway.[2]

The union was countered by the General Managers' Association, headquartered in Chicago, through which two dozen railroads worked to cap wages and subdue their workers. A federal commission, charged with probing the causes of industrial unrest that summer, cited the GMA as an example of the "persistent and shrewdly devised plans of corporations" to "usurp" power in America. A strike at the Pullman works kindled the showdown. Its founder, George Pullman, had made his fortune designing, building, and operating commodious sleeping cars. Like many a self-made millionaire, he attributed his success to clean living and hard work; unlike many tycoons, he sought to give his employees an opportunity for both, by building a model town on the outskirts of Chicago. By 1893, some twelve thousand people lived in the tidy little city of Pullman. They could walk from work on safe, tree-shaded streets, past lawns and public parks, a library and theater and other civic amenities, to modern homes and tenements. But there were snakes in Pullman's Eden. Rents and utility bills were high, to pay Pullman's hefty stock dividends. Workers faced eleven-hour days. Immigrant religions were discouraged. The village church, police, newspaper, and elections were controlled by the company. Gardening, decorating, and music making were regulated. The residents knew that company "spotters" mingled among them, reporting undesirable behavior, and that their leases gave the company the power to evict troublemakers. There was no hospital, for this was a town for productive workers, not the sickly. Pullman was "un-American," the sociologist Richard Ely concluded. "It is benevolent well-wishing feudalism."

Pullman's workers rebelled during the Panic, when the company slashed wages—but not rents. "Great destitution and suffering prevails," the *Times* reported, "but the house rent to the Pullman company must be paid." Debs recognized the fragility of his young union and opposed hasty action, but his members voted to boycott trains bearing Pullman cars. Civic delegations and union officials trekked to Pullman, seeking to forestall a confrontation. "We have nothing to arbitrate," the company declared.

George Pullman later told the strike commission that the money he would have lost in arbitration was not what moved him. "The amount . . . would not cut any figure," he said. "It was the principle involved." So what remedies, the commission asked, did the workingman have? A firm "could work a great deal of injustice to the men; no doubt about that," Pullman vice president Thomas Wickes conceded. "But then it is a man's privilege to go to work somewhere else."

The ARU launched its boycott on June 26, 1894. Freight and passenger travel came to a halt from Pennsylvania to California. Some 150,000 men walked off the job, and tens of thousands of working-class Americans wore white ribbons as an act of solidarity. It was "The Greatest Strike in History," the *New York Times* announced, and coming as it did against a background of the Commonweal marches and violent strikes by miners and textile and iron workers, it thoroughly spooked the wealthy. "The struggle with the Pullman company has developed into a contest between the producing classes and the money power of the country," Debs said. The GMA officials agreed; they set up a war room, and looked to the White House for help.[3]

As THE RAILWAY workers cheered their success, Grover Cleveland met with his advisers. The president was a Democrat from New York, with broad support on Wall Street, whose most notable accomplishments were the deals he made with J. P. Morgan and other financiers to stabilize the currency. "I do not believe that the power and duty of the General Government ought to be extended to the relief of individual suffering," Cleveland said, when vetoing an emergency farm bill. "Federal aid in such cases encourages the expectation of paternal care on the part of the Government and weakens the sturdiness of our national character."[4]

Cleveland turned to Richard Olney, the attorney general, to handle the railway strike. Skilled and ruthless, Olney had left a job as counsel for one railroad and director of two others to join the cabinet. His sentiments can be gauged by a letter he wrote advising a railroad executive not to oppose the creation of the Interstate Commerce Commission. "The Commission . . . can be made of great use to the railroads," Olney noted. "It satisfies the popular clamor for a government supervision of railroads, at the same time that supervision is almost entirely nominal. Further, the older such a commission gets to be, the more inclined it will be found to take the business and railroad view of things. It thus becomes a sort of barrier between the railroad corporations and the people."

Olney named Edwin Walker, yet another railroad lawyer, as a "special counsel" for the justice department in Chicago. And Thomas Milchrist, the U.S. attorney, sat in on the meetings of the GMA, where he asked that the railroads "report any interference with mail trains." The attorney general was itching to intervene.[5] Federal judges Peter Grosscup and William Woods, abandoning any pretext of impartiality, helped the government draft a request for an injunction and swiftly approved it. They issued what came to be called the "Gatling gun on paper," ordering all persons to "refrain from interfering" with railroad traffic and banning anyone from coercing, inciting, or even "persuading" workers to strike. Olney was nothing if not bold; he based the government's argument on the Sherman Antitrust Act, which was enacted in 1890 to fight trusts and monopolies but now was employed to crush the union.

On the evening of July 2, U.S. marshal John Arnold informed Washington that he had gone out to the rail yards and read the injunction to the striking workmen, who "simply hoot at it." The thousands of "deputies" he had recruited—toughs and drunks paid by the railroads—could not clear the tracks. Special counsel Walker (who privately called Arnold's deputies "a mob . . . worse than useless") informed Olney that it was "of utmost importance that soldiers should be distributed at several points within the city." Cleveland gave his approval.

Debs had consistently appealed "to strikers everywhere to refrain from any act of violence," the strike commission would report. Until the U.S. Army marched in, in the early morning hours of Independence Day, things were relatively peaceful. But the soldiers were a provocation. And on July 4 the striking railway men were joined by thousands of the unemployed and industrial workers celebrating Independence Day, all in a giddy and often inebriated state. As the trains tried to move within protective cordons of troops, huge crowds gathered at the crossings, blocking progress with their bodies and tipping freight cars. The first boxcars were set aflame the next day as mobs of up to fifty thousand, by some estimates, massed along the tracks. That night, someone started a fire in the deserted grounds of the White City. Whipped by warm winds, the flames consumed the Exposition's buildings. On July 6, after a railroad employee shot two rioters, hundreds looted and burned seven hundred railcars in south Chicago. "It was pandemonium let loose, the fire leaping along for miles and the men and women dancing with frenzy," the *Inter Ocean* reported. On July 7 a contingent of Illinois militia fired into a threatening crowd, killing four and wounding dozens.

There was no evidence that the ARU organized or ordered the violence. But on July 10, with the propertied classes in full bay, the federal grand jury returned an indictment charging Debs and his men with criminal conspiracy. The union offices were raided, its records confiscated and leaders arrested. A week later, while out on bail, the union leaders were charged with contempt and jailed again. Their cells were rich with vermin, said Debs. Their jailor "showed me the bloody rope with which Prendergast had been hanged, and intimated with apparent glee . . . that the same fate awaited me."[6]

Liberals were stunned by the turn of events. Cleveland and Olney were Democrats, from the party of Jefferson and Jackson. "The Federal troops had broken Debs and his strike, and there was bitterness in the air, and poverty and misery about," Edgar Lee Masters recalled. Jane Addams was struck by "the barbaric instinct to kill, roused on both sides, the sharp division into class lines, with the resultant distrust." She saw Pullman as "a modern Lear," raging after being spurned by his ungrateful "children."

Darrow had been helping the striking workers, trying to rent a hall and organize a protest meeting, even as he battled to save Prendergast. He had witnessed some of the violence. "As I stood on the prairie watching the burning cars . . . I was only sad to realize how little pressure man could stand before he reverted to the primitive," he recalled. Debs and his men needed lawyers who would serve despite public censure. Stephen Gregory signed on and Henry Lloyd, who was friendly with Debs, recommended Darrow. "I knew that it would take all my time for a long period, with no compensation," Darrow remembered. Years later, he told a friend that he wanted to turn the union down, but that his conscience forbade it: "I couldn't get away with it—with myself." And so he enlisted in the cause.[7]

CLEVELAND HAD LAUNCHED a two-tracked legal assault on Debs and his men: the contempt proceeding, in which they were accused of violating the federal court's injunction banning anyone from "inciting" workers to strike, and a criminal case that charged the union with conspiring to stop the mails and to interfere with interstate commerce. The contempt case was called first, before Judge Woods. The closing arguments took place in late September. Darrow ripped into the prosecution, scolding U.S. attorney Milchrist for labeling Debs and his men "dastardly criminals" and cowards.

"There are various kinds of cowards," Darrow said. "It was not brave for this man Milchrist to stand in a court where accident has placed him and heap vituperation on these men who cannot reply. That is not bravery. . . ."

"I don't need to take lessons in professional ethics from you," Milchrist sputtered, leaping to his feet.

"You ought to take them from somebody," Darrow told him.

Darrow challenged the government's reliance on the Sherman Antitrust Act. "Restraint of trade" was the "evil meant to be aimed at," Darrow said. "If it had been the intention of Congress to include strikes it would have said so."

No one expected that Judge Woods would admit error and reverse his own ruling, but if Darrow had any hopes of keeping Debs out of jail, he tossed them when accusing Woods of abusing power. "Every man has a right to quit his employment if he wishes. He may advise others to quit theirs," Darrow said. "In the present state of industrial progress, capital is combined necessarily in large associations. Just as necessarily must labor be combined in large masses. So long as each keeps within its rights they must be left to fight it out, and no court by hastily issued order should disarm one of them on the field of battle."

Even the *Tribune* admitted that Darrow had made "an exceedingly able argument . . . important and exciting." But, as expected, Woods found Debs and the others guilty. A law passed to limit the depredations of corporate behemoths like the railroads was instead used to promote them. The Sherman law "was applied . . . against the men whom it was meant to protect," Darrow said, "and in favor of those against whom every provision of the act was directed."

Debs was sentenced to jail for six months, and Darrow traveled to Washington to make arrangements for an appeal to the U.S. Supreme Court. There, he was admitted to the Supreme Court bar. Members of Congress friendly to labor vouched for him, and the spectator pews of the old court chamber in the Capitol were filled with men and "magnificently-attired women, blazing with diamonds," the newspapers noted, who were there to catch a glimpse of the "smooth-faced barrister" defending the notorious Debs.

"There isn't much to tell about the matter," Darrow told a *Washington Post* reporter who had asked how things stood in Chicago. "The poor people side with Debs and the rich are against him. There is the situation in a nutshell. The philosophers and dreamers are on our side too; but they haven't much influence . . . The forces of the plutocracy are so strong as to be almost irresistible."[8]

THE MARTYRDOM OF Eugene Debs moved on to its next stage: the criminal conspiracy trial before Judge Grosscup.

Woods was, as Altgeld once said, a captive of the corporations; but Grosscup, even more so. "It is an outrage that a creature like Grosscup should be permitted to sit on the bench," Theodore Roosevelt would gripe after hearing one of the judge's rulings. Grosscup would ultimately step down amid charges that he traded favors with the railroads. In a speech in the spring of 1894, he had offered a glimpse of his beliefs when he denounced labor leaders as revolutionaries, intent on imposing "tyranny." The "higher laws of civilization and advanced manhood" demanded that "this shadow on independent individuality" should be "removed effectively and at once," Grosscup said. If not, it would "destroy the basis on which business . . . can be successful."

But in the criminal case Debs would face a jury, not just the judge. When the fight began in late January, Darrow strove to put the railroads, not Debs, on trial. It was not the union that met in secret or dispatched telegrams on a private wire, he told the jurors, it was the railroads. "The obstruction of the mails might have been the result of a conspiracy. But it is not the conspiracy of these men," he said of the defendants. "If there was a conspiracy it was on the part of the General Managers' Association, which desired to use the inconvenience of the public, and the feelings of sanctity for the mails, as a club to defeat the effort that was being made to better the condition of working men."

Debs and his men "published to all the world what they were doing. And in the midst of the excitement of a widespread strike they were never so busy but that they found time to counsel against violence," Darrow told the jury. "For this, they are brought into a court by an organization which uses the government as a cloak to its purpose."

Grosscup, in his rulings, leaned toward the government. But in doing so, he added to the jury's mounting sympathy for Darrow's underdogs. So, too, did the furtive actions of George Pullman, who was subpoenaed to appear, but dodged the federal marshal sent to serve him. In the *Chicago Post*, the Irish barman Martin Dooley, the fictional creation of columnist Peter Finley Dunne, had delighted in Pullman's skedaddling:

> "Gintlemin," says he, "I must be off," he says. "Go an' kill each other," he says. "Fight it out," he says. "Defind th' constitution," he says. "Me own is not of th' best," he says, "an' I think I'll help it be spindin' th' summer . . . on th' shores iv th' Atlantic ocean."

The *Tribune*, however, offered excuses for Pullman. "It is not strange that he should be unwilling to go on the stand and be questioned by Mr. Darrow," the editors sniffed. "It is not pleasant for a person who is at the head of a great corporation to be interrogated by persons unfriendly to him and who may put disagreeable inquiries to which he has to reply."

Indeed, the railroad executives who did testify, with their haughty manners and patchy memories, left a poor impression. And Walker blundered when he insisted that the ARU produce the minutes of its 1894 convention, which had been open to the public and would yield him little. Darrow responded by demanding the same information from the managers. "That was the knockout," said Theodore Debs, the defendant's brother. "The minutes . . . would have shown who the conspirators were." After Eugene Debs, in a trim gray suit, wearing gold spectacles and a boutonniere, made an effective appearance on the stand, the government folded. On February 12, Grosscup announced that he was stopping the trial because one of the jurors had taken sick. Darrow, confident of victory, urged Grosscup to appoint a substitute, but the judge refused. It was clear what the verdict would have been. When the jurors were discharged they gathered around Debs to shake his hand. "Debs, when this trial opened I was in favor of giving you five years," said one. "Now I am anxious to set you free."[9]

Debs did not have his freedom yet. The antagonists now trudged to Washington to argue the contempt case at the U.S. Supreme Court. In a rare appearance, Attorney General Olney himself took part, jousting with Darrow and the other defense lawyers in the oral arguments.

Darrow ended Debs's case with a spirited appeal. "When a body of 100,000 men lay down their implements of labor, not because their own rights have been invaded, but because the bread has been taken from the mouths of their fellows," he told the justices, "we have no right to say they are criminals." But his remarks had little effect on justices so famous for their retrograde decisions. On May 27 the Court ruled unanimously against Debs. "No wrong," it said, "carries with it legal warrant to invite as a means of redress the cooperation of a mob."

Debs had done no such thing. And in the eyes of many Americans, in part because of the arguments and evidence presented at the trials, he and his men emerged as martyrs, Pullman as a buffoon, and Cleveland as Wall Street's toady. The president was compelled to appoint the strike commission to investigate the events of the summer of 1894. It absolved Debs and placed much blame on industry.

A furious Edwin Walker schemed to recover. He had been humiliated in the criminal case, he told Olney, but had used his influence to secure a compliant judge for the retrial. "The government will never be better prepared to try this case," he wrote. "Judge Bunn was especially assigned to this case, at my request." But Cleveland had enough of Debs. A new U.S. attorney dropped the charges. "There is not a public sentiment at this time which would sustain prosecution," he admitted.[10]

* *

As Darrow jousted in court, prickly John Altgeld had gotten into a brawl with Cleveland. The governor had used the Illinois militia to maintain order in other strikes and dispatched detachments of the guard to trouble spots during the Debs crisis. He had things under control and the deployment of the army was "entirely unnecessary and . . . unjustifiable," he told the president. "The Federal government has been applied to by men who had political and selfish motives." He accused Cleveland of doing "violence to the Constitution."

The press, again, denounced Altgeld. "This lying, hypocritical, demagogical sniveling governor of Illinois does not want the laws enforced. He is a sympathizer with riot, with violence, with lawlessness and anarchy," the *Tribune* declared. "He should be impeached."[11]

Altgeld held his ground. The president and his Wall Street allies, he declared, were a "small band of schemers . . . who have not a drop of Democratic blood in their veins, whose sympathies are entirely with the great corporations" which "treat the American republic as a foraging ground." The governor declined an invitation to celebrate Jefferson's birthday at the Iroquois Club because Olney was a guest. "Jeffersonism was the first-born of the new age of liberty and human progress," said Altgeld, but "Clevelandism is the slimy off-spring of that unhallowed marriage between Standard Oil and Wall Street." He set out to end such influence by allying the Democratic Party with the Populist movement. In doing so, Altgeld set the Democrats on a course that, over time, would transform American government and give liberalism its greatest triumphs. In this crusade, Darrow served as his lieutenant.[12]

Populism was rooted in the farms. Eastern financiers had sold Washington on a policy of tight money, based on the gold standard, that was especially tough on heavily mortgaged farmers. The railroad monopolies, meanwhile, had abused the growers by fixing shipping rates. Hard times fanned the movement, and in 1892 its presidential candidate carried six states, winning more than a million votes. Among other reforms, the Populists called for direct election of U.S. senators, a graduated income tax, and government regulation of railroads and utilities.

"We meet in the midst of a nation brought to the verge of moral, political and material ruin. Corruption dominates the ballot-box, the legislatures, the Congress and touches even the ermine of the bench," said their platform. "The newspapers are largely subsidized or muzzled, public opinion silenced, business prostrated, homes covered with mortgages, labor impoverished and the land concentrating in the hands of the capitalists. The urban workmen are denied the right to organize for self-protection, imported pauperized labor beats down their wages, a hireling standing army, unrecognized by our laws, is established to shoot them down . . . The fruits of the toil of millions are boldly stolen to build up colossal fortunes for a few . . . and the possessors of these, in turn, despise the Republic and endanger liberty."

Altgeld saw the great potential of linking urban workingmen to the farmers' cause. So did Darrow, Debs, Henry Lloyd, and William Jennings Bryan, a young congressman from Nebraska who said government should expand the supply of money by backing the currency with both gold and more plentiful silver. But Populism was not an uncontested sell in the cities. Investors and bankers feared inflation, and were adept at persuading workers that their jobs and savings could be lost in a loose-money economy. Chicago became the testing ground—"the ideal place for beginning the welding of the radical reform elements in the artisan class with the radicals of the rural district," as journalist Willis Abbot put it.

It was no easy marriage; a dispute over the party platform shattered the unity at an organizational meeting in Chicago. Republicans and Democrats dispatched toughs to Populist gatherings, who roughed up delegates as the police looked the other way. Yet Altgeld persevered, and Darrow was his instrument, serving on the Cook County central committee of the newborn People's Party.[13]

In September, the Populists held their first big rally at the Central Music Hall. Several thousand members stomped the downtown streets in a torchlight parade, and Debs and Ignatius Donnelly, a national leader, gave speeches. A week later, Darrow chaired another big gathering at the hall, where the crowd heard him read from the radical poet William Morris:

O why and for what are we waiting? While our brothers droop
and die,
And on every wind of the heavens a wasted life goes by.
How long shall they reproach us where crowd on crowd they dwell,
Poor ghosts of the wicked city, the gold-crushed hungry hell?

In October, it was Darrow's turn as headliner. Men shouted, women fainted, and thousands battled with police before being turned away from the sold-out auditorium. "It was an audience of plain people, orderly, earnest and grave of face," the *Tribune* reported, with more than a few "well-dressed comely women" eager to see Darrow. Inside, seven thousand were entertained by the Ladies Zither Club Orchestra. Then, as he rose to speak, hundreds climbed onto the stage and gathered around and behind him. He roughed up the Republicans, then turned, with relish, to Cleveland.

"I amongst the rest fondly believed that some of the pledges made in the Democratic platform would be kept. We trusted them with our aspirations, with our votes, with the political destiny of this country," he said. "We trusted that they would make some effort to correct some of the abuses that had built up a country of masters and slaves."

But "if the Administration of the Democratic Party has stopped long enough in its allegiance to Wall St. to give the workingman the slightest attention . . . I have failed to find that act," said Darrow. "The demands of the East were complied with, and the interest of the millions who labor with their hands were trampled upon, for the benefit of the few who own the property and credits of the world."

When Cleveland sent the army to break the railroad union it was "the most dangerous act ever committed by any President," Darrow said, and "a precedent which some day may furnish a door for some ambitious ruler to ride over the liberties of the people, and the ruins of the Republic, to a dictator's throne. . . .

"Mr. Cleveland has an Attorney General." The audience hissed.

"He is a Democrat." (More hisses from the audience.)

"Some of you may know his name." (More hisses.)

"Your children will not." (Laughter and applause.)

"How does the Democratic Party of Illinois stand on this question today? Where does the Democratic Party of Illinois stand, with Cleveland or Altgeld?"

"Altgeld!" the crowd shouted. "Altgeld!"

And then, in closing, Darrow turned to his hopes, and those of his fellow Populists.

> It may be that the platform of the party is not perfect. I presume that it is not. We may be out upon the sea in a leaky boat manned by visionists and cranks, that will sail but a little way before it meets the rocks and sinks forever.
>
> But as for me, I would rather sail upon a raft out into the wildest and most tempestuous sea, beneath the blackest skies, moved only by the desires and hopes of those on board than to rest securely in the staunchest ship, anchored to the creeds and errors of the past.
>
> It may be that we are dreamers . . . it may be that the land we seek is a far-off Utopia which lives only in the imagery of enthusiastic minds.
>
> But not all ideals are simply visions. We have made them real in the past, we will make them real in the days to come.
>
> Today the privileged institutions of America, fattened by unjust laws and conditions, boastfully proclaim that monopoly is king.
>
> But I hear a voice rising loud and louder from the common people, long suffering and over patient, a voice which says in thunder tones, "Not monopoly but the People are king!" And that these people, emancipated and aroused, will one day claim their own.

Darrow rushed about the city, speaking for candidates like Lloyd, who was running a long-shot race for Congress, and battling his old pals in the Democratic machine, who had formed a "People's Party Populist" ticket and tried to get it on the ballot in the place of the authentic Populists. It was an old Chicago trick, and Darrow foiled the plot.

The Populists capped their campaign in Chicago with a massive torchlight parade on November 3. Brass bands and fife-and-drum corps made the marching music, skyrockets and Roman candles lit the sky, and wagons bore transparencies—illuminated billboards—proclaiming, "The

People Are Coming." Some twenty thousand tramped the streets, carrying signs, cheering, and honking horns. Darrow was among the speakers at the rally that followed, at Tattersall's amphitheater. The crowd was so loud that he despaired of being heard. "Nothing but a trumpet or a fog horn could make any impression," he would recall. But for all the excitement that it stirred, the Populist initiative in Chicago was a crushing disappointment. "It looked as if all Chicago was there," Darrow recalled, "but if it was, most forgot to vote."[14]

In Illinois, and across the nation, the share of the vote claimed by Populist candidates rose in that off-year election. But the People's Party was inadequately funded. The major newspapers were hostile. Catholics were alienated by the socialist jargon. Leading liberals like Samuel Gompers and Henry George kept their distance. And the big-city organizations, with money, patronage, and control of the election machinery, held their own. The Republicans were the real victors, as voters disenchanted with the Democrats clung to the two-party system. "Can anything be done . . . before liberty is dead?" Darrow wrote to Lloyd. "This is one of the days I feel blue."

Lloyd tried to cheer him up. "Where the plutes are wrong is in their folly of supposing that they can cure . . . by force. They are as blind as the fools of power have always been," he told Darrow. "The radicalism of the fanatics of wealth fills me with hope." The 1894 contest had shown a way for the "Popucrats"—a coalition of the common man that would wrestle the Democratic Party from Cleveland and Wall Street and return it to the masses. "The revolution," Lloyd said, "has come."[15]

Altgeld, too, was undeterred. He decided that the vehicle to crush Cleveland was the "free silver" issue—the demand that the United States base its currency on silver as well as gold. Because tight-money policies favored banks and creditors, Altgeld "always believed that . . . the demonetization of silver was a crime against the debtor and the poor," said Darrow. As an economic prescription, Altgeld knew "that this question was magnified out of its true importance," Darrow acknowledged, but as a potent political tool, the silver issue had no rival. It became a vessel for a wide range of class and regional grievances. It was West versus East, and poor versus rich, and farmer versus banker. Tugged each way were workers and shopkeepers and middle-class professionals, whose yearning for stability warred with their resentment against the commercial oligarchs.

In the middle, as well, was Illinois. The two electoral giants, New York and Pennsylvania, were reliably for gold and Grover Cleveland, but if Altgeld could turn Illinois and the Midwest to silver, he could make his revolution. So Altgeld labored. So did Darrow, who shook off his blues and chaired the Chicago's People's Party 1895 convention, where he was chosen by acclamation to run for mayor. He had declined the nomination, citing the burden of his law practice.

The Illinois Democrats now split in two. Altgeld called for a Democratic "silver convention" to swing the party to the cause. Cleveland's supporters, known as "gold bugs," organized the "Honest Money League" in response.

The Iroquois Club was shattered. Altgeld "is a good hater, and hates Mr. Cleveland so bitterly I am satisfied he started this agitation," federal postmaster Washington Hesing, a gold bug, declared at a meeting. When Darrow stood to defend the silver movement, hecklers interrupted him, demanding to know if he was still a Democrat.

"Find one word or one line which Thomas Jefferson ever wrote in favor of a gold standard," Darrow challenged them, "or which any Democratic President ever uttered or supported up to the days of King Grover."

His foes cried, "Shame! Shame!"

"A fig for your cries of 'Shame!' It is true," said Darrow. "No person disputes the historical proposition that gold and silver were the constitutional legal money of the United States, that the mass of indebtedness that exists today, private, municipal and national, was contracted to be paid in gold and silver alike."

The meeting ended in tumult. Postmaster Hesing and former mayor John Hopkins almost came to blows in the club dining room, and might have had not Hesing grown so angry that he lapsed into his native German, mystifying Hopkins, who understood that he was being insulted but did not know exactly how.

The 1896 presidential election now commanded Darrow's attention. Altgeld set out to seize control of the party at the Democratic national convention in Chicago that July, with a platform that called for a gold-and-silver-backed currency, safeguards for the right to strike, enactment of an income tax, and other Populist planks. "It was a great revolutionary document," said Darrow, which "breathed a spirit of defiance to the tyranny of the rich." Never had a political party so repudiated its own incumbent president.

Yet Altgeld lacked a candidate; he was prevented from running for president himself. "It is a pity that Gov. Altgeld was not born on American soil," said the *New York Times*. "He is their logical candidate, as he is their actual leader." He and Darrow could only watch as Bryan roused the crowd in the platform debate, his roar reaching to the farthest corners of the Coliseum.

There were two great theories of government, Bryan said. One claimed that "if you will only legislate to make the well-to-do prosperous, their prosperity will leak through on those below." But "the Democratic idea," he said, was "if you legislate to make the masses prosperous, their prosperity will find its way up through every class which rests upon them."

Bryan defined the Democrats as the party of the little guy—the wage earners, small-town shopkeepers, miners, and farmers—and heaped scorn on the merchants of the East. "Having behind us the producing masses of this nation and the world . . . the laboring interests, and the toilers everywhere," Bryan said, and now he was stepping back from the podium, and raising his arms, as in benediction, "we will answer their demand for a gold standard by saying to them: You shall not press down upon the brow of labor this crown of thorns, you shall not crucify mankind upon a cross of gold."

There was a moment of hesitation, and then the Coliseum erupted. "Bryan did something to your spinal cord," Darrow said. It was "the molten expression of pent up wrath against evils conterminous with the government," said Masters. "Political idealism never had so thorough, so unimpeachable a presentation." Altgeld held his cards for four ballots, as Bryan slowly picked up strength and other candidates fell away. Finally, on the fifth round of voting, Altgeld announced that Illinois would vote for Bryan; it triggered the cascade that gave him the nomination. It was the unmatched trick of American political history: with a single speech, a baby-faced thirty-six-year-old congressman had seized a presidential nomination, and turned his party in a new direction. "It was the first time in my life and in the life of a generation," wrote journalist William

Allen White, "in which any man large enough to lead a national party had boldly and unashamedly made his cause that of the poor and the oppressed."[16]

Bryan faced many handicaps as he entered the fall election. He was young and inexperienced. The press was allied against him—the *New York Times* called him an "irresponsible, unregulated, ignorant, prejudiced, pathetically honest and enthusiastic crank"—and the gold bugs ran their own candidate and split the Democratic vote. Republican boss Mark Hanna raised millions of dollars and outspent his foes, twenty to one. "Never were so many fraudulent votes cast," Carter Harrison Jr. recalled. Every time Hanna ran out of money, the Republicans dispatched another trainload of currency, said Altgeld, and "debauched a continent."

Bryan barnstormed the country, halting at whistle-stops, shaking hands, giving speeches. But across the Midwest and Northeast, the factory owners told their workers that they would lose their jobs if Bryan was elected. The Republicans made Altgeld an issue, as well.

"For Mr. Bryan we can feel the contemptuous pity always felt for the small man unexpectedly thrust into a big place. But in Mr. Altgeld's case we see all too clearly the jaws and hide of the wolf," said Theodore Roosevelt. "The one plans repudiation with a light heart and a bubbly eloquence, because he lacks intelligence . . . the other would connive at wholesale murder and would justify it by elaborate and cunning sophistry."

When the Populists convened in St. Louis that summer, Darrow and Lloyd were there. The great question was whether to align with the Democrats. Lloyd, who hoped that the People's Party would become an independent, radical organization, feared it would lose its soul. But Darrow worked for fusion and so did Debs, and they urged Lloyd not to resist. He came to regret it. The Populists endorsed Bryan and, just as Lloyd feared, the Democrats absorbed the People's Party. The rising of the dirt farmers came to its end.

Darrow returned to Chicago, where, with Altgeld's help, he was nominated as a "Popucratic" candidate for Congress. He spent much of the fall campaigning for Bryan and Altgeld outside the district. He was maligned by critics as a darling of the intellectuals while his opponent, Representative Hugh Belknap, a Republican incumbent known for his campaigning skills, "goes right into the factories and among the laboring men." And, truth be told, Darrow was a flaky politician. That spring he was invited to speak at a memorial meeting for the philanthropist Baron Hirsch, a pillar of the Jewish community. The occasion called for some respectful remarks and a woeful shake of the head. Darrow would have none of it.

"The man whose picture draped in mourning stands at my side may have been great . . . but I would not select him as my patron saint," he began. There were murmurs in the audience, and the sound of chairs shifting on the stage around him.

"I do not wish to be understood as not in sympathy with this meeting," said Darrow. "But I cannot . . . understand how a man who makes millions by every scheme and financial trick can reconcile that with true humanity. Baron Hirsch gave millions to the poor, but his fortune came, ultimately, from the poor—and he never gave it all back."

A young man named S. A. Lewinsohn leaped to his feet in anger. "Fellow Jews," he said, "it seems the height of impropriety that a corporation lawyer, a professional socialist and a man who never gave a dollar to charity in his life should presume at a time like this—or anytime—to criticize the noblest Jew of his generation!" In the resultant uproar a few in the crowd, socialists no doubt, came to Darrow's rescue. But they were routed by overwhelming opposition and abandoned the hall.

Long before the election, it was clear that Bryan and Altgeld would lose. Hinky Dink Kenna, that incorrigible finagler, was caught fixing ballots for Darrow, but the Popucrats could not compete with Hanna's gold, which had bought the allegiance of far more ward and precinct leaders. Darrow lost by five hundred votes, in a race he should have won. The electorate was made up of laborers, he said, who never hesitated to call on him for free legal help but were too apathetic, or tired, or too new to America to get to the polls.

Bryan carried twenty-six states, and polled a million more votes than the victorious Cleveland had received in 1892. A switch of twenty thousand votes in a handful of states would have given him victory in the Electoral College. But he got whipped in the Midwest, failed to carry a single industrial state, and lost the popular vote by a margin of 600,000 to William McKinley.

Darrow blamed Bryan, in part, for the Democratic defeat. When they met the following spring, Darrow was "terribly raw" to Bryan, said Masters.

"You'd better . . . study science, history, philosophy and quit this village religious stuff," Darrow told Bryan before a group of fellow Democrats. "You're a head of the party before you are ready and a leader should lead with thought."

Bryan turned to the others and said, "Darrow's the only man in the world who looks down on me for believing in God."

"Your kind of a God," Darrow replied.

Bryan's success gnawed at Darrow. He despised Bryan's dull intellect and complacency. Soon, Darrow would be telling a story of how Altgeld, on the day after the Cross of Gold speech, had labeled Bryan a "damn fool."

"I've been thinking over Bryan's speech," Altgeld had sneered, according to Darrow. "What did he say anyhow?"

For thirty years, Darrow's envy and antipathy toward Bryan would build—until he was given, and took, the opportunity to destroy him.[17]

Chapter 5

FREE LOVE

A marvelous inconsistency of mind.

Darrow was almost forty. His life was as turbulent as the times. He had lost his race for Congress. His friend and patron John Altgeld had been booted from office. His law firm had dissolved. And his marriage was disintegrating.

He had been drinking Chicago in gulps; his days filled with law and politics, his nights and weekends with legal homework, club meetings, campaigns, and public speaking. But "Mother wasn't interested in the things he was interested in, and vice versa," Paul recalled. Jessie "didn't care for discussion, argument, free-thinking. She wanted to pay social calls to homes and relatives."

Darrow had tried to stick it out, but ultimately concluded that Jessie was "utterly unsuitable" for him. In a letter to his wife, he gave his reasons for leaving. "We have not been happy, and I suppose neither of us are to blame," he wrote. "I presume that we never in any way were fitted for each other . . . Of course we were too young to know it then and it is always terribly hard to correct such mistakes."

Darrow's sexual experience had been constrained by his early marriage, but now he was intoxicated by Chicago's libertine ways. "We . . . talked free love, sex and every imaginable thing," his friend and fellow lawyer Edgar Lee Masters recalled. Darrow was "full of boyishness," with a "gorgeous chuckle," said Jessie's cousin Francis Wilson. He "got into the company of the intellectual and beautiful and didn't feel that Jessie contributed to what he wanted."

Divorce was an option in Victorian America, but Darrow would need a considerable income to maintain a cosmopolitan lifestyle while still providing, as he promised, for Jessie and Paul. He had gotten valuable publicity but earned little else when representing Prendergast and Debs, and lost a financial anchor when his law firm broke apart. When asked to donate to a liberal cause in January 1895, he declined. "I . . . do not think I ought to use my money in that way," he told the solicitor. "I have not much to use."[1]

Darrow's first brush with scandal helped balance the books. In early 1895 he had joined, and profited from, one of Chicago's more notorious acts of municipal corruption. It was known as the "Ogden Gas" deal, and Altgeld's cousin, John Lanehart, helped push it through the city council. On February 26 the *Tribune* alerted Chicagoans that the Ogden Gas Company and Cosmopolitan Electric Company had each been granted fifty-year municipal franchises "that will stand for all time . . . as monuments of corruption." More than five thousand people attended a rowdy protest meeting, where squads of police were summoned to contain the crowd, and speakers denounced the aldermen as wolves, hyenas, scorpions, reptiles, freebooters, and scoundrels.

It was an archetypical bit of boodling. At the end of the nineteenth century private companies supplied the public utilities—gas for heat and light, telephones, streetcars, electric power—under franchise agreements awarded by local governments. Elected officials grew rich taking bribes to grant the franchises, or by extorting payoffs from existing utilities that wished to ward off competition. In the Ogden Gas deal, franchises for gas and electric and telephone service were awarded to corporate fronts for an elite group of Democratic politicians. "When work has been carried far enough to convince other companies that the new concern may be a serious competitor, the speculative individuals . . . will be bought out by the companies they compete with and will withdraw . . . with a handsome rake-off," the *Tribune* predicted.

John Hopkins, the city's first Irish Catholic mayor, was leaving office and looking for a sinecure. Roger Sullivan, the boss of the machine Democrats, and Levy Mayer, one of the city's sharpest lawyers, were also in on the deal. Darrow had participated in the big protest meeting, but when the boodlers needed help from an expert in municipal law, he switched sides. The Civic Federation, a good government group, sued to stop the deal, claiming the aldermen were "corruptly influenced," and Darrow and Mayer teamed up to beat the reformers in court.

"I have no doubt that many good citizens believe money was used to secure the passage of these ordinances, as during the last few years nearly everything they own has been given away," Darrow told the judge. But the separation of powers precluded judicial interference, he said. "When the City Council performs its duties carelessly or corruptly—but within its own rights—it is not the province of a court . . . The court cannot ask an alderman, 'Why did you vote for that measure?' That is for his conscience, whether he has one or not."

The court ruled for Darrow. He and Lanehart secured the operating permits for Ogden Gas and Cosmopolitan Electric. As was predicted, after several years both firms were bought out by the trusts that furnished power and light to the city, and the boodlers reaped their profits. When bought, Darrow stayed bought. He was there at the finish in 1900, leading a legal and political crusade—bankrolled by Sullivan—to put pressure on the gas trust during the final negotiations.[2]

Darrow may have received a cut, or merely earned an unsavory legal fee when saving the deal in court. He was candid enough not to make the distinction. "I undertook to serve this company . . . believing they had an ordinance procured by the aid of boodle," he admitted. "I am satisfied that judged by the higher law . . . I am practically a thief.

"I am taking money that I did not earn, which comes to me from men who did not earn it, but who get it because they have the chance to get it. I take it without performing any useful service to the world, and I take a thousand times as much as my services are worth even assuming they were useful and honest."

Darrow made this confession to Ellen Gates Starr, one of the founders of Hull House, who had scolded him in a scathing note, which he answered with a long, revealing letter. "I believe now that society is organized injustice," Darrow told Starr. In such circumstances, how does a just man live his life? There were those who believed that Morrison Swift, a mutual friend who renounced a family fortune and joined the Commonweal protests, had taken the moral path. Swift "has perhaps done some good in his way by refusing to compromise with evil," Darrow said. But in the end Swift's ways were impractical and he and other absolutists were "shunned." Darrow had chosen a different course. "I came to Chicago. I determined to take my chances with the rest, to get what I could out of the system and use it to destroy the system," he said.

He was not a child of a well-off family, like Swift and Starr. And "society provides no fund out of which . . . people can live while preaching heresy," said Darrow. So "I have . . . sold my professional services to every corporation or individual who cared to buy," said Darrow. "I have taken their ill-gotten gains and have tried to use it to prevent suffering.

"I have defended the poor and weak, have done it without pay, will do it again," he said. "I cannot defend them without bread, I cannot get this except from those who have it."[3]

Now Darrow had the money to flee his unhappy home. He left Jessie and Paul in Chicago, and roamed Europe for two months. He toured the English countryside, saw Shakespeare's grave, and wandered among the tombs in Westminster Abbey. The collapse of his marriage and his political defeats weighed on him, and he was in a gloomy mood when composing a dispatch for the *Chicago Chronicle.* "The man who believes in the cause and has the courage of his convictions finds . . . the way very lonely," he wrote. "The tide of progress . . . leaves the long coast strewn with shattered hopes, ruined plans, defeated purposes and despondent men."

Darrow was happier in France. He delighted in the whitewashed houses, the medieval nooks, and the broad boulevards of Paris. He took a boat ride on the Seine, saw Notre Dame, and visited the grave of a favorite author, Victor Hugo, at the Pantheon. Above all stood Eiffel's tower, rising "so light and graceful," like "a cobweb fastened to the earth and spun from a star." In the streets and cafés, Darrow fell hard for the French. "They laugh at the grotesque and absurd, and see all there is of life and light, of form and color, and find diversions and pleasures in little things," he wrote. "This is the philosophy of life, to make the most out of the small things that are ever near us.

"The large things are very rare, and existence would be much happier if they were rarer still," said Darrow. "The great events are deaths . . . blood and war."

In Switzerland, Darrow climbed the Lauberhorn and joined the family of a vacationing Iroquois club mate, Judge Barnum, for dinner. Darrow was a finicky eater who could not understand why tourists wasted "two mortal hours" each day at an elaborate evening meal. To her lasting delight, he grabbed the hand of Barnum's daughter Gertrude and broke from the table. "He and I took a bob-tail car to its high destination, enjoyed cottage cheese and . . . wine with a goat herd and his wife and saw the Jungfrau at her noblest," she recalled. Barnum insisted that no more happened, but of course she had to, as she was a single maid and he a married man. But there was a romantic something there, for she loved him deeply all her life.

Darrow next wrote from Venice, where he found brigades of beggars, scenes of soul-wrenching poverty, and other evidence of imperial entropy wrapped in hypnotic sensuality. "When the sun goes down and the stars and moon come out then the spell of the past falls over the magic city and all the poetry and loveliness and romance of her ancient glory comes again," he wrote. The lights of St. Mark's Square "like a fairy scene" danced upon the water. "You step into a gondola, lie back . . . [and] muse upon the glories of the past, the splendors of the ancient world, the flight of time, the mutability of human things. You think and dream and dream and think until you do not know whether you dream or think or whether perchance all that is and all that was may be but a dream."

Delight and dread danced in turn. Out on the Grand Canal, he passed a black, shrouded gondola and asked his boatman to follow it. Away from the fairy city, they came to an island graveyard, where he had the "grim satisfaction" of confronting oblivion "while I yet could come away."

"Death is too common to deserve much space," he wrote. "There was no reason why I should not meet it on the Grand Canal. For there is no island so remote, no mountain so inaccessible and no forest so dense to hide man from his all-searching gaze." All the riches of Europe were but a "digression" from the inevitability of the grave. All art a distraction. All commerce a narcotic. Darrow left his readers with a final scene of "two old, beat, yellow women, one washing chicken's gizzards and the other her feet" in the sewerage of the Grand Canal. The "shriveled crones" did "darkly stand out as the true Venice," he wrote, "against the fading luster."

On the steamship home, this latter-day Odysseus passed the time with a shipmate, the politico Chauncey Depew, who spoke of what he had witnessed at the sacred grotto in Lourdes, where a seventeen-year-old girl, her leg swollen and covered in sores, had been dipped in the holy pool and pronounced cured. "I believe the miracles of the New Testament," Depew said solemnly. "But until now I thought none like them had been wrought after that time."

"I don't believe in any miracles at all," Darrow said.[4]

Darrow was still brooding a few weeks later when he gave a speech to the United Irish Societies of Chicago. A great war would soon grip Europe, he predicted, and in that cataclysm, for Irish and Marxist and other revolutionaries, "the opportunity of the disinherited will come." Then he turned his vision toward America. "Civilization means something more than producing wealth, something besides inventing new ways to make buildings higher and kill hogs faster," he said. "All the wealth of a great city cannot weigh against the barbarism of hanging one lunatic in Chicago or burning one Negro in Texas." If war and revolution came, he told his listeners, they should "remember the long years in which the storm was rising," and "not blame the thunderbolt."[5]

In 1896, it was Paul and Jessie's turn to tour Europe, as part of Darrow's plan to obtain the divorce on the grounds that Jessie had deserted him. She was gracious, and agreed to be cited as the offending partner to preserve his professional standing. Darrow pledged to pay $150 a month—a generous amount—to support her. He signed over their house and other property, and gave her $25,000. He promised her custody of Paul, for "he is yours more than mine and he loves you more than he does me."

Jessie had seen signs. Her husband was "a man of the world," she would recall. "He wanted to be free, to have no ties." Years later, she told how "he was always good to me . . . always generous . . . I could never say anything against him in the world." But she was devastated, after seventeen years of marriage, when he walked out. "It nearly killed me to give him up," Jessie said. "But he never knew that. I never let him know."

Paul let him know. He was twelve when he and his mother were dispatched to Europe. Darrow saw them off at the station. When the divorce was filed, Paul told his father that he never wanted to see him again. Darrow had his freedom, but was racked with guilt, and wept when it was done.[6]

Had there been a corespondent in Darrow's divorce, it would probably have been Katherine Leckie, a spirited newspaper reporter who entered his life in Chicago. She was a few years younger than Darrow, the Canadian-born daughter of an English immigrant, who was working as a stenographer for the law department at City Hall when Darrow arrived there in 1889. She broke into journalism with the help of her cousin Archibald, one of the founders of the City News Bureau, who thought she was "brilliant" and "magnetic."

A friend recalled Leckie as the "warmest-hearted, reckless-souled idealist" working in Chicago's newsrooms. The anarchistic Emma Goldman valued Leckie as a "strong and ardent" soldier in radical causes. When President McKinley was shot by the anarchist Leon Czolgosz in 1901, authorities across the country cracked down on radicals, and Goldman was arrested and given the third degree. The press joined the hunt, except for Leckie, who called on Goldman in jail and pled her case with police officials. "He should be tried and convicted!" Leckie said of an officer who had struck Goldman. When her newspaper declined to print Leckie's account, she resigned.

Leckie's strength and spirit may have attracted Darrow initially, but then put him off. After leaving Jessie, he savored bachelorhood and ardently resisted when women pressed him for commitment. He became infatuated with the daughter of John W. Dowd, a family friend of Darrow's political and literary pal Brand Whitlock, who was then working in Toledo. Darrow started spending time there and urged Whitlock to commend him to "Miss Dowd," to invite her to their outings, and to accompany them on an Adirondack vacation. Darrow was dallying, as well, with the young ladies who came to Chicago to work at Hull House and the other settlements. He had bounced about town after leaving home, ultimately settling in an apartment at the Langdon—a new "model tenement" building on Desplaines Street, not far from Hull House. Several of the young women of the settlement movement—Gertrude Barnum, Mary Field, Helen Todd, Amanda Johnson, and others—were enthralled by Darrow, and the wolf in him took advantage of it. Ultimately, Leckie left Chicago for New York, for a job with a friend of Darrow's, the journalist and author Theodore Dreiser, at the *Delineator* magazine, and a life as an editor, pacifist, and suffragist.[7]

Rambling about the social and political circuit, Darrow had discovered that his roguish complexity was a lure for ladies with a taste for Byronic heroes. Many were of a breed of "new women"—bright and self-reliant girls who wanted the freedom to develop their talents in art, journalism, or other fields and fell for this mysterious, defiant soul. "No man ever had more women friends or admirers," said Natalie Schretter, who would join Darrow and his radical crowd at downtown saloons, drinking beer and eating cheese sandwiches and arguing about literature and politics as the baffled prostitutes and gamblers looked on from nearby tables. "All the gay levities Darrow had missed through a young marriage and a small town youth came to him."

Darrow relished sex, and savored the chase. His friend was "very highly sexed," said pastor Preston Bradley, who led a liberal congregation called the People's Church in Chicago. "I don't think there was one Madame X. I think there were many because Darrow did enjoy feminine company, and he looked at it as a conquest." Darrow saw sex as evidence of vitality, as well. "Hell, can he still fuck a woman?" he would ask, when judging an aged acquaintance.

Some of these young feminists embraced the doctrines of the free love movement, which called for relationships based on sexual and emotional compatibility, not repressive statutes. In Victorian America, "love as usually practiced and understood means possession—the obvious possession of the wife's person, all the way . . . to the subtle possession of her mind," wrote Mary Field. The new women sought to change that.

"The choice was between a despised, lonely and childless future, or marriage on the terms of a 'man's world,' " Gertrude Barnum recalled. She and the others "chose not to surrender our own integrity." They insisted on "a marriage of true minds" and, while searching, "took strenuous part in campaigns for the political and economic independence of women, and helped greatly in changing the status of the female of the day." But, she recalled: "What a price we paid." Darrow was a rake, but not a heel. He bedded these starry-eyed idealists, but he did not mislead them. He would "declare himself liberal-minded about associations twixt men and women, single or married," said Ruby Hamerstrom, a journalist whom he wooed, and gave them fair warning that he would "never succumb to any one woman."[8]

Darrow opened a new law office with two former associates, William Thompson and Morris St. P. Thomas, and offered a desk to Francis

Wilson, his ex-wife's cousin. He and Wilson rented two adjacent flats at the Langdon and, after pulling down a dividing wall, had the Gilded Age version of a bachelor pad. The Langdon had hardwood floors, enameled bathtubs and marble sinks, fireplaces flanked by bookshelves, and an open interior courtyard that brought in air and light. They added a red rug and drapes, an incandescent painting by the Norwegian American impressionist Svend Svendsen, and two andirons in the shape of cats, whose glass eyes flashed with each flare of the fire.

Darrow reveled in his bohemian lifestyle. "These were the days of the Roycroft influence in furniture and book binding, of stuffed chairs, fumed oak and soft leather formats; of the Ballad of Reading Gaol, of Omar Khayyám, of the rights of labor; of the melting pots," Masters wrote. "Of the rights of the misunderstood harlot . . . of the muck rake." Darrow's friends were "ramshackle star gazers; twisted and aborted sprouts of genius; world savers," Masters recalled, and "many women from thirty to forty . . . swept under the influence . . . by amorous hopes and fulfillments."

Darrow exercised his freedom "in a vast promiscuity carried on at his apartment," said Masters. "I found on the wall the pictures of martyrs who had died for liberty; and I heard him read amid feminine exclamations of wonder . . . issued from the parted lips of the six women or sometimes more draped about his feet, each wishing to be the chosen favorite." Darrow always loved to read aloud. When he got to a favorite passage he would peer over the top of the book at his adorers and grin.

Johnson, the daughter of a Chicago businessman, had persuaded wealthy investors to build the Langdon, and she was the on-site administrator. Barnum and Todd were neighbors in the building. "It was along about 1900 that he began . . . getting devilish," Wilson recalled. "Darrow liked adulation. All women gravitated toward him and he liked them. Had lots of them." For Valentine's Day in 1902, Johnson, Todd, and Barnum staged a costume ball at a nearby hall, inviting "philanthropists, philosophers, poets, painters, politicians and other patriots" to join them. Johnson, her long blond hair braided, came as a Norwegian, Barnum as an Italian peasant girl, and Todd as a Scotch lassie. Darrow, dressed as a policeman, won first prize.

Darrow and the young women and some other residents formed a cooperative living society—a kind of commune, where traveling radicals and artists would visit. Rosa Perdue, a researcher for the sociologist Richard Ely, didn't like the "peculiar people" she found there. "Their points of agreement are . . . weariness with life as lived by normal society and a desire to live a strained abnormal life," she wrote. Men and women smoked liked fiends, used "profane language as they discussed politics," and "lauded extreme socialism and anarchy." The co-op was poorly administered and forever running short of money. Darrow was the "Household God," Perdue said, and the others "content to abide in the shadow."

Darrow revived his political career with a successful campaign for the Illinois legislature, using the West Side ghetto as his base and the women at the Langdon as his campaign organizers. "He expects to be governor of Illinois and even aspires to the Presidency," Perdue told Ely. She described how Johnson, "his private secretary," had run Darrow's campaign, helping him with "most inflammatory" speeches and gathering the "lowest men and boys" from the district's saloons to parade down the streets and light bonfires in his honor. It was "a miniature French Revolution," the elated Johnson told her. Perdue concluded that Darrow was "a dangerous man."

Barnum, who arrived at the Langdon after breaking off an engagement, thought Darrow was a bit frightening, with "his Free Love theories; his radicalism." But "unlike most men, even in passionate relations with women, Darrow always made those contacts human—not just 'sexy,' " she said. "He respected each individual soul." It was a rare attitude, she concluded, among the men of her day.[9]

Barnum "was deeply in love with Darrow, and . . . it was a great disappointment that she did not win him to herself. But that is true of . . . a considerable number among Miss Barnum's intimates," Ruby Hamerstrom recalled. Darrow was "smothered" with female attention, she said. "He was continuously finding himself much more strongly entwined with them than ever intended by himself. He would have a hell of a time to extricate himself."

Hamerstrom met Darrow in 1899 at a meeting of the White City Club, an artsy group, where he gave a talk on Omar Khayyám. He was forty-two and she was twenty-six. He was taken by this girlish writer with doe eyes and a pink and white complexion, and asked her out. She was engaged to a stockbroker and declined, but he clung to her hand, refusing to let go. She agreed to join him for dinner some nights later at an Italian restaurant favored by the literary set. Afterward, as they crossed the Rush

Street bridge in the rain, Darrow paused, took one of her gloves from her hand, entwined his fingers with hers, and slid their hands into his overcoat pocket.

He told her he was smitten—but warned her he would never marry again. That was all right, she replied, as she was preparing to marry someone else. "Well," he said, "we'll have to devise ways to break your engagement." Soon, she was seeing him regularly.[10]

THE FREE LOVE movement bloomed in the years after the Civil War, when utopian dreamers and some of the early feminists pushed society to relax laws governing marriage, divorce, and contraception. By the turn of the century, libertarians of both sexes were enlisting. "All that is good in marriage, home or child-rearing rests on *free love*," wrote one of Darrow's friends, the poet and lawyer C. E. S. Wood. "When it rests on a forced appearance of love, on a forced relationship, it rests on falsity, vice and hypocrisy and no apparent social quiet can justify that . . . torture of the soul."

In 1899, Darrow served as a legal adviser to Dr. Denslow Lewis, the president of the medical staff at the Cook County Hospital, who had proposed to the American Medical Association that it publish his paper on the physiology of sex. His description of sexual practices in the Victorian era explains the appeal of the movement. A bride "too often comes to the marriage bed with inexact ideas of all that pertains to sexual intercourse," he wrote. Young women needed to be taught how pregnancy occurs and to be instructed that, in marital relations, "it is right and proper for her to experience pleasure."

"Her husband is not usually so ignorant," said Lewis, but not because anyone had instructed him. "His experience in sexual matters is due to intercourse with prostitutes. His knowledge is imperfect and often dangerous. His relations with his bride are sometime brutal." Too often, "he will come home from the club at midnight and find his wife in bed . . . Erection is speedily followed by intromission, and often before the wife is really awake, the orgasm has occurred," Lewis wrote.

"Some one should tell him the difference between a virtuous girl and a street walker," the gynecologist said. "He should know regarding the anatomic conditions. He should know that intromission is painful until dilation of the parts has occurred. He should understand that reciprocity in the mechanism of the act is not to be expected until his wife is accustomed to the marital relationship."

It was basic stuff, carefully phrased, based on years of experience treating women; but Lewis ran into fierce opposition. "I should be very sorry if in this country these matters became . . . freely talked about," one AMA discussant, Dr. Howard Kelly, told him. "I do not believe mutual pleasure in the sexual act has any particular bearing on the happiness of life."

The AMA refused to print the "nasty" article, claiming that it would run afoul of postal censors. Lewis went to Darrow, one of a few attorneys who would handle such cases. The medical society should be ashamed of its timidity, Darrow said, trying to nudge the organization to action: "Any publisher who . . . would fear to give out a paper written in good faith, for a good purpose, by a man of standing and ability . . . is not fit to publish a scientific journal." But the AMA could not be budged. Lewis was forced to publish his findings himself.[11]

It was during these years that journalist Hutchins Hapgood arrived in Chicago from the East to gather material for a book on the city's radical causes. Often, he stayed as Darrow's guest. The free love enthusiasts, Hapgood found, viewed marriage as "enslaving." They might enter relationships, but maintained the right to "follow out" desires with other partners. "This is called varietism, and was supposed to be hygienic and stimulating to the imagination," he wrote. "No doubt it was, but the time always came when human nature couldn't stand it and when one or the other broke down, and separation, sorrow and disappointment followed."

Because it undermined the elemental structures of society, the proper folk viewed the free love movement as highly subversive—"the most boiling pot on the Devil's stove"—Mary Field recalled. But Darrow was its defender. Real love is "the love of life, the love of reality, the strong love of men, the intense love of women, the honest love that nature made, the love that is," he wrote. "Not the unhealthy, immoral, false, impossible love . . . given to young girls and boys . . . to poison and corrupt."

Alarmed at rising divorce rates, the churches and good people were pushing elected officials to tighten the marriage laws. "I have noticed . . . many things said by newspapers, clergymen and others of the evils of divorce," Darrow told his friends at the Sunset Club. "I view with alarm the efforts of those who would tighten the cords that bind unwilling hearts."

"So long as the instincts of men and women are left free to act, and men and women are brought together purely by choice, very little evil can result," he said. "You may think that these things of which we speak are crimes or sins, or call them what you will, but back of all is the instinct of man . . . the heart of man."

Darrow became a legal paladin for the cause. He tilted with Anthony Comstock, the self-ordained leader of the New York Society for the Suppression of Vice, who had persuaded Congress and many states to pass the so-called Comstock Laws, which banned writing, publication, sale, and ownership of "immoral" material. When Comstock hounded Ida Craddock, a Chicago counselor who wrote sex education pamphlets for naive young couples, Darrow took up her defense; to his regret, he was not able to save her when she moved to New York and, in part as a result of Comstock's harassment, committed suicide. Darrow contributed articles to *To-Morrow* magazine, a radical journal published by the eccentric Parker Sercombe, which espoused the free love cause and employed Darrow's friend the poet Carl Sandburg. He defended Dr. Alice Stockham when she was prosecuted for circulating an informational booklet, "The Wedding Night." And, in "Woman," one of his first published essays, Darrow emerged as something of a feminist himself.[12]

"Man has always trampled on her rights," Darrow wrote. "Out of this desire to control one woman absolutely grew the institution of marriage . . . and not from any thought of a fair or equal contract."

A young woman enters the "occupation of husband-getting unconsciously," Darrow wrote, "with a smiling face, a laughing voice and a fairy step . . . She does not strive to be an individual, an entity, with high ambitions and desires, but to be a pliant, supple thing . . . to conform to another's ignoble thoughts."

Women can be lawyers, preachers, and doctors. "We know they *can* because they *have*," said Darrow. Yet "for a woman to have any other ambition than marriage is to be at once considered different from the rest of her sex; to be regarded with doubt; to be called 'strong-minded' and 'unwomanly.' . . .

"Man, looking down upon her as the plaything of an hour, the creature formed for no purpose but to serve his wants, has ensnared her with the debasing thought that he likes her best when she comes upon her bended knees," he wrote. "What woman needs to-day, first of all, is freedom; the chance to be an individual . . . to be released from the cruel restrictions and proprieties that society has thrown around her."

Darrow did more than preach. He hired Nellie Carlin, who worked with him for years, one of the first female attorneys to succeed in Chicago.[13]

"WOMAN" WAS DARROW'S first published essay on a matter outside law and politics. He was branching out, speaking and writing on philosophy and literature.

"The artist and the philosopher were growing apace through these years," said Barnum. "Evenings, Sundays and vacations were spent in delivering lectures, writing essays and stories and novels . . . He would tuck the loose notes of a favorite theme into an overcoat pocket and scurry off, late, to teach Tolstoy." Darrow made good friends in Chicago's burgeoning literary scene, like Sandburg and Dreiser and Masters, and helped launch Whitlock's writing career by bringing him to the attention of novelist William Dean Howells, the "Dean of American Letters." Journalist William Allen White visited Chicago in this period and was introduced to Darrow at a literary party that included author Hamlin Garland and two of the city's most famous stylists, George Ade and Peter Finley Dunne. Darrow stood out as "a gaunt, loose-skinned, fiery-eyed rebel," White recalled. At the Sunset Club, Darrow debated "Realism vs. Idealism in Literature and Art." At the Independent Penwoman's Club, he spoke on Omar Khayyám. At the Chicago Ethical Society, Darrow praised the poetry of Robert Burns. He honed, as well, a lecture on Walt Whitman. And there was a dark psychological essay, "The Skeleton in the Closet."

In 1899 Darrow paid the print shop at the Roycroft artisan colony in New York to produce 980 copies of *A Persian Pearl, and Other Essays*, a collection of these lectures and writings. It was well received. The *Tribune* hailed it as "a charming chaplet" of "graceful and pleasing" prose. The "pearl" of the title was *The Rubáiyát*, the series of quatrains from a twelfth-century Persian poet that Darrow had quoted in the Prendergast case. In Khayyám's poetry, Darrow recognized the values by which he lived his life. The first was agnosticism. He remained the son of Amirus and Emily, the Kinsman freethinkers, and the follower of the atheist Robert Ingersoll. When Ingersoll died that summer, Darrow was chosen to give eulogies before thousands at great memorial meetings in Chicago and Ohio. And in his essay on the *Rubáiyát*, Darrow remained faithful to the freethinkers' creed.

"There is no moment but the one that's here," he wrote. "Man has ever sought to make himself believe that these things are not what they seem; that, in reality, a death is only birth, and the body but a prison for the soul. This may be true, but the constant cries and pleadings of the ages have brought back no answering sound to prove that death is anything but death."

Man was not just doomed at death, said Darrow, he was powerless in life. Human beings were shaped by inexorable forces and, far from being captain of their fate, were "less than the tiniest bubble in the wildest, angriest sea." A man would do better to face the hopelessness of life, said Darrow, and do what he can to ease the pain of his fellow sufferers, so that "here and there some pilgrim will tell of a burden that we helped him bear, or a road we tried to smooth."

While good works occupy the time, said Darrow, so should life's pleasures. He was a hedonist. Not just a philosophical hedonist (for there was a school of philosophy, of which Darrow approved, which held that the value of any act or experience is contained in the pleasure it gives), but a sybarite who shared Khayyám's taste for the "jug of wine and thou." He lauded "the giving up of self to the enjoyment of the hour—the complete abandonment that forgets time and space and eternity, and knows only the moment that is."

Come, fill the Cup, and in the fire of Spring
Your winter garment of Repentance fling;
The Bird of time has but a little way
To feather—and the Bird is on the Wing.

Similar themes ran through Darrow's other essays. His pieces on realism, Whitman, and Burns praise the artist who confronts the frightening riddle of life, prizes love, and savors pleasure. The exception was "The Skeleton in the Closet," a chilling ode to sin and its instructive power.

"The anguish of the human soul cannot be told—it must be felt," Darrow wrote. "It is the hated skeleton that finds within our breast a heart of flint and takes this hard and pulseless thing and scars and twists and melts it in a thousand torturous ways until the stony mass is purged and softened and is sensitive to every touch."

Darrow leaves his personal skeleton nameless, though it seems to have been a sin of passion—"a flash of that great, natural light and heat that once possessed this tottering frame" which brought him "the keenest, wildest joy" like a "boiling, seething cataract." In its wake, his guilt and shame were as intense.

"We knew only the surface of the world," said Darrow. "We needed this to teach us, from the anguish of the soul, that there is a depth profound and great where pain and pleasure both are one."[14]

Darrow was influenced, as well, by Leo Tolstoy's doctrine of Christian anarchism and he responded to the war drums of the fin de siècle with a pacifist treatise, *Resist Not Evil.*

"Force is wrong," Darrow wrote. "A bayonet in the hand of one man is no better than in the hand of another. It is the bayonet that is evil."

In 1898, for the first time in the industrial age, the United States had gone to war with a European power. A generation of men who came of age after the Civil War—Theodore Roosevelt, publisher William Randolph Hearst, and others—yearned to show their mettle, and Spain's suppression of a rebellion in Cuba was a convenient cause. But Darrow opposed American imperialism. "It was never a doctrine of the founding fathers that this should be a land of conquest," he told the Sunset Club. The war was "a wild excursion of jingoism into unknown seas in foreign lands."

The United States seized the Philippines from Spain, annexed the islands, and fell into a long, grim struggle against guerrillas there. "This war against the Filipinos is murder . . . this conquest is robbery, and . . . it is imperiling the government under which we live," Darrow told an audience of workingmen. "If this war be called patriotism then blessed be treason."

"True courage and manhood come from the consciousness of the right attitude toward the world, the faith in one's own purpose, and the sufficiency of one's own approval as a justification for one's own acts," Darrow wrote. He found his own courage tested when McKinley was assassinated. In the frenzy that followed, the radical publisher Abraham Isaak was jailed in Chicago and accused of aiding the assassin. Darrow wondered if he might not be next: Isaak was a good friend, and Darrow had chaired a gathering of radicals the previous spring at which several militant anarchists spoke. Under the doctrines of the Haymarket case, he told Jane Addams, he could be arrested for inciting Czolgosz to kill.

"I would gladly avoid this if I could. I have stood in front of mobs so long that my heart is heavy and my head sore," Darrow wrote to Addams. But "the powers of capital will try to stamp out all radical thought."

"I know that Isaak and his boy . . . are perfectly innocent of any crime and are in great danger," he said. "See these people . . . and if they want me . . . I shall be ready to do all I can." The fury passed. Isaak was released. A little later, Darrow gave Isaak's daughter a job.[15]

Darrow's literary interests included journalism. When Hearst opened a newspaper in Chicago in 1900, Darrow took up his pen and joined the muckrakers—a breed of journalists, including Henry Lloyd, Ida Tarbell, and Lincoln Steffens, who were stirring Americans with reportage that exposed shameful social conditions. On thirteen Sundays in 1902, Darrow wrote "Easy Lessons in Law," an elegant series of columns in the *Chicago American* that revealed how the courts robbed the common folk of justice.

Each of Darrow's "lessons" has a mundane hero who is injured by the contrivances of the industrial age—railroads, skyscrapers, sweatshops—and turns to the law for aid. But once in court these victims find defeat at the hands of high-paid corporate lawyers, corrupt judges, and legal precedents—the "Doctrine of Fellow Servants" and the like—that place property above people.

Darrow's understated style and ice-cold irony presaged the work of twentieth-century realists in stories like that of John Swanson, a worker in a mill whose owner does not believe in unions, government regulation, or safety equipment. As a result, Swanson loses a hand in an industrial accident. "The board caught as the saw passed through, his foot slipped, he threw out his right hand to save himself," Darrow wrote. "His hand fell on the side where the waste pieces of timber were wont to drop, and the blood trickled down in the saw dust below."

Pat Connor, an Irish railway man blacklisted for his role in the Debs strike, takes dangerous work on a night train, where he is decapitated by a low bridge. "The heavy oak beam struck him just above his nose and the upper third of his skull came off almost as clean as if cut by a surgeon's saw," Darrow wrote. "He really felt no pain whatsoever."

And James Clark, an ironworker, dies in a fall from a towering skyscraper. "When the workmen went to him they found a limp, shapeless bundle of flesh and blood and bones and rags," Darrow wrote. Even the emperor Trajan insisted that nets be strung beneath the acrobats in the Roman circus. But "this was before Christianity and commercialism," Darrow noted. In court, Clark's widow receives nothing, and the judge goes on to speak at a Commercial Club banquet. "There he met some of the members of the beef trust, the railway combine and the associated banks. He spoke long and feelingly about the tyranny of labor organizations and his words were loudly cheered."

In a summary essay, "The Influences That Make the Law," Darrow told readers that these tales were drawn from real cases he had witnessed, and he warned of the pernicious interests of the era. "This is the age of iron and steel," he wrote. "Legal principles and decisions and individual rights and privileges have been as much changed, contorted and destroyed as have the old business methods that have been supplanted by electricity and steam."

The "independent artisan has been destroyed" and the legislatures were now manned by "lawyers . . . saloon-keepers and professional politicians" whose function "has sunk to the business of giving public property and privileges to the few, and executing such orders as the industrial captains see fit to give."

The legal profession, Darrow told his readers, must share the blame. "The judges are chosen from the ranks of lawyers, and by natural selection the brightest of these have been placed upon the bench," he wrote. "These have been the ones who were formerly employed by corporations and great aggregations of wealth. There is no other clientage that can yield the money and influence which the ambitious lawyer craves."[16]

LIKE MANY OF his fellow radicals at the turn of the century—when the liberal impulse was strong but the structures for promoting it were weak—Darrow rambled around the Left. He would describe himself, variously, as a reformer, a Democrat, a philosophical anarchist, a socialist, a Populist, or a progressive. He was skeptical of human creeds, and had the lawyer's knack for seeing all sides of an issue. Darrow was a "gathering point for all the 'radical notions' of the time . . . a dreamer, practical man, lawyer, politician, friend of labor, friend of women, friend of literature and of experiment," wrote Hapgood.

And if Darrow claimed no one cause, neither did any claim him. He was "regarded as 'dangerous' by the ultra-conservative, and as 'crooked' by the pure idealists, and as 'immoral' by the . . . ladies of blue stocking tendency," said Hapgood. "He is radical, idealistic and practical at once . . . with a marvelous inconsistency of mind."

"As we grow older we feel more and more the hunger for applause instead of sneers," Darrow said, as he entered his fifth decade. But for meager pay, and sneers, he continued to defend radical causes in court. In the fall of 1898, he traveled to Oshkosh, Wisconsin, to represent an old Populist ally, the union leader Thomas Kidd, who had been jailed during a woodworkers' strike. It was the Debs case, writ small. There was no attorney general claiming that the sanctity of the mails called for intervention: just local prosecutors, aping Ogden's legal tactics. But things would be bad, indeed, for American workers if any local prosecutor in a company town could use the conspiracy statutes to toss union men in jail.

Conditions were wretched in Oshkosh, a town of twenty-eight thousand dominated by seven big manufacturers specializing in the production of doors, windows, and custom millwork. The average man, typically an immigrant, earned under $1 for a day's work ($240 a year, given the seasonal nature of construction), but even that was too much for the mill owners, who started hiring women and children and paid them 60 cents for each ten-hour day. The factories were run like prison camps. "All employees are to be in their places when the bell rings and whistle blows for starting, and must not absent themselves," read the rules of the Paine Lumber Company. "Employees who quit their places . . . without our consent . . . are subject to damages . . . No unnecessary talking will be allowed during working hours."

The woodworkers called a strike. The governor dispatched units of the national guard to maintain order, and Kidd and two others were arrested and charged with criminal conspiracy. The trial began in mid-October. Darrow's strategy, as in the Debs case, was to put the mill owners on trial. For the role of the Dickensian villain, Darrow selected George Paine, the union-hating owner of the town's largest factory. Darrow recounted the steps that Paine took to break the strike: hiring Pinkerton detectives to infiltrate the union; intimidating and attempting to bribe witnesses. When he got Paine on the stand, Darrow forced him to admit he had pressured the local authorities to have Kidd indicted. And Darrow surprised everyone by calling the prosecutor, W. W. Quatermass, to the stand to testify about child labor violations in the factories.

After two weeks of testimony, Darrow began his summation on October 31.

"This is really not a criminal case," he told the jury. "It is but an episode in the great battle for human liberty."

Only collective bargaining gave workingmen the leverage that they needed to free their families from servitude, said Darrow. But Paine had refused to negotiate. "He desired that these poor slaves should come to him and petition him singly, beg him as individuals, as Oliver Twist in the almshouse held out his soup bowl," Darrow said.

"The poor devil who works there for six or seven dollars a week cannot speak loud except in case of fire, and he cannot go out excepting he raise his hand like a little boy in school, and he cannot speak to his neighbor because it hinders him in his work," Darrow said. "When the poor slaves go in there at a quarter to seven in the morning they lock the door to keep them there; and when the whistle sounds at twelve they send their guards around to unlock the doors. And when one o'clock comes again, this high priest of jailers sends his turnkey back to lock up his American citizens once more so that they cannot leave the mill until nighttime comes."

Darrow spoke for eight hours over two days without notes. He closed with a tribute to Kidd, equating the union organizer with Christ's disciples and the Abolitionists.

"Those outlaws, those disreputables, those men and women spurned, despised and accused, were the forerunners of a brighter and more glorious day," Darrow said. "Gentlemen, the world is dark . . . but it is not hopeless."

It took the jury less than an hour to acquit Kidd and his colleagues. Darrow earned only $250, though the union agreed, at his request, to print and circulate a pamphlet of his closing remarks. A Chicago newspaperman, traveling by train, came upon Amirus and spoke of the case with the old woodworker. The old man glowed at the mention of his son's name.

Darrow did not ignore his criminal practice and showed, in these years, a continuing attraction to sensational cases. One began a few days before Christmas in 1898, when thirteen-year-old Thomas Crosby shot Deputy Sheriff Frank Nye. Crosby's widowed mother, Marjorie, had struggled to keep her house through economic hard times. She hired lawyers and sued her dead husband's firm for a considerable sum it owed her. But, ultimately, the bank foreclosed on her mortgage. For weeks before the shooting, Marjorie and her son, her sister, and her aged mother had lived on nothing but oatmeal and water, shivered for lack of coal, and took turns patrolling the house with a loaded revolver. She padlocked the gate and nailed boards over the windows. For young Thomas, saving the house took on overwhelming import. When Nye arrived to evict them and used a crowbar to pry the boards away, Thomas fired once, mortally wounding the deputy. The boy and his mother were arrested and charged with murder, and their home was seized.

The trial got blanket coverage. The prosecutor was resolute: "Frank Nye was there on legal business and they knew it. The boy fired deliberately. The act constitutes murder."

When it came his turn, Darrow startled the courtroom by daring the jurors to hang the boy.

"Gentlemen of the jury, rather than have you send this boy to the penitentiary or to the reform school, to be incarcerated among criminals, where his young life would be contaminated . . . I would have you sentence him to death," Darrow told them.

His bluff worked. Thomas was acquitted, and his mother was found guilty—but of manslaughter. Darrow appealed, and the Illinois Supreme Court threw out her conviction.

The poignant tale would not be complete without a final ironic twist. A few days after the trial, Marjorie was notified that she had won a $17,700 judgment against her late husband's firm—the money she had hoped would save her home.[17]

Darrow was worried about Altgeld's declining health and spirits, and invited his friend to join his law firm, where the former governor was given top billing. The partners at Altgeld, Darrow, and Thompson stayed involved in politics and radical causes, including the plight of the Boers—the Dutch South Africans who were fighting a guerrilla war against imperial Britain. On March 11, 1902, after arguing a labor case in Chicago, Altgeld took the train to a speaking engagement in Joliet. He looked tired at the podium, but finished a forty-five-minute address in defense of the Boers by declaring that the universe, despite its swings, was ultimately just. As he stepped off the stage he was staggered by a stroke, collapsed, and died.

Darrow was called to Joliet. He put Altgeld's coffin on the train and took it back to Chicago. The body lay in state in the Chicago Public Library and thousands of mourners, despite the cold and snow, paid their respects. Darrow would give several memorial speeches in the weeks after his friend's death. Some were long rebuttals of the governor's critics. But his eulogy at the family funeral, held at Altgeld's home, was the simplest and the best.

"Liberty is the most jealous and exacting mistress that can beguile the brain and soul of man. She will have nothing from him who will not give her all," Darrow said. "But once the fierce heat of her quenchless, lustrous eyes has burned into the victim's heart he will know no other smile but hers.

"Today we pay our last sad homage to the most devoted lover, the most abject slave, the fondest, wildest, dreamiest victim that ever gave his life to liberty's immortal cause," he said.

Altgeld had made Darrow's career. He had gotten him jobs and clients and fees, introduced him to national politics, offered wise counsel, and molded his ethics and principles. Other than Amirus, no human being had done more to influence and guide Clarence Darrow. He would be missed.

"My dear, dead friend, long and well have we known you, devotedly have we followed you, implicitly have we trusted you, fondly have we loved you," said Darrow. "The heartless call has come, and we must stagger on the best we can alone."[18]

Chapter 6

LABOR'S LAWYER

Laws do not execute themselves in this world.

On a mid-November day in 1902, Clarence Darrow climbed into the elevator cage at a Lehigh and Wilkes-Barre Coal Company mine in northeastern Pennsylvania, grasped the iron bars, and sucked in his breath as he plunged into the earth. When Darrow left the cage, a quarter of a mile beneath the surface, he entered a warren of twisting gangways and steep-pitched tunnels, where bent, filthy men mined coal. Dressed in grimy overalls, their faces smeared with coal dust, standing, often, in shin-deep water, small groups of Britons, Slavs, or Italians worked by the light of the oil lamps affixed to their caps. They used hand drills and augers to open holes in the rock, which they packed with black powder and detonated. Then, with picks, they worked the shattered face, loading chunks of coal into rail cars. The air was damp, and stank of sulfur. The dust clogged the men's lungs, inducing black lung disease. Cave-ins mangled the miners, or crushed them to paste; poisonous carbonic gases killed men in moments. A mixture of coal dust and methane, known as "firedamp," fueled fiery explosions that roared down the tunnels with cyclonic power, tossing coal, timber, tools, mine cars, mules, and men. In the Pennsylvania anthracite fields, the miners died at a rate of ten per week.

Anthracite was a dense, clean-burning coal, prized for home heating, and so an essential commodity. The great financier J. P. Morgan was among those who recognized the value of "black diamond," and led the railroad interests that bought up 90 percent of the anthracite fields. They paid the mine workers, on average, a little more than a dollar a day. The miners had gone on strike, an epic confrontation was at hand, and they had hired Darrow to be their advocate.

Henry Lloyd was with Darrow on the day they toured the mine. It was a dreadful experience, Lloyd said, "like a foretaste of the Inferno."

"You might as well get used to it," Darrow told him. Heaven was reserved for Wall Street financiers. Infidels like themselves would be rooming with Satan.[1]

To SUPPLEMENT THEIR wages, the coal miners sent their daughters to work in the textile factories and silk mills that were built nearby to capitalize on the ready supply of child labor. The boys in the mining towns left school at the age of eleven or twelve to work in the breakers, towering frame buildings that housed rollers and crushers and chutes. The boys sat above the chutes and, as the coal tumbled beneath them, leaned down to pluck out worthless slate and rock. Some of the older or maimed men, their years in the mines ended, joined them—all subject to an overseer who would lash them with a stick if they dallied. They worked ten hours a day, six days a week.[2] Darrow was drawn to their plight and wrote a story—"The Breaker Boy"—published by the *American*.

> One day his little companion who always sat beside him leaned too far over as he picked the slate. He lost his balance and fell into the trough where the lumps of coal ran down. He plunged madly along with the rushing flood into the iron teeth of the remorseless breaker . . . It took a long while to stop the mighty machine, and then it was almost an hour before the boy could be put together into one pile. Several days thereafter a man in a little town in Massachusetts thought that he saw blood on some lumps of coal that he was pouring into the top of his fine nickel-plated stove—but still there is blood on all our coal—and for that matter on almost everything we use, but a man is a fool if he looks for other people's blood.[3]

THE MINERS WERE tough men. They organized unions and secret societies that included—until a Pinkerton detective infiltrated the group and helped the authorities hang twenty of them—the infamous Molly Maguires. There was more violence in 1897, during a strike organized by the fledgling United Mine Workers union, when nineteen miners were shot dead and dozens were wounded as a sheriff's posse in Latimer, Pennsylvania, opened fire on a peaceful protest march. The militia was dispatched, and the strike collapsed. The UMW had met with success during the presidential election of 1900, thanks to the leadership of young John Mitchell, who had taken over its presidency at the age of twenty-eight. Senator Mark Hanna of Ohio, the Republican campaign chairman, wanted to keep homes warm that fall and used the prospect of a Bryan victory to persuade Morgan and the operators to meet the union's demands. But the coal companies bided their time. Two years later they moved to crush the union. And some 147,000 miners walked off the job in May 1902.

"Our organization will either achieve a great triumph or it will be completely annihilated," Mitchell wrote the union organizer Mother Jones. The first two casualties were strikers, shot down by the industry's private security troops. The militia returned to the district with orders to shoot to kill. But the scales shifted in autumn's chill. As the midterm elections neared, the Republicans grew frantic about the political fallout of rising coal prices and shortages.

One railroad president, George Baer, aided the miners' cause when he assured a worried clergyman that "the rights and interests of the laboring man will be protected and cared for . . . by the Christian men of property to whom God has given control of the property rights of the country." Baer's letter, reprinted in newspapers around the nation, captured the arrogance of the robber barons at a moment when middle-class Americans were beginning to show more sympathy toward labor. "A good many people think they superintend the earth," said the *New York Times*, "but not many have the egregious vanity to describe themselves as its managing directors."[4]

In Washington, President Roosevelt grew anxious. "I fear there will be fuel riots of as bad a type as any bread riots we have ever seen," Roosevelt wrote a friend. He dreaded the responsibility of imposing order with violent measures "which will mean the death of men who have been maddened by want and suffering." The president called the union leaders and the mine owners to Washington. Mitchell was a conservative trade unionist who recognized that the union's fate lay with public opinion. He had a calm and modest deportment and deferred to Roosevelt. The operators sulked like brats. No American president had intervened in a labor dispute, except to crush strikers. "I now ask you to perform the duties invested in you as President," the coal industry's John Merkle told Roosevelt, "to at once squelch the anarchistic conditions of affairs existing in the anthracite coal regions by the strong arm of the military at your command."

Mitchell behaved "with great dignity," Roosevelt recalled. "The operators, on the contrary, showed extraordinary stupidity and bad temper, did everything in their power to goad and irritate Mitchell, becoming fairly abusive in their language to him, and were insolent to me."

Roosevelt's combative nature allowed but one response; he threatened to send federal troops to seize the mines. A week later, Secretary of War Elihu Root met with Morgan on the billionaire's yacht, the *Corsair*, to broker a deal. The miners would return to work, and a federal commission would hold hearings and impose a binding settlement. It was a momentous day. An American president had interceded in an economic dispute on behalf of labor.

"Industry had grown. Great financial corporations . . . had taken the place of the smaller concerns," Roosevelt wrote, explaining his actions in his memoirs. "A few generations before, the boss had known every man in his shop . . . he inquired after their wives and babies; he swapped jokes and stories.

"There was no such relation between the great railway magnates, who controlled the anthracite industry, and the . . . men who worked in the mines," said Roosevelt.

The result was "a crass inequality in the bargaining relation," the president said. "The great coal-mining and coal-carrying companies . . . could easily dispense with the services of any particular miner. The miner . . . however expert, could not dispense with the companies. He needed a job; his wife and children would starve if he did not get one."

"A democracy can be such, only if there is some rough approximation in similarity in stature among the men composing it," said Roosevelt. "This the great coal operators did not see."[5]

Lloyd offered to assist the miners and urged Mitchell to hire Darrow as the lead attorney. It was not a lawsuit where a jury of citizens might be swayed by a spirited appeal. The seven-man commission was led by a federal judge and had but two members with evident sympathy toward labor. It might not be "a Darrow case," Lloyd worried. Indeed, Darrow had just made headlines for calling Roosevelt a "brutal murderer" in the war with Spain. But Mitchell found he liked Darrow, put aside the objections of some of his advisers, and hired him.[6]

The opening act took place in November, at the Lackawanna County courthouse in Scranton, Pennsylvania, beneath the chandeliers of the second-floor courtroom of the Superior Court. Dressed alike in judicial black, the seven commissioners took their places in leather chairs. Mitchell, garbed in his own long black coat and black tie, bowed respectfully and read an opening statement. He was calm and forceful, though when he described the hard lives of the miners, his voice trembled. If they could earn just $600 a year, Mitchell said, the miners could leave their children in school, where they could learn the skills to better themselves.

When Mitchell finished, he took the witness stand, and Darrow led him through a brief series of questions before the coal company lawyers rose to cross-examine. It was clear, from the start, that both sides viewed the hearings as a battleground for public support. Darrow and Mitchell dwelled on the inhumane conditions, exploitative wages, and dangers of mining coal. The lawyers for the industry strove to paint the miners as selfish, violent Reds. Their lead attorney, and the toughest interrogator, was Wayne MacVeagh, a former U.S. attorney general.

"Don't you know as well as you know your name is John Mitchell that in spite of the authorities of this city, of this county, and of this state, this whole region has been treated for five months to a veritable foretaste of hell?" MacVeagh asked.

"I don't know anything of the kind," Mitchell replied.

"Well, you will before we are through with you," MacVeagh promised.

On they went, for five days, like bare-knuckled boxers in a marathon bout. Darrow, admiring Mitchell's performance, did not interfere. The most intense clashes came over Mitchell's insistence that the union had a right to employ boycotts and other forms of intimidation to keep non-union workers from taking the miners' jobs during a strike. MacVeagh had Mitchell read aloud from a roster of men who died that summer, many at the hands of union sympathizers.

MacVeagh: "You never heard that on the fifth of June a mob of your men attacked the Stanton Colliery?"
Mitchell: "No, sir."
MacVeagh: "Did you hear of a mob on that same day attacking the Hollenback breaker and burning 150 yards of fence and shooting their pistols and guns?"
Mitchell: "I did not."

"If a community . . . is aroused to a great pitch of excitement and violence, and murders are committed in consequence of the assertion of your right to deny other men the right to labor for their living," MacVeagh told him, "then I say the consequences are upon your head."[7]

But in the judgment of the reporters covering the hearings, Mitchell won the first round. And he was followed to the stand by expert witnesses who, under Darrow's questioning, described the cruel hazards of mining. "The lung when seen on post mortem is very black. It looks like a chunk of anthracite coal," said Dr. James Lenahan, the health officer for the city of Scranton. Other doctors testified to the horrible effects of poison gas and disfiguring burns, and to how their work stunted the development of the breaker boys.

"Mitchell is a wonder," Lloyd told his wife. And "Darrow is doing splendidly; he has not made a single false move." MacVeagh urged Morgan and the railroads to settle. The commission adjourned, and Darrow, Mitchell, and Lloyd traveled to Washington to haggle with MacVeagh at the Willard Hotel, where the two sides neared agreement. "We are to have something better than arbitration—conciliation," Lloyd wrote. "Darrow . . . is a master hand at this sort of thing." But the industry backed out of the deal. Hamlin Garland ran into the negotiators at the Willard and found Darrow "haggard" and Mitchell "sad, very sad."[8]

Back in Scranton, Darrow made the operators pay for their change of heart. He summoned a series of Dickensian characters to the stand to tell about life in the anthracite fields.

There was the blind and disfigured David Davis, a father of five who lost his eyes and an ear in an explosion. "My left eye was blown out clean, and my right eye was blown out on my forehead," he testified. And Harry Williams, who left school at the age of nine, told how he lost a leg in the mines at sixteen and was back at the breaker for the rest of his working life. "Poor, poor boy," one of the commissioners was heard to murmur.

Andrew Chippie was a twelve-year-old child—"a chubby little duckling of a boy," said Lloyd—sent by his mother to work in the breaker at the age of ten, after his father died in a tunnel collapse. In all that time Andrew had not seen his pay because the coal company docked his wages for rent owed by his father. "We offered as witness today a little boy *too little to be a witness.* He was eight years *old* but only about five years *grown*," Lloyd wrote his wife. "He was not too young to work in the breaker; he earned 62 cents a week."

"The Chairman ruled him out," said Lloyd. "But he couldn't rule out of his mind the tragicomic spectacle of the little wage-earner, smiling and blushing, an industrial Tiny Tim."

Then Theresa McDermott, eleven, and Annie Denko, thirteen, and Helen Sisscak, eleven, told how they worked twelve hours a day in a silk mill in violation of state law for as little as three cents an hour.

"Would you rather go to school?" asked Chairman George Gray.

"We can't, I have to go to work," said Denko.

"I would like to see your father," Gray grumbled.

"From our theory of the case the employers ought to be seen," Darrow told the chairman. "What about the employer? The father could not send them there if he did not take them."

"Laws do not amount to much, I find, up here in the mining region," said the chairman, noting the statutes that banned child labor.

"Laws do not execute themselves in this world," Darrow replied.

And then there was Henry Coll, fifty-seven, whose family was evicted from company housing that fall. It was raining, he told the commissioners, as he and wife struggled to protect her aged mother and to cover their belongings. They had to travel seven miles to find another house. His wife grew terribly ill.

"She went to bed . . . and she got choked clean and fair and died in five minutes," Coll said.

"Died?" asked the chairman, who had been stretching his legs as Coll testified, and now stopped in his tracks.

"Yes, died; yes, sir," said Coll. "I buried her yesterday . . . She died in my hands."

Tears ran down Coll's cheeks, and women in the courtroom wept. The "simple human element" was the key to the miners' case, Jane Addams recalled, "sheer pity continually breaking through and speaking over the heads of the business interests."

Just before the hearings broke for the Christmas holidays, Darrow ambushed the opposition by calling J. L. Crawford, one of the coal company presidents, to the stand. It was a tactic Darrow employed from time to time—submitting the champions of the other side to withering cross-examination—and MacVeagh had opened the door when he contended that the poor would pay the cost in higher coal prices if the miners won more money. Darrow wanted the commissioners to hear how well the operators were doing. "We are not here to show Mr. Darrow our bank account," one owner sputtered. But before the day was over, the industry acknowledged it was making fine profits and Gray announced that the commission would be governed by the presumption that the companies could afford to pay higher wages.[9]

THERE WERE SETBACKS. Darrow and Lloyd had recruited the jurist Louis Brandeis to help demonstrate how the parent railroads cloaked profits by charging their own mining subsidiaries inflated shipping fees. "These gentlemen owned the railroads and they owned the mines, and were taking money out of one pocket and putting it into the other," Darrow argued. But the commission declined to hear the evidence.[10]

And Darrow was not alone in recognizing the power of a compelling human story. The coal industry lawyers summoned a regiment of nonunion miners, officials, and townsfolk to recount the acts of violence that took place during the strike. Shop owners described the devastating effects of union boycotts and witnesses told of the beatings they received, the windows broken by rocks, and the dynamite that destroyed their front porches. George Good, a nonunion man, told how he and two friends and the sheriffs who protected them were assaulted by a mob of several thousand in the town of Shenandoah. "We began to be intercepted by women and men who began to call us 'Scab!' and to pull at our clothes and spit on us," he said. "Right behind me . . . was a woman with a hatchet trying to get at me, and a man with an axe." The brother of a deputy, trying to help the men, was beaten to death.

Darrow liked jousting with the coal company witnesses, especially General John Gobin, the national guard commander whose "shoot to kill" order had generated much sympathy for the union. The order authorized a rifleman, when meeting a "riotous element" throwing stones, to "carefully note the man attacking the column and, being certain of his man, fire upon him without any further orders." Darrow got the aged general to admit that the order could be applied, not just to armed mobs, but to rock-throwing boys and to bystanders.

"You say you had the right, where a mob or a number of people were resisting your soldier, to kill them if necessary?" Darrow asked him.

"Yes sir, I claim so," said the general.

"Did you consider that you had authority, if a boy should throw a stone at you on the street, to shoot the boy?"

"It would depend altogether upon the size of the boy."

"Can you tell your authority, sir, under the laws of this State, in reference to killing boys who stoned your soldiers?"

"Well, I never had occasion to exercise my mind on that matter," the general said.

By the time Gobin left the stand, Darrow had given the country a vivid glimpse into the minds of the authorities who suppressed industrial protests. The general conceded that the "most serious" wrongdoing he had witnessed was "the teaching of the young through that region their utter want of respect for the law."

"Did you see any mobs or riots?" Darrow asked.

"No, sir," the general replied.

"And no murders?"

"None."[11]

In the evenings and on weekends, Lloyd and Mitchell and Darrow darted about the Northeast, appearing before various political and civic organizations. Darrow and Lloyd expressed their reservations when Mitchell gave up his famous, battered felt hat and bought a new derby for a meeting with the tony National Civic Federation. Mitchell, in turn, was baffled when Darrow hooked up with the East Coast literary swells and attended a lecture by Emma Goldman. "When I was . . . younger, I hoped to reform the world, but I gave it up," Darrow told her afterward. "I love my fellow man. I'll do what I can for him, but I don't expect too much."

Lloyd admired Darrow's energy. "I am not adapted to this kaleidoscopic life. I feel distracted. Adrift," Lloyd wrote his wife. "How Darrow keeps the threads . . . I cannot imagine." It was self-preservation. At forty-five, Darrow was seeing life, more and more, as a joke with a terrifying punch line. "I think it is because it gives me something to do; busies my mind," he said, of his furious pace, "and helps me work off attacks of the blues."

After Christmas, the hearings were moved to Philadelphia, where millionaires at the saucy Clover Club gave a warm welcome to the tuxedo-clad, cigar-smoking Mitchell and his lawyers. "There is no irreconcilable conflict," the union chief told the businessmen. "As an American I believe there is no problem that we, as Americans, are unable to solve." The labor movement had come a long way from Haymarket.

At one point, the union team was visited by Mother Jones, who challenged Darrow's admiration of the "Christ-like spirit" of Eugene Debs. "Debs is a molly-coddle," Jones said. "He could have won that strike. Why didn't he burn the Pullman cars? Burn the depots? Show them he meant business."

Darrow peered at her for a moment. "And the newspapers call you the 'Angel of the Miners,' " he said.

Darrow was "universally popular. He is full of fun, courtesy and vigilance and has mastered the technicalities of the case with wonderful ease," Lloyd told his wife.

THE ANTAGONISTS BEGAN their closing arguments in early February. Baer, reading from a prepared text, gave an imperious defense of laissez-faire principles. "The perplexing question why one man should be strong, happy and prosperous, and another weak, afflicted and distressed," he said, "may be answered by Seneca's suggestion that the purpose was to teach the power of human endurance and the nobility of a life of struggle."

Darrow began speaking at two o'clock that afternoon, resumed the next morning, and did not end until evening. Every seat in the courtroom was taken; spectators lined the walls, and hundreds had been turned away. Judges and the local archbishop joined the crowd. Darrow spoke without notes. He did not take a direct road to his destination, but wandered back and forth across the path, like the waggle of a bee. He spoke of the hardships of mining, switched to the mathematics of wages, rumbled about the causes of industrial warfare, returned to the dangers that the miners faced, stirred in more statistics, and so wove, over the hours, the context for the case. Darrow capably reviewed the perplexing ways in which miners and laborers were paid, some by the hour, others by the ton. And he argued, with passion, that the unique dangers faced by miners justified their demands for better wages.

"They have come in here with broken arms, and disfigured faces, and broken legs, and with one eye and with no eyes," Darrow said. "If the civilization of this country rests upon the necessity of leaving these starvation wages to these miners and laborers or . . . upon the labor of these poor little boys from twelve to fourteen years of age who are picking their way through the dirt, clouds and dust of the anthracite coal, then the sooner we are done with this civilization and start over anew, the better. . . .

"Take these children from the breaker and shorten this day," he urged the coal operators. "You will find ways to increase the production of your breaker and ways to increase the production of your mine, and you will never miss the little boys with their black faces, and you will never be sorry that you allowed these men to live a little while longer on the face of the earth."

The short-term economics—hours and wages—were not the dominant issue. For months, the miners had been willing to settle the strike for a 10 percent raise. And it seemed likely that the commission would agree to cap the hours in a workman's day. The unsettled quarrel was over the union. Baer and his colleagues abhorred the thought of giving the miners a role in their business; it was why the operators had all those witnesses tell frightening tales of murder and riot, to portray the union as a lawless mob.

"It is well for them to say we are anarchists and criminals, that we are drunkards, that we are profligates, that we cannot speak the English language, that we are unruly boys," Darrow responded. "But it would come with far better grace from them if they could show that ever once, ever once in all their administration of these lands and of these natural bounties which Mr. Baer thinks the Lord gave to him to administer, that ever once they have considered anyone but themselves."

At times Darrow stood there, in his swallow-tailed coat, vest, and black tie, talking in conversational tones. But then he would crouch and stride across the floor, wheel toward the crowd, and thunder. He would pose, with his right hand in his pocket and his left arm raised, or wag his index finger like a rapier. As he built toward a climax he'd raise his voice, wave his right arm high, form a fist, and bring it crashing down. "In the vicinity of Scranton are at least twenty mills—silk mills, knitting mills, thread mills—where little girls from twelve to thirteen or fourteen years of age are working ten hours a day, twelve hours a day, and twelve hours at night as well," he said. "Is there any man so blind that he does not know why that anthracite region is dotted with silk mills?

"They went there because the miners were there," Darrow said. "They went there just as naturally as the wild beast goes to find its prey; they went there as the hunter goes where he can find game. Every mill in that region is a testimony to the fact that the wages that you pay are so low that you sell your boys to be slaves of the breaker and your girls to be slaves in the mills.

"I have no doubt the railroad president loves children," Darrow said. "Neither have I any doubt that the wolf loves mutton."

If it was an industrial war, if there was violence, then the operators must share the blame, Darrow said. Eight or nine men may have been killed, and "here and there dynamite was used, never once to destroy life, always to frighten," he acknowledged. But what of the widows and children of the miners killed beneath the earth, and of the Coll family and others who suffered at the hands of the industry and its stooges?

"There are all kinds of violence in this world," he said.

"I KNOW THAT we speak in a way against things that are. I believe that we dream of things that are yet to come," Darrow said, as he neared the end of his plea.

"Judge us in the light of all the impossibilities that confronted us; in the light of the severe travail through which we passed; in the light of the material which we were bound to use; in the light of the fearful, appalling odds that we faced," he asked.

"The blunders are theirs," he said, referring to Baer and the other operators. "The blunders are theirs because, in this old, old strife, they are fighting for slavery, while we are fighting for freedom. They are fighting for the rule of man over man, for despotism, for darkness, for the past. We are striving to build up man. We are working for democracy, for humanity, for the future."

When he was done, the transcript says, there was "great and long continued applause." The demonstration lasted five minutes or more, as folks crowded around Darrow to congratulate him. Mitchell was the first, grasping his lawyer's hand in thanks and approval. And "many of the capitalist women," Lloyd noted, "were quite carried away."

Darrow "began the day before with . . . the commission . . . almost openly against him. He closed with their undivided interest and admiration," said Lloyd. His friend was a man of "iron nerves and steel strength," he wrote. "After making that day and a half speech . . . he went out to dinner."[12]

The commission's final report gave the UMW much of what it wanted. "A good, substantial victory," Darrow told the press. "We didn't get all we asked, but what we did get is better than what we agreed to take last winter." There was a 10 percent raise and the adoption of an eight- or nine-hour day, depending on a man's duties. The commission urged the state to replace the industry's private police force with professional agencies answerable to the public, and to crack down on child labor abuses. But while happy with the decision, Darrow scorned the dicta. The commissioners chastised strikers for the violence and did not require that the coal operators recognize the union. In defending the "open shop" principles of industry, the commissioners had behaved in a "most cowardly" way, he told Lloyd.

It was, nevertheless, a remarkable achievement. Unions were joining the American mainstream. "The opinion of the commission is that trade unionism has come to stay and that employers must deal with these conditions," Darrow said. "That is a great victory." When Samuel Gompers was asked, years later, to pick the most crucial battle in organized labor's struggle in America, he chose the Great Strike of 1902. Mitchell's leadership, the drama of the hearings, and the arrogant behavior of the coal barons had convinced the public, and even a Republican president, that labor deserved a voice in American economic affairs.

There was a feeling, among unionists, that a tide had turned. Roosevelt was going after the trusts, and would soon call for federal income and inheritance taxes on the men he called "the malefactors of great wealth." But the robber barons would not be caught off guard again. There would be more industrial crises, and extremists on both sides, hardened in the war, would turn to kidnapping, murder, and dynamite.[13]

* *

Darrow returned to Chicago, where on February 16, six thousand people braved cold and snowy weather to welcome him, Lloyd, and Mitchell at the Auditorium. Darrow spoke, without a script, for ninety minutes. It was probably thirty minutes too long, Lloyd told his wife, but a marvelous feat of oratory just the same.

Darrow now faced a choice he had postponed as the coal commission finished its work. There was a viable movement to elect him mayor of Chicago. He was forty-five years old. If he was serious about a career in politics, this was his great chance.

It wasn't only radicals who urged Darrow to run. Carter Harrison Jr., who had been elected mayor in 1897, had parted from the Svengali who had guided his career, the Democratic chieftain Robert "Bobbie" Burke, after the jovial rascal had been indicted for pocketing public funds. Seeking revenge, Burke joined the mayor's enemies, and cast about for someone to defeat him. Darrow could win the votes of liberals and laborers, and yet the Democratic organization knew him as "a man you can talk to." And so Darrow was approached by both radical unionists and machine Democrats and urged to run for mayor.

"You now have an opportunity in this city such as comes to but few men in a generation, and seldom to the same man twice," a socialist editor, A. M. Simons, told him. It was an appealing proposition, but Darrow—immersed in the coal hearings, hundreds of miles from Chicago—was in a terrible position to weigh it. "I am told that . . . I can have the Democratic nomination by saying the word and that election would surely follow," Darrow told the *Daily News*. But "I do not know these things of my own knowledge."

Were the radical forces united and strong? His friend Thomas Kidd, the woodworkers' chief, thought not. The unions in Chicago were split into factions, and engaged in a struggle for control of the local Federation of Labor, complete with "scenes of wild disorder," the papers said, that featured "slugging and the firing of revolvers." Could Darrow believe Burke's sweet promises? Would he split the progressive vote and help elect a Republican? And, most important, did he really want to be mayor?

"I hate the fight and trouble and worry of a political campaign. I am getting lazy and like my friends and books, etc., and would rather be left alone," he told Daniel Cruice, a young labor lawyer who was helping to organize the boom. Darrow also knew that in order to be elected, he would have to forfeit his independence. "I do not believe that a fellow like me could get a Democratic nomination. By the time he got it, he would be so tied up that he would be like any other political hack."

Such questions could not be answered in Scranton or Philadelphia. So Darrow stalled. "I have been quoted as saying to friends of Mr. Harrison that I would not be a candidate," Darrow told George Schilling in a letter from Philadelphia. But Schilling should pass the word: "I have made no such statements, no pledges of any kind." The crowd of young radicals took this as a "yes," and ordered fifty thousand "Darrow for Mayor" campaign buttons. If Gompers and Mitchell supported him, and Hearst's *American* pushed his candidacy, he might even be elected.[14]

The capitalists were aghast. Should Darrow be elected, warned the National Manufacturers Association, Chicago would see "the red flower of anarchy in perfect political bloom." But many radicals also showed a lack of enthusiasm. "Mr. Darrow . . . is essentially a sentimentalist," wrote the socialist leader Daniel De Leon in the *Daily People*. "He is of that sympathetic class, among the well-to-do and professional men, whose heart does more bleeding for the woes of the workingman than its head does thinking." The working class needed to elect its own leaders, said De Leon, not look to be saved by the feckless bourgeoisie. "The road that leads over the Darrows must be blocked."[15] And Gompers and Mitchell were cool to the idea. "You ought not be wasted," said Gompers, urging Darrow to devote his "great gifts of heart and brain" to the labor movement. "Poor Darrow . . . he cannot make up his mind," Lloyd wrote, after joining an all-day meeting of Darrow's advisers at his law office on February 21. "He thinks this may be his 'opportunity.' "

As Hamlet brooded, the Harrison forces were not idle. The mayor took a bold stance on municipal ownership of the streetcar lines, depriving Darrow of that popular issue. A businessman working for Harrison paid $9,000 to teamster boss John Driscoll to undermine Darrow's union support. And word came to Darrow that the *American* would not be with him. Hearst had his own political ambitions—to win the White House in 1904—and needed Harrison in Illinois.[16] "If the *American* had seen fit to be with me, it could have been accomplished," Darrow told Cruice. But "the *American* would support Harrison to satisfy some of Mr. Hearst's political ambitions."

Darrow announced that he would not run, and Cruice was nominated by the unionists instead. In assessing the episode, it is hard not to believe that Darrow made the right choice. "I value my independence more than I do any office," he said. And that was surely true.[17]

DARROW'S PERFORMANCE IN the coal strike had brought him fame and prominence. He was now the nation's leading labor lawyer. But notoriety made Darrow a target, as well. His actions were spotlighted and his flaws magnified. When announcing that he would not run for mayor, Darrow had promised Cruice not to endorse another candidate, and "to do you some good at the right time." It was a hasty pledge, which he almost immediately broke, inspiring withering criticism.

The quandary was the streetcar war. The transit companies were maneuvering to kill all legislation that would give the city the authority to own and operate its streetcars. Darrow was a leader in the movement for municipal ownership. He knew Cruice could not win and that Harrison was far stronger on the issue than the Republican candidate. Judge Edward Dunne, a colleague in the movement, asked Darrow to endorse the mayor. In return, Darrow would get patronage jobs for his friends, and Harrison's backing should he choose to make a run for higher office. Cruice and his supporters were stunned, and then incensed, by the news. DARROW BRANDED A LABOR TRAITOR . . . A STAB IN THE BACK, read the headlines in the *Tribune*.

"When Clarence S. Darrow was defending men who had bribed juries in cases where crippled children were asking for justice from the traction companies which had injured them, it was explained in extenuation that he was acting as 'a lawyer.' I suppose it will be explained he is acting as 'a lawyer' now," an angry unionist, William Burns, sputtered at a rally. Another old ally, Altgeld's friend Joe Martin, called Darrow "a creature of purchase."

In a letter to Cruice, Darrow tried to explain. "It [was] a promise which, if I should keep . . . would mean that I would help sacrifice the rights of the people of Chicago," he wrote. Responding to accusations that he defended unions only for fat fees, Darrow offered a public accounting. He received $1,000 for his months of work in the Debs case, he said, and $10,000 in the coal arbitration. "I closed my office for four months" to represent the miners, Darrow noted. "I told them that ordinarily I would charge $100 a day but that I would take their case and when I got through they could pay me what they liked, or nothing at all. I got them a raise of $8 million and $3 million in back pay and I sent them a bill for $10,000 . . . I would have sent a corporation a bill for $50,000 for the same work."

Harrison won a fourth term. The Democrats kept control of City Hall. The results were tight enough that Darrow's decisions not to run and to endorse the mayor almost certainly made the difference. But Darrow's radical friends felt betrayed, and the episode stoked his reputation for guile and trickery.[18]

Chapter 7

RUBY, ED, AND CITIZEN HEARST

Ruby and me, we both love Darrow.

In July 1903, Darrow married Ruby Hamerstrom. For years he had vowed that no new wife would claim his freedom, and so his friends were stunned by the news. A private ceremony was performed by Judge Edward Dunne, attended only by Ruby's brother Fred and Darrow's law partner and roommate, Francis Wilson, who had been charged with quietly securing the marriage license, slipping through the doors of the bureau just before they shut for the day. There were champagne toasts and then Darrow and Ruby, evading the press, took a train to Montreal, where they boarded the steamship *Bavarian* for Europe. Darrow spent much of the voyage seasick in his berth, as Ruby read to him from a history of France. She had dreams of a six-month, or longer, trip around the world. But Darrow's investments were faring poorly, and they returned to Chicago in mid-October.

Ruby was "incurably in love," she confessed. "He seemed to be all sorts and all ages, from the boy that he never outgrew to the old man that he never became." And he was smitten. She was not a striking beauty, but pretty and fashionable. She qualified as a new woman but not so militant and, once married, content to be, as she described herself, "the weed in the knot of the tail of The Kite." She wrote for the women's sections, not the front page, and of trends and fashions, not politics or crime. "You can't really expect good Irish wit from a Swede . . . that wears French heels, I s'pose," she told Darrow's sister Jennie.[1]

Yet Ruby had wit enough to land him. "He said . . . that I was the only girl he ever liked that much who didn't take the courting out of his hands," she said proudly. In Darrow's divorce, he had to "relinquish his every last dollar's worth of property for his release," Ruby noted, but she promised she would never ask for alimony.

At eighteen, Ruby had rebelled against the dour strictures of her Lutheran home, where she had been expected to help her mother raise her six siblings. She fled from Galesburg to Chicago and the life of a newspaperwoman. Ruby had not finished high school but got work as a bookkeeper, looked for freelance assignments, and discovered a demand for stories about the doings of middle-class women—their clubs and trips and causes. She and Darrow had decided to marry in 1902, and she hoped to buy a nice house, with elm trees and a lawn.

"Just a word tonight, instead of a Christmas present, to tell you that I think you are the dearest, sweetest girl on earth," Darrow wrote her on Christmas Eve. "I love you with my whole heart and want you all to myself and I hope that this is the last Christmas so long as I live that I can not have you as I want you—all for my own."

"Goodnight dearest sweetheart," he signed the note. "Remember that you are always loved by your crazy old Clarence Darrow."

Ruby was not ruled by social conventions. She accepted Darrow's Negro friends. She liked to have a drink or two at parties or a restaurant. As women gave up their corseted, floor-sweeping gowns for more liberating fashions, Ruby was an early enthusiast. And she had a modern view of marriage. "My informant . . . told me that in addition to Darrow being a Socialist, both he and his wife are free lovers," wrote a Pinkerton detective, spying on the couple. "The wife made the statement this evening that a man had a right to desert his wife and family if he felt like it." As long as no rival made a serious claim on Ruby's place in Darrow's life ("You've got the certificate, and no one will ever get that away from you," he told her), she tolerated his infidelities. But she was conventional enough to fret about social standing, and she could be snobbish and catty; she liked nice things, and prized the wealthy and prominent company he kept.

Darrow's brothers and sisters, who had maintained a warm relationship with Jessie and Paul, tried to make Ruby feel welcome. They were open-minded; the aged Amirus had taken a far younger second wife as well. But Paul did not warm to Ruby, and she thought he was spoiled and stubborn and manipulative when exploiting his father's guilt over the divorce. Paul "appropriated every dollar available that his father permitted him to help himself to," she griped. Ruby was jealous, as well, of the hooks that Jessie still had in Darrow. She sulked after learning that Jessie left the marriage with real estate and a lovely set of diamonds and told Darrow's sisters that Jessie's controlling nature was the cause of the breakup.

Nor did Jessie much like Ruby, whom she instantly identified as a threat to her financial well-being. Darrow was still supporting Jessie with monthly payments, and would until she remarried, late in life. From Europe he wrote to assure her that there was enough money for them all, and that the stipends would continue. "I shall live where I did before or in some cheap house nearby and shall not spend money or be extravagant in any way," he promised Jessie. "So long as I live you will both come first." Ruby accepted this, Darrow promised Jessie. It was a dubious claim. The cost of maintaining a wife and an ex-wife is a reason why, though Darrow earned high fees, he was generally on edge about money. He took to speculating in the stock market, and in banks and gold mines and other ventures, but had no gift for it.

Darrow's efforts did not dispel the tension. After he returned from Europe, Darrow invited Paul to come to Washington to see him argue a case before the U.S. Supreme Court, but his son rebuffed him, just as he turned down his father's invitations to spend evenings together or to join him at the law firm. Their relationship, which had improved, took a step backward.

"I have always cared for him more than anything on Earth . . . I have tried to live an unselfish life . . . tried to consider others and do all in my power for their happiness," Darrow wrote Jessie. But his self-pity flared to anger. "Paul is too young to judge me," he wrote. "And neither to him nor anyone else shall I make any effort to be judged or understood. I shall go on with what is left of my life and try to live it as honestly and courageously as I can and pay no attention to the rewards or punishment which the world always gives without any regard to merit."

It wasn't the happiest time. Darrow's nephew Karl recalled the family's feverish maneuvering to keep Jessie, Paul, and Ruby from confronting one another at family gatherings. Gradually, Darrow drifted from his brothers and sisters.[2]

THEY HAD PLANNED to return to the Langdon, but Ruby did not want to start a new life in his old bachelor haunts. "When we came home . . . I felt I never before had seen a pigpen inhabited by humans. They all in the Langdon had used Darrow's place for a loafing place, burned all his wood [and] mopped up the ashes with beautiful velvet pillows I'd made and sent him one Christmas," she told one of his sisters. "The janitor's wife was supposed to keep the place in order, but whisked in and out very briefly, just enough to collect what was paid her."

Nor were the girls from the Langdon gracious. "One of our first callers was Gertrude Barnum, hysterically and shamelessly demanding to know how Darrow had dared to marry after promising her and all the others that he never would, and on several later occasions she came in tantrums and tears to attack us both for having betrayed them all," Ruby said. It was a rude hello to "the unwelcome stranger-bride," as she called herself, and she let Darrow know about it. The Darrows moved to a new apartment, on Sheridan Road, "more suitable and roomy and less imbedded in the soot of the West Side," she recalled.

The intensity of her new life left her breathless. "It was like wonderland," Ruby said. "I was busy learning how to manage my life, our home, making so many varied new acquaintances . . . which seemed only part of the great world I now dwelt in." She worked hard to keep Darrow happy. "He had escaped from a first marriage that had been unbearable," she explained, "and that made me careful to the greatest degree possible that he should not call me another mistake."

It is hard to find a friend of Darrow's who didn't marvel, not only that he had remarried, but that he married Ruby. The near-universal opinion of Darrow's pals is that his new wife was his intellectual inferior. They talk of her henpecking, of her "twittering," and of her insecurity and possessiveness. Ruby "is not a good sharer," one of her sisters-in-law wrote. She "would like to monopolize Clarence rather entirely."

As the years passed, Ruby took control of Darrow's life. She watched his health, served his guests, helped him with correspondence, and selected his clothes. He grew to rely upon her for the dull details of life, and she to exult in self-sacrifice. Darrow was a finicky eater who—except for a brief experiment as a vegetarian—clung to beefsteak and boiled vegetables. And so, even in the restaurants of Paris or New York, "I never ordered or ate in his presence any dish other than whatever he wished for himself," she recalled, proud of her self-abnegation.

Darrow had complained that Jessie was a poor hostess for the friends he brought home. Ruby was determined to do better. "We served . . . after dinner coffee—(in the most lovely tea-sized cups one ever would see!) There were daintily colored and arranged bonbons, fine liqueurs, in most enticing old-world glasses—exquisitely-cut finger bowls on cut glass saucers—either a low barge bowl or low wide bowl full of many-colored fruits, usually decorated with glowing cherries or strawberries dotted in among green geranium leaves here and there," she wrote. "From our honeymoon trip I had carried back in a large valise the Sheffield steel, ivory-handled knives & forks we bought at the manufacturing-plant, that he had said before we left home he wanted,—and all his favorite white-metal spoons of all sizes and serving-uses, to be polished like silver. In every respect the table was always a part of the success of the meal, as spick and span and artistically arranged as though for—any other king of my universe."

Still, he loved her. Their physical relationship was warm and satisfying. He would write her amorous notes from the road, and nestle in their big brass bed with her when home, reading aloud as they cuddled. He called her, affectionately, "Rube" or "Ruben." And she called him "D." And her loyalty to Darrow, time would show, was unshakable.

"How are you getting along with Ruby?" Lincoln Steffens asked him.

"Fine," Darrow replied, "because Ruby and me, we both love Darrow."[3]

* *

Darrow also acquired a new law partner. Altgeld's death left an empty office at the firm. He tried to lure Brand Whitlock to Chicago. "I would like you with me if it can be properly arranged," Darrow wrote Whitlock toward the end of 1902. "We need a good man who can do all kinds of work. I do not know whether you can or not. Literary men . . . are not generally the ones who can. Still, I think so much of you that I wish you could."[4]

But Whitlock was launching a political career in Toledo and so, ignoring his own insight, Darrow turned to another literary lawyer. Edgar Lee Masters was thirty-four when he joined the firm, publishing verse under a pseudonym because of the public's poor opinion of poets. His biggest achievement to this time was marrying the daughter of a railway executive. He was short and precise, "a man with a strange, rare mind," Ruby thought.

Like Darrow's, the bulk of Masters's practice was on the civil side. Though they leaned toward the underdog, Darrow, Masters & Wilson would take either the injured plaintiff or the corporate defendant as clients. That is what lawyers did. In one notorious case, Masters defended "Mother" Mary Lyons, who was charged with employing an underage girl at her brothel. He had been hired to do so by Egbert H. Gold, a lecherous rich man who kept the teen quartered at the whorehouse for his personal use. That was fine with Masters, until Gold failed to pay his fee. Then Masters sued him, and publicly exposed the man's tawdry behavior.

Masters had much in common with Darrow, maybe too much. As literary men, both were American realists. In politics, they venerated Jeffersonian principles. (Masters had a bust of Jefferson in his office.) If the poet's father, Hardin Masters, was not a bookish infidel like Amirus, he was still a roguish sort whose independent ways clashed with the "dour Puritanism" of their town. And Masters, too, had endured a childhood with an emotionally distant mother of New England stock. "Her cutting words, her flaming temper froze my heart," he recalled.

As men, Darrow and Masters craved the love and attention they had missed as boys. Each dreamed of artistic fame. In the meantime, they scrapped for fees and fought for radical causes, hung out with the literary set, and cheated on their wives. Masters was a devoted patron of Chicago's high-class whorehouse, the Everleigh Club, and wrote odes to "Maxine" and the other corseted, silk-ribboned harlots. "I had never been able to see anything wrong in erotic indulgence," he recalled. "On that subject I was as emancipated as an animal." Each was smart and both could be mean, but Darrow was better at disguising it. Masters was a hater.

At first, and for several years, the Darrows were charmed by the new law partner. Ruby recalled "mighty jolly" nights with Masters and his wife and other friends, sharing wisecracks over cocktails and dinner. Darrow had wooed him for some time, Masters recalled, and he had resisted. "I was in doubt about making an alliance with a lawyer who was in some quarters feared, in others detested, who was redolent of free love, anarchism, socialism and what not," he said. "There was something shabby about his repute, as there was a good deal shabby about his dress and his personal hygiene . . . His eyes in good humor were kindly and sleepy; in anger they were like Marat's or Robespierre's—or a rattlesnake."

Financial woes brought Masters to heel. "I had desperate hours when my bank balance was down," he confessed, and if he joined Darrow, "perhaps in a few years I could lay up enough to retire and write poetry."

Darrow was the rainmaker, and by far the better man before a jury. Masters was a fine legal technician who wrote compelling appellate briefs and kept Darrow focused on the business. "I drove the human insects out of the office as their loafing place, where they sat about discussing anarchy, free love, Bryan, the coming revolution and all such things," said Masters. "Soon the office ran as quietly as a sewing machine." Before long, they were earning as much as $30,000 each a year—the equivalent of more than half a million dollars now—and Masters had bought a fine house in Hyde Park and was taking his wife to Europe.

Their early success masked discord. Hardin Masters had practiced law, his son complained, "by ear, by inspiration, by great bursts of energy," and so did Darrow. As the lead partner, Darrow would dump cases on Masters without warning and head off to a remunerative lecture date. Once, when Darrow disappeared, it cost the firm a $25,000 payday. He had a relaxed attitude toward the obligations of partnership, as well. When short on cash, Darrow would pocket a fee—in effect, stealing from the firm. Darrow's "drawl and his sleepy ways, his humorous turns of speech, his twisted ironies made him a pleasant man to be with. He seemed an old-fashioned soul, easy and lounging and full of generosities," Masters would recall. But "he was penurious, grasping and shrewd. According to some of the descriptions of Lincoln, those who speak of Lincoln's cunning and his acting ability, I think he was more like Lincoln than anyone."

"He was a radical to the outward view [while] using that pose to play with the corporations . . . and get money," Masters recalled. "He was always gambling in the stock market and generally losing. It was this thirst for money that ruined him."[5]

And so Masters never became an intimate friend, like Altgeld, that Darrow could turn to for counsel. Lloyd was that sort of comrade, but Darrow was dismayed to discover, on the day he returned from his honeymoon, that his friend had died of pneumonia while he was away. "I loved him as I have few people and trusted him as I did almost no one else," Darrow wrote to Lloyd's widow. "I can scarcely think of anything today but this."

Masters had been with the firm a few months when he and Darrow joined in the defense of John Turner, an anarchist from Great Britain who had been seized in New York in October 1903 and ordered to be deported under the terms of the "Anarchist Exclusion Act," passed in the wake of the McKinley assassination. Masters wrote an elegant brief, and he and Darrow argued the case before the U.S. Supreme Court. "No danger exists to this country from without. No danger exists to it from the . . . acts of Jacobites within," they wrote. "The danger which now confronts the people of this country is the aggression of government."

Their appearance at the Supreme Court, however, was not a good experience. Masters got up and spoke for an hour and "was greatly heckled by members of the court." Darrow did well for fifteen minutes, Masters recalled, "then his wings wobbled." The Court unanimously ruled against Turner. "Governments . . . cannot be denied the power of self-preservation," the justices concluded.

Darrow fared better at rescuing Masters's brother-in-law, Dr. Carl Stone, who had been convicted under the Comstock laws and fined $500 for selling patent medicines, including the supposed contraceptive "Dr. Lefevre's French Female Pills," through the mail. Masters had gone to see the U.S. postal inspector on the case, who told him that "the country was full of sexual immorality" and that "the way to stop it was to have the women understand that they could not indulge themselves without taking the risks of nature."

"I could do nothing with this violent fool," Masters recalled. But by calling in favors at the federal courthouse, Darrow had "Dr. Lefevre" listed as "David Stone," and the doctor was able to escape identification until a newspaper reporter, working on an unrelated story, stumbled upon the ruse two years later. When confronted, Darrow conceded he had "done all I could to shield" the Stone family. The doctor was ruined nonetheless. "Carl gasped like an animal caught by the dogs in a thicket," Masters said. Stone drank too much, "fell into shabby adulteries," and, after contracting typhoid fever, died.[6]

On the afternoon of December 30, 1903, Helen Masters got an ominous phone call from her husband. "I just wanted to know if you . . . are home," he said, then hung up.

Many such calls were made that day, as word spread through the Loop of a fire at the Iroquois Theatre. It was Christmas week, and the city's new playhouse was packed for a matinee of the musical comedy *Mr. Bluebeard.* At around three fifteen p.m., the gaily costumed chorus opened the second act. Above them, a stagehand in the catwalks saw a bit of curtain touching a spotlight catch fire. The flames spread swiftly and, as burning sheets of painted scenery fell to the stage, the actors ran toward the stage door. The rush of air through the door sent a wave of fire roaring—like a cyclone, witnesses would say—out into the audience, igniting seats and clothing. Women and children writhed in agony and were suffocated in the fiery fumes, or trampled as they fled. For days the newspapers tried to help grieving families identify the bodies ("Boy—Lace shoes; black bow tie, with red dots; black stockings; about 10 years old"). More than six hundred people died. There were no exit signs, no fire alarm, and no sprinklers. No theater employee had been trained for an emergency. Skylights that might have vented the smoke were nailed shut. Segments of fire escapes were missing.

Chicago's building commissioner had warned Mayor Harrison and the aldermen that the city's theaters were death traps, but the matter had been referred to committee. After an inquest, the mayor, the city fire marshal, one of the theater's owners, and others were indicted. Then, on January 12, while tempers raged and even the city's clergymen were demanding retribution, Darrow published a letter in the *Daily News* asking the citizenry to show restraint.

"Had the theater been constructed . . . with the view of making life as safe as possible these dead would be still alive," Darrow wrote, making no excuses for those at fault. "It is likewise plain that if the city officials had compelled the enforcement of the ordinances . . . these lives would have been safe . . . This terrible tragedy was the direct result of an effort to save money at the serious risk of human life."

But "to send anyone to prison for this dire disaster could not bring back one of the dead," said Darrow. "It would be vengeance pure and simple and the fruits of vengeance are always evil." In Chicago, every day, working people died while raising buildings or laboring in factories and railroad switchyards. Poorer folk lost their lives in train accidents in which wealthier customers, traveling in safer cars, emerged unscathed. "The victims of our cruel greed, with maimed limbs and broken lives, are met at every corner of the street," Darrow wrote, "and every graveyard is sown thick with the forgotten dead whose lives have been sold for gold. . . .

"Grievous are the sins of this commercial, money-getting age," Darrow concluded. "It's neither just nor humane to lay all the cruelty and sin of a generation upon the shoulders of a few men, who are no more responsible than any of the rest."

Darrow had friends at City Hall and clients in the theater industry. But his sentiment was authentic. He had made similar appeals when the Harrison assassination and the Haymarket case caused comparable ferment. Eventually, the criminal charges against Harrison and most other city officials were dropped. In the civil litigation, Darrow's law firm represented families of the fire's victims. At one point, Nellie Carlin, who specialized in probate cases for the firm, "shattered all records" for a female attorney. The plaintiffs, however, received a cruel setback when federal judge Kenesaw Mountain Landis ruled against them on a technicality. In the end, very few of the victims' relatives received anything.[7]

* *

Harrison's troubles were good news, at least, for William Randolph Hearst, who was running for president and contending with the mayor's own presidential ambitions.

Purists of the Left and Right detested Hearst. The forty-year-old congressman and publisher had used his newspapers to crusade against trusts and corruption and to advance progressive causes, earning him the enmity of the moneyed class. But Hearst's raw opportunism and his role in starting the Spanish-American war alienated as many liberals. Darrow was a realist, and Hearst was a client. So he took the view of the publisher's working-class supporters in New York—"Hoist, Hoist, he's not the woist!"—and helped organize the William Randolph Hearst League in Chicago. "I cannot understand nor help regret his present political attitude," said the appalled Eugene Debs, when asked about Darrow's actions.

To curry support among midwestern Democrats, Hearst had opened the populist *American* in Chicago in 1900. The antics of those who worked in the "madhouse on Madison Street," as the Hearst building became known, added spice to the city's already formidable, fiercely competitive journalism, and not a few of Chicago's famous gangsters learned their craft in the violence that marked the circulation wars. When a band of Hearst "sluggers"—most of them former prizefighters—were arrested after destroying a newsstand, beating its proprietor unconscious, and brazenly driving off in an *American* circulation wagon, Darrow defended them. Years later, after they graduated to bootlegging, murder, and other crimes, he remained their attorney.[8]

In one sensational case, Darrow, Masters & Wilson represented Hearst in a dispute involving the famous Wild West sharpshooter Annie Oakley, who claimed to have been libeled when a wire service reported that she had been caught stealing "the trousers of a Negro" to get money for her drug habit. In fact, it was a different Annie—a burlesque dancer named Maude Fontenella who sometimes performed as "Any Oak Lay"—and the genuine cowgirl spent years profitably suing the newspapers that had carried the story. Maude was brought to Chicago by Hearst's private detectives to testify at the trial. After sizing her up, Masters got her to a doctor for a shot of cocaine before she took the stand. It invigorated the witness, but the jury found for Oakley.

In the "reign of horror" and generally chilly political climate that followed McKinley's assassination, Darrow had a hankering for a good free-speech case, he told Whitlock, and Hearst and his editors supplied one.

The *American* was then crusading against the "gas trust" that, the newspaper said, was gouging Chicago consumers. The gas interests sued, and when Judge Elbridge Hanecy sided with them, the paper ripped him in its columns and cartoons. Hanecy charged Hearst and six employees with contempt, alleging that "scandalous matter was printed . . . to terrorize and intimidate this court." The managing editor, Andrew Lawrence, and a reporter, H. S. Canfield, were sentenced to jail. There was bad blood between Hanecy and Darrow, and their exchanges in court were frequently hostile. So Darrow appealed to a more amenable jurist—his friend, the politically ambitious and liberal Judge Edward Dunne—who agreed to hear Darrow's plea for a writ of habeas corpus.

"It is for the cause they represent that powerful interests desire to place these men in jail: this yellow journal must be suppressed for through its columns has been heard the bitter cry of the outcast millions who have here found voice," Darrow told Dunne. "I care for this paper and for these men because a blow struck at them is a blow struck at the freedom of the press, which is really the greatest privilege the citizen enjoys, the greatest safeguard of human liberty."

The journalists were freed. "Public officials . . . have always been and always will be subject to criticism because of their official acts," Dunne ruled. "It is one of the incidents and burdens of a public life."[9]

HEARST PAID HIS stars well, and demanded loyalty. When the publisher launched his presidential campaign in 1904 he called on Darrow to lead it in Illinois. The job ensnared Darrow in considerable intrigue, as three groups now vied for control of the Democratic Party in Chicago: Darrow, Hearst, and Dunne led the so-called radicals, Harrison had his personal following, and the Hopkins-Sullivan machine formed the third faction. They met at the state convention, where the radical and machine forces joined, at first, to crush Harrison. The Hopkins faction imported squads of "muscular, red fisted, red faced street fighters" from local street gangs like the "Stockyard Indians" and the "Black Rabbits," to intimidate Harrison's supporters.

It was an unholy alliance. As much as he liked Darrow, his pal George Schilling told a friend, "I would under no circumstance advise that you assist him . . . The Hopkins element . . . are pirates and bandits whose only purpose . . . is to protect and extend the predatory interests of a lot of franchise grabbers." The machine men proved him right when, having disposed of the mayor, they double-crossed Hearst and Darrow. All that was missing was "the flying of the Jolly Roger," a newsman wrote. "The . . . buccaneers on the platform chortled until they shook like masses of jelly."

Darrow rallied the Hearst forces and tugged other delegates to their cause. They massed in the rear of the hall, yelling "Pirates!" and "Rotten!" at the machine men on the dais. Seizing the moment, Darrow, white-faced, his eyes intent, climbed onto a chair and offered a resolution binding the state's delegates to Hearst at the Democratic convention. It passed, and in the giddy moments afterward, Hearst's troops demanded that Darrow be nominated as the Democratic candidate for governor. The nomination was his if he wanted it. But Darrow had no desire to lead the fractious party against a Republican ticket topped by the popular Theodore Roosevelt in the fall. He shoved his way to the podium and told the Democrats that he would not accept the nomination.

In July, the battle shifted to the Democratic national convention in St. Louis. The Wall Street Democrats—the old gold and Grover Cleveland men—united behind New York judge Alton Parker and labeled themselves "the reorganizers." William Jennings Bryan had run and lost in 1896 and 1900 and was not a declared candidate, and so Hearst was the progressive alternative. But the publisher was a poor politician—he had a reedy voice and a fear of public speaking—and Bryan schemed to supplant him. When the Hopkins-Sullivan crew voted with the "reorganizers" on procedural questions Bryan challenged their credentials on the floor. "No band of train robbers ever planned a robbery . . . more deliberately, or with less conscience," he thundered. But this was not 1896. His challenge was soundly defeated, and Darrow had to plead with Hopkins for time to speak for Hearst.

It was, for Darrow, his own "cross of gold" moment. Who knew what might happen if Darrow could touch the hearts in the hall and tug them away from Wall Street and Parker? It was after midnight—still prime time in the days when sessions lasted until dawn—when Darrow rose to speak. He reminded the Democrats of the glorious days of '96, when they had campaigned in the spirit of Thomas Jefferson, for a real democracy. The forces that now led the party, Darrow said, were the very ones who had sold them out for Mark Hanna's money.

"Gentlemen of the convention," Darrow said, "even now it may not be too late to consider and to pause. . . .

"The United States is not . . . made up alone of the pawnshops that line the narrow, crooked lane which men call Wall Street; shops where human souls are placed in pawn for gold," he said. "The United States is the place where countless millions, under the clear sky and in the bright light of day, do their work and live their lives and earn their bread without the aid of schemes. . . .

"If this convention would gain the votes of the common people of the United States, that great class without whom there never was a Democratic party, they must name a man who has fought the battles of the poor," he said. "With such a man the mighty hosts of workers from the fields and prairies, from the factories and mills, from the railways and the mines . . . will bring us a victory that will be a victory indeed. . . .

"This great party will come back from the golden idols and the tempting flesh pots and once more battle for the rights of man!"

Darrow barely mentioned Hearst at all. He "enlivened the wearying crowd," the *Washington Post* reported, and "carried the galleries," said the *Tribune*. But there was, alas, no stampede. The spectators may have loved it, but those were Parker men on the floor of the convention. The Gold Democrats got their man, who was trounced by Roosevelt in November.

Darrow had taken Paul with him to St. Louis. He was trying to patch things up with his son, who had just graduated from Dartmouth. They had a long ramble that summer to Colorado, Portland, Seattle, and Vancouver and joined a Dartmouth group for three days camping in the Canadian Rockies. And in January, Paul joined his father and Masters on a trip to Cuba. To ward off seasickness, Darrow organized an onboard poker game. He feared that Paul was too serious and straitlaced. "You have all your life to work," he told his son. "Take a boat ride to Europe or something."[10]

* *

Amid the tempestuous events of that election season, Darrow published two novels and mourned the death of his father.

Amirus passed away in April 1904. The funeral was held at Darrow's brother Edward's house, and the body, in keeping with the old infidel's wishes, was cremated. Darrow's relationship with his father dominates the opening chapters of *Farmington*, a novel of boyhood, which was published the year of Amirus's death. Darrow had written it on his honeymoon, on trains and in hotels. It is the story of his life in Kinsman—a sturdy piece of American realism that preceded such better-known accounts of Midwest villages as his law partner's *Spoon River Anthology*, or his friend Sinclair Lewis's *Main Street*.

John Smith, the narrator of the novel, grows up in a small town. His father runs a gristmill, not a furniture shop, but otherwise is Amirus. "No man knew so much of books as he," says Smith, "and no man knew less of life."

Darrow draws a pastoral scene—a one-room schoolhouse, baseball, summer evenings—on which he splatters acid. For all the talk of idyllic boyhood, summer days, and willow trees, death is the foremost resident of Farmington, "the little . . . town beside the winding stream where I used to stone the frogs."

Darrow recites the inscriptions on the cool granite monuments in the cemetery. He takes his readers to Squire Allen's grand funeral, and to a burial ceremony for a young Union soldier, "glorious, brave, and noble," who went to war with a smile. We see Darrow's mother, struck down at forty-eight by cancer, "lying cold and dead" in the front room of their home. We meet his Sunday school teacher, pale and dying from tuberculosis. And we contemplate the folly of Aunt Mary, who so carefully preserved her parlor from the wear of visitors that it is spotlessly clean on the day that she's laid out in her coffin, until the neighbors track mud on her Brussels carpet, as the bluebottle flies swarm about her corpse.

"All my life I have been planning and hoping and thinking and dreaming and loitering and waiting," reads Darrow's coda. "All my life I have been getting ready to begin to do something worth the while. I have been waiting for the summer and waiting for the fall; I have been waiting for the winter and waiting for the spring; waiting for the night and waiting for the morning; waiting and dawdling and dreaming, until the day is almost spent and the twilight close at hand."

Darrow was feeling the twilight close at hand.

Darrow's critique of small-town values was so subtly expressed that the *Tribune* missed the point. "If he has any bitterness he has concealed it," the reviewer wrote, congratulating him for producing "an idyll" of boyhood. The *New York Times* saw Darrow's book with a clearer eye. Its author writes "so much truth at times that you are a bit afraid," the paper said. It called *Farmington* "real art."

William Dean Howells was delighted with Darrow's effort. "I could not lay your book down until I had finished it," he wrote. It was weakened by "grammatical solecisms," he said, "but it is also full of bottom facts and abounds in human nature." He compared it to Tolstoy's memoir of boyhood and took it to several publishing houses. But the publishers shrank from the bite of Darrow's work and concluded that the public would not buy it. Harper & Brothers found it "cold and depressing" with "unnecessary philosophizing" and decided that "the general effect is disheartening." Darrow finally got the book to a local publishing house in Chicago, whose meager sales and marketing resources confined it to obscurity.

Darrow's second novel, *An Eye for an Eye,* followed quickly. It was scrawled on vacation in the summer of 1904. The new book had quite a different setting than *Farmington,* but its fatalistic theme was much the same. "It took years of care and toil to show me that life is stronger than man, that conditions control individuals," Darrow wrote in *Farmington.* In *An Eye for An Eye,* he drew the lesson explicitly. Written in the same bleak style as the "Easy Lessons in Law" series, the novel tells the tale of Jim Jackson, an inmate on death row. From his cell, Jackson recounts the story of his crime: how he married in a hurry, lost his way at work, ran out of money, and was stuck in an unhappy marriage because the church and the law frowned on divorce. He describes how, one night in a drunken argument, he killed his wife with a poker and was tried in a city inflamed by the newspaper accounts of the crime. "I never intended to kill anybody but somehow everything just led up to it," says Jackson. "And I didn't know I was getting into it until it was done, and now here I am."

The two books of fiction, like Darrow's previous essays and his newspaper work, buffed his reputation in the literary world. He had helped set Whitlock on his path as a serious writer, and had edited a book of Altgeld's writings. In 1905 he joined with Jack London, Upton Sinclair, and other authors to found the Intercollegiate Socialist Society, a literary group for college campuses. And he was a founding member, with Hamlin Garland, of the Society of Midland Authors. But neither of Darrow's novels was commercially successful. They were imperfect, written in nooks of his life—dashed off as afterthoughts, almost. He was discouraged at the public reaction, and abandoned the art. Had Darrow found the means and the dedication, he may have emerged as another Dreiser. Garland certainly thought so.

"This is very true, very sad, and very beautiful," Garland wrote in the back of his copy of *Farmington.* "He is humorous but he is also tragic in the hopelessness of his outlook. He voiced the doubts and the questioning of our generation." *Farmington* was "only a fragment, but it is noteworthy for its diction, which has something rich and noble in its music." He urged Darrow to keep working on the book, but Darrow said he did not have the time, or money, to devote to art. "I did not tell him what I really felt," Garland wrote in his diary, "which was that to rewrite *Farmington* would be worth more than all his work in defense of criminals and fools."[11]

* *

America had entered the Progressive Era, that time in the country's history when middle-class Americans, alarmed at the excess of industry and the pervasive corruption of the Gilded Age, launched mighty crusades to curb big business and make government more powerful, honest, and responsive. Darrow, moving dexterously from populist to progressive, became a leading actor in the nationwide movement for municipal reform.

Throughout Darrow's years in Chicago, various reform movements had attempted to quell the city's rampant corruption. "Chicago under my father, and in lesser degree under me, was what is known as a 'wide open town,' " Carter Harrison Jr. acknowledged in his memoirs. Each Harrison served five terms as mayor, with the help of a roster of political allies that included "saloonkeepers of high and low degree, gamblers, dive-keepers, men about town of shady connections, the Madames of the brothels, and the owners of the less disreputable of the ten cent Flops."

The anything-goes attitude reached beyond the streets of the Levee. Factories were dangerous. The air was thick and black, and the waters polluted. The alleys were strewn with garbage and the streetcars were crowded, filthy, and freezing in winter. Shamed by critics, a group of the city's better folks organized the Civic Federation. A smaller and more focused organization—the Municipal Voters' League—followed in 1896. Of sixty-eight aldermen, it announced, fifty-seven were thieves. They were branded "the gray wolves."

Yet even in that target-rich environment there was "one man who stands out conspicuous among all the rest," wrote the muckraker William Stead. His name was Charles Yerkes, and he built and operated much of the city's streetcar system in North and West Chicago. Yerkes was hardworking and arrogant, had served time in prison for fraud, and had few illusions about his fellow man.[12] He could have profited discreetly, like the local transit barons who owned the Chicago City Railway on the south side of town, if the streetcar franchises that he purchased were not due to expire in 1903. Yerkes needed an extension of his franchise rights, and that gave the aldermen in Chicago and the legislators in Springfield a prized opportunity to auction their votes. Yerkes played the game with zest. It was Yerkes who "first made boodling a serious business," wrote Lincoln Steffens.

Yerkes wanted his franchises extended to ninety-nine years. In 1895, he offered Altgeld a bribe of at least $500,000 if the governor would approve an "eternal monopoly" bill. Yerkes was "a man of iron will, and as bold as any buccaneer who ever sailed the financial seas," Darrow recalled. And Altgeld desperately needed the money. "I knew all of Altgeld's most trusted friends; we often discussed the matter among ourselves," said Darrow. "All that was required was to withhold a veto and let it become a law." But Altgeld issued a very public veto, with a ringing declaration of the rights of the citizens to control their streets.

When Yerkes finally triumphed in Springfield, pushing a franchise extension through the legislature in 1898, former governor Altgeld joined with Mayor Harrison, the Municipal Voters' League, and angry crowds (some of whom threatened the aldermen with nooses) to block the enabling legislation in the city council. Harrison's two knavish allies—Bathhouse and Hinky Dink—opposed Yerkes, who lost in the council by a single vote. In return, the Levee lords secured the mayor's protection of the First Ward's saloons, gambling houses, and brothels. Yerkes had enough. He sold his interests and went to London, where he helped build the Underground, and offered no apologies. "I was fighting the Devil in Illinois," he said. "I fought him with fire."[13]

Municipal control of streetcars and other utilities became a potent political issue. In city after city, the citizenry called for government to run public services. Darrow acquired a national reputation in the struggle, as an ally of reform mayors like Samuel "Golden Rule" Jones and his successor, Brand Whitlock, in Toledo; Tom Johnson in Cleveland; and the socialist Emil Seidel in Milwaukee. In 1903, during Darrow's term in the Illinois legislature, the battle came to Springfield, where a measure to give Chicago the authority to run its own streetcars was imprisoned in committee by house speaker John Henry Miller and allies of the transit interests. Chicago's representatives jumped to their feet and climbed on desks, demanding to be recognized. When Miller refused to call on them, some smashed chairs and tables, waving the legs as clubs as they moved toward the rostrum.

WILD RIOT IN THE HOUSE, the *Daily News* reported. Members shouted "Coward!" and "Roll call!" and "Liar!" as "the advance of the moving host" became "threatening." Fistfights broke out. Men grappled and tumbled about the dais. Darrow knocked a foe to the floor, by one account, and dumped a wastebasket on his head. The speaker, surrounded by a praetorian guard, declared the house adjourned, beat a hasty retreat to his private rooms, and barricaded the door.

Miller's tactics had offended delegates from around the state, who joined with their counterparts from Chicago to elect a rump leader, who gaveled the house to order with a broken chair rung. Darrow reviewed the rules of impeachment. That night, the speaker caved. Darrow then joined in the successful effort to pass the bill. It was the highlight of his career in the legislature, which lasted just the single term.[14]

The struggle shifted back to Chicago, where the voters endorsed "immediate" municipal ownership at the polls in 1905, as Judge Edward Dunne was elected mayor. He hired Darrow, his friend and ally, as a special counsel to represent the city in a lawsuit that had been filed by the streetcar interests in the federal courts. Darrow's old nemesis, the unscrupulous Judge Grosscup, had ruled that the transit companies had rights to run streetcars until 1958. The city appealed to the U.S. Supreme Court, and Darrow argued and won the case.

Dunne was a genial lace-curtain Irishman who lacked Harrison's Machiavellian skills. And the voters had saddled him with a city council that preferred to negotiate franchise extensions. The mayor, seeking to please all, pleased few. Trying to get something passed, he wavered on municipal ownership, reembraced it under pressure, abandoned it once more, and endorsed it yet again. Progressives around the country were looking to Chicago to set an example, but "the Radicals" at City Hall, one journal reported, "seem incapable of really finishing anything; everything they have turned out so far has been just about half baked."

By the end of that first summer, Darrow had sent a letter of resignation to the mayor. "I have no right to say that my opinion is better than yours. It is very possible that yours is better than mine," Darrow said. "But it is not fair to me that I should be committed to a policy that I believe will fail." The resignation was not accepted, but neither was his advice. Darrow took to restating it in public as the mayor, sharing the podium, rolled his eyes in consternation. Finally, in the fall, Darrow left City Hall. "Our municipal ownership administration is very poor and will doubtless result in nothing," he wrote Whitlock. In the break with Dunne, Darrow ended his twenty years in politics as he had spent it, marching to his own drum. Inspired by Amirus, he had seen politics as a place where a young man with a good heart and a passion for a cause could change the world. He was not unselfish; he wanted, following Altgeld's prescription, to get the power and give things a twist. But now Amirus and Altgeld and Lloyd were dead—taken from him in such quick succession that he hardly had time to mourn. He had no father to honor, no captain to serve, no comrade with whom to soldier.

"You are really running for mayor," Darrow wrote Whitlock. "Well I guess I hope you will win though I cannot say why. It will mean horrible vexations of the spirit [and be] no possible good to anyone." Darrow looked more to himself. A few weeks before Dunne faced the voters for reelection in 1907, the *Tribune* published a mean satire, from an anonymous author, comparing Dunne to Mark Tapley, the Dickensian featherhead of the novel *Martin Chuzzlewit*. Dunne had all Tapley's frustrating characteristics, "except that Mark Tapley was loyal to his friends," the piece declared. The anonymous author was Darrow.

"Nothing has made me so happy in politics in recent years as the defeat of Dunne," Darrow wrote Whitlock. "He is a man without brains, backbone or guts. He is unfaithful to every person and every thing, he is the nearest to nothing of any man that I ever knew, and while municipal ownership and progressive ideas lost something in his election, they have lost nothing in his defeat."

But Darrow's friends and associates were upset by his actions, which they saw as selfish and cynical. "Dunne was weak, but he honestly stood for much if not all that Darrow pretends to advocate" and was replaced by "a spoils man who will use his position without scruple," wrote Austin Wright, one of Darrow's former clients. "A personal dislike, it does not seem to me, constitutes a good and sufficient ground for going over to the enemy."[15]

Some saw greed and cynicism in Darrow's behavior. The editors of the *American* became alarmed when Darrow took fees from both the newspaper and the International Harvester Company for negotiating an end to their journalistic crusade against the firm, which had been evading payment of its property taxes. Darrow's reputation was dented, as well, by his willingness to represent his supposed foes, the streetcar companies, in court. On behalf of the Chicago City transit firm, he led an unsuccessful attempt to kill a franchise granted to its competitor, the General Electric Railway Company.

"There was a bulge in the pockets of the aldermen who voted for this ordinance," said Darrow. "Nobody knows it better than the Electric railway company."

"Unless it be the City railway company," said the rival attorney, and the courtroom erupted in knowing laughter.[16]

Darrow's image was further smudged when another streetcar firm, the Union Traction Company, got caught bribing jurors in personal injury cases, and he agreed to defend three Irish American lawyers charged in the scandal. It was a Chicago sensation. Extra bailiffs were required to control a courtroom crowded with rowdy Celts. Fistfights broke out when a guilty verdict was announced, and the angry Irish spectators rushed the prosecutor, shouting "Dog!" and "Scoundrel!"

Darrow persevered, and two of the convictions were reversed on appeal. He then gave a job to a lawyer named Cy Simon, who was the Union Traction bagman in the case. Some months later, Masters discovered that their firm was receiving $150 a month from Union Traction to buy Simon's continued silence. And whenever Darrow represented a client in an injury case against Union Traction, Masters said, the company would invariably agree to a generous settlement. The word spread and boosted their business. "It was bribery all around," said Masters.

"Darrow has no principles," Wright told a mutual friend. "He professes to hold feelings of utmost contempt for millionaires, while his acts emphasize a greed for money."

"I once had a fondness approaching affection for Darrow," Wright concluded, "but the withering blight of his moral bankruptcy fell upon every feeling of that kind."

The journalist Hutchins Hapgood was a bit more forgiving. Darrow could best be described, he wrote, as a philosophical anarchist who, in the name of liberty, refused to be ruled by nettlesome rules or creeds. There were advantages to such a pose. "It allows a man to be an opportunist," Hapgood said, "while having a high ideal."[17]

Darrow's involvement in another scandal made the front pages across the country when the Bank of America, a Chicago thrift, went bust in early 1906. The bank had been looted by its president, former judge Abner Smith. Darrow was a cofounder and a major stockholder.

The idea for the bank was laudatory. It was to have been run for the benefit of working folks, whose pennies it would solicit by accepting deposits at neighborhood drugstores. Some five hundred families opened savings accounts. Darrow borrowed $7,000 to invest in the bank and deposited another $6,000. Masters invested $4,000. Even John Azzop, the elevator operator in their building, was persuaded to move his savings there.

But Smith never had the capital reserves required by Illinois law. And he then okayed $250,000 in ill-secured loans for himself, associates, and members of his family. Darrow and the other stockholders were fortunate in but one regard: the bank failed quickly, allowing them to save the depositors' money, if not their own. Darrow contained the scandal by alerting the authorities and announcing that he would personally guarantee the $25,000 in workingmen's deposits that were at risk. They were paid out to folks like Azzop when they showed up with their bankbooks.

"Darrow prevailed upon me to stop playing the races . . . and put my money in the bank," said Azzop, after getting his money back. "I'm going to put this on a horse," he told the press.

Masters lost his $4,000. For years he hounded and pursued Smith, who was convicted and sent to prison. The episode also added to the friction between the law partners. When Darrow used the borrowed $7,000 to embellish the bank's reserves, he had acted—though on a far smaller scale—just like Smith, said Masters. But by serving as the whistle-blower and prevailing on his friends in the press, Darrow emerged as a hero. "He participated in the fraudulent incorporation," Masters marveled, "and then prosecuted his confederate in the fraud, and escaped unexposed."

One cheerful cynic found his friend Darrow's behavior irresistible. In the fall of 1906 Elbert Hubbard wrote a satirical ode for the *Philistine*, his literary magazine.

"I love Darrow because he is such a blessed crook. He affects to be a brave man, but admits that he's an arrant coward; he poses as an altruist, but is really a pin-headed pilferer," Hubbard wrote. "People think he is bounteously unselfish and kind, whereas he dispenses and supplicates solely for Darrow & Co. He eloquently addresses the bar, bench and jury in public in the name of justice, and then privately admits the whole thing is a fraud."[18]

Others were concerned. Their knight seemed to have lost his way. In January 1907, Garland and his wife invited the Darrows to dinner. After they left, he described the evening in his diary. "I found him as grave and even more bitter than his writing indicates," said Garland. "He weakens his cause by extreme expression. His uncompromising honesty of purpose and his aggressive cynicism make him repellent to many."

"As a lawyer he was always ready to defend the under dog," said Garland, but "I was not entirely convinced that his action was dictated solely by a sense of justice. He takes a savage . . . joy in striking at society."

"I feel power but not high purpose in his program," said Garland. "We began our careers on common ground, but he has gone on—or off—into a dark and tangled forestland."

Chapter 8

INDUSTRIAL WARFARE

The cynic is humbled.

On the snow-swept evening of December 30, 1905, after weeks of planning and several bungled attempts, an ice-hearted killer named Harry Orchard wandered from a card game in the Saratoga Hotel in Caldwell, Idaho, and stumbled upon his quarry, former governor Frank Steunenberg, in the lobby.

Orchard hurried to his room and took up the bomb he had hidden in his suitcase. "It had been one of those gloomy days," Steunenberg's brother Will would recall. "Snowing and blowing all day long." Cloaked by darkness and the remnants of the storm, Orchard hurried to the Steunenberg house, just under a mile away. Working swiftly, he fastened his device to a gatepost.

It was of simple design: when the gate was opened, a bit of fishing line would tug the cork from a vial of sulfuric acid that, spilling on blasting caps, would set off dynamite. On the way back to town, Orchard passed Steunenberg, walking home. The assassin was a block or two from the warm lights of the Saratoga, with its mansard roof and turrets and busy gaming tables, when he heard the blast. It was six forty-five p.m.

Inside the Steunenberg house, the children had been watching for their father. He came into the yard, turned to close the gate, and was wrapped in a blinding flash. The explosion shredded skin and muscle on his right side, stripped him of his clothing, and threw him ten feet toward the barn. The bones of his legs were in splinters, and his right arm, with which he had reached down to close the gate, had "the inside blown completely out," a brother recalled. The windows of the house were gone. There were shards of wood and glass and bits of the victim everywhere.

His family ran to Steunenberg, but could not lift the big man, though he begged to be taken in from the cold. His flesh came away in their hands. "Someone has shot me," he said, and then, "Lord help us." They put him on a blanket and dragged him inside, where he lay writhing on a bed. His brothers urged him to tell them what happened, but he was deaf from the explosion and stared at them blankly. In the arms of his brother Will he died.

"In a very few minutes great magnificent Frank had gone," a sister-in-law wrote. "It was a mercy . . . as his agony must have been terrible."

"It is taken for granted," his sister Josephine told relatives, "that it was done by . . . the dynamiters."[1]

THE VIOLENT STRUGGLE between capital and labor in industrial-age America reached a climax out west. There were sheriffs and courts and territorial assemblies, and a parade of new states into the Union. Yet it was still a land where shrewd men could acquire power through gold, guns, or legal trickery. By the terms of its cherished myth, the West was a land of independence. But as the century turned, the pioneers and prospectors were displaced by corporations that had access to the capital and technology needed for industrial-scale mining, timber cutting, and the building of cities and railroads.

The miners were the spearhead of resistance to the new order. Absent owners like John D. Rockefeller spent no time fretting about working conditions in Idaho, Nevada, or Colorado, where their local superintendents, striving to meet corporate targets, sliced wages to as little as $1.80 a day. The frontiersmen, working their own silver claims and panning clear-water creeks for gold, raged at those who sought to make them wage slaves. "These adventurous characters, going out into a new country and plunging into the virgin, everlasting hills, where it would seem that at last all men would stand on the same footing, have suddenly discovered that amid these primitive surroundings the modern industrial system is . . . at its worst," one journalist reported. The miners—rough combative men—began to organize. The mine owners—brutal and resolved—used gunmen and militias to crush the unions. The miners responded with dynamite.[2]

"The contest verged on civil war," Darrow recalled. In radical circles, the union violence was excused. "It is a duty to stop the lesser crime of dynamite, but it is an infinitely greater duty to extirpate the greater crime of the monopolist. The one has hardly slain its tens, the other slays its thousands daily," his friend Henry Lloyd had written. "The one is spasmodic, impulsive, sporadic, exceptional . . . the other is organized wholesale destruction." There was blood to be expected in any birth. "You cannot make a revolution out of rosewater," Darrow said.

Darrow would be at the center of the reckoning. For most of eight years, from the winter of 1906 through the fall of 1913, he left Chicago and spent his energies on two renowned cases in which he defended union men charged with wide-scale, bloody campaigns of terror. His ardor for sensation bore him to a conflagration from which he barely escaped. He would win several highly publicized trials in the West, and cut one notorious deal to snatch a client from the gallows. The experience would make him a national celebrity, but it also got him indicted, and cost him almost everything: his savings, his law firm, and, very nearly, his marriage, his freedom, and his life. It was his turn in Gethsemane: the Passion of Clarence Darrow.

Darrow was among the first, in the wonder and promise of those first years of the century, to glimpse its savagery. And in the fire, his last illusions perished. It was a changed man, in some ways hollow, in others holy, who returned to Chicago.

"The cynic is humbled," wrote Lincoln Steffens, who stood by his side in the final act. "The man that laughed sees and is frightened, not at prison bars, but at his own soul."[3]

THE HOSTILITIES ERUPTED in the Coeur d'Alene territory, in the panhandle of Idaho, when workers began to organize in the early 1890s. They were met by the formation of the Mine Owners' Association, which salted spies and informants throughout their ranks. In the course of a strike in July 1892, gun battles broke out at the Gem and Bunker Hill mines, the Frisco mine was destroyed by dynamite, and President Benjamin Harrison sent in troops to restore order. A few months later, union men from around the West joined together in the Western Federation of Miners.[4]

The miners' expectations soared in 1896 when, amid the silver craze, a Democratic-Populist "fusion" ticket swept Idaho and Frank Steunenberg, a thirty-five-year-old newspaper editor and state legislator, became the state's first non-Republican governor. He was a bull of a man, tall, strong, and headstrong—one of six Steunenberg brothers who had settled in Caldwell, a whistle-stop on the Union Pacific Railroad, in keeping with their brother Albert's dictum: "We are here for the money." In addition to the newspaper and politics, they had grown prosperous investing in timber, sheep, banking, mining, retailing, and real estate.[5]

Some of the mine owners tried to make peace with their employees. But the hate ran deep, and old scores needed settling. There were whispers about an "inner circle" of union officials who were ordering beatings and executions. In 1899 several hundred miners, many wearing masks and carrying firearms, hijacked a Northern Pacific train, christened it the Dynamite Express, stopped in a series of mining towns to pick up more men, arms, and explosives, and seized and demolished the Bunker Hill mine. Steunenberg declared martial law and asked President McKinley to "call forth the military forces . . . to suppress insurrection." The army arrived again. Some seven hundred miners and supporters were arrested, hauled before secret courts, and interned in makeshift concentration camps known as "bull pens."

The WFM in Idaho was shattered. Steunenberg was damned by union men, but the grateful mine owners bankrolled his business ventures. "A little sporadic violence . . . has been met by a vastly more dangerous and more infamous infraction of the law by the constituted authorities who took their orders from the employers . . . quite as rough, quite as lawless and quite as overbearing as any of the miners," the journalist Willis Abbot reported to Lloyd.[6]

THE STRUGGLE SHIFTED to Colorado, where labor had scored some initial success with passage of a law mandating an eight-hour day. When the pro-business judges of the state supreme court declared the measure unconstitutional, the voters amended the state constitution to allow it. But the corporate interests then blocked the implementing legislation. The union men were embittered; democracy seemed a fraud. "What is the use of your ballots anyway?" WFM president Charles Moyer asked. "You might as well tear them up."[7]

In 1903, miners and mill workers in the Cripple Creek district went on strike. Governor James Peabody dispatched the state militia under the command of a mine manager named Sherman Bell. The expedition was paid for by the mine owners and the troops were there to break the union, Bell declared. His job was to "exterminate 'em." Moyer was arrested on a bogus charge of flag desecration and held for months.

As in Idaho, acts of "union violence" in Colorado were sometimes committed by provocateurs hired by the mining industry to discredit the labor movement. One miner who played both sides for money was a particularly conscienceless killer who had participated in the Coeur d'Alene troubles before coming to Colorado. He went by many names, most recently Harry Orchard. He was of medium height, with a round face and a "deep rounded barrel of a body . . . balanced sturdily on short, stout legs—a most excellent and workmanlike human machine, with the power and directness of a little Orkney bull," as one journalist described him. Those who met him were struck by Orchard's callousness. "He is without the . . . imagination of the ordinary man," a reporter wrote. The consequences of his violent acts and the suffering of his victims "simply do not present themselves to him." In November 1903, as Orchard told it, he helped bomb the Vindicator mine. That won him an invitation to Denver and entree to the leaders of the federation—President Moyer, Secretary-Treasurer William "Big Bill" Haywood, and an explosives expert named George Pettibone.

Moyer was a talented organizer—"brave and determined," Darrow would recall—with a sharp face and husky voice. Pettibone was "witty, friendly and kindly" and "something of a chemist." It was widely believed that he had blown up the Frisco mine in Idaho. The third man—Big Bill—was powerfully built and square jawed. He was "hard, tough . . . [but with] a final touch of idealism, a Jesuitic zeal that carries the man beyond himself," the journalist Ray Stannard Baker wrote. Haywood had made his mark as a rabble-rousing socialist.[8]

It was at their request, Orchard would claim, that he and an associate, Steve Adams, blew up the Independence depot of the Florence and Cripple Creek Railroad on June 6, 1904. The platform was packed with two dozen nonunion miners whose shift had just ended. Thirteen died and others were horribly mangled, their screams cleaving the summer night. And yet it was the Federation that paid the heaviest price for the bombing.

The union hall in the town of Victor was surrounded by vigilantes, and after a gun battle the miners surrendered. Sherman Bell and his militia arrived and hauled hundreds at gunpoint to the Colorado border, where they were dumped in the wasteland and told not to return.

THE WFM HAD been routed in Idaho and Colorado. Its leaders looked outside the West for allies, and helped organize the Industrial Workers of the World—dedicated to the overthrow of capitalism—in Chicago in 1905. The Wobblies, as they became known, believed in a Marxist class struggle and declared in their manifesto that "economic evils . . . can be eradicated only by a universal working class movement" led by "one great industrial union." Moyer and Haywood were joined by Debs and other prominent radicals. Haywood urged American workers to follow their Russian counterparts and "rise in revolt against the capitalist system." If western industrialists needed further motivation to take down Moyer and Haywood, the Red talk offered it. And Orchard gave them the means.[9]

As Will Steunenberg ran, sliding in the snow, to his dying brother's side on the night of the bombing, he instantly decided: "It's the Coeur d'Alenes." The next morning's edition of the *Daily Statesman*, the state's leading newspaper, barely reported the details before reaching the front-page conclusion that "a great many minds turn to the troubles in the Coeur d'Alenes and to the 'inner circle' which was said to rule by blood."

The *Statesman* was the voice of Idaho's anti-union, Republican establishment. With uncanny precision, in that first edition, it likened the Steunenberg bombing to the destruction of the Independence depot. And Sheriff Harvey Brown of Oregon, who knew Orchard, just happened to be on the special train that traveled from Boise to Caldwell that night with the state's two top Republicans, Governor Frank Gooding and soon-to-be senator William E. Borah. There were other suggestive details that led union men to believe that the bombing was the work of corporate provocateurs or a crazy loner. Orchard had not fled or disposed of the incriminating items stashed in his room and his baggage, including explosives, a sawed-off shotgun, and a postcard addressed to Moyer. After Brown identified him, Orchard had cooperatively surrendered and was formally charged less than forty-eight hours after Steunenberg stooped to close the gate.

And there were, in fact, other potential motives for the bombing. Steunenberg was a leader of Idaho's wool growers, whose war with the state's cattlemen had periodically erupted with deadly violence and histrionic murder trials. Then there was this to consider: Steunenberg's wife said he had seemed troubled in recent weeks, and particularly on the day he died. Federal investigators had targeted him for his role in a massive timber fraud conspiracy, with links to Borah, Idaho mine owners, and the family that published the *Statesman*. Idaho's Republican establishment had ample motive to want the murder case closed quickly, with blame fixed on the union. Orchard most assuredly had killed Steunenberg. But not until Lee Harvey Oswald would an assassin's motives, and his paymasters, be the topic of such dispute.

GOODING STASHED ORCHARD in the state penitentiary in Boise, where, after time in solitary confinement, he was introduced to the Pinkerton detective who had been hired to lead the investigation. J. P. McParland was a legend: the nerveless private eye who had gone undercover, risked his life, and brought down the Molly Maguires. He had drunk and bunked and schemed with the Pennsylvania coal field rebels, then testified at trials that sent twenty to their deaths. Other famous private eyes cashed in and started their own firms, but McParland stuck with the Pinkertons, who prized his anti-union zeal, and his ability to move with equal facility in the "higher or laboring classes," and among "sporting men or thieves." He was past sixty now, afflicted with various ailments and reliant on a cane. He had, of course, prejudged the case. It was the Molly Maguires all over again, and would serve as a spectacular bookend to his career.

Before he ever began to investigate, McParland declared that the "inner circle"—Moyer and Haywood—were behind the crime. Using Steunenberg's murder to dismember the union was a prime business opportunity, McParland told the Pinkertons: "It means a great deal . . . so far as the mine owners of Idaho are concerned and in fact all mine operators in the whole district."[10]

McParland knew the value of manipulating public opinion, and his conversations with Orchard, which he deftly leaked to the press, were portrayed as sacramental: the killer converted by the sage lawman, finding Jesus, and confessing his sins. "I have been an unnatural monster,"

Orchard wrote in a letter that found its way to the newspapers. "But the dear Lord regenerated me, so he could use me."[11]

Both the actual transcript of Orchard's confession and McParland's notes were kept secret for decades. In truth, it was a pedestrian interrogation, the kind conducted by coppers and DAs everywhere. "If you take my advice you will not be hung," McParland told Orchard. "If you do not you will be hung in very quick order."

The authorities knew that Orchard was "simply a tool of the Inner Circle," McParland told him. If the assassin implicated the Federation chiefs as his co-conspirators, the state would spare his life, and one day even set him free. "We would get the leaders, and that was all that the State of Colorado and the State of Idaho wished," McParland said. "I recited a number of instances which he knew of himself wherein men had become States witnesses in murder cases and not only saved their necks but also eventually got their liberty."

Orchard asked for, and McParland supplied, the precise story he needed to relate. He must describe how the Federation leaders "being men in authority, detail you to go and commit the murder, advise you how to do it, furnish you with the means," McParland said. The deal McParland offered was good for Harry Orchard, and Harry Orchard grabbed it. He hoped to be free soon, he told a fellow prisoner, and to start a new life overseas. "I awoke, as it were, from a dream," Orchard said in his confession. "And realized I had been made a tool of, aided and assisted by the members of the Executive Board of the Western Federation of Miners."

For the next five days, as McParland crafted the questions and a stenographer took notes, Orchard told how he had been dispatched to kill Steunenberg by Haywood and the others. But he did not stop there: He linked every infamous act of western labor violence to the Federation. He had bombed the Vindicator mine and the Independence depot, he said, and the home of a prominent mine owner in San Francisco. He had helped blow up the Bunker Hill mine. He had tried to assassinate Governor Peabody of Colorado, two justices of the state supreme court, and Sherman Bell. He had shot a detective in a dark alley, poisoned a mine owner's milk, and killed an innocent Denver man who stumbled into one of his plots.

Despite his alleged reconciliation with Christ, the prisoner lied from the first. His real name was not Harry Orchard, as he swore, but Alfred E. Horsley. Pinkerton operative S. Chris Thiele spent as much time with Orchard as anyone and privately scoffed at his supposed religious awakening. The killer was distilled evil, Thiele told his superiors in an agency memorandum, and he "at no time found Orchard saying that he . . . had any pity for those to whose hearts he brought sorrow." Darrow would find Orchard "remarkable . . . a man whom nothing could touch; he was above all ordinary influences: fear, hope, reward, threats; everything." Even McParland was impressed. He had known many criminals but never had he seen, until Harry Orchard, such "cold, cruel" eyes.

WITH ORCHARD'S CONFESSION in hand, McParland faced the task of arresting Haywood, Moyer, and Pettibone. "Owing to the fact that neither of these three parties had been in Idaho during this conspiracy, we cannot say that they are fugitives from justice," he warned Gooding, "and we may have considerable trouble in extraditing them."

And so Idaho kidnapped the three union leaders. To Colorado's compliant governor, McParland sold the legal fable that the three were "constructively" present in Caldwell on the night of the crime. McParland had them seized on a Saturday night and spirited away on a fast train before the Federation's lawyers could ask a court to intervene. The Union Pacific Railroad agreed to clear its tracks. Engines, watered and fueled, stood waiting along the route. Sandwiches, bottles of beer, a hundred cigars, and a quart of Old Crow were packed aboard. Cryptic messages flew back and forth. Everyone had a code name. McParland was Owl. Haywood was Viper. Moyer was Copperhead. Pettibone was Rattler. And Harry Orchard, the gifted poser, was Possum.

Moyer was grabbed, without warrant, at Union Station in Denver. Pettibone was picked up without incident at home. And the Viper was arrested in a rooming house, "stark naked and in bed with a woman," the Owl told Gooding. Haywood's bedmate was the younger sister of his invalid wife, Nevada Jane. It was to be expected, said McParland, for the Viper was a degenerate.

The abduction infuriated American labor leaders—even moderates, like Samuel Gompers, who loathed the Wobblies. AROUSE, YE SLAVES!

read the headline in the socialist *Appeal to Reason*. "It is a foul plot; a damnable conspiracy; a hellish outrage," Debs wrote. "If they attempt to murder Moyer, Haywood and their brothers, a million revolutionists, at least, will meet them with guns . . . A general strike could be ordered and industry paralyzed as a preliminary to a general uprising."

One WFM leader evaded the manhunt. Jack Simpkins, who was indicted for helping Orchard plan the Steunenberg murder, vanished. But Steve Adams, whom Orchard named as his accomplice in the bombing of the Independence depot, was seized in Oregon. McParland made his well-rehearsed pitch, and Adams signed a statement linking the WFM chieftains to Orchard's crime spree. In composing the confession, "McParland led me on step by step and showed me all that he wanted me to say," Adams later testified. He was a critical witness in the case, for Idaho law was insistent: no defendant could be convicted of a crime on the testimony of a single conspirator. Corroborating proof was required, and in Adams, the state now had corroboration.[12]

THE WFM REACHED out to Darrow in March 1906. "This is a matter which I would rather avoid . . . on account of the hard fight and the serious odds," he told John Mitchell. "However, I do not see how I can get out of it. I presume that they are trying to railroad these fellows."

After being assured that organized labor would raise sufficient funds for the defense, Darrow took the case. He traveled to Idaho at the end of May for pretrial hearings. "Public sentiment . . . is very necessary in a great case of this kind," he told Mitchell. He was genial and folksy, far from the cloven-hoofed anarchist whom Idaho expected. He informed the *Statesman* that he found Boise "a mighty nice town" and teased reporters who asked him for inside information. In court Darrow made a show of demanding a quick trial for his clients, though he knew that his union's challenge of their extradition would take months to reach the U.S. Supreme Court. "They are ready for trial," he declared. "They are entitled to trial. They demand trial."

The Supreme Court heard the extradition case in October. The Constitution permits that a person "who shall flee from justice" in one state may be extradited from others, the defense acknowledged. But Haywood and his companions had not fled anywhere. The governor of Colorado "had full knowledge of the falsity of the proceedings," the Federation argued. "This is not a case of actual fugitives." But only one member of the court, Justice Joseph McKenna, agreed. "Kidnapping is a crime, pure and simple," he said, in a lonely dissent.

The Idaho prosecutor, James Hawley, read the court correctly. He was an archetypical sagebrush lawyer: a beefy, hot-tempered, cigar-smoking cowboy with a law book in his saddlebag who grew up with the territory. In the 1892 troubles, Hawley had defended Pettibone and the other union men and helped organize the Federation. But with all the zeal of a convert, he had switched sides. He told the justices that the prisoners had other legal remedies that they could seek if they thought they were improperly snatched. "The parties abducting them could be tried for kidnapping, or the defendants could sue for damages," he said. Once they were charged on Idaho soil, the route they took was irrelevant: "They are there, and the question is are they guilty or innocent." On December 3, 1906, the Supreme Court agreed. The "vital fact" was that the defendants were now in Idaho, said Justice Harlan, in a 7-to-1 decision. "It is not necessary to go behind the indictment and inquire as to how it happened."

"Whether it was law or not, I do not know," Darrow wrote to Henry Lloyd's sister Caro. "It certainly wasn't justice."[13]

THE THREE PRISONERS were stoic when they heard the news, in part because Darrow had scored gains of his own that summer. After bidding goodbye to the Boise press in June and telling them "there will be nothing more doing" in the case until the fall, he had found his way to eastern Oregon and the door of James W. Lillard, an uncle of Steve Adams. There are two stories of how Darrow got Lillard to persuade his nephew not to testify. The first comes from the Darrow camp; it's a nice tale in which the lawyer is turned away from Lillard's door but, like a wise traveling salesman, asks for a drink of water to stall for time and make a successful pitch. The second version is from McParland. According to the Pinkertons, the defense bought Lillard with a staggering bribe.[14]

Both versions could be grounded in truth. Darrow had no qualms about paying witnesses or members of their families for helping the defense in a high-stakes case. He was reimbursing them, he would claim, for their trouble and their time. It was in character for Darrow to spend tens of thousands of dollars in this manner if the money was available, and one can easily see him sweet-talking Lillard and cinching the deal with a payoff.[15]

This much is certain: the supposedly penniless Adams suddenly repudiated his confession and hired an expensive lawyer—a former Republican governor—to win his freedom. The state responded with its own hardball tactics: it charged Adams with an unrelated murder and carted him through the forest roads to a jail in rural Wallace, high in the panhandle. There, McParland threatened to hang him unless he cooperated.

The case against Adams rested on a tale he supposedly told Orchard about visiting friends in the north woods and helping them murder a "claim jumper" named Fred Tyler. The claim jumpers were despised opportunists who, for themselves or a timber or mining interest, took advantage of a homesteader's absence to file a counterclaim for the land. "Probably never before had any one been convicted for killing a claim jumper in that part of the state," Darrow recalled.

A crucial witness was offered a lucrative federal job, and agreed to testify for the prosecution, but when McParland returned for the trial he was furious to discover that the local sheriff had been outmaneuvered, and the jury pool stocked with union sympathizers. The prosecutors did the best they could with their peremptory challenges, but in the end Darrow secured a jury with "two very doubtful, and one we are sure will never fetch in a verdict of guilty," the downcast detective reported.

Darrow was helped by the rambling opening statement made by the local prosecutor, Henry Knight, who demonstrated how much the state relied upon conjecture.

> The evidence will show that on or about the 29th or 30th day of June, possibly, 1904, Mr. Tyler left the town of Santo, or his mother's residence near that place, for the purpose of going out into the forests and taking up a homestead—or a timber claim, [Knight began. A year later,] in the month of August, or September, I think, 1905 . . . about in the month of August, or September, I think . . . the coroner with some deputy, or some deputy of the coroner, went to the place . . . I am not sure whether in exact proximity to the cabin or claim of Fred Tyler, or, at any rate near there . . . The evidence, we believe, will show that the deceased

> was shot from behind, that the bullet entered near the ear; back of the ear—one of the ears, I have forgotten which . . . Whether it was before or after breakfast I am not sure, I am not sure whether they gave him breakfast or not, at any rate it was quite early in the morning.

The frontier-flavored justice made it "about as interesting and remarkable as any case in which I figured," Darrow remembered. As Tyler's mother, clad in black, sat in court and wept, the two sides squabbled over the identification of a weathered skull and bones that had been found by surveyors in the woods. Adams had an alibi and Darrow contended that, with the countryside aflame over claim jumping, a group of vigilantes who called themselves the Jumper Killers probably shot Tyler. Indeed, the leader of the vigilantes had been arrested as a suspect at the time.

Darrow closed the case for the defense. The other union attorneys "made a very poor impression not only on the jury but on the public," McParland wrote Gooding. "Darrow is a different type of man; he gets close to the jury and makes a very earnest appeal." The real crime was not murder—it was the way the state perverted justice, Darrow argued.

Adams was nothing but "a pawn in a game," Darrow said. "Back of all this . . . is a great issue of which this is but the beginning. Because, beyond this case, and outside of this courtroom, and out in the great world, it is a great fight, a fight between capital and labor, of which this is but a manifestation up here in the woods . . . You know it; I know it; they know it."

With a target like McParland at hand, Darrow would not neglect one of his guiding dictums: the jury needs a villain. The essence of the detective's life was deception, Darrow told the jurors. Remember the Molly Maguires. "He met day after day and week after week with his neighbors and his friends, and his comrades and members of his lodge; he learned their secrets, he ate at their table, he drank at the bar with them . . . And every moment, he was working himself into the lives of these men; he was a spy, a traitor, a liar; and he was there to bring them to the gallows!" Darrow said.

"There are . . . methods that are more dangerous to the State, and are more odious to honest men, than crime," Darrow said. "It is better a thousand crimes should go unpunished . . . than that the State should lend itself to these practices of fraud and treachery."

The jury spent most of two days arguing, then told the judge they were hopelessly deadlocked. On almost every ballot, they had split 7 to 5 for acquittal. "Had it not been for two or three men we would have secured an acquittal," Darrow told reporters before fleeing the ice and chill of Wallace for a speaking tour in California. But he was content.[16]

McParland was crestfallen. Adams was "the most important witness we've got," he told Gooding. The Pinkerton approached a deputy sheriff named Carson Hicks and promised that the state would pay "liberally" if Hicks and his colleagues could cajole the prisoner to return to the prosecution. McParland began planning for a retrial, with a change of venue that would take the case from a mining community and give it instead to "true, loyal citizens."[17]

DARROW WAS NOT thoroughly cynical. If so, he could have made his life easy, and splendidly comfortable, selling his skills as a corporate lawyer. But he had studied ethics under Altgeld, who was "absolutely honest" in choosing his causes and "perfectly unscrupulous" in achieving them. The Haywood defense was now engaged in a series of unscrupulous tactics.

From the spring of 1906 through the following winter, a Pinkerton agent in Colorado known as Operative 28 kept an eye on Frank Hangs, a union lawyer who was enlisting witnesses for Haywood's defense. Hangs told prospective witnesses what he hoped they would say, and promised them money if they did so. Operative 28 was Arthur Cole, a militia officer. "Hangs was feeling me out to see if I would stand, if paid, to testify that these murders in Cripple Creek were planned" by the Mine Owners' Association, Cole told McParland. "He is talking . . . openly about me making a good piece of money." As the case neared trial, Darrow arrived in Colorado to screen the witnesses. He met with Cole, who told him that the mine owners had known in advance that Orchard was going to bomb the Vindicator and had arranged for Orchard to travel to Denver to meet Haywood, Moyer, and Pettibone and gain their confidence. "Darrow became very excited," Cole reported. He told Darrow there were other helpful things he would say "if I was paid for it" and that "Darrow appeared to be much pleased and desired me to refresh my memory." Darrow asked if Cole could testify that the mine owners were behind the

Independence depot bombing as well. "I agreed with Darrow to do these things," Cole said. "Darrow said if I would stay with the proposition I would be a valuable witness and would be taken care of in a substantial way." The Pinkerton operative agreed to perjure himself for $500 and claimed to have been paid $50 by Darrow as an advance.

It is hard to weigh the tale. Cole was a mine owners' man, telling McParland what he wanted to hear. Or perhaps a wary Darrow was stringing Operative 28 along, for at some point the defense caught wind of the plot and Cole was exposed as a spy.[18] McParland was crestfallen. He had hoped to entrap Darrow and reveal, with a dramatic flourish in the courtroom, a conspiracy to suborn perjury. But in the end, he came away with nothing.[19] Darrow's only comment came in his autobiography. While "investigating rumors" in Colorado, he wrote, he came upon many "marvelous tales" from people "impelled by all sorts of motives."

THE PROSECUTION HAD its own ethical contortions, which undoubtedly stirred Darrow's willingness to break the rules. "We are here employed by the State," Hawley had told the jury in Wallace. "Not a bit of corporate money jingles in my pockets." It was a lie. The state of Idaho could not easily come up with the funds it needed to abduct and prosecute Adams, Haywood, Moyer, and Pettibone, so Gooding had turned to the state's banks—especially those owned by the mining industry—for loans. Borah and Hawley pitched in as fundraisers, with Hawley telling one mine owner that this was their chance "to rid the West entirely" of the Federation, whose "foul crimes" had done "so much to retard our progress, and which is a menace to our future." In response to such pleas, the mining companies donated $5,000.

Word of the fundraising reached Washington, alarming President Roosevelt. "That Haywood and Moyer have been at the head of a labor organization, the members of which have practiced every form of violence, including assassination . . . is not to be disputed," the president wrote his attorney general. He dismissed the kidnapping of the three WFM leaders as a "failure to comply with . . . formalities." Gooding was engaged, said the president, in the noble work of "saving civilization." And yet Roosevelt recognized the liabilities of having mine owners bankrolling the prosecution of union leaders.

"Such action would be the grossest impropriety," Roosevelt wrote in a letter hand-delivered to Calvin Cobb, the publisher of the *Statesman*, who was in Washington lobbying for the prosecution. "If the Governor or the other officials of Idaho accept a cent from the operators . . . I should personally feel that they had committed a real crime." The governor rushed to refund the $5,000 and promised the president that "the mine owners will not be asked for a dollar, nor permitted to take any part in the prosecution." But Hawley and the others simply shifted their fundraising to Colorado and other states, where mining and commercial interests quietly contributed the tens of thousands of dollars needed to destroy the Federation.

Roosevelt's own behavior, it turned out, was also of the "grossest impropriety." Just days before the Supreme Court heard the oral arguments in the extradition case the president had hosted the justices at the White House, where he read aloud from a letter he had written condemning Moyer and Haywood as "undesirable" citizens. The incident became public in the spring of 1907.[20] Labor and the Left erupted. Socialists and unionists, who had been forming "Moyer-Haywood conferences" around the country, chose May 4—the Saturday before the trial was to begin—for a national day of protest. A hundred thousand marched and cheered in Boston and almost as many in New York, where they waved red flags and sang the "Marseillaise." Thousands wore badges that said, "I am an Undesirable Citizen."[21]

Roosevelt's most malodorous intervention was still to come. It was triggered by a cable from federal investigators in Idaho alerting the White House that the "civilization" which Governor Gooding was "saving" was rotten to the core. The Haywood prosecution, the investigators said, was being used to deflect attention from pervasive corruption.

"Investigations will show Steunenberg to be leading member timber frauds," they said. Borah was "morally if not criminally connected. Cobb of *Statesman* and Governor Gooding both use all influence against investigation. Cobb morally and probably criminally connected." Attorney General Charles Bonaparte quickly confirmed, and wrote the president, that the findings in the cable were "well-founded."

The news stunned Roosevelt. If it became public it could ruin all the productive work that Cobb, McParland, and the others had done to paint Steunenberg as a saintly victim. Worse yet, it gave credence to the defense's contention that Orchard might have had other paymasters. The findings offered an alternative "motive for the persons involved in these timber frauds to kill Steunenberg," the attorney general advised Roosevelt.

The Haywood prosecution, moreover, was depending on Borah's arts of persuasion. The "new U.S. senator" cited in the cable was a favorite of the president and a darling of the press. With "keen blue eyes, a powerful square chin, a frank straightforward manner and a winning boyish smile," Borah beat down his foes with "the dazzling force of a thunderbolt," the *New York Sun* reported. He was a self-made man who had married a governor's daughter and profited from his ties to the mining industry as he rose from hick lawyer to corporate attorney and, eventually, to the Senate. "This is the work of my personal enemies," Borah told Roosevelt—and, he said, of the Federation. But the miners had not caused Borah's troubles. The investigation was launched by Roosevelt's own land office personnel in response to widespread swindling in the Northwest. A similar prosecution in Oregon had been applauded by the White House, and its prosecutors lauded as heroes.

Gooding moved to get the White House to quash the investigation. He sent Roosevelt copies of Pinkerton reports which revealed that the prosecution had another spy—Operative 21—embedded in the defense who warned that Haywood's legal team had gotten wind of the probe. "Everything should be made subservient to this great trial," Gooding wrote, urging Roosevelt to rein in the investigators.

Roosevelt caved. There were no lectures on propriety this time. If he had any qualms about Gooding's news that the state of Idaho had used a Pinkerton detective to infiltrate the defense staff and corrupt the jury selection process, the president of the United States never voiced them. He ordered Bonaparte to seal the indictments until Borah had finished hanging Haywood. "I have sacrificed, or at least, endangered, some of the chances of a successful prosecution of the Steunenberg frauds," Bonaparte reported back to Roosevelt, "in order . . . not to injuriously affect the chances of the prosecution in the Haywood case."

Operative 21—a Pinkerton detective by the name of Johnson—was a deep-cover man for the agency. He had arrived in Idaho in the days after the assassination posing as a socialist agitator and wormed his way onto the local defense team. There he was assigned the task of surveying the people on the voting rolls, from whom the Haywood jurors would be chosen.[22] Canvassing was a vital practice in a big trial. Teams of investigators from both sides would roam the countryside posing as salesmen or lost travelers, engaging the locals in casual gossip and turning the conversation to the case at hand. They would compile lists of each prospective juror's age and occupation, political affiliation, and views about the case, unions, capital punishment, and other topics. Armed with the data, the lawyers would know what questions to ask to reveal a juror's bias, and whether to spend one of their peremptory challenges to keep him off the jury.

Having Operative 21 handling this chore for the defense gave the prosecution a twofold advantage. His work for the defense, and other secrets, was available to the state. At the same time, he could feed misinformation to Darrow. A juror the defense might otherwise covet, having been maligned by Operative 21, might be challenged.[23]

On May 16, the governor invited the press corps to the penitentiary and introduced them to Harry Orchard. The eastern reporters—who had come to Boise hoping to find Dodge City and discovered Harrisburg with mountains instead—were grateful. For weeks they could salt their coverage with accounts of the day they had gazed into the soul of America's deadliest killer.

"I have received no promise of immunity from anyone," Orchard told them. "I have been moved only by a desire to do right."

The *New York Times* led the coverage, as it would throughout the trial. The newspaper was the voice of Manhattan's economic royalists and its editors had given the assignment to their chief Washington correspondent, Oscar Davis, a Roosevelt enthusiast. Gooding personally escorted Davis to the interview. Orchard was dolled up in a gray suit with patent leather shoes. "His complexion is as fresh and pink as a child's," Davis wrote. "There was irresistibly a feeling in him of serenity and sincerity."

At the time of the killer's arrest, Orchard's eyes had been uniformly described—by reporters, witnesses, and even McParland—as empty, cold, and cruel. Davis now found them "round, blue and shining, ready to twinkle merrily at the slightest suggestion." Orchard was not permitted to speak about the case, and talked instead of the lessons he learned from his Bible. By the end of that twenty-minute interview, Davis had bought the prosecution patter. He announced to his readers that Orchard had undergone a spiritual conversion, wished only to repent, and was testifying with no thought of saving his neck.

A few reporters retained their professional skepticism, noting in their copy that McParland had had more than a year to train Orchard. And some even failed to see the merry twinkle in Harry's eyes. The *Denver Post* reported that Orchard "is admittedly a man who has played with all parties. At one time he owned mines himself. At another time he was a member of the Western Federation. At another he worked for the Thiel Detective agency. At still another time he was employed by some associated mine owners." His confession, the paper said, "is almost too complete."

And one prominent journal singled Darrow out for tribute. The *Mirror*, published by William M. Reedy in St. Louis, carried a laudatory profile, written by one M. L. Edgar. Darrow's "tireless mind roams through the world and space seeking out the reason of things . . . His control over men, over affairs, his power in a court and before a jury lies in his sincerity, his perfect truthfulness and his kindness," Edgar wrote. "He could have been on the winning side, in the sunshine of favor, on the lips of those who make reputations. He could have been rich out of the coffers of privilege. But he chose what is called the thorny way."

It was a glowing, perceptive account, obviously written by someone from Chicago who knew Darrow well and had ample opportunity to study him. A poet perhaps. The profile would be picked up and cited by other writers in the weeks to come. No one asked who M. L. Edgar was. And so it must be noted how, several years later, the poems of the *Spoon River Anthology* were first published in the *Mirror*, written by a close friend of Reedy, who delighted, throughout his life, in the use of noms de plume. "M. L. Edgar" was no doubt Edgar L. Masters, Darrow's poetic partner in law.[24]

Chapter 9

BIG BILL

I speak for the poor, for the weak, for the weary,
for that long line of men who, in darkness and despair,
have borne the labors of the human race.

Big Bill Haywood went on trial for his life on May 9, 1907. For more than a year, he and Pettibone and Moyer had been imprisoned in the Ada County jail, down the stairs from the courtroom. Moyer was his same intense self and Pettibone still the "Happy Hooligan," as his friends knew him. He had taken up leatherwork in jail, and on one piece burned a motto: "So live that every day you can look every man in the face and tell him to go to hell." Big Bill seemed bigger than ever. He had exercised regularly, dug a vegetable garden, and studied Marx. Haywood had lost an eye in an accident when young and to focus had to turn his head. It gave him, the *Times* reported, an "unfairly" furtive expression, since the truculent union leader was nothing if not blunt.

Haywood's extended family joined him in the courtroom, and rare was the newsman who missed the tableau of blond, ten-year-old Henrietta sitting in her father's lap. The actress Ethel Barrymore performed in Boise in a traveling theatrical trifle that summer and sat in on a session of the trial. She appreciated Darrow's stagecraft: "He had all the props: an old mother in a wheelchair and a little girl with curls."

The courtroom was plain and rectangular. Its most notable feature was its intimacy. Instead of sitting off to one side, the jurors were seated directly in front of and slightly below Judge Fremont Wood's bench, looking out toward the room. From the chairs in which they softly rocked, they could gaze squarely at the witness, who sat in an armchair on a raised platform, facing them, some fifteen feet away. In the pit between the jury and the witness chair were tables for the press, court stenographers, and lawyers. It was crowded (the defense routinely had half a dozen lawyers besides Darrow at its table) and hot. At any one time the spectators would include gunmen, celebrities, or whiskered socialists. There were pitchers of water and inkwells, the jurors' broad-brimmed cowboy hats hanging on pegs along the wall, and blue and white spittoons. Witnesses would raise their hands, swear to tell the truth, spit, and take the stand.

It took a month to select a jury. Four venires, with more than 250 potential jurors—"talesmen," as they are called—had to be summoned. The prosecution and the defense hoarded their peremptory challenges, and grilled the candidates about their occupations, political and religious beliefs, union affiliations, newspaper subscriptions, and opinions of President Roosevelt. The prosecution labored to keep unionists off the jury; the defense to bar the suspiciously large number of bankers. By repeatedly asking about "probable cause" and "reasonable doubt" the defense began its work of indoctrinating the jurors.

Hawley and the other attorneys stayed in their seats when conducting the voir dire. Darrow, dressed in homely clothes, with baggy trousers and unshined shoes, chose to stroll around the courtroom or to drape himself over the back of a chair, or lean into the box to question a man. His soft drawl and relaxed approach irritated Hawley, who complained to the judge: "That is no way to examine a juror." Hawley wanted Darrow to drop the "confidential exchange of views." There was method in Darrow's manner; he believed that a juror's decision was inevitably based on emotion, not intellect. The more he could, in quiet conversation, weigh a man's heart, the better. Watching Darrow at work picking jurors, Haywood said admiringly, was like watching a man "killing snakes."

Even Darrow had a hard time with one sluggish serpent. Harmon Cox had a daughter who worked as a scab for the local telephone company when its operators went on strike. The defense didn't want to waste a peremptory challenge, but old man Cox resisted Darrow's attempts to portray him as biased. Darrow sat on the edge of the defense table, twirling his eyeglasses, launching question after question. "I challenge this juror for incompetency," Darrow declared. "He is ignorant and no man should be tried for his life by such a man on the jury." He looked plaintively, in appeal, to Borah, who sat on the edge of his own table, jauntily tapping his foot. "State your challenge," Borah said. "And cut out your stump speeches."

It cost the defense a peremptory challenge to rid themselves of Cox. But killing snakes is an inexact science, and all the lawyers had bad days. By the time the last two jurors were chosen both sides were out of challenges, and cattleman O. V. Sebern and builder J. A. Robertson joined the jury almost as an afterthought. At first glance, the state appeared to have won the opening skirmish. Sebern had sat on a jury that hanged a man. Lee Schrivener had once worked as a sheriff, and Samuel Russell as a justice of the peace. Robertson had leased a room to Steunenberg in the governor's first term, and Thomas Gess had known Steunenberg for more than a decade. All twelve men were farmers or ranchers; eight were Republicans and one a Prohibitionist. None of the jurors were wage earners and just one had ever—briefly and long ago—belonged to a union. Their average age was around sixty.[1]

"I AM GOING back to Idaho . . . to begin the fight of my life," Darrow had told Brand Whitlock, just before he and Ruby left Chicago. They had traveled to Boise via a long train ride over desert wastes, where Darrow could not decide which was worse: to shut the window and roast like a shoulder of pork, or to open it and choke on "the clouds of powdered alkali." They arrived at the end of April and found a rented cottage, with a garden of lilacs and roses. Darrow liked the food, especially the tenderloin steaks. "Except for the hard work, intense worry and suffering and the bitter opposition," he recalled, "it was a pleasant place." Ruby remembered the icy reception given them by the "respectables," with their "air of ultra goodness, whose skirts were drawn aside from such persons as attempted to decree what their friends—mine owners and bosses and bull pen inventors and goaders and crucifiers of slaves—should grant as additional pay. THAT was an unheard of impertinence."

Darrow soon won the respect of even the royalist press. At the start of the trial, the *New York Sun* correspondent noted the lawyer's "tilted eyebrows, sardonic mouth and long and rather unkempt hair." A month later the same reporter found Darrow "a man of intellect and subtlety" with "an old shoe manner" and "a capacity for getting inside the skin of a witness that is possessed by few lawyers. There is nothing theatric about him. He never strikes an attitude. He never explodes. He stands before a witness and just bores into his mind, gently, shrewdly with every appearance of wanting merely to know just the truth and nothing more. . . .

"He knows how to browbeat, too; when he thinks it will serve his turn," the correspondent wrote, "but he adapts his method to his man and seldom makes a mistake."

On the third weekend in May, Darrow appeared at the Columbia Theatre to lecture on Walt Whitman. It was a big event for Boise and a welcome diversion for the out-of-town reporters, who were growing tired of the local recreation: a municipal swimming pool, bush-league baseball, and the ongoing prosecution of the Great La Fayette, a traveling healer who proposed to cure gallstones with snake oil and a mysterious manipulation of the wrist. The Pinkertons, Senator Borah, and Judge Wood were there, leaning forward in their seats to catch each word, and a knot of socialist and capitalist scribes, mingling like "the lion and the lamb." Darrow had even "had his hair manicured for the occasion," the *Sun* noted. "The result was . . . a sacrifice of the pictaresque." All agreed that Darrow "had made a good talk." Then "the whole bloodthirsty crew poured out of the theatre and strolled slowly home under the stars discussing the philosophy of Walt Whitman."[2]

With his twenty years of experience handling Chicago's raucous corps of reporters (where he was a member of the press club), Darrow was adept at massaging scribes. He even joined them in the opening weeks of the trial, filing a bylined story of five or six paragraphs for each day's edition of the *Times*. "McParland is a well-preserved well-fed man, 65 or 70 years old," he wrote in one dispatch. "He never goes out in the street without a bodyguard. No one can see why this is necessary but the old detective evidently feels it is best to be on the safe side."

Should the laborites resort to violence, one "substantial man" of Boise told the *Times*, "the solid men of this State" would put three hundred armed men on the street. To impress Barrymore, McParland lifted up his mattress at the Idanha Hotel and revealed a dozen rifles.

Darrow's rivalry with the Federation's regular lawyer, Edmund Richardson—each called himself the lead attorney—was exacerbated by the size of the defense team, which made everything unwieldy. Of the dozen lawyers, the most noteworthy addition was Edgar Wilson, a former congressman who had been, for many years, Judge Wood's law partner.[3] Among other things, Darrow and Richardson quarreled over the techniques used by Darrow's investigators—one of whom had suggested that they exploit Borah's weakness for women by planting a comely secretary as a spy in his office. At one point, Darrow threatened to quit. "I certainly can not stay in it with the understanding that he is leading counsel and that he will give directions," Darrow wrote his clients. Adjustments were made and he stayed on, with a guarantee that he would make the final closing address.[4]

THE STATE OPENED its case on June 4. The jurors were freshly shaved. Nevada Jane was wheeled to Haywood's side with red roses in her lap. Haywood looked drawn and anxious; he had suffered agonizing pain in the previous forty-eight hours and been treated with shots of morphine.[5]

To keep the defense guessing, Hawley's opening speech revealed as little as possible. But it was clear that the state would have Orchard tell of all his bloody deeds to demonstrate that Haywood was the linchpin in a conspiracy that stalked victims throughout the West. The WFM was responsible not only for the death of Steunenberg, said Hawley, but "of scores of others besides." Darrow was on his feet, objecting at the first mention of violence outside Caldwell. "That . . . hasn't anything to do with this case," he protested. Haywood was not even a member of the union when, years earlier, Orchard had ridden the Dynamite Express through the Coeur d'Alenes. The only issue, he argued, was whether Haywood helped kill Steunenberg. But the judge overruled the objection. The state could try to prove the existence of a conspiracy, said Wood, and he would strike out any extraneous information later. This was no consolation for Darrow, who believed that "nothing can be stricken out of a human consciousness after being once let in." And so he or Richardson leaped up each time Hawley introduced another of Orchard's alleged degradations. They got under Hawley's skin, interrupted his train of thought, and signaled the jury that this was all a matter of conjecture, not fact.

Darrow was mendacious when, while recounting how McParland persuaded Orchard to confess, Hawley referred to "this gentleman, who will be on the stand."

"You mean McParland?" Darrow asked.

"Yes," said Hawley.

"Or Orchard?"

"Both of them will be on if you desire."

"I didn't know which. You said gentleman," Darrow said, drawing out the word.

"That may be very cunning, those kind of remarks, but they are entirely out of place," Hawley said. "This gentleman to whom I am referring was Mr. James McParland, the terror of the evil-doers throughout the West, and whose very presence in any community is security for the good order of that community."

"That will be proven, I suppose?" asked Richardson.

Hawley had been selected as the "goat"—the foe Darrow chose for needling and vilification. Darrow would be so persistently mean, in the coming weeks, that Hawley's son would threaten to thrash him.

HARRY ORCHARD WAS called to the courtroom late on the morning of the second day. He was neatly barbered, plump and pink, and barely recognizable—if not for the five gun-toting guards who conveyed him to the witness chair. There was a rustling in the courtroom as people rose to get a better view. "Sit down!" shouted one of Orchard's larger bodyguards, silencing the crowd. A man with a bundle beneath his coat (it turned out to be a spare set of overalls) was seized, wrestled from the room, and searched. The hired guns of each side eyed each other warily.

"How he beamed whenever he was escorted down the aisle to the witness chair," Ruby remembered. "So genuinely enjoying the limelight." Hawley told Orchard to begin at the beginning, and "put it in narrative form." For much of that day and the next, the killer told his tale. He'd had months of McParland's deft coaching to revise and rehearse—to emphasize facts that could be double-checked and to artfully fudge the rest. He had written it down, and polished it, for an "autobiography" that he sold, with the state's contrivance, for $1,000 to *McClure's* magazine.

"It was a revolting story of a callous degenerate," Haywood recalled, "and no one will ever know how much of it was true."

Richardson had claimed the honor of cross-examining Orchard. Tall and bald, with a cropped red mustache and impeccable clothing, he was almost fustian. Darrow believed that important witnesses in major cases were so well rehearsed that "as a rule it is futile to go over in cross-examination the testimony already given." But Richardson chose to batter the witness with a barrage of questions. "Although Mr. Richardson was an able man, he was somewhat lacking in subtlety," Darrow recalled. "Orchard remained perfectly cool and . . . repeated on cross-examination the story already told."

Like Darrow, many of the newspapermen gave Richardson poor reviews. But his cross-examination raised many matters for the jurors to consider. Orchard acknowledged a host of sneaky, unmanly sins that breached the Western code of honor. He admitted to being a bigamist, an ore and powder thief, an informer, and a liar with a history of embellishing his criminal prowess. "I have told some people about things I have done that I never did," he conceded.

"It was your habit to lie about everything, wasn't it?" Richardson asked him.

"Yes . . . whenever it suited my purpose," Orchard replied.

Richardson established that Orchard was a double agent, working for the railroad and mine owners in Cripple Creek. And he suggested that Orchard bore a private grudge against Steunenberg, for when the federal troops arrived in the Coeur d'Alenes in 1899, Orchard had been forced to flee, after selling his interest in the Hercules mine. The owners of the mine who remained behind became quite rich. The destitute Orchard had visited one of them, Gus Paulson, and seen all the wealth he had forfeited just before he left for Caldwell to kill the governor.

At times, Orchard contradicted himself, or had to be rescued by the prosecutors. But because he generally kept his cool, he was ruled the victor of the showdown—and his reputation for credibility, forged that week, survived for decades. Mesmerized by Orchard's monotone performance (and encouraged by Borah and McParland), many of the reporters abandoned their professional skepticism.[6]

"Never a man like this sat in the witness chair before," Oscar Davis wrote in the *Times*. In the months before he killed Steunenberg, Orchard had yearned to escape the slaughter, yearned to buy a ranch, yearned for "an end . . . of the bloody calling," Davis said. But the evil inner circle would not allow it. Haywood was "insatiable of blood, vindictive, savage, revengeful" and drove poor Harry on. "It was kill, kill, kill with him, kill and never cease," and Orchard was merely the "obedient murder machine" who "did as he was told." Until, with McParland's gentle guidance, Orchard had made his spiritual journey "beyond caring."

Orchard was "telling this story on his own account, not to secure immunity or pardon or commutation of sentence," Davis asserted. "The man now sitting in the witness chair at the Haywood trial is not a criminal." Indeed, between Richardson and the assassin, "Orchard is now the stronger moral force," the *Times* reporter announced. "It is indeed a modern miracle."[7]

Harry Orchard was, of course, nowhere near "beyond caring." William Pinkerton, in a private agency memo, derided the notion that Orchard had found Jesus, or was "saved" by divine grace. The killer was "a human demon" and "a murdering scoundrel" and the "only reason why" this "cold blooded desperado" gave any information at all, Pinkerton wrote, "was to save his own worthless hide." Yet McParland, Hawley, and Gooding would fulfill their part of the bargain. To the dismay of many in Steunenberg's family, Orchard would escape the noose and get special privileges in the penitentiary, where he lived in a comfortable little cottage, making money from various enterprises. The fate of the actual killer was a trifling matter, said Hawley, when compared to the need to crush the union. "From that time on," Hawley said proudly, still trying to win Orchard his freedom two decades later, "there has not been . . . trouble of any kind occasioned by the action of the Western Federation."[8]

For all its artful telling, Orchard's testimony had a glaring weakness: there was no corroboration. McParland and his men—given that they'd had a year to do their work, and had infiltrated Haywood's defense team—were remarkably ineffective.

They could show that Orchard knew Haywood, had stayed at Pettibone's house, and had worked as Moyer's bodyguard. There were hotel records and eyewitness testimony to place Simpkins—a member of the union's executive committee—with Orchard as he stalked Steunenberg, and two bank drafts sent to Simpkins from Haywood. And there was a telegram sent from the Federation's Spokane law firm on the day after Orchard's arrest, informing the Caldwell authorities that lawyer Fred Miller was on his way—before Harry ever sent for him. If Orchard wasn't working for the Federation, why did it rush to his defense?

This evidence, and other bits and pieces, established Orchard's familiarity with the members of the "inner circle," but was far from enough to convict Haywood of murder. Simpkins was a union organizer, Idaho was his territory, and as treasurer Haywood routinely sent bank drafts to his officers and organizers. Besides, Orchard had admitted to being broke, stealing from cash registers, and borrowing from friends in the weeks before the murder: If he was Haywood's prized assassin, being bankrolled via Simpkins, why was he out of money?

Orchard's own words had revealed him as a cheat, thief, bigamist, and perjurer. He worked for what side would pay him, in a war where the use of spies and double agents was common. The state had dressed him up, but there was no way the jurors could not conclude that he was a thoroughly corrupt and villainous individual, with a supreme motive to lie. "We had little corroborating evidence," Hawley would later complain. He and Borah began to prepare excuses. They were "greatly disappointed in some of the witnesses brought here by Detective McParland," the *Denver Post* reported. "The State has been misled by Pinkerton detectives who promised to produce indubitable evidence to connect Haywood."[9]

The prosecutors introduced hotel ledgers and bank records and witnesses from around the West to confirm the dates and destinations of Orchard's travels. Colorado authorities testified that they found an unexploded bomb like the one that killed Steunenberg buried at the gate of a state supreme court justice, just where Orchard said it was. And witnesses put Orchard in the neighborhood on the day when the San Francisco home of Bunker Hill mine owner Fred Bradley was bombed. But when Hawley and Borah rested their case, in late June, there was very little implicating Haywood. "Many witnesses appeared . . . to substantiate much that Orchard said about himself, but none supplied the direct positive connection between the assassin and Haywood," wrote the *Boston Globe*'s John Carberry. Even the *Statesman* had to admit that "many who have been following the case . . . cannot see how the evidence tends to connect Mr. Haywood sufficiently to convict him."[10]

On June 21, the defense made a motion for a directed verdict of acquittal. "The statute of the state of Idaho ought to mean something," Darrow told Judge Wood. "No man's life can be taken from him, no man's liberty can be taken from him, upon evidence which comes from such a polluted source as this—an informer, a traitor, an assassin, an accomplice."

Years later, Wood acknowledged that Darrow was correct. The judge almost stopped the trial right there. One of the things that stopped him was the presence of his former law partner, Wilson, on the defense. If he had halted the trial, the judge said, it would have given substance to those who questioned his impartiality. The defense had fallen victim to its own schemes.

DARROW OPENED Bill Haywood's defense on the morning of June 24. He approached the jury and, with no flourishes or preliminaries, began to speak in his "slow, mellow drawl." At times he would lean forward, until their noses almost touched. Sometimes he'd pause to consider, and wipe his glasses. He spoke in the "straight simple language of the hills and mines," one reporter said. He "gave them a talk much in the same manner that the good old deacon in the little Methodist church you used to attend led the class meeting," said another.

McParland and Orchard had worked hard at constructing their saga. Now it was time for Darrow to present a counternarrative. His tale was of sturdy Americans, working in dangerous conditions for up to twelve to fourteen hours a day, forced to live in company housing and to buy their food at extortive prices in company stores, and, when injured, to seek care in company hospitals where the owners found little difficulty getting the wounded to release the company from damages. "Their teeth fell out, their bones twisted, they became helpless, crippled and paralytic," he said. "The machinery was unsafe, the smelters vomited forth poison and death."

And so the miners had drawn together, and immediately "met the enmity and the opposition and the force and violence of every kind of the mine owners' association," Darrow said. Onto this violent stage, with its vigilantes, gunmen, informers, and spies, wandered Harry Orchard. He was "a cheap soldier of fortune—a shoestring gambler who never degraded himself by work," said Darrow. He was "a gentleman miner—who mined the miners." He was a "monumental liar." Or maybe he was demented,

Darrow said, and believed in the fantasies he related on the witness stand; it would account for his preternatural calm.

Orchard was working as a spy when he started killing in Colorado. Detectives protected him from the military units that patrolled the district, and gave him the means to travel to Denver, to "become acquainted, to talk . . . and ingratiate himself" with the WFM leaders, Darrow said. There was peace in Cripple Creek, until Orchard destroyed the Independence depot. Then union miners were shot, beaten, rounded up at gunpoint, and deported from the state. Cui bono? Who benefited? The mine owners, not the union.

Orchard was broke, "a tramp," working as a con man and a petty thief when he crossed paths with Simpkins in Idaho, and drifted toward Caldwell. "He had been pursuing Governor Steunenberg and swearing vengeance upon him for years . . . He fixed this bomb and it was exploded in the most cowardly way that a coward could kill a man," Darrow told the sagebrush elders. "And after manipulations with McParland for a sufficient length of time he was persuaded that the easiest thing for him to do was to lay his crimes onto somebody else, and so he did it, and . . . he is going to get the biggest reward for killing these men, if he lands them, than he ever got for anything in his life. He is going to save his own miserable neck."[11]

SOME OF THE defense testimony was strong, including that of several boardinghouse keepers, who told how Orchard was a frequent, and furtive, visitor of K. C. Sterling, an industry detective. Morris Friedman, who had worked as McParland's stenographer in the Pinkerton offices in Denver, told how the agency had planted a dozen detectives, who acted as spies and provocateurs, in the Federation ranks. But some witnesses cut both ways. Lottie Day, one of Orchard's landladies, told the jury that she had heard him condemn "that devil of a Steunenberg" for costing him his stake in the Hercules mine. "I loved one woman, and only one woman," Orchard had told Day, "and if I had retained the mine I could have had her." It was good stuff. But when Hawley cross-examined Day, she also furnished damaging details of Orchard's ties to Haywood.

The defense concluded with testimony from its own marquee witnesses: Moyer and Haywood. The city was buzzing with rumors that Moyer, who had been feuding with Haywood, was ready to join the prosecution; at one point Pettibone had to step between the two men to prevent a fistfight. But when he took the stand, Moyer shrouded his anger. Calmly, he told the jury that it was Simpkins who hired attorney Fred Miller to defend Orchard in the hours after the assassination, and not Haywood. It was crucial testimony, because Miller's telegram to the Caldwell jail had been brandished by the state as evidence of Haywood's involvement. Moyer testified for a day and a half, putting himself at considerable risk. The evidence against Moyer was weak, and by exposing himself to cross-examination he could help the prosecution build a case against him. "I hope that will please the Goddamn revolutionists!" Moyer told Pettibone when he returned to their cell.

When court reconvened that afternoon, Big Bill, the revolutionist, took the stand. Richardson had been roasted for failing to crack Orchard during cross-examination. Borah, who worked harder at ingratiating himself with the reporters, got off far easier after flunking his opportunity to nail Haywood. The courtroom, stifling hot that week, was packed with fan-wielding spectators filled with "expectation," but Borah's assault on Haywood lasted just a single afternoon. "The prosecuting attorney did not succeed in entrapping Haywood into any significant admissions," wrote the *Globe*'s Carberry. "Haywood made an admirable witness."[12]

THE FOUR LEAD attorneys—Hawley and Borah, Richardson and Darrow—gave their closing speeches in the last days of July. Boise baked, and the judge added evening sessions to free the trial's participants from the worst of the afternoon heat.

Hawley was most distressed by the torrid temperatures, and asked the jury to excuse lapses caused by fatigue, a splitting headache, and his ongoing struggle with stomach illness. For much of two days, he gave a standard prosecutor's talk: an annotated account of the crime and the evidence. He lied at least twice, when assuring the jury that only state funds had been used by the prosecution, and declaring that Orchard was not motivated by a promise of lenient treatment. "Generally we take the statement of a man who is an informer with many grains of allowance," Hawley told the jurors. But with Orchard, "it was the saving power of Divine Grace . . . that finally impelled him to make this confession."

The verdict of the press was that Hawley's speech had been able, "in its way." Richardson countered with a summation that took two days. He had the counsel table moved to give him room, for he liked to back off as far as he could and crouch as he approached the jury, speaking softly until, almost in their laps, he rose to his full height and thundered.

Maybe Orchard was working for the mine owners, Richardson told the jury: Cui bono? But if he wasn't a tool of the industry, he no doubt acted alone. Orchard had "a homicidal mania" that "compelled him to go out . . . and kill," Richardson said. "That mania was greater at times and less at times . . . As he wavered in the pursuit of his victim sometimes the victims escaped and sometimes they did not." He selected his targets "either because of some fancied grievance of the organization of which he was a member, or because of some fancied grievance which he had on some other account," said Richardson. "When some obstacle would occur . . . or when his mania would have a cessation, a retrocession of feeling . . . he would abandon temporarily the enterprise upon which he had been engaged. And then when the surge of hate and desire of the mania would come over him again, it would seek . . . gratification."

The Denver lawyer mopped the sweat from his face, analyzed the evidence, and kept his oratorical flourishes to a minimum. Not so Darrow.

Of all Darrow's courtroom speeches, his summation in the Haywood case was arguably the most brilliant, and dangerous. Conventional wisdom called for a careful dissection of the prosecution's case. And Darrow did much of that. But primarily he sought to put it all in context: to place Haywood and Orchard and Steunenberg in the grand sweep of history—to catalog capitalism's sins and justify the miners' rebellion, even to the point of bloodshed. If its central purpose was to save Haywood's life, it was a perilous gamble.

"Preaching socialism and trying a law case are entirely different matters," Richardson said later. "Darrow's closing speech before the jury . . . was rank. It was enough to hang any man, regardless of the fact of his innocence or guilt."[13]

Yet Darrow had spent months observing, from a few feet away, the twelve men in the jury box. Now, he wagered, he could touch their hearts. On Wednesday morning, July 24, he took his favored position, at the iron foot rail, an arm's length from the jurors. His jacket was unbuttoned; he wore no vest. His hands were shoved in his pants pockets. "He stood big and broad-shouldered, dressed in a slouchy gray suit, a wisp of hair down across his forehead, his glasses in his hand, clasped by the nose piece," Haywood recalled. "While he spoke he was sometimes intense, his great voice rumbling, his left hand shoved deep in his coat pocket, his right arm uplifted. Again he would take a pleading attitude, his voice would become gentle and very quiet."

Harry Orchard was everything that the men of the West despised. He "never did a courageous thing in his life, not one," Darrow said.

> If his story is true he sneaked through the dark passages of the mine . . . when he blew up the Vindicator. If his story is true he sneaked back in the darkness and put the box of powder under the [Independence] station and ran away in the night when he killed fourteen men. . . .
>
> If his story is true he met a man coming out of a saloon, drunken at midnight and killed him without a chance or a word . . . If he has told the truth he sneaked up the back stairs and poured arsenic or strychnine in milk to poison a man and his wife and little babe. If it is true, he went up in the night and he laid a bomb at Steunenberg's gate and then he ran back in the darkness. . . .
>
> Will you show me the act that was not the act of a sneaking craven coward in this man's life?

"What do you think?" Darrow asked the twelve men. "Has he been promised anything . . . for delivering these three enemies of the Mine Owners' Association? . . .

"He is living, isn't he? He looks fat and sleek and healthy and not in any danger of any sudden death.

"If, to save his miserable carcass, he had not turned to kill three men, the grass would have been growing above his grave for twelve months past," Darrow said. "Is there any doubt about that?"

Darrow was on the move, pacing back and forth before the jury, or leaning forward and speaking to them, one by one. At calculated moments he let loose, waved his arms, offered his exaggerated shrugs, or crouched, twisting, like a boxer. At one point he stopped, turned to the jury, and confided, "I am going to take a chance, and talk about religion." He ridiculed the testimony about Orchard's conversion and scorned the "sickly slobbering idiots" who viewed it as a sign from God. "I do not believe in miracles," he said. "You can't take his crooked brain and his crooked, dwarfed soul, and make it over again in a second."

Shortly before noon court was adjourned, to wait the cooler breeze of evening. Long before the six p.m. start, the room was packed. Some four hundred people were turned away. By special arrangement, the court had saved fifty seats for a group of "young women school teachers" from the country.

Darrow's references to Christianity were spurring protests from some in the audience, and the bailiffs had to quiet them. In time, sucking on lozenges to ease his hoarse voice, Darrow left the Good Book behind. As Haywood watched approvingly, with a flushed face and a hard-set jaw, Darrow told the tale of the Federation's struggle.

> If for any reason a thousand men deliberately determined to go and blow up the Bunker Hill mill then it needed blowing up. You need not tell me that a thousand of Idaho citizens, the brawn and sinew of Idaho, were criminals and murderers. Men don't act that way. They only act that way upon great provocation. . . .
>
> I don't mean to tell this jury that labor organizations do no wrong. I know them too well for that. . . .
>
> But I am here to say that in a great cause these labor organizations—despised and weak and outlawed as they generally are—have stood for the poor, they have stood for the weak. . . .
>
> They stood for the father who was bound down with his task; they stood for the wife threatened to be taken from the home to work by his side; and they have stood by the little child who has also been taken to work in their places, that the rich could grow richer still. And they have fought for the right of the little one to give him a little of life, a little comfort while he is young.
>
> I don't care how many wrongs they committed—I don't care how many crimes these weak, rough, rugged, unlettered men, who often know no other power but the brute force of their strong right arm, who find themselves bound and confined and impaired

> whichever way they turn, and who look up and worship the God of might as the only God they know. I don't care how often they fail, how many brutalities they are guilty of.
>
> I know their cause is just.

The second session ended at nine p.m. Many in the press were astonished; they could not decide if they had seen Darrow "skillful, artful, accomplished, weighing the effect of every word," Carberry wrote, or "reckless by risking his cause upon the chance of inflaming the passions of the jurors."[14] The trial resumed on Thursday morning, and once more Darrow spoke all day, his voice hoarse and husky. Around four p.m., trembling, wrought with emotion, he neared the end, and began his famous peroration. He seemed to stumble as he approached the jurors, this last time, and apologized to them for his failing strength. They stopped rocking in their chairs, and hung on every word as he spoke once more of Harry Orchard.

"I don't believe that this man was ever loyally in the employ of anybody," Darrow said. "I don't believe he ever had any allegiance to the Mine Owners' Association, to the Pinkertons, to the Western Federation of Miners, to his family, to his kindred, to his God or to anything human or Divine.

"He was a soldier of fortune ready to pick up a penny or a dollar or any other sum in any way . . . to serve the devil if he got his price, and his price was cheap," said Darrow. "He never did get a good price for trying to kill a man until McParland got a hold of him . . . and told him the value of killing a man . . . his life for Haywood's."

"There is nothing in this case but Orchard. Orchard, an unspeakable scoundrel; Orchard, a perjured villain; Orchard, the biggest coward on record; Orchard, shifting the burden of his sins upon these men to save his life," he told the jurors. "If you men can kill my client on his testimony, then peace be with you."

As for Haywood, "I don't claim that this man is an angel. The Western Federation of Miners could not afford to put an angel at their head. Do you want to hire an angel to fight the Mine Owners' Association and the Pinkerton detectives and the power of wealth? Oh, no gentlemen; you better get a first class fighting man who has physical courage, who has mental courage, who has strong devotion, who loves the poor, who loves the weak, who hates iniquity and hates it more when it is with the powerful and the great," said Darrow. "An angel would not be fitted for that place and I make no claim of that.

"But he is not a demon. If he were a demon or a bad man he would never be working in this cause, for the prizes of the world are somewhere else," Darrow said.

He had been speaking, over two days, for eleven hours. He was almost sobbing now and his cheeks, and those of many in the courtroom, including some jurors, were tracked with tears. He grasped the edge of the table for support.

> I have known Haywood—I have known him well and I believe in him. I do believe in him. God knows it would be a sore day to me if he should ascend the scaffold . . .
>
> But . . . other men have died in the same cause in which Bill Haywood has risked his life. Men strong with devotion, men who love liberty, men who love their fellow-men have raised their voices in defense of the poor, in defense of justice, have made their good fight and have met death on the scaffold, on the rack, in the flame, and they will meet it again and again until the world grows old and gray.
>
> Bill Haywood is no better than the rest. He can die, if die he needs. He can die if this jury decrees it; but, oh, gentlemen, don't think for a moment that if you hang him you will crucify the labor movement of the world; don't think that you will kill the hopes and the aspirations and the desires of the weak and poor.
>
> You people who are anxious for this blood, are you so blind as to believe that liberty will die when he is dead? Do you think there are no other brave hearts and no other strong arms, no other devoted souls who will risk all in that great cause which has demanded martyrs in every age of the world? There are others and these others will come to take his place; they will come to carry the banner where he could not carry it.
>
> Gentlemen, it is not for him alone that I speak. I speak for the poor, for the weak, for the weary, for that long line of men who, in darkness and despair, have borne the labors of the human race. The eyes of the world are upon you—upon you twelve men of

> Idaho tonight. Wherever the English language is spoken or wherever any foreign tongue known to the civilized world is spoken men are talking and wondering and dreaming about the verdict of these twelve men that I see before me now.
>
> If you kill him your act will be applauded by many. If you should decree Bill Haywood's death in the great railroad offices of our great cities men will sing your praise. If you decree his death, amongst the spiders of Wall Street will go up paeans of praise for these twelve good men and true who killed Bill Haywood. In every bank, almost, in the world, where men wish to get rid of agitators and disturbers, where men hate him because he fights for the poor and against the accursed system upon which they live and grow rich and fat—from all those you will receive blessing and praise, that you have killed him.
>
> [But] there are still those who will reverently bow their heads and thank these twelve men for the life and character they have saved. Out on our broad prairies where men toil with their hands, out on the wide ocean where men are sailing the ships, through our mills and factories, down deep under the earth, thousands of men and of women and children—men who labor, men who suffer, women and children weary with care and toil—these men and these women and these children will kneel tonight and ask their God to guide your judgment. These men and these women and these little children—the poor, the weak and the suffering of the world—will stretch out their hands to this jury and implore you to save Haywood's life.

Darrow's last few words were barely audible. He seemed to stagger to his chair. Haywood and his other lawyers surrounded Darrow, and even Borah elbowed his way in to offer his compliments. It had been a golden moment, and Darrow had done it justice.

Now it was Borah's turn. That night a thousand people, dressed in their finery, crowded the courthouse and the lawn outside to hear Idaho's young lion. To Darrow, the scene evoked Lord Byron's lines on the ball in Brussels on the eve of Waterloo:

There was a sound of revelry by night,
And Belgium's capital had gather'd then
Her beauty and her chivalry, and bright
The lamps shone o'er fair women and brave men.

Borah attacked like Wellington's cavalry, swinging a saber. Darrow was his target.

"If I were fighting for the cause of labor, I would not seek to engender hatred and ill-will, faction against faction, or class against class. I would not inveigh against law; I would not inveigh against society; I would not inveigh against every man who owns his home or his farm; I would not inveigh against Christianity," Borah said. "Without such things the laboring man goes down into slavery and dirt."

And there was something the jurors should remember about Orchard, said Borah. Repugnant and vicious—yes, but. . . .

"There is another peculiarity about this homicidal maniac. As the greatest reader of the human heart once said, 'There must be method in his madness.' In all his scurrying here and there, killing where he would and where he could, he always lit upon the enemies of the Western Federation of Miners," the prosecutor said. "Maniac? A very necessary maniac."

After an hour Thursday night, Borah resumed the next morning, and finished his summation that evening. Haywood's mother and Steunenberg's widow, overcome by emotion, needed to be helped from the courtroom.

"You have no doubt often in this case been moved by the eloquence of counsel for the defense," Borah said. "But as I listened to the voice of counsel and felt for a time their great influence, there came to me, after the spell was broken, another scene . . . I remembered again the awful thing of December 30, 1905 . . . I felt again its cold and icy chill, faced the drifting snow and peered at last into the darkness for the sacred spot where last lay the body of my dead friend and saw true, only too true, the stain of his life's blood upon the whitened earth.

"I saw Idaho dishonored and disgraced. I saw murder—no, not murder, a thousand times worse than murder—I saw anarchy wave its first bloody triumph in Idaho."

Borah's peroration did not match Darrow's (the senator wrote a more dramatic finish for a published version), but he had linked the bits of circumstantial evidence into a chain that enveloped Haywood—or at least observers thought so. In the shorthand and immediacy of the newspapers, all that came before was forgotten, and Haywood's fate now rested upon this final face-off: Darrow versus Borah. And Borah had won.

Borah had shown "wonderful lucidity" and "deadly precision," Davis wrote. "It was a display of intellectual power that amounted almost to revelation . . . The dingy courtroom was lighted up by a flame of living fire as this man stood there pleading the case of outraged law."[15]

When the senator ended his speech that Friday night, a consensus had formed. The best the defense could hope for was a hung jury, or a compromise verdict of second-degree murder.[16]

Darrow had, typically, soared high and low throughout the trial. He "was a man of moods," said his friend, the Chicago labor leader Anton Johannsen. "He would have faith in the morning and be despairing in the evening." At one point Darrow strode into the jail grinning, and shouted to his clients: "We've got the sons of bitches!" At another he was so downcast that the irreverent Pettibone ordered him to cheer up because "You know it's us fellows that have to be hanged."[17]

The jury began to deliberate late Saturday morning, and Darrow remained at the courthouse, fearing and expecting, like most, a quick guilty verdict. As the hours went on, he remained anxious, and appeared to be hoping for a hung jury. "It takes only one," he told a reporter. The press and the lawyers settled in, drawing chairs together as makeshift beds. According to the courthouse scuttlebutt, the jury had taken a quick vote, and gone 10 to 2 for conviction. The Associated Press carried the story to the waiting nation; it seemed but a matter of time before the two holdouts were converted.

Just before ten p.m., the judge went home. The courtroom was swept of the newspapers and sandwich wrappings and cigar butts, and locked up for the night. Darrow could not sleep; he roamed the streets with friends and reporters, finally settling in a house across the street from the courthouse. At midnight the rumors were again specific. One of the holdouts had caved; it was now 11 to 1, and Haywood would surely hang.

On Sunday morning, before seven a.m., telephones started ringing in Boise. The jury had reached its verdict. No audience gathered at this early hour, just reporters and lawyers. Darrow was among the first to arrive, his eyes red and his skin ashen. Haywood was brought up from the jail, still dressed in yesterday's clothing, testament to a sleepless night. Borah was missing, but Governor Gooding stood in the doorway.

The morning sun streamed through the courtroom windows, heralding another hellish day. Darrow put his arm around his client and said quietly, "Brace up there, now, Bill."

Haywood sat erect, red-faced, his arm hooked upon the high back of his chair. The jury was brought in, looking grim.

"Have you agreed upon a verdict?" Wood asked.

"We have," said the foreman. There was fumbling with the envelope. The judge looked at the verdict and handed it to his clerk to be read. Darrow covered his face with his hands.

"State of Idaho against William D. Haywood," the clerk intoned. "We the jury in the above entitled cause find the defendant, William D. Haywood, not guilty."

An instant of shock; then pandemonium.

"Bill, you're free, you're free, do you know it?" Darrow told him, grasping Haywood by the hands. Richardson rose to make a motion, but couldn't get the words out. "The defendant will be discharged," Wood declared, "and the jury dismissed." Hawley departed; Gooding disappeared.

Haywood gleefully shook hands with the jurors, who crowded around the labor leader and his lawyers.

"I want to say, Mr. Darrow, that I like you. I liked the way you handled this case," said juror Russell. "I believe you are honest and what you said went a long way with me."

"And you, too, Mr. Robertson, were with us," Darrow told the aged Scot. "I was afraid of you. I was afraid you could not forget that Gov. Steunenberg was your friend."

"So he was, Mr. Darrow," Robertson replied. "But do you suppose that after Harry Orchard, that wretch, killed him that I could sit and see him try to throw it off on Mr. Haywood? No, sir." He walked off chuckling at the way he had fooled the lawyers.

"Mr. McBean," said Darrow, reaching to pull the juror into the circle. "We never could figure just where you stood."

"Mr. Darrow, I didn't know myself," he replied. "When the state got through I was in doubt. And when you finished I was in doubt. The judge said if any of us had doubts we must acquit. I said that is good enough for me."

And Darrow told Foreman Gess, "I didn't know as you liked my attack on Mr. Hawley, as I believe he and you are old friends."

"Oh, that's all right," Gess replied. "I know how lawyers are."

Ruby was searching for Darrow, squeezing her way through "a solid jam of humanity on every street . . . trying to get to the winners, shouting, surging, waving, smiling, crying aloud their joy over the victory." As she made her way down Main Street she saw Borah, "in the doorway at the foot of the stairway that led up to his office . . . one shoulder leaning against the wall, hands in pockets, feet crossed, hat tilted to one side, the picture of abject despair."

Haywood, grabbing Darrow's hat instead of his own in his excitement, rushed from the courtroom. He went first down the stairs, to greet his codefendants.

"That's good," said Moyer, who never stopped shaving as he heard the news.

"Give my regards to Broadway," said Pettibone.

Then Haywood went to the hospital, where his mother was being treated for exhaustion and a Federation lawyer, John Murphy, was dying of tuberculosis. Murphy's two withered arms reached up. He knew his friend well. He placed his hands on Haywood's cheeks and said, "Bill, you are a great big-hearted fellow. In your hour of triumph be humble." In a walk through Boise the next day, Darrow told Haywood much the same thing—to stay out of trouble and keep a low profile—but his client rejected the advice. "His arguments had no weight with me," he said. "Darrow had been employed as a lawyer and not as a mentor."[18]

McParland railed at Darrow, and undoubtedly was the source for reporters who variously assigned the verdict to bribery, corrupt bailiffs, or cowardly jurors. Davis blamed the verdict on the judge's instructions, and Roosevelt on the jurors' fear of union retaliation. But Cobb set blame on the president. The Idaho authorities had foolishly heeded Roosevelt's call for a fair trial, the publisher griped, and "spoiled a good hanging."[19]

Chapter 10

FRAILTIES

He was always . . . the lone wolf.

Darrow was back in Idaho in early September, preparing to defend Steve Adams in a retrial of the north woods murder case. The exaltation he felt at the Haywood verdict had faded amid a series of troubles. "Your letter came today just when I needed it. For I was blue as the devil," Darrow wrote Brand Whitlock. "The enemy, stung by my victories, have been firing hot shot into me—and some of my associates, jealous . . . have been helping them."

Darrow had been snubbed by Haywood when Big Bill's victory tour roared through Chicago, and lost a public spat with the press over whether he excused violence at the trial. (Darrow denied it; the transcript clearly showed he had.) "This is the mad brawling of an anarchist," the *Tribune* told its readers. "The Idaho jury heard the most unseemly, abusive, inflammatory speech ever delivered in an American courtroom . . . It was a long tirade against religion, morality and law [for which] Mr. Darrow has only scoffs and sneers."

Darrow was "an infidel, a misanthrope, a revolutionist, a hater of the rich, a condemner of the educated and the polite, a hopeless cynic," said the *New York Sun*. He had "grown gray and rich . . . in the service of labor, and no man living has been able to coin more money out of popularity with workingmen." The harsh opinions offered in the press were abetted by Richardson, whose feud with Darrow had erupted again in the last weeks of the trial. "I will try no more cases with Clarence S. Darrow," said Richardson. He called Darrow "a most persistent and disgusting newspaper advertiser."

"Mr. Richardson was . . . very egotistical, arrogant and exceedingly jealous," Darrow, in turn, told reporters. In the end, Pettibone and Moyer stuck by him, and Richardson left the defense. But Darrow was feeling the searing caress of fame. It was one thing to be the hometown bad boy, another to be a national symbol for godlessness and anarchy. When he failed to stand at a Spokane restaurant as the band played "America," Darrow was hissed by the crowd. He wrapped himself, as best he could, in the comfort of martyrdom. "I don't know as either of us are entitled to any sympathy for what we have lost for our convictions," he wrote Debs. "We have likewise gained much."[1]

Then, on the eve of the Adams trial, Darrow became suddenly, gravely ill. He was in Boise when he was struck by flulike symptoms and terrible pain. The city's only specialist lanced his ear, hoping to drain an abscess, and the worry displayed by Ruby to friends back in Chicago made its way into print. C. S. DARROW IS ILL; TUMOR ON BRAIN, the *Tribune* announced, erroneously. THE MAN WHO DEFENDED HAYWOOD MAY SOON FACE THE OMNIPOTENT JUDGE, said the *Washington Post*. The press linked his physical and spiritual ailments. "That the illness . . . was aggravated by events subsequent to the Haywood trial is little doubted," the *Tribune* reported. "Where he had enemies he had made them more bitter . . . He found himself unable to disregard criticism . . . with the serenity which was characteristic. It never had worried Darrow before that his views, beliefs and statements condemned him in the minds of the great majority of his fellow citizens. This time it did."

Darrow was warned that the infection might spread to the mastoid bone and then to the brain, with a risk of meningitis. The doctor left the wound open, for irrigation and drainage, and told Darrow to watch for swelling. It was a potentially fatal condition. The physicians of 1907 did not have X-ray machines to assess such an illness or antibiotics and sulfa drugs to cure it. He left the hospital on October 6, but only for a day. Four days later he appeared in court for a hearing on the Pettibone case, bundled in a heavy overcoat. He returned to the hospital immediately and did not depart before mid-October, when he went to San Francisco seeking the advice of a specialist. Ruby was put in charge of irrigating the ear, boiling water to sterilize the instruments, sharpening the points of the hypodermic needles, and giving Darrow injections of codeine to help him sleep at night.

Darrow had tried to keep the second Adams trial in the mining country around Wallace, but the judge approved the prosecution's motion for a change of venue to rural Rathdrum. On October 30, against the advice of his doctors, Darrow arrived to take charge of jury selection. He would remember this time as "one continuous orgy of pain." They boarded with a local family, in a cottage near the courthouse. "I was becoming used to the hypodermic," he recalled. "It took more and more to put me to sleep."

The prosecution launched its case on November 5. It had difficulty getting witnesses to testify after a bomb at his own gate tore former sheriff Harvey Brown apart, so the jury listened as the lawyers recited testimony from the transcript of the first trial. On two days in mid-November, Darrow cross-examined McParland before a standing-room-only crowd. He had the detective tell of his exploits as a spy for hire to illustrate how McParland trafficked in deception. And he pressed McParland on the promises the detective made to induce Adams to testify.

The showdown was cut short, however, so that Darrow could be taken to Spokane for treatment. The doctor there prescribed rest, but rest was not an option. "There was scarcely a moment in court when I was not in pain," he recalled. "When the pain was unbearable, as it often was, we had to resort to the hypodermic."

As in the first trial, Darrow set the claim jumper's death in the context of frontier justice. The pioneers had "subdued" the forest, Darrow said, and then "the coming of the jumpers led the older settlers to indulge in the carrying of firearms and to hold meetings at which jumpers were discussed and the best means of getting rid of them. It was almost open warfare." Anyone might have killed Tyler. Hawley sprung a surprise toward the end, introducing letters written by Adams that had not been offered as evidence at the first trial. "I was glad to hear of your belief in my innocence," Adams had told his family. "I wish to God that I was, but I fell in with bad company and was led to commit a number of most vile sins."

Darrow gave his closing address on November 23. "If there ever was a cause or justification for poor men standing together, this is such justification," he told the jury. "These powerful interests that are back of this case are not interested in Steve Adams . . . The pretense is made that a man is being prosecuted for one crime when the whole civilized world knows it is a delusion and a lie . . . He is being tried because he went back on McParland and repudiated his statements." Back in Boise, the *Statesman* told its readers that the state's case was "100 percent stronger than at the first trial." But the jury declared itself hopelessly deadlocked. The eight members who voted for acquittal had not been able to budge four jurors who believed Adams was guilty. Another good hanging spoiled. Calvin Cobb aimed his fury at Darrow, the "blood-stained figure of anarchy" who "stalks into our courts and brazenly justifies murder."[2]

THREE DAYS AFTER the Adams verdict, Judge Wood called Pettibone to trial. There was a good reason to rush: the defendant was fatally ill. The prosecutors wanted to hang him, and his lawyers wanted to win him a few months of liberty before he died.

As in Rathdrum, things moved quickly. Hawley led off for the state, telling the story of Steunenberg's death. He characterized Pettibone as the counselor, paymaster, and armorer for the federation's campaign of terror. Once more, Harry Orchard took the stand. He had "remembered" further details in the intervening months, including the sensational claim that Moyer, Haywood, and Pettibone had bragged about belonging to a secret "inner circle," in which killing was a prerequisite of membership.

There was speculation before the trial about how Darrow would cross-examine Orchard. Richardson's attacks had failed to shake the witness, but surely Darrow could not forgo some attempt to shatter Orchard's poise? Darrow treated Orchard differently. He did not pick at Orchard's story, looking for inconsistencies. The best thing to do was let Harry Orchard show his detestable self. After Orchard would admit to burning down a business for the insurance money or shortchanging farmers for their milk, or stealing another man's wife, or blowing up a mine, Darrow would ask:

"You didn't know Pettibone then?"

"No," Orchard would reply.

"Nor Moyer or Haywood?"

"No."

Darrow's "cross examination was rigid and effective," the Associated Press reported, "in that the witness was pictured as an inhuman monster, a murderer, bigamist, perjurer, gambler, thief and incendiary." Darrow closed his cross-examination on a Saturday evening by describing each of

Orchard's confessed crimes in minute detail and asking, "You did that, did you not?"

"Yes, sir, I did," Orchard replied. The witness looked miserable, perhaps realizing that without Oscar Davis to tell it otherwise, the world would lose its sympathy for the merry-eyed murder machine. Indeed, the humbled press corps had dropped their lavish testaments to McParland's skills and the "miracle" of Orchard's religious conversion. "Mr. Darrow with dextrous hand drew for the jury not the picture of a repentant murderer aiding justice, but invested Orchard with the crimson-stained robes of a craven assassin," said the *Globe*. He had compelled Orchard "to depict himself as a despicable slayer of men . . . an inhuman fiend . . . and a wretch who lay in wait for his victims and shot them in the back."

But when court reconvened on Monday, Darrow was not there. Nor on Tuesday, Wednesday, and Thursday. It was almost time to open the defense, and the lead attorney was in agony, confined to bed. Darrow made it to Friday's session of the trial, looking far from well. He questioned a witness that day and Saturday, with short, raspy inquiries and ill-tempered insinuations. He got a brief reprieve for the Christmas holiday but was required to return to court on December 26 to make the opening argument for the defense. He did not have the strength to stand on his feet. Nor to raise his voice. He got permission to sit as he made his remarks.

A chair was set in front of the jurors. As a hushed courtroom strained to hear him, for two hours, Darrow spoke slowly, and at times with obvious effort. He apologized for his infirmity, and announced that this would be his final appearance at the trial.

Darrow had wired his friend C. E. S. Wood in Oregon, asking him to "answer quick" if there was a "first class ear expert" in Portland. But instead of traveling to the cold and wet Northwest, Darrow and Ruby left for Los Angeles on December 27. An old pal, the writer James Griffes, had made arrangements for the couple. Darrow was admitted to the California Hospital, to be treated by Dr. John Haynes, and Griffes found a bungalow for them near the Church of the Angels. They were accompanied by Billy Cavanaugh, a stonecutter from Chicago who had met Darrow in Boise and acted as a bodyguard and companion.

In California, Darrow received good news. On January 4, the jury acquitted Pettibone, and Hawley announced that the state would drop the charges against Moyer. Having heard the evidence twice, said Judge Wood, it was clear there was "nothing" beyond Orchard's testimony to connect Moyer to Steunenberg's murder. Pettibone left the courthouse clinging to the arm of his wife; he would die from cancer the following summer. Haywood missed the funeral.

To the surprise of no one, Orchard pleaded guilty to the murder of Frank Steunenberg and was sentenced to hang. But Harry did not swing. Pinkerton detective Chris Thiele reported to his superiors how Hawley used "his influence" to "have the Pardon Board commute Orchard's sentence." The bargain was kept. Yet despite the efforts of his promoters—Detective McParland, Prosecutor Hawley, and Governor Gooding—Orchard never did walk free. He was a "human demon," and "I do not believe there is a Governor in the world who would dare liberate a murdering scoundrel like this," William Pinkerton wrote McParland. The assassin died in prison at the age of eighty-eight. Steve Adams was tried one last time, in Colorado, for the murder of a mining company official, and acquitted.

"While the thinking world has taken one view of these cases, the juries have taken another," the *Statesman* concluded. Fair enough. But the states of Idaho and Colorado had staged five trials in their efforts to sustain the tale of a murderous "inner circle." Two of the three Adams trials ended with hung juries, the other in an acquittal. The trials of Haywood and Pettibone—the two instances where jurors had an opportunity to watch Orchard testify and judge him—ended in verdicts of not guilty. Despite its home court advantage and star witness, the finest prosecutors and a compliant press, the mine owners' money, the Pinkerton spies, a permissive Supreme Court, and the unconscionable meddling of Theodore Roosevelt, the state had failed to prove that the union killed Frank Steunenberg.

MEANWHILE, DARROW WAS suffering through another month—his fourth—of grueling pain. The usual procedure for mastoiditis was to remove a portion of the affected area, drain the wound, and keep the infection from spreading. But the doctors were stumped by the absence of characteristic swelling or fever, and balked at subjecting him to the hazards of an operation. On January 2, the newspapers in Los Angeles reported that Darrow's condition was critical, and that he had resolved to return to Chicago. Then, on the day that he and Ruby were preparing to leave, Darrow felt a lump behind his ear. The surgeons operated the next day.

Darrow recovered, though he lost his hearing in that ear. But his troubles were not over. A panic had swept Wall Street in October. Banks failed, speculators hoarded gold, and desperate investors killed themselves. The resultant depression lingered for months, crushing businesses and throwing millions out of work. Darrow lost his investments in bank stocks, and Ruby received urgent cables from an Illinois associate who had helped persuade him to invest in a Mexican gold mine. Darrow had sunk much of his savings in the Black Mountain mine and should withdraw his money immediately, the man said. But the doctors in California told Ruby that Darrow should not be subjected to such a shock. She shoved the telegrams under a cushion, and more money was lost. When she finally informed him, he stood up "like a rocket and paced back and forth, jerking himself from the arms of those strong men trying to subdue his emotions," Ruby remembered. "Toward me he turned an unforgettable look, charged with . . . accusation."

Darrow demanded to know if she realized that "I had thrown away his life savings, his dream of retiring," Ruby said. "Now he would have to begin all over and be a slave to the irksome law work." He had nursed hopes of moving to New York or London to be a man of letters. He sank back onto the bed and told her: "I will never forgive you for this. We're wiped out. We're broke."[3]

Back in Chicago, Edgar Lee Masters was feeling the effects of the market crash as well. He had developed a fine opinion of himself and his talents, convinced that the acts of lesser men—"the cords of the Lilliputians," as Masters put it—kept him from fulfilling his great promise.

Darrow, Masters & Wilson had done well. "Business had poured into our office, and we could have become rich on it," Masters recalled. Yet his rambunctious sex life cost him money, and his wife Helen was pressing him to buy a home commensurate with their social status. And though the Haywood case carried a supposed fee of $50,000, the Federation was strapped for funds. By June 1907, the law firm had received just $14,500. His defense of the union took Darrow away from the office for much of two years. "He neglected the most important cases," Masters griped, "and the result was that they ceased to come." Hearst was behind on his payments to the firm, the American economy was crumbling, and according to Ruby's frantic messages, the rainmaker was on the brink of death.

In November, Masters had written Darrow, alerting him to the firm's troubled finances and demanding money. The partners had an agreement, Masters reminded him, to divide the fees. Darrow was to get 55 percent, Masters to get 25 percent, and Cy Symon and Frank Wilson 10 percent each. But Darrow and his son Paul were overdrawing money from the firm's account to cover their losses and pay Jessie's expenses. According to Masters, Darrow owed him $1,725, plus a share of the balance due from the union. More important, the firm needed its marquee name back in Chicago, generating business.

Darrow answered the letter from Boise. He expressed his "regret" that the firm was "hard up" and that his absence "hurts the business," but was wounded by his partner's demands and defended his decision to stay and save Adams and Pettibone. "I could see no way to stop; there was none," Darrow wrote. He told Masters that "if you look the books over you will find that the amount of money I have put in from business I got . . . has more than paid what I took out." His partners should be grateful, Darrow wrote. Money was "scarce," he was getting old, and he and Paul "have been pressed" by their investments. He threatened to quit the firm if Masters continued to badger him.

"I would not give up our association in the office for money," Darrow wrote. But "I cannot at my time of my life afford to lose what I have . . . I would feel very badly if it was necessary to quit . . . but I am absolutely obliged to hold what I get here until the pinch is over."

Masters seethed over the holidays, and in January, with Darrow in the hospital, took a different tack. He wrote the Federation, asking for a full accounting of the money paid and owed. It was merely a matter of year-end bookkeeping, Masters assured the union, regrettable but necessary because his partner's illness had made "any business conferences with him impracticable." The WFM declined to comply. It would deal only with Darrow, the union said: "He is the only party we recognize." The response infuriated Masters, and fed his suspicion that Darrow was cheating him.

Darrow limped back to Chicago in February, his head swathed in bandages, with one eye peering out. By his account, the partners settled their dispute, after accepting a payment from the union "for much less than my contract entitled me to." Masters recalled it differently. "He was gone from Chicago for 26 months. He returned at last a sick man," Masters recalled. "The first thing he did on arriving was to beg off on the payment he owed the firm. My share was $9,000. I told him that I would not press it, but that he would have to pay it sometime."

Masters gnawed on the grievance. The two partners were much alike, and no more so than when it came to money. Both made it handily, spent it lavishly, professed its unimportance, and fought like wolverines over every dollar when their comfort was at stake. The Haywood case was the beginning of the end for their law firm, and their friendship. "What a rotter Masters was," Ruby recalled. Knowing Darrow was ill, Masters "ignominiously and brutally accused" him "of having extracted from the firm's earnings." And all that time, she said, Masters was roosting in his corner office, writing poems and plays on the firm's time.[4]

A YEAR AND MORE passed before Darrow paid off some $10,000 to $15,000 in personal debts. Paul married a Vassar graduate who worked as a telephone operator in his father's office and headed west to Greeley, Colorado, to run a coal gas plant. It would eventually be a fine investment, but Darrow's piece of the deal required that he help fund construction of gas lines and other works. Darrow and Ruby moved into an apartment by the University of Chicago, and for a year purchased nothing but food and essentials. "We both slaved, yes slaved," she recalled.

Darrow thought to move his practice to New York, perhaps as a stop on his way to London. "I have been in a hard struggle for two or three years on account of some very heavy losses, and am paying up debts to hold my gas plant in Colorado," he wrote, turning down a solicitation from a liberal cause. "As soon as I am out of the woods, I intend moving to New York, but I have been obliged to refuse to make contributions for some time."

Darrow had sworn off politics, and seemed more cynical than ever. "It is not possible to accomplish anything," he wrote Whitlock. "The people are not ready and after you are done they will return to their vomit.

"The only thing worthwhile is to develop your own individuality and leave something that will do a little to liberalize the few who knew and cared because you lived," said Darrow. "I am strongly thinking of leaving [Chicago] before very long and . . . would have done it before if I had not lost all my money."

To supplement his law practice, Darrow struck out on the lecture circuit, most lucratively for the beer and liquor industry, for whom he argued the case against Prohibition. America had always been a hard-drinking country. But the deleterious effect of alcohol on the poor and working classes inspired a middle-class constituency for reform, led by groups like the Women's Christian Temperance Union and the Anti-Saloon League. As a libertarian, Darrow had fought such concerns since his early days in Chicago, and he barnstormed Illinois that spring, speaking against a statewide referendum that would let counties and townships ban alcohol. That Chicago would stay "wet" was never in doubt, but in a notable defeat for the saloon-keepers, hundreds of small jurisdictions declared themselves "dry" on Election Day. The growing alliance between suffragists and Prohibitionists alarmed Darrow and soured him on the feminist cause.

His public speaking caused more tension at the firm. "Darrow took to the lecture platform, speaking for the liquor interests," Masters recalled. "He was much away and naturally did not turn his fees as a lecturer into the law office treasury . . . My own burdens were heavier in consequence. I remonstrated with him repeatedly, but to no avail. He was the business producer and therefore he was in a position of authority."[5]

For all his muttering, Darrow's troubles did not quell his sense of idealism. He was back in Chicago for just a few months when horrific events in Springfield, Illinois, brought him into the newborn civil rights movement, and a role as a founding director of the National Association for the Advancement of Colored People.

It was no easy time for African Americans, or their white allies. The Supreme Court had given a legal imprimatur to segregation in 1896, in *Plessy v. Ferguson*. When Roosevelt had invited the Negro leader Booker

T. Washington to dine at the White House in 1901, South Carolina senator "Pitchfork" Ben Tillman captured the sentiments of many of his fellow Americans. "The action of President Roosevelt in entertaining that nigger will necessitate our killing a thousand niggers in the South before they will learn their place again," Tillman complained.

But Darrow was a friend to Chicago's small black community. He attended a Negro church on New Year's Eve, consulted a black physician, and occasionally went bicycle riding with an African American man whom he knew. In 1899, Darrow had advised the "Chicago Colored Citizens," a group that hired a private investigator to travel to the South and investigate reports of lynchings. The crusading black journalist Ida Wells-Barnett took the information and composed "Lynch Law in Georgia," a pamphlet that described how Samuel Hose was tied to a stake, tortured, disemboweled, and burned alive, and a friend, the aged preacher Elijah Strickland, hanged—and how the residents of Newman, Georgia, fought one another for blackened scraps of flesh and bones, as souvenirs.

In 1901, Darrow had created a stir in Chicago by asking: "Is there any reason why a white girl should not marry a man with African blood in his veins?" He urged blacks to assert their rights. "These lynchings in the South and these burnings in the South are not for the protection of the home and the fireside; they are to keep the Negroes in their place," Darrow said. "The South never means to recognize any such thing as social equality. . . .

"You must respect yourselves or nobody will respect you," he told the members of a black men's club. It would be a long, hard struggle, and "many of you must suffer, and many must die before the victory will be won." There was a split in the black community, between accommodating leaders like Booker T. Washington and militants like W. E. B. Du Bois. Darrow came down on the side of the militants, urging them to demand full equality.[6]

Northerners clung to the notion that race was a Southern problem. Then, on the night of August 13, 1908, twenty-one-year-old Mabel Hallam, the white wife of a Springfield streetcar operator, claimed that she had been raped by a black construction worker. It was a lie, but a mob of between five thousand and ten thousand people stormed the jail, and rioted when they learned the sheriff had spirited the prisoner away. The militia was deployed, but it could not stop the razing, looting, and burning of the Levee and the Badlands, the city's black neighborhoods. Two African Americans were seized by mobs, tortured, and hanged. Most of the black population fled; a few took up arms and shot from rooftops and upper stories, killing four white men.

The riot commanded national attention, for the city was the site of Abraham Lincoln's home and tomb. Darrow was among the first to express outrage. "Today, within the shadow of the monument raised to the great Liberator's name, defenseless Negroes are murdered, families are driven from their homes . . . and the ruthless hand of vengeance and destruction is raised against every man, woman and child whose face is black," Darrow wrote in the *American.* It would be easy to blame the riot on "hoodlums" and "drunkards," Darrow wrote, but to do so would be a mistake. The Springfield riot was a sign that a "dark stain" of racism gripped all American society. "North and South—men of place and influence—have freely parroted words of venom and hate against a poor and helpless race, until in churches, clubs, factories, shops and on the streets the word is passed from mouth to mouth that life is not safe unless the black is hanged or burned by the righteous mob.

"Time was when these lynchings in the South awoke the righteous indignation of the North. But those days have passed. The friends of the Negro have gone to their last long sleep and on this question of color the North and South are one."

Two weeks later, William E. Walling, a wealthy socialist who had rushed to Springfield for a firsthand look at the scene, published an appeal for a "large and powerful body of citizens" to come to the aid of American blacks. He asked Darrow for his help, and liberals like Jane Addams, John Dewey, Florence Kelley, Lincoln Steffens, William Dean Howells, and Oswald Villard enlisted in the cause. Darrow was on the program when, at a conference in New York in May 1910, the NAACP was founded. He spoke in the evening at Cooper Union—the site of Lincoln's landmark speech against slavery. The abolitionist Theodore Parker had said, in the years before the Civil War, that "the arc of the moral universe is long, but it bends toward justice." Martin Luther King Jr. would like the image; so did Amirus Darrow's son. "God's and nature's laws are working, and working toward equality, and broadly and slowly and imperceptibly, perhaps, toward justice," Darrow said.[7]

As Darrow worked his way out of debt, his client list was the usual assortment—a rich glimpse of the social, legal, and economic disputes at the century's turn.

On behalf of his friend William O. Thompson—who was married to one of the young ladies—Darrow conducted shuttle diplomacy among the three comely daughters of a local King Lear, a wealthy capitalist whose fortune needed dividing. One brother-in-law took to loitering near the mansion with a revolver. When he was banished by the family, his wife rushed to join him, crying, "I still love him" and—to the delight of the gossips of tony Hinsdale—"suffered a heart shock and fell in a swoon" on the lawn. The affair seemed destined for a scandalous legal confrontation until Darrow helped them reach a settlement.

Sex and money were the culprits again when Darrow went to the aid of the wealthy Anna Boysen, who had been arrested in a rooming house with her young skating instructor, Rudolph Hough, and charged with illegal cohabitation. The warrants for the arrest had been procured by Boysen's mother, Helen Leet, who insisted that Anna was a floozy given to drink, drugs, and carousing and could not be trusted to administer her finances. But Darrow told reporters that Anna had been deserted by her husband, and that Leet was taking advantage of her daughter's predicament to steal her money. Anna and Rudolph were just good friends, Darrow insisted. Once again, he got the warring sides to settle.

Darrow took the case of lawyer Charles F. Davies, who was charged with blackmail after accepting a $3,200 payment from Charles Foster, a prominent Cadillac car executive who had four wives. And then there was the juicy divorce of Sidney Love, a broker whose spectacular financial collapse was accompanied by accusations that he married an English heiress for her money, and whose story delighted headline writers ("Love Will Try Again"). Darrow represented William Henley, a former judge and railroad president accused of embezzlement, and John Ericson, the city engineer, who allegedly distributed public funds to his friends. He defended distillery operators charged in federal court with tax evasion. He took a $500 fee from local theatrical interests that wanted to have underage actors exempted from child labor rules. And he unsuccessfully represented the crooked directors of a Kankakee, Illinois, manufacturing firm that was sued for defrauding investors. Some clients were seriously unsavory. Darrow represented Willis Rayburn, one of three men—including Nicholas Martin, the private secretary to Alderman Hinky Dink Kenna—charged with bribing juries. And he went to court for Simon Tuckhorn, a pimp, gambler, and lieutenant of Mont Tennes, the gambling kingpin.[8]

THE ARMIES OF the Progressive movement were finding it hard to know what to think about Darrow. He was invariably crossing them up—heroic one day, contemptible the next.

In November 1908, the criminal court clerk, Abram Harris, and a number of hangers-on were indicted for election fraud. Harris hired Darrow, who noted that the charges were filed under the new statute that created a direct primary election system. He decided to challenge the law. VOTE TAINTERS SEEK LOOPHOLE, the *Tribune* declared. The direct primary was a prized accomplishment of reformers in the Progressive Era, for opening up the party nominating process to the voters. Now Darrow was arguing for the other side.

"A decision favorable to Attorney Darrow's contention means the death of the primary law . . . and a chaos in Chicago and Cook County politics," the paper reported. Darrow, "who has been rated as one of the leading high brows in political thought, has permitted himself to fall into a condition of skepticism." When the trial judge rejected Darrow's argument, he and his partners took the case to the Illinois Supreme Court, and won. The law was overturned, the special prosecutor was dismissed, and Darrow's clients walked free.

But in the same weeks that Darrow was undermining electoral reform, he endeared himself to liberals by representing a Russian revolutionary named Christian Rudowitz.

The case had its roots in the doomed Revolution of 1905, when workers rose against the czar, Nicholas II. Hundreds of protesters were killed outside the Winter Palace in Saint Petersburg when the imperial guard opened fire. Martial law was declared, and Cossacks were dispatched to slaughter socialist sympathizers.

A month after the Cossack raids, on a gloomy night in January 1906, three horse-drawn sleighs crossed the snowcapped Baltic landscape to the home of Theodore Kinze. Masked men armed with muskets entered the house, accused Kinze's wife of being a government spy, shot her and her parents, and set the place on fire. Rudowitz, a young carpenter, fled to Chicago to escape the subsequent reprisals.

The czarist government asked U.S. officials to extradite Rudowitz, and he was arrested in November 1908. He admitted that he had participated in the socialist meeting that condemned the Kinze family to death. Informers were shot and their houses burned, he said, in retaliation for the Cossack atrocities: "It was right that they should die also." But he insisted that he had not been one of the executioners.

The evidence against Rudowitz was weak. Mrs. Kinze's brother declared at the time of the murders that he could not identify the killers, but "official Russia reached the conclusion that this deposition . . . did not prove as much as was desirable," an immigration expert noted, and recollections were "refreshed." The facts "which seem truthful are vague and those which are definite have the earmarks of having been manufactured."

A movement to free Rudowitz was organized in Chicago. Debs, Addams, and others enlisted. The Political Refugee Defense League was established, with headquarters at Hull House, to circulate tens of thousands of pamphlets with the title: "Shall America Soil Her Hands in Blood?" Darrow led a team of lawyers and law professors. They filled the three-hundred-page record with authenticated accounts of czarist torture, killings, and other cruelties. At the extradition hearing, Darrow took on the job of examining Rudowitz and made the closing statement. The room was crowded with adults and children, "many of them carrying scars of the Cossack's lash," the papers reported.

"It has been the policy of this government since its birth to grant political exiles an asylum," Darrow said. "If that rule cannot hold in this case, then . . . none of the oppressed who have rebelled against tyrannical rules of other countries can look to this country."

The record proved that the killings were a revolutionary act, he argued, and that Rudowitz deserved asylum. "The struggle for freedom now in progress in Russia is the greatest revolution in the history of the world," Darrow said. "It is the greatest drama and tragedy of modern times, and will not end until the people of that country have been given freedom."

The U.S. immigration commissioner was unmoved. But the case was now a national cause. Addams wrote to Roosevelt. Sam Gompers led a delegation of AFL officials to the White House. There were protest meetings on college campuses and some four thousand socialists held a masquerade ball in Chicago—young women in scandalous short-skirted costumes or even "Turkish trousers"—singing out the "Marseillaise" and heckling actors portraying Uncle Sam, the czar, and his executioners. Darrow traveled to Washington and submitted a long brief to the State Department. On January 26, as one of the Roosevelt administration's final actions, Secretary of State Elihu Root announced that Rudowitz would be freed.[9]

IT WAS AROUND this time—in the latter part of 1908 or early 1909—that the fifty-one-year-old Darrow met the thirty-year-old Mary Field. They were introduced at a protest rally. It may have been a Rudowitz meeting; in later years, she could not remember. ("Somebody was jailed, or somebody was striking or somebody wanted higher wages.") After Darrow finished his speech, his old Desplaines Street neighbor Helen Todd brought them together.

Todd was working with the Elm Street settlement house, trying to save young David Anderson from the gallows. She prevailed on Darrow to take the case, and he argued that the state should not be executing a nineteen-year-old who, even if guilty of shooting a policeman, had been represented by a disbarred lawyer. Days before the hanging, the governor and the parole board heard Darrow's plea, and commuted the sentence to life imprisonment.

Mary was a veteran of the settlement world, a social worker with literary ambitions and socialistic leanings. She was spirited, clever, idealistic, and pretty—just the kind of independent "new woman" to whom Darrow was drawn. Darrow cheated on his "silly little" wife, and had "many affairs," Mary's sister Sara recalled. "But always his . . . love affairs were with intellectual women."

In a letter to a friend, Columbia University professor Randolph Bourne described the "new woman" of the era as if he were writing about Mary. "They are all social workers, or magazine writers in a small way. They are decidedly emancipated and advanced, and . . . thoroughly healthy and zestful," he said. "They shock you constantly . . . They have an amazing combination of wisdom and youthfulness, of humor and ability, and innocence and self-reliance, which absolutely belies everything you will read in the story-books or any other description of womankind . . . They enjoy the adventure of life; the full, reliant audacious way in which they go about makes you wonder if the new woman isn't to be a very splendid sort of person."

Mary was one of three daughters of a rigid Baptist father and a devout Quaker mother. The girls inherited their mother's gentle idealism and their father's will. Mary defied his order that she attend a small religious college, borrowed money, and enrolled at the University of Michigan—a stunning act of independence for a young woman in the 1890s. He banished her from their home.[10]

Like Darrow, Mary worked as a teacher for a time, in a one-room school in rural Michigan. After hearing Debs speak one night, she applied to Hull House, where Addams passed her name to Graham Taylor at the Chicago Commons. There, she gave English classes, and taught parenting to immigrant mothers and helped deliver babies. "I came to the Commons in a glow of enthusiasm for service among the plain people," she recalled. "I was so happy." She thought Addams was "very wise," but Saint Jane did not return her regard—she viewed Mary as saucy and irreverent.

Mary had several suitors in Chicago, including a Russian diplomat, a police inspector who presented her with the comb of a notorious murderess, and a wealthy young man who gave her a set of pearl-handled golf clubs and an engagement ring. She called off the marriage when, in an argument at a party, he slapped a cocktail from her hands; it reminded her of her father's cruelty. Another affair ended ruinously when her lover—a black-haired Irish newspaperman who lived at the Commons and took her to anarchist lectures—disclosed he was betrothed to another woman. Mary had "peaks of ecstasy and elation" that could be followed by "descents into the valley of despondency," her sister Sara said.

Mary's breakup with the journalist helped feed a disillusionment with settlement life. "I grew to doubt everything," she wrote Taylor. Charity work seemed but a palliative, insufficient without greater social change. She feared that the "good is the enemy of the best." Taylor hoped a move would do Mary good, and she was named co-director of the Maxwell Street Settlement House, in a neighborhood of impoverished Jewish immigrants known as "Little Russia." There, in the spring of 1908, she gained some notoriety when Lazarus Averbuch, a student in her English class, was shot five times on the doorstep of the city police chief.

Chief George Shippy claimed Averbuch forced his way into his vestibule and attacked him. But Chicago's radicals raged at what they suspected was an unjustified shooting of an innocent beggar. Mary joined in the legal strategy meetings, helped arrange for the disinterment and autopsy of Averbuch's body, and sheltered his sister Olga at the settlement.[11] "Chicago had its spree and its excitement and its hysterics . . . things quieted down . . . [and] it was forgotten," Mary recalled. But the Averbuch incident had been a "blow upon the settlements. They were criticized for harboring young radicals, and particularly anarchists," she said. "It gave them the name of nurseries of communism." Concluding that her "usefulness had been impaired," she left Maxwell Street and the Commons.

Mary knew Darrow by reputation. But though he topped the bill at big public rallies, he was not a daily part of settlement activities, nor did he attend the endless sessions where protests or programs were planned. "He was always called the lone wolf. He never went to those meetings," she recalled. "He used to go off with a little group of people and read Tolstoy . . . a group of fellow travelers in the suburbs that has sympathy with the poor people."

Mary was entering her thirties now, considered herself a modern woman, and agreed with Darrow that enlightened adults should be able to pair up, unfettered by religious and social conventions. She was drawn to him, turned to him for favors, and aided him in his work. When an itinerant gypsy family begged her for money to avoid arrest, Mary asked Darrow for the $10 or $25 they needed. He laughed at the uselessness of jailing gypsies, and reached into his pocket. "He never carried money in a billfold. He always had it rolled in funny little bunches in his pocket," Mary recalled. "I always asked him if he blew his nose on his money because it always came out like a dirty handkerchief."[12]

Mary took dictation, typed his letters, and helped him with clients. They stole away to join Sara on a holiday and visited her in Cleveland, where her liberal beliefs and charity work as the wife of a Baptist minister had brought her to the attention of Progressive mayor Tom Johnson and his circle. Mary saw Darrow's flaws. He was "inclined to be stingy" with money—making her take streetcars instead of cabs—and could be sloppy, short-tempered, and crude. But all that paled before his "infinite compassion." Moreover, he was famous and his life was exciting, and he shared her militancy for the cause of labor. "I have never known anybody like him," she recalled. "You couldn't help but love a person like that."

Darrow took her to lunch at workingmen's cafés, and occasionally to dinner, and, ultimately, to bed. He called her Moll or Molly. She called him Darrow. "He had lots of girls," she recalled. "Women all liked him. And he understood women." At the same time, he was a married man, wary of scandal and "very cautious." There was a tension in Darrow's marriage. He "often used the phrase, 'women's biological excuse for existence' and was contemptuous of childless women," his friend Natalie Schretter recalled. "Women who otherwise adored him bristled with distaste when he would make those biting remarks, especially as everyone guessed that the dearest dream of his wife—to have a child—could never be fulfilled."

Mary had few illusions about their relationship; she was a convenience. On a sweltering day in July 1909, she was overwhelmed with panic when, after fainting on a downtown sidewalk, she realized she had no proof of identity aside from some papers she was carrying for Darrow. She phoned him, but he had left for the day, for home and Ruby. She was alone and hungry and could not even afford to buy a train ticket to Cleveland to see Sara. She wept hysterically at "the sudden and blinding realization that my life meant nothing to anyone."

Mary resolved to leave. Darrow was gracious, and caring in his way. He gave her money to move to New York, sent her cash to live on, and called on Dreiser and other friends to get her assignments as a magazine writer. She found a flat overlooking the East River and joined the bohemians of Greenwich Village, alive with "atheists, cubists, poets, free-thinkers, free-lovers, women with bobbed hair and intellectuals . . . philosophers, artists, reporters and musicians," one writer observed. Here were Goldman and Ben Reitman, Steffens, John Reed, Hutchins Hapgood, Mabel Dodge, and Max Eastman. Mary and her friends stayed up late, debating momentous issues over cheap red wine or cups of strong coffee in the city's cafés. She sold three stories for $1,200 and vacationed in Provincetown, Massachusetts, where she shared a house with Gertrude Barnum and met Eugene O'Neill. In time, she was invited to join the feminist Heterodoxy Club. "This is a precarious living, off the fruits of one's pen, yet there are always the friends who come to one's help," she told Sara. "I know I can always ask Clarence Darrow freely for aid."

Darrow teased her in his letters ("We will have to stop praising you pretty soon, or you will lose your head, poor little Miss Field") and said how much he missed her ("Damn if I wouldn't like to see you, Molly dear") and visited her in New York when he could. He and a friend picked up Mary and an actress for a weekend of Broadway, dinners, and a picnic in the country where Mary and the men took off their shoes and strolled barefoot through the grass. They listened to Darrow read from Bret Harte's Western tales, and he stopped her from plucking violets because "It's a shame to break up their little love affairs." And "so we left them," Mary reported to Sara, "aching demurely as violets do."

Then Darrow returned to Chicago, and once more she felt the pain of "having no one who cares a damn."

So THE LOVERS parted—for a time. Mary was more than just one of Darrow's "girls." She had come to represent vitality and ardor to an aging, somewhat lost, hero who had just returned from a brush with death. The reminders of his own mortality were insistent. In September 1909, while on a speaking tour in the state of Washington, he was again seriously ill. And in November 1909, his sister Mary passed away. For a year she had lost sleep over a lawsuit she had filed against their late brother Hubert's business partners; Darrow took over the case, and won the judgment. A few days after her death, he hosted a séance at his apartment, trying to make contact with her spirit. With a group of other radicals, he welcomed and listened to Swami Abhedananda, an Indian holy man. Darrow began to daydream about founding a "colony" in California, where intellectuals could write and reflect and practice their free love creed.

"He talks at some length to me regarding coming to Southern California to live, in a sort of retirement, and of purchasing a place where he could live and work, surrounded by such congenial friends as he might choose," said Henry Coit, a California banker in a letter to a friend. Darrow hoped to build the retreat along the path of a planned streetcar line from Pasadena or in the mission town of San Juan Capistrano, and profit as the value of the real estate grew. "If I had the courage I would move to California," Darrow wrote his friend, San Francisco editor Fremont Older, "but I still have to earn some money and am a little afraid to make the change."

Yet middle-aged restlessness could not fully explain his relationship with Mary, which would last the rest of his life. Darrow was a self-confessed failure at the art of writing letters—except when he sat down at his desk after everyone had left the office for the day and opened his heart to her.

"Dear Mary," he wrote on March 15, 1910, "I miss you all the time. No one else is so bright and clear and sympathetic to say nothing of sweet and dear, and I wonder how you are and what you are doing in the big city. I don't hear from you—please write."

He was "tired and hungry and wish you were here to eat and drink with me and talk to me with your low sweet kind sympathetic voice," Darrow wrote. "I shall send you more money next week."

So things stood. And then, on the first of October in 1910, a bomb destroyed the *Los Angeles Times*.[13]

Chapter 11

LOS ANGELES

I dread the fight and am in the dark.

David Douglas and Charlie Hagerty were tending the huge printing press called the "Old Guard" in the moments after midnight on October 1, 1910. General Harrison Gray Otis, USA (Ret.), the militant owner of the *Los Angeles Times,* liked to christen his presses and adorn them with martial symbols. Otis was a union hater, and the "Old Guard" had been named to honor the nonunion pressmen who broke a printers' strike in 1890. It bore the image of a Roman soldier and the *Times* motto, STAND FAST, STAND FIRM, STAND SURE, STAND TRUE.[1]

It was a busy night at the *Times.* A new press had been installed, requiring a reconfiguration of the basement pressroom. There was confusion, and the paper missed its early deadlines. At one a.m., there were still more than a hundred employees in the block-long building at the northeast corner of Broadway and First Street. It was a warm night, and the pressroom windows were open. Late-night passersby could look down on the illuminated scene and hear the presses roar.

C. G. Varcoe had been sitting on a windowsill along Broadway watching the printers work as he waited for a streetcar. Then, growing impatient, he strolled down the hill toward Spring Street. He was halfway down the block when he heard a piercing blast. Turning, Varcoe saw "a column of debris and smoke" rising above the *Times* building. It was followed by a second rumble, "and immediately with the second explosion came the column of flame."

The second detonation had a dull *whump*, like the sound of gas igniting. But there was no mistaking the initial blast. "The first one had," Varcoe said, "the distinctive crack of dynamite."

The explosion, directly above him, threw Douglas to the basement floor. Dazed, he stumbled to his feet. There was a sizzling and a cracking noise, and dust and darkness all around. His corner of the pressroom lay just below "Ink Alley," a street-level passage that opened on Broadway, where barrels of flammable ink were stored. The blast pulverized concrete, snapped iron beams, and slung the floor of the alley down into the basement. Groping through the oily smoke, Douglas found a stairway and escaped. He never saw Hagerty again.

Harry Chandler's office adjoined Ink Alley on the ground floor of the *Times* building. He was the assistant publisher of the newspaper, and the son-in-law of its owner. Chandler had just left for home that night when the explosion obliterated the room and tore the head and limbs from the torso of his dutiful stenographer, J. Wesley Reaves. The next floor up, in the composing room, foreman Simeon Crabill was delivering corrected proofs to a typesetter when a blast that would "jar you inside" parted the boards and timbers beneath his feet. The floor over the alley, he saw, was gone, replaced by a gaping, volcanic opening with "just one solid sheet of flame, shooting up, shutting out the exit." Crabill watched as John Howard, a copy cutter, raised his arms in mute appeal, and was swallowed by the inferno.

Crabill ran north through a hall of linotype machines, each with its own gas burner, used to keep the lead type pliable. Scattered about were cans of gasoline to clean ink from the printing plates, as well as saturated rags and paper. He was enveloped in a panicky group of men who bore him toward the open doors of an elevator; they could not see, in the acrid gloom, that the car itself was stuck far below. Crabill and others tumbled into the black shaft, colliding with the walls and cables, and each other, as they fell to the basement. "I heard them shrieking for help," Crabill recalled. "It was all dark in there . . . the darkest night on earth right at that spot." He came upon a conveyor belt used to carry bundles of newspapers to the street, wormed his way up the chute, and fell through its now-burning opening to the sidewalk. "As I looked back the whole Broadway front was a solid mass of flames," he said.

The newsroom of the *Times* was on the third floor. Most of the staff had left for the night, but a small crew was on duty to update later editions and cover breaking news. "My God, they have got us at last," said C. Harvey Elder, the assistant city editor, as he and his colleague Charles Lovelace felt the pulse of an "instantaneous blast" of light through the windows along Broadway. Plaster fell from the ceilings, and the arc lights swung wildly above them.

Otis was a despised figure among union men, and the *Times* had been leading the Los Angeles business community in a fierce, violent struggle against labor that summer. There were racks of rifles in the tower rooms and shotguns in the newsroom. San Francisco's unions had been warned by Bay Area companies that they could not compete with the southland's nonunion shops, and a General Campaign Strike Committee, led by Olaf Tvietmoe of the building trades council and Darrow's old friend Anton Johannsen, was assembled. Tvietmoe, known as "the Old Man" or "the Viking," was "a leader among men of his ilk, unscrupulous, defiant of law and audacious in execution," said James Noel, a city prosecutor. Sluggers sent nonunion workers to the hospitals with broken limbs and fractured skulls. The local ironworkers wrote and asked John J. McNamara, treasurer of the national ironworkers' union, to dispatch "a good live one . . . not a kid glove man" to organize a campaign to sabotage the city's nonunion iron and structural steel works.

"It was war from the jump," the *Times* said. The newspaper and the Merchants and Manufacturers Association, an anti-union lobby, led the forces of capital. The M&M hired detectives, spied on the strike's leaders, and pressured local politicians and judges. Its attorney, Earl Rogers, prepared a new law banning protests and picketing, and pushed it through the city council in mid-July. When union men defied the ordinance, dozens were arrested.

California was just one front in the struggle in the steel industry—more than a hundred explosions had torn up nonunion job sites in New England, the Middle Atlantic states, and the Midwest in the two years preceding the *Times* disaster. "Never before . . . has there been the same kind or class of insurrection," wrote the press lord E. W. Scripps. "Both sides have adopted . . . tactics of warfare."

Elder and Lovelace rushed from stairwell to window, looking in vain for a fire escape, and wound up in a room adjoining the corner tower. As the flames burst from openings on either side of them they joined Harry

Crane, a telegraph operator, on a windowsill. A group of passing sailors, out on a night's liberty, tore down an awning from the building across the street and offered it as a net. Lovelace leaped and shattered his hip, but the awning saved him. He would live, and have the unique experience of reading his name, mistakenly listed among the dead, in the newspapers. Crane turned back from the window just as a section of the burning structure came crashing down; he vanished into a plume of sparks and flame.

Finally, Elder—who had been horribly burned—crawled out on the ledge, hung by his hands until the heat seared his skin, and dropped. He struck the end of the canvas awning, which tore, and his leg broke as he hit the street. "His back and front were seared and scarred, the skin and flesh hanging like ribbons," John Beckwith, a reporter, recalled, but Elder urged his rescuers to leave him be, and try to save others. "There is a lot of boys in there yet," he told them. His colleagues carried him to a nearby hospital, where he remained conscious and talked with friends for a time before dying that morning.[2]

My God, they have got us at last. Like poor, doomed C. Harvey Elder, many in Los Angeles instantly blamed the unions for the blast. The paper's grieving employees, rallied by Chandler, gathered at an auxiliary plant that had been readied for just such a day and put a one-page edition on the street that Saturday morning, placing the death toll at twenty-one, with a headline that read UNIONIST BOMBS WRECK THE TIMES.

In the next day's paper, the seventy-three-year-old Otis, a great fierce walrus of a man who had hurried back from a trip to Mexico, denounced the bombers with characteristic vitriol: "O you anarchic scum, you cowardly murderers, you leeches upon honest labor, you midnight assassins, you whose hands are dripping with the innocent blood of your victims, you against whom the wails of poor widows and the cries of fatherless children are ascending to the Great White Throne, go look at the ruins wherein are buried the calcined remains of those whom you murdered."

As a young man, Otis had worked as a union printer, but his military service during the Civil and Spanish-American wars, and life as a pioneer, entrepreneur, and Republican Party functionary, had made him one of labor's most outspoken foes. He named his staff his "phalanx" and designed the *Times* building as a fortress, with a statue of a screaming eagle on the highest battlement. Otis was for the "open shop." He "preached that the right to work for whom you please is an inalienable right," said Noel, "and that the right to employ whom you please on such terms as you may agree upon with him, is also an inalienable right."

As the champion of southern California conservatives, and chieftain of a small group of rapacious local business leaders, Otis skewered socialists, Democrats, and liberal Republicans in his choleric screeds and provoked equally vivid responses. Otis "sits there in senile dementia with gangrene heart and rotting brain, grimacing at every reform, chattering impotently at all things that are decent, frothing, fuming, violently gibbering, going down to his grave in snarling infamy," said Hiram Johnson, on his way to election as governor as a progressive Republican that fall. "Disgraceful, depraved, corrupt, crooked and putrescent—that is Harrison Gray Otis."[3]

The hunt for the killers moved swiftly, on skilled police work, luck, and the blunders of the bombers.

Around noon on Saturday, a suitcase was discovered on the grounds of "The Bivouac," the Wilshire Boulevard home of General Otis. While opening it the police heard a whirring sound and ran. They were sixty feet away when the bomb went off, digging a crater and breaking windows in the neighborhood. Another ominous package was discovered by members of the household staff and family at the home of Felix Zeehandelaar, the secretary of the M&M association. This bomb did not explode. A passing motorman carried the bundle to the street, where he carefully unwrapped the newspaper and found sixteen sticks of dynamite wired to an alarm clock. Stamped on the dynamite were the date and place of its manufacture: "Giant Powder Co., Giant, Calif., Sept. 20, 1910."[4]

Within hours, employees at the Giant powder works, across the bay from San Francisco, were interviewed. The company's clerks instantly recalled the three furtive gentlemen who had purchased ten fifty-pound cases of 80 percent dynamite in late September—a far too powerful concentration for their purported purpose, to blow up tree stumps. Thomas Branson, a secretary at Giant, had not liked the looks of the men. "Take a good look at that bugger," he had told a colleague, nodding at one of the trio. "You will probably have to identify him some day." The Giant clerks had demanded references from the three strangers, and saved their names and addresses.[5]

On October 15, the investigators got another break when a landlord stopped in to check on the tenants who were renting a house he owned in San Francisco. The building was deserted, except for a stack of crated dynamite. Chemists matched the explosives with that used in the Zeehandelaar bomb.

By mid-October, then, the police had acquired the descriptions of three fugitives who had plotted to bomb the *Times* and other West Coast targets. Two of the men were identified as Bay Area radicals David Caplan and Matthew Schmidt. They were friends of Johannsen, Tvietmoe, and other union officials. As they searched for Caplan and Schmidt and hauled Tvietmoe and others before a grand jury, the authorities worked to identify the mysterious third suspect, a thin-faced man who had gone by the name of "Brice" or "Bryson."

The Zeehandelaar bomb was again the key. On the day of the *Times* disaster, William Burns, the head of a nationally known detective agency, happened to be in Los Angeles to speak at a banking convention. Mayor George Alexander called on Burns at his hotel and pleaded with him to find the bombers. The detective, a burly, red-haired sleuth with a talent for self-promotion, examined the "infernal device" found at Zeehandelaar's house, and recognized its features. For months, Burns's agents had been working for the industrialists back east, where "open shop" construction sites—skyscrapers and bridges being built by nonunion workers—were being bombed. The device Burns saw in Los Angeles looked just like an unexploded bomb that was recovered from an Illinois bridge site.

It took no imaginative leap to suspect that officials in the International Association of Bridge and Structural Iron Workers, headquartered in Indianapolis, were behind the bombing campaign. Herbert Hockin, a member of the union's executive board and planner of the bombings, had quarreled with his brethren over money and become an industry informant. By mid-October, he had identified "Brice" as James B. McNamara—an out-of-work printer whose brother was John J. McNamara, the popular treasurer of the ironworkers union. The brothers were a study in contrasts. James, twenty-eight, with his narrow face and ragged mustache, seemed feral, surly, haggard with nervous energy. John, thirty-four, was the natural politician—clean-shaven with a ruddy complexion; handsome, bluff, and intelligent, and blessed with apparent kindness.

James McNamara had arrived in Los Angeles from San Francisco with a suitcase of dynamite on Thursday, September 29. The following evening, at around five thirty p.m., he planted his infernal device in Ink Alley, about thirty-five or forty feet in from Broadway, among a dozen or more five-hundred-pound wooden barrels of ink. He then bought passage on the *Lark*, the overnight train to San Francisco, and was leagues away when the bomb went off. "The strikes I witnessed . . . and the rank injustice that grew out of them made a deep impression on me, and when the opportunity presented itself I was more than willing to respond," James McNamara recalled. "I saw real war on the industrial field." Tvietmoe, he said, was "instrumental" in his West Coast assignments. As they searched for James, detectives put his brother John and Ortie McManigal, another union saboteur, under surveillance. But the sleuths lost track of them and the "wrecking crew" launched eight more attacks, including a Christmas Day bombing of the Llewellyn Iron Works in Los Angeles.

Finally, on Saturday, April 22, 1911, police and industry detectives seized John McNamara at union headquarters in Indianapolis and yanked him before a local police court, where a compliant judge okayed an illegal extradition order. The union's officers were outraged to discover Burns and Walter Drew—the steel industry's union-busting lobbyist and security cop—among those searching their offices. The authorities carted away boxes of incriminating correspondence, eighty-six sticks of dynamite, and bomb-making materials, including a collection of alarm clocks. Both sides believed their worthy ends justified illegal means. The kidnapping of John McNamara was an "unlawful thing," Drew acknowledged, in a letter to Burns. But "this we did in the interests of justice, and personally I would do it over again."

McNamara was taken on the *California Limited*, a high-speed train, to Los Angeles. On board were his brother James and McManigal, who had been seized with a suitcase of dynamite on their way to their next job and held without counsel for ten days in a house near Chicago. McManigal made a full confession, but James tried to bribe his guards, offering them $5,000, then $10,000 and ultimately $30,000 for his freedom.

They might as well take it, he told them, or the money would go to Clarence Darrow.[6]

FROM THE MOMENT the leaders of organized labor asked him to take charge of the McNamara defense, Darrow feared that the case would be a debacle. He knew about union slugging and had high regard for the Burns agency. In an off-the-record conversation, Darrow told a newsman, Ernest Stout, there was "absolute proof" of the brothers' guilt, and that he was "sure they were going to be hung." Darrow would never take the case, Stout informed his editors, because "he felt he had no chance in the world of winning."

"Let them get a younger man," Darrow told another reporter. But he seemed to be conducting a debate with himself. "I have enough money," he said. "Of course, I am not rich, but I am getting to a point in life where I do not wish to undertake such a task . . . I want rest. Of course the fee attached to a case like the Los Angeles affair is a big one."

Darrow had just celebrated his fifty-fourth birthday when he heard of the McNamara arrests. He had promised Ruby not to risk his health in another ordeal like the Haywood case. And he knew that if he left Chicago again for trials that could last years, it would destroy his law firm. "You don't know how I dread to undertake this case with all the responsibility and trouble," he wrote Caro Lloyd, the sister of his late friend Henry. Yet Darrow's faith in labor was still strong. He had been an informal adviser to Gompers and the unions for more than a decade. The McNamaras may have been flawed representatives of the cause, but there was this: representing bad guys is what defense lawyers do. And Darrow had seen too much of the robber barons, their tactics, and the way they corrupted American government to nurse any illusions. As in Idaho, the state would align with industry and take industry's money, and bend every standard of ethical behavior to put a rope around the brothers' necks.

Darrow also relished fame, and the McNamara case was a famous case indeed. And he needed a big fee. He was $25,000 in debt, he told Paul, for his reckless investment practices had caught up with him again. In another dubious gold mine deal, he and three associates had pledged $300,000 to buy the Alto digs in Calaveras County, in northern California, and been swindled of $175,000. He had lost money, as well, in an Illinois brick company, and was still sending money to the Greeley gas company. The firm had promise, but its receipts were disappointing. "It seems to me that Greeley won't make us very rich," he told his son.

During their earlier stay in Los Angeles, Ruby had enjoyed California's warm nights, fruit trees, and abundant flowers, and was willing to listen to Darrow's "talk" about moving there. But by now she was aware of her husband's deficiencies as a speculator. "Maybe a ranch will be a better gamble than a mud mine or an imaginary wheat field," she told his sister Jennie. Of one business deal that Darrow had turned down, Ruby reported, "It's the only wild cat scheme that I . . . [ever] knew Clarence to resist."

"He had a period where he was eager for money. Part of it he wanted for sinking into the Greeley gas company," his old law partner Francis Wilson recalled. "He . . . thought he could win the case in a couple of months and get the money."[7]

Sam Gompers, meanwhile, was digging himself a hole. "That organized labor had anything to do with it, I most emphatically deny," the AFL chief said, while the ashes of the *Times* were warm. "I will never believe any of the boys placed or exploded that dynamite."

At first, Darrow said he was only giving advice. His health would not allow him to represent the McNamaras, he told reporters, then left for Indianapolis to meet with forty of the nation's labor chieftains. The following morning, leaders of the bricklayers and the teamsters, the ironworkers and the machinists, the barbers and carpenters and other trade unions heard Darrow out. They pressed him to take the case, and he was blunt. The fight might be necessary, but it would be arduous and demand all of organized labor's attention, energy, and fundraising ability.

On April 26, Darrow wrote to Whitlock. "I go at it, if I do, with fear and forebodings—I dread the fight & am in the dark. If I could avoid it I would, but how can I—they are my friends & in trouble & have an insane faith in me & I don't see how I can disappoint them much as I tremble at the plunge," he said. "I feel like one going away on a long & dangerous voyage."

Gompers came to Kankakee, where Darrow was trying a case, to see him. Darrow said that to properly defend the McNamaras, he would have to move to California and forfeit all other work and income. Defending the brothers would cost the unions more than $300,000, Darrow said, with $50,000 of that as his fee. Gompers blanched, but acceded. Darrow received a retainer of $5,000, and the AFL announced to the press that Darrow would conduct the defense.[8]

Darrow arrived in Los Angeles on an overnight train from San Francisco in late May after meeting with Tvietmoe and Bay Area labor leaders and radicals. Before leaving for the coast, he and Ruby had dined with Hamlin Garland. Darrow was "bitter, bitter and essentially hopeless," Garland told his diary. "I can not find that he has any ideals or convictions left."

In Los Angeles, Darrow joined the irrepressible Johannsen, who had been running the citywide strike for Tvietmoe. He met with his clients, and began to assemble a team of lawyers and investigators. "From the moment I met him I knew I was in the presence of an actor who would never forget his public role, never remove his makeup," a reporter, Hugh Baillie, noted. "He could shamble, or stride vigorously, as the occasion demanded, use his smile as a gesture of gratitude or as a formal grimace. He could weep at will—real tears." Baillie found arrogance, as well as pretense. "When he spoke, you listened. He expected it, and talked in the leisurely manner of a man who knows he won't be interrupted," the newsman recalled.

The rest of the legal team was drawn from the California bar. The local attorneys were an eclectic but impressive lot, and all would play noteworthy roles in the upcoming drama.

A highly regarded defense attorney, forty-seven-year-old LeCompte Davis, lent his expertise on the city's criminal court system. He was a former prosecutor, and a seasoned defender who was known for his spirited efforts in fraud and murder cases. He shared many of Darrow's political and literary tastes, and his wife, Edythe, got along with Ruby: the two couples would socialize and go on trips together.

Job Harriman, fifty, was a different kind of cat entirely. He was a devoted socialist who had come to California from Indiana, run for governor in 1898, and shared the socialists' national ticket with Debs as the vice-presidential nominee in 1900. Harriman was a dreamer who in the years ahead would organize utopian colonies in California and Louisiana. During the strikes in the summer of 1910, he had defended those who were arrested under the city ordinance that banned them from picketing, demonstrating, or "speaking in public streets in a loud or unusual tone." The socialists then named Harriman as their candidate for mayor, and he had surprised Los Angeles with an effective campaign.

Joseph Scott, forty-four, was the English-born son of a Scottish father and an Irish mother. He was a pious Catholic, a father of eleven children, a lifelong Republican, president of the local Chamber of Commerce, and director of a local bank. He was welcomed by Darrow for his respectability and appeal to Catholic jurors. And Cyrus McNutt, seventy-four, was a former Indiana judge and law professor who had come to Los Angeles to retire a decade earlier, but found himself drawn into the practice of law. He was kindly, a staunch Democrat, and could help stop the evidence seized in Indiana from being used against the McNamaras in California.

Harriman had secured a fine suite of offices on the ninth floor of the elegant Higgins Building at the corner of Second and Main Streets, overlooking St. Vibiana's Cathedral. The ten-story concrete Beaux Arts building, with its mosaic-tiled floors, lobby clad in Italian marble, and soaring ceilings, had just opened to the public. It was designed to be "absolutely fire and earthquake proof," a selling point in the wake of San Francisco's 1906 quake. It housed the anti-Prohibition campaigns of the Association of Liquor Dealers and the offices of the Women's Progressive League, which held luncheons on its rooftop.

After settling these initial matters, Darrow returned to Chicago to dissolve his law firm and then moved to Los Angeles with Ruby at midsummer. They rented a house on Bonnie Brae Street. Davis and his wife held dinner parties to introduce the Darrows to "a set of intellectual, social people of excellent standing," Ruby recalled. She was less enthused about the dinners hosted by the Catholic Joe Scott and his Jewish wife, where the guest lists leaned heavily toward "priests and politicians."

In July, Darrow reported to Paul that he had "a good crowd with me" in Los Angeles. "Am a little more hopeful," he said, "but it is tough enough and desperate—shall be surprised at nothing." The members of the defense team were fine men, but none was close enough to Darrow for him to confide in, or to save him from rash mistakes. Two friends who might have done so declined his invitation to join him in Los Angeles. One was Whitlock, who was now mayor of Toledo. The other was Charles Erskine Scott Wood.[9]

TALL AND HANDSOME, with a grand tousled mane, Erskine Wood was another rebellious libertarian laboring in the law. He had graduated from West Point and served ably in the West. After picking up a law degree from Columbia University he settled in Portland, Oregon. There,

Wood developed an epicurean delight in wine, gardening, artwork, food—and women. Though married with five children, Wood bristled in the grasp of respectable society, and carried on a series of adulterous affairs. Like Darrow, he was a man of contradictions. He came from a family of privilege, and represented banks, railroads, and other avaricious clients. Yet he defended Emma Goldman and the Wobblies on free speech cases. Politically, Wood argued for "absolute personal liberty"—a benign kind of anarchy—and endorsed free love.

"I rebel against the suppression of the individual, the lack of freedom and the falsity, the hypocrisy of the smooth successful life. I rebel against all the ideas of sex that it is wicked, low, vulgar, that it is to be suppressed and made little and base . . . I rebel against the praise of submission to authority and I preach the gospel of rebellion," Wood wrote in his journal. "Deliver me from your smooth-shaven, flabby-cheeked human octopus, the rich respectable man."

The local newspaper, the *Oregonian*, smelled hypocrisy. "It is the habit with Mr. C. E. S. Wood to boast that he is 'an anarchist,' " one editorial noted. But this "unusually elastic" man was "exceedingly fond of the rich among whom his select associations lie. No moth flies more industriously about the arc lights."

Darrow admired Wood. They had met before the Haywood saga and worked together in the defense of a San Diego banker who was under investigation for fraud in Portland. In the course of that case, Darrow offered his philosophy about billing. "You are the one who prevented this indictment . . . it should stand a good fee," Darrow wrote his friend. "Of course, the law is a con game and there is no way to tell what a thing is worth and yet this service has been valuable to him, and I feel that no one else could have done it."

It was Darrow who forced Wood to confront his contradictions. In the spring of 1910, Mary Field's brother-in-law, the Reverend Albert Ehrgott, was hired by a Baptist congregation in Portland, and her sister Sara and the couple's two young children prepared to move from Cleveland to Oregon. Portland was a provincial burg—"a little town of little minds," as Louise Bryant put it. Sara was near tears, and Darrow sought to console her. He agreed that, when it came to intellectual discourse, Portland was "pretty benighted," but told her: "There is one man there of our stripe. He is a great liberal, a poet and an artist."

One June day, as she was working in her garden, a taxi plowed through the mud of her unpaved road, and out got Darrow.

"I want you and your husband to come to dinner and meet my friend Wood that I've told you about," he said.

"Oh, Darrow," she said, still resisting. "I haven't got any decent clothes."

"Oh, I'm sure you can arrange it all right, and were going to dine in a very bohemian place. You can wear any old thing at all." He smiled and drawled, "You know I have never been a fellow that dressed up very much."

Wood had begged off too, saying he had promised to spend the evening with his wife. "Can't you get out of it?" Darrow said. "Why don't you just lie to her? I find that's the easiest way."

Wood was not enthralled with the notion of spending a night with a minister and his wife, but Darrow assured him, "Listen, she's one of us." They went to a restaurant called the Hofbrau, and Wood brought along his secretary, who, Sara would later discover, was then his mistress. After the dinner, the Reverend Ehrgott left for a meeting but the rest retired to Wood's office, with its great solid desk and plush Oriental rug, where Darrow read to them from a book of Galsworthy short stories.

Sara had volunteered to work on the Oregon suffrage campaign. Its headquarters was convenient to Wood's office, and he asked her to edit his poetry. There, he read to her from a book about free love. It was not "an advocate of a sort of merry-go-round of partners," but a "philosophical" volume, which helped persuade her that "I was not doing the selfish thing in considering that I must be free, but was also preparing a freer and better life for the children," she recalled. "Of course, the psychologist might think that this was wishful thinking." After weeks of sexual tension, they began their affair. Sara was twenty-eight; Erskine, as she called him, was thirty years older.

Wood thought of himself as nobler than Darrow, and turned down his requests to join in the McNamara defense. Darrow was doing what good Chicago lawyers did: looking for alibis, massaging witnesses, trying to decipher the prosecution case, and concocting alternate causes for the explosion. Though the grand jury that investigated the bombing found not "a scintilla of evidence" to support the theory of a gas explosion, Darrow plunged ahead, hiring experts and paying for a detailed model of the *Times* building, which he hoped to blow up, to promote that explanation. Wood thought him "unscrupulous."

"He is not making this fight for the cause of Labor—nor for the McNamaras—but for C. Darrow," Wood told Sara. "And in this he is like the most of us lawyers. We prate of our fight for justice. We are fighting for our own glory and profit. Darrow's glory and Darrow's pocket is what he is fighting for."

Wood had many contacts in the West, and had heard about Darrow's tactics in Idaho. "He will use bribery where safe, perjury where safe," Wood told Sara. "He will manipulate and marshal labor all over the United States at psychological moments to appear in masses and mutter threats, arousing a bitterness, a recklessness meant to intimidate the jury in Los Angeles."

Wood's suspicions were fed when Darrow asked him to vouch for Larry Sullivan, a detective known for his willingness to corrupt or intimidate witnesses. Sullivan was one of several dubious investigators hired by the defense, including lawyer John Harrington, a roly-poly figure from Chicago, and Bert Franklin, a hard-drinking former U.S. marshal in Los Angeles who was placed in charge of investigating jurors.

And then there was Mary, whose editors had sent her to cover the McNamara trial. Darrow had tried to warn her away, noting that he was the subject of constant scrutiny. She felt hurt, but came anyway, resolving not to seek his company, and was surprised when he welcomed her lovingly to Los Angeles and turned to her for comfort, companionship, and sex. It was a reckless act—the move of a man tangoing with despair, seeking relief from relentless pressure. And Mary soon discovered why. Upon arriving in California, Darrow had found that all he feared about the case was true. The McNamaras were "guilty as hell," he told Mary. He had "not a shadow of a chance" to prove their innocence, and feared they'd be put to death.

"My God, you left a trail behind you a mile wide!" he told James McNamara.[10]

Darrow tried to turn the state's star witness—Ortie McManigal—via a trick he had employed in the Haywood case. With an appeal to working-class solidarity, and wads of cash, Darrow persuaded Ortie's wife and uncle to try to get him to repudiate the confession. They visited the jail and browbeat McManigal, and his wife threatened to take the children and leave him. He weakened, but ultimately refused to flip. "My wife has sold herself for a few thousand dollars of union money," he told a *Times* reporter, between sobs. "The union's attorneys in their efforts to save the necks of the McNamaras have broken up my home." The bomber cut a deal worthy of Harry Orchard. In return for testifying, McManigal was freed, given employment by the state, and awarded "quite a substantial sum of money" by the grateful steel industry.[11]

Harrington and Sullivan were sent to San Francisco to buy off witnesses. And Ruby's brother Bert was called in to help, and given the task of spiriting Kurt Diekelman—a hotel clerk who could testify that James McNamara was in Los Angeles at the time of the bombing—to Chicago. Yet the Burns detectives frustrated Darrow's agents in almost every instance. And Judge Walter Bordwell allowed District Attorney John Fredericks to deploy the grand jury to intimidate the defense. McManigal's wife and uncle were subpoenaed and threatened with contempt of court, and Harrington was interrogated. Even square Joe Scott grew furious at the state's tactics. He waved his fist in a detective's face and threatened to beat his damned head off.

Burns was no stranger to intrigue—a few months later, the U.S. Justice Department would charge that the detective had stacked the jury lists in a federal case in Oregon. "Weed out the sons of bitches who will not vote for a conviction," Burns had told his agents. "No man's name goes into the box unless we know that he will convict." His operatives now sought jobs in Darrow's offices. Detective Guy Biddinger met Darrow in the bar of the Alexandria Hotel and agreed—for $5,000—to inform on the prosecution. Some of the information he funneled Darrow was true, other bits were false: all was tailored to sow discord. Darrow's offices were "filled with detectives in our employ," city detective Sam Browne bragged later. Darrow was too "close-fisted" with his staff, and they happily agreed to spy for the prosecution. "When a man needs to pull off crooked deals, it pays to be liberal," Browne said. "Several of Darrow's supposedly trusted men came to me for money. I slipped them some."

Soon, Darrow was seeing traitors everywhere. "We are having a fierce time," he wrote Gompers. "Burns's whole force utterly regardless of personal rights is everywhere in evidence intimidating, hounding, bulldozing—the grand jury kept constantly in session to awe every one who comes as our witness." Money was an issue. "There is no way to try this case with a chance of winning without a great deal of money," Darrow told Gompers in July. "The other side are spending it in every direction. Then they have all the organized channels of society—the state's attorney—grand jury—police force, mayor, manufacturers association. Every one is afraid of the line up and there is little light anywhere. . . .

"You know I never wanted to come. It is filled only with trouble for me," Darrow said. "If the necessary things can not be done I must know that . . . I am very sorry to put any extra trouble on you—but what can we do? We all seem to think that organized labor must make this fight and I suppose it must."

Plans were made to launch a national fundraising campaign—docking each union worker in the country 25 cents for the McNamara defense fund. McNamara stamps and buttons were sold, and a motion picture was produced to raise money in working-class communities. But later that summer Darrow wrote to Tvietmoe, saying that of a promised $350,000 only $170,000 had been raised. He insisted that he needed $20,000 a month, and threatened to "quit the game" unless the AFL met its financial commitments. "I am simply not going to kill myself with this case and then worry over money and not know what to do," Darrow said. Tvietmoe wired Gompers: "Darrow is anxious . . . Start machine. Keep flame burning."

Gompers responded. He pressed union leaders to raise money, and put his own prestige on the line. In the fall, he traveled to Los Angeles to meet and have his photograph taken with the brothers. James was a "jovial and yet deep-thinking, studious fellow," Gompers told reporters, and John was "bright, intelligent . . . firm in his convictions, and yet as gentle as the gentlest woman."

When he met the boys in jail, Gompers said, John had taken his hand and assured the AFL chief: "Sam, tell the boys I am innocent."[12]

As in Boise, Darrow's foes in California included the press, the local establishment, and the president of the United States. And as in Idaho, the local elites were neck deep in corrupt schemes to rob Americans of their natural resources. In Idaho the game was timber; in L.A. it was water.

The dreamers of the golden dream were building harbors and stretching roads and streetcar lines in every direction, but their great aspirations were seemingly capped by the meager local water supply.

William Mulholland, the city's water superintendent, looked to the Owens River valley, a land of family farms and ranches on the eastern slope of the Sierra Nevada, more than two hundred miles northeast of Los Angeles, as the solution. One of Roosevelt's legislative accomplishments, the Federal Reclamation Act, was the vehicle. The law was designed to water the arid lands of the West, largely through power and irrigation projects, and the Owens Valley was originally seen as a superb prospect for an agricultural reservoir and canals. But Fred Eaton, a former Los Angeles mayor, hatched an elaborate scheme to corner the valley's water rights and build an aqueduct to the coast. As an intimate pal of both Mulholland and Joseph Lippincott, the regional chief of the new Reclamation Service, the piratical Eaton was well suited for the job. He and Mulholland launched a clandestine campaign (Eaton liked to brag of his "curves" and "Italian work") to buy up land and water rights, and many landowners were deceived into thinking they were dealing with a federal irrigation project. Eaton then made a fortune selling the water to Los Angeles. Lippincott received a plump consulting contract from the city. Shrugging off the objections made by colleagues over his "illegal, vicious" and "repugnant" actions, Lippincott assured his superiors that "the greatest public necessity" required the divergence of the valley's water to Los Angeles. The project was approved.

"I got away with it," Mulholland said.

Not yet. The need to raise funds to build the aqueduct brought the plot to light in 1905. With the enthusiastic support of the *Times*, which had spread Mulholland's alarms about a city-killing "drought," the public approved municipal bond sales in the 1905 and 1907 elections. The *Times* forgot its former opposition to municipal ownership of public utilities, and skewered critics of the aqueduct as "freaks and pests." The rival *Express* revealed why: Otis was an investor in the San Fernando Mission Land Company, a syndicate of the region's most powerful men, including bankers, utility chiefs, publishers, and the railroad magnates Henry Huntington and E. H. Harriman, that was buying up land in the San Fernando Valley. It would soar in value when the aqueduct passed through on the way to Los Angeles.

In the next six years, a group including Otis, his son-in-law Harry Chandler, water board member Moses Sherman, and banker Otto Brant took over the leadership of the syndicate, buying more and more land in the San Fernando Valley.[13] The state's Progressives—who had just elected Hiram Johnson governor—were seduced as well. With the aqueduct, "we have the assurance of a growth in population, commerce and consequently in land values that will be the wonder of the world," wrote Meyer Lissner, the governor's political lieutenant in Los Angeles. "The man who invests $100,000 here right now with any sort of judgment can take out a million within a few years." He plotted, with Johnson, to craft a new congressional district that would be dominated by Los Angeles and protect "our aqueduct."

Only the radicals stood in the way. The aqueduct was a major issue in Job Harriman's campaign when he declared his candidacy for mayor that spring. He and his socialist allies vowed to halt the distribution of the Owens Valley water to the Otis-Chandler syndicate and other land speculators. Harriman had to be stopped, and his clients, the McNamaras, discredited and convicted.[14]

Oscar Lawler, a lawyer working for the M&M in Los Angeles, joined Walter Drew, the steel industry's point man on the case, in orchestrating an approach to Washington. Drew was underwriting the costs of the McNamara case and loaning detectives to the prosecutors in Los Angeles and Indiana. His men burglarized the union offices in Indianapolis and installed a dictograph—a crude listening device—to eavesdrop on its president. They illegally acquired John McNamara's phone and bank records, tailed his former secretary, covertly photographed union correspondence, brawled with union officers, and shadowed newspapermen. He and Lawler feared that Indiana officials would cave to local political pressure and surrender the evidence seized from McNamara's office. "Strenuous efforts are being made, by bribery and every other means known to guilty persons and corrupt associations, to spirit away witnesses and destroy evidence," Lawler wrote in an encrypted message that Drew hand-delivered to Attorney General George Wickersham.

When the Justice Department balked, reluctant to act like an industry tool, Lawler urged Drew to tap "every possible influence among senators and various large business interests." Otis was assigned to write the White House. "The explosion of the *Times* building was only an incident in the carrying out of the general purpose to establish a reign of wholesale terrorism and intimidation," Otis told his friend, President William Howard Taft. On October 17, the president met with Lawler and Otis in Los Angeles. Lawler, who had worked with Taft in Washington, laid out the arguments. Taft ordered the federal prosecutors in Indianapolis into action, and they began an investigation and secured the evidence that had been seized in the ironworkers' offices.[15]

WORD OF THE Taft administration's decision to intervene reached Darrow within days, adding to his gloom.[16] For despite all his efforts, he was losing the battle to select a jury.

The lawyers had begun the arduous task on October 11 in a newly constructed courtroom on the eighth floor of the Hall of Records. It smelled of fresh paint, and workmen still labored outside. In the audience were "a motley crowd" of Wobblies, trade unionists, and socialists. Darrow had requested that the brothers be tried separately, and the state elected to try James McNamara first.

"Darrow . . . searches the hidden motive in a marvelous way," Mary's sister Sara, who had joined her in Los Angeles, told Wood. "Questions which the prosecution object to he puts aside and then asks after a while in another way and in juxtaposition to something else, so that dressed in new words and out of its environment . . . the prosecution does not recognize it. . . .

"He gains the confidence of the man he is examining and draws him out by subtle as well as apparent methods that are remarkable to watch. He finds out his religious persuasion . . . he goes into his heredity and environment," Sara wrote. "Whatever he is or is not, he is sure good at this work."

And yet Darrow was frustrated by Judge Bordwell, who consistently declined to recognize bias in potential jurors. He compelled Darrow to use peremptory challenges and threatened him with contempt when he complained. Fredericks, meanwhile, quietly paraded his cast of witnesses through the courtroom, where they could identify James McNamara—and he could see them. It unnerved the defendant, and his lawyers. "They've brought that fellow here to identify me," James would tell Darrow. Then news arrived that Frank Eckhoff, a friend of the McNamaras who could corroborate key parts of McManigal's confession, would testify for the state. Darrow "expects to lose and this fact is nearly crushing him. He is very blue all the time now and really looks ill," Sara wrote. "Waving all his mistakes and failings aside it is a sad thing for an old fighter to lose his greatest, and possibly his last case." They had, Darrow told Sara, "not a ghost of a chance" of winning.

Sara was on the scene because Wood had persuaded the editors of two Oregon publications to carry her dispatches from the trial, in part so he and his "hungry little mistress," as she called herself, could enjoy a tryst. She had no training as a journalist and had never been in a courtroom, but in early October she arrived in Los Angeles, where Mary had rented a typewriter and an apartment on Ingraham Street, about a mile from the courthouse, for $35 a month. It had nice furnishings and fresh linens twice a week, but it was tiny: a single space served as living and dining room and bedroom, with a Murphy bed that folded down from the wall.

Sara was shocked when she learned, on her first evening in town, that Darrow and Mary had resumed their affair.

"You know how CD laid it on thick about how he would be watched . . . Yet the first thing he does is invite us to a public dinner in a fashionable place and walk way home to our apartment *with his arms around us* most of the way," Sara wrote Wood. "I don't enjoy his familiarity at all."

Darrow angered Sara for the way he played with Mary's feelings. She grew angrier yet when, after Mary left them alone in the apartment one day, Darrow grabbed Sara in a lecherous embrace. The scene was repeated a few days later when Sara turned up at the Higgins Building to interview a member of the defense team. Darrow lured her into his private office, locked the door, and once more tried to seduce her. In each case, flustered, she managed to extricate herself.

"His attitude toward women," she told Wood, "is disgusting in the extreme." Sara had a way of tweaking her lover's jealousy with tales about men who sought to bed her and it is possible that she embellished her encounters with Darrow. But Wood responded with ire.

"Darrow is above all things selfish, with a not necessary adjunct to selfishness, vanity, and a side development, avarice," Wood wrote.

When Mary first proposed to cover the trial, Wood explained, Darrow "did not need Mary to feed his vanity, for he is a general at the head of an admiring swarm. He feels amply idolized in the centre of a great stage. He feared she would compromise him with the world and he is in such a matter a coward."

But then "Mary arrives, he finds she is discreet . . . He is glad she has come, has a spasmodic return of physical passion which makes him even gay and adoring," Wood wrote. "She is delighted, forgets all and idolizes."

"Now for prediction," Wood concluded. "When he is sated he will treat her like a sucked orange."

"A woman's body is nothing more to Darrow than to the Sultan—a delicious morsel to be taken everywhere, found and forgotten," Wood wrote. "A woman's mind is nothing to him except that the adoration of a brainy woman is more subtle flattery. But he'd take flattery from a chorus girl."

Darrow was displaying the manic behavior he'd shown in the Haywood trial. He would arrive at Mary's flat, alive with great plans for the day, and take the sisters on delightful excursions. On other days he would mope, bark rudely, and curse. "Due to his age and to the fact that he places his heart and his soul in the interest of his defendants," Darrow was "unable to stand the terrible responsibility . . . and he lost faith and hope and became discouraged," Johannsen recalled. He "seemed to be in constant fear that his clients would be . . . sent to the gallows."

At some point Ruby discovered her husband's California philandering, adding to Darrow's anxiety. She blamed Mary and other camp lovelies for throwing themselves at him and dismissed his affairs as meaningless rutting. His old Sunset Club friend W. W. Catlin found Darrow "far more cynical and callous" than when he knew him in Chicago. "The idea of loyalty to a principle seems rather to amuse than inspire him now," Catlin told Wood. And "as to woman, especially, he is now rather gross where he formerly was fine."[17]

During the summer and fall, as Darrow fenced with the prosecutors, he had tried, through various intermediaries, to see if Fredericks was open to a deal.

"It was borne in on me day by day that this man I knew who trusted everything to me could not be saved," Darrow recalled. As he grew to know the McNamaras, "I heard these men talk of their brothers, of their mother, of the dead; I saw their human side," said Darrow. "I wanted to save them."[18]

Then, in mid-November, Lincoln Steffens came to town. The dapper little muckraker had just returned from Europe, where he had dined with Burns in Paris and been persuaded that the McNamaras were guilty. In London, an English labor leader had challenged Steffens to write about not whether union leaders turned to violence, but why. Steffens liked the idea. He lined up the necessary newspaper clients and headed for Los Angeles. "Dear Dad," he told his father, "I am to write for my newspapers the situation back of the McNamara trial; not the trial itself, but the cause, consequences, and the significance thereof.

"It's a delicate job, somewhat like handling dynamite, but somebody has to tackle it hard," he joked. "Why shouldn't I be the McNamara of my profession?"[19]

On November 19, Steffens joined Darrow on a trip to Miramar, the sprawling La Jolla estate of the wealthy press lord E. W. Scripps. Despite his great fortune, the self-described "old crank" was something of a radical who sympathized with the workingman. Scripps had plans to publish a newspaper called the *Day Book* in Chicago and wanted Darrow's help promoting the journal among working-class audiences. He believed Darrow was a realist, a man like himself, guided not by weakly "altruistic sentiment" but by "contempt and hatred for . . . the sins of our class." He thought Darrow had great "physical and moral courage" and concluded that the lawyer's famous cynicism was a mask.

Scripps gave his visitors a tour of the private auto speedway he had built on his property and introduced them to Berkeley zoologist William Ritter, the founding scientist at the new oceanographic institute that the Scripps family was financing. Later the three men retired to the great study, where the publisher considered his visitors and thought them an odd pair: Steffens the "little litterateur" and Darrow "a great big brute of a man, with every fiber coarse, but sturdy." Scripps read aloud from a "disquisition" he had written, defending "belligerent rights" in industrial warfare. They spoke of Harriman's mayoral campaign, which had stunned the city by triumphing in the October 31 primary and was now in a runoff with Mayor Alexander. Darrow sketched a pessimistic outline of where things stood in the trial. The case against James McNamara, Darrow said sorrowfully, was a "dead cinch."

Steffens was moved, and inspired to act. He would not merely write about the case, he would help Darrow settle it. Over breakfast the next morning, Steffens outlined his idea to Darrow. He proposed to call on "the big men" in town and let them know that a deal could be had. He would try to persuade them, he said, that it was in their interest to end their costly war with the unions. Darrow consented. "I hate to have a man hang that I undertake to defend," he said, "and I cannot bear to think of this boy being killed." But he was not without skepticism. The fate of James McNamara, he suspected, would not be an issue. If McNamara pled guilty before the December 5 election, it would discredit Harriman. And the men with the greatest motive for vengeance—the Otis-Chandler crew—so feared the effects of a socialist victory on their plans for the aqueduct and other business schemes that they would trade blood for money.

The hitch, Darrow told Steffens, was John McNamara. Labor might deliver an itinerant printer like James to San Quentin, but not John, a national leader. His confession would humiliate Gompers and disgrace the unions. Drew and the steel industry, who were bankrolling the prosecution, would insist that John plead guilty too. But off Steffens went with a promise to be discreet, and an understanding that Darrow would deny the whole endeavor if Fredericks exposed the negotiations.

The first call that Steffens made on Darrow's behalf showed their appreciation for the leverage offered by the political situation: it was Lissner, the governor's savvy operative, whom the state's frantic elite had named to rescue the campaign against Harriman. Lissner immediately recognized the opportunity and, with the help of a friendly go-between, persuaded Chandler to sign off on a deal that would imprison James for life and set John free. Chandler and Otto Brant—another of the partners in the aqueduct scheme—brought the proposal to Fredericks, who insisted on hearing it from Darrow. They spoke the next day in court.

"What is this gink Steffens trying to do?" Fredericks asked.

"This fellow would plead guilty," Darrow told him, nodding at James, "if the other fellow could be turned loose."

Fredericks rejected the offer. John McNamara would have to plead guilty too, the district attorney said, or "We will hang them both." But the talks went on, and a greater number of interested parties were called into the circle. Drew was notified and told Fredericks that the steel industry didn't care about the fate of the McNamaras, as long as they made full confessions. He was most concerned about public opinion and saw no need to give labor a martyr. "The important thing is the effect upon the public mind," Drew told Fredericks. "I hardly believe JJ intended to kill twenty-one people and would personally be willing to see the murder case dismissed on condition of a full confession." But he was insistent on guilty pleas from both brothers. Otherwise, "it will always be said that JB . . . sacrificed himself for his older brother and that both were innocent."[20]

Darrow summoned Older to Los Angeles for advice. They had lunch with Steffens, and Darrow told the editor that the case for James was "utterly hopeless" and that, in the end, they would probably have to, as Older put it, "throw John J. to the wolves" as well. Older told Darrow what he already knew: that his career as a labor lawyer would be over if he pled the brothers guilty. Labor was paying the bills, Darrow conceded, but he had been employed "to save these men's lives." Darrow sent a wire to Gompers, asking that he send a representative like Tvietmoe or Nockels to California from Atlanta, where the national labor chiefs were gathered at the AFL convention. And that weekend he sat down with his clients.

The McNamaras had no illusions about their chances. In court that week, after Bordwell issued yet another unfavorable ruling, James had murmured to Darrow: "You might as well get a rope." Each brother agreed to plead guilty, but only if it saved the other. James would confess if the state would drop its charges against John, and John would plead guilty to save James from hanging. There the bargaining stood—initiated, progressing, but not conclusive—on the morning of Tuesday, November 28, when Bert Franklin, Darrow's top jury investigator, was arrested on the corner of Third and Main streets, in the act of bribing a juror—as Darrow stood there, watching it go down.[21]

Franklin was a former federal marshal and detective, an undistinguished hanger-on with the local courthouse gang. He had been given the job of taking the lists of potential jurors and compiling reports on their loyalties, backgrounds, and beliefs. But he did more than draw up the book. As in Idaho, the defense team sought to frighten off undesirable jurors by warning them of the expected length of the trial, or of the violent passions the conflict would unleash. And, in league with someone on the McNamara defense who supplied the money, Franklin set out to buy jurors.

In early October, Franklin made a $400 down payment to juror Robert Bain, a seventy-year-old Civil War veteran who agreed to take $4,000 to vote not guilty. Just to be sure, the brazen Franklin approached a half dozen other jurors and reached a second $4,000 deal with a former sheriff's department employee named George Lockwood, who alerted Fredericks. As he paid off Lockwood, Franklin was arrested by Detective Sam Browne—just as Darrow crossed Main Street to join them. Browne pushed Darrow aside and hustled Franklin away. A few moments later, at the courthouse, Darrow asked the detective: "My God, Browne. What is all this?"

"You ought to know what it is," Browne replied. "It's bribery."

"My God, I wouldn't have had this happen for the world," Darrow said. "If I had known this was going to happen this way I never would have allowed it to be done."[22]

Franklin's arrest spurred huge headlines in the city's newspapers. "We gave him no such sum of money for any such purpose," Darrow told reporters, and the initial news stories did not mention Darrow's presence at the scene. But it was a huge blow and stoked Darrow's desire to settle the case. He told Steffens to assure "your people," as he liked to call the business leaders, that the defense still wanted a deal. Nockels arrived in Los Angeles and was briefed. Steffens convinced a roomful of civic leaders to accept the settlement. And Fredericks, after consulting his political advisers, agreed on the final terms. The state would accept James McNamara's plea and ask the judge for clemency, said Fredericks, if John pleaded guilty to the lesser charge of ordering the Christmas, 1910, bombing of the Llewellyn Iron Works.

Now the brothers had to give their consent. On Thursday, which was Thanksgiving Day, their supporters treated the McNamaras to a fine turkey dinner, with dessert and cigars, in the city jail. The brothers spent the rest of the day listening to Darrow and the other lawyers.

"I am thinking of you, J.B.," said Darrow.

"Yes," said James, "and I am thinking of you, Darrow." Both of them knew the plea would injure labor, and that labor would look for, as Older had put it, "a goat."

James held out for most of the day, knowing how John's confession would hurt the union cause. Davis warned him that unless he pled guilty, the state would hang John too. And Darrow promised him that if the brothers pled guilty, the state would not prosecute Tvietmoe and the other California labor leaders. Joseph Scott had a priest summoned, who spoke quietly to James. Ultimately, John McNamara threatened to plead guilty on his own, if need be, to save his brother's life. "I was overwhelmed by a two hundred thousand dollar defense, with a constant nightmarish fear, that there was great danger of taking the San Francisco 'labor leaders' with me," James recalled. On Thanksgiving night, Davis went to see Fredericks at home. The district attorney brought out cigars, and they confirmed the deal.[23]

SOMEHOW, THE SECRET kept. Reporters were puzzled when the next morning's session was postponed until the afternoon and then convened with two notable features: the grim expressions of the defense attorneys and the unusual presence of John McNamara, who had not been attending his brother's trial.

James and John chewed gum. Darrow sat at the end of the long defense table, looking anxious and gnawing on a pencil. First James and then John withdrew their pleas of not guilty and, when asked by Bordwell, declared themselves guilty.

The judge ended the short session, and Darrow tried, without much success, to put himself between the reporters and the McNamaras. Darrow looked stricken, like a hunted animal, the *Times* reported. "I did the best I could," he said. "I am very tired, worn and sorrowful . . . I hope I saved a human life out of the wreckage."

Darrow made his way through the crowd of sullen socialists and laborites, out to where, the *Times* chortled, the gutters of Los Angeles were littered with discarded Harriman campaign buttons. Darrow had done a lawyer's duty. With time running out and the defense staggering from reversals, he took advantage of the opportunity created by Harriman's campaign to save James McNamara's life, and perhaps John's as well. "All this evidence is against them, and I didn't know it when I undertook the case, and now . . . I must save these men," Darrow told Sara, who had clung to Larry Sullivan, weeping, when the brothers pled guilty.

Harriman had not been warned. Later that day, he and his campaign manager, Alexander Irvine, met with Darrow at their offices. Why was he not informed? Harriman asked. They didn't have the heart to tell him, Darrow said.

"Was it part of the bargain that this plea should be made before the election?" Irvine asked.

"It was to be made at once," Darrow acknowledged.

Friends of labor—even tough men like Gompers and Johannsen—were staggered by the news.[24] Martyrs were useful, and some union leaders, like Johannsen, blamed Darrow and the brothers for not taking the battle to the limit, even at the cost of a life or two. "That's the way they are, you fight for them and they turn on you," Johannsen told Hapgood. "But I love them, the poor slaves."[25]

Gompers was dozing on a train when a reporter came aboard at a New Jersey station and told him. "I am astonished at this," Gompers sputtered. "We have had the gravest assurances given to us by everyone connected with the trial, either directly or indirectly, that these men were innocent . . . The cause of labor has been imposed upon by both supposed friends and enemies."[26]

Darrow and Nockels sent wires to Gompers, explaining the necessity of the plea. "There was no avoiding step taken today," Darrow wrote. "When I see you I know you will be satisfied that all of us gave everything we had to accomplish the best." But Gompers would never forgive Darrow. Labor needed a fall guy. "Angered and injured," said Steffens, "it seeks somebody to blame and kill."

His friend Peter Sissman later asked Darrow why he had not kept fighting in court, hoping, perhaps, for a hung jury. "Whose lawyer was I?" Darrow asked Sissman. "The McNamaras had the right to know the case looked bad and they would probably hang . . . I felt they had the right to choose to save their own lives."

From the beginning, Darrow was candid with Gompers about the difficulties they faced in Los Angeles; the cost of the case, and his fear they would ultimately lose. He apparently thought these were winks enough.

He never did tell Gompers that the McNamaras were guilty, Darrow said, "for Mr. Gompers never asked me." Furthermore, he said, "as their attorney I could not have told Mr. Gompers without their consent."

Which may not have been forthcoming. "I was fighting for my life . . . I would have been a fool to confide my guilt to anyone, and it would have been unfair to Gompers to make him carry around any secret confession of mine," said James McNamara. At some point, as the evidence against them accumulated, the interests of the brothers ran counter to the interests of the labor movement. "I am sorry to have put [Gompers] in a fix by sticking to my defense for so long," James said, but "I was working to help in my way, and I could not turn down the money for defense when it came without putting the noose around my neck."[27]

The shock that Gompers showed at the news of the guilty plea seems genuine, but it is hard to believe he was so out of touch as to not suspect the McNamaras. The documents seized in Indianapolis show that the bombing campaign was a topic of correspondence among union leaders across the country. If Gompers did not know, it was because he didn't want to know, and because others, like Darrow, were shielding him.

Franklin's arrest had wreaked havoc in the McNamara defense and was, several critics maintained, the real motivating factor in Darrow's eagerness to cut a deal. Bordwell said as much after sentencing the brothers to prison. "The public can rely on it that the developments of last week as to the . . . attempted bribery of jurors were the efficient causes of the change of pleas," he announced.[28]

Some questioned whether Darrow pled the brothers guilty to save himself. "Darrow is very dangerously near the jury and witness corruption and he is very apprehensive that the connecting link exists," Lawler told the attorney general. "He has induced the defendants to assume their present attitude for the purpose of using it as a bargain on his own behalf." If so, Darrow played his cards badly. On January 29 he was indicted for bribery.[29]

Chapter 12

GETHSEMANE

So fade our dreams, so fall our ideals, so pass our stars.

On a dreary night in December 1911, cowed by shame and fear, Darrow showed up at Mary Field's apartment and sat down at the kitchen table.

He pulled a bottle of whiskey from one overcoat pocket and a revolver from the other. Warily, she brought two glasses and he poured.

"I am going to kill myself," Darrow said. "They are going to indict me for bribing the McNamara jury. I can't stand the disgrace."

Mary had to talk fast. Suicide would be wrong, she said. It would be an admission of guilt and cede victory to his enemies. He must fight on.

She persuaded her distraught lover to put the gun away. He slipped it in his pocket, picked up the bottle, and walked out into the rain.[1]

On Election Day, Judge Bordwell had sentenced James McNamara to life imprisonment and given John McNamara a fifteen-year term in San Quentin. When the ballots were counted, Job Harriman had lost the mayor's race by thirty-four thousand votes.[2]

Otis could not keep from crowing. "The confession of the McNamaras and the defeat of Harriman . . . saved our city from the disgrace and disaster of socialistic rule," said the *Times* on New Year's Day. "Boycotting, picketing, assaulting and dynamiting are at an end . . . Industrial freedom reigns supreme."[3]

Attention now turned to the jury-bribing case. The McNamara defense team had paid Bert Franklin's bail, but it seemed just a matter of time before he cut a deal with the prosecutors. "I have practiced long enough to know the influence of a threat of the penitentiary on a man. And I feared just what . . . happened," Darrow recalled. "That he would be offered his liberty to turn me over." It was a gloomy holiday season. In letters from Los Angeles, Darrow and Ruby conveyed their anxiety even as they sought to reassure their friends and families that everything was fine. "There is nothing to worry about," Ruby told Paul. His father was "more than half anxious to be arrested and given a hearing and a chance to set himself right publicly." But even as she wrote, her bravado crumbled. Darrow was counting on Paul to "stand by . . . him," she wrote. "I am going to stay with the thing and stand by D to the last ditch . . . So be game yourself . . . and depend on whatever is necessary."

Franklin agreed to testify for the state in mid-January. To Mary and members of his family, Darrow suggested that it might be "for the best" if he was convicted. Labor would have its martyr. He would have time to write in prison, to "do my best work and perhaps it is necessary." But then he waved away such thoughts. "Still I shall resist," he said.

And then Darrow did one of the harder, but smarter, things in his life: he hired Earl Rogers to defend him.[4]

"Bert, we do not want you, we want those behind you," the prosecutors told Franklin. And he boasted, accurately, to reporters: "You can take it from me. Bert Franklin never will go to the penitentiary."

But the state lacked corroboration. There were no witnesses to the incriminating conversations that Franklin claimed to have had with Darrow, nor was the money trail conclusive. And so, like their counterparts in the Steunenberg case, the prosecutors decked the crimes with the ornaments of conspiracy. They spent much of their time and money investigating tangential matters that made Darrow look awful but had nothing to do with the charge of bribery. The defense that Earl Rogers led was tailored to defeat this kind of case. A wandering presentation by the state gave a savvy defense attorney an opportunity to drench a jury in distraction. And if there ever was a lawyer who could beguile and bewilder jurors, ever an attorney who could transform a courtroom into a circus, it was Rogers. "He believed implicitly in showmanship," his daughter Adela recalled. "Dad always held the center of the stage."

Rogers was the son of a preacher man, a rascal and a dynamo and a drunk. Lean and handsome, with black hair and penetrating blue eyes, he was a superb assayer of courtroom psychology. He came to court meticulously dressed—in fawn waistcoat, spats, a rich cravat, bat-winged collar, and a gardenia boutonniere. At home he favored Chinese robes or a wine-red velvet dressing gown. He twirled a walking stick, tucked a handkerchief in his sleeve, and, instead of eyeglasses, relied on a lorgnette, which he would hold to his eyes to stare down a witness, then twirl on its ribbon and flip into the pocket of his cutaway coat. Elegant, but no mannequin.

Rogers roamed the courtroom as he questioned witnesses, gesturing and dashing and amusing the jurors with sarcastic asides that brought prosecutors to the brink of fistfights. "If the seat next to me was vacant, I might find Rogers in it," the young newsman Hugh Baillie recalled, "asking questions of a witness while he read my dispatches and attempted to edit them." Rogers's smiles could be kind or wolfish; his voice like an electric bolt, or mellow as virgin oil. John Barrymore studied Rogers for acting tips. He was famous for his dramatic and at times precedent-setting use of forensic evidence—as in the case where he brought the pickled guts of a homicide victim into court to demonstrate how a bullet had traveled through the entrails.

Once, in a trial on Catalina Island, the only eyewitness to a murder swore that he sat at a card table, calmly watching as the accused killer shot a player in the game and then pointed the gun at him. At the peak of his closing address, Rogers pulled out a Colt .45 and aimed it at the district attorneys, who dove beneath their table. It was the only human reaction in such a situation, Rogers told the jury: the witness must be lying.

Rogers represented more than his share of sleazy Angelinos—fat little millionaires who shot their wives, corrupt railway magnates, notorious gamblers, and the like. Every crime reporter in the city relished the story of how Rogers, after winning one client his freedom, declined to shake hands and barked: "Get away from me, you slimy pimp. You're guilty as hell."

He was a frontier type—an individualist who had no qualms about helping the M&M crack down on the striking workers in the summer of 1910. Yet he was a Democrat, with a streak of populist in him, born perhaps from recognition of his own weakness. He was apt to vanish on benders, forcing the teenaged Adela to comb the better brothels of the town in search of the daddy she adored. One day the booze would get him, and Rogers would die in a flophouse—a victim, his daughter wrote, of "the strain, the pressure, the strange immoral mesmerism of criminal law." But he was still at the peak of his powers in 1912.[5]

Before asking Rogers to represent him, Darrow took Ruby to the small town of Hanford, where they watched him clinch a case involving a contested inheritance. Mrs. Darrow's haughty ways quickly enrolled Adela, then seventeen, in the women-who-hate-Ruby club. And though Rogers told his daughter that Darrow's lax grooming habits were in part a calculated tactic to demonstrate solidarity with the common man, she found the rumpled suits and dirty fingernails offensive.[6] Friends of both men were confounded at the news of their collaboration. "The thing that . . . shocked me was that you should employ such a notorious corporation corruptionist and all around capitalist retainer," Debs told Darrow in an otherwise affectionate letter. It was no doubt a sign of peril, Debs wrote, that Darrow had been "driven to engage the lead-wolf, to escape the pack."

Rogers, for his part, was accosted by pals like Lawler and *Times* reporter Harry Carr. Rogers had been in his office, across the street from the *Times*, on the night of the bombing. He had burned his hands helping victims flee the inferno and lost a friend in C. Harvey Elder, the editor who jumped from a window. But "they've caught Darrow in a trap, a nasty, cold-blooded, planned, baited trap. I am against traps," Rogers told Carr. "An informer is the chief witness against him. I am against informers."

"You obstinate, sentimental Irish bastard," Carr said.[7]

The siren Fame drew Rogers to Darrow's side, and admiration for the champion of underdogs. It surely was not money. The AFL had stopped payment on the final $10,000 draft that Darrow requested in the McNamara case.[8] The Darrows would have to survive on their own while trying to save something for Ruby to live on, should he be imprisoned at San Quentin. The two counts of bribery would be tried separately, and even if Darrow was acquitted in the Lockwood case Fredericks could try him again on charges of bribing Bain. Years might pass before he was receiving rather than paying out legal fees, and only then if he was not disbarred. "Hard times are coming on," Darrow told Paul. "I may never be able to make any more money."

The Darrows left the house on Bonnie Brae and took a flat far from town, in Ocean Park, near Venice. They tried to cap expenses at $90 a month, and Darrow asked Paul if they could reduce the monthly payment to Jessie from $75 to $50. "They had no right to do this to me," Darrow wrote his brother-in-law, Howard Moore. "But the evidence against me is strong . . . I may have to leave you all for a time." He took long walks on the beach with friends, railing at his predicament. "You may say that I am assuming Darrow to be guilty. I am," his friend Catlin wrote after one such visit. "Darrow said no word to me of innocence."

The Darrows ate at home or in cafeterias, and Ruby darned their clothes and tracked their few expenses. Two pairs of cheap stockings. A 29-cent collar. An 85-cent nightgown. Two 50-cent vests. "Ruby writes as though they are reduced to bread and water," wrote Darrow's sister-in-law Helen. His sister Jennie, in turn, urged Ruby to watch Darrow's diet—to serve him only light food, "not hearty meals that will clog the system with poisons." She warned Ruby that her brother might withdraw, and be "stony and unemotional as the sphinx" under the strain.

"We don't plan for even a day at a time, and cannot tell when we ever will," Ruby wrote a friend. "He is 54 years old and he is *Poor.* I am doing *Everything* myself in a little apartment." And yet, Ruby said, "No matter what happens, there is no woman in the world that I would trade shoes with." The Darrows were grateful when their old friend Jim Griffes invited them to suppers of canned corned beef and potatoes, and late-night debates about free will. LeCompte Davis and his wife remained loyal as well. And an admirer, Dr. Perceval Gerson, led another group that befriended the Darrows. They named themselves the "Heart to Heart Club" and treated Darrow to dinners of pounded steaks, biscuits, lemon pie, and literary discussions.[9]

Darrow assembled a list of books to take with him to the penitentiary. "What a hell of a trap I'm in," he told Gerson. The doctor, a believer in nonviolence, suggested that Darrow resist not evil. "State the facts of the case and take the consequences without resistance," he told Darrow.

"Gerson, you're right, but I can't do it," Darrow replied. His freedom and livelihood were at stake.[10]

Darrow needed $25,000, he figured, to meet his legal expenses.[11] "So many people think I have money when really I have been in debt all my life," he wrote the mine workers' John Mitchell. "Surely I have served long and faithfully and . . . the unions would not let me go to prison without a defense." But Mitchell wrote back that "it is absolutely impossible for the miners to do anything at this time."[12] Darrow begged Gompers for aid. "In every crisis I have stood by labor and my convictions and always given my best," Darrow reminded him. "I am in serious trouble . . . I need help to protect my liberty." The AFL chief waited a month before sending a frigid reply. "I can not see how we can raise any money," Gompers wrote. It was Darrow's own fault. "Believing, aye, almost firmly convinced of the innocence of the McNamaras we strained every nerve to raise as near as possible the amount of money you suggested . . . Upon learning that they were guilty, the first intimation of which was conveyed to the rank and file as well as to the officers of the labor movement through their confession, I am free to say to you that in my judgment any general appeal for funds to defend you . . . would fall upon indifferent ears."[13]

Darrow was wounded, as well, by the silence from Toledo, where Brand Whitlock seemed to have abandoned him. "Mr. Darrow is so crushed," Mary wrote Whitlock. "You, I am sure, can say something to help him." Ruby wrote Whitlock as well. "Are you, that he has always deemed one of his bravest and strongest fellow soldiers, turning deserter?" she asked. "HOW CAN you have remained silent so long!" she demanded. "Are you ALL GOING to sit on the fence and see this man marched past you to prison?"

At one point, Gerson grew alarmed at Darrow's drinking. "Let him alone," Rogers told the doctor. "The liquor is good for him at a time like this."[14]

Darrow was indicted at the end of January. Fredericks gave him the courtesy of not arresting him at home. He went to court, was formally charged with bribing Bain and Lockwood, and released on $20,000 bail. If convicted on both charges, Darrow would face up to thirty years—the rest of his life—in prison. "Darrow . . . pale and nervous as a man of his highly sensitive organization must be under a prolonged strain . . . endured the ordeal with fortitude," the *Examiner* reported. He straightened up, lit a cigarette, and forced a smile for the reporters.

"This will be a real fight," Rogers promised the press. "There will be no milk and water methods in this trial." The newspapers confirmed his prediction when a series of leaks from the prosecution apprised Californians that Darrow had been found at the scene of the bribery. "Well, boys, is everything fixed?" he was said to have asked, with his arms draped around Franklin and Lockwood. It was a blatant lie that would not be repeated in court, but it troubled Darrow, who had great respect for the "spiritual weight" of public opinion on jurors.

By pleading not guilty, Darrow formally denied the charges. And in his private correspondence with those closest to him—Everett, Jennie, Mary, Paul—he said he had done nothing wrong. "There is no right to get me," he wrote his son. But legally guilty could be morally right—certainly in Darrow's code of ethics, where the motive and not the act was the controlling measure of morality. In explaining what happened, Darrow chose his words carefully. "Can't make myself feel guilty," Darrow told Everett in a telegram. "My conscience refuses to reproach me."

"As you know the ax has fallen," Darrow wrote Edgar Lee Masters. "Well, I chose my life and must stand the consequences." Masters took this as a confession. [15]

Many of Darrow's friends rallied around him. Older wired, "Keep your courage high." And Gertrude Barnum sent a telegram saying, "History repeats itself. Big men in the patrol wagon. Little men in the band wagon." Cy Simon, the Chicago jury briber he had taken into his office, offered to do "anything at all" and take "any sort of chance" to help the man who had rescued him from an identical predicament. John Jones, writing as a representative of "a large number of the Colored Lawyers in Chicago," pledged their "unmovable and unchangeable faith and confidence in your innocence." And from San Francisco came a telegram from Mary. "Your indictments come on Tom Paine's birthday. Humanity's friends travel the same road," she wrote. "Keep up your courage. Friends are with you."

Debs wrote, saying how "exceedingly touched and pained" he was by Darrow's dilemma and offering him hard-earned advice. "The thing of most vital concern to you now is that Darrow, above all others, shall stand by himself and be strong enough, even in his present situation, in which he is being tried by fire."

Darrow's pride had constrained him from asking friends for money.

But once labor deserted him, he had no choice. He wrote to Erskine Wood, begging him for $500 or $1,000. Three days later, embarrassed, he wrote Wood again and withdrew the request. Wood sent a check anyway. "I need it so badly I will keep it," Darrow told him. "I hope you will get the money back. I believe you will."

"I have no sense of pride or shame, only rage, and would cheerfully sit on every street corner in the land . . . with a tin cup," Ruby wrote to Older. She drew up a list, which was sent to Masters, of prominent men who "must be made to understand" the financial crisis that the Darrows faced. Masters set out to solicit money and to collect depositions that could be used as character references. Many were helpful, but one jurist—federal judge Kennesaw Mountain Landis—declined, telling Masters that "they had caught Darrow at last, and he was glad of it."[16] Scripps distanced himself as well. Like many, he presumed Darrow was guilty. "No one will believe that Franklin could have handled such sums . . . without the knowledge of the chief counsel for the defense," wrote C. D. Willard, a municipal reformer in Los Angeles, to the publisher.

February brought a fresh crisis. Portly John Harrington, threatened with prosecution, made a deal to corroborate Franklin's tale. The ardent Oscar Lawler was now working as a federal special prosecutor, and at his direction Harrington took a hotel room that had been outfitted with a dictograph by Robert Foster, a detective working for Walter Drew and the steel industry. Darrow and Harrington met repeatedly, with Harrington trying to get Darrow to make an incriminating statement for the hidden microphone, and Darrow, suspecting a trap, striving to avoid it.

"Are you going to testify against me, John?" Darrow asked.

"I would not say a word, but, my God, Darrow, I won't perjure myself for any man," said Harrington.

"I am sorry you have that in your head," said Darrow. "I will give you anything you ask within reason. I wish you would name the amount. Don't desert me on this thing."

The episode came to an inconclusive end, though not until the state leaked a sensational account of the "Dictograph Trap" to the newspapers.

Drew, who was in constant contact with Fredericks, told a henchman in late February that Darrow would plead guilty and "tell all he knows" about Gompers if spared a prison sentence. This story was also fed to the press. "He is a man of great sensitiveness and already he has suffered terribly," the *Times* said. "Will he go further and appear in court for weeks while . . . his inmost secrets are bared?" The roguish defense investigator, Larry Sullivan, thought not. Darrow "will either plead guilty or commit suicide," Sullivan predicted in a letter to Wood.[17]

But it was far from rare for a defendant or a go-between to explore the terms of a plea bargain with a district attorney and then reject them. His foes no doubt leaked the tale to further the perception of Darrow's guilt. It was never a real possibility, he later insisted. "I had no information to give," Darrow said, though he noted that this was "as much as Franklin or Harrington had." He could have "told them any story that I saw fit," he recalled. "I could have purchased my liberty at the price of my honor." But he did not.

Honor did not keep Darrow from other intrigues. In April, with the start of the trial just a few weeks away, he and Ruby joined a gathering of friends in San Francisco. At one point, Johannsen pulled Wood aside and asked if he would help them kidnap Harrington. Both Darrow and Rogers had waylaid witnesses in their careers. While certainly illegal, it was—like stealing evidence or paying witnesses exorbitant amounts as "expenses"—a not-unheard-of tactic. "I am sure Darrow knows of it," Wood wrote Sara.

Wood told Johannsen he would take no part in it. Anton was philosophical. He admired Wood's strength, Johannsen said. Darrow, on the other hand, was a weak man—too soft to either stand by his principles or to prosper at wickedness. Darrow had "departed on a piratical course," Johannsen said, but was, in the end, "too flabby to be a pirate."[18]

THE TRIAL BEGAN on May 15. There was no apparent irony in the day's *Herald,* which noted how Ruby had been accompanied up the hill to the courthouse by "Miss Mary Field of San Francisco, who is making a stay in this city and spending most of her time with Mrs. Darrow." In the turbulent weeks at the end of the McNamara trial, Mary and Darrow had ended their affair. Mary was "widowed," Wood decided. Sara concurred. Her sister had once seen Darrow "as a Napoleon who was changing the map of Labor's world," Sara wrote Wood. "So fade our dreams, so fall our ideals, so pass our stars."

But Mary still had an emotional tie to Darrow, and he to her. She was in Los Angeles to cover the trial for *Organized Labor*, a union newspaper, and to stand by him, Ruby notwithstanding. "My heart aches . . . for him," Mary wrote Sara. "He is such a sensitive man . . . it cuts him cruelly."

Ruby smiled bravely as she greeted the reporters and vowed "to help my husband in any way I can." But inside the courtroom she wiped at tears. She slipped into a chair inside the rail, behind her husband, whose "face was haggard," the newspapers noted. The muscles of his cheeks "twitched unceasingly," and the lines in his face "told of nights of sleeplessness and worry."

Darrow could be grateful for one turn of events. He might be up against the same prosecutors who beat him in the McNamara case, but not the same judge. Judge George Hutton was nothing like the martinet Judge Bordwell. The young and earnest Hutton had just four years' experience on the bench.

Jury selection went swiftly as Rogers, Frederick, and the assistant district attorney—Joseph Ford—identified the biases of the talesmen. By the end of the first week, Darrow joined the questioning—hoisting a leg upon a chair and leaning on his knee with folded arms, speaking soothingly as he "began to impress his subtle personality upon the jurymen." Even the *Times* admitted that Darrow was "remarkably effective."

"You realize that this is an important case to me and that all I want is a fair and impartial trial?" Darrow asked one candidate as the other talesmen looked on from the jury box.

"I do," said the mesmerized man.

It took but ten days to select the jury, a time otherwise marked by news, illustrative of the passions gripping the state, of an assault on Emma Goldman and her lover, Ben Reitman. The two anarchists had been ridden out of San Diego by a reactionary mob that abducted Reitman, took him to the desert, stripped him and abused his rectum and testicles, soaked him in tar, and beat him as he ran their gauntlet.[19]

The selection of one juror proved especially significant. Young Fred Golding was a partner in a local lumber company and, as an up-and-coming businessman, likely to be challenged by the defense. He was also, however, a believer in conspiracies, which he detected in the way that Franklin was arrested. Rogers encouraged Golding, for this was a line of argument the defense would press during the trial. Franklin's arrest was "like a stage play . . . with an orchestra playing," Rogers suggested.

Yes, Golding said: "A man like Darrow would not carry out any such affair in the daytime."

Yet Fredericks, presuming that Golding's loyalties as a businessman would win out, let him join the jury. It was a calamitous mistake. Time and again, Golding would vex the prosecutors, until they despaired at ever winning his vote. And Darrow, after the trial, would pay Golding $4,500—some $55,000 in today's currency—or more.[20]

FREDERICKS MADE HIS opening statement on May 24. After giving a chronology of the Lockwood bribery, he declared that it was but "one of a series of efforts" in which Darrow "endeavored to defeat and obstruct justice" in the McNamara case "by offering and paying money to other jurors . . . [and] to witnesses."

Rogers jumped up, trembling with ersatz outrage. "The rules of evidence will not and do not permit the introduction of any such evidence," he announced. "We believe we can sustain our position beyond any peradventure." When Fredericks tried to continue, Rogers filled the day with objections and exceptions. It is fair to conclude that the jury failed to get the full impact of the prosecutor's address: even Fredericks lost his train of thought and had to ask the court reporter to read back what he said.

Lockwood took the stand the next day. He was a gray-bearded, sixty-four-year-old former policeman who had once worked with Franklin in the sheriff's office. He told how Franklin had approached him, saying that they both were at a stage of life where they needed money "sufficient for our wants in our old age" and offering him $4,000. When Lockwood asked what he was to do, Franklin told him: "Vote not guilty."

But before Lockwood could finish, Rogers was up and at it again. That day's *Examiner* had published a front-page story in which Walter Drew's detective, Robert Foster, bragged that "I will convict Darrow with the dictograph evidence." Rogers now condemned it as a brazen attempt by the steel industry and the prosecution to influence the jury, whose spellbound members watched agog as he strutted and declared it "one of the most outrageous things that ever happened in jurisprudence!"

Rogers knew that Fredericks had a temper and, sure enough, the prosecutor lost it. "This has gone about as far as a man with red blood in his veins can stand," he told the judge, then demanded: "Are we going to trial in the case of Clarence Darrow for bribery?"

"Yes, we are going to try him squarely and we are going to try him without interference of Robert J. Foster or any member of the steel trust or the erectors association," Rogers proclaimed. "We do not want to go on with this kind of thing, coming up day after day against us, with every attempt to intimidate and prejudice our witnesses, to give us the most queer trial in America!"

When Lockwood resumed, his testimony seemed almost anticlimactic. He had alerted Fredericks, he said, who had plotted to trap Darrow in the act. An initial attempt at Lockwood's ranch failed when, to the disappointment of the detectives hidden around the grounds, Franklin did not bring Darrow or the money. The payoff was rescheduled for November 28.

On the downtown corner, Franklin had handed $500 to Lockwood and $3,500 to C. E. White, a mutual friend who was to hold the balance until the verdict was secured. Lockwood then dropped a $500 bill—a signal for the police to move in. Finally, Franklin sensed trouble. "The sons of bitches. Let's get out of here," he told Lockwood. They moved up on Third Street to the sidewalk along Main, where detective Browne stopped them, just as Darrow arrived.

Rogers did not spend much time cross-examining Lockwood. "It was a trap," he said contemptuously. "It was put on as a performance." That was sufficient to ignite Fredericks, who demanded that Rogers be punished for contempt. "If the prosecution has any right in the world in endeavoring to keep the Courts pure and decent . . . they have a right to be protected from a man who comes in here and makes a statement such as that," Fredericks told the judge.

Given the whoppers that the district attorney was telling in court—he had just finished denying that Drew and Foster were helping him build the case against Darrow—his anger was unjustified. Moreover, it was just what Rogers wanted. For the jurors immersed in the details of the trial, the stagecraft of Earl Rogers was drowning the impact of otherwise damaging testimony. "Hell seethed and erupted," Adela recalled. From afar, Drew recognized what was happening. The whole dictograph controversy, he griped to a hireling, "was a trumped-up affair for the purpose of distracting attention."[21]

When Franklin was called to the stand, he entered the courtroom "looking jaunty and confident," the newspapers said. As they strolled along a Los Angeles sidewalk on the previous October 4, he testified, Darrow told him, "It is time for us now to get busy with the jury." They huddled the next day at the Higgins Building, where Darrow said: "We have been talking the matter over and have decided that $5,000 would be a proper amount to pay . . . for jurymen." Franklin was to keep $1,000 and pay $4,000 to each corrupted juror. It was Darrow who suggested that Bain was a likely target, and who wrote out a $1,000 check for an initial payment. A few weeks later, said Franklin, Darrow instructed him to bribe Lockwood. There were no witnesses to these conversations, he said. Otherwise, he seemed credible.

Franklin was the prosecution's most important witness, and it was absolutely essential that Rogers dent his story. But on the eve of his cross-examination, Rogers prepped for the duty by going on a bender. His employees and daughter searched his favorite bars and brothels and ultimately discovered him, shit-faced, in a whorehouse.

Darrow was looking for him too. "Is he drunk?" Darrow asked Adela, when he caught up with her.

"If he is, you're enough to drive anyone to it," she replied.

"I knew it," Ruby sniffed. "He drinks secretly all the time. I can smell it on him."

Yet Rogers had awesome recuperative powers. He strode into the courtroom at the appointed time, neatly dressed and shaved, with a haircut and a manicure.

Darrow chewed nervously on a piece of paper as Franklin finished up his direct testimony. He said that Job Harriman had gone to the bank and withdrawn $4,000 in $500 and $1,000 bills that morning, which Darrow then gave to Franklin. He described the fiasco on Main Street and said Darrow had warned him, "Bert, they are on to you" before Browne tugged him away. Had Darrow not intruded, Franklin said, he might have tried a "stunt"—seizing Lockwood himself, delivering him to the detectives, and accusing him of soliciting a bribe.

"You would have pulled off your stunt of turning Lockwood over to the police," Rogers said, as he began the cross-examination. "That was your first attempt to get out of your crime by charging somebody else, was it?"

There were benefits in hiring the "lead wolf," who had worked for the

M&M and had sources all over town. In an astounding exchange, Rogers got Franklin to concede that he had not merely been promised immunity, evaded jail, and had his fines paid for him—he had been personally cajoled to turn on Darrow by a committee of the city's leading businessmen led by General Otis's good friends Felix Zeehandelaar and Reese Llewellyn, whose properties had also been targets of the union bombers. The corporate leaders had promised to reward Franklin if he testified against Darrow. "My future in this city was going to be a very difficult one," Franklin said, "and I felt that those men, being friends of mine, would later on assist me . . . among businessmen."

Ford objected to the line of questioning—a foolish move, for it allowed Rogers to respond with a speech, spelling things out for any juror who missed the point.

"Now we have . . . the chief witness for the prosecution, before he appears upon the stand . . . going up to the office of the Merchants & Manufacturers Association and there meeting a portion of their directors, their strike committee," said Rogers.

"He must have been impressed by this body of distinguished gentlemen . . . assuring him of . . . things that would doubtless happen in the future," Rogers said. "We have a right to know whether or not they were his friends, personally, or whether they were his friends because, perchance, he might come on this stand and testify in this case against . . . the champion of their opponents."

Rogers was absent from court the next day—"resting," the newspapers said. But Juror Golding raised his hand, asked the judge for permission to examine Franklin, and peppered the witness with questions that suggested the case was a frame-up, causing Franklin to respond with an unappealing testiness.

In deference to a summer heat wave, the trial was moved to a bigger, better-ventilated courtroom, where Fredericks set out to show a pattern of corruption in Darrow's behavior. Guy Biddinger, the Burns detective, told how Darrow had given him $700, and discussed ways to hijack evidence. McManigal's uncle related his efforts to get Ortie to retract his confession. Kurt Diekelman, the hotel clerk, gave his account of how Ruby's brother had spirited him to Chicago. And when Johannsen denied that the McNamara defense had conspired to get David Caplan's wife out of the state, he was confronted with coded telegrams he had sent updating Darrow's team on Flora Caplan's flight. Several talesmen from the McNamara trial were called to the stand, and told how they were offered bribes by Franklin. Witnesses traced the path of a $10,000 check from the AFL that Darrow and Tvietmoe had cashed in San Francisco for mysterious purposes. And the debonair Detective Browne, in his soft Southern accent, described his encounter with Darrow after Franklin's arrest.

"Browne, this is terrible, for God's sake," Darrow told him. "Can't you do anything for us?"

"You ought to have known better than to employ a man like Franklin; he is always drunk," Browne replied.

"Do the best you can and I will take care of you," Darrow had promised. It was, said the state, another attempt at bribery.

To cap its case, in late June, the prosecution called Harrington to the stand. Filling the witness chair with his bulk, Harrington told how the previous September, as they talked on the porch at the Bonnie Brae house, Darrow had pulled a roll of bills from his pocket, said it was $10,000, and vowed to use it to "reach" a couple of jurymen. "He said he had the check cashed in Tvietmoe's bank in San Francisco so that the money could not be traced," Harrington testified. "I told Darrow not to attempt such a thing, it would be his ruin."

"I guess you are right," Darrow had told him. "I won't do it." But on the day that Franklin was arrested, said Harrington, he recalled the incident and asked if Darrow had cause for worry. "Yes," Darrow told him. "My God, if he speaks I am ruined."

Darrow prepared his loved ones for the worst. "I am afraid there is no way to win," he wrote Paul. In court, Darrow was "increasingly glum and grim; he felt mortified and resentful, heartbroken and trapped," said Baillie. "He told me he thought that even Rogers believed him guilty."[22]

Rogers parried, once again, with mischief and disruption. Harrington was an attorney and knew what made a good witness. During the cross-examination, instead of looking at Rogers, he addressed his answers directly, and earnestly, to the jury. Rogers "padded about the courtroom with the stealthy tread of a panther," trying to break Harrington's gaze, the *Examiner* reported. He urged Darrow, who was also up and wandering the room, to "make him look you in the eye."

Inexplicably, Fredericks lost it. "May it please the court," he told the judge. "We would like to have Mr. Darrow keep his seat."

Why? "We maintain that Mr. Darrow is attempting to use hypnotism on this witness," Fredericks said.

Hypnotism? "At the mention of the mystic Svengali art," the *Examiner* reported, "a shout of laughter" went up from the spectators and the jurors. In moments of high tension, humor can trigger hysterics. Even the *Times* conceded that "the laughter and applause . . . exceeded anything" that longtime court employees could recall. The judge was forced to call a recess.

Fredericks was still smarting three days later, when Rogers and his co-counsel, Horace Appel, ganged up on him in an effort to obtain the transcripts of the dictograph recordings.

"Darrow never told me outright in words that he had anything to do with the bribing of jurors," Harrington had conceded, when asked about their exchanges.

"If he had four or five conversations with Mr. Darrow . . . and Mr. Darrow told him that he had nothing to do with the bribery," said Rogers, then the jury should see the transcripts.

Transcriptions were the confidential property of the state, Assistant District Attorney Ford replied, and "the public interests would suffer by disclosure of it at this time."

"There is no such thing in a criminal case," Appel argued. "The public interests will suffer, Your Honor, if an innocent man is convicted by suppression of the evidence."

"There won't be any innocent man convicted," said Fredericks, unable to stay still. "It will come out at the right time."

"Yes, it will come out as you are coming out," said Appel, "and your conduct of the case."

Fredericks had no use for Appel, a brilliant but crazed individual (he would end his days in an asylum) whose swarthy looks and accent reflected a Jewish-Mexican ancestry. He was from a different caste and adept at needling the prosecutor. A few days earlier, he had called Fredericks "cowardly."

"Stop it!" Fredericks now told Appel. "I have stood this thing just as long as I am going to stand it. And I will stand it no longer."

"Captain Fredericks!" said the judge. "Sit down."

"If this is going to be a court of justice let us have a court of justice and if it is going to be a fight, then I will have a fight," Fredericks said. He picked up a heavy glass inkstand and prepared to hurl it at Appel.

Rogers and Ford and the bailiff threw themselves on the furious prosecutor, and Rogers cut his wrist in the resultant scuffle.

"Do you include me in that?" Rogers asked Fredericks when the prosecutor was subdued.

"I do, Mr. Rogers," was the reply.

Rogers threw out his chest, waved his bloody wound, and embraced martyrdom. "I just saved Captain Fredericks from committing a crime," he said, "and I do not deserve it."

On it went like a Keystone farce, with eruptions over which side had gunmen planted among the spectators, or whether Burns called Rogers a son of a bitch, or if the detective hid a sword inside his cane, or why Fredericks was a bigot for moving to dismiss a Mexican American bailiff who was popular with the jurors. "Now you can pick up your ink bottle," Rogers taunted. Rogers, Fredericks, Ford, Appel, and Burns were all fined for contempt of court—and Rogers was briefly jailed—as Hutton tried, without much success, to keep order.

The judge was "a dear, sweet, weak, kind loving fellow," Mary decided, but his rulings were "the laughingstock of the bar."

* *

Fredericks rested his case in early July, and Rogers began Darrow's defense by reading the affidavits that Masters had collected from former mayor Carter Harrison Jr., an array of judges, past mayors, and U.S. senators, and other prominent Chicagoans. The city was like a rowdy clan whose siblings fight viciously among themselves but rally to one another's side if threatened by an outsider. And Chicago was not about to let an upstart like Los Angeles mess with a favorite son.

Several witnesses—most notably Job Harriman—were called to rebuke Franklin's testimony. A dozen men told how Franklin and Harrington—until they were flipped by the prosecution—had sworn that Darrow had nothing to do with the bribery plot. And a Harriman adviser, socialist Charles Hawley, testified that he telephoned the Higgins Building on the morning of November 28 to summon Darrow to the campaign headquarters, a half block from where Franklin was arrested. It gave Darrow his reason for being at the scene.[23]

The West Coast union leaders increasingly felt that their fate was linked to Darrow and put aside their anger over how he had conducted the McNamara case. There was no evidence, Johannsen had decided, that "Darrow was guilty of anything dishonorable or dishonest" in the McNamara settlement. Darrow had merely "broke down and lost faith and became a victim of his own cynicism." Now the labor leaders strove to rebuild his nerve.

One night after dinner, Mary and Darrow accompanied Tvietmoe, Johannsen, and others to their hotel, where the union leaders, with whiskey and song, labored to help "poor broken Darrow" forget "his pain, his sense of failure."

Tvietmoe paced the room, Mary recalled, "big thumbs looped in the armholes of his vest," quoting verse from a Wild West poet.

More than half beaten, but fearless
Facing the storm and the night
Breathless and reeling, but tearless
Here in the lull of the fight;
I who bow not but before thee
God of the Fighting Clan,
Lifting my fists I implore thee,
Give me the heart of a man!

"That's a God damn son of a bitch of a poem!" said Johannsen. "Say it again!"

Tvietmoe did so.

"God damn it!" said Johannsen. "Pass the whiskey."[24]

Darrow's progressive allies were starting to drift back too. Lincoln Steffens urged Whitlock to end his silence, and Whitlock responded with a letter that soothed Darrow's hurt.[25] And in St. Louis, Bill Reedy took a stand on Darrow's behalf. Darrow "saw Capitalism as a monster devouring the men slain in manufacture and transportation, or killing them in slow starvation," Reedy's *Mirror* declared. "If he tried to save the McNamaras by 'fixing' the jury he did it under the conviction that the trial was but a battle . . . and . . . he was only doing what the other side would do. . . .

"Let us say he was caught in lawless acts. Very well . . . He saved the lives of his clients at the sacrifice of his own career," Reedy argued. "Such a man in the dock for an idea must command a great deal of admiration . . . Beset by enemies he battles alone."[26]

Not totally alone. Rogers now called Steffens to the stand.

"When the fight is on there is a call, not for an umpire, but a friend," Steffens wrote his sister Laura. "That's why I'm here with Darrow. What do I care if he is guilty as hell; what if his friends and attorneys turn away ashamed of him and the soul of Man—Good God, I'll look with him, and if it's any comfort, I'll show him my soul, as black as his. Sometimes all we humans have is a friend, somebody to represent God in the world."

Steffens's task was to demolish a motive for the crime. For if Darrow had agreed to settle the case, why would he bribe a juror?

There was no doubt that the plea negotiations were under way before Franklin was arrested. At issue was Darrow's state of mind after Fredericks told him that both McNamaras had to go to jail. Had the state's insistence that both brothers plead guilty spurred Darrow to turn to bribery? Or did Darrow believe that, as he told Older, he could ultimately "throw John J. to the wolves" as well? Impeccably neat, precisely spoken, Steffens told the jurors that Darrow had assured him a week before the Lockwood bribery that "if it was necessary . . . J.J. must go." Darrow and Steffens shared "a feeling of elation that the thing had been consented to and agreed upon," he said.

Fredericks treated newspapermen with disdain, was a foe of progressives, and just didn't like Steffens. He called him "Stinkin' Leffens" and deplored his "sloppy palaver." He underestimated his opponent.

"As I understand it, you are an avowed anarchist. Is that correct or not?" Fredericks asked, starting his cross-examination by pointing a finger in the witness's face.

"No, that is not true," Steffens replied. "I am a good deal worse than an avowed anarchist."

Fredericks was puzzled, thrown off track. "You are a good deal worse than an avowed anarchist?" he asked.

"Yes sir," said the witness. "I believe in Christianity."

There was laughter from the standing-room-only crowd. Fredericks grew irritated and launched a flurry of accusatory questions, but Steffens calmly parried, and cooled himself with a palm leaf fan. "Time after time Mr. Fredericks sought to get the witness to admit that the culmination of the McNamara case was caused by the arrest of Bert Franklin for bribery," the *New York Times* reported. "As often Steffens insisted that all parties concerned in the defense had agreed to the settlement before the bribery."

"While District Attorney Fredericks did the best cross-examining of his career," the Los Angeles *Record* reported, he "was easily frustrated by the writer's coolness and biting wit."

When Fredericks gave up, the judge let the jury ask questions. Golding was, again, most helpful. He wanted to know whether Darrow "appeared like a guilty man, frustrated in bribing a juror—or an innocent man?"

"An innocent man," Steffens answered. Why, when Steffens had suggested that they get Fredericks to drop the bribery case as part of the McNamara negotiations, Darrow had refused, saying: "Leave this case out of the settlement."[27]

By the end of July, as Darrow prepared to take the stand, he was feeling better. Whole segments of the prosecution's case had crumbled. Its tracing of the $10,000 check from the AFL to Darrow to Tvietmoe was tantalizing—but the money trail ended in San Francisco. And the notion that Darrow had taken great pains to launder the bribery money through Tvietmoe contradicted two other elements of the district attorney's case: that Darrow paid Franklin to bribe Bain with a check from the office account and bribed Lockwood with six $500 bills, and a $1,000 bill from Harriman's safe deposit box—two easily traced transactions.[28]

Ruby suffered a breakdown from the stress. But as the summer passed, the newsmen covering the trial saw Darrow shake off his gloom and take a more active role in his defense. He got Biddinger to concede, for example, his motives in infiltrating the McNamara defense. "I wanted to create trouble in your ranks; that is what I was after," the Burns detective said. This and other admissions about the prosecution's tactics in the McNamara case reduced Darrow's sins to the status of mutual shenanigans.

Rogers had held the bridge, dismaying their foes with his bluffs and diversions, but he never stopped reminding his client that the verdict would rest on what the jurors thought of Darrow. As the trial neared its end, Darrow had two compelling forums—as a witness in his own defense, and as a lawyer pleading for liberty in his closing address—to persuade them of his innocence.

Darrow took the stand on July 29 and spent more than a week answering questions from Rogers, Ford, and Fredericks. The flush in his cheeks was his only sign of emotion, and the trial's observers gave him high marks. From the first, leaning on an arm of the witness chair, his legs crossed, Darrow showed himself "a master hand of narration," the *Times* said. "He used simple words and from time to time gazed directly at the jurors, challenging, as it were, their right to believe he would be guilty." The paper noted how Darrow, conceding various points in the interest of fairness, seemed to rise above the squabbling duo of Rogers and Fredericks. "This attitude, whether natural or the result of studied art, is not without weight," said the *Times*. "It was apparent that some of the jurors seemed considerably impressed."

On November 28, Darrow said, he had arrived at his office at about eight thirty a.m. He was at his desk but a short time, he said, when he was summoned by Hawley's phone call to Harriman's campaign headquarters. It was then, as he walked along the street, that he saw Franklin. "I never had any conversation with him in reference to anything improper or unlawful or corrupt with Lockwood," Darrow testified. "He never received any thousand dollars from me for any juror." Darrow said he was "very much shocked" by Franklin's arrest, and "at first I didn't think what to do." Dazed, he wandered back to the courthouse, where he ran into Browne.

"What does it mean?" Darrow said.

"We arrested Franklin for jury bribing," Browne replied.

"That could not be possible," Darrow said. "If I had ever dreamed of any such thing it could not possibly have been."

The check he gave Tvietmoe, said Darrow, was to pay for legal expenses in San Francisco, where the city's labor leaders had been hauled before the grand jury and both sides were scouring the city, trying to secure witnesses. And Harrington? "From the first time he opened his mouth he wanted money," said Darrow. "About half what he said was about getting more money out of me while I was under indictment . . . threatening me."

Finally, there was the question of motive.

"As we went on in the preparation of this case it kept growing on all of us that there was no possible chance to win," Darrow said. "It grew on us from day to day and from week to week, the exact condition we were in and that our clients were in, which a lawyer never knows at once, the same as a doctor learns that the patient is going to die."

As far as Darrow was concerned, the case had been settled on the weekend before Franklin's arrest, when John McNamara agreed to accept a ten-year sentence. No documents had been signed, and they still had to persuade James McNamara to accept his brother's decision. But it was over, said Darrow. He had no motive to bribe Lockwood.

Darrow had an uncomfortable moment when Ford produced a coded telegram that Darrow had sent to an ironworker's lawyer in Indianapolis on November 29, authorizing the expenditure of $1,000 in the ongoing tussle to recover the evidence seized at the union headquarters there. If the McNamara case was all but settled, why did Darrow care about the Indianapolis evidence?

There was nothing, of course, to prevent Darrow from seeking insurance in case the deal fell apart. (Or, for that matter, to tamper with the jury. As Fredericks would later argue, "Clarence Darrow did not put all his bait on one hook.") But Rogers had labored long to persuade the jurors that Darrow had no motive. So Darrow had to explain. "I was always interested in regaining the letters, telegrams and files," he said. The U.S. authorities in Los Angeles and Indianapolis were building a federal case against the ironworkers' union and organized labor. "It was up to me to do what I could to protect everybody else."

All in all, Darrow had given a fine performance. And the rebuttal phase of the trial ended on a promising note when Golding, once more taking advantage of Hutton's willingness to let jurors join in, asked Job Harriman if Franklin's arrest had not been part of a conspiracy to defeat the socialists in the mayoral election, and thus ensure that Otis and the others would get the Owens Valley water for their real estate.

"There are lots of people directly interested" in the fate of the aqueduct who were "interested also in the settlement of the McNamara case . . . Mr. Brand . . . Mr. Chandler. Mr. Otis," Golding said helpfully. "Did this occurrence down at Third and Los Angeles, which might have probably been taken advantage of by some unscrupulous people . . . to their own advantage . . . lose you any votes?"

Yes. "The men involved in the negotiations, not excluding the District Attorney, saw that there was developing in this city a tremendous political power in opposition to them," Harriman told the jury. "I am convinced that if the plea of guilty had not been made or entered until after the campaign was over, that we would have been elected."[29]

During Darrow's testimony, "the courtroom was filled by an eager crowd of spectators. Women largely predominated," the *Times* reported. Johannsen called them "Darrow's harem."

Mary was among them, writing "as vindictively and heatedly as I could" as a journalist, and helping Darrow as a friend. But her position was awkward, and painful. Darrow had been moved by Ruby's loyalty, and when he did feel "the need of physical nearness" he had other women to console him. There was one "young girl . . . warm and intense," Mary reported in her journal, to whom Darrow could "tell secrets, troubles, joys . . . as one might pour the jewels and colored stones into the lap of a child."

"When it's all over, I skidoo," Mary wrote Wood. "I hate to lose Darrow's presence but I hate worse to be out of harmony with my environment."

"They are planning big doings for Darrow when the verdict comes in," Mary wrote. "But as for me—I don't want the crowds . . . Success scares me—its vulgarity, its mediocrity, its unwillingness to be tested." As the fickle crowd drifted back to Darrow, she believed her work was done. "The palms and hosannas are for the multitudes," she told Wood. "Only a few, a very few go into the Gethsemanes."

Darrow had one more night in the Garden before reaping the hosannas. On Monday, August 12, Joe Ford began the closing arguments with a savage assault. J. B. McNamara was not to blame for the carnage of the *Times* bombing, Ford said. Darrow was. "The unfortunate Brice, the poor deluded Brice, when he placed that bomb of dynamite that hurled twenty unsuspecting souls into eternity, knew that if he were caught that he could get a smart lawyer, like Clarence Darrow," said Ford. The law provides that each man is entitled to a proper defense, the deputy district attorney said. But "to the disgrace of our civilization, many criminal lawyers have enlarged this privilege. They have extended it into an excuse for committing all sorts of chicanery and fraud," he said. And Darrow was among the worst. "He has used it as an excuse for subornation of perjury on the part of witnesses, for the bribery of judges and juries."

Darrow's beliefs about crime and justice encouraged depraved behavior and turned innocent lads to fiends, said Ford.

"Picture in your mind . . . gentlemen . . . that fateful October morning . . . that fiery furnace at First and Broadway," said Ford, turning to face Darrow. "Picture if you can the poor father . . . caught like a rat in a trap, praying upon his scorched knees.

"Ah well for that poor doomed wretch, that he could not lift the curtain from the future . . . and see that the man who had poisoned the mind of poor Brice would also some day poison the mind of his own little babbling boy, and that same . . . boy would be led into a life of crime and would some day dangle from the gallows," said Ford. "Well for that father that he could not see his little innocent baby daughter, lured into a life of infamy and shame by some wretch who believed that there is no such thing as crime."

Ford stretched out his arms toward Darrow, mimicking children pleading. "Ah well and truly may these little helpless children stretch forth their hands to this defendant and say, 'Give, oh, give us back our murdered father.' "

Poor Brice? Give us back our murdered father? Darrow was furious and on his feet. "Is it the ruling of this court that counsel may say *anything*?" Darrow asked Hutton. But the judge declined to rein Ford in; it was for the jury to weigh, he said.

Ford continued. When Darrow saw that Franklin's arrest had placed him in jeopardy, he turned coward, said the prosecutor. "Mr. Darrow, fearful in his heart that the Franklin bribery would be investigated to the bitter end, hoped that the plea of guilty would stop further prosecution" and so "sacrificed J. J. McNamara in order to save himself."[30]

Rogers showed up for his closing address in a black frock coat with a black stock at his throat, looking—the ladies said—like Patrick Henry. Speaking in his soft, persuasive voice, he used charts to demonstrate how the prosecutors had failed to corroborate Franklin's testimony. For an afternoon, and all the following morning, he ridiculed the state for its reliance on Darrow's other escapades, which even the press now dismissed as "collateral" charges.

"The District Attorney wasted two months of your time trying to show that Darrow did some dirty work in the McNamara case," Rogers said. "Who testified that he ever bribed a juror?"

But the emotional highlight of Rogers's address came when he told the jury: "Let's see what kind of man Darrow is. . . .

"Go into the mines of Pennsylvania, ask the man there with the lamp on his cap who gave him his education. He'll tell you that he was a breaker boy, working 14 hours a day, picking slate from coal on the breaker, and that the strike came—and Clarence Darrow got him his rights, shortened his hours, lightened his labor, raised his wages. Ask the firemen on the railroads, the clerks in the Chicago department stores. Who arbitrated their strikes? Lightened their lives? And they will tell you—Clarence Darrow. Who carried the fight of the city of Chicago against the street railways to the Supreme Court and won it? Clarence Darrow."

"Rogers had the jury with him as he spoke," the *Examiner* reported. "The silence was absolute, broken only by his solemn words of warning." Rogers turned to Ford's most vicious accusation, that Darrow was responsible for the moral climate that led to the *Times* bombing. He stood before the jury and spoke solemnly. "I saw those charred bodies taken out of there, no bigger sometimes than the buckets in which they carried them. I saw the weeping women and children," Rogers said.

"When all men in this country get their rights, when all have work, when all are equal, there will be no dynamiting . . . but so long as there are hungry babes while others are living on the fat of the land there will be violence.

"I do not favor violence. I have fought the labor unions all my life. I drew up the famous anti-picketing ordinance. Yet if I had walked the streets all day long offering to sell my hands or head to feed my hungry, crying baby, and could not get work, and knew there were others living on bees knees and humming birds tongues, and giving monkey dinners, I'd commit violence," he growled. "I'd tear the front off the First National Bank with my fingernails."[31]

Rogers finished before noon. And a thousand people jammed the courtroom in the Hall of Records that afternoon to hear Darrow speak in his own defense. Hundreds more struggled with the bailiffs without success. Every chair and every foot of standing room were filled. Women fainted and men gasped for breath.

Darrow had been working on his closing remarks. On a Sunday in early August, Mary joined him on an auto excursion with his friends Fay Lewis and Jim Griffes. "Darrow sang all day, sang and talked to himself his speech—and joked," she told Wood. "So you see his state of mind." At the courthouse, during breaks, Darrow walked "up and down muttering to himself, rehearsing the essential features."

As Darrow approached the jury, the scuffling and pushing in the back of the room stopped. The courtroom was still. He hesitated, then began, his eyes wandering across the jury box, peering at the men who would jail or free him.

"Gentlemen of the jury, an experience like this never came to me before, and of course I cannot say how I will get along with it," he said, his hands thrust into the coat pockets of his now-familiar gray suit, his hair disheveled. "But I have felt, gentlemen, after the patience you have given this case for all these weeks, that you would be willing to listen to me, even though I might not argue it as well as I would some other case. I felt that at least I ought to say something to you twelve men. . . .

"I am a defendant charged with a serious crime. I have been looking into the penitentiary for six or seven months," he said, "and now I am waiting for you twelve men to say whether I shall go there. . . .

"I am not on trial for having sought to bribe a man named Lockwood," he told the jurors. "I am on trial because I have been a lover of the poor, a friend of the oppressed, because I have stood by labor for all these years, and I have brought down upon my head the wrath of the criminal interests of this country.

"Whether guilty or innocent of the crime charged in the indictment, that is the reason I am here, and that is the reason that I have been pursued by as cruel a gang as ever followed a man," he said. "If the district attorney of this county thought a crime had been committed, well and good, let him go ahead and prosecute. But has he done this? Has he prosecuted any of the bribe takers and givers? And who are the people back of him . . . who have been hot on my trail? Will you tell me, gentlemen of the jury, why the Erectors' Association and the Steel Trust are interested in this case way out here in Los Angeles? . . .

"Are these people interested in bribery? Why, almost every dollar of their ill-gotten gains has come from bribery. . . .

"Suppose I am guilty of bribery—is that why I am prosecuted in this court? Is that why, by the most infamous methods known to the law and outside the law, these men, the real enemies of society, are trying to get me inside the penitentiary?

"No that isn't it, and you twelve men know it," he said, his voice breaking. "I have committed one crime, one crime which is like that against the Holy Ghost, which cannot be forgiven. I have stood for the weak and the poor. I have stood for the men who toil. And therefore I have stood against them, and now is their chance. All right gentlemen, I am in your hands."

It was a riveting start. Tears ran down his cheeks; the jurors were enthralled. "Darrow rose to the occasion," the *Examiner* reported, "and summoning all of his old time fire and eloquence, made the supreme effort of his career." He had not denied his crime—he would do so directly but once in his speech. As always, he was nudging the jury toward another place, toward questions of justice and fairness. He turned to the collateral accusations.

"I am going to be honest with you in this matter. The McNamara case was a hard fight.

"Here was the district attorney with his sleuths. Here was Burns with his hounds. Here was the Erectors' Association with its gold," he said. "We had to work fast and hard. We had to work the best we could. . . .

"I was doing exactly what they were doing, what Burns admitted he was doing . . . what Sam Browne says they did, when he testified that they filled our office with detectives."

Darrow laughed at the claim, made by Ford, that the state had the right to pursue such tactics—but not the defense. "Isn't that wonderful, gentlemen?" he asked. "The prosecution has a right to load us up with spies and detectives and informers and we cannot put anyone in their office?" But for all the district attorney's advantages, he told the jury, the prosecution had a flimsy case. "They had detectives in our office. They had us surrounded by gumshoe and keyhole men at every step—and what did they secure? Nothing, nothing," Darrow said.

"If you twelve men think that I, with thirty-five years experience, general attorney of a railroad company of the city of Chicago, attorney for the elevated railroad company, with all kinds of clients and important cases—if you think that I would pick out a place half a block from my office and send a man with money in his hand in broad daylight to go down on the street corner to pass $4,000, and then skip over to another street corner and pass $500—two of the most prominent streets in the city of Los Angeles; if you think I did that, gentlemen, then find me guilty. I certainly belong in some state institution. . . .

"I am as fitted for jury bribing as a Methodist preacher for tending bar," Darrow said.

But if the barons of industry could dispatch their private armies to crush the unions, bribe, cheat, and spy, he asked, didn't the workingmen have the right to fight back?

"I would have walked from Chicago across the Rocky Mountains . . . to lay my hands upon the shoulder of J. B. McNamara and tell him not to place dynamite in the *Times* building," he told the jurors. "All my life I have counseled gentleness, kindness and forgiveness for every human being."

But "there was a fierce conflict in this city, exciting the minds of thousands of people, some poor, some weak, some irresponsible, some doing wrong on the side of the powerful as well as upon the side of the poor—and this thing happened. . . .

"Until you go down to fundamental causes, these things will happen over and over again. They will come as the earthquake comes. They will come as the hurricane that uproots the trees. They will come as the lightning comes," he said. "We as a people are responsible for these conditions, and we must look results squarely in the face." In the audience, Anton Johannsen found himself weeping.

James McNamara "had nothing to gain," Darrow said. "He believed in a cause, and he risked his life in that cause."

"Whether rightly or wrongly, it makes no difference . . . I would not have done it. You would not have done it. But judged in the light of his motives . . . I cannot condemn the man."

"None of the perpetrators of this deed was ever morally guilty of murder. Never."

So ended the first day. He resumed the next morning, after another mob scene at the courtroom doors. Hysterical women had grasped at his hands, like some holy man or prophet, as he made his way into court.

He began by speaking about Harrington and the dictograph. The prosecution may have thought their eavesdropping tool was a nifty new toy, but it clashed with the spirit of the West. It was sneaky—a tool of weasels and moneyed tricksters.

"Think of it a moment," said Darrow. "Wouldn't it be better that every rogue and rascal in the world should go unpunished than to say that detectives could put a dictograph into your parlor, in your dining room, in your bedroom and destroy that privacy which alone makes life worth living?"

The state's admission that the trap had been set by Walter Drew's operative confirmed Darrow's claim that he had been targeted by the oligarchs because he was a friend of working folks. "Do you want to tell me that the Erectors' Association, that would be guilty of a shame like this, would not be guilty of plotting my ruin?" he asked the jurors.

The people of California differed on much, but this they knew: their state had long been in the grip of corrupting enterprises like the Southern Pacific Railroad, known for buying politicians and judges.

The courtroom was silent now.

"I know I could have tried the McNamara case, and that a large class of the working people of America would honestly have believed, if these men had been hanged, that they were not guilty," said Darrow. "I could have done this and have saved myself . . . I could have made money."

But "if you had hanged these men . . . you would have settled in the hearts of a great mass of men a hatred so deep, so profound, that it would never die away," he said. "I took the responsibility, gentlemen. Maybe I did wrong, but I took it, and the matter was disposed of and the question set at rest. . . .

"I acted out the instincts that were within me. I acted according to the teachings of the parents who reared me, and according to the life I had lived," he said. "But where I got one word of praise, I got a thousand words of blame and I have stood under that for nearly a year. . . .

"I know the mob. In one way I love it, in another way I despise it," he said. "I have been their idol and I have been cast down and trampled beneath their feet. . . .

"No man is judged rightly by his fellow men," said Darrow. "We go here and there, and we think we control our destinies and our lives, but above us and beyond us and around us are unseen hands and unseen forces that move us at their will."

After all, Darrow said, finishing softly with a bit of verse, *Life is a game of whist. From unknown sources / The cards are shuffled and the hands are dealt.* Jurors looked at the floor; two of them were crying. The judge, struggling to contain his own emotions, traced figures with his finger on his desk.

"I have taken the cards as they came; I have played the best I could," said Darrow. "I know my life, I know what I have done. My life has not been perfect; it has been human, too human."

But "I have felt the heartbeats of every man who lived," he said. "I have tried to help in the world. I have not had malice in my heart. I have had love."

FREDERICKS SHOULDERED THE task of closing the case for the prosecution. He asked the jurors to think of justice, the sanctity of the jury system, and the need to preserve the rule of law.

Darrow's "oration" had been "plausible, eloquent . . . But that, my gentlemen, only reflects the ability of the man, and has mighty little to do with his guilt or innocence," he said.

The key to the case is to "find out who furnished Franklin the money," said the district attorney. "Now let us look. Someone connected with the defense, certainly. That circle can be drawn." And "of all the men in all the world who might have been there at that particular time, isn't it strange that as the officer of the law put his hands upon the felon Franklin, that felon's boss—Darrow—should come right up and stand by his side?

"Can logic, tears or wails or fears convince you that Clarence Darrow was there by accident? Ah, nonsense! Nonsense! Absurd!"

Fredericks finished on a Friday. On Saturday morning the judge charged the jury. It began its deliberations just after nine a.m.

Darrow looked haunted. He remained in the courtroom, pacing nervously, hands shoved deep in his pockets. Ruby wept, ceaselessly. Fredericks retired to his office.

Hardly any time passed before the jury called for the bailiff. It had taken thirty-five minutes and three quick ballots for the jurors to reach a decision. Darrow smiled at the sounds of cheers and clapping in the jury room. It was a good omen. So was the short deliberation. And so was the fact that Fredericks stayed away, sending Ford to get the results.

The twelve men filed back into the box. They had indeed reached a verdict, they told the judge. "Not guilty," said the foreman. Darrow sighed deeply. Johannsen let out a victory whoop. Ruby hugged her husband and his friends crowded around. "Oh, I can't talk. I can't talk. I am so happy. It is wonderful," Ruby said. "I knew it. I knew it."

Several jurors and bailiffs and then Judge Hutton came to congratulate Darrow. "Hundreds of thousands of Hallelujahs will go up from as many throats when they hear of this," Hutton told him.

"Look this way," the photographers shouted as their flashbulbs lit the room. "I can't look all ways at once, gentlemen," the happy Darrow told them. The crowd of well-wishers pushed him back against a wall. "Thank you. Thank you, friends!" he called out. It was a "long, hard ordeal," he told reporters, and he vowed to go on, fighting for the needy.

The *Examiner* polled the jurors. It was a simple chore to reach a verdict, they declared: the evidence was lacking, and the prosecution had not proved its case. "Darrow has been dealt with very unjustly," one told the paper. "He should never have been put on trial unless there was evidence enough to convict him."

The celebrants lingered in the courtroom, not wanting the moment to end. Then they made their way to a workingman's café just down the street from the courthouse. It took Darrow half an hour to get there, as he was repeatedly stopped by admirers who demanded to shake his hand. Mary treasured a photograph taken at the victory party. It showed Darrow and wife Ruby sitting at a table with a crowd behind them. Standing between them, joyous, was Mary.

Within hours, however, their joy was tempered by dismay. Word came from the courthouse. Fredericks had announced that his office would proceed with the second bribery count, and put Darrow on trial for buying the vote of juror Robert Bain.[32]

Chapter 13

THE SECOND TRIAL

A sensitive man must bribe to save.

Twenty years later, when her fervid adoration of Darrow had been somewhat allayed by time, Mary Field Parton admitted to her diary that even she—the lover who shared his secrets and his bed during those searing months in California—suspected he had bribed the McNamara jurors.

At the time, Mary vowed to everyone—even her sister Sara, to whom she confided all—that Darrow was innocent. But one night in January 1934, in the pages of her leather-covered notebook, she summoned "memories burned in with red hot rods" from the time when he was "crushed and weighted with the desertion of friends, with betrayal, with the impending doom of jail."

"Bribing a juror to save a man's life?" Mary wrote. "He wouldn't hesitate . . . If men are so cruel as to break other men's necks, so greedy as to be restrained only by money, then a sensitive man must bribe to save."

THE DISTRICT ATTORNEY had no choice but to soldier on. "The loss of this case has greatly injured Fredericks," Larry Sullivan wrote Erskine Wood. "The public condemnation . . . is general and vigorous."

The average Californian may have believed that society had been compensated for the *Times* bombing by the long prison terms given the McNamara brothers, Harriman's defeat, and the price Darrow paid during the first bribery trial. As Darrow put it, "even savages do not compel their prisoners to run the gauntlet more than once."[1] And the city's ruling clique had reason to be content; the Owens Valley aqueduct would bring fortunes to the men who bought land on the water's route to the sea. But Fredericks had political ambitions; he would eventually run for governor. And so he pressed ahead. "The district attorney told me when I was out there that he would wear you out," former senator Richard Pettigrew wrote to Darrow. "It is clear persecution."[2]

As the news of the Lockwood verdict spread, Darrow received congratulatory telegrams and letters from around the country. Working-class resentment over the McNamara case was fading. On August 31, he took the train to San Francisco. He was met at the station by a brass band and hundreds of cheering supporters and smiled through his tears at the welcome. Darrow rode through the city at the front of the Labor Day parade, sharing an automobile with Tvietmoe, Mayor P. H. McCarthy, and other labor leaders. "One figure dominated the marching hosts above all others. Time and again his name rang out, flashing along the line from end to end and back again—Darrow—labor's big-hearted champion," the *San Francisco Daily News* reported.

At Shell Mound Park, on the shore of the bay, a band struck up the "Marseillaise" and the musicians escorted Darrow to the podium, shoving and pushing their way through the crowd, which refused to stop cheering for a full ten minutes after he took the stage. "He was dusty and travel marked," one newsman wrote, "and those who knew him prior to the strenuous days of the McNamara cases commented on the change wrought in his face and bearing."

Like many of Darrow's speeches, his talk that day strolled and wandered before it got around to soaring. He had never much liked parades, he told the crowd. If he walked he got tired and dusty; if he rode he felt guilty about those who walked. And "the great question between capital and labor cannot be solved by marching," he said. Darrow dismissed many of the remedial bandages that he and the labor movement had battled for: eight-hour-day laws, women's suffrage, child labor legislation. "We are busy patching and tinkering, and doing a poor job patching and tinkering at that."

The working class must seize the earth's natural resources and the means of production, he said. "There can never be any proper distribution of wealth in the world while a few own the earth—a few men own the mines, the railroads, the forests, while the great mass of men are bound to compete with each other for a chance to toil," Darrow told them. "There will never be a solution until all men are capitalists and all men workingmen . . . there can be no peace without it." It was a banner day, but Darrow could not hide his hurt at how Gompers had forsaken him. He urged the workingmen and -women to "stand together in these contests and . . . not run away from comrades who, they believe, have made a mistake."[3]

Darrow's next stop was Portland, where Mary had preceded him. She and Sara made the rounds of newspaper offices, working as an advance team to drum up interest and shape the coverage. Darrow arrived on September 10 before leaving for Nevada and Utah, where he was to meet with Charles Moyer and confer on a copper mining strike. He concluded an otherwise dark and gloomy speech on a note of optimism. "The earth is moving, the universe is working, all the laws of creation are working toward justice, toward a better humanity, toward a higher ideal, toward a time when men will be brothers the world over," Darrow said.[4]

Sara and Mary could not help but be impressed. "She still believes *so entirely* in him. And God knows I am glad she does," Sara wrote Wood, who shared her suspicion that Darrow had conspired to bribe the jurors. "What is the truth—our illusions or our cold and careful speculations and analysis?" Sara wrote. "Who knows?"

"I don't forgive Mr. Darrow's wrong to society," she told her lover, "but I can forgive the man out of which it came because from his composite has come his great good."[5]

THERE WAS A lull that fall between the drama of the first trial and the battle that lay ahead. In the interim, Darrow and his friends turned their attention to romantic intrigues and the complications of their free love beliefs. Darrow had made it clear to Mary that he would not leave his wife, despite what Ruby called "our present strained uncertain mental and physical vibration."

And so Mary found a measure of solace in the arms of Lem Parton, a journalist who courted her in San Francisco, who took her dancing in working-class halls, on hikes through the California foothills, and for long walks along the waterfront. She was, Lem told her, a "little sparkling elf-eyed lady with that dear devilish little pagan smile, which puts the old bunk world to flight."[6] Darrow kept his hooks in Mary from afar. "I do miss you," he wrote in October, quoting lines of poetry and offering to send her money. "How I wish I were there," he wrote, several weeks later. "How I will miss you if you are not here."[7]

Sara, deeply in love with Wood (and pregnant, for a time, with their child), sought a divorce from her husband, Albert Ehrgott, but he refused to cooperate. Wood had loaned Albert money and posed as his friend, even as he seduced his wife. Now the minister threatened to expose the adulterers. "I warned you a long time ago and begged you to avoid inoculating my wife with your 'free love' philosophy," Ehrgott wrote Wood.[8] Sara went to Darrow for help, and he urged her to establish residency in Nevada, where a friend of his was a local judge and would grant her a divorce. Before leaving, Sara crisscrossed the state of Oregon giving speeches and organizing women in that fall's campaign for suffrage. Oregon voters gave women the vote that year but Sara, physically and emotionally drubbed, ended it in a sanitarium in Pasadena, California, seeking to recover from exhaustion and the onslaught of tuberculosis.

Wood was not ready to leave his comfortable hearth or wife and fulfill his promises to Sara. As a serial adulterer, Wood thought it important, moreover, to settle the terms of his involvement in the freethinkers' colony—the literary commune—that he and Fremont Older were now organizing near Los Gatos, a village in the foothills of the Santa Cruz mountains. Darrow, Mary, Helen Todd, and Lincoln Steffens had all signaled their interest in joining.[9]

Wood had concerns. "I want you to understand this is no joke about my being an anarchist and necessarily as such a believer in all freedom including free love," he wrote to Older. "I despise marriage as an institution. I consider it a superstition and a bond and absolutely hurtful to society and obscuring the true relation of sex—union because of absolute affinity and mutual attraction.

"At my age, I hardly expect to run a red light district or a harem, but if I should be attracted to a woman and desire her as a companion I should not hesitate to put her under my roof, and whether she was my literary companion, my secretary, my cook, my mistress, or all these together I would consider my own affair," he told Older. "I am not at all sure that the colony would be prepared to go so far in practice though they might in theory. I am very sure Mrs. Darrow would not in either theory or practice."[10]

Indeed, Ruby was everyone's concern. Each couple or individual at "the ranch," as they called the commune, would have their own home but would share common areas with the rest, the better to inspire thought, debate, and creativity. The chemistry was therefore quite important. Mary was willing to put up with Ruby, but Wood was not. "I hate to seem to pick out one person always as an example, but it has come to my knowledge recently that Mrs. Darrow is objectionable to Lincoln Steffens, as we know she is to Helen Todd, yourself, [and] Mrs. Older," Wood told Older. "Are we, for love of Darrow and because of his need for companionship and consolation, to introduce into this colony a personality that may negate the whole purpose?"[11]

Sara, too, had little use for Ruby—especially after Darrow had dispatched his wife to visit her at the sanitarium. Ruby stayed for two hours. "She is all that the Olders say, and that is pretty terrible—a pitifully shallow suspicious mind that reminds one of a narrow coffin from which she is forever removing the lid and exposing some ancient idea long since a corpse to those of us who do not accept conventional morality, ethics and standards," Sara told Wood.

"Isn't she awful?" Mary wrote Sara. "It is she—the revelation that she was the woman he loved—that stabbed me to the very quick. And he loves her yet—best of all—I believe. Poor, ignorant, cheap, tawdry little creature."[12]

Darrow also visited Sara at the sanitarium and, notwithstanding her health, his relationship with Mary, and his friendship with Wood, once more propositioned her. Sara was troubled, emotionally and intellectually. According to the philosophy of sexual freedom that they embraced, she told Wood, Darrow was acting as a free agent, responding to his nature, and should not be condemned. Yet he evoked revulsion just the same. So she made sure, when he came, that another woman was always in the room with her. Sure enough, his visits tapered off.

"I wish I could admire him more at short range," she wrote. "But he looks at *all* women with one idea. When he sees a woman he sees *sex*. That's *all*. I hate it. It's abnormal."[13]

As THE LOVERS coped with the discovery that little in love is free, the Bain case was moving toward trial.

In the happy days that followed the Lockwood verdict, the Darrow camp had presumed that the second trial would be a formality and shrugged off ominous signs.

The first was the dynamite case in Indianapolis, where the federal government was proving that the McNamaras had not acted alone, and demonstrating how the *Times* bombing was but part of a nationwide union conspiracy to use terror as a weapon. On December 28, three weeks before Darrow's trial was to begin, the jury found thirty-eight of the forty defendants—including Olav Tvietmoe—guilty of a conspiracy to transport explosives with illegal intent. The verdict spurred huge headlines in Los Angeles and across the country.

Mary had caused her own sensation in Indianapolis. Writing for a union journal, she denounced the "farce" of a trial "in which money, prestige, power, was the prosecutor of want and obscurity." There was a hullabaloo in court, and the judge banned Mary from the courtroom. "The judge is a tyrannical vinegar bottle, dyspeptic, lean as an empty pea pod, for years a petty politician and . . . a prosecutor of the bitterest type," she complained.[14] With her usefulness ended in Indiana, Mary returned to Los Angeles to resume work as Darrow's operative: interceding with potential witnesses, or posing as a cosmetic saleswoman or a harried mother (using Sara's daughter as a prop) to gain entry into the homes of potential jurors and gauge their sympathies. Lem was dismayed. "This whole business seems sinister and hopeless and you seem too fine and sweet," he wrote her.[15]

A new cast of players also promised to make the second trial more than a perfunctory exercise. Wheaton Gray, the counsel for the M&M, had been installed as a special prosecutor. Unwilling to admit that Earl Rogers had outfoxed him, Fredericks blamed Judge Hutton for his defeat. ("We simply could not overcome the damnable atmosphere that counsel on the other side created in the courtroom," he said. "As long as the court allowed them to do it we were helpless.") A new judge—William Conley—would steer a different course. Whenever the lawyers "appeared on the point of indulging in inflammable personalities, Judge Conley put a quick stop to them," the *Times* noted. There would be no "shilly shally" this time. Indeed, when the defense tried to read the forty testimonials to Darrow into the record, Conley cut the number to five.

The facts of the case contained a significant difference from those the state presented in the Lockwood trial. Bert Franklin had given Robert Bain a $400 bribe *before* Darrow and Steffens began to negotiate the McNamara guilty plea, and so the defense could not claim, as it had in the first trial, that Darrow had no motive for corrupting the jury.[16]

And no sooner did the trial begin than it was resolutely clear that Rogers would not dominate this courtroom. Rogers was in awful shape, pale and shaking in court. After ineffectually cross-examining Bain, the lawyer disappeared for several days. Word was passed to the press that he was recuperating from an "illness" in a sanitarium. Rogers was "always uncertain at critical times," Darrow griped in a letter to Paul.

Darrow understood the danger that lawyers face when representing themselves in court—their judgment is distorted, and every argument seems self-serving. Nor was he happy with the jury, which, he suspected, contained some hostile members. But he tried to pick up the slack, firing questions when Franklin, nervously jiggling a big gold watch, took the stand. Looming before the witness, with his hands in his pockets and head thrust forward, Darrow caught his former employee on several inconsistencies. He brought out the terms of the deal that Franklin struck with the city's capitalists and got him to plead forgetfulness on some important details.[17]

The defense wasn't losing, but it wasn't winning. Rogers returned to the courtroom with a flourish on February 6, announcing his intent to continue in Darrow's defense though it meant risking death. With a nurse and a doctor standing by in an anteroom, Rogers—seemingly unable to rise from a wooden swivel chair, his arms dangling at his sides—cross-examined Lockwood and had him relate how Fredericks had schemed to entrap Darrow and then rewarded Lockwood with a job on the county payroll.

"Franklin would never have come out to bribe you at all if you hadn't called him up and made arrangements at the orders of Fredericks," Rogers said.

"Probably not," Lockwood admitted.

"You got that job as a reward for testifying against Darrow . . . didn't you?" Rogers said.

At the lunchtime recess, a concerned Conley came down from the bench and ordered Rogers to withdraw. "I can't, Judge . . . I'm going to do it if it kills me," Rogers told him. But, threatened with a contempt citation, he left for two more weeks.[18]

Behind the scenes, the maneuvering continued. On February 12, George Schilling wrote to Darrow from Chicago, saying that a friend of John Harrington had offered, for "considerable money," to keep Harrington from testifying. The approach had been made by an investigator named Cooney, who shared an office with Harrington in Chicago and had testified in the Lockwood trial. If well paid, Cooney promised to "fix things up so that neither he nor Mr. Harrington would be witnesses."

Was it an authentic offer? Could Cooney really deliver Harrington, or was he trying to fleece the defense? Was it a government sting? Schilling and Ed Nockels discussed the matter with William Thompson, Darrow's former law partner, and all agreed that the offer should at least be conveyed to Los Angeles. "We feel you ought to know these facts, and if it will be desirable for Mr. Nockels to come to Los Angeles in regard to this . . . send a telegram," Schilling wrote. In the end, nothing came of it. Harrington was called to the stand and testified as he had in the first trial. But Schilling's letter throws further light on Darrow's ethical standards, and what he and his associates were willing to consider.[19]

Opening for the defense, Darrow stressed evidence cited in the first trial: that the $1,000 check he gave to Franklin was dated October 4—two days before the October 6 date on which, according to Franklin, they first discussed bribery. "He received the check . . . before he says there was ever any conversation about bribing anybody," Darrow told the jury. It was merely Franklin's regular pay. From the witness stand, Steffens and Older then walked the jury through the chronology of the McNamara negotiations, asking, this time: Why would Darrow make plans to plead the brothers guilty if he already knew that Bain was in his pocket? And LeCompte Davis testified that Darrow had wanted to strike Bain as a juror, and relented only at Franklin's insistence.[20]

The Darrows had left Venice for a cramped apartment closer to downtown, with a roll-away bed in the dining room. Darrow tried to keep their spirits up, laughing when he could at their predicament. One night, when they visited their friend Frances Peede's house for dinner, Darrow asked her: "Frances, is this the dining room?"

"Yes," she replied.

"Where is the bed?"

On the day Steffens testified, he and Older and Darrow and Johannsen telephoned Mary at five p.m. and said they would be there in an hour for dinner. "With red wine, cigarettes and general friendship the evening sparkled. It occurred to me that here was a group of people all in tune like some fine violins. Maybe years and years had been taken in just tuning up and—then we met! And the result was harmony," Mary said.

"Older told tales of prisoners with such loving tenderness," Mary wrote Lem. "Darrow was brilliant with his Mephistophilian wit. Jo dramatic. Steffens mercurial. Steffens and Jo stayed til very late. Steffens finally getting Jo to repudiate force . . . Not that Jo will change permanently, but he saw the logic of Steffens' position."[21]

In typically dashing fashion, Rogers returned to the trial at the end of February, pushing open the doors, tossing his hat and coat aside, and striding to the front of the courtroom to take charge of the questioning when Darrow was on the stand.

Fredericks was summoned as a rebuttal witness by the prosecution to furnish his account of the McNamara plea negotiations. He swore that what ultimately caused Darrow to plead the brothers guilty was the news that the prosecutors had Bain, as well as Lockwood, in hand. At the mention of Bain's name, said Fredericks, Darrow had broken into a sweat and almost immediately agreed to a deal.

But Fredericks perjured himself when denying that he had cleared the terms of the McNamara plea bargain with Drew. And when he got the opportunity to cross-examine his adversary, Darrow demonstrated how Fredericks had given a quite different timeline of the McNamara negotiations, when it suited him, in the Lockwood trial.

"I demand the right to explain!" Fredericks shouted at the top of his voice. Then Ford and Darrow went at it, and the judge tried vainly to still them all.[22]

The closing arguments began on March 4. Gray opened for the prosecution with the subtlety of an Otis editorial.

"He is a moral idiot," Gray said of Darrow. "Think of the number of people Darrow has an influence over in the United States! Think of the number who follow his leadership! He is the God of their idolatry; the dime novel hero of their worship.

"As soon as he gets his fox-like eyes on them, and breathes a few assuring words to them, they believe he can do impossible things," said Gray. "Clarence Darrow is the greatest power for evil in the United States today!"[23]

As the hour approached for his own closing argument, Darrow and his supporters believed that another acquittal was at hand. Unless the government had "fixed" the jury, Wood told Sara, Darrow would triumph. "I think I will win," Darrow wrote, returning a $3 donation to a workingman named Meyers.[24]

A thousand people tried to squeeze into the tiny courtroom on Wednesday, March 5, to hear Darrow speak. The "sweating, shouting, shoving mass of humanity" swept the bailiffs aside and pushed at the doors; women fainted in the crowd and were carried along, upright, unable to fall, until a "flying wedge of deputy sheriffs" cleared a path. The deputies had to rescue Darrow, Steffens, and Judge Conley.

Darrow began his argument in the afternoon, and much of it ran parallel to his address at the Lockwood trial. "I am not here because they think or because they care whether the allegations of this indictment are true or false," he said, "but because . . . I have committed the unpardonable sin; I have dared to oppose the mighty and strong and to speak in defense of the poor and the weak. . . .

"The forces that control in this United States, the great forces of evil, want to destroy me," he declared.

As always, Darrow chose to demonize a target in the prosecution, and Gray was an opportune target. Few of his adversaries ever came in for the disapprobation that Darrow had for the special prosecutor. He called him fat, piglike, corrupt. "Harry Chandler . . . has visited Gray's pen a good many times and poured many a pail of swill down his trough!" Darrow said. Gray and his fellow prosecutors "have raked up every gutter-snipe and sewer-rat they could find and bribed them that their masters might get me!" said Darrow.

"It is my sad duty to make Gray immortal," said Darrow. Gray's "great frame should go down into the earth and take its place to feed the worms . . . so that the dead might do some good, although the living had not. And here I come and I thrust immortality on him, because he must live in the future as the man who rented himself to persecute me."

In the Lockwood trial, Darrow had suggested that the McNamaras were not "morally guilty." Now he went further. There were, on that particular day, no greater outcasts in the United States. But, though it put his own freedom in jeopardy, he defended the brothers. "I want to say to this jury, even if it costs me my liberty, that the placing of dynamite in the *Times* alley was not a 'crime of the century.' It was not even a crime," Darrow said. "Under the laws of God, which consider motive everything, they were not guilty of murder. . . .

"Do you want to know who is responsible?" he asked. "It is the men who have reached out their hands and taken possession of all the wealth of the world; it is the owners of the great railroad systems; it is the Rockefellers, it is the Morgans, it is the Goulds; it is that paralyzing hand of wealth which has reached out and destroyed all the opportunities of the poor."

Here was the grand statement on the roots and causes of industrial violence that Steffens and the McNamaras had thought to make in the fall of 1911. Here was Darrow's justification for bribing jurors. Here was his attempt to pay back labor, whose cause he had fumbled.

"Here is J. B. McNamara. If there is no other man on earth who will raise his voice to do justice to him, I will do it, even if I am pleading for myself," said Darrow. "He was a working man. He was a fanatical trade unionist. He believed in force. . . .

"Out of willfulness or wickedness? No. Because in his brain was burning the thought that he was doing great good to the poor and the weak.

"He had seen those men who were building these skyscrapers, going up five, seven, eight, ten stories in the air, catching red hot bolts, walking narrow beams, handling heavy loads, growing dizzy and dropping to the earth, and their comrades pick up a bundle of rags and flesh and bones and blood and take it home to a mother or a wife," Darrow said.

"He had seen their flesh and blood ground into money for the rich. He had seen the little children working in factories and the mills; he had seen death in every form coming from the oppression of the strong and the powerful; and he struck out blindly in the dark to do what he thought would help. . . .

"He listened to the cries of the weak, and he could hear nothing else.

And he did it; and serious as the consequences have been to me . . . I shall always be thankful that I had the courage to take that step to save his life.

"I may be in the penitentiary, or I may be dead; but some time the world will understand that you cannot settle the great question of poverty; that you cannot settle the great conflict between capital and labor; that you cannot settle it by sending men to jail and hanging them by the neck until they are dead."[25]

Darrow spoke for two hours that Wednesday afternoon. "He was master of the courtroom," the *Examiner* said. "With sharp wit and biting sarcasm, and vitriolic characterizations, he fired volley after volley."[26]

The *Times*, however, was unforgiving. "Snapping and snarling," the paper reported, "Clarence Darrow fought back yesterday in an argument envenomed with fury." His attacks on Gray, the newspaper suggested, had alienated the jurors.[27]

Darrow completed his address on Thursday morning, reciting verses from Swinburne and from the Neihardt poem he had sung with Mary and the labor leaders: "More than half beaten, but fearless / Facing the storm and the night / Breathless and reeling, but tearless / Here in the lull of the fight; / I who bow not but before thee / God of the Fighting Clan, / Lifting my fists I implore thee, / Give me the heart of a man!"

"I believe in the law of love," he told the jurors at the end, as many in the courtroom wept. "I believe it is the greatest and most potent force in all this great universe. I have loved peace, and I have had to fight almost from the time I have opened my eyes—I have been fighting, fighting, fighting.

"And it is for this, gentlemen, that I am here today, because I haven't condemned, I haven't judged; I have loved my fellow man; I have loved the weak; I have loved the poor; I have loved the struggling; I have fought for their liberties, for their rights, that they might have something in this world more than the hard conditions that social life has given them.

"I could have hunted with the wolves. But I did not," he said. "I have brains enough to know that that path is easy. I know that all the good things in the world come to those who play with them. I have passed it aside . . . I could have done nothing else . . . I was born with the feelings I have. I have lived them the best I could.

"I could travel no other road," he told them, weeping with them now. "I come to you worn and weary and tired, and submit my fate."[28]

In a certain light, Darrow could look Lincolnesque, no small plus in Illinois.

Darrow with his son, Paul, and his father, Amirus. Said Darrow of his dad: "To his dying day, he lived in a walking trance."

Chicago at the turn of the century, shortly after Darrow arrived. The "smooth-faced" young man rose through the city's rough legal and political scenes at a pace that the newspapers called "phenomenal."

Clarence Darrow's great mentor, Illinois governor John Peter Altgeld. "His character was that of the dreamer, of the idealist," but "there was mixed with that . . . the practical touch of the politician," said Darrow. "He knew how to play to those cheap feelings which the politician uses to inspire the vulgar mob."

Railway union leader and socialist Eugene Debs, who hired Darrow after the federal government crushed a successful strike against the Pullman company and the nation's railroads in 1894. "He never felt fear," said Darrow. "He had the courage of the babe who has no conception of the word."

VOL. XXXVIII.—No. 1961.
Copyright, 1894, by HARPER & BROTHERS.
All Rights Reserved.

NEW YORK, SATURDAY, JULY 21, 1894.

TEN CENTS A COPY.
FOUR DOLLARS A YEAR.

THE VANGUARD OF ANARCHY.

In the wake of the great Pullman strike, the cover of the July 21, 1894, edition of *Harper's Weekly* showed John P. Altgeld in a fool's cap and a gang of Populist leaders bearing Eugene Debs as the king of anarchy.

Darrow's longtime lover, Mary Field Parton. She would have been content to be "his loving mistress," her sister Sara said, if Darrow were not "running after these disgustingly brainless women all the time."

(Right) **T**he radical muckraker Lincoln Steffens, who joined with Darrow in progressive causes and stuck by him through perilous times. "Sometimes all we humans have is a friend, somebody to represent God in the world," Steffens said. It was he who christened Darrow "the attorney for the damned."

(Left) **L**awyer and poet Edgar Lee Masters. In 1903, he formed a law partnership with Darrow, which ultimately collapsed in enmity. In the end, they were too much alike.

In the winter of 1902–03, Darrow represented the striking United Mine Workers before a presidential commission investigating the dire working conditions of anthracite coal miners. He called a number of child laborers and injured miners to testify, including "breaker boys" like these. Lewis Hine, who took these two photographs *(above and below)* at a Pennsylvania Coal Company mine in Pittston, Pennsylvania, wrote, "The dust was so dense at times as to obscure the view. This dust penetrated the utmost recesses of the boys' lungs. A kind of slave-driver sometimes stands over the boys, prodding them into obedience." *(Right)* **M**uckraker Henry Demarest Lloyd, union leader John Mitchell, and Darrow. For their ardent work representing the mine workers before the presidential commission, they became known as "the miners' trinity."

Union officials George Pettibone, Big Bill Haywood, and Charles Moyer in the yard outside the Boise, Idaho, jail, awaiting their trials for the assassination of former Idaho governor Frank Steunenberg by a bomb planted at his front gate.

(Left) Harry Orchard, the bomber and key witness. Not until Lee Harvey Oswald shot President John F. Kennedy would the motive and paymaster of an assassin again be cause for such bitter, unresolved contention.

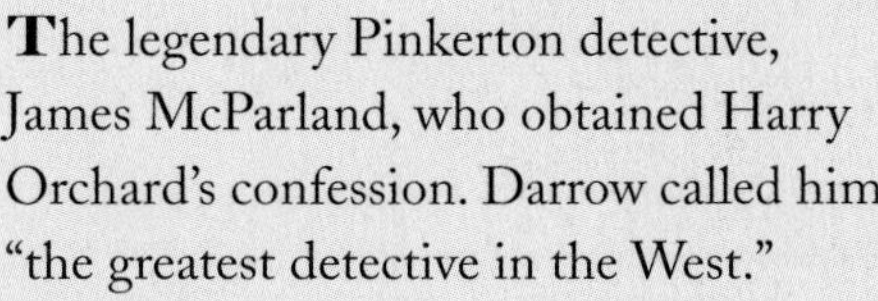

The legendary Pinkerton detective, James McParland, who obtained Harry Orchard's confession. Darrow called him "the greatest detective in the West."

Prosecutor and, later, governor James Hawley, in the Wild West getup that appealed to his constituents. In court during the Haywood trial, Darrow baited him so often that Hawley's son threatened to thrash him.

A closer look at Darrow in action, questioning a witness during the Haywood trial. Behind him is Big Bill. The bald-headed man to the right of Haywood is co-counsel Edmund Richardson, who clashed with Darrow over the conduct of the trial.

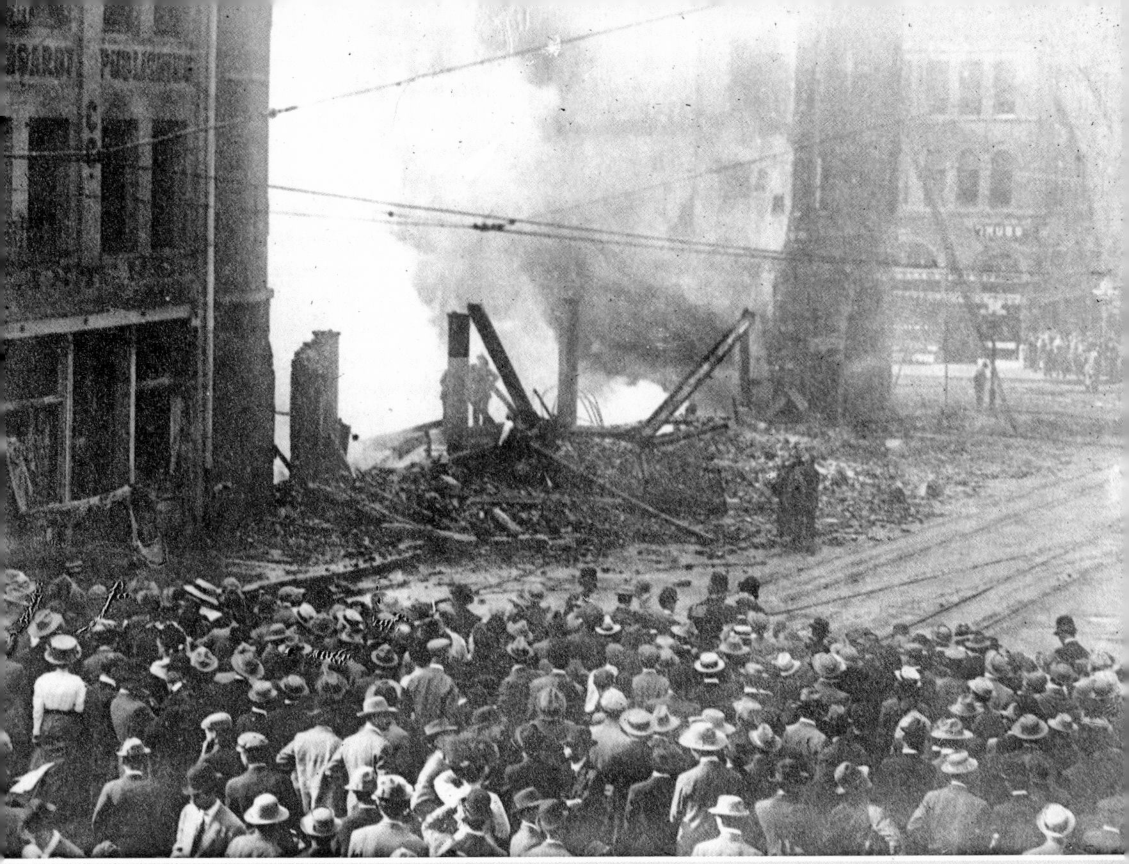

Crowds gather in downtown Los Angeles on October 1, 1910, to see the smoking ruins of the Los Angeles Times Building, where a union bomb claimed the lives of twenty men.

Union bombers John J. and James B. McNamara in prison at San Quentin. “I saw war” in capital’s cruel treatment of labor, said Jim McNamara, who placed the bomb in Ink Alley at the *Times*. The deal that Darrow cut to save their lives almost cost him his career, his marriage, and his freedom.

Darrow entering his plea of "not guilty" to charges that he bribed the jury at the McNamara brothers' trial. "The forces that control in this United States, the great forces of evil, want to destroy me," he told the jurors at his trial.

(Above) **I**n this photograph, taken at the celebration following Darrow's acquittal in his first bribery trial, he and his wife, Ruby, sit at a table, and a happy Mary Field stands between them.

(Left) **E**arl Rogers, Darrow's lawyer in the bribery trials. The defense he crafted, with its drama and hysterics, was tailored to foil the prosecution's case.

Darrow back at work in Chicago, captured by a *Daily News* photographer, on his way to court on a downtown street.

The capsized *Eastland* at its berth on the Chicago River. It was the worst disaster, in terms of lives lost, in Chicago history. Darrow led a successful defense of the ship's engineer, who was blamed for the tragedy despite his heroic efforts to save lives.

Darrow, speaking to Judge John Caverly. To the left are Richard Loeb, in a light-colored jacket and tie, and Nathan Leopold, in a dark tie and suit, facing execution for killing young Bobby Franks for "the thrill" of it in 1924. The man in glasses to the left of Leopold, whose face is partially obscured by the lamp shade, is prosecutor Robert Crowe.

Leopold, Loeb, and Darrow in the courtroom. Leopold is the scarier-looking, but he managed to live a productive life in prison and was paroled after three decades behind bars. Loeb met an early death, knifed in jail by another inmate.

William Jennings Bryan, arriving in Dayton, Tennessee, in July 1925 for the Scopes Monkey Trial. Bryan enlisted in the prosecution to promote his campaign to bar the teaching of evolution in public schools. His presence drew Darrow into a sensational and historic showdown with Bryan and the fundamentalists over academic and scientific freedom.

(Right) **J**ohn Scopes, the defendant, welcomes Darrow, his lawyer, in this photograph staged for the press. Between them, leaning to get into the picture, is Tennessee attorney John Neal, another member of the defense team.

(Below) **T**he streets of Dayton became a circus, hosting all sorts of festivities and attractions, including this sermon from the traveling evangelist T. T. Martin, a determined foe of evolution.

The greatest legal face-off in American history took place on a small wooden platform on the lawn of the Dayton courthouse, in the shade of the trees. Here Bryan, on the witness stand, is answering Darrow, who seems to be plucking at his suspenders.

Dr. Ossian Sweet, who was charged with murdering a white man while defending his Detroit home *(below)* from a racist mob. Darrow asked the all-white jury to put themselves in Sweet's place and to recognize that black men, too, have a right to self-defense.

In 1932, an emotionally troubled Thalia Massie claimed she was raped by a group of native Hawaiian youths. Her husband, Thomas, a naval officer at Pearl Harbor, led a lynch gang that kidnapped and murdered a young Hawaiian man in revenge. Darrow agreed to represent the killers because he needed money after losing all his savings in the stock market crash of 1929. Besides, he told the press, he had always wanted to see Hawaii. It was his last high-profile case.

Clarence Darrow, circa 1902. At forty-five, he was one of the nation's foremost labor lawyers, a defender of radicals and dissenters, a populist and progressive reformer, and almost mayor of Chicago. And his worst, and best, days were still ahead of him.

It was not the speech of a flabby pirate. Even Johannsen thought Darrow showed guts. "This took courage and faith," the union organizer said. "And it was stated at the time and place where there was imminent danger, and it was made against the advice of some of his eminent counsel."[29]

The jury began its deliberations at nine p.m. on Thursday. There was no quick verdict this time. "An air of gloom" settled on Darrow as the hours passed. At least some of the jurors, it was apparent, believed him guilty. Inside the jury room, two factions talked and argued all of Friday, and after the jurors retired that night, word reached reporters that the count stood 8 to 4 for conviction. Darrow had sat in the courtroom all day with Ruby and Steffens, Mary and other friends, enduring the pressure.

"Hour in, hour out—every little while the room would thrill with a rumor and the news would flash back and forth and soon an Extra would be out," Mary wrote Lem. "The strain of that waiting was terrible."[30]

On Saturday morning, the *Times* greeted Los Angeles with an editorial, attacking Darrow for "wanton words of glorification of his miserable self."

"How can he sleep with the shrieks of the McNamara victims ringing in his ears?" the editors asked, no doubt mindful that the judge allowed the jurors to read the daily papers. "How can he drink with the blood of twenty innocent men surging to the rim of his cup?"[31]

Shortly before noon, the jurors reentered the courtroom and told Conley they were helplessly deadlocked. The judge declared a mistrial. For Darrow, it was less than vindication. He left the courtroom quickly, snapping at reporters. "He seemed a beaten man," Baillie said.[32]

There had indeed been four holdouts, who told reporters they were not convinced of Darrow's involvement. The eight who pushed for a guilty verdict said that Darrow's closing argument justifying the *Times* bombing was a factor in their decision. His radical philosophy, they concluded, could easily have led him to bribery. It was the verdict reached by Mary Field, and confided to her diary. And one that Darrow himself seemed to give when talking to his friend and investigator Victor Yarros a few years later.

"Do not the rich and powerful bribe juries, intimidate and coerce judges as well as juries? Do they shrink from any weapon?" Darrow asked. "Why this theatrical indignation against alleged or actual jury tampering in behalf of 'lawless' strikers or other unfortunate victims of ruthless Capitalism?"[33]

Like Harry Orchard, Franklin had been caught at the scene and cut a deal with the authorities. In each case, it was reasonable to assume that someone had sent the miscreants on their missions. But where was the evidence that proved it was Haywood, Pettibone, or Darrow? Logic may have argued that the defendants were guilty—but not proof. In all of the Idaho and California trials, it is hard to argue that the verdict was unjust.

WHICH STILL LEAVES a question to be answered. Did Darrow participate in the bribery scheme?

Almost assuredly.

Two years later, when Los Angeles was preparing to put Matt Schmidt and David Caplan on trial for their role aiding James McNamara, a *Times* reporter came upon Johannsen and asked him if Darrow would play a role in the defense of the two co-conspirators. Johannsen had the odor of liquor on his breath. He was untypically candid. He dismissed Darrow as a "sentimental [expletive]" who "got off lucky."

In his correspondence with his family, Darrow did not assert innocence—only righteousness. "Can't make myself feel guilty," he wrote his brother Everett. "My conscience refuses to reproach me." Guilty of what? Reproach him for what? "Do not be surprised at anything you hear," he told Paul.

It might well have taken place just as Bert Franklin and John Harrington testified—with Job Harriman and Olav Tvietmoe joining Darrow in an orchestrated plot. The three men certainly wanted to save the McNamaras from the gallows. They hated the corrupt capitalists. They believed such tactics were justified—especially, in Darrow's case, with lives at stake.

Many of Darrow's friends reached the conclusion that he knew what Franklin was up to. "While Darrow has naturally my human sympathy there goes with it the old Greek sense of . . . justice," Wood wrote to Sara. "He played the game. He made his own code of morals. He took the risk."

"I never had any doubts on the subject," journalist Hugh Baillie recalled. "In my opinion Darrow was guilty—on the evidence . . . on his attitude and appearance during the trials; and on the basis of my private conversations with him."

The "laws of God . . . consider motive everything," Darrow had said. He was under intense pressure that fall and clearly unable to master his ego, libido, and emotions. It's more than possible that he seized a reckless way out. For the fact is that Franklin bribed jurors. And somebody gave him the money to do it. Fredericks reached a reasonable conclusion that the McNamaras' lead attorney must have been in on the crime. And if Franklin was an agent of some other McNamara supporter—a radical like Harriman or a labor leader like Tvietmoe—it is hard to see him working without Darrow's knowledge. "It would not be until after he had consulted with Mr. Darrow and knew it was all right to do so," Ford argued. And "then Mr. Darrow would be guilty whether he personally gave the money to Franklin or not."

And yet Franklin had testified—stunningly—that he approached four other potential jurors without ever informing Darrow. He was running around town offering bribes to old acquaintances, several with law enforcement connections, heedless of the risks. "If he went to those . . . without my knowledge or direction," Darrow asked in court, why not Bain and Lockwood?

If not Darrow, who? There is a scenario that, without relieving Darrow of responsibility, moves him away from the center of the plot. It was Rogers who, in his closing argument, fingered Tvietmoe as the architect. "Tvietmoe is the last man who had the money," Rogers said, referring to the AFL's $10,000 check. Tvietmoe was "the Viking" who ran the rough stuff for labor on the West Coast. It is useful to consider how the whole "dynamite conspiracy" was built around clumsy winks. Union violence was orchestrated in secret and okayed by a select few, in part to keep the "lily whites" in the movement free from taint or legal danger, Johannsen explained. Maintaining deniability for higher-ups was important.

Darrow's active part in the conspiracy may have ended when, with his own nod or wink, he gave Tvietmoe the check. Even Fredericks told the jury that Darrow "did not know the details." The defense detective, Larry Sullivan, acknowledged that he knew when Franklin bribed Bain—and told their friend Wood, in a private letter, that Darrow did not.

That was the pattern in the Haywood case. Subalterns like Frank Hangs did the dirty work—finding witnesses who would concoct testimony for a fee and helping them craft their stories. Only at the end were the aspiring perjurers brought, with a wink, before Darrow.

And if the bribery plot was, like the *Times* bombing itself, a Tvietmoe operation—which was the prosecution's original theory—it would explain why, even as Darrow and Steffens labored to settle the case, Franklin plowed ahead. Darrow kept the McNamara plea negotiations a secret, and neither Franklin nor Tvietmoe nor Harriman had an inkling on the morning of November 28 that there would be no need for a jury. They had every reason to continue with a plot to bribe Lockwood.

From this perspective, what Darrow blurted to detective Sam Browne that morning makes sense. According to Browne, Darrow showed shock and ire at how—not whether—the crime occurred: "My God," he said. "If I had known that this was going to happen *this way* I never would have allowed it to be done."[34]

Whether at the center of the bribery plot or at its periphery, Darrow believed that great political movements have philosophers, who provide the intellectual foundation, and men of action, who transform theory into force. And "both are useful," he said. Though his enthusiasm for a cause was generally tempered by his skepticism, and his action generally limited to court, Darrow defined himself as a little of each. In Los Angeles the man of action, the aspiring pirate, went too far.[35]

Did Darrow pay for it by spending two years of his life in purgatory? Undoubtedly. And it made him a better lawyer. "The cynic is humbled," as Steffens said. Darrow felt hurt that was real, not theoretical. He believed, more than ever, that life is a hopeless, savage, and pointless exercise. But his heart moved him, more than ever, to try to save others from the pain. Darrow was fifty-five when the second trial ended, broke and disgraced. But for the rest of his life he would make amends, score his greatest triumphs, and die an American hero.

AT THE TIME, however, the mistrial was a disaster. Though saved again from prison, Darrow was left with the taint of guilt. There was no tide of congratulations, no bouquets of flowers.

"This is not vindication," Wood wrote Sara. "Poor Darrow. Poor Mary."[36]

"It was a fluke all around," Darrow told Paul. He blamed "two or three . . . damn chumps of farmers" on the jury. And in a letter to Wood, Darrow attributed the result of the second trial to a series of "accidents such as sometimes comes in a case." The daily pounding by the *Times* played a role, he said, as did fallout from the Indianapolis convictions. The jury was "very bad" and "I really had no lawyer. Rogers broke down the first day."[37]

Fredericks kept Darrow in limbo before finally signaling that the state would not seek a third trial and allowing the Darrows to leave for Chicago. He wrung one last humiliation from Darrow before the indictment was dismissed, compelling him to sign a fawning letter that the district attorney could display to union voters in California. "You were absolutely fair," the letter from Darrow to Fredericks said. "I know you had no personal animus, or feeling either against my clients, whom I was defending, or the great army of labor unions who were assisting them. You personally refused at all times to adopt any measures or follow any course for the purpose of creating public sentiment against labor unions."[38]

On April 4, the *Tribune* reported that Darrow was on his way back to Chicago, but only for a time. The famous attorney, the paper said, planned to "retire to a ranch in northern California and devote himself to literature." The free love colony seemed closer than ever. But that same day, in Los Angeles, his friends received an urgent telegram from Darrow. Ruby had disappeared.[39]

"Mary and I believe she has done this purposely to frighten him and show him his need of her," Sara wrote to Wood. "She has been painfully jealous of everybody here and hates the Pacific Coast; has vowed they would stay in Chicago while Mr. D has vowed they would return."

Ruby had reason to detest California and cause to resist the move to Los Gatos. She knew of her husband's philandering, and of what the other members of the proposed artistic colony thought of her. Before the Darrows came to Los Angeles, "she was not aware of his diversified interests in women as she has been here. Also, he has drawn closely about him that group of intellectual radicals with whom Mrs. D has had nothing in common," Sara wrote. "Her one desperate idea seems to have been to hold him by any means she could."[40]

And so, when the train carrying them home from Los Angeles stopped at a small California depot, Ruby got off, and left Darrow behind.

Chapter 14

GRIEF AND RESURRECTION

To see the cherry hung in snow.

Ruby's remonstration got Darrow's attention. He and she were reconciled. But the price she exacted was steep. He abandoned his dreams of a literary life, and the belvedere where he and his friends would gather, like cicadas in the California sunshine. "The Darrows have gone back to Chicago to remain," Fremont Older's wife, Cora, told Erskine Wood, updating him on plans for the colony. "He would like to but she is greatly opposed."

Darrow owed her. "For all Ruby has done for me and is doing, she never could get more from me than her own if she were to take all I had," he told her brother.[1]

Darrow admitted, as well, to a feeling of shame when he thought of California. "I . . . long to go—but with the longing comes the horrible revulsion," he told Mary.[2] "It is so hard to go back to the scene of all the indignities, insults and humiliations . . . When I think of it a black cloud comes over the sky and I can't get out from under it." Any hopes that his enemies might mellow ended that fall when the *Los Angeles Times* called attention to an accusation in a sensational divorce case that Darrow had made love to a Pasadena woman in California. She was described as "a musician, and full of temperament," and he had been spotted hugging and kissing her, and leaving her home at night.

Mary was on his mind in those first months back. He had no law practice and made money by touring the small towns of the Midwest, giving lectures for $100 and a cut of the gate. At night in his hotel, he would write long letters to her. "I am up here making a couple of speeches and as lonesome as hell," he wrote from Montevideo, Minnesota, on the Fourth of July. He was wasting his time on the "little jay towns and jay people," he said. "I am blue and lonesome tonight and wish I could see you. . . .

"The only feeling in the world that can make you forget for a little time is the sex feeling," he wrote.

Darrow greeted the news of Mary's June 1913 marriage to Lem with the same mixed feelings she did. Mary loved her husband ("Oh, he has the heart that Darrow hasn't," she told her diary), but knew she was surrendering to conformity. "Mornings I shall put on a house frock and link the corners of my mouth to my ears," she wrote Sara. Woman's "purpose is Man. In him—always to all women some man is Man—she moves and breathes and has her being," Mary said. "I include myself, damn it!"

Darrow was happy for her. "I am sure it will be all right and if not you will both have sense enough to stop it," he said. But he urged her to retain some independence: "Mary don't settle down to the *conventional* married lady, but write, write." Two years later, when she told him she and Lem were expecting a baby, he wrote: "Life isn't worthwhile, and still we keep producing it [but] there is no joy like a child, perhaps no sorrow too." Darrow's feelings for Paul were heartfelt. They were business partners in the Greeley gas venture, and Darrow a happy grandfather who made time to spend holidays and summer vacations in Colorado. He wrote to Mary of "the consolation that Paul has brought."[3]

Chicago's radicals were glad to have Darrow back. The Lawyers Association of Illinois, a group he and John Altgeld had helped found as an alternative to the staid bar association, held a banquet in his honor. More than two hundred people attended.

"They have robbed him of his fortunes; they have robbed him of his fair name, but they have not destroyed his character," said the Reverend John Gillan, a Catholic priest who often sent impoverished parishioners to Darrow for legal help. "Did he ever refuse to take up a case? No. They had no money; they were poor; they were down-trodden; they were suffering, but it was always a glad welcome, always a hand extended; never a refusal."

Darrow was moved. His chest heaved as he listened, and when it was his turn to speak, the members of his audience had to strain to hear. He began on a self-deprecating note. "I have not so very long ago heard considerable objections to myself," he said, of his trials in Los Angeles. "I have a suspicion that neither my enemies nor my friends have told the exact truth . . . and still a stronger suspicion that I shall not tell it either. . . .

"At times I felt that I stood alone in the world, and it is not a bad feeling," he told them. "And it is well enough for a man once in a while to feel that he stands alone and is ready to fight the world. It is good for your courage; it is good for your character."[4]

Darrow was invited to speak, in those first weeks back, at the Elizabeth Cady Stanton guild, the Society for Rationalism, and the Walt Whitman fellowship, where the women in the audience scandalized the editors at the *Tribune* by lighting "dainty cigarets" after dinner. Hamlin Garland found him "vigorous and full of fight." He gave talks in New York and other eastern cities, visited with Gertrude Barnum, and wrote to the unbridled Mabel Dodge Luhan, whose bohemian friends at her Greenwich Village salon had welcomed him and urged him to relocate. "The lure of New York is still in me. It is a dangerous place for me to visit," Darrow said. "But . . . the habit of procrastination is . . . strong and old with me."

Darrow was not back for long before an old friend from the Secular Union, the socialist Peter Sissman, suggested they be law partners. If he didn't return to the courtroom, Sissman told him, it would be a "tacit admission" of guilt. Darrow agreed to split the proceeds of the new firm equally with Sissman, whose civil practice subsidized them both at first. Over time, they would be joined by the scholar Victor Yarros, who worked as a researcher and investigator, and two young attorneys, William Carlin and William Holly, who would never forget the experience.

Darrow tried his first significant case in June. He took it mainly to advertise that he was back. It was an arson case in which the star witness was the firebug himself—testifying under a grant of immunity against the men who hired him to burn down their woolen goods store. Darrow told Paul there was "not a chance to win" and the jury quickly found his client guilty. He fared better in the defense of the defendant's secretary, a naive young lady charged with perjury for helping her employer manufacture an alibi. Darrow secured a promise for a pardon from the governor, then made it redundant by getting her acquitted. "I must have made a good speech," he told Sissman, "because the jury was in tears and even the judge turned his face to the wall."[5]

A fine array of scoundrels made their way to his door. The million-dollar forger Peter Van Vlissingen and a doctor who poisoned his wife with chloroform—Dr. Haldane Cleminson—got Darrow to plea for reductions in their sentences. When real estate dealer Carleton Hudson was exposed as a con man—"J. Rufus Wallingford, the Count of Coxsackie"—he hired Darrow to keep him from jail. And Darrow persuaded then-Governor Edward Dunne to pardon Newton Dougherty, a former superintendent who had fleeced the Peoria public schools of $700,000. Darrow saved the seventeen-year-old killer William Rahn from the gallows, not by pleading the boy innocent by virtue of insanity but by presenting evidence of mental deficiencies and persuading a judge to show mercy. A year later, Darrow used the strategy again and kept Russell Pethick, the crazed delivery boy, from the noose.

The work was therapeutic. "I am fairly happy, for me," Darrow told Older. "I believe I have got over the self-pity." But some saw a waste of his talents. Darrow had an "irresistible impulse . . . to help stupid and ungrateful persons who were totally incapable of applying or using the excellent advice that he always gave," said lawyer Harold Mulks.

Darrow was his old provocative self when he addressed the Women's Law League, a gathering of what the newspapers called "pretty lawyeresses." Women were not so clever, and could "never expect the fees that men get," he said. Why not give up on corporate law, he asked them, and build a practice "you can have solely for your own? . . .

"The poor man . . . charged with murder . . . can't get a decent lawyer to defend him . . . Make that your field," Darrow said slyly. "You won't make a living at it, but it's worthwhile and you'll have no competition."

He stayed in the public eye. It must have been pleasant to see himself portrayed as a hero in *From Dusk to Dawn*, a silent movie made by socialist filmmakers, based loosely on the McNamara case. (Very loosely. The workers win.) Segments of the ninety-minute drama, which mixed staged scenes and documentary footage, had been filmed during the trial in Los Angeles, with Darrow and Job Harriman re-creating their roles in court. It had a national release, and a half-million people saw the film in New York alone.[6]

And in early 1914, Darrow joined another of Chicago's well-known defense lawyers, Charles Erbstein, in the sensational defense of rich, petite Louise Van Keuren and her lover, the impecunious but dashing jeweler George Penrose.

Louise was charged with murdering her husband when he broke into the front door of an apartment as Penrose snuck out the back. In court, she wept, moaned, and collapsed on cue, and then posed for photographers. She had not recognized her husband, Darrow insisted, though the dead man had been shot from so close that he had powder burns on his face.

It took the jury an hour to free Louise. The prosecutor, W. W. Witty, took his loss philosophically and, when reporters asked for his reaction, offered a Chicago maxim: "You can't convict a woman of murder in Cook County, especially if she is a pretty woman."[7]

DARROW HAD NO such advantage in the toughest criminal case he handled in those first months back from California. An attractive white woman was the victim, and the defendant, Isaac "Ike" Bond, was an African American.

Ida Leegson was an artist, working as a nurse to pay for her studies, who had placed an ad in the newspaper, looking for work. On an October afternoon she set out to meet a potential client. The next morning, her body was found on the prairie. She had been raped and strangled.

The search for the killer was a travesty. The initial description of the suspect was of a short white man. Then came reports that a black man had pawned Leegson's watch in a shop on State Street, and witnesses told police of seeing a tall "copper-colored" Negro in the company of a white girl. The sensational news of her death, her naked body, and the race of her killer ("Negro Her Murderer . . . Girl Tortured for Hours") made front pages across the country. It was soon open season on dark men in the Midwest. Bond, a former deputy, was questioned by police in Gary, Indiana. He went to the Chicago pawnshop to clear himself, but instead the owner fingered him as the murderer.

Critics like Edgar Lee Masters often looked for baser motives—money, publicity—in Darrow's willingness to defend the misbegotten. But there was no percentage in representing Ike Bond in Chicago in 1914. The city was roiled by prejudice and hate, and would erupt in an ugly race riot in the summer of 1919, in which thirty-eight people would die. Bond "had no money, his friends had none either, and no compensation was to be counted on," Yarros recalled. But Darrow took the case. "Most identifications are of little value unless a witness has been acquainted with the subject," Darrow believed. "If a man is black that is identification in itself, in most minds."

The jury was "seething" after the prosecution gave the gory details of the rape and murder. Respectable white folks—a pawnshop clerk, a railroad cop, a streetcar motorman—swore they had seen Bond in Chicago at the time of the killing. Bond's black friends from Gary tried to give him an alibi. "The material upon which he had to rely for a defense was the testimony of several ignorant, illiterate and stupid" witnesses who gave "incoherent, rambling, uncertain and contradictory statements," Darrow's friend Mulks recalled. "It is practically impossible to conceive of a case where a sentence of death would appear more inevitable."

But in closing, Darrow challenged the all-white jurors to confront their own prejudices. His eloquence worked its magic. Though they brought in a verdict of guilty, the jurors spared Bond's life. Of the dozens of men Darrow saved from the hangman, Bond's rescue was one of the more miraculous. Privately, even he was certain that Bond was guilty.

A few months later, in a public forum, Darrow explained his tactics. "You try to throw around the case a feeling of pity, of love, if possible, for the fellow who is on trial," he said. If the jurors can be made to identify with the defendant and his "pain and position" they will act "to satisfy themselves." At this point, the case is won, Darrow said. Juries will furnish their own rationalization. "If a man wants to do something, and he is intelligent, he can give a reason for it," said Darrow. "You've got to get him to want to do it . . . That is how the mind acts."

The ordeal in Los Angeles had changed him. That "sad, hard experience made me kindlier and more understanding and less critical," Darrow would say. "He had been on the ropes," said Francis Wilson. "He knew what it was to suffer." Not too long after the Bond trial, Darrow saved the life of nineteen-year-old Edgar Hettinger, a psychiatric patient who had slashed the throat of a woman because he wanted money for a bicycle. Darrow persuaded a judge to accept a guilty plea, and the troubled young man escaped the noose. And when the Chicago police arrested a chronic petty criminal called "Booster" on what they called "general principles," Darrow took up his defense. It did not matter that "Booster" had a long record, Darrow told the judge. The police have no right to harass citizens. His client had been arrested while walking down a sidewalk. "He had done no wrong. He is accused of disorderly conduct and there is no evidence," Darrow said, and Booster went free.[8]

Darrow's life was percolating again. "He is surrounded by the maim, the halt and the blind and to get an audience with him is like getting an audience with King George," Mary told Sara after a visit to Chicago. "I cannot see that his prosecution in any way hurt him, except financially. His name draws an immense audience. His practice—half charity—is tremendous."[9]

He was no longer America's leading labor lawyer, but Darrow played a role in one more notorious working-class tragedy. On Christmas Eve, 1913, in the copper-mining community of Red Jacket, Michigan, hundreds of children and their parents jammed the second-floor meeting room of a community building, the Italian Hall. The party had been organized by the wives of Finnish, Italian, and Slavic miners, members of the Western Federation of Miners who had been on strike for six months.

The boys and girls were standing in long lines to see Santa Claus or opening their gifts when a man in the crowd yelled "Fire!" The revelers panicked and rushed for the staircase that led down to the street. Some fell, causing those behind them to tumble as well. Children were trampled and squeezed to death as bodies blocked the stairway, rising to its ceiling, crushing those below them. It was over in minutes, but it took rescuers hours to disentangle the dead. Incredibly, seventy-three people—including fifty-nine children—had been killed. That night, Charles Moyer, the head of the WFM, blamed the mining industry for the tragedy.

Bill Haywood had gone to the Wobblies, and George Pettibone was dead. But Moyer still led the WFM. When the miners went on strike that summer, he had hired Darrow as a union negotiator. The two of them met with Governor Woodbridge Ferris, and Darrow tried to broker a settlement with the mining companies. Each side offered some minor concessions, but violence overran the talks. The mining companies hired ruffians and detectives and organized a vigilante group called the "Citizens' Alliance." Two union men died when company gunmen surrounded a boardinghouse and opened fire, and on Labor Day a fourteen-year-old girl participating in a protest march was shot in the head. Union assassins retaliated, murdering three strikebreakers in early December. Then came Italian Hall. The local newspapers accused Moyer of exploiting the tragedy, and he was cornered by a mob in his hotel room, shot in the back, dragged through the streets, shoved on a train, and told not to return.

Before his abduction, Moyer had asked Darrow to speak at the funeral for the Italian Hall victims. After the incident, Darrow, perhaps fearfully, declined. Instead he and John Mitchell went to plead with Ferris, who made a last, unsuccessful attempt to bring the two sides to an agreement. Ferris was disconsolate, but Darrow told him to take heart. He, too, had wrestled with unbending zealots. "About all I know," Darrow wrote, "is that through constant agitating for more justice, something comes."[10]

Twenty years earlier, the American public would have blamed the violence in Michigan on Reds and anarchists. But the *Los Angeles Times* bombing, the 1911 fire at the Triangle Shirtwaist Factory in New York, the Italian Hall disaster of 1913, and the Ludlow Massacre in Colorado in 1914 spurred a national soul-searching.[11] President Woodrow Wilson appointed the Commission on Industrial Relations, and among those summoned to appear as witnesses were J. P. Morgan, Andrew Carnegie, General Otis, and many of Darrow's friends and associates, including Wood, Haywood, Gompers, and Johannsen. Darrow preceded John D. Rockefeller Jr. as a witness, and the famous industrialist had to cool his heels as the commissioners, enjoying themselves, devoted three sessions over two days to sparring with the radical lawyer. He described the government's machinations and misuse of the Sherman Act in the Pullman strike and the kidnappings of J. J. McNamara and the Western Federation leaders. The best lawyers seek the best fees, Darrow explained, and so the legal system was tilted toward wealth. "I don't think we live in a free country," he said, "or enjoy civil liberties."

"Are you a believer in bloodshed?" one of the commissioners asked him.

"Neither a believer nor disbeliever in it," Darrow said. "Suppose blood was shed and property destroyed, but liberty was saved, then what?" he said. "There are things to consider besides property and other things to consider besides bloodshed. The liberty of the man, which is one thing worth defending."

The commissioners wanted to like Darrow and were troubled by his general hopelessness. "There is no moral purpose in the universe that we can see," Darrow told them. "The righteous man suffers the same as the unrighteous. The good is crucified as often as the evil, and evil triumphs as often as the good."

"Is it not better to look at the doughnut than the hole?" one asked of him.

"We differ in our temperaments," Darrow admitted. "My emotions are quickly reached and my sympathy is quickly touched, and I have a lot of imagination—which has caused me a lot of trouble."[12]

His ordeal in California had left deep furrows. Privately, Darrow was struggling. Life was just a weary journey to "death and annihilation," he wrote Mary, and the wiser human beings found their own brand of "dope—intellectual, spiritual or physical"—with which to endure. "No one can find life tolerable without dope. The Catholics are right, the Christian Scientists are right, the Methodists are right, the drunkards are right, the dope fiends of all kinds are right," he wrote. "For some of us the dope must be good and strong and shot into the arm."

He had been reading the German philosophers Arthur Schopenhauer and Friedrich Nietzsche, whose theories he stirred into his Spencer and Jefferson, the fading influence of Tolstoy, and what he was learning about genetics, sociology, and human behavior from a group of scientists, mostly from the University of Chicago, whose gatherings he dubbed "Biology Class." They met to discuss books and papers, listen to speakers, and keep abreast of new discoveries. "Nietzsche is . . . influencing me against the rabble with its cruelty, its littleness, its prejudices, its hatred, its stupidity," he wrote Mary.

In June 1914 the Austrian archduke Franz Ferdinand and his wife were assassinated by a Bosnian gunman in Sarajevo, triggering events that brought Europe to war. Before it was over, the Great War would claim the lives of 14 million people—a human catastrophe beyond conception for those who lived though it. It put an end to the Good Years, as they were called, when the general glow of prosperity and good feelings was interrupted only by spectacular disasters like the San Francisco earthquake, or the sinking of the *Titanic*. Now people grew glum as the stock market crashed and the economy fell into recession. Darrow was ahead of his countrymen in exhibiting feelings of dread and despair.

In October 1914, Darrow delivered a lecture on war to the Society of Rationalism at the Germania Theatre in Chicago and conveyed his grim perspective. The dreamers who had brought such optimism to the era before the war had been revealed as frauds, Darrow said. The German socialist who had called his French counterpart "comrade" would "run a dagger into him" now, he said. "All the theories have fallen down—religion, socialism, trade-unionism, capitalism, education—every theory has been swept away."

The "small feelings" of life are "swallowed up in a strong emotion," Darrow said. "Men are not kept alive by intellect—they are kept alive by the will to live, the will to power, the deep instincts and emotions. . . .

"We feel sorry for the poor peasant that dies on the field of battle in Europe . . . seized by strong emotion, goes into a battle, fighting like a demon, and dies," said Darrow. But "if he had not gone to war, he would have lived fifty years in cold, in rags, in hunger, in toil and suffering, and brought forth a dozen others to live the same kind of life that he had lived.

"Did he win, or did he lose, by having that one great emotion which meant his death?"

Darrow had come a long way from *Resist Not Evil*, in which he had argued that man "with his higher intellect and better developed moral being is . . . susceptible to kindness and love." The Otises and McNamaras of the world could do that to a man.[13]

It was embryonic philosophy; Darrow was a synthesizer, who tended to think things out as he went along. He was writing and lecturing about Voltaire and was influenced by Romain Rolland's *Jean-Christophe* novels, a saga of a musician who must balance the call of genius with the uninspiring demands of a dull, materialistic world, and by *Folkways*, a study of how natural instincts and social customs become law, by the American sociologist William Sumner. "I wonder what I really do believe, anyhow," he told Mary.

Death continued to dominate his days. Many in Chicago knew Darrow as a friend, but he was deft at masking his real feelings. Outwardly he would charm, while "every other emotion or estimate was most completely concealed," Ruby said. Among the exceptions were his closest intellectual companions: his brother-in-law, the gentle naturalist John H. Moore, with whom he discussed the mysteries of eternity, and George Burman Foster, a tall and elegant philosophy professor at the University of Chicago with whom Darrow debated and caroused.

In the summer of 1916, the gentle Moore saw his wife Jennie off on a shopping trip and went to the Wooded Island, in Jackson Park. There, where he had liked to go to watch the birds and wildlife, he shot himself. "The long struggle is ended," he wrote in a suicide note. "Oh, men are so cold and hard and half-conscious toward their suffering fellows . . . Take me to my river. There, where the wild birds sing and the waters go on and on, alone in my groves, forever."

Darrow gave the eulogy. Moore "was my brother and my friend," Darrow said. "His was a tender heart, a noble brain, and a nature so sensitive and fine that in his imagination he lived the lives of every thing that breathes—and men like him cannot die old."

Darrow's letters to his friends were now dabbled with notations that he was "blue" or "in the dumps" or "longing." He spoke of life's "dark maze" and muttered "we are so long dead." He told Mary that "every thing is such a dull gray to me" and "I fear it grows grayer as the time comes for it to turn black" and that "nothing is important but death." A winter snowstorm made him feel "that the warmth of the crematory would be welcome."

Darrow's friendship with Foster was a relief and an exception. They were a year apart in age, had been raised in strict midwestern towns, and now, in their late fifties, did "the things they should have gotten out of their system when they were 18," as Foster's wife put it. They would stagger in at midnight from a tour of the Fifty-seventh Street art colony or a masquerade ball and eat cold baked beans as they rehashed the night's events. "They were as young as the youngest," an acolyte, Natalie Schretter, recalled. "Girls never thought of them as old men." After Sunday evening debates, Darrow and Foster would retreat to a nook at the Kunz-Remmlers restaurant with a small circle of pals, to continue the discussion. One night, after Darrow had lectured on a certain radical pamphleteer of the American Revolution, a rich and pretty widow was invited to join them. She made both men's wives nervous until she asked, "Is Tom Paine a Chicago man?" and was instantly dismissed.

Two years after Moore's death, Foster was struck down by illness at the age of sixty. Darrow gave that memorial address as well. His friend "had the head of a god and the heart of a child," Darrow said. He loved him "as I seldom loved any other man. . . .

"At a time like this, the mortality of things is brought home to all, and there is no chance to close our eyes," he said, and quoted verse from "A Shropshire Lad."

And since to look at things in bloom
Fifty springs are little room,
About the woodland I will go
To see the cherry hung in snow.

"All that is left for us is to go out and see the cherries hung with snow," Darrow told the mourners. "Get what you can—get it kindly—because that is the best—but get it while the day is here, for the night comes apace."

His friend was gone. "The winter will be longer and colder, and the summer shorter now that he is dead," said Darrow. "The stars in heaven will never shine so bright again. The day will lose its old time glory. The sun will fade faster, the twilight fall quicker and the night close deeper since he is dead."

Darrow "was at his best," Margaret Johannsen told Sara. "I sat, unconscious of having a body until I felt the tears rolling quietly down my cheeks."[14]

Death was Darrow's near-constant companion at work, as well. The 2,500 men and women and children who went aboard the steamship *Eastland* early on the morning of July 24, 1915, didn't mind a bit of drizzle. They were factory workers and their families, eager to be ferried on the grand lake steamer to a Western Electric company outing in Michigan City, Indiana.

They did not know that the *Eastland* had a history of instability. As the crew prepared to get under way the ship dipped to starboard, toward its dock on the Chicago River. Chief Engineer Joseph Erickson issued orders to take on water, for ballast, to trim the ship. Now the *Eastland* rocked to port, and unsecured equipment and frightened picnickers slid along the deck. The musicians, playing ragtime on the promenade, dug in their heels to stay in their chairs. The ship rocked back up, there was a pause—just long enough for the frightened families to sigh in relief—and then the *Eastland* took one slow, final roll toward the river and capsized.

Sirens blew; thousands of Western Electric employees, boarding other steamships, looked on, horrified. Trapped below deck, the passengers stumbled and clawed at one another, trying to flee the flooding boat. The river was filled with frantic folk, weighed down by their heavy, soaked clothing, many of whom had never learned to swim. In moments, 844 people died. In loss of life, the sinking of the *Eastland* surpassed both the Iroquois Theatre fire and the Great Chicago Fire of 1871 as the greatest disaster in the city's history. Captain Harry Pedersen survived the day, but the police had to take him into protective custody to save him from being lynched on the wharf. Pedersen, Chief Engineer Erickson, and several corporate officers of the two companies that owned and operated the *Eastland* were indicted by a federal grand jury.

Once more Darrow bucked the mob. He agreed to represent Erickson, who had stayed at his post below deck as the ship capsized, flooding the boiler so it would not explode, until the water reached his neck. Erickson and the others were charged with conspiring to operate an unsafe ship. Darrow sought an alternate theory of events and proposed that the *Eastland* had toppled from an underwater obstruction. It was a possibility that had first been raised by federal officials, and Darrow hired divers to survey the site. Three submerged pilings, left behind from construction of a streetcar tunnel, were discovered at the steamship's berth, as well as an accumulation of debris. Darrow had a model of the ship made and a three-dimensional relief map of the river bottom, and tried to swing the blame back toward the city of Chicago, which was supposed to maintain a safe waterway.

The testimony at the trial, which was held in Grand Rapids, Michigan, in early 1916, absolved Erickson and the others, but not entirely for the reasons that Darrow presented. The prosecution's own experts established that the *Eastland* was simply a dangerous ship. On the day it capsized, it had fresh concrete flooring, the weight of 2,500 people, a load of new coal, and fifteen tons of lifeboats and rafts that had been added to its upper decks as part of new safety requirements inspired by the loss of life on the *Titanic*. And the *Eastland*'s builders had used poorly designed water tanks for ballast. When Erickson tried to trim the vessel, the incoming water sloshed back and forth in the ballast tanks, making matters worse.

It was a rare case, Darrow would recall, in which he had a sudden flash of insight in court. The engineering and the mathematics were so daunting, Darrow realized, as to be far beyond the comprehension of a lake boat's crew. "The prosecution wants to put these steamboat . . . sailors in prison" for not knowing what only a few experts in the world could explain, he argued. Judge Clarence Sessions agreed. It was a terrible accident, he ruled, but "there is no proof which tends, even in a slight degree, to fasten such guilt on any of the respondents."[15]

THE GREAT WAR cleaved wounds in the radical community. Socialists like Debs and pacifists like Jane Addams decried the slaughter, which they blamed on militarists and industrialists from both sides. But other liberals and progressives, like Gompers and Darrow, condemned Germany. In the spring of 1915, Sara visited Chicago, and she and Darrow had a heated quarrel. "Imagine Sara and I fighting when either one of us would go to hell for the other," he told Mary. But "here was Germany preparing for years to destroy civilization . . . to make the world Prussian. They trampled Belgium under foot violating their written word. They invaded France and Poland. They ran their submarines under ships and destroyed them without warning . . . The world had to submit to Germany and to go back to barbarism, or fight. . . .

"There can be no peace while Prussian militarism lives," he wrote, "and I want to see it destroyed."

Darrow's old flame Katherine Leckie, Addams, and other pacifists took advantage of Henry Ford's offer to finance the journey of a "peace ship" that would tour European ports. Darrow was asked to join them but turned down the invitation. "I can make a damned fool of myself without leaving Chicago," he said.[16]

"Can't help being glad U.S. is getting into the war," Darrow wrote Paul when President Wilson brought America into the conflict. "It is time Germany was licked."[17]

Darrow enlisted with Gompers in a campaign to rally labor behind the war. He joined groups like Labor's Loyal Legion, the American Alliance for Labor and Democracy, and the National Security League. He toured as a speaker, wrote essays, and contributed to a pamphlet called "The War for Peace," published by the government's new Committee on Public Information. Teddy Roosevelt praised his patriotism, and wealthy industrialists served beside him. He was "right in it with the fellows who have always been against me," he told Paul, but if they needed to raise money for the gas business, he noted, that might be helpful.

A special target was Chicago's Republican mayor William "Big Bill" Thompson, who was pro-German and antiwar. Darrow compared him to "a biting adder . . . that lies lurking in the grass," and said that Thompson and other opponents of the war were being used by German agents "in a conspiracy of treason." In October, Darrow spoke on "Loyalty Day," when 150,000 people gathered in Grant Park for fireworks, anthems, and martial rhetoric. "I believe in liberty; I believe in the greatest possible freedom of speech and of the press, but I know this: the rules for war and the rules for peace . . . cannot be the same," Darrow said. "This country is at war and this country will win and you are playing with fire when you fight us in the rear."

In a New York speech to the National Security League, Darrow sounded Prussian himself: "Be it said to the honor and glory and idealism of America, that she accepted the gage of battle from the German empire and prepared to fight! . . .

"It ill becomes any American to criticize the President in this great crisis," he said. "The United States never had a greater, wiser, more patriotic President than Woodrow Wilson, and it is for the people of the United States, not to condemn or criticize, but to support and uphold him in this, the greatest crisis of our nation's life!"[18]

Darrow's friends were thunderstruck. They saw his stand as a betrayal, and some believed that Darrow, along with Gompers, had joined in the patriotic fever to bleach the stains of the McNamara debacle. Gene Debs was chagrined. Darrow "is war mad," Johannsen reported. Dr. Gerson wrote Darrow a letter of protest. Austin Wright called Darrow "the prostitute." Few felt so betrayed as Mary.

"Darrow is following the flag. Too bad. Too bad that old General Otis is dead, not to sit on the platform with Darrow!" she wrote Sara. "Oh, but now is Darrow thrice forgiven his sins! Though his sins be scarlet they shall be white as wool . . . once he bathes in the muddy waters of patriotism."

In the summer of 1918, Darrow took advantage of a British offer to speak in England and tour the battlefields of France. The trenches seemed a foolish destination for a sixty-one-year-old man. But he promised Paul he would "try to keep away from the submarines and bullets" and sent Jessie a letter with reassuring instructions about money, "in case anything happens."

"I can't miss it," Darrow told Mary. "The lure is too strong." As their ship skirted the German U-boats, he spent pleasant hours on board playing bridge with the young sculptress Nancy Cox-McCormack, who delighted in his "droll" humor. Darrow gave speeches to labor crowds in England, met with H. G. Wells, visited the fleet, and praised the quiet determination shown by the British. "They fought and died and held the invaders back," he wrote, in one of a series of dispatches for the *Chicago Journal.* It is difficult to tell how much his writing was restrained by censors, or by self-censorship, but he labored dutifully as a propagandist. "It is true that our Allied airplanes are now dropping bombs on German cities," he wrote. "But let it never be forgotten that the bombardment of open towns, the destruction of non-combatants, the violation of all the rules of the game was begun by Germany."

Darrow did not mention the shock he had received at the site of so many young men in England with an empty sleeve or a trouser leg pinned up. Crossing the channel to France on a troop ship, he was struck by the quiet on board as the soldiers struggled to master their dread, except for the one despairing soul who hurled himself into the sea.

"France is beautiful even in her sorrow," Darrow told his readers. But privately he noted the obliterated villages, so torn and blasted that he could not tell where the streets and buildings had once stood. He saw the ambulances with their shelves of wounded stacked in agony, and the filthy soldiers huddled in the trenches. For the *Journal*, he described the Allied warplanes as "uncanny birds, whose hearts are engines, whose bodies are wood and steel . . . and whose talons are machine guns." In his private correspondence, he likened them to "great buzzards looking down on the carrion that was dead on every field."

Aboard ship, on the way back to America, Darrow composed a long description of what he had seen, which he sent to Mary. The lands of

France and Belgium "for endless miles were filled with shell holes, covered with broken guns, discarded helmets, empty shells—and graves, graves everywhere. Graves inside of barbed wire fences with a white cross marking the spot; graves alone in the fields and by the side of the road. Some soldiers, too, with no cross or grave." He had eaten dinner in a dugout with a general and his staff, who paid no attention to the German artillery shells that fell nearby. "They were used to it, and had accepted it as one more way to die." Darrow was frightened, but determined not to show it. "I hadn't the courage to run—what would the others say?"

He was seduced by the immediacy of war, the intoxicating sense of life in the moment. "The battlefield haunts, the cannons and graves and trenches and supplies and hospitals haunt me. The waste and suffering and hatred haunt me . . . all the horrible hash of life and death," he said, and still he felt an irresistible yearning to go "back into the maelstrom."

"God, what a mad, wild fight it is!" he wrote, and wondered if he could obtain a position in a military hospital in France. "It . . . lures me—and makes me ask questions about life and wonder more and more why people take it so seriously—why I do above all of them—and why we shouldn't want peace and death."

Darrow contemplated the dreary existence that waited for him with Ruby in Chicago: toothaches and "nagging" and financial woes and meddlesome people.

"I felt when I left London that I was running away from a pestilence. Here I am a week out in the ocean thinking of it all and of the submarines under the ocean waiting to get us, of the million dead and half million worse than dead in England," he wrote. "And I wish the ship would turn around and take me back."[19]

Chapter 15

RED SCARE

You can only be free if I am free.

Darrow's contrarian nature, and his fearlessness expressing it, would ultimately win him absolution from his radical friends. For even as he publicly supported wartime restraints on speech, he was working behind the scenes to defend individual dissidents. And once the war was over, there was no stronger defender of individual liberty, sexual freedom, civil rights, and dissent.

The government's enhanced powers to regulate speech and public protest were rooted in the Espionage Act of 1917. The law and its companion legislation, the Sedition Act of 1918, gave the authorities the power to ban newspapers and other undesirable material from the mail and made it a crime to use "disloyal, profane, scurrilous or abusive language" about the government, the Constitution, or the flag. Its most noteworthy victim was Eugene Debs, who was tried and imprisoned for criticizing the war effort.

Darrow was not exempt from scrutiny. Using spies and informants, intercepting mail, searching without warrants, and tapping telephones, the government's agents kept tabs on him and his friends and associates. "Radicalism was strongly injected into the convention of the International Ladies' Garment Workers' Union," one intelligence agent reported to his superiors at the War Department. "Clarence Darrow, radical attorney, in his speech declared that Attorney General Palmer is 'a liar, hypocrite and traitor to the people.' "[1]

Darrow joined several civil liberties groups and served as legal adviser to the most effective organization, Roger Baldwin's National Civil Liberties Bureau. It was an outgrowth of the pacifist American Union Against Militarism and would morph, over time, into the American Civil Liberties Union. On the ACLU's behalf, and that of the Socialist Party, Darrow joined a delegation of lawyers who traveled to Washington in July 1917 to protest censorship. "Although Darrow supported the war and most of us concerned with the problems of civil liberties did not, he joined in without criticism," Baldwin recalled.

"I have been heartsick over the frenzy that is sweeping over the country, have been speaking and working on it," Darrow told Mary.

Darrow represented Theron Cooper, a pacifist in Chicago, and Schulim Melamed, an anarchist who was slated for deportation. He advised former senator Richard Pettigrew, who was charged with making antiwar comments in the press. When hundreds of Wobblies were carted off to jail, Darrow helped raise funds for Bill Haywood's bail and eventually took the case of Vincent St. John, one of the arrested leaders. He testified for the defense at the trial of once and future congressman Victor Berger and four other Socialist Party officials accused under the Espionage Act, and contributed to a Supreme Court brief on behalf of Emma Goldman, who had been convicted of opposing the military draft.[2]

In August 1917, Darrow met in Washington with President Wilson and his aides, who saw the value of having radicals who would endorse the war. If carefully handled and brought on board, Darrow could be an "agency for good," his advisers told the president. Wilson and Darrow had a "philosophical" discussion about the wartime limits on expression, in which Darrow sought guidelines for dissenters and the press. There was just no way to draw a definite line, Wilson told him, but he promised to be fair and to work on a "good sense" solution.

In the summer of 1918, Darrow was back to Washington again, "urging the officials to be more lenient and human" to the Wobblies and others "who, if they had the power, would be as cruel as the rest," he acknowledged to Mary. "I don't know if I did any good. I saw the president and the attorney general and others, but whether they remember what I said after the next visitor arrives I don't know. Probably they will not."

After the Armistice, Darrow went once more to the capital, to plead for Debs's release. He came to Washington from Atlanta, where he had visited Debs in the federal penitentiary. He didn't get an audience, but left

Wilson a letter. "I gave my time and energy without reserve to support the Allies' cause," Darrow reminded the president. "Debs . . . is courageous, honest, emotional and loving . . . He is sixty-four years old and in prison for speaking what he believed to be the truth and now, when the war is over and the danger is passed, he should be released. . . .

"I am most anxious that this Government, which has always tolerated differences and upheld the freedom of thought and speech, should show that stern measures were only used for self-protection," Darrow wrote. But the Wilson administration, fearing that releasing Debs would make the president look soft and expose him to conservative criticism as he pushed for ratification of the Versailles peace treaty, rejected the appeal.[3]

The autocratic trends in American life, a legacy of the war, bothered Darrow. "The modern policy of our government . . . has . . . brought on an era of centralization and power which is rapidly crushing the individual," he told Erskine Wood. Darrow was settling in politically as a fervent libertarian. To the mechanizing effect of industry and the suffocating conformities of society, he added a new target: the state. He opposed Prohibition and picked up the tempo of his attacks on capital punishment. He maintained a high regard for Wilson, but opposed the president's proposal to reshape the world with a League of Nations.

"I am one of the old-time democrats who believe in states' rights and abhor strong centralized governments," Darrow told Wood. "Now it is proposed to virtually make one government that will reach around the world. It would be the death of liberty."[4]

In court, Darrow was an attorney of choice for nonconformists. He handled the divorce of Crystal Eastman, the suffragist lawyer who, as a feminist principle, insisted that she would take no alimony from her wayward husband, just as she had never taken his name. Darrow tried, but failed, to save Ben Hecht, the Chicago reporter turned novelist, playwright, and screenwriter, from a hefty fine when he was charged with writing a "lewd, lascivious and filthy" novel. Darrow represented Joseph Marino, a gypsy chieftain accused of selling one of his daughters for $2,000 and then stealing her back. He tried, without success, to win parole for Evelyn Arthur See, the convicted leader of a "love cult," who had been imprisoned for luring young girls to serve as "priestesses." And, a decade after the courts ruled that New York officials could forcibly quarantine "Typhoid Mary" Mallon for carrying the typhoid bacilli, Darrow took a similar case to the Illinois Supreme Court, trying, without success, to get sixty-five-year-old Jennie Barmore freed from indefinite house arrest.

It was Darrow who rescued William Thomas, a fifty-five-year-old University of Chicago sociologist and author of the book *Sex and Society*, who had committed the decidedly unpatriotic act of dallying in a hotel room with the twenty-four-year-old wife of an army officer serving in Europe. Darrow could not save the professor's job, but he won him an acquittal in court. He was outraged that a federal investigator, having seen Thomas and the young woman doing nothing more than cuddling on a train, would assign himself to ruin their lives. A week later, Darrow was back at it, trying to preserve the reputation of another kind of officer—a "major general" in a charity that, like the Salvation Army, organized itself along military lines—who had been charged with fraternizing with the wife of a subaltern. "He was supposed to be my spiritual adviser in time of trouble, he did it by making desperate love to me," said the lady. "You know, I am of an affectionate disposition."

Darrow's most notable defense of sexual freedom occurred in November 1915 when he saved Frank Lloyd Wright from prosecution for violating the Mann Act, a federal "white slavery" law that made it a crime for unmarried couples to travel across state lines. Wright was still recovering from the tragedy that took place at his Wisconsin bungalow, Taliesin, fifteen months earlier, when a crazed workman set fire to the house and, using a hand ax, slashed and killed Wright's lover, two of her children, and four of Wright's friends as they rushed from the flames. He had found solace in the love of a tempestuous sculptress, Miriam Noel, but her haughty ways alienated a housekeeper, who tattled to federal authorities and turned over stolen love letters, which soon appeared in the newspapers.

Noel regally received reporters in a white Grecian gown and proclaimed her love. "It's all true," she told them. "Frank Wright and I are . . . capable of making laws of our own." Darrow no doubt agreed, but the couple's boldness was not helpful as he tried to persuade the federal government not to prosecute. He provided investigators with threatening notes that the housekeeper had written to Wright and the case was ultimately dropped.

In the midst of the Wright controversy, Darrow had his own lusty impulse. Sara came through town on a mission for the suffrage movement and stopped to see him at his office. Once again he propositioned her.[5]

One old friend who was tainted by scandal did not get Darrow's help. Edgar Lee Masters had stewed for a decade over the $9,000 he claimed he was owed from the Haywood case. Although Darrow "seemed generous, in fact he was inordinately selfish, penurious and greedy," Masters said. "He was fleet, false and perjured and had boxed every compass in Chicago."

In early 1916, Masters lashed at Darrow in verse. He sent a poem called "On a Bust" to Reedy at the *Mirror.*

A giant as we hoped, in truth, a dwarf;
A barrel of slop that shines on Lethe's wharf,
Which at first seemed a vessel with sweet wine
For thirsty lips. So down the swift decline
You went through sloven spirit, craven heart
And cynic indolence. And here the art
Of molding clay has caught you for the nonce
And made your shame our shame—Your head in bronze!

"I get 'The Bust.' It means Clarence Darrow or nobody," Reedy wrote Masters. "It is a scathing thing and, while I recognize its truth, somehow I feel sorry that you did it."

Masters was riding high at the time—in late 1914 Reedy had announced that the lawyer-poet was the author of the Spoon River poems, which were published to critical acclaim and phenomenal commercial success. Masters finally had his fame. He bought himself a country home and hired more servants. The attack on Darrow was published in the eagerly anticipated follow-up, *Songs and Satires*, which every critic in America would see.[6]

Darrow was furious, but with formidable—Masters would say "reptilian"—cunning, he took revenge in actions whose malice were all the more impressive for the long sweep of time in which they unfolded. Darrow steeped Masters in flattery, bought copies of his books, talked him up in the growing literary circles of the Chicago Renaissance, and sent adoring women his way. "He seemed magnanimous," Masters recalled. But the poet's marriage was not surviving what he dismissed as "lighthearted adulteries." He left his wife, Helen, but she refused to divorce him. It was at this point that Darrow, assuring Masters that he had nothing but affection toward him, started acting as a confessor and adviser to them both.

Masters wrote Darrow, worrying that "in a time of storm, rain is likely to fall and flowers can be splotched from the spatter."

"Of course you know me well enough to know that I would never . . . try to make you any trouble in court or out," Darrow told his old partner. "My relations with both parties might make it possible for me to assist both of you which of course I will do without any thought of compensation, except friendship."

Masters discovered what was in store for him when Helen filed suit for support. The dispute—and the poet's womanizing—were splashed in the press. Masters staged a reconciliation, but he and Helen quarreled and he struck her. That too made the newspapers. In the final divorce agreement, the author lost his house, his country home, his children, and his fortune. Darrow "unquestionably waited for a chance to revenge himself," Masters concluded. "He approached me extending his hand with an ingratiating smile." Too late, Masters saw what happened. Helen "is in the hands of Darrow, avaricious and sordid," the poet told a friend. "He is revenging himself for the poems I wrote on him . . . I'll make that son of a bitch the most detestable figure in American history."

There were lulls in Masters's hatred. In 1922 he wrote two laudatory poems, the shorter of which read:

This is Darrow,
Inadequately scrawled, with his young, old heart,
And his drawl, and his infinite paradox
And his sadness, and kindness,
And his artist sense that drives him to shape his life
To something harmonious, even against the schemes of God.

More characteristic was what Masters told Carter Harrison Jr. of Darrow some twenty years later. "He was a dishonest mind and man. He was a quitter and a betrayer both of men and women and causes," the poet wrote. "They will try to get a bust of him and make him an heir of fame, but what he did in life, his dishonesty and his treachery and his selfish grabbing and living will seep up from the grass of any pedestal and fill the circumambient air with feculence."[7]

When he wrote his autobiography, Masters never mentioned Darrow by name. In Darrow's autobiography, Masters is not mentioned at all.

Time was dealing harshly with all of Darrow's friends. Mary suffered an emotional breakdown after the birth of her daughter, and her husband, Lem, left her for a time, to be treated for depression. And Sara, while on an outing with Wood in the fall of 1918, drove her car off a cliff in California. Her leg was almost severed, and her son Albert was killed.

"That which is overtaking you is retribution, nemesis . . . a vindication of those fundamental truths you so ruthlessly cast aside," her former husband, the Reverend Ehrgott, told the despondent Sara. He blamed her, Darrow, Wood, and Mary for killing his son and shattering his family with their careless theories.

"You remember that day when like two happy children we were digging together in our garden back of our splendid new home, suddenly a shadow fell over us—it was Clarence Darrow. That fateful night he introduced us to CES Wood," Ehrgott wrote Sara. "But for your infatuation for CES Wood and his scandalous conduct toward you . . . Albert would be with us still, abounding with life to his very finger tips. He is sacrificed on the altar of Anarchy, Atheism and Free Love."

"Poor girl," Darrow wrote to Sara. "Life is nothing but foolishness, a burden and a tragedy. Death is peace. It is nothing." He offered Sara the wisdom of his long-dead mother: "All the rest is a delusion and a dream."

His own marriage remained troubled. "I am lonely—loneliness all the time," he wrote Mary.[8]

* *

Millions were slaughtered in the shambles of Flanders, Picardy, and the other battlegrounds of World War I. America entered the war late and its civilian population was spared, yet still it suffered 300,000 casualties.

The advances of recent decades—the airplane, the car, the telephone, and the radio—were no longer novelties; they were in general use, serving as accelerants, shrinking time and distance. And in war, when mixed with more insidious technology, they brought death on a heretofore unimagined scale.

Against this backdrop, scientists and philosophers offered disconcerting propositions. In 1905, Albert Einstein had proposed his Special Theory of Relativity. When it was confirmed by scientists in 1919, it assailed the notion of absolute truths. The writings of Dr. Sigmund Freud gave psychological causes—excuses, the righteous called them—for human behavior. Nietzsche's readings of a godless world, built in part on the works of Darwin, took his disciples "beyond good and evil." In its deterministic vision of a struggle among classes, Marxism-Leninism discarded the concepts of religion, rights, and individual liberty. In popular culture, dizzying social change occurred. Joyce and Eliot and Stravinsky and Picasso and others brought a new sensibility to the arts. Women and blacks began their march toward full emancipation. And the "Roaring" decade, as it came to be known, shocked traditionalists with its jazz joints, short skirts, movies, and speakeasies.

America had caught up to Darrow. He would spend the 1920s defending Reds and Negroes, corrupt politicians, bootleggers, and criminal fiends. He made cynical wisecracks and promoted his humanistic strain of atheism and—instead of being condemned—was lauded for it. In the Roaring Twenties, he fit right in.

DARROW BROKE WITH the Wilson administration in a speech in Chicago in late 1919. The existential threat of war had passed, he told his audience, but the government retained the habit of repression. On the two days before he spoke, federal and state authorities had raided homes and meeting places in fifteen cities in search of communists and anarchists, in what came to be known as the Palmer Raids. It was the beginning of the Red Scare.

"A strong element of society, under the cry of a sort of super-patriotism, is today doing all that can be done to crush the liberties of the American people," Darrow warned. "They would leave it an offense to speak and to write and to print . . . they would seize those whom they believe to be against them, send them to jail, because they are violating the powers that be. . . .

"Eternal vigilance is the price of liberty!" Darrow told the audience, quoting Thomas Jefferson and Wendell Phillips. "No man can speak his convictions, no man can write them, and no man can print them with the fear of the jail in his heart! He must speak them freely and unafraid. Even if he speaks extravagantly and wildly and foolishly, he must be left to do it freely."[9]

It was a gutsy speech, which Darrow backed with action. When a band of violent anarchists asked for help, he went to their aid. The case had its roots in a bloody incident in Milwaukee during the war when, as an organist played "America," the anarchists and police exchanged gunfire at a loyalty rally organized by an evangelical minister. Two anarchists died. Several weeks later, the police were called to the minister's church after a suspicious package was found on the property. The parcel was taken to the station house, where, as police milled around, it exploded, killing eleven people.

In this enflamed atmosphere eleven Italian anarchists were put on trial, not for the bombing, but on assault charges stemming from the initial shootout. Though only two of them had been seen with guns, all were convicted of assault with intent to murder and sentenced to twenty-five years in prison. Darrow and Sissman took the appeal, and Darrow made the oral arguments before the Wisconsin Supreme Court. It reversed the verdicts of nine of the defendants. The sentences of the two remaining anarchists were commuted by the governor three years later.[10]

Anarchism returned to the news in June 1919, when a soft spring night in Washington, D.C., was ripped by an explosion on the doorstep of Attorney General Mitchell Palmer. The police concluded that an assassin had tripped and blown himself to pieces. Scattered in the debris were copies of a handbill from "The Anarchist Fighters" with the promise "There will have to be bloodshed." Reports soon reached Palmer of other explosions around the country at the homes of judges and other prominent men.[11] The June bombings were not the only sign of disorder. A wave of mail bombs aimed at members of Wilson's cabinet, U.S. senators, and others had been stopped by an alert postal inspector. Race riots ripped Washington, D.C., and Chicago. Wobblies fired on a parade in the state of Washington, and in the resultant chaos one of the union gunmen was hauled from jail by a lynch mob and hanged. A general strike in Seattle, national coal and steel strikes, and a police strike in Boston led a long list of ugly labor disputes. And in 1920, a bomb killed twenty-nine people on Wall Street.

Palmer was a square-jawed former congressman and judge who hoped to succeed Wilson in the White House. The bombing of his R Street townhouse gave him a personal motive and a political opportunity to crack down on American radicals. Federal and state authorities raided meeting places, seized and deported immigrants, and put U.S. citizens on trial for treason. "America won't be a safe place to live in after a while," Darrow told his old friend Neg Cochran after a second set of mass raids on New Year's Day in 1920. By mid-January Darrow was in Washington, lobbying against "this mad crusade against freedom," as he described it in a letter to Debs.

America's Reds, inspired by the revolution in Russia, welcomed the confrontation. Meeting in Chicago in the summer of 1919, in characteristic disarray, the militants broke from the staid old socialists. The new American Communist Labor Party was led by native-born Reds like millionaire William Bross Lloyd, journalist John Reed, and former New York State assemblyman Benjamin Gitlow, and dedicated to the overthrow of capitalist rule. Emma Goldman and other noncitizens had been herded out to Ellis Island and put on a "Soviet ark" for Europe, but the Americans had rights and looked to Darrow to defend them. He quickly agreed, not because he shared their beliefs ("I am getting afraid of everyone who has conviction," he told Mary. "I presume when the Soviets get to boss the world they will snuff out what little freedom is left"), but because of the bedrock liberties at risk.[12]

The first to go to trial, in early 1920, was Gitlow, who had been charged by New York officials with "criminal anarchy" for writing and publishing a "Left Wing Manifesto" in a radical newspaper. The essay outlined Marxist beliefs and predicted that the workers would one day rise against the capitalist order, but stopped short of urging its readers to start building barricades, shooting police, or throwing bombs themselves. Gitlow was the son of Russian immigrants, raised on the Lower East Side of New York in a home and community steeped in radical ideas. At their first meeting, he made it clear to Darrow that he would not recant. "I know you are innocent," Darrow warned him. "But they have the country steamed up." He persuaded Gitlow not to take the stand, where he would be subject to cross-examination, but his client insisted on exercising his right to address the jury. Darrow knew what that would mean. "Well, I suppose a revolutionist must have his say in court even if it kills him," he concluded.

Darrow expected the prosecution to excite the jurors with fearful descriptions of revolution, and so he tried to move the case along. "I want to say . . . so that it may save time, that my client was the business manager and on the board of this paper, and there will be no attempt on his part to deny legal responsibility for it," he announced. But Judge Bartow Weeks allowed the prosecutor to call witnesses to Gitlow's actions (one of whom was arrested for her beliefs as she stepped down from the stand) and others to describe the violence inherent in revolutionary doctrine. Darrow then told the court that, though the defense would offer no testimony, Gitlow wished to address the jury.

It did not go well. Gitlow rambled on in the pedantry of a true believer ("Now, the Russian workers set up a form of government known as the dictatorship of the proletariat . . ."), which spurred Judge Weeks to repeatedly interrupt him, causing Darrow to object, over and again. Finally, Gitlow ended with a brave flourish: "I am not going to evade the issue. My whole life has been dedicated to the movement which I am in. No jails will change my opinion."

Darrow tried to sway the jury with a closing argument that portrayed Gitlow as an intellectual whose ideas posed no threat, were protected by the First Amendment, and stood within American traditions. George Washington was a revolutionary, he reminded the jurors. So were Jesus Christ and John Brown. "This country, with its institutions, belongs to the people who inhabit it. Whenever they shall grow weary of the existing government, they can exercise their constitutional right to amend it, or their revolutionary right to dismember or overthrow it," said Darrow, quoting Lincoln's first inaugural address.

"That was Lincoln," Darrow said. "If Lincoln would have been here today, Mr. Palmer, the Attorney General of the United States, would send his night-riders to invade his office and the privacy of his home and send him to jail.

"I would place no fetters on thought and actions and dreams and ideals of men, even the most despised of them," Darrow continued. "Whatever I may think of their prudence, whatever I may think of their judgment, I am for the dreamers. I would rather that every practical man shall die if the dreamer be saved."

But if Darrow made an impact with his closing address, it did not survive the bracketing it got between Gitlow's talk and the prosecutor's patriotic exhortation. The jurors were mannequins and the judge "a fiend," Darrow told Mary. "There was no chance."[13]

The jurors took just three hours to find Gitlow guilty, and Judge Weeks sentenced him to five to seven years of hard labor.[14]

DARROW RETURNED TO Chicago, but he was back in the courtroom in April, defending Reds in nearby Rockford.

The Rockford case showed how far the government was prepared to go with its witch hunts. The Palmer Raids in that small factory town began at five p.m. on Friday, January 2, and continued into the predawn hours of Saturday. The police found no guns or bullets or dynamite, just a large number of immigrants, including young girls and teenage boys whose names—like Lukashevich—the locals had difficulty spelling. By the middle of the following week, the dragnet had expanded to include the town's "intellectuals," targeting a socialist former alderman; Dr. Alfred Olson, a town physician whose "reading has been along the line of works of a radical and Socialist character"; and Alice Beal Parson, a local club woman.

The account of Parson's arrest offered a glimpse of what the good people thought was dangerous behavior. "The radical utterances of Mrs. Parson have been town talk for a long time," the local newspaper reported. "Her activities and associations with those inclined toward revolutionary proceedings were known to all her acquaintances and friends who deplored the situation deeply, but their admonitions and friendly counsel are said to have been of no avail. She appeared to glory in her fanaticism, they said, and to live largely for the purpose of devouring 'Red' literature." For this, she was prosecuted.[15]

The immigrants were held for deportation and the American citizens were charged under an Illinois law—a newly passed statute that prohibited citizens from advocating not just violent revolution, but "reformation" of their government via writing, speaking, joining a group, organizing meetings, or carrying banners and flags.

The prosecutors and the defense lawyers agreed to a test case, and Arthur Person was chosen to stand trial. He was a simple factory hand, a Swedish American immigrant who was arrested without resistance as he returned home from work one day and, when asked why he was a communist, told the police that he believed the United States should be run for the workingman. He had become interested in communism through conversations with Dr. Olson, his family doctor. His wife was "known as an extremist also" and "would have been taken into custody too, but for the fact that her . . . little children needed her care," the paper reported.

The prosecution put on witnesses—a newspaper reporter and a government investigator—who had attended the chaotic birth of the Communist Labor Party the previous summer but knew nothing of Person. Darrow got a laugh—and scored a point—when a local stenographer told the jury that the treasury of the Rockford communists had been all of thirty cents. "That would be only a dime apiece for the lawyers," Darrow said, nodding at his two co-counsels, "if the treasury has not been swelled to any extent since."

The key issue in the trial was whether Person recognized that the party he joined was advocating violent revolution. It was reasonable to believe, Darrow contended, that Americans like Person thought change would arrive in some golden future through perfectly legal means.

"Behold a party of seven obscure people going out to conquer the world with thirty cents," Darrow told the jury. "What did these people do? Talked and dreamed . . . just as all these poor idealists have always done. . . .

"The enemies of this Republic are not the working men who give their lives and strength," said Darrow. "The danger to this country is not from them. It is from those who worship no God but greed; it is from those who are so blind and devoted to their idol of gold that they would destroy the Constitution of the United States; would destroy freedom of speech and the freedom of the press. . . .

"This man is obscure, he is unknown, he is poor, he has worked all his life, but his case is one that reaches down to the foundation of your freedom and to mine," Darrow said. "If twelve men should say that they could take a man like him and send him to prison and destroy his home . . . you should hang this courthouse in crepe and drape your city hall with black."

The jury deliberated for six hours and returned a verdict of not guilty.

And Arthur Person, wrote one journalist, "went home to his wife and children and has been just as harmless to the government of the United States as before."[16]

As GRATIFYING AS the Person victory was, he was but a minnow in the Red Scare. The true catch—Lloyd and other leaders of the Communist Labor Party—was prosecuted in a national show trial in Chicago, which began in May and lasted all summer.

The government crackdown on the Left was succeeding. Lloyd and his friends had not even had a year to organize their little cadre of Reds before they were tied up in court, jailed, or deported. Gitlow was dispatched to Sing Sing. Reed was in Russia, where he would soon die of typhus. That left Lloyd as the final prize.

The Harvard-educated millionaire was the son of Darrow's old friend Henry and had inherited his father's flair. When he was not seized in the January raids (he was spending the holidays at the family estate in Winnetka) he had invited the authorities to come and get him. "Violence is the only way," Lloyd told a newsman. He was pleased to be indicted.[17]

Lloyd had condemned Darrow's work for the Allied governments during the war, and when Darrow was described as a socialist in the newspapers, Lloyd had disowned him in letters to the editor. "These are times of stress that show what men really are," Lloyd wrote. "The Socialist Party has many burdens to bear, but I am thankful to say Clarence Darrow is not one of them." Yet he recognized Darrow's gifts and did not object when the other nineteen communists facing trial hired him. The bigger the stage, Lloyd thought, the better the propaganda.

The prosecution was led by a special counsel, Frank Comerford, who claimed to be an expert on the Bolshevik threat. Because Lloyd and the others had carried out most of their activities in public, it was easy for the prosecution to demonstrate their membership in a revolutionary body. "We want a mobilization plan and an organization for the revolution," Lloyd had told a Milwaukee audience in 1917. "You want to get rifles, machine guns, field artillery and the ammunition for it; you want to get dynamite. Dynamite the doors of the banks to get the money to finance the revolution."

Darrow gave the closing speech for the defense. He spoke for two days. "Throngs crowded the courtroom. The heat did not stop them. They wanted to hear Darrow," the *Tribune* reported. The issue was "whether this jury will stand by the convictions of the Fathers and, so far as you can, stop this mad wave that threatens to engulf the liberty of the American citizens," Darrow said. With that opening salvo, he was off. He "shouted, pleaded, thumped the table, then spoke softly," the *Tribune* reported. "He was coatless, but the perspiration was dripping from him. His shirt was wringing wet as he worked himself into a frenzy."

"There is something that I believe in more than I do in my country, and that is human freedom. I have loved America first of all because she stood for it," he said. "You make us a nation of slaves, and I love it no more. . . .

"I am not here to defend their opinions," Darrow said, with a nod toward the defendants. "I am here to defend their rights to express their opinions."

Truth is elusive. What is right today can be wrong tomorrow. What matters is the freedom to keep searching.

Find the rebel guilty and "you will be finding yourself guilty," said Darrow. "You will be joining yourself with the hunters and the hounds and the wolves that have chased to their death every man who dared to raise his head above his fellows, who dared to see a vision that a sordid man cannot see.

"Today it is these twenty men. Tomorrow it will be somebody else," said Darrow. "You can only protect your liberties in this world by protecting the other man's freedom. You can only be free if I am free."

He finished the next morning.

"I have always loved this country. I love its broad prairies. Its great mountains; its noble rivers; its dense forests," he told the jurors. "I love the freedom that has come from new ideas, from a Constitution founded and made by rebels and protected by rebels; from a Constitution born in strife and contumely and rebellion. . . .

"I love it because over its vast areas one can find a free breath of pure air; because of its intellectual freedom, one may love, he may speak the thoughts that are in him; he may develop himself; he may work for humanity; if he will he may be free, and without freedom nothing is of value. I love it for these and for these I will fight."

But "I know the tendency of security and ease and power," said Darrow. "I know that freedom produces wealth and then wealth destroys freedom. I know that the nation that is not watchful of its liberty will lose it. I know that the individual that will not stand for his rights will have no rights. . . .

"This is freedom. It is the freedom we believe in. It is the freedom we work for, and gentlemen it is the freedom I urge you, with all the force I can urge, to preserve.

"I ask you to say that men shall be free."

It was a terrific speech, but Darrow didn't move the jury. Comerford did. If the jury were to acquit the defendants, the prosecutor said, then it might as well tear down the Stars and Stripes and wave the Red flag; throw down the busts of Lincoln and Washington and raise those of Lenin and Trotsky; strip Christ from the crucifix and venerate Judas, and disinter the heroes at Arlington and replace them with Benedict Arnold. He finished by reciting, aloud, the lyrics of "The Star-Spangled Banner." The jurors took but a few hours to agree on the defendants' guilt.[18]

So ended the last of the show trials. It was now midsummer, 1920. The country was getting its first taste of the prosperity, and splendors, of the decade ahead. The sense of danger had faded. In the course of the trials, the Reds had been revealed as ineffectual "dreamers," as Darrow described them, not communist shock troops. Public sentiment shifted as the press conveyed Darrow's arguments and those of the other libertarians who came to the dissidents' defense. In the coverage of the trials and a series of congressional hearings, Americans were shown how their government had arrested thousands of people without warrants and held them in crude lockups, denying them access to due process or counsel. "A more lawless proceeding is hard to conceive," said one federal judge. "I can hardly sit on the bench as an American citizen and restrain my indignation."

It was bad news for Palmer. Even the ultraconservative *Tribune* took offense at the "legal lynching" and the repressive methods employed by the attorney general's youthful and eager adviser, J. Edgar Hoover. Liberals and labor rallied, and Palmer's campaign for the Democratic presidential nomination foundered. Lloyd and the Chicago defendants were pardoned by Illinois governor Len Small in 1922. Gitlow served three years in prison, and then he too was pardoned, by New York governor Al Smith.

In the Red Scare trials Darrow was an "unleashed old Lucifer . . . sooty with the dust of the abyss" but "fulgurant with the untarnishable glow of the archangel," wrote Arturo Giovannittie in the *Liberator.* His "great frame shook and trembled as if under the blasts of an internal upheaval, his fists rose and fell as if brandishing unseen swords."

Darrow's radical friends welcomed him back. "Darrow is false to everything," Anton Johannsen told Erskine Wood, "except humanity."[19]

Chapter 16

ALL THAT JAZZ

I have lived a life in the front trenches, looking for trouble.

The life story of a single mobster, "were it known in every detail, would disclose practically all there is to know about syndicated gambling as a phase of organized crime in Chicago in the last quarter century," an Illinois crime commission reported in 1928. "That man is Mont Tennes." When federal authorities hauled Tennes into court, Darrow was his lawyer.

Mayor William "Big Bill" Thompson was "congenitally demagogical," Darrow's associate Victor Yarros would recall. The mayor served three terms during World War I and the 1920s. He was "indolent, ignorant of public issues, inefficient as an administrator, incapable of making a respectable argument, reckless in his campaign methods," and indebted to a series of corrupt Republican bosses, most notably Fred Lundin. But when Lundin and the boys were charged with bribery and extortion, Darrow was their lawyer too.

Bootlegging, gambling, and corruption flourished during the Thompson-Lundin era, as did a new breed of gangster drawn to Chicago by the palms-out stance at City Hall and the spectacular riches offered by the sale of illicit beer and liquor during Prohibition. The mob hits and Tommy-gun shoot-outs of Johnny Torrio, Big Jim Colosimo, Dion O'Banion, Bugs Moran, and Al Capone added mythic chapters to Chicago history. And Darrow helped make it happen. When one of the Hull House ladies chastised him, demanding to know how he could represent such reprobates, "I told her, for the money," said Darrow, "and because I hated jails and the good people." But it's a chapter in his life he left out of his memoirs.

The first great rogue to hire Darrow was Tennes, a visionary bookmaker who introduced technology to interstate gambling. Tennes placed spotters at the country's major horse tracks, gave them telegraph keys, and had them wire the results of each race to Chicago. The scheme would not be possible without the cooperation of the police and public officials, which Tennes purchased. "His alliances with and wars of violence against competitors . . . involve the name of every gambler of any consequence in Chicago for this period," the crime commission reported. "His control over politicians and officials for purposes of protection . . . even to use police raids for the destruction of competitors . . . exhibit a marked continuity." Mont endured gang wars, bombing campaigns, and assassination attempts before the arrival of the deadliest predator—Capone—finally spurred him to retire.[1]

Tennes was still atop the game, however, when federal authorities led by Judge Kenesaw Mountain Landis targeted him in 1916, and Darrow agreed to defend him. Darrow looked at the evidence the feds had gathered, reckoned that Tennes could survive, and advised him to exercise his Fifth Amendment right. "I'd rather not answer that; I might incriminate myself," Tennes said, over and over. Landis was thoroughly irritated. Soon Darrow was advising a flock of Mont's men, who would gather in his office in the morning before court to be taught, with varying success, how to take the Fifth.

"I must refuse to answer that question for fear of incriminating myself," Hank Troy told the judge. "You see, I've been retained by a lawyer."

Landis called Bud White, one of Troy's friends, to the stand.

"Do you know Troy?" the judge asked.

"Yes, sir," the man replied.

"What's his business?"

"I have to refuse to answer that . . . because I might incriminate him," White answered, and flushed when the spectators laughed.

"Bud, you can buy a great many things from a lawyer, but you can't buy that," Landis said.

"Well your honor, I can't tell you," White said. "I might incriminate . . . myself."

Landis had a long-standing disdain for Darrow. He thought he was "smart and tricky" and "a crook." When he asked Tennes how he could afford Darrow, the gambling czar said he'd pay the lawyer with money from his winnings.

"Don't do it," Landis told Tennes. "Don't give Mr. Darrow that money covered with dirt and slime, with the blood which has come from a lot of young fellows about this town who are being made criminals. See if you can't get some clean money." The judge's taunts, and the widespread coverage of his unsavory clientele, smudged Darrow's reputation. But his work saved Tennes and his bookies from jail.[2]

The next infamous addition to Darrow's roster of clients was Oscar De Priest, an African American alderman who ran the South Side's Black Belt for the Thompson-Lundin machine.

Like many black citizens of the city, De Priest was a refugee from the South. He made his way to the Midwest as a laborer and bookkeeper and amassed a tidy fortune in real estate. He was the first black man to serve on the city council, where he introduced a measure to grant civil rights to his constituents. It was not well received. Race relations were "as nearly perfect as human nature will permit," the *Tribune* assured its readers, three years before the devastating race riot of 1919 tore the city apart. "Thoughtful Negroes know this."

In 1917, De Priest was snared by state's attorney Maclay Hoyne, a crime buster conducting an Ahab-like pursuit of Thompson. Hoyne's men raided City Hall, hauled off files, and sought a warrant to arrest the chief of police. A police captain testified that "vice conditions have flourished unchecked in the riotous cafes of the black belt" with "black men and white women, and white men and black women" indulging in "unspeakable orgies" between "midnight and dawn, drinking and dancing indecent dances." Few were surprised. On the sidewalks of south State Street "midnight was like day," the poet Langston Hughes wrote. "The street was full of workers and gamblers, prostitutes and pimps, church folks and sinners." But Henry "Teenan" Jones, a black nightclub owner, was pressured into testifying and told how De Priest collected payoffs in return for delivering protection from the police.

De Priest arrived at the Criminal Courts Building in a limousine, escorted by notables from the South Side. Preachers, businessmen, and women's clubs supported him, for the city's black community, knowing the corruption that existed at all levels of Chicago society, wondered why their leader had been singled out. He too hired Darrow. In court, Darrow described De Priest as a little guy, being boxed around by the big men who ran things in Chicago. Yes, he got payments from Jones and others, but they were campaign contributions, De Priest told the jury. The allegations against him were the concoctions of his political enemies. He might have used his clout to intimidate a few street cops, but he had no pull at police headquarters. "Gambling is a horrible crime," Darrow drawled. "Why doesn't our industrious state's attorney attack it in the women's clubs, where they play bridge and whist for money and prizes?"

The jury took seven hours to acquit De Priest. In 1928, he was elected to Congress and became the first black man to serve in the House since Reconstruction.[3]

HOYNE WAS FURIOUS but persevered. And obtaining the indictment and resignation of his next target—Police Chief Charles Healey—was a notable accomplishment. The chief was charged with taking $1,000 a month in graft from the poolrooms, brothels, and saloons. The state had incriminating records seized from City Hall, and wiretap transcripts of Healey's phone conversations. Among the prosecution witnesses was Tom Costello, the chief's bagman, who agreed to testify in return for leniency. Healey had been on the take, said Costello, since 1898. They had manufactured evidence, sold protection, and auctioned off promotions to crooked cops. It looked like a rock-solid case.

Healey was a stand-up guy and refused to implicate Thompson. On the witness stand, he claimed to not remember things. "My client stated some things that were not correct," Darrow was compelled to explain. "I deny that he lied."

The defense was based on equal portions of cynicism and sentiment. Healey was no mastermind, Darrow told the jury, just a flawed cop who had tried to keep his head above the waters of corruption. The chief was frail and old, and had a modest home and a blind, devoted wife. He was a victim of the political rivalry between Hoyne and Thompson. Costello was the real schemer, framing Healey to save his own hide. Why, the chief's miserable performance on the stand was proof, said Darrow, that Healey was not bright enough to organize a grafting ring.

"The state has told you he was a poor witness, and he was," said Darrow. "Costello was a good witness; one of the cleverest."

"I . . . confess that if I were mayor of this city, and knowing Healey as well as I know him now, I wouldn't make him chief of police," said Darrow. "It takes a clever man to be chief of police and keep out of jail—and this man is a child in the hands of Costello."

The trial was a sensation, with the kinds of twists that lent defense attorneys "an aura of sulfur," said lawyer Charles Erbstein, who worked with Darrow for the defense. There is no ready contemporary record that Darrow, as was said in the years after his death, would insert a thin piece of wire in a cigar to have jurors focus on the long, dangling accumulation of ash instead of the prosecution or its witnesses. But Erbstein accomplished much the same thing, with a broken watch that took endless noisy winding.

In the end, it was pathos that carried the day. "In poor man's suit, baggy pants, floppy jacket, stringy tie," Darrow "sang his song of humanity to the jurors," Ben Hecht recalled.

"Mr. Healey is old, broken physically and mentally," Darrow told the jury. "He has labored under a strain the last few months such has sent other men to the insane asylum, suicide, or drink." The state's attorney's tactics were what should be condemned, not Healey, Darrow told the jurors. They shouldn't, just couldn't, send the poor old cop to prison for a few venial sins, for succumbing to temptations such as all men do. This was Chicago.

Hundreds who braved a winter storm heard Darrow ask the jury to deal with Healey as you wish others to deal with you at the grave and serious times of your life. It was sentimental slush. And it worked. After eight weeks of testimony, the jury set Healey and his codefendants free. The chief cried and trembled after hearing the verdict and embraced Darrow. "My one thought now is to get home to my wife and sit with her by the fireside," Healey told the press, in character to the end.

"The verdict in this trial was a mighty big surprise," Hoyne grumbled.

Hoyne must have thought back to the Healey verdict—and Darrow's machinations in the McNamara trial—when the state unearthed a conspiracy to bribe jurors in the next big corruption case. Francis Becker, a chief examiner for the Civil Service Commission, was defended by Darrow after being charged with shaking down saloons and whorehouses. In May 1918, a jury acquitted him. A few weeks later Hoyne charged the jury foreman and two other men with soliciting bribes. No money was passed and there was no evidence that Darrow knew anything about it, but he felt the need to reassure Paul. "You may be absolutely sure there isn't the slightest thing in it," Darrow wrote his son.

Hoyne was now 0 for 3 against Darrow but finally prevailed when a jury convicted William Miller, a Thompson man in the governor's cabinet, for selling the answers to licensing exams to unqualified doctors and pharmacists. There was a limit, after all, to Chicago's cynicism. Even with the answers, some of the quacks had failed the test.[4]

"Law and the pursuit of . . . justice leave but few illusions," said Erbstein.[5]

DARROW HAD BEEN paid a $1,000 retainer and $100 a day in the Healey case. The firm was grossing $100,000 a year. He was back. "Am called for everywhere and by all kinds of people, from preachers and bankers and governors—up to . . . burglars," he told Paul. His work for the Thompson-Lundin gang was interspersed with his speaking tours on behalf of the war effort, defense of communists in the Red Scare, learning to drive a car, his first ride in a "Flying Machine," and a palette of clients whose cases offered a taste of Chicago in the Jazz Age.[6]

Joseph Weil, aka the "Yellow Kid," was a debonair con man with a Van Dyke beard and a knack for persuading people to give him their money. His biggest score was said to have been for $250,000, from a swindle in which he and his confederates created a phony stock brokerage, complete with tickers, secretaries, and receptionists. In another variation, they rented a building and got dozens of pals to pose as the customers and employees of a busy bank, with stacks of fake cash, a line of tellers, and—a nice touch—printed stationery and deposit slips. The Kid apologized repeatedly as he and his mark waited to see the "bank manager," but the bustle convinced the victim that this was a well-run financial establishment. The man handed over $50,000, and was flummoxed when he returned and found an empty building.

But not even Darrow could save Weil when he was caught posing as a mining engineer for Standard Oil and swindling a Fort Wayne banker out of $15,000. While awaiting trial on that charge, Weil and his pals took another Indianan for $110,000. Their photographs were carried across the country and soon men from all over—a Michigan doctor, a Montana rancher, a banker from Wyoming—who valued their money more than their dignity showed up in Chicago, claiming to have been fleeced.

"I am not holding up my client as a saint," Darrow told the jury, in something of an understatement. But of the victims, Darrow said: "All these men were out for a pot of gold . . . I don't see any reason for wasting sympathy."

The jury saw it differently. The Kid went off to Joliet in style, with a diamond stickpin in his cravat, a Killarney green overcoat, tan shoes, and an emerald velour hat "of gay and rakish tilt," the papers noted.[7]

Darrow maintained his practice of defending heartbroken individuals, rich and poor, whose love affairs led them into conflict with each other or the law. He got hefty fees for handling messy divorces or probate cases for heirs to the Cole circus, McCormick reaper, and Rockefeller oil fortunes. And his defense of George Munding, the "riding master to the city's uptown society," earned front-page coverage.

Munding, believing his fiancée was unfaithful, had shot and killed her as she stood outside the paddock of her riding academy in Hillsdale. "Picture this poor man," Darrow told the jury, "as one adrift in a rowboat on the sea of elemental emotion. The sea overwhelmed him, as it has overwhelmed many another, and he sank. He was a poor, helpless victim of environment and heredity and the passion that has driven men mad since Cleopatra's day." Munding dodged the hangman, and received a prison term.

And then there was Emma Simpson, who smuggled a revolver into a Chicago courtroom, pulled it from the folds of her dress, and shot her adulterous husband four times as they quarreled over their impending divorce.

Spectators screamed. The judge gaped. A bailiff threw his arms around Ms. Simpson.

"You've killed him!" screamed the court reporter.

"I hope so," Emma said.

Later, she smiled for the newspaper photographers. "My life has been besmirched," she told the press. "I have always loved . . . Elmer, and he has always repaid me with faithlessness."

Simpson was the niece of a streetcar magnate and could afford to retain Darrow. The city waited as Elmer lingered, for a month, on his deathbed. "I guess I nagged her too much," he told his doctors. When at last he expired, the state charged Emma with murder and said it hoped to hang her.

Emma showed up in court for her trial, "attired in the customary subdued though fetching raiment of the feminine defendant—plain linen frock, white pumps and sable sailor" hat, one of the newspaper sob sisters wrote. Darrow announced that Emma was temporarily insane. Friends and family members told of her erratic behavior. And Emma did her part. When the prosecutor introduced the handgun as evidence Emma stood, screamed "Take it away!" and, after a dramatic pause, certain that every eye in the courtroom was upon her, collapsed to the floor.

Darrow employed an "honor defense"—telling the all-male jury that women, like men, should be excused by the unwritten law that forgave the killing of adulterers. Ladies, after all, were even more susceptible to emotion. "Women will take a bunch of old love letters, tied with faded ribbon, and relive an early romance," Darrow said. "To men an old romance would be dust and ashes."

Why, the shooting "was a crazy act," said Darrow. "Does it seem to you, gentlemen, that a person in his or her right mind would pick out a court, a temple of justice, where a dozen persons are gathered, to do a murder?" he asked the jury. Darrow could not resist: "It is not only murder but . . . contempt of court."

Well, you can't convict a pretty woman for murder in Cook County, especially for bumping off a cheating louse like Elmer. The jury took half an hour to find Emma innocent. She spent fifty-one days in a mental hospital and was given her freedom.

The good people were outraged. "Sentimentality is lawless. The disease in America is endemic," the editors at the *Tribune* sputtered. "We need some drastic moral therapy."[8]

THE GOOD TIMES rolled on. Darrow was adding to his near-perfect record of saving clients from the death penalty. If he could not persuade a judge or a jury he'd keep at it, and prevail with an appeal or a pardon.

And so George Vogel, a cheap hood who shot a police sergeant in the back one night at Paddy the Bear's saloon, escaped death row when Darrow persuaded the jury that his client acted in self-defense. When troubled Reinhold Faust was caught lighting a bomb in an opera house, an act that he believed would end America's war with Germany and convince a bank to give him $100,000, Darrow reached a deal with the prosecutors to get him psychiatric treatment. J. Ellsworth Griffin was acquitted, in one of the briefest murder trials in Cook County history, after Darrow argued that Griffin had, in a drunken argument, pulled the trigger while wrestling for a pistol with his business partner.

In a case that spurred headlines across America, Darrow got the courts to rule that Emily Strutynsky was insane when she gunned down her parish priest at confession. She had knelt at her confessor's feet in the guise of a penitent, pulled out her gun, shot him through the mouth, chased him around the altar, firing until he fell, and hurdled his body in her bid to escape before being tackled by two female parishioners. The congregation was making preparations to lynch her when the police arrived at the church. Darrow got her sent to an asylum. Four years later, she escaped the grounds, hurled herself into the Kankakee River, and drowned.

In 1920, a gang of gunsels tried to rob the State Exchange Bank in Culver, Indiana. The townfolk responded and met the bandits with a volley of bullets. One Hoosier was fatally wounded in the shoot-out. Four robbers were caught, and charged with capital murder. Darrow agreed to defend them. The trial was conducted in rural Warsaw, where crowds flocked to the courthouse with picnic baskets. Men stood on stepladders to peer through the court windows, and there were fistfights over seats. "This is no vaudeville," the judge lectured the spectators. "I never saw such a crazy crowd. You are completely off your base, people."

Darrow played the humanist. "These boys, not one of them intended to kill," Darrow said. "They intended to rob. Their moral guilt is fixed by their intent."

The jury found them guilty but spared their lives. "I went down to a small town in Indiana to defend four young fellows who tried to get money out of a bank without having deposited any," Darrow told Mary. "I worked ten days to save their lives—nothing else—and the jury did it—much to the regret of the whole community."[9]

Ends generally outweighed means in Chicago, and Darrow's success returned him to high standing. For his sixty-first birthday, Darrow was given another banquet in his honor, by a far more prosperous and notable crowd than the preachers and radical lawyers who had welcomed him back from Los Angeles five years earlier.

Carl Sandburg was among those who spoke. There was a "big honesty of shiftiness about Darrow," said the poet, with the insight into the city and its sons that made him famous. "There are times when you cannot be right without being shifty. And this faculty of his, the power of being . . . everything in general and nothing in particular, just about hits him off."

Then the poet read a verse in tribute.

Let the nanny-goats and the billy-goats of the shanty people eat the clover over my grave.
And if yellow hair, or any blue smoke of flowers is good enough to grow over me, let the dirty-fisted children of the shanty people pick those flowers.
I have had my chance to live with the people who have too much and the people who have too little, and I chose one of the two and I have told no man why.

"On the whole the years have passed rapidly," Darrow said when it came his time to speak. "So quickly have they sped that I hardly realize that so many have been checked off." There was rheumatism to remind him, and "the Lord never seemed to know much about teeth," Darrow said. A dentist had manufactured a complex bridge for him, he confided, with four false teeth. "These new ones do good work," he said. "They never hurt me. I generally wear them in my pocket. . . .

"The fact is, age does not necessarily bring wisdom; it may here and there bring caution, but not always that," he told the crowd. Man's awful cruelty dismayed him. Life's meaninglessness saddened him. The sensualists had it right. "Neither the old nor the young can live long without pleasure . . . The denial of this is death or worse than death," said Darrow. "I could never resist temptation . . . Why live without joy?"

He closed on a serious note.

"I have lived a life in the front trenches, looking for trouble," he said.

"The front trenches are disagreeable; they are hard; they are dangerous; it is only a question of days or hours when you are killed or wounded and taken back. But it is exciting. You are living; and if now and then you go back to rest, you think of your comrades in the fight; you hear the drum; you hear the cannon's voice; you hear the bugle call; and you rush back to the trenches and to the thick of the fight. There, for a short time, you really live. It is hard, but it is life.

"This is life . . . to play the game, to play the cards we get; play them uncomplainingly and play them to the end. The game may not be worth the while. The stakes may not be worth the winning. But the playing of the game is the forgetting of self, and we should be game sports and play it bravely to the end."[10]

MAURICE "MOSSY" ENRIGHT was one game sport who played it bravely to the end, which came on the night when, on the street in front of his home, he was riddled with bullets in a gangland slaying. Enright was a convicted murderer, labor racketeer, and union enforcer. His motto was "Spare the rod and you'll spill the beans."

"Moss slugged and shot and intrigued his way into prominence where prominence comes hard," the *Daily News* said. "But last night it was his turn . . . as he was stepping out of his new swell automobile to enter his new swell home for dinner."

Enright was a man of many friends—five thousand showed up for the gangland funeral—and enemies. When the police rounded up the "usual suspects," the count exceeded fifty. Among those interrogated were Timothy "Big Tim" Murphy, former legislator, president of the gas workers union, and onetime Enright protégé; Michael "Dago Mike" Carozzo, the leader of the street sweepers' union; and Vincenzo "Sunny Jim" Cosmano—all members of a labor faction that had been feuding with the deceased. Carozzo asked to remain in his cell when two hot-blooded women, both claiming to be his wife, and previously unknown to each other, arrived to bail him out. The police were fortunate when young James Vinci, paling at the sight of the noose, confessed to driving the murder car and named the three as the killers.

Darrow knew them all. The Irish-born Enright was a union man who had worked, for a time, as an investigator for Erbstein. Murphy was an old friend of Mont Tennes and a veteran goon from the bone-breaking days of the Hearst circulation wars. Cosmano, who was named by Vinci as the triggerman, hired Darrow to serve as his lawyer. State's attorney Hoyne's chief foe was delay. Over time, witnesses in Chicago had a way of vanishing. And when Darrow kept asking for continuances (as he was then defending Lloyd and the local communists) the newspapers raged. But the courts agreed to the postponement and, sure enough, the witnesses went away. The big men were freed. Only Vinci was convicted of Mossy's murder, and his conviction was overturned on appeal.

The Enright assassination marked "the beginning of a new epoch in the evolution of the Chicago underworld," the *Tribune*'s Philip Kinsley wrote. Ruthlessness had replaced honor. There were no "more or less courageous gun battles and fights in barrooms," said Kinsley. "The scene shifts from this time on to the ways of the stealthy Sicilians, the hired gunmen who followed their victims for weeks, if necessary, shooting with sawed-off shotguns from automobiles into the back of an unsuspecting man."

Cosmano and Murphy prospered, but only for a time. Sunny Jim was shot in the gut in a tussle with Big Jim Colosimo's gang, which in turn became (after Colosimo was gunned down one night in the lobby of his café) Johnny Torrio's and Al Capone's "Outfit." And the tall, well-tailored Big Tim, though he seemed to live a charmed life, eventually met Mossy's fate. He answered the door one night and was machine-gunned on the steps of his home at the age of forty-two, leaving a meager estate of $1,000. "He had always been a good spender," his widow sighed philosophically.[11]

IN JANUARY 1920, the good people triumphed, and the United States began its thirteen-year experiment with Prohibition. Darrow had opposed the temperance movement for decades, as a matter of good business, since he represented various beer and liquor interests, and conviction, as an intrusion on personal freedom. "A man would be better off without booze, but the same is true of pie," he told audiences.

The ban on alcoholic beverages was supposed to correct human behavior and curb crime. It did just the opposite. Speakeasies flourished, smugglers made fortunes, people kept drinking, and Americans lost respect for law. The trade in illicit liquor was staggeringly lucrative, sustaining organized crime and breeding crops of gangsters who stippled the streets with gunfire. "You can hardly be surprised at the boys killing each other. The business pays very well, but it is outside the law and they can't go to court like shoe dealers or real estate men or grocers when they think an injustice has been done them or unfair competition has arisen in their territory," Darrow said. "So they shoot."

Given his philosophical leanings, Darrow had no qualms about defending the bootleggers—even killers like Bugs Moran, Frank McErlane, Terry Druggan, Frankie Lake, George "Red" Barker, and William "Three-fingered Jack" White. But his willingness to serve such villains dismayed his admirers. He was called a "pitiable spectacle" by federal judge Evan Evans, who said that the "dangling purse" of the rumrunners had ruined a great lawyer.

Darrow suffered defeat in the trial of Michael "Mike de Pike" Heitler and his confederates, who were convicted of buying some of the remaining stock of proscribed bourbon from the Old Grand Dad distillery, selling it to speakeasies in Chicago, and having corrupt friends on the police force steal it back in bogus "raids." His next clients were more respectable—wealthy Chicagoans who were offered the leftover inventory of the Grommes & Ullrich distillery if they purchased "shares" in the business. Several bought hundreds of cases for their basements. "Your honor, a bootlegger is one who professionally buys or sells liquor," Darrow told the judge. "The defendants . . . were not professionals." Hoarding liquor was a universal custom for those who liked a snort. "Don't you know that hundreds of Chicago families have as much as $30,000 or $40,000 worth of liquor in their cellars?" Darrow asked. None of the defendants was convicted.[12]

Occasionally, Darrow's success would have tragic repercussions. Joseph Kyle, a wealthy Realtor, left the mob-owned Derby Cafe in the early morning hours with a couple of pals and three young women who were variously described as "dancers" or "cabaret girls." His racy Templar speedster careened through Chicago before caroming into a farm truck, killing the aged driver, C. C. Hudson. When the police arrived at the scene, Kyle tried to bribe them.

A coroner's jury cleared Kyle of wrongdoing and the state's attorney stepped in, suspecting that the Colosimo gang had corrupted the inquiry. Kyle hired Darrow, whose closing argument—that his client had spent most of the night in question washing his yacht—somehow failed to win the jury's sympathy. Kyle was sentenced to the penitentiary, but freed after Darrow persuaded a judge to overturn the verdict as part of a negotiated settlement in which Hudson's family received $12,500.

"Well," Darrow told reporters, "everybody seems to be satisfied." Not everyone. Five years later, after another all-night tour of roadhouses with a young lady, Kyle crashed into a milk wagon, critically injuring another innocent driver.[13]

Some of Darrow's gangland clients, like Murphy and Cosmano, had Runyonesque qualities. But the hellions of Rock Island, Illinois, were downright Gothic. For more than two decades, the warring factions filled the streets with bullets and bombs as the dead-eyed John Looney, in the guise of a newspaperman, sought to install himself as thane.

Looney was "the stormy petrel of Rock Island politics and journalism—an eccentric, brilliant man, posing as reformer and moralist, who kept the town in terror," said the *Tribune*. He ate raw liver, spread on soda crackers, and believed he had demonic protection. He ran whorehouses and speakeasies. Looney shot it out on a downtown street with a rival publisher, whose presses were dynamited. A few years later, he was hauled into City Hall and beaten by a corrupt rival—the mayor—as the police looked on. The next night a riotous mob incited by Looney besieged the police station. The governor had to send in the National Guard.

In 1922, Looney's son was killed when rival gangsters drove up in two automobiles and opened fire on a busy downtown street. "It's come," Looney shouted and ran for cover to a nearby doorway. His son pulled a pistol but wasn't fast enough. It is hard to see what motive lured Darrow to Rock Island to defend the men who killed Looney's boy, other than the $30,000 that reportedly was paid him. In any event, he couldn't do much for George "Crimps" Holsapple and Anthony Billburg and their accomplices. Darrow tried to play "the part of the grand old man, gentle in every respect," a newspaper reported. But the whole town had seen the attack, and the jury was not swayed.[14]

Darrow marked his seventh decade with some fine diversions. He took two months off in the summer of 1921 and retreated to Fish Creek, Wisconsin, to write a book on the causes of crime. He had been suffering from a digestive ailment and was told he might need surgery, but the rest seemed to cure him. In 1922, Darrow celebrated his sixty-fifth birthday by touring Europe and the Holy Land, traveling across Canada to visit Paul and his family in Colorado, and wintering in Florida. He attended World Series games and, in 1923, in the middle of a trial, took off on a junket to the Kentucky Derby.

Darrow joined in the effort to kill the proposed new Illinois constitution, which called, among other things, for Bible reading in public schools. He wrote an article for H. L. Mencken's magazine, the *American Mercury*, on the "ordeal of Prohibition" and spoke out against the city health board's new regulations on venereal disease, which allowed its inspectors to arrest and publicly stigmatize the infected. And he and Ruby opened their apartment to Sinclair Lewis when the Nobel Prize–winning author visited Chicago to conduct research for his novel *Arrowsmith*. "When many people imagine I'm in a secret and sinister conference with the Reds, or indignantly fighting the censorship of burlesque show posters . . . or lecturing with a flushed face on capital punishment," Darrow told editor George Nathan, "what I'm really doing—and having a grand time doing it—is getting a lot of friends over to my house in Chicago and reading aloud to them."[15]

Then, at sixty-six, Darrow returned to the arena for the biggest political corruption trial yet. The prosecutors in the state's attorney's office had worked their way up the ladder and nailed Lundin himself. The Chicago school board was the venue for his larceny. He and the boys demanded kickbacks for just about everything that it purchased: land, buses, boilers, doors, insurance, furniture, coal—even lightbulbs.

The "Poor Swede," as he was known, was a goggle-eyed salesman of patent medicines who had risen through Republican ranks to become a master political strategist and a congressman. The newspapers called him "the silent power" behind Thompson and "the long-recognized czar" of city and state politics. "To hell with the public," Lundin said, when one school board member questioned the size of a kickback on textbooks. "We are at the trough now and we are going to feed."

Lundin was done in by a double cross. In 1920, to get rid of Maclay Hoyne, the Thompson-Lundin team had promoted the candidacy of Robert Crowe, a young judge, for state's attorney. Crowe replaced Hoyne but almost immediately turned on his benefactors, and Lundin and a dozen cronies were indicted.

Darrow's liberal allies were distressed by his willingness to defend a chiseler like Lundin. It was then that his old friend from Hull House came to his office and demanded to know why he took such clients. "I said that I had fought for many things that her people believed in but I had never seen the time that one of them had sent me a case where there was a fee," he told Mary. "They had sent poor men to me, that no one else would look after, but if one had money they sent them to a respectable lawyer. . . .

"Any how," he wrote, "it never occurred to me that I should refuse to defend anyone. All I care about is the hard work . . . it is awful to have nothing to do but to think . . . It is better to love money, and try to get it."

The trial was a long humiliation for Lundin. The prosecutors portrayed him as corrupt, and his lawyers cast him as a dupe. With his shrugs and quips, Darrow created an atmosphere of "sympathy and amused tolerance," wrote the *Tribune*'s Kinsley. But Darrow's cross-examinations were fierce, unearthing the motives of the prosecution's witnesses. The case was nothing but a "political persecution," Darrow said.

And, indeed, the evidence tying Lundin to the scams was thin. Day after day, as temperatures soared, the prosecutors offered evidence that the school board overpaid its suppliers. But "the supposed captain of this piratical ship is mentioned so seldom in the evidence that it is hard to remember that he is the chief defendant," the *Tribune* admitted. Thompson flew back from a Hawaiian vacation to testify for the defense. And Lundin took the stand, speaking directly to the jurors, denying wrongdoing. Darrow closed for the defense.

The prosecution's case, he said, was all "cobwebs, doubt, mystery, haze . . . a weird, intangible composite, a mythical nothing," said Darrow. Prosecutors take the scent like hunting dogs. Politicians claw for power. Lawyers twist the truth. "We all do it," Darrow told the jury. "I am too honest to tell you that I'm not dishonest." But this was different. "I never knew Lundin until I came into this case. I am not going to tell you he is the best man I ever saw. I don't know. Some men fool you," Darrow said. But "I heard his story here. He never once hedged, sidestepped or ran away. He met his accusers face to face."

The jurors ordered lunch, and cigars, and returned not-guilty verdicts for Lundin and his fourteen codefendants. "Shouts burst from a hundred throats" as the verdicts were read, wrote Kinsley. "Men climbed on chairs and yelled. Women cried."

"What's the matter with Lundin?" someone shouted, and the boys chanted the customary response: "He's all right!"

The reporters gathered around. "Truth crushed to earth will rise again," Lundin told them. Then he turned to his weeping wife and said, "C'mon, kid. Let's go home."[16]

Thompson, wounded by the scandals, decided not to run for reelection.[17] But Crowe, smarting from his loss in the Lundin trial, soon had a case that, he was certain, even Darrow could not win.

Chapter 17

LOEB AND LEOPOLD

But fetch the county kerchief, and noose me in the knot.

Of the infamous villains whom Darrow defended, none were so patently evil in the eyes of Americans as the teenaged killers Nathan Leopold and Richard Loeb. They were spoiled geniuses—rich kids who claimed no God but Self and insisted, by virtue of their intellectual primacy, on living free from any moral code. They were homosexuals. They were Jews. They kidnapped and murdered a child whose body, the state alleged, was molested before and after death. They did it, they said, for the thrill. In the course of their trial came hints of other grisly offenses they were said to have committed—abduction, murder, mutilation. Leopold and Loeb were truly heartless fiends.

And celebrities. Once Loeb and Leopold were captured, newspapers across the country relentlessly pumped the story of the wealthy thrill killers. Crowds cheered them and girls swooned at the sight of handsome Dickie Loeb, with his hair slicked back like Valentino. Ruby Darrow thought they were "adorable." Thousands of people tried to get seats in the courtroom, pushing against a line of police and tearing a door from its hinges. It was another "crime of the century," with the riddle not whodunit—but why.

"Babe" Leopold was nineteen, the scion of a rich shipping and manufacturing family, a University of Chicago law student about to transfer to Harvard. He was short and slight and brilliant, a promising ornithologist and linguist. "Dickie" Loeb was eighteen, the youngest graduate in the history of the University of Michigan. His father was a wealthy lawyer and executive at Sears, Roebuck. Dickie was taller, better looking, and charming.

The two young men, with their stylish suits, luxury automobiles, and pompadours, had been handed every opportunity that a fulsome nation, victorious in war and awash in prosperity, could give them. And so the death of fourteen-year-old Bobby Franks, the boy from their Kenwood neighborhood whom they lured into a car and bludgeoned and strangled in May 1924, became an emblem of modern times.

The postwar era had brought fast girls and cars, hip flasks, and speak-easies. The Franks murder "stirred in everybody a shivering suspicion that the kind of civilization that we have set up is producing more problems than we can handle," said the editors at *Life* magazine. Here was the fruit of surrender to sensation. Here, said respectable folk, is where the teachings of Darwin and Freud and Einstein—where moral relativity, science, and atheism—must lead. Leopold "denies any feeling of remorse," the defense psychiatrists noted. "He states that he has no feeling of having done anything morally wrong as he doesn't feel that there is any such thing as morals . . . Anything which gives him pleasure is right."

"I did it because I wanted to," said Loeb.[1]

THEY HAD BEEN drawn to each other as precocious undergraduates—sixteen and fifteen years old—at the University of Chicago. Both had been raised by cold and distant parents and abused by governesses. Loeb needed no justification for his acts, but Leopold had constructed an elaborate rationale. He was a weakling and socially inept—it was one reason he idolized Dickie, the frat man and garrulous carouser. To console himself, Leopold fell back on his intellectual superiority. He had studied Nietzsche, who proposed that superior individuals were exempt from the rules constraining the average man. He and Loeb, Babe decided, were beings of just that sort. They would show the world by committing the "perfect" crime.

But the Nietzschean "supermen" managed to drop Leopold's eyeglasses—with their distinctive frame—near the culvert where they hid Franks's body, in a nature preserve by the Indiana border. The police traced the spectacles and brought Leopold in for questioning. As a birdwatcher who regularly tramped the preserve, he had already emerged as a figure of interest. Babe told the prosecutors he had tripped on a hike and no doubt lost his glasses when they slipped from his breast pocket. But no matter how he threw himself to the floor, he could not re-create the accident—the eyeglasses stayed in his coat.

Two resourceful *Daily News* reporters, meanwhile, interviewed the members of Leopold's law school study group, obtained notes typed on Babe's Underwood typewriter, and matched them to the typing on a ransom note sent to the victim's family. And the Leopold family's chauffeur undermined the killers' alibi. In the early morning hours of Saturday, May 31, they confessed. For the next two days, Leopold and Loeb chatted freely with the detectives and newsmen who accompanied them on grisly scavenger hunts around town, as spectators gathered to watch. "They had a great day of it yesterday, and they responded to the trailing crowds' morbid interest by showing off in sophomoric fashion," the *News* reported. "They quarreled for the spotlight, aired their young eruditions, swaggered and posed before the worshipful Boswells, talked the cant of their intellectual set."

Here was the bridge over the Jackson Park lagoon, where they tossed the typewriter into the water. Here was the hardware store where they bought the murder weapons: a heavy chisel and some rope. Here was where they buried the bloody blanket that they had used to lug Bobby's body to its hiding place. The corpse lay in a foot of water for only a night before it was discovered by a passing workman in the first light of morning.

"We have a hanging case," Robert Crowe announced.[2]

THE CRIME HAD no overt allurement for Darrow. These defendants were young men of privilege, not underdogs. Besides, he was sixty-seven years old. But he was a ferocious foe of hanging, and then there was that fathomless empathy. When Darrow spoke at the Lincoln Center settlement house in Chicago that weekend he was no doubt thinking of the teenaged suspects when he chose to recite the A. E. Housman poem "The Culprit."

Housman's work was "thought, and it is poetry, and it is music," he told the crowd, then softly chanted:

The night my father got me
His mind was not on me;
He did not plague his fancy
To muse if I should be
The son you see.

The day my mother bore me
She was a fool and glad,
For all the pain I cost her,
That she had borne the lad
That borne she had.

My mother and my father
Out of the light they lie;
The warrant would not find them,
And here 'tis only I
Shall hang so high.

Oh let not man remember
The soul that God forgot
But fetch the county kerchief
And noose me in the knot
And I will rot.

For so the game is ended
That should not have begun.
My father and my mother
They had a likely son,
And I have none.

The newspapers had aroused the good folks of Chicago with the ghastly news that Bobby Franks was the victim of a pedophile. Darrow spoke, nonetheless, for compassion and understanding. "Sex . . . is the strongest and the deepest emotion of life excepting possibly one," he said. "And, its very strength and its very depth and its very eternity makes it one that often goes awry."

Character is just "a different tip of the balance one way or the other;

a little change in the elements," he told the audience. There but for the grace of God goes any man's beloved son.

That night the Darrows were awakened by the doorbell. As Ruby later told it, she got up from bed and found "four men seeming like masked desperados, clutching at their upturned coat-collars . . . forcing themselves forward." It was a delegation from the boys' families, led by Jacob Loeb, Dickie's uncle. They crowded into Darrow's bedroom and pressed him to take the case.[3]

Darrow knew Loeb. He also knew Jacob Franks, the father of the victim, a former pawnbroker who had grown rich, in part, by the money he made buying John Altgeld's shares in the Ogden Gas deal. And Darrow knew, without doubt, that he would be bucking the mob. But he persuaded himself that the youths were "kindly" and the victims of "strange and unfortunate circumstances." In his account of the trial in his memoirs, he would slice a year off their ages. He took the case, agreeing to serve with Benjamin and Walter Bachrach, the Loeb family lawyers.

"I went in to do what I could, for sanity and humanity," Darrow recalled. He viewed the case as a vehicle with which to assault America's treatment of crime, and in particular its use of capital punishment. And he certainly looked forward to getting paid by two wealthy families. "I will of course get a fair and substantial fee," he told Paul. "The families are fine people and will do what is right."[4]

AND SO LEOPOLD and Loeb met their lawyer. "My first impression was horror," Leopold recalled. "On the other side of the bars stood one of the least . . . impressive-looking human beings I have ever seen.

"The day was warm and Darrow was wearing a light seersucker jacket," said Leopold. "Only this one looked as if he had slept in it. His shirt was wrinkled, too, and he must have had eggs for breakfast that morning. I could see the vestiges. Or perhaps he hadn't changed shirts since the day before. His tie was askew . . . and his unruly shock of lusterless, almost mousey hair kept falling over his right eye. Impatiently he'd brush it back with his hand . . . He looked for all the world like an innocent hayseed, a bumpkin. . . .

"Could this scarecrow know anything about the law?" Leopold asked himself. "He didn't look as if he knew much of anything!"

The killers had seen to it that the prosecution had the requisite evidence to hang them. Their only apparent course was a plea of not guilty by reason of insanity. Yet the two young men had lived lucid lives for months, made plans for summer vacation, socialized with friends and family, and displayed no signs of craziness as they carried out minute preparations to collect a $10,000 ransom. Once in custody, they had spoken frankly and intelligently—arrogantly, in fact—about their deeds to the state's prosecutors and psychiatrists, and explicitly rejected any notion that they were ill.

The defendants were arraigned and pled not guilty. The case was set for arguments on July 21 and trial on August 4. "Never did I have a more hectic life," Darrow recalled. His apartment was crammed with legal and medical experts. "This case is quite perplexing, and will most likely be a hard struggle to save the lives of the boys," he told Jessie.[5]

As the trial approached, Darrow became convinced that his clients would do best to embrace a time-honored tradition: to offer a plea of guilty and throw themselves on the mercy of the court. In Chicago there was precedent for treating young criminals mercifully: no teenaged killer who pled guilty to murder had ever been executed. If Dickie and Babe were stockyard toughs who had killed a neighborhood boy and confessed, Crowe would almost certainly have cut a deal to clear the case, and sent the pair away for life.

The problem was finding someone to accept the plea. Crowe would not: he was running for reelection that year, and his office was working overtime to keep the city frenzied. Nor could Darrow wager that a jury would be merciful to his monsters. That left the judge. Darrow had known the sixty-three-year-old John Caverly for decades, since the jurist was a lawyer for the Democratic machine, giving Hinky Dink Kenna and Bathhouse John advice in the First Ward. "Johnny is a good boy," Kenna had told former mayor Carter Harrison Jr. "He ain't shanty-Irish. He comes from good people, has an education, is a good lawyer and is clean. That is what we want him to be." Even after he became a judge, Caverly was a fixture at the raucus First Ward balls, and when the mobster Big Jim Colosimo was gunned down in 1920, Caverly served as an honorary pallbearer.

Darrow saw Caverly as "kindly and discerning in his views of life"—a Catholic whose sympathies might lead him to spare the defendants. The defense would present an array of medical testimony, Darrow decided, but not to a jury. He would offer it to Caverly as mitigating evidence. It was a rare strategy, but Darrow had employed it to save lives before. "Boys, we are going to ask you to do something that may strike you as very strange," Darrow told Loeb and Leopold, swearing them to secrecy. "It's the only way . . . We're going to plead you guilty."[6]

On July 21, Darrow was recognized to offer what motions he might make. "It is unnecessary to say that this case has given us many perplexities and sleepless nights," he said, speaking softly. "We want to state frankly here that no one in this case believes that these defendants should be released. We believe they should be permanently isolated from society, and if we as lawyers thought differently, their families would not permit us to do otherwise."

The reporters leaned forward to catch every word. What was he up to? Darrow reached under his jacket and tucked his thumbs in his suspenders. He tossed his shoulders back. "After long reflection and thorough discussion we have determined to make a motion in this court . . . to withdraw our plea of not guilty and enter a plea of guilty," Darrow said.

Reporters dashed for telephones. A bailiff called for order as the spectators voiced their shock. Loeb and Leopold seemed indifferent—Darrow had broken the news that morning—but Jacob Loeb, head bowed, was weeping. Nathan Leopold Sr. sat stiffly, lost in pain.

"Your honor," Darrow told Caverly, "we dislike to throw this burden upon this court, or any court. We know its seriousness and its gravity, but a court can no more shirk responsibilities than attorneys. And, while we wish it could be otherwise, we feel that it must be as we have chosen. . . .

"The statute provides that evidence may be offered in mitigation of the punishment, and we shall ask at such time as the court may direct that we may be permitted to offer evidence as to the mental condition of these young men, to show the degree of responsibility they had and also to offer evidence as to the youth of these defendants and the fact of a plea of guilty as further mitigation," said Darrow. "With that we throw ourselves upon the mercy of this court and this court alone."

It was, said the *Daily News*, "a sensational turnabout."

"If these boys were poor, I am confident I could get a verdict of acquittal," Darrow said, working the reporters who gathered around him after court was adjourned. "Their wealth is a tremendous handicap." He saw the need to relieve the pressure on Caverly, and so Darrow had the Loeb and Leopold families issue a public statement. They would not use their money "to stage an unsightly legal battle . . . in an attempt to defeat justice," they promised. "There will be no large sums of money spent, either for legal or medical talent."[7]

"You have no doubt been surprised at the turn we have taken in the Loeb-Leopold case," Darrow wrote Paul. "We have concluded it is the most hopeful way of saving the boys' lives." But his expectations were low. "It is doubtful if any way will accomplish it," Darrow told his son. "The papers have been so rotten that the feeling runs high."[8]

IN THE MIDST of that chaotic summer, Mary Field Parton arrived. Her husband, Lem, had called upon his friends in journalism to get her what both hoped would be a career-boosting assignment.

"Left for Chicago on 20th Century. Full of hope!" she wrote in her diary on the train from New York. "Get a story from Darrow on this strange murder . . . Loeb and Leopold, rich boys, precocious, everything to live for—kill a little boy of 14, 'for the thrill' they say. Whole country, foreign countries, avid for news—for explanation . . . Darling Lem put this one for me."

Mary arrived in Chicago on June 17 with her nine-year-old daughter, Margaret, in tow and was welcomed by the "same old Darrow . . . chuckling at the human race whose elephant feet and ostrich head he so loathes—and pities." But her dreams of a big exclusive were misplaced. "Terribly disappointed," she wrote in her diary on June 20. "Darrow will not give me anything. Nor will he see my position. I too am employed . . . Oh hell—he is like all business men! Business first."

A few days later, Mary dined with Darrow, University of Chicago sociologist Ellsworth Faris, and "some dame friend of Darrow's." It was "a stupid, tiresome Babbitty affair," she told her diary. "Cheap, stale jokes! Soggy wit! Dull puns. Invited to a banquet and taken to a one-arm lunch counter!" She blamed the presence of Darrow's other dame. He was "at his worst when he is with two women," she wrote. "With one, his wisdom, his philosophy, his companionship is possible," but otherwise he "treats women as playmates rather than workmates."

Lem, in a letter, tried to cheer her up. "Don't be unhappy, Mary, about not turning up the big yarn. It was clearly understood that this was a short-end gamble, and it is understood that Darrow is in a position where it might be ruinous for him to play any favorite," he wrote. But as high as she had been on the journey to Chicago, Mary was that low returning to New York.

At some point, Ruby learned of the visit. As she remembered things, Mary had arrived with a suitcase, demanding access, and Darrow had ordered a bailiff to send the "bloodsucker" packing. "She had a mealy, insinuating and misleading manner," said Ruby. But unless Mary was lying to her diary—and recognizing Darrow's tendency to reach out for solace in the tension of a big trial—there was probably more to the visit than Ruby knew, or admitted.

At home in New York, Mary kept track of the case and worked to knit a magazine piece from the string she had collected. "Wise Darrow—of course no jury could try that case without prejudice . . . I'll bet the judge gives them life," she told her diary. "Wise saturnine Darrow."[9]

CAVERLY CALLED THE sentencing phase of the case to order on July 23. Like many of the big trials in Darrow's career, it took place in sweltering weather. The sixth-floor courtroom was tightly packed, and a few electric fans gave meager relief. Pillars blocked the view of many spectators. Still, hundreds of people were turned away, and out-of-town reporters begged for the little pink ticket, signed by the judge, that would give them access. Young women, hoping to glimpse "Angel Face Dickie," as the Hearst papers called him, lingered for hours at the "bridge of sighs" that spanned the alley between the county jail and the Criminal Courts Building.

Leopold and Loeb smoked cigarettes, lighting one from another, as they waited to enter the courtroom. "Are you nervous?" someone asked Babe. "Do I look it?" he asked, with a raspy laugh. As the trial went on, the newspapers would describe the defendants' attitude as "chipper" and "debonair," "jaunty" and "facetious." Of the two killers, Loeb seemed slightly more worried. Leopold made plans to write a book before their hanging and was drafting the protocol for an experiment in which, after his body was hauled down from the gibbet, scientists could try to contact his spirit. He was certain they would fail.

Crowe opened the proceedings with a florid description of the wealthy ingrates who had committed such a repellent crime. The "cautious, crafty, cruel and vicious" youths had committed "the most cruel, cowardly, dastardly murder ever . . . in the annals of American jurisprudence," he said.

Because he could identify them, Bobby Franks was "struck four times over the head with this cold chisel," said Crowe, "and then the man in the back seat grabbed this little, fragile, dying, innocent boy and pulled him back, shoved a gag down his mouth . . . and so held him until life left this little fragile body."

The prosecutor was trying not so much to persuade Caverly as to keep the public pressure on him. That became abundantly clear when Crowe described how Leopold had boasted that his wealthy family could hire slick lawyers, bribe jurors, or "get a friendly judge" to evade justice. The prosecutor would return to the "friendly judge" comment time and again in the course of the trial. The implication was as evident as it was ugly: if Caverly was to rule in the boys' favor, it would be because he was bought by their families' wealth and influence.

The judge didn't like it, and Darrow, sensing that, responded. Crowe had displayed "poor grace" when giving a speech that "meant only to appeal to the passion of man," said Darrow, thumbs in his suspenders, rocking on his heels. It was a "lurid painting . . . made for nothing excepting that a hoarse cry of angry people may somehow reach these chambers." The defense would have objected, Darrow told Caverly, except that it knew the judge would disregard Crowe's tactics, and instead do "what is just, fair and merciful."

Indeed, Darrow was as cool as Crowe had been hot. He shoved his hands into his pants pockets, and gazed hard at the floor. It was all a matter of precedent, Darrow said. "We shall insist in this case, your Honor, that terrible as this is—that terrible as any killing is—it would be without precedent if two boys of this age should be hanged by the neck until dead," he said. "It would be without precedent . . . if on a plea of guilty this should be done."

The themes had been sung; what followed was adornment and elaboration. In the coming weeks, Crowe would call dozens of witnesses to illustrate, in detail, the horror of the crime. And Darrow would parry, call for calm, offer more palatable explanations for murder, and return, again and again, to the age of his two lost boys. "His arguments and pleadings had for their purpose the building up of an atmosphere in which the judge might feel justified in following a tradition, and the public would acquiesce," Victor Yarros said.

Crowe began the first day with the coroner, who described the victim's wounds. Then the prosecutor brought the boy's parents to the stand. It was the first time that the public had seen Flora Franks since her son's funeral. She was a figure of "listless sorrow . . . tragic and valiant . . . like some graven thing in mournful bronze," the *Tribune* said. Stoically, the parents identified the bits of clothing—a sock, a buckle, shoes—that Bobby had been wearing on the day he died.

Dickie Loeb marveled at his own cold heart. One would think, he said to himself, that this wrenching testimony would evoke some kind of sympathy. But "I did not have any feeling," he discovered. "There is nothing inside me."

When he was finished with the bereaved parents, Crowe summoned an army of detectives, doctors, tradesmen, maids, and other witnesses—thirty-three on the second day alone. A metal filing cabinet was carted into the courtroom, to contain all the evidence. Darrow decried the spectacle and, in all but a few cases, declined to cross-examine the state's witnesses. He did choose to grill the sixty-eighth person Crowe called to the stand—a police detective who claimed to have heard Leopold's boast about a friendly judge.

Darrow wheeled in his seat and demanded of Leopold: "Did you say that, Babe?"

"Hell no!" Leopold told him.

Darrow rose, swung his chair around, and leaned upon it. He pressed the detective for witnesses, notes, or other supporting evidence. Leopold could, by now, recognize when Darrow was shifting from "leonine" into "tiger" mode. When the copper hedged, Darrow pounced.

"Who was with you?"

"Nobody but he and I," the detective acknowledged.

"Did you make any memoranda on it?"

"Not at that time . . ."

"Mr. Officer," he said. "Don't you know that this story of yours in reference to a 'friendly judge' is a pure fabrication made for the purpose of intimidating this court?"[10]

On the morning of Monday, July 28, the *Herald Examiner* offered, with a banner front-page headline, the INSIDE STORY OF LOEB AND LEOPOLD; FIRST FULL REPORT OF ALIENISTS. The newspaper devoted six pages to a summary and excerpts of an eighty-thousand-word report prepared by Drs. Karl Bowman and H. S. Hulbert on the mental condition of the two defendants.

Most Americans, by 1924, were familiar with the plea of insanity—and generally willing to spare the life of a crazed wretch who, babbling or hallucinating, was found with a bloody instrument in hand. Many were fascinated by the theories of Freud, Jung, and other pathfinders of psychiatry. The themes that the trial explored—childhood and adolescence, juvenile delinquency, sexual identity, and the nature of evil—would be lasting preoccupations in twentieth-century America. Darrow released the report—and another by psychiatrist William Healy—so all the papers had the story.

As a boy, Nathan Leopold had been sexually abused by an ignorant and dominating nanny described by the doctors as "insane" and "oversexual in unusual ways." With a variety of threats and prurient inducements, she kept Babe from his family and friends, and taught him to lie and steal. Nathan's intellectual ability far outpaced his physical development, and at school he was scorned by his classmates as "Crazy Bird" or "Flea." He repressed the homosexual urges that stirred in puberty and, in doing so, crushed most other feelings in the process.

"While yet a child he began to strive to be the cold-blooded egocentric intellectualist, turning gradually . . . to a deliberate overthrowing and eliminating of God, conscience, sympathy, social responsibility and loyalty as being thoroughly unnecessary to him and unworthy of him," the psychiatrists wrote. The result was a pitiably soulless individual. "The split between the intellectual process and the emotional process is very striking." It was an "essential feature" of dementia praecox or, as it was now being called, schizophrenia.

Nathan's love for Richard Loeb was the one emotion he could not suppress. In fantasies, Leopold saw himself as a strong and handsome slave, willing to fight and die for a masterful king. In Loeb he found that master—a superior intellect like himself, but with the physical gifts that Nathan lacked. "It was a blind hero worship," Leopold told the doctors, and he wrote, many years later, that "my motive, so far as I can be said to have had one, was to please Dick." But the relationship was not all one-sided. In a crisis, the powerful slave could "take the reins," the experts said. And in some of his fantasies Nathan was a rapist.

Richard Loeb also had a "split personality," in which his intellectual capacity far exceeded his emotional maturity, which remained at the level of a child. He too had been coddled by an "insane" nanny—a "particularly repressive and jealous governess" who had "peculiar" ideas about sex and a "paranoid" fear of men, and so repressed her sexual urges. She coveted Dickie's love and, as he moved through puberty, kept him away from girlfriends and other boys his age. He had entered college at the age of fourteen before learning about sex.

To escape his nanny's strictures, Loeb became an accomplished liar, cheat, and petty thief. In his fantasies, he was a criminal mastermind, often beaten and imprisoned, but able to outwit his captors. He was obsessed with criminal behavior, stalking strangers and enlisting Nathan in acts of vandalism, auto theft, arson, and burglary. After killing Bobby Franks, Loeb had infiltrated the ranks of young reporters who were covering the crime and led them to scoops. Loeb was troubled at how his life had developed; unlike his friend, he contemplated suicide. But when asked if he could kill again, Loeb said yes. There was "nothing inside me" to prevent it, he told the doctors.

"There wasn't a sunnier, pleasanter, more likable fellow in the world," Leopold said. "His charm was magnetic—maybe mesmeric is the better word . . . But then there was that other side to him . . . He wasn't immoral; he was just plain amoral—unmoral. Right and wrong didn't exist. He'd do anything—anything."

It was after a nighttime burglary of a University of Michigan fraternity house in the fall of 1923 that the pair reached a compact to commit the perfect crime. Sexually, Loeb seemed indifferent to Leopold. He thought Babe a bother and a bad influence, and once contemplated killing him. But Dickie needed Nathan as "an audience," and agreed to continue their lovemaking if Leopold would join him in criminal activities. Just as he had when his nanny had enticed him to climb on her back and put his penis between her legs, Nathan felt an overwhelming thrill when performing that act with Loeb. Dickie would feign drunkenness, and Babe would furiously pretend to rape him. And so they negotiated. In return for being Dickie's accomplice, Babe could have sex a certain number of times, or after each criminal deed.

"Each boy felt inadequate to carry out the life he most desired unless he had someone else in his life to complement him, to complete him,"

Hulbert declared. "The psychiatric cause for this is not to be found in either boy alone, but in the interplay or interweaving of their two personalities."[11]

ROBERT CROWE WAS not about to let exculpatory material into the record without a fight. When Darrow called Dr. William White, a prominent psychiatrist, to the stand, Crowe rose to object, demanding that Caverly halt the proceedings.

"What is the defense trying to do here?" Crowe asked. "Are they attempting to avoid a trial upon a plea of not guilty with the defendants before twelve men that would hang them, and trying to produce a situation where they can get a trial before one man that they think won't hang them?"

It was a rhetorical question. Everyone in Chicago knew that this was exactly what Darrow was trying to do.

"There are not degrees . . . in responsibility," Crowe argued.

Darrow's entire case rested on Caverly's ruling, and he showed great restraint in not joining the debate. Crowe was trying to bully Caverly, and Darrow, who believed that the outcomes of trials rested on such elemental factors as likability, let the prosecutor continue, trusting that Crowe would antagonize the judge. It was only after Caverly asked for legal briefs and argument the next day that Darrow responded with an hourlong address.

"I understand," he began, leaning upon the bar in his wrinkled seersucker suit, that "the position of the State's attorney is that the universe will crumble unless these two boys are hanged. . . .

"I must say that I have never before seen the same passion and enthusiasm for a death penalty," he said.

"If I thought that hanging them would prevent any further murders I would probably be in favor of doing it," Darrow said. "But I have no such feeling. I know the world will go on about the same in the future as it has in the past."

It was all about precedent. "The defense in this case has met these issues perfectly squarely," Darrow said, raising his voice and jutting out his jaw. "We have not invoked any harsh and strained laws to save the lives of these defendants, and we protest against any such rules of law being invoked to kill them."

Caverly listened thoughtfully, tapping his teeth with a pencil. "A man may be wholly, or nearly wholly, defective, and still it doesn't come under the definition of legal insanity," Darrow said. "There are many conditions and diseases that come far short." He was swaying back and forth now, like a grizzly on its hind legs.

There was precedent, Darrow said, and he cited his own defense of the crazy Russell Pethick, the grocery boy who had slaughtered a young mother and her toddler son. As in the Pethick case, the condition of Babe and Dickie was such "that we did not wish to go before a jury with the full defense of insanity . . . but it was such as we believed would appeal to any court as a ground for clemency and mercy in the case of these two unfortunate lads."

Yes, he had called them "unfortunate lads." No doubt he believed it. His speech led the papers the next morning, and the uncritical coverage was a signal to Caverly that a merciful verdict might not be met with public execration.

In a salute befitting the Windy City, a reporter for the *Herald Examiner* declared that Darrow had shown himself as "the greatest figure in the greatest moment of the greatest drama of life and death in the history of American jurisprudence. . . .

"Darrow, of counsel for the defense. Darrow, greatest criminal lawyer in America. Darrow going into action," the newspaper gushed. "Hamlet has his epitaph: 'He was a man; take him for all in all, I shall not look upon his like again.' "[12] The judge overruled Crowe's objection and let the trial proceed on Darrow's terms.

White and the other experts took the stand to state their conclusions and answer questions about the content of the psychiatric reports. The study of hormones and glands and their effect on human behavior was in its infancy, but Darrow was fascinated by the notion that the release of natural chemicals made the human machine run in certain ways. And so more doctors were summoned to describe the abnormalities of Leopold's pineal gland and Loeb's slow metabolism.

The world was paying attention, even if it was difficult to decide just what, in the scattershot testimony of the experts, the defense was trying to say. "Mr. Clarence Darrow may be said to have opened a new chapter in the criminal courts," the editors of Great Britain's *New Statesman* wrote. "His witnesses went all out in the direction of the new psychiatry:

Freud, Behaviorism, endocrine glands, split personality, *folie à deux,* basal metabolism and the rest of it—every theory and term that, during these eventful years of psychological enterprise, has been heard in the babel of the schools. Much of it, perhaps the greater part, was pretentious or merely grotesque; but not a little was very interesting, and part of it undeniably significant."

Crowe countered with his own experts, who declared the boys sane. But under Darrow's persistent cross-examination, they acknowledged that they had been rushed and were working in far from ideal conditions when they examined the defendants for just three hours in a chaotic session on Memorial Day weekend. In some cases, Darrow read from textbooks they had authored, in which they wrote how controlled clinical conditions were essential elements of a competent observation. At one point Darrow accused Dr. Archibald Church—whom he knew quite well, and had worked with since the Prendergast trial—of conspiring with Crowe to hang the boys. "You know better than that," the doctor told him, shaking his finger at Darrow, who, chastened, withdrew the question. But he did get Church to admit that there were more than a dozen detectives, prosecutors, and others in the state's attorney's office when the doctors observed the youths.

"Too many," Church admitted, "for an ideal consultation."

"Did you ask any questions to find out evidence of mental disease?"

"No," Church conceded.[13]

THE CLOSING ARGUMENTS began on August 19, when two of Crowe's assistants recited the details of the crime with such savagery that Jacob Franks fled the courtroom and Nathan Leopold shuddered with tears. Word spread that Darrow was to begin speaking on the afternoon of Friday, August 22. Two thousand men and women showed up at the courthouse in what the *Herald Examiner* described as a "maelstrom of rioters who trampled upon each other, clawed at the police and deputies, tore each other's clothing, cursed and, for a critical half hour, threatened wholesale bloodshed." Caverly needed the help of three bailiffs, who formed a wedge, to get into his courtroom. The howling from the corridor was so persistent that Darrow threw up his hands and suspended his remarks while more police were called to clear the halls.

Darrow spoke to three distinct audiences. The most important, of course, was Caverly. Here he was direct, using statistics to build the weight of precedent. "I told your Honor in the beginning that never had there been a case in Chicago where on a plea of guilty, a boy under twenty-one had been sentenced to death," Darrow said, waving a solemn finger. "If these boys hang, you must do it . . . It must be by your deliberate, cool, premeditated act."

Indeed, "in the last ten years 350 people have been indicted for murder in the city of Chicago and have pled guilty," he said, and "only one has been hanged."[14]

Arms folded, Darrow looked up at the judge.

"Your Honor will never thank me for unloading this responsibility upon you, but you know that I would have been untrue to my clients if I had not concluded to take this chance before a court, instead of submitting it to a poisoned jury," Darrow said. "I did it knowing that it would be an unheard-of thing for any court, no matter who, to sentence these boys to death."

For the most part, Darrow ignored the detailed testimony of the psychiatric experts—disappointing some advocates of the new science. There was no need for it, he said; it was patently clear from the bizarre nature of the crime that Leopold and Loeb were gripped by forces beyond their control. "It was the senseless act of immature and diseased children . . . wandering around in the dark and moved by some emotion that we still, perhaps, have not the knowledge or the insight into life to thoroughly understand." Crowe and his aides sat silently. Caverly leaned forward, resting his chin on his clasped hands, listening intently.

The judge was the most important audience, but there were others whom Darrow addressed. As in many of his famous closing arguments, he sought to teach his fellow Americans a larger point of law or politics—in this case, the evil of capital punishment. "My God! This world has been one long slaughter house from the beginning until today, and killing goes on and on and on and will forever," he exclaimed. "Why not read something, why not study something, why not think instead of blindly calling for death?

"Kill them! Will that prevent other senseless boys or other vicious men or vicious women. No! It would simply call upon every weak-minded person to do as they have done."

The final audience was Chicago. Darrow wanted to touch Caverly's heart, but he knew the judge was a politician and that this speech must move public opinion. As he neared the end of that first day, Darrow played on the emotions of the city's parents, whose hearts were filled with sympathy for Jacob and Flora Franks, but also with horror at what had happened to the Loebs and the Leopolds.

"I know that any mother might be the mother of a little Bobby Franks, who left his home and went to his school and whose life was taken, and who never came back," Darrow said. But "I know that any mother might be the mother of Richard Loeb and Nathan Leopold, just the same."

Walking back and forth before the bench, wiping the sweat from his neck with a handkerchief, he brought all the familiar gestures into play: striking his palm with his hand, tugging at the armholes of his vest, wagging his fingers, and tossing his shoulders. "I remember a little poem," Darrow said. And here, in a voice so low that only those in the front of the courtroom could hear him, he recited the Housman verse that he had read, back in May, at the Lincoln Center event.

And so the game is ended
That should not have begun . . .

Darrow stood in the tight space before the bar. "No one knows what will be the fate of the child they get or the child they bear," he said.

His voice was tight with emotion now.

"I am sorry for these fathers and these mothers. The mother who looks into the blue eyes of her little babe cannot help wonder what will be the end of this child, whether it will be crowned with the greatest promises which her mind can imagine, or whether he may meet death from the gallows," he said. "All she can do is to raise him with care, to watch over him tenderly, to meet life with hope and trust and confidence and to leave the rest with fate."

Women in the audience—including Judge Caverly's wife and sister—wept. The defendants had stopped laughing; he had touched even their cold souls. They blinked back tears, and Leopold stumbled from the courtroom, his head bowed. In his cell that night, Loeb wrote a letter to his lawyer.

"Only the tears in my eyes as you talked and the feeling in my heart could express the admiration, the love, that I have for you," Loeb wrote. "I have gone thru so much of my life a play actor—but I am sure you know when it is the heart that is speaking. A heart, Mr. Darrow, with a thick coating of deceit, of selfishness, but a heart that way down deep must, because I am the son of my father and mother, have some good in it, and my message comes from there."[15]

JUDGE CAVERLY HAD scheduled a morning session for Saturday, and so, again, Darrow spoke for half a day. The crowds, alarmed by the reports of Friday's riot, stayed away. Darrow, in the calmer setting, was solemn.

"I can picture them, wakened in the gray light of morning, furnished a suit of clothes by the state, led to the scaffold, their feet tied, a black cap drawn over their heads, placed on a trap door . . . so that it falls under them and they are only stopped by the rope around their necks," he said. "Do I need to argue to your Honor that cruelty only makes cruelty? That hatred only causes hatred? That if there is any way to . . . soften the human heart, which is hard enough at its best, if there is any way to kill evil and hatred and all that goes with it, it is not through evil and hatred and cruelty; it is through charity, and love and understanding?"

He dropped his arms, as if in futility. "I am asking your Honor not to visit the grave and dire and terrible misfortune . . . upon these two boys," he said. "I do not know where to place it. I know it is somewhere in the infinite economy of nature . . . I know it is there, and to say that because they are as they are you should hang them, is brutality and cruelty, and savors of the time of fang and claw." Tears were streaming down his face.

AND AT THE age of sixty-seven, Darrow spoke all day on Monday. An entire day, two sessions of court, two lives at stake.

He talked about each of the defendants at length. Dickie Loeb, in the hands of his mad governess, "had no pleasures, such as a boy should have, except in what was gained by lying and cheating." And there grew in his brain—"dwarfed and twisted"—a hunger for crime. Darrow's voice cracked a bit and his eyes glistened as he ventured back to his own childhood.

"Before I would tie a noose around the neck of a boy I would try to call back into my mind the emotions of youth . . . I would try to remember how weak and inefficient was youth in the presence of the surging controlling feelings of the child," he told the judge.

"It is not enough to take a boy filled with his dreams and his fantasies and living in an unreal world, but the age of adolescence comes on him . . . the most trying period of the life of a child . . . when the call of sex is new and strange . . . moved by the strongest feelings and passions that have ever moved men. . . .

"This boy needed more home, needed more love, more affection, more direction," Darrow said. "He needed to have his emotions awakened. He needed to have guiding hands along the serious road that youth must travel."

Then Darrow turned to Nathan Leopold.

"He was just a half boy—an intellect, an intellectual machine going without balance," Darrow said. "At 17, at 16, at 18, while healthy boys were playing baseball or working on the farm, or doing odd jobs, he was reading Nietzsche, a boy who never should have seen it." In his last years, Nietzsche suffered from mental illness. "His own doctrines made him a maniac," said Darrow. "And here is a young boy, in the adolescent age, harassed by everything that harasses children, who takes this philosophy and swallows it, who believes it literally, lives his life on it."

Darrow was, in retrospect, a uniquely apt lawyer for Leopold and Loeb. He had the audacity to treat judges and juries to original sermons on an intellectual plane far higher than the usual courtroom wrangling, and to do so in a captivating way. People listened to his reasoning, despite its strangeness, its theory, its difficult demand for mercy.

"I am trying to trace causes. I am trying to trace them honestly. I am trying to trace them with the light I have," he said. "I am trying to say to this court that these boys are not responsible for this . . . and asking this court not to visit the judgment of its wrath upon them for things for which they are not to blame. . . .

"Sometimes, your Honor, a boy of great promise is cut off in his early youth. Sometimes he dies and is placed in a culvert. Sometimes a boy of great promise stands on a trap door and is hanged by the neck until dead."

After the noon recess, Darrow resumed his place before the bench. He began again, speaking calmly. The courtroom was packed "like a black hole. Hardly a breath of air moved in it," the *News* said. But the crowd stayed with him, listening to every word. Judge Caverly toyed with his pencil, his face flushed, from time to time, with the heat and the emotion.

"Ninety men have been hanged by the neck until dead, because of the ancient superstition that in some way hanging one man keeps another from committing a crime," Darrow said. He looked around dejectedly. "The ancient superstition. . . .

"We have not grown better than the ancients. We have grown more squeamish; we do not like to look at it, that is all," he said.

But "in ninety men hanged in Illinois from its beginning, not one single person under 24 was ever hanged upon a plea of guilty—not one."

He cited, one final time, Crowe's crack about a "friendly judge." He leaned across the shelf separating him from the judge, as close as he could get. "Your Honor, that is a blow below the belt," he said. "It was carved out of the air, to awe and influence the court."

Americans had lost a measure of innocence in the Great War, Darrow said. Man grew coarse. Humanity became hard. Could it come as a surprise that boys were cruel?

"I have spoken about the war. I believed in it," Darrow said. "I approved of it; I joined in the general cry of madness and despair. . . .

"Right or wrong, justifiable or unjustifiable . . . it changed the world. For four long years the civilized world was engaged in killing men. Christian against Christian, barbarians uniting with Christians to kill Christians; anything to kill. It was taught in every school . . . the little children played at war.

"Do you suppose this world has ever been the same since?" Darrow asked.

"How long, your Honor will it take for the world to get back in its human emotions to where it stood before the war? How long will it take the calloused heart of man before the scars of hatred and cruelty shall be removed? We read of killing one hundred thousand in a day; probably exaggerated, but what of it? We read about it and rejoice in it; it was the other fellows who were killed. We were fed on flesh and drank blood. . . .

"I have been sorry, and I am sorry for the bereavement of Mr. and Mrs. Franks," he said, "for those broken ties that cannot be mended. All I can hope and wish is that some good may come from it.

"But as compared with the families of Leopold and Loeb, they are to be envied. They are to be envied, and everyone knows it.

"I do not know how much salvage there is in these two boys. I hate to say it in their presence, but what is there to look forward to? I do not know but what your Honor would be merciful if you tied a rope around their neck and let them die; merciful to them, but not merciful to civilization, and not merciful to those who would be left behind. I do not know; to spend the balance of their days in prison is mighty little to look forward to, if anything."

He wiped tears from his eyes with the back of a trembling hand as once more, softly, he read a verse from Housman.

Now, hollow fires burn out tonight,
And lights are guttering low;
Square your shoulders and lift your pack,
And leave your friends and go.
Don't ever fear, lads, naught's to dread
Look not left nor right;
In all the endless road you tread,
There's nothing but the night.

"Whether the march begins at the gallows or when the gates of Joliet close upon them, there is nothing but the night," said Darrow.

"None of us are unmindful of the public; courts are not, and juries are not," Darrow told the judge. He was coming to the end. "I have stood here for three months as somebody might stand at the seacoast trying to sweep back the tide. I hope the seas are subsiding and the wind is falling and I believe they are. But I wish to make no false pretense to this court. The easy thing and the popular thing to do is to hang my clients. I know it.

"Men and women who do not think will applaud. The cruel and the thoughtless will approve," he said.

Through the open windows came the muffled noise of the streetcars, and of passing automobiles. But inside the courtroom, the only sound was of Darrow's voice. And now it was breaking.

"Your Honor stands between the future and the past," he said. "I know the future is with me, and what I stand for here; not merely for the lives of these two unfortunate lads, but for all boys and all girls; all of the young, and as far as possible, for all of the old. I am pleading for life, understanding, charity and kindness and the infinite mercy that forgives all. I am pleading that we overcome cruelty with kindness and hatred with love.

"I know the future is on my side," he said, stretching his arms in supplication to the bench. "You may hang these boys; you may hang them by the neck til they are dead. But in doing it you will turn your face toward the past. In doing it you are making it harder for every other boy."

Or "you may save them," he told Caverly, "and it makes it easier for every child that some time may sit where these boys sit. It makes it easier for every human being with an aspiration and a vision and a hope and a fate.

"I am pleading for the future," Darrow said. "I am pleading for a time when hatred and cruelty will not control the hearts of men. When we can learn by reason and judgment and understanding and faith that all life is worth saving, and that mercy is the highest attribute of man."

He stood sorrowfully, wiping more tears from his eyes. It was almost four p.m. "I feel that I ought to apologize for the length of time I have taken. This may not be as important as I think it is, and I am sure I do not need to tell this court, or to tell my friend Mr. Crowe, that I would fight just as hard for the poor as for the rich.

"If I should succeed in saving these boys' lives and do nothing for the progress of the law, I should feel sad, indeed. If I can succeed, my greatest award and my greatest hope and my greatest compensation will be that I have done something for the tens of thousands of other boys, for the other unfortunates who must tread the same way that these poor youths have trod, that I have done something to help human understanding, to temper justice with mercy, to overcome hate with love.

"I was reading last night of the aspiration of the old Persian poet, Omar Khayyám. It appealed to me as the highest that I can envision. I wish it was in my heart, and I wish it was in the heart of all, and I can do no better than to quote what he said:

So I be written in the Book of Love,
I do not care about that Book above.
Erase my name or write it as you will,
So I be written in the Book of Love.

And so he ended, with his beloved *Rubáiyát*, in a voice so soft and tremulous that only he and Caverly and a few others could hear him. For a time the audience waited in silence. A minute. Two minutes. He leaned over and, eyes tearing, shuffled the papers before him. He nodded his head, and sat down.[16]

DARROW BELIEVED THAT the study of criminal justice was at a turning point, and that he represented a wiser and more compassionate future. And maybe as the Progressive Era drew toward its end, he had reason to believe it. It was nice to think so.

His faith was misplaced. The future had nothing but worse in store—a new world war to eclipse the old one, tactics to torment civilians, crazed theories of racial and religious supremacy, death camps and atomic fire. Over time, Darrow's America would be ripped by witch hunts, race riots, drug-fueled crime, and reborn enthusiasm for dispatching millions of citizens to its broken prisons. Thousands, including innocents and teenagers, would be sent to death rows, to gallows and gas chambers, firing squads and electric chairs and gurneys with poison drips. The future, this day, was not Clarence Darrow's. The future was Robert Crowe's.

He began by deriding Darrow as "the distinguished gentleman whose profession it is to protect murder in Cook County." He ridiculed White and the other defense psychiatrist as "the three wise men from the East who came on to tell your honor about these little babes." And, almost immediately, he resumed his attempt to bully Caverly. "If a jury were sitting in that box and they returned a verdict and did not fix the punishment at death, every person in this community, would feel that that verdict was founded in corruption," he told the judge.

For parts of three days Crowe ranted, until his nasal voice faded to a hoarse croak. He shouted and stamped and waved his arms. "Now he thrust his face, purple with the strain of his apoplectic speech, into the faces of Loeb and Leopold, now he strode before Judge Caverly, shaking his fist as he put all his lung power into some climax or other," the *Daily News* said. "It was all climax . . . There were no valleys in the speech, just peaks . . . strident, impassioned, almost delirious."

Crowe marched upon Leopold. "I wonder now, Nathan, whether you think there is a God or not," he snarled. "I wonder whether you think it is pure accident that this disciple of Nietzschean philosophy dropped his glasses—or whether it was an act of Divine Providence to visit upon your miserable carcasses the wrath of God!"

The killers "are as much entitled to the sympathy and mercy of this court as a couple of rattlesnakes, flushed with venom, coiled and ready to strike," Crowe told the judge. "They are entitled to as much mercy . . . as two mad dogs." They were "perverts" with "a desire to satisfy unnatural lust." For the first time in the trial, Crowe accused the boys of raping the dead or dying Bobby Franks. "Immediately upon killing him they took his trousers off . . . His rectum was distended," the prosecutor said. "This little naked body lay in the water all night long with running water going over it, and that is why there wasn't any other evidence . . . There was no evidence of semen, but it was washed away, I contend."

When the defense objected and a debate erupted over the coroner's report (which was ambiguous on the issue), Caverly had the courtroom cleared of all female spectators. "I have asked the ladies to leave the room . . . I want you to leave . . . There is nothing left here now but a lot of stuff that is not fit for you to hear."

And finally, as he drew toward the end, Crowe found a target on which to blame the crime, the disorder, and the chaos of the times.

"I want to tell you the real defense in this case, your Honor. It is Clarence Darrow's dangerous philosophy of life," Crowe said. "It would be much better if God had not caused this crime to be disclosed. It would have been much better if it went unsolved . . . It would not have done near the harm to this community as will be done if your Honor . . . puts your official seal of approval upon the doctrines of anarchy preached by Clarence Darrow."

Then Crowe made a terrible blunder. He ended his address by hauling out, one last time, the specter of the "friendly judge." The killers "have laughed and sneered and jeered" throughout the trial, Crowe said. "If the defendant, Leopold, did not say that he would plead guilty before a friendly judge, his actions demonstrated that he thinks he has got one."

Darrow leaped to his feet and objected. Judge Caverly flushed, and ordered the court stenographer to make sure to take the words down carefully. Crowe sensed the judge's anger, stammered on a bit, and sat down.

Caverly fumed in silence as Crowe took his seat. Caverly fumed in silence as the lawyers went through the formalities of applying the testimony from the murder case to the other count, of kidnapping. Caverly fumed in silence until Crowe announced, "The state rests." And then the judge let him have it.

"The court will order stricken from the record the closing remarks of the State's Attorney," Caverly said, as the startled reporters and spectators looked up, "as being a cowardly and dastardly assault upon the integrity of the court . . ."

"It was not so intended, your Honor," Crowe said.

" . . . And it could not be used for any other purpose except to incite a mob and to try and intimidate this court. It will be stricken from the record."

"If your Honor please . . . ," Crowe said.

"The State's Attorney knew that would be heralded all through this country and all over this world, and he knows the court hasn't an opportunity except to do what he did . . . This court will not be intimidated by anybody at any time or place as long as he occupies this position."

It is not easy to dismiss the thought that after all the weeks of testimony and all the hours of argument, the lives of Nathan Leopold and Richard Loeb were saved in the end by Robert Crowe's intemperance. As he left the bench that day, Caverly seemed more concerned about showing that he could not be bullied than about the public backlash if he sent the youths to jail.[17]

So it was. On September 10 they gathered again in the little courtroom to hear Caverly read his decision. As he began, the judge sounded like he was prepared to hang the youths. They were not insane, he declared. And while the killers were "abnormal," Caverly said, that came as no surprise. "Had they been normal they would not have committed the crime." The testimony of the psychiatric witnesses was a valuable contribution to criminology, said the judge, but would not affect his decision. "The court is satisfied that neither in the act itself, nor in its motives or lack of motives, or in the antecedents of the offenders, can he find any mitigating circumstances."

Loeb and Leopold looked pale and stricken. Then Caverly swiveled. "In choosing imprisonment instead of death, the court is moved chiefly by the consideration of the age of the defendants, boys of 18 and 19 years," he declared. Darrow had read Caverly correctly. Precedent was the key. "This determination," said the judge, "appears to be in accordance with the progress of criminal law all over the world and with the dictates of enlightened humanity. More than that, it seems to be in accordance with the precedents hitherto observed in this State.

"The records of Illinois show only two cases of minors who were put to death by legal process," said the judge, "to which number the court does not feel inclined to make an addition."

Darrow had won. He was delighted and relieved. "Well, it's just what we asked for," he told the reporters who gathered around him as Leopold and Loeb were taken back to their cells. "But it's pretty tough," he added. "It was more of a punishment than death would have been."

Not too much later, a reporter caught up to Darrow in the lobby of his hotel on a speaking trip to Omaha, and asked him what fate awaited his clients. Darrow slouched on the plush red divan, stared awhile at his "stern black shoes," then said: "They'll never get out. Probably both be dead in 10 years. Suffering from dementia praecox. Getting worse."

When friends asked him privately what he would do if he was the judge, he replied: "For the good of society and for the good of the boys, I'd deal with them quite differently. Loeb would be quietly, painlessly put to sleep—not as punishment, for he is already doomed and life holds nothing for him. Death would be a merciful release.

"But Leopold's case is different. He has scientific genius of high order; he may be another Darwin. I would, of course, restrain him, but in a place where he would have all laboratory facilities. Keep him confined until he has saved himself—through work."

Darrow's sympathy for the youths was not contrived. Over the years he visited and wrote them, from time to time, and offered advice on how to get by behind bars. In the last few hours before he was taken to Joliet, Leopold wrote a long letter of thanks to his attorney.

Some of what Leopold wrote was chilling, as when he praised Darrow's intellect. "This one attribute of Man has always appealed to me more strongly than any other, and since you happen to possess more of it than any other man whom I have had the pleasure of meeting, this alone would cause me to bow down in abject hero-worship," the killer wrote. "It would be an inconsistent 'Superman' indeed who did not reverence his superior."

But Darrow's compassion had touched even Leopold. "Grant then intellect and courage . . . and we haven't begun to describe you," he wrote.

"What of that heart in which there is room for all the world even including murderers and State's Attorneys? What of that spontaneous sympathy and understanding which instantly goes out from you to the most dastardly criminal? It were sacrilege for me who so utterly lack them, to attempt to measure them. But even lacking them, I can admire and wonder in awe."

Darrow had suggested throughout the trial that this might be his last criminal case. He vowed to spend his retirement leading a public campaign against capital punishment. The paycheck he expected from the families would finance his golden years of writing and travel.[18]

His health was a worry. After hearing Caverly's decision, Darrow and Ruby had joined Leopold's father and brother on the evening train for Charlevoix to meet with Loeb's parents and recuperate at the family estate. They arrived after midnight and Darrow, complaining of chest pains, went to bed until noon.

No mention was made of money, and thirteen months passed, said Ruby. Then one evening Darrow came home "weary-looking, sat down on the edge of the big brass bed . . . glancing up at me standing at service as usual," and told her he had met with Jacob Loeb, and accepted a meager settlement.

Loeb had told him: "Clarence, you realize that the world is full of lawyers who would have paid a fortune for the chance of distinguishing themselves as representatives in this case."

"You know I couldn't let it be said that I haggled about the price," he told Ruby.

In reality, the settlement took three months—not thirteen. On December 9, the Loeb and Leopold families offered Darrow $65,000, and he signed his acceptance. The Bachrachs received another $65,000, and the deal was approved by a bar association committee in January.

Darrow was sore. He had suggested at one point in the negotiations that his work was worth $200,000, at which point a representative of the families had complained of feeling faint. It was a lot of money, Darrow acknowledged, but when the families "with an aggregate wealth of ten million dollars came to me pleading for me to take the case . . . nobody fainted then."[19]

Chapter 18

THE MONKEY TRIAL

The state of Tennessee don't rule the world yet.

Williams Jennings Bryan resigned as secretary of state in 1915 to protest President Wilson's decision to take sides against Germany in World War I. It was the most prestigious office that Bryan ever held and he had schemed to get it, but he was appalled at the brutality of warfare in the industrial age. He moved to Florida, where he made a fortune in the real estate boom, switched his focus to religion, and reemerged in the 1920s as the country's foremost critic of Charles Darwin's theory of evolution.[1]

Bryan was a devout Christian, and his populist beliefs went strongly against the notion of "survival of the fittest," which had been cited by the robber barons to justify the injustice of their era. He saw natural selection as "the law of hate—the merciless law by which the strong crowd out and kill off the weak." And his wartime studies persuaded him that German militarism, inspired by the teachings of Darwin and Nietzsche, was responsible for the carnage. He followed the Leopold and Loeb case closely, took note of their debt to Nietzsche, and added the death of Bobby Franks to the toll.[2]

Bryan's alarm found a ready audience. In many Baptist, Methodist, and Pentecostal congregations in that broad swath of the southern and western United States known as the Bible Belt, the faithful yearned for a return to simple verities. There was a feeling that something was wrong, that the truths of their childhood had been taken from them. These self-anointed "fundamentalists" believed that the Bible was the Rock of Ages—written by God and given to man, an infallible guide to good behavior and the path to paradise. And in Genesis they found a story of creation, and man's place at the center of the universe, that made no mention of apelike ancestors.

Bryan had joined with the religious conservatives in support of Prohibition. Now he toured the country alerting crowds to "the Menace of Darwinism." He wrote newspaper articles, visited colleges, and addressed state legislatures, urging them to ban the teaching of evolution in the public schools. Critics found his moral outrage selective. Bryan had always been cool to the issue of civil rights, and defended the Ku Klux Klan from attacks at the 1924 Democratic convention. "How petty, mean and contemptible Bryan . . . is," Eugene Debs wrote Darrow, the following summer. "This shallow-minded mouther of empty phrases, this pious canting mountebank, this prophet of the stone age."

Darrow was always watchful of Bryan, and composed an open letter that was printed in the *Chicago Tribune* in the summer of 1923. "I have . . . followed Mr. Bryan's efforts to shut out the teaching of science from the public schools," Darrow wrote. "A few questions to Mr. Bryan and the fundamentalists if fairly answered might serve the interests of reaching the truth." He followed with a questionnaire that listed Old Testament tales—the garden of Eden, Noah's ark, the whale and Jonah, and others—and asked Bryan if he believed they were literally true. Some of Darrow's queries were rooted in science ("Are there not evidences in writing and hieroglyphics . . . which show that man has been on the earth more than 50,000 years?"), but others were sarcastic ("Did God curse the serpent for tempting Eve and decree that thereafter he should go on his belly? How did he travel before that?"). Bryan declined the bait. "I am not worried about an atheist" like Darrow, he told reporters.[3]

TENNESSEE EMERGED AS the battleground for the anti-evolution cause in early 1925. A rural state representative named John Washington Butler, the clerk of the Round Lick Association of Primitive Baptists, introduced a bill making it illegal for public schools "to teach any theory that denies the story of the Divine Creation of man as taught in the Bible, and to teach instead that man has descended from a lower order of animals."

Folks like Butler bridled when the public schools used textbooks that challenged their faith in Genesis. One of the nation's most popular biology texts—*A Civic Biology* by George W. Hunter—was in use in Tennessee high schools. Later generations would find much to deplore in Hunter's claim that the Caucasian race was "the highest type of all," or in his argument that progeny of feeble-minded and "immoral" families are "parasites" who should be kept from breeding. But that was not what bothered the fundamentalists. They objected to the section on evolution.

"Geology teaches that millions of years ago, life upon the earth was very simple, and that gradually more and more complex forms of life appeared," the text said. "The group of mammals which includes the monkeys, apes and man we call the primates." The fundamentalists wanted the mighty Lord of Genesis in the classroom, not monkeys. "Man's spiritual nature is not even referred to, and the child would very readily get the idea that the proof of man's connection with the monkey was complete and the Bible record false," Bryan said.

The cocklebur vote had shown its clout in recent years: freethinking professors had been expelled from the faculty of the University of Tennessee. Butler's legislation passed the Tennessee House with little fanfare. The *Nashville Banner* noted how the representatives that day "covered a wide range of territory, from a local measure to prohibit suck-egg dogs from running at large . . . to a general measure prohibiting the teaching of evolution." The House action stirred a few editorial writers to object, but the Senate fell in line. The bill was signed into law by Governor Austin Peay, who, with atrocious misjudgment, pronounced it a matter of no consequence. "Probably the law will never be applied," he said.[4]

After defending Leopold and Loeb, Darrow had spent much of the fall of 1924 and the early months of 1925, as he liked to say, loafing. At the end of September he made a sentimental trip to Kinsman, where the local bar association, apparently not recalling his aversion to poultry, held a chicken dinner in his honor. Judges and childhood friends joined a crowd of eighty people, and Darrow spoke for about an hour, of how fate and chance had taken him from the Western Reserve to national celebrity.[5] He remembered his first case in court, which was held in the shadow of a coffin that hung on the wall awaiting the demise of its farsighted owner, the marvelously named Riverious Bidwell. Darrow told how his legal practice in Chicago had been transformed by his fascination with criminal law. There was little to keep an attorney awake at night when the stakes were merely credit or property, he said. But in criminal law "you are dealing with flesh, blood, reputations, shame, disgrace, honor" and with "wives, fathers, mothers and children." It was "vital" work, though "wearing on your nerves and sympathies," he said. "You must learn to endure criticism and to be callous to spiteful remarks."[6]

The Leopold and Loeb case had added immensely to his fame. Darrow was traveling widely, speaking to large audiences. He presided at a liberal campaign rally that brought ten thousand to Madison Square Garden in New York in 1924.[7] He decried capital punishment in debates before audiences of three thousand at the Metropolitan Opera House and seven thousand in St. Petersburg. He spoke on Prohibition in New York, on crime in Philadelphia and Miami, and on capital punishment in Montreal and New Orleans.

Mary came to see Darrow in New York and found his room thronged with admirers. "The incense was burning," she told her diary. "The Great One was enveloped in praise." He was regularly in New York alone, and often they would meet at his hotel. From Florida, where he and Ruby fled to escape a Chicago winter, Darrow wrote to her: "There is enough of me left to remember you . . . as long as I can remember anyone and with all the love of the old days."[8]

In early May of 1925, the American Civil Liberties Union issued a press release decrying the signing of the Butler Act and offering to defend any teacher prosecuted for teaching evolution. "We are looking for a Tennessee teacher who is willing to accept our services in testing this law," the ACLU announced. "Distinguished counsel have volunteered their services. All we need now is a willing client." On May 4, the *Chattanooga Times* reported how the ACLU was "agitating for a test case." A few miles up the road, in the valley town of Dayton, the story caught the eye of George Rappleyea, a spirited thirty-one-year-old engineer with bushy hair and Coke-bottle glasses. He was a transplanted Yankee worried about the lingering economic torpor brought on by the closing of the local ironworks and, truth be told, missing the razz and dazzle of New York. Why not take the ACLU up on its offer? Rappleyea asked a group of fellow idlers gathered in wire-backed chairs around a wood-topped table at Robinson's Drug Store ("Stationery—Soda—Cigarettes—Kodaks—Candies") the following afternoon. Why not stage a showdown in Dayton? It would garner their town some lucrative attention. At the very least it would liven up the summer. Little did they know.

From its inception, the Scopes trial was conceived and promoted and staged as a circus stunt. No one presumed that a Dayton jury would have the final say on the matter. All agreed that John Scopes, a twenty-four-year-old high school science teacher who was summoned to Robinson's pharmacy from a nearby tennis court and coaxed to stand trial, would be found guilty—giving the ACLU a martyr whose conviction it could take to a higher court. The local constable, prosecutors, and superintendent of schools were among those sipping Coca-Cola and working on the scheme at the drugstore, for Dayton was that kind of small town. F. E. Robinson was not just the druggist, but doubled as the textbook vendor who supplied the schools with *A Civic Biology.* His sales were made easier by the fact that he also chaired the Rhea County board of education, and so purchased the texts from himself.

"You have been teaching 'em this book?" Rappleyea asked Scopes as they paged through a volume of *A Civic Biology.*

"Yes," said Scopes.

"Then you've been violating the law," said Robinson.

Scopes agreed to take the fall. "Justice of the Peace will find him guilty and he will appeal," Rappleyea promised in a telegram to the ACLU.

Yet lawyers being what they are—constitutionally combative and not much caring to lose in the glare of public attention—the staged skirmish evolved into a genuine struggle and then, to Dayton's delight, a national spectacle. The schemers had originally presumed that ol' Judge Godsey, a corpulent retired jurist, would defend Scopes. But then Bryan agreed to lead the prosecution. And that compelled Darrow to shoulder his way onto the Scopes defense team.[9]

THE SIXTY-FIVE-YEAR-OLD BRYAN'S once glorious and vibrant baritone was diminished by age, and the tousled head of hair of his youth had thinned to a monkish fringe. He was slowed by diabetes. But he still had the fight of a snapping turtle, a species that, with the dome of his forehead, beak nose, and broad mouth, he somewhat resembled—especially when, in deference to the temperature, he took to wearing a collarless shirt.

It would be, Bryan prophesied, "a duel to the death" between Christianity and "this slimy thing, evolution." He stepped off the train—the Royal Palm Limited from Miami made an unscheduled stop for him—at the Dayton depot like a figure out of Kipling, with a pith helmet and a leather satchel. Hundreds of people waited and, in a caravan of automobiles, paraded him through town. He spoke the next night at a mountaintop retreat to an audience gathered on a lawn, as thunder growled and bolts of lightning split the sky behind him. At a dinner at the Hotel Aqua, hosted by the Dayton Progressive Club, Bryan announced his plans to campaign for an amendment to the U.S. Constitution to prohibit the teaching of Darwinism in any public school. He leaned across the table to where a stagestruck Scopes was sitting and told the teacher: "You have no idea what a black and brutal thing this evolution is."

He also displayed his prodigious appetite: "John, are you going to eat your side dishes?" he asked and helped himself to the defendant's corn and potatoes.[10]

With Bryan in the fray, "Darrow was keen to be included," Scopes remembered. "Deeply religious people he was afraid of because he said the next step was fanaticism," Mary recalled. "With fanaticism came persecutions and abridgement of liberty."

Darrow had discussed the case with the liberal lawyers Arthur Garfield Hays and Dudley Malone, the journalist H. L. Mencken, and others. He feared, at first, that the Civil Liberties Union would prefer a counsel who wasn't such a lightning rod for strife. Indeed, the ACLU hoped that a respectable lawyer like former New York governor Charles Evans Hughes would present a "quiet, strictly legalistic" case, Scopes recalled.

Mencken wanted none of that. He was, like Darrow, a pronounced libertarian and religious skeptic. In addition to his newspaper work for the *Baltimore Evening Sun*, Mencken was editor of a hip, style-setting magazine, the *American Mercury*. His slashing copy helped make the Scopes case a national phenomenon. "Bryan . . . is a bit mangey and flea-bitten, but by no means ready for his harp," Mencken wrote. "The fellow is full of such bitter, implacable hatreds that they radiate from him like heat from a stove. He hates the learning that he cannot grasp. He hates those who sneer at him. He hates in general, all who stand apart from his own pathetic commonness. And the yokels hate with him, some of them almost as bitterly as he does himself.

"This year it is a misdemeanor for a country school teacher to flout the archaic nonsense of Genesis. Next year it will be a felony. The year after the net will be spread wider," Mencken warned. "The clowns turn out to be armed, and have begun to shoot."[11]

Mencken met up with Darrow in Richmond, where Darrow was speaking to the American Psychiatric Association, and urged him to head for Dayton. And why not? The drugstore conspirators were displaying their own love of hoopla, choreographing fistfights at town meetings and staging gunplay on Main Street for the benefit of visiting reporters. John Randolph Neal, a defrocked University of Tennessee law professor, had gone to Dayton, nudged Godsey aside, and declared himself the lead defense counsel. Rappleyea was trying to get former secretary of state Bainbridge Colby or English novelist H. G. Wells to serve on the defense.

Darrow saw his chance to outflank the ACLU. He and Malone sent a telegram to Neal (with a press-pleasing dig at Bryan's Florida land deals) offering their services: "We have read the report that William Jennings Bryan has volunteered to aid the prosecution, and in view of the fact that scientists are so much interested in the pursuit of knowledge that they cannot make the money that lecturers and Florida real estate agents command, in case you should need us, we are willing, without fees or expenses, to help the defense of Professor Scopes in any way." Neal quickly accepted the offer.[12]

Bryan was sure he could defeat the man he liked to call the nation's foremost atheist. Darrow "is an outspoken believer in evolution and has the courage to carry the logic of evolution to its legitimate course," Bryan wrote a Tennessee associate. "He will furnish us with abundant material." The faint hearts at the ACLU tended to agree. Scopes had accepted Neal, Darrow, and Malone "before we got our grip on the case and without any consultation," griped the ACLU's Forrest Bailey, in a letter marked "Confidential" to journalist Walter Lippmann. "We did the very best we could to undo it." In the holy chuch of liberalism, Darrow and Malone were irreverent "fakes," Mencken explained to a friend. "Darrow is hated by all Liberals as a renegade. Malone is simply an Irishman who likes a fight."

Reporters were pulled aside and reminded of Darrow's faults. "The report that Mr. Darrow is an atheist . . . has led to grave shaking of heads," wrote Philip Kinsley in the *Tribune*. "The spectacle of Mr. Darrow being questioned by Mr. Bryan before a jury of Tennessee hill men, almost certain to be old fashioned religionists, is not pleasant." That seemed a silly thought—when did lawyers put each other on the stand? But Darrow felt the need to tell the press: "I am not an atheist. When it comes to the question of knowing whether there is a God, I am ignorant."

The decision was left to Scopes. The "yokel"—as Mencken called him—showed his mettle at an ACLU parley in New York. "The arguments against Darrow were various: that he was too radical, that he was a headline hunter," Scopes recalled. Nevertheless, "I wanted Clarence Darrow." The thing was a circus already. Bryan's entry had guaranteed that. "We should expect a gouging, roughhouse battle . . . a real gutter fight," said Scopes. "Darrow had been in many such situations." And so Hughes and Wells remained on the sidelines and Colby—aghast at the signs of hellzapoppin'—withdrew on the eve of the trial.

"There shortly will descend upon Dayton, Tenn., the greatest aggregation of assorted cranks, including agnostics, atheists, communists, syndicalists and new-dawners, ever known in a single procession," the *New York Post* reported. "Greenwich Village is on its way . . . Men of science are being smothered in the rush of long-haired men and short-haired women, feminists, neurotics, free thinkers and free lovers . . . The vital issues on trial in Tennessee are being lost in the stampede of professional martyrs and a swarm of practicing egoists."

The best that the ACLU could do was add Hays, its counsel, to the defense team. It proved to be a fortuitous choice. Hays was bright and combative. He and Darrow had complementary talents, became lasting friends, and would join in the defense of civil rights and liberties in several notable cases to come. Before he left New York, Scopes was feted at a City Club dinner, where Manhattan's liberals gathered to raise money. Mary went as Darrow's escort and sent Sara a description of Darrow's speech. "His position is that only those men, and women, who bring light to man's darkness are important: the great men of science—Darwin, Pasteur, Pavlov—men of knowledge who dispel superstition, fanaticism, disease, cruelty, who make the human race more intelligent," she wrote. The cause of labor, which he had upheld so long, left men as it found them, "jungle creatures fighting for a bone more, a breathing spell more—but not the least bit more intelligent about their bondage, as addicted to their religions and fetishes, their political and social myths, as ever." At the end of the night Darrow gave her "a little silver—not enough—for taxi fare," she noted caustically. But she was back for breakfast the next day, and a ride along the Hudson. And Darrow promised to "skin the pants off old Bryan."[13]

THE MONKEY TRIAL now became the talk of the English-speaking world. Dayton was swept and dusted, and hung with billboards and bunting. ("Read Your Bible" said a sign on the courthouse—no good omen for the defense.) The streets were jammed with flivvers; the sidewalks with gawkers and grifters. Traveling tent shows came to town. Chimpanzees did tricks, and hucksters sold lemonade, an infinite variety of monkey souvenirs—and redemption.

"The sweetheart love of Jesus Christ and Paradise Street is at hand," one proselytizer promised. "Do you want to be a sweet angel?" He listed the terms of a heavenly contract ("Forty days of prayer," "Itemize your sins and iniquities") and guaranteed results ("If you come clean, God will talk back to you in voice"). Even the public privies were decked with religious banners. And from the rich bottomland and the precarious farms of the Cumberland ridges came the Bible-toting folk of the soil in buggies and high-wheeled cars, women in their bonnets and gingham, men in slouched felt hats and overalls—there to swear to the power of the Book, the faith of their fathers, and the unchallengeable, literal authority of Genesis.

There came, as well, the legions of Mammon. Robinson hung a sign ("Where It Started") outside the drugstore and supervised the distribution of a promotional pamphlet—*Why Dayton of All Places?*—that had been printed to drum up business.[14] Mencken, who had christened himself a "consulting Man of Vision" for the defense, was unimpressed. "I am leaving for the Hill of the Skull," he told a friend. "I shall put up at Chattanooga to avoid the hookworm," he promised. "I hear that 100 bootleggers and 250 head of Chicago whores will be in attendance."[15]

Summoned by "the sportive gods of news," as one of them put it, scores of reporters arrived, with their cheap suits, smart-aleck ways, and illicit whiskey, from the big-city papers of the East, Midwest, and South. Many of them slept on cots (and shared the single outhouse) at Bailey's hardware store, which they christened the "Press Hall" and filled with the clacks and dings of typewriters. Telegraph wires were strung from the upper floors of the redbrick Rhea County courthouse, and two dozen telegraph operators at the local Western Union office prepared to move 400,000 words a day. Microphones were set about the cavernous, freshly painted courtroom—the second largest in Tennessee, folks noted proudly, and newly scrubbed of tobacco juice—so that the trial could be broadcast by radio: an American first.[16]

There was more at stake, obviously, than Scopes and his eighth-grade biology class. Modernity was on trial. The headline in *Time* magazine promised, "Light vs. Darkness." And the Dayton prosecutors, thrust into the spotlight, focused on their duties. A regional attorney general, Thomas Stewart, led the Tennessee team, with Dayton's own Wallace Haggard, the Hicks brothers—Sue and Herbert—and the lovable rascal Ben McKenzie and his son Gordon. Bryan brought his son, William Jr., to the trial as well.

"I congratulate you on getting into it . . . The advertising this case will bring you will be worth untold money," the Reverend Ira Hicks, a minister, wrote his brothers. "You will have no trouble in making the evolutionists who take the stand look like a joke." Accomplished Red hunters sent the prosecutors dossiers on Darrow, Malone, and the ACLU. "From a friendly suit," wrote Kinsley, "this case has suddenly changed to a cold, stern fight."[17]

THE KEY TO that midsummer's showdown was, from the first, the issue of scientific testimony. The prosecutors always knew what their strongest argument was: the public's right to run its own schools. A teacher had broken a law. End of story. There was no need, really, to debate Darwinism at all.

"It is the *easiest* case to explain I have ever found," Bryan wrote to Sue Hicks. "While I am perfectly willing to go into the question of evolution, I am not sure that it is involved. The *right* of the *people* speaking through the legislature to control the schools which they *create* and *support* is the real issue as I see it."

Darrow, of course, had grand matters to place before the country—issues of academic liberty, free thought, and scientific inquiry. He hoped, by calling scientists to the stand, to educate the public and alert them to the threat posed by rural zealots with their silly lockstep creed. And the defense was aided by public expectations. The country was looking forward to a spectacular debate on Monkeys and Man, led by the titans Darrow and Bryan. A cut-and-dried case that addressed only the question "Did John Scopes teach the theory of evolution?" would make it look like Bryan and his team had fled the field. So Bryan set out to collect an array of experts of his own. "We can confine the case to the right of the legislature to control the schools and easily win," Sue Hicks wrote his brother Reese. "However, we want both legal and moral victory if possible."

The prosecutors felt cocky because Judge John Raulston, who would preside at the trial, had been "somewhat indiscreet," as Hicks put it, when plotting the case with them. But the churchmen whom Bryan solicited were not so confident. They worried about how the Yankee press would describe their faith in virgin births and talking snakes. One by one, Bryan's experts declined his invitation. And so, as the trial approached, the prosecutors returned to their initial strategy. They spoke no more about moral victories, and went to work on the judge, intent on keeping experts off the stand.

Raulston was a deeply religious man, born in a mountain vale called Fiery Gizzard, down near the Alabama border. He was a lay preacher in the Methodist Church and had taken a few turns speaking at revivals. And he was an ambitious man who knew his constituents and shared their pride and insecurities. "Scientific testimony for either side would be impertinent and incompetent," Hicks told him. "We have no desire to . . . allow the defense to turn loose a slush of scientific imagination and guesswork on our people, upon whom . . . these great lawyers from the north and northwest look with pity and compassion, denominating them a set of ignoramuses."

"If we can shut out the expert testimony, we will be through in a short time," Bryan wrote a friend on the eve of the trial. "I have no doubt of our final victory."[18]

Darrow had visited Dayton at the end of June to take his turn before the Dayton Progressive Club. "He was somewhat disarmed to find the people, not dogmatic and intolerant, but open minded and of sound judgment," Haggard told Bryan. Indeed it was so. Aside from the heat, Darrow thought Dayton a lovely little market town and he went to work wooing its residents. "He drawled comfortably and hadn't any airs," Scopes remembered. "He gave the impression he might have grown up in Dayton, just an unpolished, casual country lawyer."

Dayton charmed reporters as well. "The streets are asphalt, the electric lights work indoors and out . . . the girls are peaches and wear flapper clothes, the young fellows are stylish and collegiate," wrote Jack Lait for the Hearst news service. "An airplane . . . roars over the town and no horses shy and no yokels stare."

Colby and Malone were in Dayton as well, and it was this trip that "convinced Colby he would be happier elsewhere," said Scopes. The defendant and his lawyers had visited a courthouse in the mountains so Darrow and Colby could get a feel for local justice. "It was a rape case, and the defendant appeared to be a half-witted young fellow who wasn't sure what was going on," Scopes recalled. "His accuser was a young woman who seemed to know too well what was going on . . . She said she was pregnant and . . . as a means of escaping an embarrassing situation . . . had conveniently accused the poor devil of raping her."

A court-appointed counsel was botching the defense before an audience of gun-toting hillbillies. Colby was "overcome at the poverty, the ignorance and the uncleanliness of the inhabitants." But Darrow, outraged, muttered, "I am going to defend that boy" and headed toward the bench. Neal and Scopes blocked him, told him that an outsider would only alienate the jury, and muscled him into the car.[19]

Some wondered if Darrow was up to the task. Edgar Lee Masters wrote to Mencken, previewing the showdown. "I fear that you will find that Darrow is not the man to fight Bryan," Masters wrote. "I have seen Darrow perform over and over again. He must have the stage set, a complaisant judge or a fixed jury to be bold and even there his forte is a speech, such as it is. He fails in cross examination due to his lack of concentration, patience, sequences of plan, pugnacity and will. I have seen Darrow quit cold more than once where he could see that it meant labor to fight, and where the publicity was doubtful, or adverse. In a word he lacks character."

Mencken didn't disagree, but Darrow's flaws were irrelevant, the newsman replied. Everyone understood the strategy. "The way to handle it is to convert it into a headlong assault upon Bryan. He is the central figure, not that poor worm of a school master," Mencken wrote.[20]

DARROW RETURNED TO Dayton on Thursday, July 9, the eve of the trial. He had turned sixty-eight that April, and age had surely weathered him; his famously unruly forelock was cut short and rather than falling across his brow stayed plastered to his scalp. Yet there were still signs of the younger man in the cavernous, piercing eyes and mighty cheekbones. His arrival at the depot was not so lonely as a later generation of dramatists would have it (in *Inherit the Wind*, "A long ominous shadow appears . . ."). Newsreel cameras, photographers, and a scrum of reporters recorded the scene. Darrow wore a quality suit, a straw skimmer, and a short white necktie that, in the style of the time, fell halfway down his chest. And, of course, there were the galluses, which were there as courtroom props—to snap with emphasis, or to hook his thumbs into during an emblematic shrug—as much as to secure his trousers.

On the day before he left Chicago, Darrow encountered his friend Natalie Schretter at the railway station. She was with a young female lawyer whom Darrow much admired, and he sat himself between them on the train. He joked and chatted the whole way into town, on topics that ranged from Nietzsche to Kinsman. Darrow was "exuberantly happy—as gay as his bright red necktie" about the coming fight, Schretter recalled. He fondly described Amirus as "a real village cracker-barrel Nay-Sayer" and told the two young women, "His one wish was that his father could have come to Dayton with him."

With the rest of the visiting defense attorneys and the scientists who had come to testify on Scopes's behalf, Darrow stayed the night in an empty, bat-ridden, and dilapidated eighteen-room house on the outside of town, known locally as "the Mansion" and rechristened "the Monkey House." It was painted a faded yellow, with weathered brown trim. On the first night, it had neither power nor running water. "Shaving and washing were out of the question; food not even remotely on the horizon," the writer Marcet Haldeman-Julius, a friend of the defense, recalled.

Ruby arrived, checked out the Monkey House, and persuaded a

banker to move to his mountain cabin and let the Darrows have his home in town. Bryan and his wife were installed in the house of a local pharmacist. Mary Bryan had a poor opinion of the defense. Scopes, she wrote, "carries himself wretchedly . . . his whole appearance is simpering, weak and gawky." Neal "has the appearance of being suddenly frightened up out of the grass like a startled rabbit." Hays "is as forward and self-asserting as the New York Jew can be . . . His eyes are filled with shrewdness." And Darrow "has a weary hopeless expression, which might well prove his lack of faith. He wears rather soiled suspenders and his favorite attitudes are shrugging, and thrusting his hands under his suspenders . . . He speaks very calmly and deliberately and is full of sarcasm and bitterness."

Ruby shared Mary Bryan's prejudices toward Jews, but that was about all. She recalled, with a touch of acid, how the Great Commoner's wife, whose health had been failing, was "wheeled into the courtroom by her nurse . . . [with] her dainty white gown, her beautiful countenance and graces and almost-saintliness." There was no socializing. "I am not aware that [the Bryans] had any intention to be rude to me, but certainly they glanced the other way any time we were at all near each other."[21]

Mencken, with his suitcases, typewriter, and four bottles of Scotch, renounced the hazardous drive from Chattanooga—"The trip out and back gave me the worst scare I have had since the battle of Chancellorsville," he told his future wife—and checked into a boardinghouse, where he sat in his underwear each evening and crafted dispatches for the *Sun*. "Exactly twelve minutes after I reached the village I was taken in tow by a Christian man and introduced to the favorite tipple of the Cumberland Range: half corn liquor and half Coca-Cola," he wrote. "It seemed a dreadful dose to me, spoiled as I was by the bootleg light wines and beers of the Eastern seaboard, but I found that the Dayton illuminati got it down with gusto, rubbing their tummies and rolling their eyes."[22]

Yet there were those who saw the shadows of the place, and darker forces at work. Seven years earlier in the little burg of Estill Springs, some sixty miles from Dayton, a prosperous black farmer, Jim McIlherron, had shot into a group of white youths who were pelting him with rocks, killing two of his attackers. A white mob murdered a black minister who tried to help McIlherron escape, captured the fugitive, chained him to a hickory tree, tortured and castrated him with red-hot irons, and roasted him alive as two thousand tormenters, drawn by the chance to "have some fun with the damned nigger," cheered at his agony.

"One hundred percent Americans are now endeavoring to persuade hilarious and sarcastic Europe that Dayton, Tennessee, is a huge joke and very very exceptional. And in proof of all this the learned American press is emitting huge guffaws," wrote W. E. B. Du Bois in the NAACP journal, the *Crisis*. "The truth is and we know it: Dayton, Tennessee, is America! A great, ignorant, simple-minded land, curiously compounded of brutality, bigotry, religious faith and demagoguery, and capable not simply of mistakes but persecution, lynching, murder and idiotic blundering. . . .

"Dayton, Tennessee, is no laughing matter. It is menace and warning. It is a challenge to Religion, Science and Democracy."[23]

* *

THE TRIAL OPENED on Friday, July 10. To get to the redbrick courthouse, with its soaring clock tower and Romanesque arches, the spectators strolled through an arcade of refreshment stands selling fried chicken sandwiches, shucked corn, and watermelons, past booths where they could purchase religious tracts, including some from an itinerant Georgia preacher which insisted that blacks were not human. There were two or three stray souls in town "with obvious mental irregularities of a religious tendency" who would "chatter volubly to any one who will listen to them," the *Times* reported, and arcade games, including one in which the challenge was to "Hit the Nigger Baby." Further along, the town's children were delighted by trained monkeys, and their parents charmed by the blind minstrels Will Grissom and Charlie Oaks, who filled the square with spirituals and country ballads. On the courthouse lawn a platform had been erected in the shade of a big maple tree, with rows of benches, and loudspeakers to convey the proceedings to the overflow crowd. Pits were dug to roast sides of beef.

A thousand spectators climbed the central staircase to the second floor, where they jammed the courtroom, filling every seat and foot of standing room. They cheered Bryan, their hero, when he walked in. They waited patiently as Judge Raulston (wearing his best suit and accompanied by his wife and two daughters, Maryantha and Rose Comfort) gave the newsreel and newspaper cameramen full rein. And they bowed their heads as a fundamentalist preacher, L. M. Cartwright, opened court with a prayer that seemed to last for all eternity. The temperature soared as the day progressed. Like most men in the courtroom, Darrow doffed his jacket, showing lavender suspenders and a tan silk shirt, while Bryan joined those who waved palm-leaf fans distributed by a toothpaste company, on which was emblazoned the urgent question: "Do Your Gums Bleed?" It was the twenty-ninth anniversary, the newspapers noted, of Bryan's Cross of Gold speech.

Judge Raulston "is a pleasant faced man with a deep dimple in his chin," wrote Mary Bryan, "who tries to make everybody comfortable and happy and wants to do the fair thing." The morning was spent perfecting the indictment, which was suspect due to its hasty passage in May. It required a reading from the first chapter of Genesis and the following instruction from Raulston to the grand jurors, which ended any doubts of how the judge was leaning: "The school room is not only a place to develop thought, but also a place to develop discipline, power of restraint, and character," he told them. "If a teacher openly and flagrantly violates the laws of the land . . . his example cannot be wholesome to the undeveloped mind."

Nor was it difficult, that first morning, to foresee that the issue of expert testimony would dominate the trial. When Darrow asked the judge for adequate time to summon scientists from their far-off campuses and laboratories, Stewart warned that any such testimony "will be resisted by the state as vigorously as we know how." If the prosecution was persuasive, noted Kinsley, "Darrow's case in Dayton is gone."

In the afternoon, a jury was selected: ten farmers, a gray-haired schoolteacher, and a clerk. They might as well "have been recruited from the Anti-Evolution League," the *Tribune* noted. Darrow went through the motions of questioning the panel. "You say you couldn't read. Is that due to your eyes?" Darrow asked one farmer. "No, I am uneducated," the man replied. Darrow accepted him as a juror.[24]

DARROW SPENT MUCH of the weekend at the Monkey House, conferring with the other defense attorneys and dueling, in the press, with

Bryan. Mencken and friends snuck up on a gathering of "Holy Rollers," and he treated his readers to a glimpse of the "barbaric grotesquerie" that they witnessed as the hill folk spoke in tongues, and jerked and leaped and babbled as if possessed by demons. Will Rogers, considering the spectacle from afar, accused the celebrants of unfairly infringing on the entertainers' turf. "Ye Gods," he wrote. Up against the show that was going on in Dayton, "What chance has a poor comedian got?"[25]

To everyone's delight, Friday's formalities gave way to a roaring battle on Monday, when Neal rose and urged the judge to quash the indictment. He and Hays gave a number of specific and technical reasons why the Butler Bill violated the Tennessee constitution, and the prosecutors replied. There was an uneasy moment when McKenzie made a crack about "outside" lawyers, and then on Monday afternoon Darrow rose for the defense.

It was a terribly hot southern day. "The peasants pack into the courtroom like sardines in a can, eager to see Darrow struck dead," Mencken wrote his fiancée, Sara Haardt. "I have a window picked out and shall jump 40 feet when God begins to run amuck." It was likely, Darrow knew, his lone opportunity to speak on the issues that had brought him to Dayton. In order to keep Bryan from ending the trial with a grand, soaring speech, the defense planned to waive closing arguments.[26]

Darrow began with some genial banter, thanked the court for bestowing on him the honorary title of "Colonel," and praised the locals for the courtesies that he and the others had received. Then his tone changed, and the mood in the courtroom was transformed as he pointed at Bryan and blamed him "for this foolish, mischievous and wicked act." Darrow was off, lashing out at the fundamentalists "with a hunch of his shoulders and a thumb in his suspenders," challenging "every belief they hold sacred," the *Times* reported. "He prowled around inside the big arena of the courtroom, his voice sinking to a whisper at times, again rising in a burst of rage as his head dropped to his chest and thrust forward. He knew that he was defying the lightning."

If the Butler Act was upheld, said Darrow, "we will establish a course in the public schools of teaching that the Christian religion as unfolded in the Bible is true, and that every other religion, or mode or system of ethics is false."

"Would that be constitutional?" he asked. "If it is, the constitution is a lie and a snare and the people have forgot what liberty means. . . .

"Here we find today as brazen and as bold an attempt to destroy learning as was ever made in the middle ages, and the only difference is that we have not provided that they shall be burned at the stake," Darrow said. "But there is time for that, Your Honor," he said mockingly. "We have to approach these things gradually."

Darrow was best with grand and sweeping themes, and here he had to argue technical points of law: Did the introductory "caption" of the act, as required, match its substance? Was the law properly crafted and uniform in application? Was the indictment sufficiently specific? But though the content was sometimes dry, Darrow's performance made the afternoon memorable. He paced like a big caged cat. He tugged at his galluses. A small tear at the elbow of his shirt got bigger with each gesture, until his sleeve was in tatters.

"He would stop and brood a minute, hunching his shoulders almost up to his ears, and then they would drop, his hand would shoot forward and his lower lip protrude as he hurled some bitter word at his opponents," said the *Times*. Or he would pause, gently swaying, his thoughts coming slowly, and then "launch himself, a thunderbolt of indignation, words streaming from him in a torrent of denunciation." Occasionally, for emphasis, he would bring his right palm down on his left with a resounding smack.

The audience was mesmerized. The only sound, aside from his voice, was the clicking of the telegraph keys that were carrying his speech to millions of Americans.

He had nothing against the Bible, Darrow said. "I know there are millions of people in the world who derive consolation in their times of trouble and solace in times of distress from the Bible," he told the court. "I would be pretty near the last one in the world to do anything or take any action to take it away." But using government to impose a religious creed on Americans was terribly dangerous. "There is nothing else, Your Honor, that has caused the difference of opinion, of bitterness, of hatred, of war, of cruelty, that religion has caused."

Faith "is one of those particular things that should be left solely between the individual and his Maker," Darrow said. America's freedoms are not preserved for one sect of Christians. "To think is to differ." The constitution protects all creeds, even the "Mohammedan" and "the Buddhist" and "the Chinaman."

"Can a legislative body say, 'You cannot read a book or take a lesson or make a talk on science until you first find out whether [what] you are saying [is] against Genesis?' " Darrow asked. "Can it say to the astronomer, you cannot turn your telescope upon the infinite planets and suns and stars that fill space, lest you find that the earth is not the center of the universe and there is not any firmament between us and the heaven? Can it? It could—except for the work of Thomas Jefferson, which has been woven into every state constitution of the Union, and has stayed there like a flaming sword to protect the rights of man."

Faith and science are not exclusive, he argued. A man or woman could accept Darwin's teachings and still love God. "There are people who believed that organic life and the plants and the animals and man and the mind of man . . . are the subjects of evolution," Darrow said, "and that the God in which they believed did not finish Creation on the first day, but that he is still working to make something better and higher still out of human beings."

But then "along comes somebody who says, 'We have got to believe it as I believe it. It is a crime to know more than I know.' And they publish a law to inhibit learning," Darrow said. "It makes the Bible the yardstick. . . .

"Are your mathematics good? Turn to First Elijah two. Is your philosophy good? See Second Samuel three. Is your astronomy good? See Genesis, Chapter Two, Verse Seven. Is your chemistry good? See . . . Deuteronomy . . . or anything else that tells about brimstone. . . .

"You can close your eyes," Darrow warned his countrymen. "But your life and my life and the life of every American citizen depends after all upon tolerance and forbearance . . . If men are not tolerant, if men cannot respect each other's opinions, if men cannot live and let live, then no man's life is safe."

After two hours, Darrow was nearing the end. The Tennesseans leaned forward, disturbed but attentive. Bryan sat tight-lipped. Judge Raulston interrupted, tried to stop Darrow. It was getting late—end tomorrow. Darrow ignored him. Finished the lesson.

"If today you can take a thing, like evolution, and make it a crime to teach it in the public school, tomorrow you can make it a crime to teach it in the private schools, and the next year you can make it a crime to teach it to the hustings or in the church. At the next session you can ban books and the newspapers. Soon you may set Catholic against Protestant, and Protestant against Protestant, and try to foist your own religion upon the minds of men.

"If you can do one you can do another," he said. "Ignorance and fanaticism is ever busy and needs feeding . . .

"After awhile, Your Honor, it is the setting of man against man and creed against creed until—with flying banners and beating drums—we are marching backwards to the glorious ages of the 16th century when bigots lighted fagots to burn the men who dared to bring any intelligence and enlightenment and culture to the human mind."

It was done. Darrow was content. The crowd did not applaud, but his friends gathered around and praised his work. "The clanging of it was as important as the logic," Mencken said later. "It rose like a wind and ended like a flourish of bugles." Even Masters was impressed. "At last Darrow has his hour," the poet wrote to a friend. "He is a grey eyed infidel, and all his life he has been talking this stuff; now he can empty his mind of it on a good occasion."

Darrow adjourned to Robinson's drugstore for ice cream. A mighty summer storm swept through Dayton that night, knocking out the town's electric power. "I ain't going to say exactly that this is a judgment," a townsman by the name of Buckshot Morgan was alleged to have told a reporter. "But it certainly is powerful mysterious."[27]

Raulston had promised to rule on the defense motion to quash the indictment on Tuesday morning. But he was delayed by Monday night's blackout and extended his deadline until Wednesday. As they waited the two sides were drawn into a noisy scrap about religion.

Darrow began it by interrupting the minister, who was about to offer the daily benediction.

"I object to prayer," said Darrow.

"It has been my custom since I have been judge to have prayers in the courtroom . . . I know of no reason I should not follow up this custom," Raulston said, dismissing the objection.

"Just a minute," said Darrow. "We took no exceptions on the first day, but seeing this has persisted in every session and the nature of this case being one where it is claimed by the state that there is a conflict between science and religion . . . I do object to the turning of this courtroom into a meeting house."

"Such an idea extended by the agnostic counsel for the defense is foreign to the thoughts and ideas of the people," said Attorney General Stewart.

"Those prayers we have already heard, having been duly argumentative . . . help to increase the atmosphere of hostility to our point of view, which already exists in this community by widespread propaganda," Malone replied.

"I would advise Mr. Malone that this is a God-fearing country," said Stewart.

"It is no more God-fearing than that from which I came," said Malone.

Raulston reached for a Solomon-like settlement. He would expand the list of clergymen who offered prayers. It would ultimately include a rabbi, and even a Unitarian.

The defense experts, meanwhile, were arriving in Dayton. One night after dinner, zoologist W. C. Curtis adjourned with Darrow to the mansion porch, where they continued a discussion begun at the table about mortality. Curtis had been diagnosed with cancer and told he had no more than a year to live. He was living with "the expectation of death," he recalled. The two men talked quietly, and Darrow was able to lift the man's spirits. "I can never be quite so lonely again having known you," Curtis told him in a letter that summer. He thanked Darrow for sharing a creed—"that those who strive to live righteously as they see it in this life need not fear the future."[28]

THERE WERE COURTESIES all around on Wednesday morning. Hays offered his hand to Stewart, who had apologized for intemperance. And Darrow declared that he took no offense at being labeled an agnostic. "I do not presume to know, where many ignorant men are sure," he said. "That is all agnosticism means."

Then, as expected, Raulston declared that the indictment was proper, and the trial lurched into gear. The jury was sworn in. Stewart and Malone made opening statements. The prosecutors summoned schoolboys and other witnesses to the stand to establish that Scopes had indeed taught the theory of evolution.

"He said that man had a reasoning power that these animals did not," said one young scholar.

"There is some doubt about that," Darrow said, to general laughter.

The evidence was lacking; even Scopes could not recall just what he had taught his students. But Darrow was not looking to win on a technicality; he wanted the knockout. "Your honor, every single word that was said against this defendant—everything was true," he stipulated. Then the defense called its first witness—zoologist Maynard Metcalf from Johns Hopkins University—and things came to a halt. The jury was sent out as Metcalf explained just what he would say if allowed to testify. Raulston listened, Stewart objected, and the judge scheduled arguments on whether the experts could testify for Thursday.[29]

Bryan led off the afternoon session on Thursday with the sweeping argument that his admirers, who swamped the courtroom, expected. He drank deeply from a jug of water, and then walked forward with a fan in one hand and Hunter's textbook in the other. He stood erect, defying the heat with a starched collar and a small black bow tie. The loop of a heavy chain drooped from his watch pocket. "I never saw him quite so agitated," Mary Bryan wrote her daughter. "He trembled when he stood up."

"Has it come to a time when the minority can take charge of a state like Tennessee and compel the majority to pay their teachers while they take religion out of the heart of the children?" Bryan asked. "Parents have a right to say that no teacher paid by their money shall rob their children of faith in God and send them back to their homes skeptical, infidels, or agnostics or atheists."

From the first, Bryan played to the crowd, with stale jokes that won laughs from his adorers. He cited Darwin's claim that humanity descended from the Old World branch of apes. "Not even American monkeys," Bryan sniffed, "but from Old World monkeys."

"I hope the reporters get the 'Amens' in the record," Darrow interjected when the crowd responded with joyous ejaculations.

"The Bible is the Word of God. The Bible is the only expression of man's hope of salvation," Bryan preached. "The Bible, the record of the Son of God, the Savior of the world, born of the virgin Mary, crucified and risen again—that Bible is not going to be driven out of this court by experts who come hundreds of miles to testify that they can reconcile evolution, with its ancestor in the jungle, with man made by God in his image."

It was a fair speech. A good speech, even, for a Sunday pulpit. But it fell far short of the moment. Bryan had not routed the defense, put a dent in Darwin, or effectively dealt with the legal question he supposedly was addressing. "Once the voice had in it the qualities of brazen trumpets but the resonance had gone from the brass. Once it had . . . the qualities of a stringed instrument, but today the strings were loose and discordant. Once it had the booming note of the drum, but today the drum showed that it had been punctured in many places, and its hollowness was evident," wrote William O. McGeehan of the *New York Herald Tribune*. The larger jury—the national audience—was unimpressed, and the Great Commoner sensed it. "Mr. Bryan seemed to feel that he had swung and missed. The brethren and sisters . . . looked sorrowful and disappointed."[30]

Mencken called Bryan's effort "downright touching in its imbecility . . . Once he had one leg in the White House, and the nation trembled under his roars. Now he is a tinpot pope in the Coca-Cola belt, and a brother to the forlorn pastors who belabor half wits in galvanized iron tabernacles behind the railroad yards. . . .

"When he sat down he was done for, and he knew it," Mencken wrote. "He sat into his seat a wreck."

Bryan fretted more as Dudley Malone gave a triumphant rebuttal. He began with a fine trick worthy of a Yankee lawyer. Throughout the trial, no matter how stifling the heat, heedless of Raulston's urgings that the lawyers doff their coats, Malone had kept his jacket on. No matter how many handkerchiefs he soaked, mopping sweat from his face and scalp, the coat stayed on. The locals had taken it as a sign of madness, discussed it at length, and settled on begrudging admiration. Now, with a marvelous flourish, Malone removed his jacket, carefully folded it, and laid it down. Had there been any doubt about the import of the moment, it was gone.

Bryan had famously promised "a duel to the death," Malone reminded his listeners. "Is our weapon to be taken from us, so that the duel will be entirely one-sided?"

Expert testimony was required, Malone argued, because of the word *and* in the statute. The prosecution was required by the wording of the Butler law to show that Scopes had taught about the descent of man *and* taught a theory incompatible with Divine creation. But the defense would show that the theory of evolution was perfectly compatible with Scripture, he said. "Keep your Bible. Keep it as your consolation. Keep it as your guide," Malone told the true believers. "But keep it where it belongs, in the world of your own conscience, in the world of your individual judgment . . . in the world of theology."

Malone's speech was what Bryan's was not: relevant, persuasive, and alive. And loud. "It roared out of the open windows like the sound of artillery practice," Mencken wrote, "and alarmed the moonshiners and catamounts on distant peaks." He was arguing for fairness, and for something with popular appeal for Dayton and its merchants—a chance to extend the trial.

"The truth always wins, and we are not afraid of it," Malone said. He faced Bryan and asked why the prosecution was so fearful.

"We are ready," Malone taunted. "We feel we stand with progress. We feel we stand with science. We feel we stand with intelligence. . . .

"Where is the fear? We meet it!" he said. "Where is the fear? We defy it."[31]

MALONE'S SPEECH WAS received, the court reporter noted in his transcript, with "profound and continued applause." Among those applauding, said a Chattanooga paper, "were many Daytonians who had come to scoff, and left to think." Malone was, they said to one another, a northern Patrick Henry. "The last effort of the orator of the Cross of Gold had been, what they call on Broadway, a flop," said McGeehan. "The speech of Dudley Field Malone was a wow."

It was left to Stewart to close the debate. He did so, slyly mixing law with politics. The defense may quibble about the word *and*, he told the judge. But when a statute was confusing, Stewart said, "the cardinal rule of construction is that the intention of the legislature must prevail." And everyone in Tennessee knew what the legislature intended when it passed that bill: no evolution.

Don't let the Yankees confuse you, he told Raulston. "When science treads upon holy ground, then science should invade no further," said Stewart. "Why have we not the right to bar the door to science when it comes within the four walls of God's church?" The people—the voters—were watching. "Let us not make a blunder in the annals of the tribunals of Tennessee."

Stewart had begun with reasoned tone, but by the end he was shouting like the evangelist Billy Sunday, crouching and waving his arms. The trial was matching its hype. It was the "day of days," a Chattanooga paper reported. Darrow would recall it as "a summer for the gods."

THURSDAY NIGHT at the Monkey House, Darrow warned his experts not to celebrate: "Today we have won, but tomorrow the judge will have recovered and will rule against us." And on Friday, Raulston did just that. "The evidence of experts would shed no light on the issues," he announced.

"Tennessee closed the door against science today," wrote Kinsley. "Fundamentalism has won." A happy Mary Bryan wrote her daughter: "As matters now stand, the case is clearly lost to the defense."

Darrow fumed. Hays raised a caustic objection. Stewart took exception to the manner in which Hays objected. "Well, it don't hurt this court," said Raulston, trying to soothe things.

"There is no danger of it hurting us," said Darrow.

"No, you are already hurt as much as you can be hurt," Stewart gloated.

"Don't worry about us," Darrow shot back. "The state of Tennessee don't rule the world yet."

But it seemed, at the time, like bravado. And as the morning went on, Darrow's anger got the better of him.

"Has there been any effort to ascertain the truth in this case?" Darrow demanded of the judge when Raulston ruled against him on a minor matter. "I do not understand why every request of the State and every suggestion of the prosecution should meet with an endless waste of time, and a bare suggestion of anything that is perfectly competent, on our part, should be immediately overruled."

"I hope you do not mean to reflect upon the Court?" said the judge.

Darrow plucked at his cornflower-blue suspenders. "Well, your honor has the right to hope," he said.

"I have the right to do something else, perhaps," said Raulston.

"All right," Darrow dared him. "All right."[32]

MENCKEN LEFT TOWN on Saturday.

"The trial has blown up," he wrote Haardt. "Holy Church is everywhere triumphant." The greatest journalist of the era, the ferocious iconoclast who, more than any other, had transformed *State of Tennessee v. John Thomas Scopes* into a national frolic, left town before the final verdict. In doing so, he missed the biggest story of his life.[33]

It is difficult to fault Mencken or the other newsmen who departed. Raulston's ruling was the latest in a series of setbacks the judge had dealt Scopes. And that weekend word made its way around town: the judge was sure to cite Darrow for contempt when court resumed Monday. The defense would be fortunate, it was said, if the trial did not end with both Scopes *and* his attorney behind bars.

Meanwhile, a delegation of Dayton businessmen spent Saturday searching for Mencken, intending to convey their anger at the way he had portrayed them as rubes in his dispatches. It gave rise to a story that he fled a tar and feathering. Absurd, Mencken told Sara. He had magazine deadlines to meet, and was tired of the food, sick from the heat, and exhausted by the work. "I have just got back from Dayton, and am all in. Two weeks of infernal weather, with very little sleep," Mencken wrote a friend on Sunday. "This evening I shall lay in eight cocktails, eat a big dinner, and then stick my nose into the malt."

But, most of all, Mencken thought the fireworks were finished. "Darrow has lost," he told his readers.

"There may be some legal jousting on Monday . . . but the main battle is over, with Genesis completely triumphant."[34]

AT THE MONKEY HOUSE on Saturday, stenographers took down statements from the defense experts to build a record for the appeal. Bryan and his wife went to visit Lookout Mountain. Scopes went dancing. And Darrow made a strange phone call—or so it seemed—to the Jewish scholar Rabbi Louis Ginzberg, whose Sabbath he interrupted. His friend Darrow wanted to know: "Where did Cain get his wife?"

Sunday evening Darrow sat down with Hays and Harvard University geologist Kirtley Mather, who knew his Bible as well as his rocks. The two lawyers asked Mather to play the role of William Jennings Bryan, and together they conducted a mock interrogation, quizzing the professor about Adam's rib, Jonah and the whale, and other biblical tales.

It was the trap that Darrow had tried to set with his public letter to Bryan in 1923. If Bryan insisted that the Bible must be taken literally, he would have to defend some mighty strange things. But if the Commoner strayed from a literal interpretation, he opened himself up to the defense team's contention—that Creation may have included evolution.

"I'm going to put a Bible expert on the stand," Darrow told Charles Francis Potter, a Unitarian minister who had journeyed to Dayton to help the defense. "A greater expert than you—greatest in the world—he thinks." Darrow asked Potter to page through a Bible, looking for "all the unscientific parts." He gave him a sheaf of telegrams that the defense had received with advice from supporters around the country. "See if there are any good ideas we can use," Darrow said.[35]

Putting an opposing champion on the stand was an unusual tactic, but Bryan should have seen it coming. Darrow had done it several times in his career. And the notion was in the air: Darrow's hometown *Tribune* openly speculated, on the weekend before the showdown, about what he might do if given the chance to cross-examine Bryan. Darrow had dared Bryan, in the press, to submit to questioning "in open court under oath." And the defense, in fact, had already shown its hand in court—on Thursday, when Darrow quizzed Ben McKenzie about his beliefs.

It happened when McKenzie was ridiculing the defense contention that evolution and Genesis were reconcilable. "They want to put words in God's mouth," McKenzie said, "and have Him say that He issued some sort of protoplasm, or soft dish rag, and put it in the ocean, and said 'Old boy, if you wait around for 6,000 years, I will make something out of you.' "

The audience laughed. But Darrow rose to challenge him. "Let me ask a question," Darrow said. "When it said, 'in His own image' did you think that meant the physical man? . . . You think men must believe that, to believe the Bible—that the physical man as we see him looks like God?"

"The reason I believe that firmly is because the Bible teaches it," said McKenzie.

"Let me ask another question," said Darrow. "You said there was the first day, the second day, the third day . . . do you think they were literal days?"

"We didn't have any sun until the fourth day," McKenzie acknowledged. But he sensed where this was headed and swiftly extricated himself.[36]

AND SO IT happened that on Monday, after Raulston had cited Darrow for contempt of court and Darrow had, with elaborate and suspicious humility, apologized, and the judge had just as elaborately—reciting poetry and prayer—forgiven him, and after Hays had spent long hours of the morning reading excerpts from the experts' affidavits into the record, the proceedings were moved for a few final chores to the speaker's platform of rough-hewn wood that had been erected on the north side of the courthouse for preachers and performers.

It was just too hot, and the crowd too large, for the courtroom, Raulston said; he had been warned that the floor was showing signs of collapse. So tables and chairs were carried to the outdoor stage; thousands of spectators sat in rows of makeshift benches or stood in the shade of the maple trees on the two-acre lawn, and reporters leaned from the courthouse windows.

"The change from the hot stuffy courtroom was a very agreeable one," Mary Bryan wrote, though she was disappointed that Darrow had not been found in contempt. "I would not have wept if he had spent the night in jail. He has been so abusive, so bitter and so venomous all the way through."

After the usual verbal tilt, Darrow persuaded the judge to have the "Read Your Bible" sign removed from the courthouse wall. Then Malone whispered to Scopes, "Hell is going to pop now!" and Hays was calmly telling the judge, "The defense desires to call Mr. Bryan as a witness . . ."

There was a split-second pause as Hays talked on and three thousand souls tried to grasp what he had asked. Then, Scopes recalled, "all of the lawyers leaped to their feet . . . the judge blanched and was at a loss for words. Everyone seemed to be talking at once." After a bit of argument—for nothing was accomplished in Dayton without argument—Raulston allowed Bryan to take the stand.

Indeed, Bryan demanded to testify. He was still hurting from the whipping he'd gotten from Malone on Thursday. And he was angry at the charge, made by the defense and widely circulated, that he was hiding behind the judge's rulings, afraid to fight for his beliefs. It was a terrible decision. Darrow's legal talents were well known and freshly honed; Bryan had not been in a courtroom for twenty-eight years. Darrow frequently joined in debates; Bryan's public appearances were always monologues. Darrow had rehearsed that weekend; Bryan was seemingly caught by surprise.

But "it was his one opportunity to recoup the glory," Scopes wrote. "He underestimated Clarence Darrow."[37]

For the next two hours, penned on that small stage, Darrow and Bryan would be but three or four feet—often, just inches—apart. Darrow would stand with arms folded, or slouch in a chair, or lean, half-sitting, on the court reporters' pinewood table. Bryan glared from an office swivel chair that had been carried out for use as the witness stand; he clutched a palm-leaf fan in his fist. By the end they would be standing, shouting insults, pointing fingers, or shaking fists in each other's faces.

"You have given considerable study to the Bible, haven't you, Mr. Bryan?" Darrow began. "Do you claim that everything in the Bible should be literally interpreted?"

"I believe everything in the Bible should be accepted as it is given there," Bryan replied. "Some of the Bible is given illustratively. For instance: 'Ye are the salt of the earth.' I would not insist that man was actually salt, or that he had flesh of salt . . ."

"But when you read that Jonah swallowed the whale—or that the whale swallowed Jonah, excuse me please—how do you literally interpret that?"

"When I read that a big fish swallowed Jonah . . . I believe it. And I believe in a God who can make a whale and can make a man and make both do what he pleases."

For Bryan, so far so good. The fundamentalists in the audience heartily approved his defense of Jonah. The men were smoking. Children played on seesaws made from the rough wood benches. Bryan was calm and contemptuous as Darrow probed, looking for a weakness, Scopes said, like "a hawk after prey."

"You don't know whether it was the ordinary run of fish, or made for that purpose?" Darrow asked.

"You may guess. You evolutionists guess," Bryan responded.

"But when we do guess, we have a sense to guess right," said Darrow.

"But do not do it often," said Bryan.

The Commoner thought things were going well. The crowd was with him. He was enjoying himself. He leaned to one side and a little bit forward, resting an elbow on the arm of his chair. "One miracle is just as easy to believe as another," he said.

Small boys walked through the crowd selling soda pop. An airplane sailed overhead. The judge relaxed and picked up an afternoon newspaper, with its account of Darrow's apology.

"Do you believe Joshua made the sun stand still?" Darrow asked.

"I accept the Bible absolutely," said Bryan.

Stewart objected. He could see where Darrow was going. If Joshua was said to have made the sun stand still, then the authors of the Old Testament must have believed that the sun was in motion around the earth—an error corrected by Copernicus and Galileo. The questioning, Stewart said, "has gone beyond the pale of any issue that could possibly be injected into this lawsuit." But Bryan and Raulston, pleased to be providing the crowd-pleasing showdown that folks had been clamoring for, brushed the objection aside.

> DARROW: "Have you an opinion as to whether whoever wrote the book, I believe it is . . . the Book of Joshua . . . thought the sun went around the earth?"
> BRYAN: "I believe that he was inspired."
> DARROW: "Can you answer my question?"
> BRYAN: "When you let me finish the statement."
> DARROW: "It is a simple question . . ."
> BRYAN: "You cannot measure the length of my answer by the length of your question."
> (Laughter in the courtyard.)

DARROW: "No, except that the answer be longer."
(Laughter in the courtyard.)
DARROW: "Do you think whoever inspired it believed that the sun went around the earth?"
BRYAN: "I believe it was inspired by the Almighty, and He may have used language that could be understood at the time . . . instead of using language that could not be understood until Darrow was born."
(Laughter and applause in the courtyard.)

Still no blood. Darrow prowled on. He brought up the story of the Great Flood and of Noah, who was said to have gathered all the animals, two by two, in an ark that rode out the storm. Seventeenth-century scholars had fixed the date of man's creation at around 4000 B.C.

"You believe the story of the flood to be a literal interpretation?" he asked.

"Yes, sir," said Bryan.

"When was that flood . . . about 4004 B.C.?"

"That has been the estimate," Bryan said. The calculations, made by a Protestant bishop in 1650, were included as annotations in the well-known King James Version of the Bible. At first, Bryan hesitated to defend them.

"I never made a calculation," Bryan said.[38]

But Darrow fired his questions rapidly.

DARROW: "A calculation from what?"
BRYAN: "I could not say."
DARROW: "From the generations of man?"
BRYAN: "I would not want to say that."
DARROW: "What do you think?"
BRYAN: "I do not think about things I don't think about."
DARROW: "Do you think about things you do think about?"
BRYAN: "Well, sometimes."
(Laughter in the courtyard.)
POLICEMAN: "Let us have order."

I do not think about things I don't think about. The exchange made Bryan look silly, pathetic, ignorant. *Do you think about things you do think about? Well, sometimes.* It has echoed through history for almost a century. *Laughter in the courtyard.*

Now Stewart tried, again, to stop the fight.

"I am objecting to his cross-examining his own witness," the prosecutor said. But the judge left it up to Bryan.

"I want him to have all the latitude he wants," Bryan said. No one would say he ran away. "For I am going to have latitude when he gets through."

"You can have latitude and longitude," said Darrow.

It was a silly pun, but it drew a laugh from the spectators. The people of Dayton "forgot for a moment that Bryan's faith was their own," wrote a newsman. "The crowd saw only the battle."

Again, Stewart objected. McKenzie was on his feet too. And again, Bryan insisted on continuing. Darrow and his colleagues "did not come here to try this case. They came here to try revealed religion," Bryan said, rising from the swivel chair to address the crowd out on the lawn. "I am here to defend it, and they can ask me any questions they please."

Bryan's loyalists applauded, but it was a poison gift. Their approval only spurred their hero on.

DARROW: "Great applause from the bleachers."
BRYAN: "From those whom you call yokels."
DARROW: "I have never called them yokels."
BRYAN: "That is the ignorance of Tennessee, the bigotry."
DARROW: "You mean who are applauding you?"
(Applause.)
BRYAN: "Those are the people you insult."
DARROW: "You insult every man of science and learning in the world because he does not believe in your fool religion."

But Bryan had lost his way. He was now defending not the wisdom of the Good Book, but a three-hundred-year-old pseudo-history created by a long-dead Irish bishop. And each of Darrow's goading questions revealed more of Bryan's closed-mindedness, and his ignorance of science and history. It made Bryan look stupid. The farmers in their overalls may have loved him for it, but no thinking person could escape the conclusion.

"Don't you know there are any number of civilizations that are traced back to more than 5,000 years?" Darrow asked.

"I have no evidence of it that is satisfactory," said Bryan. His face was red. He glowered at Darrow. "No evidence that I have found . . . would justify me in accepting the opinions of these men against what I believe to be the inspired word of God."

So, asked Darrow, "whatever human beings, including all the tribes that inhabited the world . . . and all the animals, have come onto the earth since the flood?"

"Yes."

"Do you know a scientific man on the face of the earth that believes any such thing?"

"I don't think I have ever asked one the direct question."

"Quite important, isn't it?" Darrow's arms were crossed, and he tapped his gold-rimmed spectacles against his biceps.

"Well, I don't know that it is," said Bryan. "I have been more interested in Christians going on right now."

"You have never investigated to find out how long man has been on the earth?" Darrow asked.

"I have never found it necessary."

"Don't you know that the ancient civilizations of China are 6,000 or 7,000 years old, at the very least?"

"No, but they would not run back beyond the creation, according to the Bible."

"Have you any idea of how old the Egyptian civilization is?"

"No."

Bryan was getting tired. And more so after, at Bryan's insistence, Darrow let him make a rambling speech about comparative religions. Now Darrow drew him back to specifics.

"Do you think the Earth was made in six days?" he asked Bryan.

"Not six days of 24 hours," Bryan replied.

Again, the wary Stewart saw where they were headed. Bryan was abandoning a literal interpretation of the "days" of Genesis. To those who were familiar with Bryan's personal views of evolution, this was not surprising—but Stewart knew that the audience, and the crowd of reporters, would see it as a faith-shaking concession.

"What is the purpose of this examination?" Stewart demanded of the judge.

Bryan, finally, sensed danger. He lashed out at Darrow. "The purpose is to cast ridicule on everybody who believes in the Bible," Bryan said.

"We have the purpose of preventing bigots and ignoramuses from controlling the education of the United States, and you know it, and that is all," said Darrow.

"I am trying to protect the word of God against the greatest atheist or agnostic in the United States," said Bryan, up on his feet and waving a finger at Darrow. "I want the papers to know I am not afraid."

Darrow promised Raulston to wrap things up. He had only a few more questions, he told the judge.

DARROW: "Do you believe that the first woman was Eve?"

BRYAN: "Yes."

DARROW: "Do you believe she was literally made out of Adam's rib?"

BRYAN: "I do."

DARROW: Did you ever discover where Cain got his wife?"

BRYAN: "No sir; I leave the agnostics to hunt for her."

DARROW: "There were no others recorded, but Cain got a wife."

BRYAN: "That is what the Bible says."

And now, as they approached the two-hour mark of the debate, Darrow returned to Bryan's admission that the "days" of Genesis may have lasted more than twenty-four hours.

Goaded by his adversary, Bryan struggled to explain. "I do not see that there is any necessity for construing the words 'the evening and the morning' as meaning necessarily a 24-hour day," Bryan said.

"You think those were not literal days," said Darrow.

"I do not think they were 24-hour days," said Bryan. "I think it would be just as easy for the kind of God we believe in to make the earth in six days as in six years or in six million years or in six hundred million years. I do not think it important whether we believe one or the other."

"The creation might have been going on for a very long time?" Darrow asked.

"It might have continued for millions of years," said Bryan. There was a collective gasp—some claimed they heard shouts of disapproval—from the crowd.

Bryan had conceded one of the defense team's most important arguments. For if a Christian was not bound to a literal translation of Genesis, and could construe that God took hundreds of millions of years to make the world, why couldn't he construe that God's creation of man took ages as well? And if so, then the Bible and evolution, faith and science, were indeed reconcilable.

Bryan had "agreed that no intelligent person would accept the Bible literally," Hays recalled. "It seemed to many that Darrow demolished the fundamentalist case, for if anything is conceded to interpretation, the fundamentalist authoritarian position is destroyed."[39]

Darrow's job was almost finished, as he took one last shot at the wounded prey. There was an unanswered riddle from his old list of Bible questions. To ask it now was cruel and gratuitous—an obvious play for cheap laughs. But he went ahead and read aloud from Genesis, the story of Eve and the apple.

"Do you think that is why the serpent is compelled to crawl upon its belly?"

"I believe that," said Bryan.

"Have you any idea how the snake went before that time?"

"No, sir."

"Do you know whether he walked on his tail?"

The laughter of the crowd brought Bryan to his feet. "Your Honor, I think I can shorten this testimony. The only purpose Mr. Darrow has is to slur at the Bible," he shouted. "I want the world to know that this man, who does not believe in a God, is trying to use a court in Tennessee to slur at it."

"I am examining you on your fool ideas that no intelligent Christian on earth believes," Darrow yelled back. They were both on their feet, shaking their fists. And with that Raulston adjourned the most memorable session of any American legal case, ever.

"The followers of Darrow rose up and swarmed to his side, anxious to seize the hand of their champion," said Hays. "Bryan stood apart, almost alone, a strained tired expression on his face as he looked into the twilight that was closing about him."[40]

For those who witnessed the great duel under the maples, there was no escaping the conclusion that Bryan had blundered terribly.

BRYAN IS WORSTED, read a headline in the *Chattanooga News*. His concession on the length of days was "a real victory for the defense," the paper reported. Bryan's answers, the *News* editorial said, had been "grossly inadequate. His personal knowledge of science was not of a nature particularly responsive to a hostile examination." It was a charitable conclusion.

Mary Bryan felt that "Papa stood by his guns very manfully" under Darrow's abusive questioning. But things had gone badly, she wrote her children. The Infidel had fired so many questions so fast that Papa's "answers made him appear more ignorant than he is." And "of course, it went out over the country."

Indeed it did. A narrative of Bryan's fall in a man-to-man duel with Darrow was irresistible to the skeptics of the press, with their innate contempt for jay towns and fun-killing preachers. "I made up my mind to show the country what an ignoramus he was and I succeeded," Darrow wrote the absent Mencken. Darrow went back to the Monkey House, leaned back in a chair on the porch, and let the newspapermen do their work. They had found a third act for their modernist script: teacher persecuted. Titans grapple. Freedom triumphs. And out across the country—or at least in the bigger towns and cities—an American population that venerated science and progress saw in Bryan not a great moral leader. They saw instead a crank.

"There was no pity for the helplessness of the believer come so suddenly and so unexpectedly upon a moment when he could not reconcile statements of the Bible with generally accepted facts," the *Times* reported. "There was no pity for his admissions of ignorance of things boys and girls learn in high school, his floundering confessions that he knew practically nothing of geology, biology, philology, little of comparative religion and little even of ancient history." The newspaper was describing the reaction of the crowd in Dayton, but the words applied to the millions who had followed the trial from home. "And finally, when Mr. Bryan, pressed harder and harder by Mr. Darrow, confessed he did not believe everything in the Bible should be taken literally, the crowd howled."

Across America, the crowd howled. And Bryan had further gall to drink. Stewart called on him that night and told him the trial would end the next morning, without giving Bryan an opportunity to put Darrow on the stand. Stewart had skillfully managed the case, to the considerable frustration of the defense attorneys, until Bryan's performance wrecked things. Stewart could not stop it as it happened, but he was determined to halt it now. He absolutely refused to let Bryan match wits with Darrow again.[41]

It rained on Tuesday, and the trial moved back into the courtroom, where further disappointment awaited Bryan. The jury was brought in and both sides asked it to return a guilty verdict, so that the case could move on to higher courts. Bryan had labored for weeks on a monumental address—it was to be a capstone of his career—but there would be no more long speeches, and he was left to implore the remaining reporters to include a text of his remarks in their coverage. Raulston fined Scopes $100.

"The papers are prejudiced against us and may not say so," Herbert Hicks wrote his brother Ira. But "we gave the atheist Jew Arthur Garfield Hays, the agnostic Clarence Darrow, and the ostracized Catholic Dudley Field Malone a sound licking."

But at trial's end, the crowd surged to congratulate Darrow. He "was delighted as a boy and seemed as shy," one account noted. Bryan was "a weary, heartbroken man," wrote another correspondent. And so ended what Bryan called the "little case of little consequence."[42]

Most of the participants and reporters left Dayton that evening, but not the two titans. They each had speaking engagements to honor in Tennessee and wanted to rest and enjoy the scenery. Darrow was the featured guest at a dance thrown by Dayton's young people, where he danced a waltz with Malone's handsome wife. Bryan kept to his fervent schedule with no apparent signs of discouragement. Five days after the trial, Darrow was sightseeing in the Smoky Mountains near Knoxville when a reporter tracked him down with the news that Bryan, while napping in his borrowed bed in Dayton, had died in his sleep.

Darrow managed to compose a suitable public tribute to his old foe. But when it was suggested that Bryan died of a broken heart he murmured, "Busted heart nothing; he died of an overstuffed belly."

"The lapse of time leaves heroes stranded," the *Nation* reported, in its farewell tribute. It was Bryan's great flaw "that his heart was much stronger than his head . . . He was lost when pinned down to detail.

"Always the heart swept him on, with no check from a reasoning hand," the magazine said. "And when Clarence Darrow got him on the witness stand he revealed himself as a pathetically sincere and pitifully ignorant old man."[43]

Bryan's funeral was a national event. He was still, Will Rogers wrote, the tribune of the little folk. His death gave a hyperdramatic coda to the Scopes trial, further cinching its claim on history. He was buried at Arlington National Cemetery, his coffin draped in an American flag. And the poet Vachel Lindsay wrote:

Where is that boy, that Heaven-born Bryan
That Homer Bryan, who sang from the West?
Gone to join the shadows with Altgeld the Eagle,
Where the kings and the slaves and the troubadours rest.

Chapter 19

SWEET

That is all there is to this case . . .
Take the hatred away and you have nothing.

When he arrived in Tennessee in the summer of 1925, Darrow was a famous man; by the time he left, he was an American folk hero. He had been known for much of his professional life as a radical, a rebel, and a champion of underdogs. Now, after winning Chief Healey and Fred Lundin their freedom, saving the lives of Leopold and Loeb, and besting Bryan in the Bible Belt, he emerged as an American archetype: the legal sorcerer who won hopeless cases.

The Monkey Trial had captured the American imagination. Ernest Hemingway slipped a mention of Bryan's demise into *The Sun Also Rises*. Inspired by the events in Dayton, Sinclair Lewis began work on *Elmer Gantry*, a tale of a corrupt preacher. There was a slice of Darrow in the lawyer Billy Flynn in the 1926 play *Chicago*. And "Get Clarence Darrow!" cried editor Walter Burns when *The Front Page* debuted on Broadway in 1928. There was no need to explain the joke to Manhattan theatergoers: it signified the depth of the editor's predicament. Darrow had become, Lincoln Steffens would write in the *Saturday Review*, the "Attorney for the Damned." Or, as *Vanity Fair* christened him, "The Great Defender."

The Scopes trial "was inconceivably dramatic: two ancient warlocks brought jaw to jaw at last," wrote Mencken. "It was superb to see Darrow throw out his webs, lay his foundations, prepare his baits. His virtuosity never failed. In the end Bryan staggered to the block and took that last appalling clout. It was delivered calmly, deliberately, beautifully. Bryan was killed as plainly as if he had been felled with an axe. He rolled into the sawdust a comic obscenity."[1]

Darrow's friends rejoiced. "Nothing is dangerous which the whole world is laughing at, and the world is laughing at Tennessee and Mr. Bryan," Erskine Wood wrote in his diary. In Europe, Brand Whitlock shared a similar sentiment in his journal: "This chance, Darrow made the most of, rendering Bryan ridiculous."[2]

When Darrow arrived back in Chicago, he could have demanded staggering fees for whatever fat and easy cases struck his fancy. Instead, he worked almost a year for meager wages saving Negroes charged with murdering a white man.

THE KILLING OCCURRED on September 9, 1925, but the tension that caused the event began to build the day before, in a modest middle-class neighborhood on the east side of Detroit. At mid-morning a truck filled with furniture moved up to the curb at the corner of Garland and Charlevoix Avenues, where young black men carried furniture into a two-story brick bungalow. The house belonged to Dr. Ossian Sweet, twenty-nine, and his twenty-three-year-old wife, Gladys. With their baby daughter, they were the first African American family to settle in this white neighborhood and had no illusions about how they would be welcomed. Among the furnishings were a sack of firearms and a satchel heavy with some four hundred rounds of ammunition.

Earlier that summer, Dr. Alexander Turner, another black physician, had been confronted by a mob as he tried to move into his purchased house in a white neighborhood in Detroit. Rocks and bricks shattered the windows of his car and home and, at gunpoint, he was compelled to sign a deed and relinquish ownership of the property. Turner was but one of a number of black homebuyers who met violence when they tried to move outside the city's cramped "Black Bottom" ghetto. In several cases, the blacks or police had to ward off racist mobs with gunfire.

Sure enough, a crowd of several hundred white people gathered at the corner of Garland and Charlevoix that evening; some rocks were thrown, and those in the house heard shouted vows to get the "niggers." A contingent of Detroit policemen kept the whites in order, and the night passed without violence. The Sweets went shopping for furniture for their new home on Wednesday, and Ossian spent the afternoon seeing patients at his medical practice in the black quarter of the city. But alarmed by reports that the mob would return, he asked his brothers—Henry and Otis—and a group of friends, and some friends of friends, to help defend his home.[3]

At nightfall on Wednesday, the crowd was back, lining the sidewalks and lots across the streets. Inside, the black men tried to calm themselves with a game of whist and waited for a dinner of fresh ham, greens, and sweet potatoes. Gladys was baking a cake for dessert. Then, as Otis and a friend arrived in a taxi, the first rock hit the house. Ossian opened the door to let his brother in and saw the crowd surge toward the house. Stones rained on the roof and porch. Someone shouted, "The people! The people are coming!" A bedroom window was broken. The men armed themselves and took firing positions throughout the house. Another pane shattered. And, down in the dining room, Ossian heard volleys of gunfire.

Some twenty shots were fired. On the lawns and sidewalks across the avenues, men ducked and women screamed and ran to collect their children. Two of the Sweets' white neighbors went down, hit by gunshots. One of them, a foreman at an auto plant named Leon Breiner, was smoking his pipe when a bullet hit him in the back. He bled to death before doctors could save him. A dozen Detroit policemen who had been stationed about the corner were stirred into action by the fusillades, and an officer fired at the armed black men on the second floor. Inspector Norton Schuknecht, the burly, double-chinned officer in charge, chuffed up the steps of the Sweet house and, incongruously, rang the doorbell.

"Jesus Christ!" he exploded, when Ossian let him in. "What in hell are you fellows shooting for?"

"Why, they're ruining my house," Sweet stammered.[4]

News of Breiner's death spread quickly. The crowd swelled into the thousands, black motorists on nearby streets were assaulted, and the police had to deploy an armored car and hundreds of club-wielding officers to keep the house protected. The Sweets and their friends were stripped of their weapons—a shotgun, two rifles, and seven handguns—and pushed from the house, out the back door and across the yard, into a paddy wagon parked in the alley. Only the drawn guns of the police kept the whites at bay.

Ossian and Gladys and nine of their friends and family members were taken to police headquarters and questioned that night. Most tried to obfuscate, but Henry Sweet, twenty-one, the doctor's brother, told his interrogators how he crouched at the front window with a rifle and, with the stones "pouring down like rain," fired two shots "to protect myself." If he had not acted in self-defense, Henry told the authorities, "probably, I would have been dead by now."

The white prosecutors saw things differently. The blacks had provoked things by moving into a neighborhood where they were not wanted. The crowd on the corner was tiny and tame. The threat "was not sufficiently serious to justify taking a life," the prosecuting attorney would claim later. "If a man threatens to slap my face, I have no right to kill him." All eleven black men were charged with assault with intent to commit murder, and with first-degree murder for the death of Leon Breiner. In the parlance of the law, they had maliciously conspired "to shoot to kill without legal justification or excuse."

THE SWEET BROTHERS, grandsons of slaves, had been raised in the South. Ossian was born in central Florida in 1895, the oldest surviving boy of ten children in a family of hardworking farmers. At the age of thirteen Ossian was sent north, to a Negro college in Ohio. To help pay his tuition, he got summer jobs in Detroit. In 1917, he entered medical school at Howard University in Washington, D.C., and after graduation moved back to Michigan, where he opened his practice, met and married Gladys, and joined Detroit's professional black elite. He tended the sick and injured at the Negro hospital, opened a pharmacy, and took Gladys to Europe, where he studied advanced medicine in Vienna and Paris.

Otis, a dentist, joined Ossian in Detroit, as did Henry, a college student. They were part of the great migration of African Americans who made their way north in the years around World War I, fleeing the Jim Crow era in the South, manning the factories, and packing the cramped black ghettoes of New York, Chicago, Detroit, and other cities. Almost a million blacks made the journey, one-tenth of the nation's Negro population.

"The great majority of people came here absolutely broke . . . you saw families coming here with their old clothes, and a basket and a bundle . . . just getting here, you know," the black lawyer Charles Mahoney recalled. "They lived where they could and they worked for what they could get . . . They had no experience, they had no money, they had no contacts. They were just here . . . They came because it was better, you know. They came looking for hope."

Three or four families shared a single apartment. Homes took in so many lodgers that they might as well have been hotels. Stables, garages, and cellars were converted into rented rooms. A growing number of the new arrivals, like the Sweet brothers, were college educated and middle class. They vowed to secure their rights.[5]

The NAACP was a symbol of this militancy. Since the days of its founding, the organization had grown more professional and aggressive. In 1920 James Weldon Johnson—lawyer, poet, journalist, songwriter, diplomat, and educator—took over as the NAACP's executive secretary, as its chief operating officer was known. He was the first black man to hold that office. Johnson hired Walter White, a young blond-haired blue-eyed Negro novelist as assistant secretary and sent him and others around the country to catalog incidents of injustice. The results of their investigations were printed in the *Crisis*, edited by the brilliant Du Bois.

Almost a century after they were written, the NAACP's accounts of racial barbarity retain the power to sadden and revolt. As awful as is the image of a mob hanging a Negro from a light post, the reality is worse. The victims rarely met their deaths with a quick snap of their necks: they were tortured, mutilated, and burned alive. Often, the blacks lost their ears, fingers, or teeth, which were kept by their killers, or their killers' children, or sold as souvenirs. Five dollars a tooth. Two bits for a link from the chain.

White was twenty-four when he joined the NAACP. Within months he was in southern Georgia, where a black man named Sidney Johnson killed a white man who had beaten him. A mob seized two random blacks and shot them seven hundred times, then, over a period of time, killed seven more innocent African Americans. Mary Turner, the widow of one of the dead men, threatened to swear out warrants for his killers. She was eight months pregnant, but her affront was not forgiven. The mob hung her upside down from a small oak tree, splashed her with gasoline, and set her on fire. She declined to die and was hauled back up, and her unborn child cut from her womb with "a knife, evidently one such as is used in splitting hogs," White wrote. "The infant, prematurely born, gave two feeble cries and then its head was crushed by a member of the mob with his heel. Hundreds of bullets were fired into the body of the woman, now mercifully dead." Johnson was finally trapped in a cabin and died in a shootout. His corpse was castrated, dragged through town behind a car, tied to a tree, and burned.[6]

The race riots were lynchings on a grander scale, accompanied by widespread killing, looting, and burning of Negro neighborhoods. Hundreds of blacks died in massacres at Elaine, Arkansas, Ocoee and Rosewood, Florida, and Tulsa, Oklahoma, and in urban rioting in Chicago, East St. Louis, and Washington, D.C. Ossian Sweet had witnessed both kinds of atrocities. When he was a small boy, the rape and murder of a young white woman had enflamed the white community in his Florida town, terrifying the Sweets and other black families, until a Negro teenager confessed to the crime. He was tied to a tree and burned alive. And Sweet was in Washington in 1919, studying the healing arts at Howard, when reports that a white woman had been raped by a black man triggered four days of rioting, beatings, and gunfire in the nation's capital. He had relatives living near Ocoee, where the black section of town was torched and its inhabitants hunted down in 1920. These events and other like them were foremost in his mind on the night of September 9, as the stones came through the windows of his home.

"I was filled with a peculiar fear," he would testify. "The kind no one could feel unless they had known the history of our race."[7]

JAMES JOHNSON WAS tracking the events in Detroit that summer. The city had become a stronghold of the reborn Ku Klux Klan. Tens of thousands of the hooded bullies had marched brazenly down Pennsylvania Avenue in Washington that August. In Detroit's mayoral election in 1924 the KKK ran its own candidate, staged an outdoor meeting that drew fifty thousand people, and appeared to have won until its foes, employing the election machinery, had thousands of votes ruled invalid. A Klan-supported candidate was back in the fall of 1925, challenging Mayor John Smith. All-white neighborhood "improvement associations" were organized, and lawyers wrote racial covenants that banned blacks from white communities. The NAACP had warned its local branch to protect "colored householders from mob violence."

The NAACP's lawyers were preparing to argue a segregation case before the Supreme Court that fall, and Johnson needed a compelling controversy to call attention to the issue and help him raise money for the legal defense team. When he read about the Sweets in the New York newspapers, Johnson wired the Detroit branch asking for details. He got its request: send Walter White.

Like Johnson, White was a remarkable man. He was fair-skinned enough to pass as white—which immeasurably aided his investigative work—but chose to live life as a Negro. He was an indefatigable networker, hosting a cultural salon that brought friends like Mencken and Lewis in contact with Paul Robeson, Langston Hughes, and other African American artists.[8] White saw the potential to raise consciousness and cash with the Sweet case. He informed the defendants and their supporters in Detroit that the NAACP would pay for a top-notch white lawyer to represent them if they surrendered control to his organization. The Sweet brothers, whose lives were in jeopardy, jumped at the chance. "I expressed our insistence on the retaining of the very best lawyer available," White told Johnson. "I pointed out that this cast no reflections on the colored lawyers, but that it was a question bigger than Detroit . . . for it was the dramatic climax of the nation-wide fight to enforce residential segregation."

Now the NAACP needed an attorney to fulfill its promise. On October 7, Johnson sent a long telegram to Darrow in Chicago. "This issue constitutes a supreme test of the constitutional guarantees of American Negro citizens," the NAACP director wrote. "Defense requires ablest attorney of national prestige."

After leaving Tennessee, Darrow had traveled a bit—visiting Paul in Colorado and the Haldeman-Julius farm in Kansas. "I had determined not to get into any more cases that required hard work and brought me into conflict with the crowd," Darrow recalled. "But I could not rest. I get tired of resting." Now Darrow happened to be in New York for a reunion of the Scopes defense team and the journalists who covered the trial. Hearing this, Johnson grabbed White, Arthur Springarn, the chair of the organization's legal committee, and Springarn's law partner, Charles Studin, and headed for Arthur Garfield Hays's home, where Darrow was staying.

Springarn and Studin were dark-complexioned white men, and White was a light-complexioned black man. As Darrow told them of his reluctance to take the case he turned to Springarn and assured him: "I know full well the difficulties faced by your race."

"I'm sorry, Mr. Darrow," Springarn said. "I am not a Negro."

"Well, you understand what I mean," he told Studin.

"I am not colored either," Studin replied.

With a certain degree of exasperation, Darrow turned to White. "I wouldn't make the same mistake with you," he told the blond-haired black man.

"I smiled and told him I *was* colored," White recalled.

Darrow chuckled. After some hawing he agreed to take the case. Hays signed on as well. Both men agreed to accept the fees the NAACP was offering: $5,000 in Darrow's case and $3,000 for Hays. A white Detroit lawyer and three black attorneys from the city who had been representing the Sweet group in preliminary hearings were also retained. Herbert Friedman, a friend of Darrow's from Chicago, volunteered his services.

"It is a thrilling situation there and we have got a very hard fight on our hands," White told a friend. "With Mr. Darrow as our chief counsel, we have got a fighting chance to win."[9]

THE NAACP ANNOUNCED Darrow's participation on October 15. "The atmosphere of the case changed when Darrow came in," Otis Sweet recalled. "That's when you built up a little hope."

The Sweet case would win but a fraction of the publicity and attention given the Monkey Trial. But Darrow's participation caused many in white America to consider the issues raised by the shooting. "This was no ordinary murder trial," David Lilienthal wrote in the *Nation*. "Back of it all was the whole sensitive problem of race relations, intensified a thousandfold by the recent Northern migration of the Negro."

The sturdy old saw "a man's home is his castle" reflected the belief that an individual may use deadly force when defending himself, his family, or his home. So two questions ruled the case: Did Negroes have the same right of self-defense as white people? And if so, had the Sweet defendants been truly threatened? The trial was set for October 30, leaving Darrow and Hays little time to prepare. They were fortunate that the judge was on their side.

Judge Frank Murphy was a long way from the U.S. Supreme Court seat he would one day occupy, and a few years away from terms as Detroit's mayor and Michigan's governor. By the fall of 1925, however, he had made a mark as an up-and-coming liberal leader who had won his robes by assembling a coalition of Irish, Italian, and other ethnic voters, the swelling black electorate, Jews, and white professionals, and become presiding judge of the city's criminal courts. It was the same kind of coalition that governors Al Smith and Franklin D. Roosevelt forged in New York, then built across the nation. "A liberal wave is just beginning to gather momentum," Murphy told a friend. "Public opinion moves in cycles. We are on the upward swing." When Darrow looked up at the mahogany bench in the Sweet trial, he saw a red-haired lawyer with progressive beliefs, a devout and sentimental Irish Catholic with a political debt to the black community. Where other judges saw the Sweet case as a "graveyard," Murphy saw an opportunity.

Not that he was reckless. Murphy could have dismissed the case, but he wanted white Detroit to believe that justice had been served and preferred "that they be acquitted by the jury," a local NAACP official told White. But Murphy "is only awaiting the opportunity to take a definite stand in favor of the defendants," the official wrote. "I have been advised, confidentially, that Murphy expects to run for mayor two years hence, and will use this case to win the Negro vote."[10]

It took Darrow and Wayne County prosecutor Robert Toms a week to choose a jury. Toms was a proud and ambitious man, tall and affable, whose decision to press the case was supported by the judges who, at preliminary hearings, allowed it to proceed. He admired Darrow and treated him with deference, in part not to rile him. At one point, Darrow complained. "Toms, you aren't treating me fair in this case," he said. "You're so darned nice I can't get going."

Toms had Schuknecht and his policemen and a troop of residents from the neighborhood who would swear that the few white people who gathered around the Sweet house on the night of the shooting had been well behaved. Darrow had a group of frightened blacks who had lied to the police and answered even their own lawyers evasively. "On the face of it, our case was not strong," Hays said. "Shooting from various windows indicated a concerted plan . . . We took their stories one by one and they didn't wholly jibe."

Toms found twelve men to his liking in a single day. Then it was Darrow's turn. He had no deep-pocketed union like the AFL to pay for research on potential jurors—he had to rely on his own skill and intuition and what gossip the local lawyers brought in. But Murphy could be counted on to rule his way on challenges for cause, and state law gave Darrow 330 peremptory challenges. So he took his time, working his way through the panels of candidates, asking about their profession, faith, subscriptions, memberships, and political leanings, and their opinions on black folks, property values, and the like.

"Every question he asks," Murphy told a friend, "sets up a chain reaction in the mind of every man in that box. Just watch their faces. They are doing more thinking about this subject of race than they have ever done before in their lives. Darrow is trying his case now. He is preparing that jury to appraise and interpret all the evidence which will be presented later on. The prosecution knows this but they don't know how to stop him."

Wearing his familiar gray suit, Darrow slouched with his hands in his pockets or slowly roamed the marble-floored courtroom, with its marble wainscot and gray and ivory walls, speaking in a low voice to the talesmen. "He's got the court—judge, clerk, attendants—all with him, most of the jurors are eager," White wrote Johnson. "He ever so often makes some droll remark that sets the entire courtroom to laughing and instantly all tension is relieved."[11]

Darrow pushed too far with one prospective juror when, after almost satisfying himself, he asked the talesman where he got his news. The *Nation*, he said, and Toms promptly had the man excused. "You have to know where to stop," Darrow told friends that night. "One question too many and you lose a desirable juror. I should have known enough to refrain."

In the midst of the process, Mayor Smith crushed his Klan challenger in the municipal election. It was a good omen. Darrow and Hays found three Klansmen in the jury pool and sent them packing as well. Jury selection ended on Wednesday, November 4—the day after the election—with a collection of ethnic Catholics, immigrants, and workingmen on the panel.[12]

On the first day of testimony, Toms put his key witness on the stand. Aside from any prejudice against blacks he may have harbored, Inspector Schuknecht had a motive for declaring that all was peaceful outside 2905 Garland Avenue on the night Breiner died: he was there with specific orders to prevent what took place.

No one could have seen it coming, Schuknecht assured the jury; the crowd on the corner numbered no more than a dozen. No one was shouting, no rocks were thrown; all was quiet when suddenly, without provocation, the blacks opened fire.

Darrow began his cross-examination before lunch and continued until court adjourned that evening. As Darrow fired questions, the inspector conceded that within a block of the Sweet house "a couple hundred people" had gathered on the night of September 8, and that "quite a number of automobiles" were cruising by and unloading passengers at dusk on September 9, prompting him to blockade the street. And, toward the end, as Schuknecht sagged under the strain of his long day on the stand, he admitted that he found a half a dozen or more stones on the porch and roof of the house. Darrow asked him to describe the front bedroom. What besides the furniture was there?

"A small stone," Schuknecht acknowledged.

"Did you find any broken glass?"

"Yes . . . ," the inspector testified. "We found the stone on the inside, and I believe it was thrown from the outside."

Toms was aggrieved. "You cannot ask for anything better than that, can you?" he muttered.

Toms called other police officers and residents of the neighborhood to buttress Schuknecht's claim that the blacks were not in danger. But the testimony seemed contrived—too good to be true. And one witness let slip why.

When Toms questioned him about the size of the crowd, Dwight Hubbard stumbled. "There was a great number . . . I won't say a great number—there were a large . . . there were a few people there," he testified.

"When you first started to answer the question . . . you started to say you saw a great crowd there, didn't you?" Darrow asked him when his turn came to cross-examine.

"Yes, sir."

"Then you modified to say a large crowd, didn't you?"

"Yes, sir."

"Then you said a few people . . ."

"Yes, sir."

Hubbard had been coached by the police, Darrow said, and instructed to testify that only a few people had gathered. Wasn't that so?

"Yes, sir," the man, now thoroughly miserable, admitted.

Afterward, Toms conceded that his witnesses were inferior—in terms of education, intellect, aplomb, and appearance—to the Negro defendants. Steadily, the estimates of the size of the crowd given by the prosecution witnesses inched upward—toward and beyond one hundred. Two youngsters admitted that they heard glass breaking as boys threw stones at the Sweet residence.

"I heard some noise . . . it may have been stones, or mud . . . hard dirt, you know, striking something . . . maybe it was against this house," one witness conceded.

"You knew sounds of something striking a building came from that direction . . . ," Darrow said.

"Well, it seemed like it, yes," said the witness.

"And you knew the sounds of breaking glass came from that direction?"

"Yes."

"And they came about the same time?"

"Yes."

"And after that—the shooting?"

"Yes."

It was grueling, and at times depressing, work exposing the prejudices of human beings. One night, in a discussion about the defendants, a tired Darrow asked Hays, "What difference does it make whether or not these people go to jail?"

Hays was surprised. If Darrow felt like that, Hays asked him, why was he defending them? "I dunno," said Darrow. "I suppose I'd be uncomfortable if I didn't."

From the prosecution witnesses Darrow drew the story of the Waterworks Park Improvement Association, an all-white group that lured hundreds of people to a protest meeting at the elementary school across the street from the Sweet house a few weeks before the shooting, at which speakers urged them to drive the black residents out. "I don't believe in mixing people together that way, colored and white," one neighbor explained.[13]

Darrow and Hays meshed well, White said: "Hays the logician, relentless, keen, incontrovertible; Darrow the great humanist, pleading with fervor for decency and justice and tolerance, breathing into the law romance and beauty and drama." One of Hays's central missions was to keep them from being snagged by a legal trick or an obscure precedent. One day Toms asked Darrow if he wasn't going to join them in the judge's chambers, where Hays was arguing a point of law. "Nooo, I guess not," Darrow said. "I can't be bothered with the books. Let Arthur take care of that."[14]

DARROW HAD NO trouble filling his time in Detroit. Watching Darrow had become an event for the smart set. He would meet Hays and White and others to wind down and plot strategy at his quarters in the Book Cadillac Hotel, and then join journalists, vivacious young actresses, and other celebrities at a large round table. The girls were "young, attractive, on their toes with the gait of the world," Ruby wrote. Darrow held court, "beaming with his own happiness."[15]

On one evening he made the trip to Ann Arbor, where, after dining at a fraternity house on campus, he addressed more then four thousand students at his alma mater. He spoke to some 1,500 black people who gathered at a YMCA in Detroit and addressed the Detroit Federation of Labor. A young theologian, Reinhold Niebuhr, was in the audience, and came away impressed. Darrow made the crowd "writhe as he pictured the injustices and immoralities of our present industrial system," Niebuhr wrote, though "the tremendous effect of his powerful address was partially offset by the bitterness . . . I suppose it is difficult to escape bitterness when you have the eyes to see and the heart to feel what others are too blind and too callous to notice."[16]

Darrow also joined Hays and White at gatherings of the city's Penguin Club, a hangout for silk-stocking liberals. It was there he spotted Josephine Gomon. The thirty-three-year-old "Jo" was the daughter of a college professor. By the time she met Darrow she had worked her way through the University of Michigan as a switchboard operator, graduated with a degree in engineering, taken a job teaching physics at City College in Detroit, married, and had five children. After seeing two friends die in childbirth, Gomon became a champion of family planning and got into politics. She was an adviser to progressive leaders like Harriet McGraw and Judge Murphy and attended the Sweet trial as often as she could.

Darrow nurtured the relationship by chatting with Gomon during breaks in the trial and by walking her to her car after court ended for the day. Her diary offers a glimpse of Darrow's seductive advances. "Women fall into two classes for him—those he is interested in and those he isn't," she wrote. "He treats all the former with the same flattering attention as if they were the only woman—each of them—that he had ever found worthy of notice. And he is quite sincere. He enjoys women—especially young ones."[17]

THE DEFENSE BEGAN to present its case on Monday, November 16, when Hays gave the opening statement.

"Our defense is based upon a sacred ancient right, that of protection of home and life," Hays said. The prosecution had told the story of what happened outside 2905 Garland Avenue, Hays told the jurors, now the defense would let them see what happened inside the house. At one point he had Ossian Sweet rise in the dock so the jurors could look at him as Hays described the doctor's long journey, in the teeth of prejudice, to the day he proudly bought a home for his wife and daughter.

Darrow and Hays called African American witnesses to describe the other instances in which black families had been driven by mobs from their homes, and friends who told the jury about the mounting fear in the Sweet home those two days in September. Philip Adler, a white reporter for the *Detroit News*, told how he was driving by early on the night of the shooting and saw a crowd of four or five hundred people gathered at the corner. Thinking they were drawn by a newsworthy fire or traffic accident, he stopped, and some in the mob told him they were there to get the Negroes out. Before the gunfire, he said, he heard a continuous pelting sound, like hail on a roof. And though they did not base their entire defense on the theory, Hays and Darrow suggested that Breiner may have been hit by a stray round fired by police.[18]

On November 18, Ossian Sweet took the stand and gave what the *Nation* called "a vivid picture of the fear-ridden mind of a black man, terrified by a hostile crowd of whites." When Toms objected to Sweet's account of the racial violence he had witnessed in his life, Darrow responded: "This is the question of the psychology of the race . . . of how everything known to a race affects its actions." The judge allowed the testimony.

"A car had pulled up to the curb," Sweet said, recounting the events of September 9. "My brother and Mr. Davis got out. The mob yelled, 'Here's niggers! Get them! Get them!' As they rushed in, the mob surged forward. . . .

"It looked like a human sea. Stones kept coming faster. I was downstairs. Another window was smashed. Then one shot—then eight or ten from upstairs. . . .

"When I opened the door and saw the mob," Sweet told the jury, "I realized I was facing the same mob that had hounded my people through its entire history."[19]

THE CLOSING ARGUMENTS began on November 24, the Tuesday of Thanksgiving week. Darrow began in the afternoon session. Extra police were called to handle the crowd. "A deep silence fell over the crowded noisy courtroom," wrote Lilienthal. "The old man with the unutterably sad face and the great stooped shoulders seemed no mere lawyer pleading for hire. He seemed, instead, a patriarch out of another age, counseling his children, sorrowing because of their cruelty and hatred."

The Sweet defense team's duty in the trial was to show that the shooting was justified. And they had been successful; it now seemed clear that a threatening mob had surrounded the doctor's house that night. The witnesses who claimed that all was calm were lying, Darrow told the jurors, and any thinking man knew it.

"Every one of them . . . perjured themselves over and over and over again to send twelve black people to prison for life," Darrow said. "The almost instinctive hatred of the white for anything that approaches social equality is so deep and so abiding in the hearts of most white people that they are willing to perjure themselves on behalf of what they think is their noble, Nordic race. . . .

"I don't need to take any pains to prove to you what was the cause of this trouble down at Charlevoix and Garland, do I?" he asked. It was racism, pure and simple. "If you don't know it, you are stupider than any people I have ever seen in the jury box yet, and I have seen some daisies in my time. . . .

"Is there anything criminal about Dr. Sweet?" he asked them. "Would you be afraid to meet him in an alley? Not a minute. You know there is not the first element of criminality in him." The real criminals, Darrow said, were out on the street that night. But the jurors had to get past their own racism to see it.

"How many of you have close friends who have African blood in their veins? How many of you have visited their homes? How many of you have invited them into your home to dine with you? If no, why not? Is it anything except a long feeling of race distinction that has come to us? We know not where it came from or how deep it is. Is there anything else? You know there is not."

Hands thrust into his pockets, or thumbs stuck in the armholes of his vest, speaking conversationally, he reminded the jury of witnesses like Hubbard, who admitted during cross-examination how they had been coached. Darrow's voice was "a low rumble; in it resounded all the misery his tired eyes had seen," Lilienthal recalled, except when "suddenly the voice . . . rang out like a brass gong" and "every muscle of the huge body was tense and strained."

The mob on Garland Avenue was "gathered together just the same as the Roman Colosseum used to be filled with a great throng of people with their eyes cast on the door where the lions would come out," Darrow said. "They were gathered together just as in the old days a mob would assemble to see an outdoor hanging, waiting for the victim with their eyes set on the gallows.

"You gentlemen know the danger. One man might not bother about driving a Negro out of his home, but get 100, 500, 1,000—one man gathers from another, and mob psychology is the most dreadful psychology that man has to contend with," Darrow told the jurors. "It is like starting a prairie fire, this gathering of a mob. Somebody comes along and throws a match into the dry stubble, and it spreads and spreads and spreads and the wind fans it and the flames make the wind and finally the two together, spreading and spreading, will pass all obstacles and devour everything in its way.

"Before you know it, if it is not quenched, if the power of the state is not placed upon it, it has spread from neighbor to neighbor, it draws into its grasp the wicked and even the innocent, it draws into its grasp the evil and the good, until by mob psychology it sweeps all before it and destroys life and property and liberty, because each gathers force for the other until the power is irresistible."

At that, Darrow stopped, and court was adjourned for the day. "It was wonderful. Eloquent. Logical. People wept and jurors were moved," Jo Gomon told her diary.

That evening, after another Penguin Club event, Darrow tried to lure Gomon to his room. "Do you mind if I walked to the street car with you?" he asked, taking hold of her arm and drawing her through the lobby of the Wolverine Hotel.

"I'd be delighted but I'm driving," she said.

"Then you'll drive me home?" he said. "Come up to my room. I'm expecting a couple of interesting fellows over and we'll read poetry."

But then Harriet McGraw and another friend who had accompanied Gomon that night joined them at the car. "You seem to be well protected," Darrow said regretfully. "I was looking forward to having a nice long talk with you."[20]

MURPHY HAD AN ambitious agenda for Wednesday. It was the day before Thanksgiving, and he wanted to finish the closing speeches and give the case to the jury. With luck, they might even get a quick verdict. Darrow resumed, challenging the jurors to step outside their skin.

"Put yourselves there, gentlemen, that is all I ask you, put yourselves there, with the history of your race back of you, with the stories of assaults and lynchings and destroying homes back of you, put yourselves there, with the injustice that has been inflicted upon blacks for all these centuries, and which is pursuing them still."

Acquit my clients, Darrow told the jurors, and repair the damage caused by America's shameful original sin. "He seemed to be pleading more that the white man might be just, than that the black be free; more for the spirit of the master than the body of the slave," said Lilienthal. But there were moments as well when, "aroused and angered, his head lowered like a fighter coming out of his corner, he turned upon the prosecutors, his arms swinging, eyes narrowed and pitiless. . . .

"There are no more underground railroads or fugitive slave laws or whipping posts," Lilienthal wrote. "But there are mobs and torches and trees hideous with swinging black shapes and there is suspicion, prejudice, hatred. And on the new battlefield, fighting a subtler foe, and one that may perhaps never be defeated, is Clarence Darrow, son of the Abolitionists."

Black people would one day gain equality, Darrow predicted. He urged the jurors to help them make the journey.

"Do you think that these people, simply because their color is black, are to be forever kept as slaves of the white? Do you think that all the rights which you claim for yourselves are to be denied them?" he asked.

"I do not believe it . . . Oh no. There are colored people of intellect, and colored people of courage, and colored people who risk their fortunes and their lives for their independence," he said. "You cannot get rid of them, gentlemen, they are here. . . .

"The world moves slowly, but it is forever grinding, and it grinds down injustice and wrong and prejudice and hate, even though it is by the slow and cruel process of years," he said as he closed. "I ask you—more than everything else—I ask you in behalf of justice, often maligned and down-trodden, hard to protect and hard to maintain, I ask you in behalf of yourselves, in behalf of our race, to see that no harm comes to them."

It was not the argument of a cynic.

After a brief recess, Toms sought to bring the case back from the lofty place where Darrow had raised it.

"Darrow doesn't want to look at it as a criminal case, but as a cross section of human nature," said Toms. "But that's not what we are here for."

"It isn't your business" to settle the nation's racial problems, he told the jury. "This courtroom is just a tiny speck in the world. We are not going to change anything here. . . .

"What an insignificant figure Breiner has been in this argument, and yet we started out to find who killed him."

Toms turned to address Hays and Darrow.

"All your specious arguments, Mr. Darrow, your artful ingenuity born of many years experience—all of your racial theories, Mr. Hays, all your cleverly conceived psychology, can never dethrone justice in this case," Toms said. "Leon Breiner, peaceably chatting with his neighbor at his doorstep, enjoying his God-given and inalienable right to live, is shot through the back from ambush. And you can't make anything out of those facts, gentlemen of the defense, but cold-blooded murder."

DARROW AUTOGRAPHED BOOKS when the court adjourned for lunch. Then he invited Gomon to dine with him. They both were disappointed when Ruby arrived in the courtroom.

"Aren't you going to lunch, D?" Ruby asked her husband.

"No, I don't want anything. Haven't you had lunch?"

"Certainly not, and the Hayses want us to go out with them."

"Tell them I'm busy. Can't possibly get away. Have to see some people. And I don't want any lunch anyway. You go with them," he told her.

She tried to persuade him to eat a little something at least. "I don't want anything," he snapped. Once Ruby left the courtroom, Darrow returned to Gomon. "A married man isn't even supposed to know when he wants to eat," he chuckled. "Well, I guess we can go now. How about it? Do you know some place where we can get some wine?"

Darrow collected his coat and hat, and he and Gomon set off for their private get-together. To their dismay, they ran into Ruby and Hays and his wife in the lobby.

"Where you going Clarence? Change your mind about lunch?" Hays asked. Yes he had, said Darrow. They would have to "get this party over with," he murmured to Gomon.

"Ruby was a hair shirt to him," Toms noted. "He used to complain, volubly and occasionally profanely."[21]

MURPHY MET HIS timetable. By three thirty that afternoon, the jury had been charged and began its deliberations. The great throng of Negro spectators lingered in the courtroom and spilled out into the corridor. But the quick verdict that many had expected proved elusive. The jurors argued, asked the judge to clarify some questions of law, and debated until two a.m. on Thanksgiving morning. After a few hours' sleep, they resumed their disputation, broke for a turkey dinner, and kept at it until eleven p.m.

"All Thanksgiving Day colored people remained waiting and watching, many of them going without Thanksgiving dinner in order to be on hand," White reported. At times, angry shouts, profanities, and the scraping of chairs could be heard through the closed door of the jury room. "I'll stay here twenty years, if necessary, and I am younger than any of you," one man was heard to shout. The jurors told the judge they were deadlocked, but Murphy held them for another night.

Darrow, Hays, and White had their holiday supper at the black community's YMCA, where Gomon joined them after leaving her children with her husband. They then returned to the courthouse, where a helpful clerk—"fairly well lit" on illicit whiskey—opened up a nearby courtroom. "We took a bottle of scotch and adjourned," Gomon told her diary. At one point that evening, after she expressed her opposition to Prohibition, Darrow reached over and took her hands and said, "We are affinities. To think that I should ever hear such an opinion from a woman."

At one thirty Friday afternoon, some forty-six hours after the jury began its deliberations, Murphy declared a mistrial. All twelve jurors agreed that eight of the defendants were not guilty, and five jurors had accepted Darrow's plea to acquit all eleven defendants. But seven jurors voted over and over again to convict Ossian and Henry Sweet and one other man for a lesser charge of second-degree murder.[22]

Darrow was disappointed, yet satisfied with the outcome. If it wasn't the big triumph that the NAACP had hoped for, the jury's skeptical reaction to the prosecution case made it highly unlikely, he believed, that Toms would ever get a conviction. After a few days' reflection, Hays reached the same conclusion. "I expect the victory to be complete the next time," he wrote Johnson.

Given this reassurance, the NAACP leaders were reluctantly content. "We have got to go over the whole thing again," White told a friend. But "it was a magnificent fight and all decent public opinion has been swung to our side." Besides, the mistrial would allow them to keep the fundraising machine running. In the end, the Sweet trial would help bring in $75,000 to the organization.[23]

Back in Chicago, Darrow handled, without pay, the defense of Fred Curry, a penniless fourteen-year-old Negro youth who had stabbed an Italian American boy in a racial scuffle at school. Curry was thirteen at the time of the fight but was indicted in adult court for manslaughter. Darrow persuaded a judge to keep the case in juvenile court, and the boy was sent to a reformatory.

In mid-December, Darrow traveled to New York, where Mary caught up with him at his hotel. He hosted Hays and the NAACP officials to plan strategy for the retrial of the Sweet case and gave a speech on Darwin. Darrow's old newspaper friend Neg Cochran stopped by to see him. So did Dudley Malone, Carl Sandburg, and a slim and beautiful sister of the poet Edna St. Vincent Millay. Judge Murphy was in town and joined the group for a raucous lunch with cigarettes and a fine, illegal, well-aged bottle of whiskey. That evening, Mary and Lem had Sandburg, Darrow, and Cochran to their house for dinner and then she drove Darrow to a Jewish center in Brooklyn for another speech on evolution. In the car on the way back to Manhattan, Mary and Darrow analyzed his fame. "Mary, I am terribly famous and goddamn unimportant," he said. He rounded out his visit to New York with a speech that drew four thousand people to a fundraiser for the NAACP in Harlem. Before he left, Darrow told White that he would handle the retrial without charging a fee, if need be, and would pay his own expenses.

Darrow and Ruby spent the Christmas "hollow days," as he called them, with Paul and his family in Colorado, but in January he was home and traveling widely again—to New York, Michigan, Missouri, Pennsylvania, Maryland, and Washington, where he testified before Congress on the folly of capital punishment. If deterrence was the goal, as some of the congressmen argued, then the government should return to public hangings, Darrow said, with a school holiday so that children could attend.[24]

In March, a few weeks before his sixty-ninth birthday, Darrow returned to Ann Arbor to debate the League of Nations with the Harvard law professor Manley Hudson. Ruby was not with him, but Jo Gomon was. Instead of taking the direct train home to Chicago, he drove with Jo and her friends to Detroit. She sat with him in the car, and he held her hand. "If you are really fond of me, I can forgive you for thinking me an old fool," he told her.

Darrow wasn't much interested in the talk or opinions of Gomon's friends—just her. "I like pretty women and women with brains, but I rarely meet the latter," he explained. And then there were the "impossible" ones—the type "who thinks she has brains, and hasn't." Such women were "natural reformers," he said. "It is as much a part of them as clothes. They don't know how to enjoy life."

But Gomon wasn't like that. "You belong to a small group of women that a man can talk to and love too," he told her. Gomon blushed and Darrow chuckled. It was long past midnight when they sat down in a restaurant at the Michigan Central station in Detroit. Even at that hour, well-wishers gathered around. Darrow told a few stories, then caught a late train for Chicago.

Gomon admired Darrow, and was flattered and confused by his attention. "It is not only embarrassing—it is most annoying—even humiliating to have intellectual interest and conversation continually fall back onto the personal," she told her diary. "Some of my lady purists would call Darrow an old reprobate because of his harmless and perhaps senile flirtations."

Darrow was pressing her to come visit him in Chicago. As unlikely was the notion of a love affair, she knew that she could hold hands for only so long. "I am no infant, and to go on playing the part is not going to always save me from embarrassing situations," she wrote. "The obtrusion of sex on interesting social life can be somewhat circumvented by ignoring the fact—but not entirely." Recognizing this, she was drawn to Darrow nonetheless. "Behind [his] commonplace advances there stands always discernible the giant intellect and compelling personality." Ruby had seen this act before and recognized what was happening with her gallant cavalier. When Darrow returned to Detroit she politely, but obviously, made sure she was around when Gomon was present.

"Mrs. Darrow doesn't like me," Gomon told Darrow after Ruby had canceled a social engagement.

"You can't blame her, can you?" Darrow replied. "You know what I think of you."[25]

THE RETRIAL WAS scheduled for April with several changes in the cast. Darrow was back, and so were Judge Murphy and Toms. But Hays was busy in New York, and at Darrow's urging the NAACP hired Thomas Chawke, a top-notch criminal defense lawyer in Detroit. Chawke insisted on $7,500 and a guarantee that the defense would conduct the kind of investigation into the backgrounds of the potential jurors that Darrow had not had in the first trial.[26]

The most significant change, however, was the identity of the defendant. Instead of trying all eleven black men, Toms had singled out Henry Sweet, who had confessed to the police that he fired a rifle from an upstairs window. Darrow was content; both he and Toms wanted a clear-cut victory and attributed the November mistrial to the jury's inability to allot guilt or innocence among so many potential culprits.

The trial got under way on April 19. "In examining the prospective jurors, Darrow and Chawke probed pretty thoroughly into their lives," the *Free Press* reported. Armed with information gathered by Chawke's investigators, he and Darrow took five days, methodically working their way through 197 candidates, before settling on a jury.

Toms had no surprise witnesses; he stuck with the roster that he used in November. "I am not prepared to show who fired the shot that killed Breiner . . . there is no way to find out," he told the jury in his opening statement. "Either Henry Sweet did, or he aided and abetted the man who did. We will show that Henry Sweet fired shots."

The testimony followed the pattern set in the first case. By the end of the week, the defense had "succeeded . . . in drawing from witnesses admissions that a crowd had gathered in the vicinity, that stones were hurled at the Sweet residence prior to the shooting, and that people in the neighborhood were opposed to the presence of Negroes," the *Free Press* reported. Darrow and Chawke were helped by the failure of several prosecution witnesses to remember and repeat the stories they told in the first trial, leaving them vulnerable on cross-examination.

One new feature from the second trial was the admission by a prosecution witness named Andrews, under tenacious questioning by Darrow, that speakers at the Waterworks Park meeting had urged residents in the neighborhood to use violence, if necessary, to keep the blacks out.

Q: "Did the speaker talk about legal means?"
A: "I admitted to you that the man was radical."
Q: "Answer my question. Did he talk about legal means?"
A: "No."
Q: "He talked about driving them out, didn't he?"
A: "Yes, he was radical, I admit that . . ."
Q: "In what way was he radical?"
A: "Well I don't—I myself do not believe in violence."

Q: "I didn't ask you what you believed in. I said in what way was he radical . . . You did not rise in that meeting and say, 'I myself don't believe in violence,' did you?"
A: "No, I'd had a fine chance with 600 people there."
Q: "What? You would have caught it, yourself, wouldn't you? You wouldn't have dared to do it at that meeting . . ."
A: "I object to violence."
Q: "Did anybody—did *anybody* in that audience of 600 people protest against advocating violence against colored people who moved into the neighborhood?"
A: "I don't know."
Q: "You didn't hear any protest?"
A: "No."
Q: "You only heard applause . . . You heard nobody utter any protest, and all the manifestation you heard was applause at what he said?"
A: "Yes, that is all."

Toms tried to perform some repairs under redirect examination but only made things worse.

"Did he *advocate* violence?" Toms asked.

"I said this man was radical," the witness replied.

"I know you did. Did he advocate violence?"

"Yes," the witness said.

Darrow said later that his pinning of Andrews was just a matter of chance. Lawyers flail around on cross-examination, he said, and sometimes they find a prize.

The journalistic chorus had changed. White was replaced by James Johnson. And Lilienthal's part was sung by Marcet Haldeman-Julius, who, like her predecessor, left a vivid account of a trial that, because the defendants were black, did not command the attention of white newspaper editors.[27]

Marcet was struck by the African Americans who came to court each day. "There were toil-bent people and successful-looking businessmen; artists stamped with modernity, and a wistful, wrinkled little woman whom Judge Murphy thoughtfully decreed should always be admitted and safely seated. But however they varied, those faces . . . there was in them all the same vigilant anxiety," she wrote. "All hung on Darrow's every word and marked well Judge Murphy's every ruling. Only occasionally allowing themselves a low contemptuous laugh at some too flagrant prevarication or an approving murmur at a quick and just retort, they listened for the most part silently."

Chawke proved more than able. His staccato questioning forced a flustered police lieutenant who had initially denied that there were an unusual number of cars cruising the neighborhood on the night of the shooting to admit that the police closed off the street because, as the officer finally, and glumly, acknowledged, "there was a considerable amount of traffic."

Though Chawke had viewed the case as just another murder trial, and taken it largely for the fee and the publicity, he told Marcet that his heart was touched, as the trial proceeded, by the plight of the black defendants. "He became, once he got into it, more and more deeply interested in all its implications; more and more concerned for the issues involved," she wrote. It showed in Chawke's closing address, which preceded Darrow's, on May 10. "I arise to present this man's defense to you," Chawke told the jury. "I appreciate the high honor which he has done me in selecting me to assist in a defense in the charge of a crime which is made, not only against him, but against ten others of his race."

Darrow began the next morning in a relaxed, conversational manner. "There is nothing but prejudice in this case," he told the jury. "If it was reversed, and eleven white men had shot and killed a black while protecting their home and their lives against a mob of blacks, nobody would have dreamed of having them indicted . . . They would have been given medals instead. . . .

"That is all there is to this case," he said. "Take the hatred away and you have nothing."

To meet the demand of those who wanted to hear Darrow speak, dozens of folding chairs had been brought into the courtroom, and filled every inch of space. "The serried rows of colored faces that packed the courtroom from the rail to the back wall, watching and waiting, were like so many tragic masks," Johnson wrote. "The rugged face of Clarence Darrow, more haggard and lined by the anxious days, with the deep, brooding eyes, heightened the intense effect of the whole."

"His voice went on and on, always interesting, always fascinating, always holding the attention of judge, jurors and audience," Gomon told her diary. Sometimes he spoke with his hands in his pockets, his shoulders up in a characteristic shrug. He would point a finger, or throw his arms out wide, and swing them in half a circle. "He remained a tower of ceaseless energy, every muscle of his body strained and eager."

Sweet "bought that home just as you buy yours, because he wanted a home to live in, to take his wife and to raise a family," Darrow said. And "no man lived a better life or died a better death than fighting for his home and his children."

Some of the Negro spectators were quietly weeping.

"I do not like to speak of it in the presence of these colored people, whom I have always urged to be as happy as they can. But it is true. Life is a hard game, anyhow, but when the cards are stacked against you it is terribly hard. And they are stacked against a race for no reason but that they are black," he said. "Their ancestors were captured in the jungles and on the plains of Africa, captured as you capture wild beasts, torn from their homes and their kindred; loaded into slave ships, packed like sardines in a box, half of them dying on the ocean passage; some jumping into the sea in their frenzy, when they had a chance to choose death in place of slavery."

It was almost five p.m. when he stood at last before the jury, worn from the long day of intense intellectual exercise, and lifted his arms out toward them, hands outspread.

"I believe the life of the Negro race has been a life of tragedy, of injustice, of oppression. The law had made him equal, but man has not," Darrow said. "I know there is a long road ahead of him, before he can take the place which I believe he should take. I know that before him there is suffering, sorrow, tribulation and death among the blacks, and perhaps among the whites. I am sorry. I would do what I could to avert it. I would advise patience; I would advise toleration; I would advise understanding."

Now he was leaning over the jury rail, his voice a hoarse whisper.

"I have watched, day after day, these black tense faces that have crowded this court. These black faces that now are looking to you twelve whites, feeling that the hopes and fears of a race are in your keeping," said Darrow. "This case is about to end, gentlemen. To them, it is life. Not one of their color sits on this jury. Their fate is in the hands of twelve whites. Their eyes are fixed on you, their hearts go out to you and their hopes hang on your verdict.

"That is all. I ask you, on behalf of this defendant, on behalf of these helpless ones who turn to you . . . I ask you in the name of progress and of the human race, to return a verdict of not guilty in this case." His face was white and tense from exhaustion as he sat down.

Johnson was unequivocal in his praise. "For nearly seven hours he talked to the jury. I sat where I could catch every work and every expression of his face," Johnson wrote. "It was the most wonderful flow of words I ever heard from a man's lips. . . .

"When he finished I walked over to him to express . . . my appreciation and thanks," Johnson recalled. "His eyes were shining and wet. He placed his hands on my shoulders. I stammered out a few words but broke down and wept, and I was not ashamed of my tears."

TOMS GAVE THE final closing argument the next day. He cast Breiner as a victim not of fear, but belligerence.

Even if there were five hundred people gathered around the corner that night, Toms said, people had a right to be curious, to gather outside on a warm night, to talk with neighbors and watch the excitement. "Did you ever do it? In the middle of the summer, did you ever go over to the corner store for a paper or a cigar without your coat on? Maybe in your slippers. Maybe you took a youngster along with you, and you met some neighbors over in the drug store, and you stopped to chat about the ball game that day, or how rotten the Tiger pitcher was, or how bad business is; maybe walked back with your neighbors," Toms said. "Would you like to be called a cowardly crowd for doing that, if you happened to pass the home of a Negro?"

The Waterworks organization should not be cast as a racial hate group, Toms said, any more than the NAACP. It "wasn't unreasonable," he contended, for the community association to want to maintain the racial purity of their neighborhood. If the Waterworks organization could be branded as violent and hateful, Toms argued, then it was equally fair to characterize the NAACP as "a scheme for forcing colored people into white neighborhoods . . . a scheme for grabbing public offices for colored people . . . a scheme for securing marriage with the white race."

It was not fear that led Henry Sweet to pull the trigger, Toms insisted. It was hate. It was arrogance. The Sweets and their friends were uppity. Rocks were thrown, but just two broke panes of glass. Photographs of the house, taken the next day, showed no other damage. A hedge was not trampled. A rosebush was in bloom.

"There is no legal justification . . . They had no right, morally or ethically, or legally, to kill Leon Breiner just to impress on the white people that they didn't propose to be driven out," said Toms. "And that is just what happened."[28]

THE JURY RETIRED to deliberate at one thirty that afternoon. Darrow and Ruby left the courthouse with Chawke, Gomon, and others for lunch at Cohen's, a speakeasy. They stayed for three hours, drinking Scotch whiskey and port. Ruby got very drunk.

A judge "recited poems and stories," Gomon told her diary. "Darrow recited about the girl whose lover kept a livery stable, and about the Beautiful Persian Pussy."

Then Darrow and his entourage piled back into taxis and returned to the courthouse. He stopped in the press room and lit a cigarette, and he and Toms had shots of Scotch. His eyes were gleaming, "like bright blue agates set into the face of an old, old statue," a reporter recalled. He asked the newsmen, "What do you think? Will we win or lose?"

Shortly after five p.m. the jury had its verdict.

"Do not let passion interfere with your acceptance of this verdict, whatever it may be," Murphy warned the audience. He seemed to be prepping the Negro spectators for disappointment: "Accept it courageously and with a good will."

The prosecutors assumed a magnanimous air, Johnson recalled, while the members of the defense team were "seized with apprehension." Johnson put a hand on Henry Sweet's arm and vowed that the NAACP would stand by him "to the end."

The foreman said, "Not guilty."

"The effect is electrical," Johnson reported. Everyone is shaking everybody else's hand. Negro women are sobbing convulsively. Darrow and Chawke are speechless. Toms is stunned."[29]

"Lawyer Darrow has again gilded his unique reputation by securing an acquittal against heavy odds," *Time* magazine reported. "There is a peculiar consistency in his defense of the hopelessly lost, of the rich and poor alike, of the underdog who is under because of inexorable gyrations of fate."

"I cannot hardly realize yet that we succeeded in convincing them that we were right," Darrow told Johnson two days after the verdict. Johnson wrote back: "I agree . . . it sometimes seems like a dream from which we are to awake."

The case was a huge victory for the NAACP. The publicity it garnered and the money it raised from black and liberal donors in 1925 and 1926 helped cement the organization's position as America's leading civil rights group, and allowed it to build the superb legal defense team that, over thirty years of litigation, would persuade the federal courts that separate was not equal.

Many of the trial's white participants profited from their experience. Hays and Chawke buffed their reputations. Judge Murphy won his wager on American politics, became a genuine liberal hero, and rose to the Supreme Court, where he championed civil liberties and penned the great dissent in *Korematsu v. United States*, decrying the internment, by the president who had named him to the court, of Japanese Americans during World War II.[30]

Jo Gomon resisted Darrow's entreaties. Perhaps she learned that while he was sweet-talking her in Detroit, he was also wooing a lady in Chicago. On Darrow's last night in Detroit, he spoke at a Penguin Club dinner and, ill and weary, rambled about "dope" in his cynical way. "He seemed to lose some of the marks of greatness, and became for me suddenly an old man with dirty ears," she told her diary. "I had a picture of Mrs. Darrow too drunk to properly supervise his bath the night before, and pitied her marriage to an old man . . . Her brains are capable of appreciating only his fame, and little of his intellect. And reflected glory is not so gratifying without the vigor of sustained interest in personality and sex."

Robert Toms did not suffer. The prosecutor waited for months before dropping his cases against the other Sweet defendants but ultimately did so, as he had promised. When he first ran for election to the bench, Toms asked Darrow to return to Detroit and campaign with him in black precincts. Darrow did, and Toms won. He capped his career at Nuremberg, Germany, where he was one of the judges who presided at the postwar trials of Nazi war criminals.

Years after the Sweet trials, Toms told an interviewer that "I can put myself in that house on Garland Ave. that night, and I can imagine the terror that must have crept through every occupant . . . I can't say that it was an unjust verdict at all."

Nor would he challenge the witnesses for the defense who had testified that there were four or five hundred people outside 2905 Garland Avenue on that warm summer night. The Sweets and their friends "panicked, that's what happened," Toms said, warming to his tale. "They spread themselves around the house and when the stones began to fall . . . Bang! Bang! It didn't take much to start the shooting."

The Sweet trials had a salutary effect on the city of Detroit, he said. "I think it taught the fringe of the white people who were in foment. I think it taught them that they couldn't have the support of the law in blocking the Negro from living where he wanted."

"Sociologically, I mean, leaving all legal aspects aside, I think it was probably a fortunate thing," Toms said. "Of course, this doesn't say much for Mr. Breiner, who was shot. But, after all, what's one soldier in a war?"[31]

The Sweets paid for their victories. First Ossian and Gladys lost their baby girl to tuberculosis. Then Gladys died of the disease. Henry earned a law degree at Howard University and practiced briefly before he too succumbed to tuberculosis before the age of forty. Their family believed that Henry and Gladys contracted the disease while awaiting trial in the county jail, and gave it to her baby.

Before Gladys died, Ossian moved her into the house on Garland Avenue, and afterward he lived there many years. But his personal and professional life was erratic. Burdened by debt, Sweet sold the property in 1958. And in 1960, ill and disturbed, Ossian Sweet took his own life. One soldier in a war.[32]

Chapter 20

CRASHING

Here is the kind of damn fool I have been.

Darrow did not pause long to celebrate his victory in the Sweet case. In two weeks he was off to Tennessee, to argue the Scopes appeal before the state supreme court. It was a stressful exercise, with foes before and behind him. His critics had been horrified by the carnival in Dayton, and schemed to remove him from the legal team.

"It will not be our cause on trial," George Rappelyea wrote his co-conspirator Forrest Bailey at the ACLU. "It will be a case of the State of Tennessee vs. Clarence Darrow, the man who spiritually and literally crucified Bryan."[1]

But Bailey had a hard time finding someone to bell the cat; Darrow was a public hero. "We are constantly receiving criticisms and protests concerning the Darrow personality and the harm it may do us," Bailey told one ACLU supporter, "but feel inhibited from passing these on directly to Mr. Darrow."

Inevitably, word got back to Darrow, and he acceded to the suggestion that a distinguished Tennessee lawyer be added to the appeals team. But now Hays had his back up. "I don't think you can accept the services of Darrow and Malone in the trial of the case and then suggest ousting them," Hays told ACLU counsel Walter Nelles. "I am not willing to have conservative lawyers . . . reap the benefit of work done by liberals or radicals. . . .

"I never yet have found any conservative lawyer who, at the beginning, wanted to undertake a case which *might* reflect discredit upon him. When it turns out differently and there seem to be some publicity or honor to be had, then offers of assistance come," Hays said. Nelles and the others surrendered, but only as far as the Tennessee appeal. The ACLU insisted that Darrow withdraw before the case went to the U.S. Supreme Court.

In the end, it was Tennessee's lawyers who disgraced themselves before their state's high court, ranting against scientists and intellectuals and jabbering about the specter of communism. Darrow was nothing but dignified. "The schools of this state were not established to teach religion, they were established to teach science," he told the justices.

"We must learn, and we will learn, and what we have today is the result of knowledge, of investigation, of science," he said. "It will be a sad day, both for education and religion, when the sword is tied to the cross."[2]

Darrow returned to Chicago to pack for a vacation in Colorado. The victories of the last three years had been as draining as they were glorious, and he needed a rest. In June he headed for Greeley. It was there that he suffered a coronary episode—a heart attack, it seems, brought on by an arterial blockage—and was hospitalized in Denver. Darrow and Ruby lingered in Colorado as he regained strength. "I had rather a serious breakdown . . . and am very slowly recovering," he wrote Whitlock. "I must not work or indulge in any feverish activity. Of course it is time that I had a permanent breakdown for I will be 70 next April and have led a very strenuous life."

Ruby tried, with little success, to get him to stop smoking. His doctors told him to postpone a planned European vacation and to spend the winter in the South. The Darrows settled on Fairhope, Alabama, a liberal colony on Mobile Bay. Mary saw him in New York before he left. "Darrow looks very old and even more tired. Sags like an old bag out of which almost everything is taken. Jokes as usual, simple rustic jokes. Criticizes none. Asks nothing. People come to strut before him and puff their breast bones and ruffle their feathers. He sits humbly, with head bowed, silent," she told her diary. She saw him off at the station and, as she watched him board the train, was struck by a premonition of death.

In January, word came from Tennessee. The court had given Scopes the victory, but on a technicality: the defendant was freed because Judge Raulston, and not the jury, had fixed the amount of the $100 fine. The justices upheld the anti-evolution law, but instructed the prosecutors to drop the "bizarre" case that had proved so embarrassing. Though never enforced, the law stayed on the books. It would take another forty years before the U.S. Supreme Court overturned an anti-evolution statute.

But the law, Darrow knew, follows folkways. And the showdown on the courthouse lawn was not forgotten. Darrow did not give fundamentalism its death blow in Dayton—it is, after all, in the nature of religious fanatics to ignore objective truth—but he had exposed it to ridicule. The timorous politicians of the South continued to sanction intolerance, and commercial textbook publishers ducked the issue. But away from the clout of the Bible Belt churches, Americans had no problem honoring the poetry of Genesis in Sunday school, and the findings of Darwin in science class. Darrow never made but a modest claim about the outcome, which was inarguable. "Somebody had to make a fuss about it," he wrote Mencken. "I was interested in waking up the country as to what they had to meet and think we succeeded. I do not know how much farther [the fundamentalists] can get, but they will never pull off anything else without a fight."

Darrow despised fanatics, not faith. Nor would he deny to lost mankind what solace it might find in religion. In the weeks after Dayton, Darrow declined an invitation from Manhattan's liberals to speak on the topic "Is Science the Enemy of the Church?" It was the "dense ignorance" of the fundamentalists, and "their persistent endeavor to destroy all freedom of thought," that had led him to the Monkey Trial, he said.

"I would hate to put myself openly in the way of declaring that the church is the enemy of science," he wrote Oswald Villard. "Life is so hard that I am satisfied for some time to come, perhaps forever, the great mass of men will turn to some kind of faith to make it easier. I am not at all certain that humanity at large could live without it."[3]

For a moment in 1926 it seemed Darrow might enter another famous case. He had offered advice to Nicola Sacco and Bartolomeo Vanzetti, anarchists sentenced to die in Massachusetts for murdering guards in a payroll holdup. It seemed a trumped-up charge to liberals, who rallied behind the men. Darrow "is an anarchist, and has for the ruling beast our feelings," Vanzetti told his defense committee. "There is the probability that the dogs, knowing to have to face a fearless and merciless man of genius, may yield." But Vanzetti's legal team was cool to the idea and persuaded him to drop it because, he told a friend, of the "resentment and hostility that [Darrow's] personality and his coming from Chicago would arise in the black-gowned hangers."

Darrow did scheme, with Fremont Older and Lincoln Steffens, to win Jim McNamara his freedom. He offered to go to California himself, though, he told Older, "I am not well and my heart is not good." Steffens was dispatched instead. "I don't expect to die in the near future," Darrow reassured Older, "still I know that it won't be very long and I know of nothing I would rather accomplish than this."[4]

Darrow kept an office, and loaned his name to a law firm—Darrow, Smith, Cronson & Smith—organized by several former Chicago prosecutors. He went downtown when he could but bemoaned the "stream of poor crippled useless people on the way to their graves" who crowded the waiting room for help he could no longer give them. "Hell, Mary," he wrote her, "I am sorry not to be cheerful. I really am cheerful. I am eternally saying things witty and clever and laughing at fate. Still I don't seem to be in that mood today."

In August 1927 Darrow returned to court, responding to an alarm raised by Chicago social workers over the impending execution of two black men—Stonewall Clark and Ernest Holt—who had been sentenced to death for murdering a white grocer during a $4 robbery. The *Defender* praised his "love of humanity," but the most Darrow could do, in a questionable case, was broker a deal to preserve the duo's lives. He persuaded Judge Emanuel Eller to grant them a new trial on the condition that they would plead guilty and accept a sentence of life imprisonment.

A few days later, Darrow and Ruby left for Europe aboard the White Star liner *Majestic*, where he spent the trip reading and playing cards and shuffleboard. In England, he had a pleasant visit with A. E. Housman. But after Darrow left, the poet sniffed a bit at this American who had brought him pamphlets of his closing arguments. "Sure enough," Housman told W. H. Auden, "there were two of my poems—both misquoted."[5] From Britain, the Darrows went to Paris and Geneva. He was chased by bad news from home. California had rejected Jim McNamara's appeal. Sacco and Vanzetti had been executed. And his brother Everett had died. Everett's wife, Helen, was bitter that Darrow had not taken the opportunity, when passing through New York, to visit them one last time. "Clarence did not come out," Helen told Jennie. "Everett was much disappointed, he had written him telling him he wanted to see him. Too bad he could not have spared an hour from his lawyers and friends."[6]

In Belgium, his old pal Whitlock returned home from golf one day and found the Darrows waiting. "He is now 70 and retired after a long life spent in fighting for all the most hopeless causes and standing by the underdogs," Whitlock told his diary. "I was very much touched by his coming this long way, with much difficulty, to see me." Darrow still liked to read aloud, and that night chose the work of a black poet, most likely Langston Hughes, whom Darrow had met at James Johnson's salon in Harlem. Ruby had the irritating habit of repeating, out loud, the last line of each poem after Darrow finished, "as in a litany," Whitlock wrote. It nettled Whitlock, though he concluded that she was a "nice, admirable little woman" who looks after Darrow, "with all his whims . . . devoutly."[7]

The Darrows returned to America in October. He went promptly to Cincinnati to testify as a character witness for George Remus, the "King of the Bootleggers," who was on trial for killing his wife. Remus had practiced law in Chicago for years before cheating Prohibition had made him a millionaire. He claimed he shot his wife after he had been cuckolded by a federal agent and sobbed when a witness told the jurors that the late Mrs. Remus had a murder contract on her husband's life. The jury took nineteen minutes to find him not guilty, by reason of temporary insanity. "American justice! I thank you!" he shouted.

Back in Chicago, Darrow stirred a ruckus when he told a largely Jewish audience that the concept of a chosen people, and the Zionist dream of a Jewish state in Palestine, was bunk. "There are no such thing as races," Darrow said. "There is a difference caused by climate [or] long living in particular localities, but [humans] are all made alike." Zionism was an "absurd enterprise," said Darrow. The Middle East was a dry and barren land. "No sane person would ever think of going to Palestine, except for religion. It has been the home of myth . . . and fable and sleight-of-hand ever since we knew it. . . .

"I love idealism," said Darrow. "I am something of a dreamer myself, but there are some things that are not worth dreaming about." He described his own visit to the Temple Mount in Jerusalem, where he saw a young man "with the idealism that people like myself always recognize—the far-off look of the dreamer who is thinking of something beyond the world and of some justice somewhere, sometime.

"I saw him beating his fist and his head against a wailing wall," said Darrow, "wailing for the lost Jerusalem, wailing for lost Zion, wailing for the glory and grandeur that once was there, wailing for the past, like everyone else, for the past to come back out of the dark and the dawn, and it never comes, and it never can."[8]

Darrow saw Mary twice that fall. On one visit she welcomed Darrow, Steffens, and others to dinner, and resented her role as housekeeper and cook, waiting on the gentlemen. "Lions are hard to entertain," she told her diary. "They get used to homage." A second visit, a week later, went better. She had Darrow to herself at dinner and accompanied him to a speaking engagement in Brooklyn, holding his hand in the backseat of the car.[9]

Darrow returned to New York in December, but not to hold hands. The fascist Benito Mussolini had taken power in Italy, and his success roiled the Italian American community. After a series of confrontations in the spring of 1927, two American fascists from the Bronx were assassinated. Mussolini himself sent flowers to their funeral, and the bodies were brought to Italy, placed in silver caskets, and given a state burial. In July, the police in New York charged two men—Donato Carillo and Calogero Greco—with the murders.

The Left rallied behind the defendants, and Darrow and Hays led the defense. Alexander Rocco, a comrade of the victims, claimed to have seen Carillo and Greco join in the killing. But Darrow got Rocco to admit that the description of the killer he originally gave police did not fit either of the defendants. Luigi Alfano, a witness who was not affiliated with either side, declined—despite furious efforts by the prosecutors—to identify the defendants. He didn't want the conviction of innocent men on his conscience, he told the court. And a third man, under Darrow's questioning, admitted that he had been working as a fascist spy.

"Darrow rendered each of them useless in a few hours of cross-examination," one newsman wrote. Darrow's own chief witness was a Mussolini sympathizer who had split from the dead men's organization, the Fascist League of North America. He had seen the attack up close and emphatically denied that Carillo and Greco were the killers. The defendants testified on their own behalf, and had alibi witnesses placing them at their homes in Brooklyn.

The New York press was delighted to have Darrow working a sensational murder case. "Deep furrows have been cut by time in Darrow's majestic face," one feature writer wrote. "His hair looks as if he had it cut twice a year, and then with a scythe. His pants are never pressed. . . .

"But Darrow would be a majestic figure no matter how he dressed. He towers over six feet. His head sticks forward, always in sort of an onward rush at his adversary. His broad, square shoulders know how to shrug with finest sarcasm. . . .

"Everything is natural, unaffected and perfectly timed . . . The only waste motion in Darrow's technique is an occasional habit of scratching himself behind the ear," the story said. "Now and then he has been known to scratch his head. But this is a Will Rogers head scratch, which has its definite effect upon the judge, jury and audience. He scratches his head in such a way as to bring out more clearly, more sarcastically, a certain bit of cross-examination. The scratch behind the ear, however, apparently has no purpose whatsoever."

In his closing address, Darrow attacked Mussolini's rule. "Fascism was born in bloodshed," Darrow said. "Of course these defendants hate the regime in Italy, as all men do, and they had the courage to say so."

The jury deliberated eight hours and found Carillo and Greco innocent. The judge praised the verdict. After the holidays, Darrow was the guest at a "victory luncheon." He had two reasons for taking the case, he said. "The first reason is that I detest Mussolini and everything he stands for," said Darrow. "The second was the example of the Sacco-Vanzetti case, where I felt that prejudice, passion and feeling were largely responsible for the verdict. I didn't want to see it happen again." He had been promised $10,000, but agreed to accept $1,000 from the defense committee. "He received their love, if not their fee," said Mary, who was his escort.[10]

Darrow then left for Vermont to pay off a twenty-year-old debt. When Paul was a student at Dartmouth College he had lost control of a horse, which ran down and killed a five-year-old boy. Paul had written to the distraught mother, at the time, pledging to do anything to ease her sorrow. In 1927, after her nephew John Winters was condemned to death for murder, she approached Darrow, who was giving a lecture at Dartmouth, and told him of Paul's promise.

"One of the boys came to me and told me the lady wanted to see me and told me what it was all about. I told the boy that she must be crazy, that no such thing could have happened," Darrow wrote his son. "She came in and showed me your letter (it was a very nice letter) and said that you were in no way to blame. I am sorry that this has bothered you all these years. . . .

"It is very doubtful if anything can be done," Darrow told Paul, but he scheduled an appearance before the Vermont Supreme Court. The courtroom and the hallways outside were crowded with lawyers and local residents hoping to see him. Darrow asked why a key witness had taken several days to identify Winters as the killer. He challenged rulings of the trial judge, who had allowed the jury to see a staged rearrangement of furniture at the crime scene but excluded evidence that the blood found on the defendant's clothing may have been his own. "Blood is an important factor in a murder case," said Darrow. "I don't know what the jury would have done with the evidence. But it had a right to it." The justices agreed, spared the defendant's life, and granted him a new trial. Winters then pled guilty to second-degree murder and went to prison for twenty years.[11]

Darrow spent most of 1928 on a ten-month speaking tour. He mixed his usual debates and lectures with appearances to benefit the NAACP and, in the fall, the Democratic presidential candidate, Al Smith.[12] In May, he mixed business with sentiment and returned to Ohio to represent a notorious local bootlegger, James Munsene, who was on trial for attempting to bribe the Trumbull County sheriff. Munsene was an Italian immigrant who had settled in Warren and made his way as a grocer and nightclub owner. He tracked Darrow down when Darrow was visiting Kinsman and persuaded him to take the case. It was Munsene's third trial on the charge: the first two had ended in convictions but were overturned on appeal.

The trial was conducted in the Ashtabula County seat, in Jefferson, where Darrow had practiced law as a young man. It was the first time, he told the local papers, he had tried a case with women on the jury. One potential juror, a member in good standing of the Women's Christian Temperance Union, chastised the great infidel as he questioned her. She was excused.

Darrow quizzed witnesses and raised many questions about the sheriff's warm relationship with the Ku Klux Klan, which was active in northeast Ohio and didn't much like Italian immigrants. After a weeklong trial the jury was deadlocked. Darrow returned in 1929 and defended Munsene at his fourth trial. That jury was deadlocked as well, and another mistrial declared. Finally, in 1930, Darrow persuaded Munsene to plead guilty and pay a fine. Munsene went on to fame as a racketeer and nightclub owner and was shot to death by gunmen in 1941.[13]

DARROW WAS FEELING better than he had for months. That summer he roamed New England and the Dakotas, seeing sights and making speeches. "Clarence retires somewhat after the fashion of a fly that can't really stay away from the fly-paper long," Ruby wrote Dr. Gerson. "I have caught the knack of care-taker and general proxy for many a step and stretch and strain that saves taxing his none-too-fit heart—alas."

Ruby "watches over Clarence, day and night, like a baby, and Clarence delights in it," the critic George Nathan wrote. "She answers all his telephone calls, makes or breaks all his appointments, writes and answers three-fourths of his letters, lifts him out of taxicabs (when the occasion demands), tells him when his socks are falling down, pours his and his friends' drinks for him, answers any possibly embarrassing questions that interviewers may put to him, tells him what he should eat and if it tastes good to him. . . .

"Without Ruby, he would be completely lost—and he knows it," Nathan wrote. "She tells him several times a day that he is the greatest and finest and most adorable man she has ever known and that she loves him to death."

Hoover whipped Smith in the November election, which Darrow blamed, in part, on women voters who had gone against the "wet" candidate. "To any woman he is the best, the most helpful, the most understanding friend. But the collective woman! Here he lets emotion color his views," said Mary, after listening to one of Darrow's tirades. "Against the collective woman he rages as he would like to against the little piss ant wife whose pettiness and jealousies have galled him."

Yet when feminist Margaret Sanger was persecuted for her advocacy of sex education and birth control, Darrow spoke at a rally on her behalf in Boston in 1929. She arrived with a gag around her mouth and Harvard historian Arthur Schlesinger read her speech. The next day Darrow was in court, as a witness, speaking in defense of Theodore Dreiser, who had been charged with violating obscenity laws when writing *An American Tragedy*. The jury found Dreiser guilty.

"The powers of reaction and despotism never sleep," Darrow told Roger Baldwin. "We have to be very watchful."[14]

IN JUNE 1929 the Darrows were off to Europe once again. They went to Paris and to Germany, where Darrow was examined by heart specialists. They took a motor tour of Wales and Scotland and the English countryside. From Montreux, in Switzerland, Darrow wrote his grandchildren in the nonsense style he liked to use.

"Eye have bin thinking how lucky it waz that Eye got U to kum to Chicago so I woodent be so far away from U when U kum. Eye dident think about kumming to Europe but now I am 4 thosand miles aweigh but if U haddent kame to Chicago eye would now bee 5 thousand miles awa and what wood we have dun then. You kan sea yourself." He signed it "Ur Grand Dad."

Darrow seemed set in retirement. His investment in the Colorado gas company, with Paul's sweat equity, left them with small fortunes when they sold the business in 1928. Paul moved back to Chicago. Darrow loaned $8,000 to Mary and Lem (without telling Ruby); helped fund treatments for two friends suffering from cancer; and wrote to the ACLU and the NAACP to announce that he was adding them as beneficiaries in his will. "Do you need any money?" he asked W. C. Curtis, after hearing the news that the zoologist's son had contracted polio.

Darrow had always liked to speculate—railroads, copper companies, banks, gold mines, and Latin American stocks were among his favorites—even though he often took big losses. "Here is the kind of damn fool I have been," he had written Paul after a previous catastrophe. He had invested $10,000 on a tip "from a friend of mine who knows," who "had word direct from Guggenheim who is a relative about the supposed copper merger." The copper stocks "went up a minute, then went down fast" and Darrow was stuck scurrying for cash to cover margin calls.

"We are not very good speculators, and had better go slow in the stock business," Darrow told Paul. Now "I am going to quit forever," he vowed. "I think we both should and this time I will stay sworn off."

Of course, he did not. But he was wise enough in the bull market of 1929 to see what was going to happen. "Things can't keep going up forever," he warned Paul in August. "I don't like the look of things. All stocks are far too high," he told his son in September, and "if there are big drops you might get caught very badly." In early October he wrote Paul again: "Everybody is crazy and most of them will lose their money."

Paul assured his father that he was acting responsibly. And even after the stock market took its first great plunge, Darrow and Ruby remained in Europe. In their absence, Paul tried to recoup his losses by buying what he reckoned were bargains, only to keep losing as the economy cratered. Darrow's savings slipped from $300,000 before the crash to $125,000 afterward—and that he had to give to Paul, who was deep in debt and struggling to meet his margin calls and interest payments. "Use all I have," he told his son.

"I am in a predicament right now," Darrow told Walter White. "Really it is not so much that I am but Paul is and you know that I think more of him than myself. Anyhow I am obliged if possible to get in some money to save what is left." Ruby was furious at Darrow and at Paul. Her aged husband had to go out on the road, giving lectures and debating and after picking up a check for the night's work immediately sending it to his son. She scolded Paul for not realizing "how almost sacred his life savings have been to us two, and how impossible to replace." Darrow had told her that "he begged you to be careful," she wrote Paul, "and had been worried and fearful all along and firmly prophesized the disaster . . . but couldn't get you to see his attitude."[15]

WHITLOCK WAS IN Cannes working on a book, and somewhat surprised when the Darrows arrived and announced they would be staying weeks, not days. He liked his walks along the sea with Darrow at first, but railed in his diary about Ruby's "utter provincial ignorance" and the way she fluttered about her husband, even fixing his food on his plate. Before long, Whitlock tired of Darrow as well. Sick and fretting over money, Darrow was not good company. "I didn't invite them here or encourage him to come; they came on their own, but for some odd reason seem to expect me to entertain and amuse them," Whitlock wrote. "Mrs. D is wholly uninteresting, crude . . . with no redeeming wit . . . D. is brilliant, but impossible, and intellectually vain and with all his radicalism, nihilism, atheism and all the rest, the most intolerant . . . There is something sinister and diabolic about him, something baffling, frustrating and unwholesome.

"He . . . sneers at everything and has an insatiable appetite for approval and flattery. His manners are those of his rural middle west of his youth. He goes slouching along slovenly and unkempt, his hands in his pockets, spitting now and then and demolishing everything that is, in that soft and rather musical voice of his. He has a taste in literature, though limited to the literature of revolt and pessimism and a sympathy with the poor and outcast, which I like in him, but he has no genuine culture."

Whitlock was relieved when the Darrows took off for visits to see H. G. Wells (a free love advocate who was living with a mistress, Whitlock noted disapprovingly) and Somerset Maugham, and in time Whitlock regretted his ill will. But he couldn't hide his relief on March 8, 1930, when he saw the Darrows off on their ship home. "The *Saturnia* lay off Cannes all afternoon," he wrote. "I, from our window, watched her sail away, with relief, because the Darrows were aboard. Darrow has many virtues and is clever but he is *dificil* and trying and it has been a *corvee* to have to see so much of him this winter."[16]

Darrow was confronted, upon arriving home, with his shattered finances. "It has been twenty years at least since I have had to ask anyone for any help and had no idea that I ever should again," he told White. Darrow went on speaking tours and, in debate, took on some younger opponents—like G. K. Chesterton—whose wit he could no longer match. He swallowed hard, and wrote Mary and Lem about the loan he had given them. He had secured it with stock in the Southern Pacific Railroad, and wondered "just how much is owed the bank and the rate at which it is being paid and whether you have any difficulty keeping it up," since he needed to sell some shares for cash. "The truth is I got pretty badly hurt with all the rest in last year's failure and the disappointments since."

He reminded them to answer via his next-door neighbor, who had agreed to take mail that Darrow didn't want Ruby to see. "Poor great Darrow, unafraid of God, of public opinion, of custom of prejudice—brave enough to stand alone—yet cowed before a little insect of a woman," Mary wrote in her diary.[17]

Darrow announced, as well, that he would return to the courtroom at the age of seventy-three to defend gangsters George "Red" Barker and William "Three-fingered Jack" White. They had been rounded up in Chicago in Judge John Lyle's campaign to use the city vagrancy statutes to arrest "public enemies." Darrow's partners had taken on several infamous underworld clients in recent years, including Myles and Klondike O'Donnell, John "Dingbat" Oberta, and George "Bugs" Moran. Now he would join them on the gangster payroll.

"I can't somehow reconcile your representation of these men with your excellent record and their atrocious records," Lyle scolded Darrow in court.

"If the authorities wish to harass the lawless they should do it legally," Darrow told him. "There is no such charge in law as a 'public enemy.' "

Darrow also joined the appeals team for the reprehensible David Stephenson, the grand dragon of the Indiana Ku Klux Klan. Stephenson had doubled as the state's political boss in the mid-1920s and was one of Indiana's most powerful individuals when he was convicted of murdering Madge Oberholtzer, a twenty-eight-year-old social worker. In her dying declaration, Oberholtzer said she had been drugged, kidnapped, and repeatedly violated, and had taken poison to escape her captivity and disgrace.

"While I have not believed in the Klan, I think that the conviction was absolutely wrong," Darrow wrote Stephenson. "The ideas that you have apparently stood for are as far away from my views as one can possibly imagine, but I believe in fair play and I have a very strong feeling that you have not had it." Despite Darrow's aid, Stephenson's appeal failed.[18]

In the spring of 1931, Darrow was invited to participate in his last great civil rights case. On March 25 an Alabama posse chasing a group of black men who had brawled with some white hoboes pulled nine black youths and two white girls, dressed as boys, from a freight train near Scottsboro. It would have been scandalous for Ruby Bates, seventeen, and

Victoria Price, twenty-one, to admit to riding the rails with black men. They claimed, falsely, that they had been raped. So began the nightmare of the Scottsboro Boys. It would last for almost twenty years.

The black men escaped lynching but were rushed to trial, with incompetent counsel, in less than two weeks. Eight of the nine, all of whom were under the age of twenty, were convicted by all-white juries and condemned to death. There was a mistrial in the case of the final defendant, a thirteen-year-old boy: though the prosecutors had asked only for life imprisonment, seven jurors insisted that he be executed.

At the NAACP, White made the worst call of his career. Despite requests for help from local black leaders, he held back, worried by reports that the defendants might be guilty. His inaction allowed the legal arm of the American Communist Party—the International Labor Defense—to get to Scottsboro first. They signed up the unschooled and desperate African Americans as clients and promised to appeal the verdicts. The ILD called Darrow and asked if he would take the case. He notified White, who was finally moved to act and offered Darrow $5,000 to represent the boys for the NAACP.[19]

The rivalry between the groups was intense. In December, Darrow and Hays traveled to Birmingham to see if they could forge a common front. In the course of a long night of negotiating that ventured on "bedlam," the two men agreed to disassociate themselves from the NAACP and work with the ILD as private attorneys, under no organization's flag. But the communists would not bend. Darrow and Hays were welcome to join the communist team, and take communist direction, or go home. They went home.

The ILD would score some successes away from Alabama, but its communist ideology alienated the state and helped doom the defendants to years in prison. "The trouble with these fellows is that they think only of the cause," Darrow told Erskine Wood in a letter. "They may be right, but no lawyer can accept this doctrine. The client, of course, comes first."[20]

It was a dismal experience for Darrow. Until he could explain what happened in Birmingham, good friends accused him of deserting the defendants. He then faced the humiliating task of writing to his friends at the NAACP and begging them for time to pay back $1,000 that he owed them from his unearned retainer.

"The truth is that before these terrible times I had about $300,000, in what seemed perfectly good securities. They are not now worth more than ten and are not paying dividends," Darrow told White, in what the latter called a "most pathetic" plea. "Paul had about the same but he owed quite a large amount and for a year I have been giving him every cent I could to save what he had. The debt is now reduced to about $10,000 but the value of his stock has been reduced much more. . . .

"I had intended returning $1,000, but it looks from here as if I was broke entirely," Darrow wrote White. It took him until the summer of 1933 to refund all the money.[21]

Chapter 21

CLOSING

The old ghosts creep out of the dimming past.

Just before one a.m. on September 13, 1931, on the island of Oahu in the territory of Hawaii, a car full of late-night partygoers were startled to see an intoxicated young woman step out into the glare of their headlights on a desolate stretch of Ala Moana Road. She waved them to a stop. "Are you white people? Thank God," said Thalia Massie. "Please take me back to my husband."

Thalia's face was badly swollen, as if she had been beaten. She told the Good Samaritans that she had left a party at a Waikiki inn and, as she walked along the sidewalk toward the beach, was grabbed by a group of Hawaiian men, struck in the face when she struggled, and dumped in a clearing on the side of the road. A lady in the car asked the obvious question, but tactfully. Had the abductors hurt Thalia in any other way? "No," she said.

It was after Thalia Massie got home and was reunited with her husband that she declared she was raped. He was a lieutenant in the U.S. Navy, and the news moved quickly through the great base at Pearl Harbor. The rumors were lurid, and untrue. "They had violated her in every respect and . . . orifice," one sailor recalled. "They kicked her and broke her pelvis and they bit the nipple practically off one of her breasts . . . They broke her nose. Blackened both of her eyes, of course. On her face was a perfect imprint of a rubber heel, where they stomped on her."[1]

The navy and the Hawaiians had an uneasy relationship, dating back to America's seizure of the islands in the 1890s. And then there was this: Thalia was white, and her alleged ravagers were brown. Admiral Yates Stirling, the southern-born commandant in Hawaii, was informed that the wife of one of his officers had been gang-raped by "dark-skinned . . . half-breed hoodlums." He resisted his initial impulse, which was "to seize the brutes and string them up on trees."

Thalia was twenty years old. Her parents were Granville Roland Fortescue, a cousin of Teddy Roosevelt, and Grace Bell Fortescue, a doyenne of Washington, D.C., society. Thalia had been but sixteen when she married Tommie Massie, a Kentucky-born Naval Academy graduate about to join the fleet. Her wedding photograph showed a doll-like innocent with large eyes and dark blond hair. When five Hawaiians were arrested and charged with Thalia's rape, the news sent navy officials, members of Congress, and many of their constituents into an ugly fury. The islands were portrayed as a steamy hell where brown savages preyed upon the wives and daughters of American servicemen. Naval officials threatened to pull the fleet from Pearl Harbor, a move that would devastate the local economy. In Washington, Admiral William Pratt, the chief of naval operations, declared that indolent Hawaiian officials had sanctioned a plague of sexual assaults on white women—forty was the fanciful number that he cited.[2]

But there were elements of Thalia's account that didn't add up. At first, she told the authorities that she could not identify her abductors or their car. Yet when the boys were arrested and presented to her she claimed to recognize them, despite her shock and the haze of painkillers. As the night went on, and the police radio blared the number of their license plate, she "remembered" it as well. The recovery of her memory was convenient to the point of dubious. She had extremely poor vision and wasn't wearing her glasses on that moonless night.

The crime had taken place amid a series of personal and family crises for Thalia. She was sullen, often drunk, and had a disputatious attitude that put off many of the navy wives. Thalia was flirtatious with men, which tormented her husband, who was away from port for weeks at a time on submarine patrols. The Massie maid told investigators that Thalia welcomed one young navy lieutenant to her home and went away with him overnight when Tommie was at sea. Tommie struck Thalia in his rage and threatened her with divorce. "He had been violent with me. I had plenty of bruises, I can tell you," she later confided to Darrow. Her attempts to have children ended in miscarriages.

At the Waikiki party, Thalia had quarreled with Tommie and gotten into an alcohol-fueled argument with one of his superior officers, whose face she slapped before stalking out of the tavern. Indeed, her whole group was rowdy drunk that night, a fact suppressed to prevent "embarrassment to the Navy," Governor Lawrence Judd told Washington officials, and "to eliminate any possible ground for any juror to conclude that Mrs. Massie had been on a drunken party where she might have been beaten."

After telling her story to the police, Thalia had been taken to the hospital. Though she claimed to have been raped six or seven times by her abductors, the doctors found no bruising, nor swelling, nor semen when they examined her vagina. She did not become pregnant and abort a child, as she later claimed. Her doctor did not believe that Thalia was raped and urged Tommie to drop the matter and transfer from Hawaii. Witnesses had seen Thalia, staggering down the sidewalk, being followed by a white man. None of her fingerprints were found on the suspects' car. And the tire tracks discovered at the clearing where Thalia was taken may well have been made by the local police who, in an act of stunning incompetence, or malfeasance, had driven the defendants' auto there and run it back and forth across the crime scene.[3]

There was also a question of timing. If the five Hawaiians had abducted Thalia, they would have had just twenty to thirty minutes to cross the city, find and grab her from the sidewalk, drive to the clearing, take turns raping her, and travel to a luau in another part of town. None of their clothing had blood or semen stains and, though offered freedom and a $5,000 reward, none of the five would testify against the others. "An analysis . . . makes it impossible to escape the conviction that the kidnapping and assault was not caused by those accused," Judd's investigators would decide.

Many in Hawaii questioned whether Thalia had been raped at all. It was well known that young white women from the mainland came to Hawaii "to lie on the beach at Waikiki and get an all-over sun tan, and . . . let the bronze, handsome young athletes and surf riders teach them how to ride the waves, play . . . ball with them and . . . have the boys rub them down with coconut oil," wrote the *Tribune*'s Philip Kinsley, who was sent to Hawaii to cover the trial. The "fast young service set" lived in "lovely bungalows with great red hibiscus flowers in the doorways, and there is much drinking among them."

Two of Hawaii's foremost defense attorneys agreed to represent the five young men. On December 6, 1931, the trial ended in a mistrial after the jurors failed to reach a verdict. Six days later, one of the defendants was shanghaied, beaten, and flogged. And on January 8, another defendant, Joe Kahahawai, was snatched from the courthouse grounds in Honolulu and hustled into a waiting car by two men waving a counterfeit warrant. Two hours later the police found him, shot dead, bound, and wrapped in a bedsheet, in the back of a fleeing Buick sedan that they forced to a stop on a seafront highway overlooking Hanauma Bay. The living occupants of the car were Tommie Massie, a navy seaman named Edward Lord, and Thalia's mother. The trio and another enlisted man—Albert Jones—were charged with murder. They asked Darrow to defend them.[4]

BACK IN THE States, the newspapers called Kahahawai's death an "honor killing." *Time* magazine told how Thalia had been "roughly seized and ruthlessly raped by a band of five brown-skinned bucks." But Darrow recognized what had happened. His friends at the NAACP, where he still served on the board of directors, had spent their lives investigating such crimes, and demanded that Admiral Pratt be rebuked for his "unqualified endorsement of lynching."[5]

And so at first Darrow was reluctant. "I had so long and decidedly been for the Negro" and this was a case "at variance with what I felt and had stood for," he told a friend. Darrow ultimately agreed to go, he told himself, because he might bring healing to the troubled islands. And because he had always wanted to see Hawaii. But most of all he took the case because he needed money.

His decision triggered a debate in the civil rights community over whether Darrow "is at heart loyal to the cause he espouses," wrote the African American editors of the *Chicago Bee*, "or whether his interest in them wanes at the sight of sufficient monetary consideration."

Darrow was troubled by such commentary. "I have occasionally in the past represented people of wealth, and there has always been criticism," he wrote a friend who objected to his decision. "I don't know what I should have done if now and then a fairly well to do client had not come my way; the ravens have never called on me." He set his price at $30,000. "Please do not tell anyone what you are to receive," Ruby wrote her husband, who was traveling when the $5,000 retainer arrived in Chicago, "or again you'll be eaten alive by those who will think they may as well get some of it."

DARROW AND RUBY sailed from San Francisco. It was his first trip back to California since the bribery trial. He took a young New York lawyer, George Leisure, who had tried a case in Honolulu and volunteered to assist him without pay. They arrived in Hawaii on March 24 and Darrow, bedecked in leis, immediately sought to cool passions in the islands. The territorial legislature was considering a bill that would add rape to the list of crimes punishable by death in Hawaii. It was an awful idea, said Darrow, for it would only encourage rapists to murder their victims, since the penalty would be the same, and dead girls tell no tales.

Ruby glowed for years over the way that island society—the good people—welcomed them with lunches and receptions. And it was important, as things turned out, for Darrow to meet Governor Judd and Thalia's physician, and the Chamber of Commerce types like Walter Dillingham, a leader of the haole elite. Darrow also spent evenings with the out-of-town reporters; he jawed with Charles Banks, an old Chicago newspaperman he found in Honolulu, and spoke to George Wright, a former Allegheny College professor who edited the *Hawaii Hochi* and had, from the start, defended Kahahawai and the other suspects.

Darrow visited the beach and let Duke Kahanamoku, the Olympic swimmer, and a crew of Waikiki beach boys give him a ride through the cresting surf on an outrigger canoe. But he turned seventy-five that spring. On several occasions, the sun and the work and the *okolehao*, the local moonshine, took their toll.[6] Darrow was disarmingly frank about his motives. "He has told us candidly and with a smile that he wanted to take the trip to Hawaii and was offered an attractive fee," Wright wrote in the *Hochi*. "The present case . . . in no sense detracts from his record as an idealist . . . it is the bow that a great actor makes when he has been called before the curtain, after the play is over."

Darrow found obstacles in Hawaii. The first was a new prosecutor, John C. Kelley, "rugged, powerful, afraid of nothing . . . a shrewd, keen lawyer," as the mainland papers reported. Another was the Hawaiian character. If he hoped to get a jury of sympathetic whites, Darrow was disappointed. Racial mixing was tolerated, even prized, away from the navy base, and huge crowds had attended Kahahawai's funeral. Leisure warned Darrow that they must, by all means, avoid being seen as "coming to the rescue of The White Race."[7]

"I kept every white man I could," Darrow said later, and the final roster of jurors looked promising, with seven whites, three Chinese, and no pure Hawaiians. Yet Darrow was troubled, and told Leisure they had little hope for success. He began to direct his remarks, via his friends in the press, at the population back home in hopes of obtaining pardons. "He . . . frankly confesses that he has difficulty in trying to understand the mentality of these oddly mixed island jurors," Russell Owen wrote in the *Times*. For a lawyer whose strength was his ability to manipulate a jury's emotions, not knowing "the mentality" was indeed a problem.

Prosecutor Kelley, nattily dressed in a white tropical suit, opened with an account of Kahahawai's murder. Massie had set out on the morning of the killing dressed as a chauffeur, disguised with a fake mustache. Mrs. Fortescue had served as a lookout, and Jones had forced Kahahawai into the car. They all then drove to Fortescue's rented house, where they tried to make Kahahawai confess. It was there, Kelley said, as Kahahawai sat on the edge of a bed, that he had been shot and his body toted to the bathtub, where his blood ran down the drain.

Though the weapon was never found (before he was arrested, Jones gave it to Thalia's sister, who threw it into a pool of quicksand), the slug had no doubt come from a .32 automatic pistol that Jones had purchased, Kelley said. With a flourish, he showed the jury the bullet, and how it matched the expended .32 caliber shell and clip of .32 caliber ammunition found on Jones when he was arrested. Over four days, the prosecution demonstrated that the murder was a carefully planned crime, and not some act of temporary insanity. A police officer, describing the discovery of Kahahawai's body, told how he had praised a younger colleague for chasing down the Fortescue car with a hearty "Good work, kid!" Massie had thought the officer was talking to him and replied, "Thank you very much."

"Darrow at times appeared confused by the inflexions of speech and the English used," the *Hochi* reported. "Twice one of the local lawyers had to explain . . . answers."[8]

Darrow launched the defense on the afternoon of Thursday, April 14. He stood with folded arms and bowed head, as his calm, thoughtful questions took Massie back over the events of the night that Thalia was attacked. The young lieutenant replied in short, clipped sentences. He spent much of the time staring at the floor. The spectators could see his jaw muscles tighten, and he spoke in "a voice suggesting that of a frightened schoolboy," one recalled. Massie choked up, and Mrs. Fortescue sobbed, when he told how Thalia had been raped.

The day's session ended before Massie's tale reached the kidnapping of Kahahawai, and he did not disappoint when he returned to the stand on Saturday morning. He told the court how, at gunpoint, Kahahawai had confessed to raping Thalia—"Yes, we done it," the young Hawaiian supposedly said—and at that point, Massie testified, his mind was filled with an overwhelming image of his wife being raped. He remembered nothing more, Massie told the court, before their car was pulled over by the police on the bluffs above the ocean.

Massie's blackout was an exceptionally fortunate development, for the defense had a problem: it was not Massie who fired the fatal shot. Years later, Jones would confess that he had killed Kahahawai, when the "black bastard" made a sudden move. But Jones could not claim, to a sympathetic jury, to have been driven to insanity by rage and shame over a young wife's ravishment. Massie could. It was "Mr. Darrow's idea to let Tommie take the rap," said Jones. "Tommie had a motive and the reason. After all, it was his wife."

Darrow finished his presentation by calling Thalia to the stand. She spoke "like a hurt child," Owen wrote, "and with uncontrollable fits of silent weeping she told a story that brought tears to the eyes of many of the women in the room." Thalia twisted and tugged on a handkerchief and buried her face in her hands. And when she looked up, after describing the assault, her features were "distorted in agony."

The trial's unforgettable moment belonged to Kelley, however. The previous summer, a few weeks before she was attacked, and when her marriage to Massie seemed to be disintegrating, Thalia had sought psychological counseling from Professor E. Lowell Kelly at the University of Hawaii. After two or three sessions, Kelly informed Tommie that his wife needed psychiatric help. When the professor read about her in the newspapers, "I could not but doubt the validity of her accusations," he recalled. Indeed, his files still held a confidential questionnaire that Thalia had answered, in which she detailed the problems in her marriage. It contradicted the tales of marital sweetness that Tommie and Thalia told on the stand.

After Kahahawai was murdered, the professor discussed his ethical quandary with a colleague and concluded that doctor–patient privilege kept him from saying anything. But the colleague passed the word to Kelley, who got Thalia's files from the university when Kelly was away on a trip to Maui. Now, after some seemingly innocuous questions, Kelley asked Thalia if her husband was always kind to her. Yes, she said. Then Kelley asked her if she had sought psychological help the previous summer.

"I went to see Professor Kelly," she replied.

Kelley handed her a sheet of paper from her file. "Is this your handwriting?" he asked.

Thalia looked at the prosecutor with murderous rage. "Where did you get this?" she asked.

"I'm asking the questions," Kelley said, and he repeated the question. "Has your husband always been kind to you?"[9]

"Don't you know this is a confidential communication between doctor and patient?" she shot back. "You have no right to bring this into the courtroom." She had been transformed, as all watched, from troubled child to cold, furious woman. And as everyone looked on in astonishment, she ripped the paper to pieces. Her supporters in the audience began to applaud. Tommie and the other defendants joined them. The judge called for order.

"Thank you, Mrs. Massie, at last you have shown yourself in your true colors," said Kelley. He released her from the witness stand, and she staggered and fell into Tommie's arms, wailing, "What right has he got to say that I don't love you?"

Kelley had begun his cross-examination on April 20 at eleven forty-two a.m. By eleven fifty he was finished. So was the defense.[10]

In the end, Darrow rested his argument on the "unwritten law" that, for centuries, had absolved a man for killing a rival who stole his woman.

"There is, somewhere deep in the feelings and instincts of a man, a yearning for justice, an idea of what is right and wrong, of what is fair between man and man, that came before the first law was written and will abide after the last one is dead," Darrow told the jurors. Over and over Darrow asked them, "If you put yourself in Tommie Massie's place, what would you have done?"

He was dressed in a new, crisp Palm Beach suit but looked tired, and a bit unsure. Many of the leading players in the drama were there, including

Admiral Stirling, Thalia, and Kahahawai's parents. He spoke, all told, for four hours. At lunch he took a nap, then finished with a flourish in the afternoon heat. He used his array of gestures—crouching and twisting and shifting his voice from a gentle whisper to a roar. Leisure was amazed by Darrow's "tremendous" powers of concentration.

"If this husband and this mother and these faithful boys go to the penitentiary, it won't be the first time that a penitentiary has been sanctified by its inmates," Darrow told the jury.

"Take these poor pursued, suffering people, take them into your care, as you would have them take you if you were in their place," he begged.

But the jury had more to consider than mercy, said Kelley, who took but an hour to argue for justice on behalf of the dead Joe Kahahawai.

"Three able men and a cold, calculating woman let a man bleed to death in front of them, inch by inch," he argued. "They aren't kids. They're brought up in an atmosphere of guns. They're taught the art of killing, also of first aid. But they let him die, dragged him into the bathroom like a dog and let him die. . . .

"A killing is a killing, and under certain circumstances is murder," he said. "If the serpent of lynch law is permitted to raise its head on these islands, watch out, watch out."

The jurors wrestled diligently and arrived at a compromise after two days of deliberating. They found the four defendants guilty of the lesser charge of manslaughter and asked the court to show lenience in the sentencing.

"He talked to us like a lot of farmers," one of the jurors said of Darrow's closing appeal. "That stuff may go over big in the Midwest, but not here."[11]

Yet Darrow knew that while one trial was over, the greater trial, for public opinion, went on. There was an equilibrium in the moment that he thought he could exploit. The guilty verdict had restored Hawaii's pride and humbled the naval and commercial interests that, after seven months of turmoil, wanted to get on with the business of making money and defending America. Thalia had been revealed as less than reliable. The imprisonment of Massie and Mrs. Fortescue and two navy seamen, the road through the appeals courts, and the retrial of the remaining Ala Moana rape defendants all promised more months of turmoil. And Japan's growing militancy and the strategic importance of Hawaii were compelling reasons for officials in the Hoover administration to end the drama.

The elements were there for a deal, and Darrow now put his connections to the business elite, the territorial officials, and the navy brass to use. He knew the pressure Judd was under: members of Congress were threatening to put the islands under military rule. Via his attorney general, Judd had offered to reduce the sentences to one year, but the defendants declined. Darrow called on him. "What are you going to do?" he asked. "Full pardons are indicated in the circumstances."

"I'll commute the sentences to one hour," Judd replied.

Darrow thought it through. "So be it," he said. He conveyed the news to Admiral Stirling, who insisted that commutation wasn't enough. Darrow returned to Judd seeking full pardons, but the governor was feeling tremendous "personal guilt" for bowing to the pressure and refused to bend any further. Darrow went back to the defendants. They agreed to take the deal.

On Wednesday, May 4, Darrow's four clients suddenly appeared in court and were sentenced to serve up to ten years in prison. But they were smiling as they left the courthouse and walked over to the Iolani Palace, where Judd commuted their sentences to one hour. They finished the time in the governor's office and returned to the drydocked navy cruiser in Pearl Harbor where, for their safety, they had been held since their arrest. Darrow told reporters that Tommie and Thalia would leave Hawaii and not press for a retrial of the rape case. It would be "a useless waste of public money and would not be for the best interests of the community," he said.

Kelley was not part of the deal and sent men to Pearl Harbor to serve a subpoena on Thalia, but navy personnel blocked them—at one point physically as Thalia fled through the galley and the hold—until the Massies were safely in their cabin on a cruise ship heading for San Francisco. "The courtroom records in Honolulu would show that Clarence Darrow lost this trial," said Leisure. "But he felt we had gone to Honolulu to save four American citizens and . . . brought . . . them back on the steamer with us to the mainland." Mrs. Fortescue stood at the rail with a lei around her neck, waving goodbye to the crowd at the dock as an orchestra played "Aloha oe."[12]

"All Hawaii recognizes this is the best way out," wrote Owen. Others were not sure. Wright, the *Hochi* editor, expressed a different opinion in a letter to Darrow. "You are right as between human beings, right in the desire to save from suffering, in the denial of society's right to punish,"

Wright wrote. "You have been consistent to the end. And you have won your fight—won it with distinction."

"But in every battle won there are the vanquished," said Wright. "I belong to Hawaii, and Hawaii has been beaten and shamed and outraged."

"I think Mrs. Massie was mistaken in her identification, and that Massie lied when he said Kahahawai confessed," said Wright.

"The Navy in this case typifies arrogance, intolerance, superiority. It has lied and slandered Hawaii," said Wright. "They could not afford to lose face and yield to what they so contemptuously regarded as 'nigger justice.' "[13]

Thalia, in a festive blue dress, had beamed on the day of her sentencing. But she had told her story from the stand twice, and neither jury had wholly believed her.

Now something needed to be done about the outstanding charges against the remaining rape defendants. Kelley and Judd agreed to have an independent review conducted by the Pinkerton agency, whose detectives interviewed dozens of people in Hawaii and across the United States in a three-month investigation. Its verdict was definitive. "We have found nothing in the record of this case, nor have we through our own efforts been able to find . . . sufficient corroboration of the statements of Mrs. Massie to establish the occurrence of rape," the agency concluded.

Massie's close friends told the Pinkertons that "the thought is now that she may not have been raped at all . . . and has told the story to excite sympathy from her husband, and having told the story stuck to it, believing her husband, who is a southerner, would not leave her under such conditions." In February 1933, after the findings of the Pinkerton investigation were made public, Kelley made a motion to drop the charges against the remaining Ala Moana defendants.

Judd was still being pressed, from Capitol Hill, for a pardon. He noted, when deciding against it, Darrow's tactics in the trial: "There is no credible evidence—no evidence at all—that Lieutenant Massie was the person who fired the shot that killed. . . .

"Honesty of defense required a disclosure of the fact . . . The indulgence of pardon should not be extended to people who have consistently refused to disclose, on oath or otherwise, what really transpired," he concluded. "Punishment has been relieved. Vindication is not due."

Darrow always insisted that Thalia told the truth. And certainly someone had taken her from Waikiki to the isolated clearing along Ala Moana Road, where she was assaulted. Did a Hawaiian or navy patron of the tavern offer her a ride and press her for sex, then strike her when she refused? Did she cry rape to cloak a romantic assignation that turned ugly? Was Tommie furious at her escapade, and did he add to her injuries? The Pinkertons could not say. But Darrow felt sorry for her, and thought she was smart, and liked her sass. And she shared his distaste for the good people.[14]

When she heard the news that Kelley had dropped the charges, Thalia griped to reporters. Darrow urged her to keep still, but she refused. "Naturally it made me mad when Judd and Kelley and the Pinkertons and the rest of the tribe practically called me a liar and cast all sorts of innuendos in the newspapers," she told him. "Silence on my part looked suspicious.

"I am sure that you will agree that I was right," she wrote. "I mean, darling, you're so idealistic and believe in turning the other cheek, but one must be practical."

As the years passed, Tommie and Thalia showed themselves to be very troubled individuals. They had not been away from Hawaii for long before Tommie wrote Darrow, informing him that the couple would separate. "For five years and more I have tolerated more from Thalia than any human being would have," he said. She had a "marvelous" intellect, Massie wrote, but there was "a massive difference in her moral code and mine. . . .

"She feels great malice because I have *never* believed in her," Massie wrote. The two of them now pelted Darrow with letters, each arguing their case. She called Tommie a "selfish weakling" and chronicled his excessive drinking, physical abuse, and fling with one of her distant relatives, a "dreadful little slut."

"You probably won't believe the things I have told you," Thalia wrote Darrow. "You have always thought Tommie was a little tin god. Just because he has beautiful manners! That's how he gets by . . . I don't give a damn whether you believe me or not; I don't give a damn about anything any more . . . we'll all be dead pretty soon, and who will care? . . .

"I do not, at the present time, intend to divorce him," she told Darrow. "If I do everyone will . . . say I'm rotten to do such a thing after what *they think* he did for me."

But Thalia relented, and the couple announced their separation in October 1933 and were divorced in Reno, Nevada, four months later. She was hospitalized that night, after becoming hysterical and collapsing at a nightclub. In April, on an ocean liner bound for Italy, she slashed her wrists but survived. In June 1934, Thalia was examined by Dr. William White, the superintendent at St. Elizabeths Hospital in Washington, D.C. She confessed to several suicide attempts and he found that she suffered "attacks of great fear . . . accompanied by feelings of unreality." She remarried, divorced, and ultimately took an overdose of pills in 1962.

Tommie's career in the navy came to a dismal end when he suffered a mental breakdown in 1940 while serving on the battleship *Texas*. His medical records show a succession of symptoms and illnesses—hallucination, paranoia, delusion, schizophrenia, psychosis, and manic depression—which rendered him unfit for service. He was discharged before the war began, lived uneventfully in southern California, and died in 1987.[15]

Darrow's financial woes were eased by his fee in the Massie case, as well as by the publication of a bestselling autobiography, *The Story of My Life*. The book was well received by reviewers despite the fact that, as Darrow conceded to a friend, it was as much "propaganda" as biography. Scribner's had outbid several publishing houses for the rights, and the famous Max Perkins was the editor. He flattered Darrow profusely, then suggested that the philosophical sections were a bit repetitious, and could he thin them out? Darrow had started working on the book in 1929, writing chapters in longhand. These penciled first drafts were not heavily edited, at least by Darrow; many went right into print, a testament to his lucidity of thought and powers of concentration. Ruby did the typing and conveyed messages to the publishers. "This quality of thought and expression seems so much a part of the author that he is unable (and unwilling!) to rearrange—or reform—parts and passages—just as he would not know how to remold himself; and would not allow anyone else to alter beyond changes that now appear on galleys herewith returned," she informed them.

There were no great revelations, and a lot of philosophizing. Chapters were devoted to his most famous cases—the Debs, Haywood, McNamara, Leopold and Loeb, Scopes, and Sweet trials—but as many were given to his beliefs on crime, law, capital punishment, Prohibition, religion, and other matters. He was careless when relating dates, spelling people's names, and telling how things went. (It is McParland, not McPartland; Hughitt, not Hewitt; he came to Chicago in 1887, not 1888; he didn't call Bryan to the stand in Dayton, Hays did, etc.) Darrow promised a "plain, unvarnished account of how things really have happened," but his readers are as served by his warning that "autobiography is never entirely true."

The Kinsman chapters were charming, and reminiscent of *Farmington*. "The house was small, the family large, the furnishing meager, but there were books whichever way one turned," he remembered. But his account of his resignation from the Chicago & North Western railroad was fictitious. His repeated defeats in election campaigns, and involvement in lost causes, went unmentioned. An extra chapter on the Massie trial was published in *Scribner's Magazine* in 1932 and added to later editions of the book. He continued to insist, knowing it was not true, that Massie fired the shot that killed Joe Kahahawai.

An interesting feature of Darrow's autobiography is what, and whom, he chose to leave out. There is no mention of Gertrude Barnum, Mary Field, and his other loves, though that's to be expected. But Darrow also omits, in the telling of his story, all the sociopaths he saved, the women who shot their cheating husbands, the con men, the gangsters, drunk drivers, labor sluggers, corrupt businessmen, and crooked politicians who were his clients. Forgotten or omitted are William Goudy, Edgar Lee Masters, Cy Simon, Olav Tvietmoe, Anton Johannsen, Samuel Gompers, William Randolph Hearst, Robert Crowe, Mayors Carter Harrison Jr. and Big Bill Thompson, Fred Lundin, Chief Charles Healey, "Three-fingered Jack" White, Mont Tennes, Vincenzo Cosmano and the boys, Emma Simpson and the other homicidal ladies, the Bank of America, the Scottsboro Boys, the Iroquois Theatre fire, the *Eastland* disaster, and the Ogden Gas scandal. Darrow's two wives and son are mentioned, but almost as afterthoughts.

Darrow's account of the McNamara case was curt and defensive. "Before I left Chicago I knew nothing about the facts," he claimed. After arriving in Los Angeles, he wrote, it quickly became clear that the case was hopeless, and more so after Bert Franklin was arrested for bribery. Darrow's foremost obligation was to save his clients' lives, he argued. "By every emotion of my life, by the rule of my profession, by every human instinct, I was bound to act as I did, and consider my clients only, and I am glad that I did not stop to think of consequences," he said. "My life is made up, and must stand as it is. But I was in a terrible crisis that I faced almost alone."

Darrow did reveal how, during his first bribery trial, a hulking cop killer named George Bissett whom Darrow had once defended in Chicago arrived in Los Angeles and offered to murder Franklin. Darrow gently dissuaded him and sent him home. But as for the bribery charge, "I feel confident that no reader will blame me if I do not unduly dwell on this part of my story," Darrow wrote. "As I write the old ghosts creep out of the dimming past and dance around me as if in glee, and I am anxious to drive them back and lock them up where I cannot see their haunting faces or hear their mocking jeers."[16]

THE MASSIE TRIAL had further fanned Darrow's fame, and made his name quite marketable. He performed on the radio, defending (unsuccessfully) Benedict Arnold in a dramatization for $5,000. And he earned a nice fee from Hollywood for narrating a motion picture documentary on biology called *The Mystery of Life*. Its profoundly untitillating explanation of reproduction nonetheless drew the attention, and the scissors, of the censors. But "because of the recent Darrow-Massie trial in Hawaii," the documentary "is far more valuable than it was a year ago," its distributor told its salesmen.

"Remember that you are selling Darrow (America's biggest draw according to *Variety*) and you are selling him to the MASSES, not the CLASSES," Universal Pictures told theater owners. "Remember to sell DARROW, and do not stress the evolution angle of the thing or make it sound educational."

"I really need the money," Darrow told the critic George Nathan, showing him the advertising copy for the movie. "If you don't believe I needed the money, look what I let myself in for. Good God."

Darrow's uncertain health and finances did not prevent him, at the age of seventy-five, from returning to court in two last capital cases, and saving two boys from execution.

James "Iggy" Varecha was seventeen when he shot and killed a salesman in a robbery and, an hour later, kidnapped and raped the twenty-year-old niece of a Chicago police commissioner. Though Varecha was an escapee from a mental hospital, he was judged sane by the state's doctors. Varecha pled guilty, thinking his life would be spared, but his lawyer had not obtained assurances from the judge. Varecha was sentenced to die in the electric chair. It took three bailiffs to restrain him in court.

Darrow was aghast that the state would execute someone with the stated mental capacity of an eleven-year-old and took the appeal. Stooped and gray, his voice barely a whisper, Darrow strode back and forth in the well of the court, waving his arms as he pleaded for Varecha's life. "His father and mother are illiterate. All his brothers and sisters, with one exception, are defective," he argued. "This boy is not to blame. Organized society had its chance to keep him off the streets, but it failed to do so. He was just a young animal, turned loose on the streets in the shape of a boy." In time, the Illinois Supreme Court granted Varecha a new trial. This time, the plea bargain was properly sealed. He was sentenced to one hundred years in prison.

Darrow fought, as well, for the life of Russell McWilliams, who had also been but seventeen when he killed a streetcar operator in a Rockford robbery. McWilliams was drunk when he shot the man five times. Like Varecha, he had made the mistake of pleading guilty and asking for mercy from a court, which sentenced him to die. Three times Darrow won McWilliams a reprieve, and three times a judge confirmed the penalty. So Darrow begged the state pardon board to urge the governor to commute the sentence. His strength was failing that day, and he asked to speak from a chair. "It is not the policy of this state to kill children," Darrow told the board. "The mind of the child is not the mind of the man." On Darrow's seventy-sixth birthday, Governor Henry Horner spared the boy's life, three days before he was scheduled to be electrocuted. McWilliams was a model prisoner, and was paroled in 1951.

"The powers seemed bent on taking his life," Darrow wrote Graham Taylor. "I just can't understand them. I am much alarmed for fear they will cut down what we have so far made the limit of taking life, which is still 18. I am sure it will take the efforts of all of us to keep back the tide of hatred that seems to be overwhelming us."[17]

It was absolutely fitting that, before he died, Darrow took bold stands for individual liberty in the face of political and corporate gigantism. "Ideas have come and gone, but I have always been a champion of the individual as against the majority and the State," Darrow wrote in his autobiography. "Of all the political leaders of the past, Thomas Jefferson made the strongest appeal to me." It was a thought that Franklin Roosevelt and his aides might have pondered before giving Darrow a public platform, resources, and license to critique the president's New Deal.

Darrow had supported and spoken for Roosevelt in the 1932 presidential campaign. Roosevelt had promised "bold persistent experimentation" to fight the effects of the Great Depression, which had left 13 million Americans out of work. President Herbert Hoover's mishandling of the crisis had led Darrow to quip that "I used to be taught that anybody could be President; it begins to look as if they could, too."

And so it seemed to Roosevelt's staff that Darrow was a safe choice to chair a special board to review the operation of the National Recovery Administration, which was established in the first hundred days of Roosevelt's presidency. Its symbol was a blue eagle, which shops and businesses—even dancing girls—displayed to show that they were following "codes" of behavior drawn up and administered by the NRA and its industrial councils. It was, said one historian, the center ring in the New Deal circus, and its ringmaster—a retired army cavalry officer who combined the qualities of military leader and sideshow barker—was the colorful, irrepressible, and impetuous General Hugh Johnson. His deputy was Donald Richberg, one of Darrow's old pals from the Chicago reform movement. At a time when the country needed a cause to join, the NRA offered hope.

Yet, as with any government agency, particularly one that invited commercial interests to help draft its codes, the NRA's operations reflected the influence of the bigger corporate lobbies. The agency allowed companies to join together to fix prices, wages, and hours. This soon led other businesses, unions, and consumers to squawk. Evasion and cheating were reported. "The excessive centralization and the dictatorial spirit," wrote

Walter Lippmann, "are producing a revulsion of feeling against bureaucratic control of American economic life." Congress responded and, led by Senators William Borah of Idaho and Gerald Nye of North Dakota, convinced the White House to name a National Recovery Review Board, with Darrow as its chair.

Masters tried to warn Roosevelt of what was to come. Via a friend, the poet got a letter to the president's private secretary, Marguerite "Missy" LeHand, savaging his former law partner.

"Money and publicity have been his life objects and to get them he has sacrificed parties and friends and principles all along," Masters wrote. "I do not refer to Darrow's malodorous career, to his indictment for jury bribing in California, nor to his dubious reputation as a lawyer in Chicago, but rather to his insidious and subtle faculty of playing fast and loose with labor and capital," said Masters, "to his bewildering shifts and changes in which he has flirted with democracy, socialism, the single tax and anarchism; to his faithless attitude toward friends, leaders like Bryan and others."

Darrow had spent a lifetime "winding serpent-like where there was food, and winding safely away when there was danger, and never shot, or so completely exposed, that he was ended," said Masters. He was sure to turn and "fang" the administration now that they had let him "inside the breastworks . . . clothed in the armor of a pretended intellectual independence."

Masters conveyed similar sentiments to Mencken. It can't be that bad, Mencken replied. Richberg had suggested Darrow. And surely FDR, the sly fox, had "a Machiavellian purpose" in appointing an aged gent whose faculties were eroded and whose time was clearly past, and whose thoughts would not be taken seriously. Darrow was just an old pussycat, entranced by the "catnip" of the press, Mencken said.

The "Darrow review board" began its work in March 1934. He and Ruby installed themselves in a suite at the Willard Hotel, where the staff, led by Washington lawyer Lowell Mason, held nearly sixty public hearings and reviewed three thousand complaints. The first report, released in May, exploded on Washington like an artillery round. It charged the NRA with fostering monopolistic practices that favored influential interests at the cost of the little guy. It didn't matter that, as Richberg, Mencken, and others pointed out, the report was philosophically incoherent. So was much of the reasoning behind the NRA. The slap to Roosevelt was a great political story and the two loquacious and leathery foes—Darrow and Johnson—were irresistible copy, especially when they took a car ride together around Arlington, ostensibly to bury the hatchet, and discussed anthropology, murder, religion, and the hereafter.

Darrow's mandate expired in June, and he got a cold shoulder from Roosevelt. A White House assistant was delegated to write Darrow that "the President asks me to acknowledge receipt of your final report, which he did not have a chance to look into before his departure, and to act for him in accepting your resignation."

"I hear from Washington that Darrow is wandering around in a fog, scarcely knowing where he is at or what he is doing," Mencken wrote Masters. "His report will take its place among the comic documents of all time. When it came in the Brain Trust boys threw back their ears and howled with delight. They took two weeks to answer it, not because answering it was difficult, but because they were constantly impeded by their own laughter."

That was the White House spin. But reforms were enacted and by the end of the summer Johnson was on his way out of office. The NRA never recovered its élan. And in the spring of 1935, a year after Darrow's report, the Supreme Court ruled, unanimously, that the NRA represented an unconstitutional excess of federal power.[18]

Darrow was exhausted by the NRA assignment. But Hays pleaded with him to take on one more duty. After getting assurances that he could rest at Hays's Long Island home during the trip, Darrow agreed to serve as the chair of the American Inquiry Commission, an ad hoc group opposed to Hitler and Nazi rule, at hearings in New York City in early July. The Nazis "threaten the lives of some of the leading men in Germany who are now in concentration camps," Hays had written Darrow. "Now is the time for the inquiry to be held."

Darrow's had been a public voice against fascism for years. It was a prime reason he defended Carillo and Greco. The previous December, Darrow had joined Preston Bradley and Louis Mann at Chicago's Washington Boulevard Temple in a forum on Nazism.

Hitler had taken power in January 1933. He immediately issued emergency decrees, claiming dictatorial powers "for the protection of the People and the State." The Führer never hid where he was going. "Curbs on personal liberty, on the right of free expression of opinion, including freedom of the press, of associations, and of assembly; surveillance over letters, telegrams and telephone communications, searches of homes and confiscations of as well as restrictions on property, are hereby permissible," the Nazis declared. Opposition parties were dissolved. Political foes were assassinated. The first concentration camp was opened at Dachau that spring. The Nuremberg Laws, which stripped Jews of their citizenship, and the nationwide pogrom called Kristallnacht were still months or years away, but Darrow and the others recognized what was happening.

"One inferior man, with energy and daring and nerve, is able to convert Germany almost into a morgue filled with Jews," Darrow warned. "The thing which shocks me . . . when many people have thought that human beings were growing more intelligent, when we believed that men and women were broader and more understanding and more liberal, there should come a man with the power and strength to make a warfare upon a race out of the clear sky; and the most destructive warfare, as I read of it, that has ever been carried on against the Jews. . . .

"It amazes me and scares me," he said. "For where it can be done against any people or any religion, no people of any sort or of any religions can be safe."

In July, with Hays and Malone, a U.S. senator, and other notables beside him, Darrow listened as a series of witnesses before the commission told of Nazi outrages in a hearing room in downtown Manhattan.

"Hitler is a very dangerous man, and should be destroyed," Darrow told reporters as the members of the commission paid a visit on Mayor La Guardia during its lunchtime break.[19]

THOSE WHO SAW him were struck by how tired Darrow looked. He had to write to Baldwin and beg off a simple assignment when the ACLU asked him to sign a petition protesting labor conditions on the West Coast. He was "scandalously old," Darrow told Baldwin, and in ill health. He did not have the strength to study the controversy and "did not dare go into a matter that I so vaguely understood."

"Darrow is right," Baldwin told his staff. "He is too old to go into such matters. Let him alone after this."[20]

Darrow was suffering from arterial blockages and damage from his earlier heart trouble, which sapped his strength. The effects of arteriosclerosis and lapses in the flow of oxygen began to affect his brain.

"What a tragedy it is—Darrow with his mind gone, groping around trying to make a living lecturing," Older wrote Lem Parton. "That is the worst news I have had in years."[21]

Ruby wrote to Jim McNamara at San Quentin, describing their stay in Washington. It was "a Big Comeback indeed," she said, but it was the last time Darrow would be "mingling with and being counted in with those who help to make the wheels go around." Darrow's health was so "variable," said Ruby, that they never knew which mornings he could rise, and which days he'd be forced to stay in bed. Often, he found it impossible to climb stairs, or an incline. At times, even at rest, he gasped for breath "in a quiet little way, trying not to admit his trouble." Other times he felt stronger. In November, Darrow was back east on the lecture circuit "to keep the poor bank balance from sinking too far," she reported.

Darrow had never recovered his full hearing after the mastoid operation. Now his eyes were dimming. He felt too frail to take the train to the Loop, where the crowds might knock him down. They had moved his big black desk and the other office furniture to the apartment on the Midway, but his hip ached, which made it hard to sit. Ruby took control of his correspondence.

"He comes home and welcomes the bed in the back room, where he almost lives, with books and papers and what mail he cannot shirk," she told McNamara. "I have a little typewriter that I tuck under my arm and trot to his bedside balancing it on my lap, letting him tell me what to say."[22]

In March 1935, Darrow summoned the will to make the trip to Washington and testify before Congress on the NRA. It did not go well. He drifted, and snapped like a turtle.

Darrow sensed he was rambling. "If you get tired, I wish you would tell me. I am getting to the garrulous age," he told the committee.[23] In September, he kept a lecture engagement at a local church, but asked if he could remain in his chair as he spoke.

From time to time, he made a bit of a stir. The reporters called him up for a comment when Dickie Loeb was murdered in prison. He criticized the prosecutorial tactics that led to the convictions of Al Capone and Bruno Hauptmann, the kidnapper of the Lindbergh baby. And, in 1936, a few days short of his seventy-ninth birthday, he argued his last case—that of Jesse Binga, a black banker convicted of fraud.

There were few bright spots in the last months of Darrow's life. His friend Fay Lewis came to call in February 1938, but was alarmed when no one answered the door.

"I imagine father was home, but they never answer the door because he is in no condition to see anyone," Paul wrote Lewis. "His mind is practically gone and it is necessary to have a day and night nurse. He is up almost every day around the house—most of the time walking alone [I mean without help] but some one is with him constantly to see that he does not fall.

"He talks considerably but says nothing that we can understand. Once in a while I can catch a word or two but no connected words that give me any idea of what he means. He has been this way for most of the last six months. I took him out for a ride the last Sunday in January. The last two Sundays he has not been well enough to go."[24]

He needed around-the-clock care, as his once tall and broad-shouldered frame withered, in his dying, to ninety pounds. He was given morphine, at first at night, then all the time. The cruelest stroke, for those who loved him, was the loss of his powers of analysis and expression. "The wonderful intellect has crashed," one friend wrote another. For six months, Darrow rambled about his Hyde Park apartment, raving and muttering.

On March 5, 1938, Binga was freed. The great lawyer had won his final appeal. But Darrow was too ill, and senescent, to comprehend the news.

He left the living on March 13, a few weeks short of his eighty-first birthday—a small, wizened corpse of just a few score pounds.

In Ohio, an enterprising newspaper editor dispatched a reporter to Kinsman, which "never really understood" the "gaunt village lad who grew up to a strange greatness."

Ruth Root, who had sat beside young Clarence in class at school, allowed that "he was a good man, I reckon, but folks didn't like the way he believed. Myself, I never could see how he could plead for those murderers."

"Funeral service?" said her friend Florence Flowers. "I thought they'd just toss him off a cliff."[25]

IN THE WEEKS after his death, Ruby Darrow was compelled to give up their Midway flat and to sell his library and belongings. She was stunned to discover, in those Depression days, how little the estate commanded. The books, well pawed and annotated, went to Kroch's Bookstore on Michigan Avenue for a few hundred dollars. The grandfather clock that Ruby thought was worth hundreds sold for $50 at auction. The Oriental rug she had valued at $300 was bought for $70. His pocket knife, which he used to sharpen pencils for the crossword puzzles he enjoyed, went for $1.50.

A WINTER RAIN was falling on March 19 as an automobile braked to a halt on a stone bridge spanning the lagoon in Jackson Park, on the lakefront in Chicago. The weather fit the season, which was grim with news of war; the newspapers carried photographs of Londoners in gas masks at civil defense drills, and told how the Nazi legions had marched into Vienna.

One of the passengers—the lawyer's son—stayed in the car; the other, his business manager, emerged and walked to the rail, where he opened a metal box, leaned out, and spilled cinders and ash and cremated bone into the water below. He returned to the car and it rode away, and was swallowed in the lakeside traffic.[26]

ACKNOWLEDGMENTS

This book would not be, except for the love of my wife Catharina. It is dedicated to my son John and daughter Caitlin. They are a generous and supportive family, fine traveling companions, and not too bad as research assistants.

I have a wonderful friend and agent in David Black, and I benefited from the help of a remarkably talented team at Doubleday, led by Kris Puopolo, Bill Thomas, Stephanie Bowen, Nora Reichard, and Rosalie Wieder. I thank Kris, especially, for her exacting standards, literary vision, and unflagging encouragement.

I thank the Darrow family for its help, especially William and Judy Lyon, who opened their basement archives to me.

At the Library of Congress, Jeff Flannery and his colleagues in the manuscript reading room and its companion divisions were superb guides. With their help, I explored the Clarence Darrow Papers and the microfilm or original collections of the American Civil Liberties Union, the NAACP, Sam Gompers and the AFL-CIO, the Pinkerton detective agency, Theodore Roosevelt, Brand Whitlock, Woodrow Wilson, William Jennings Bryan, William Howard Taft, Louis Brandeis, Henry Demarest Lloyd, Elmer Gertz, and others. At the Library I found essential resources like the transcript of the Anthracite Strike Commission hearings, Harry Orchard's confession and detective James McParland's correspondence from the Steunenberg murder case, the Pinkerton report from the Massie case, the original transcript of Darrow's closing remarks (with his edits for publication) from his second bribery trial, and, among the Gertz papers, the transcript of the second and third day of Darrow's closing address in the Leopold and Loeb trial, which some scholars thought was lost.

Since I was a boy of twelve, I have owned a copy of Irving Stone's biography of Darrow. I was moved to write my own story of the great man's life after discovering in 2005 that the University of Minnesota had acquired a huge cache of his private correspondence from his heirs. It was found, along with a subsequent collection held by Ruby Darrow's family, by Minneapolis attorney Randall Tietjen, who is editing a forthcoming book of Darrow letters. The lion's share of the correspondence came online in 2010 when the university's law library opened hundreds of these documents—most of them previously unavailable to scholars—to the public. Katherine Hedin and Michael Hannon and their colleagues have done a first-rate job assembling their collection as a digital archive that includes letters, trial transcripts, photographs, and secondary sources. It was there, for example, that I found Darrow's instruction to his son Paul to pay $4,500 to a juror from the bribery trial.

The treasure hunt provides much of the fun when writing a biography. After Darrow's death, his wife Ruby sold his papers to Irving Stone, who then sold the collection to philanthropist Leo Cherne, who donated most of it to the Library of Congress. At Boston University, I discovered that Cherne's papers contain a trove of correspondence that he did not give to the Library, including revealing letters from Tommie and Thalia Massie, and from Darrow's friends and family during the bribery trials. Another invaluable resource for Darrow scholars is the papers of Mary Field Parton, his longtime friend and lover. The full collection, including her diaries, is at the University of Oregon, and has never been used in a full-scale life of Darrow. Going page by page through her diaries, I found Mary's acknowledgment, to herself, that the man she so loved and admired may indeed have bribed the McNamara jury. In the Karl Darrow papers at the American Institute of Physics in College Park, Maryland, I found poignant accounts of Darrow's mother's death from cancer, and other glimpses of the Darrow family, related in letters from Amirus and Mary Darrow.

Chicago is an essential stop for a Darrow scholar. A smaller selection of Mary's correspondence with Darrow, which includes his long and expressive letters, is at the Newberry Library. The Newberry also has his first wife Jessie Ohl's scrapbooks, a file of correspondence by Edgar Lee Masters, and the papers of Darrow scholars Arthur and Lila Weinberg. I made use of other collections there as well, including those of Eunice Tietjens, Ben Hecht, Wallace Rice, May Walden, Graham Taylor, Robert Bergstrom, Bernard Brommel, and Mayor Carter Harrison II. Along the way, I came to know and enjoy the city and its people. The University of Chicago has a small Darrow collection and papers of George Schilling. Northwestern University has a second Gertz collection, with a set of Leopold and Loeb transcripts. The Chicago Historical Society holds more Leopold and Loeb material, including the papers of Hal Higdon and Nathan Leopold, and other fascinating collections. The Chicago Public Library has a minor Darrow collection as well.

The National Archives in Chicago and in Washington, D.C., and College Park, Maryland, hold important files on the Red Scare, the Pullman Strike, Leopold and Loeb, the Massie case, the Haywood and McNamara prosecutions, and the *Eastland* disaster. John Mitchell's papers are at Catholic University in Washington, D.C.

Darrow's disastrous California experience is well chronicled there. I read the 10,000-page transcript of the first bribery trial, and volumes from the prosecution of David Caplan and Matt Schmidt, at the Los Angeles Law Library, just a few feet across Broadway from where the Los Angeles Times Building was destroyed by James McNamara's bomb in 1910. The Huntington Library in San Marino holds the papers of Charles Erskine Scott Wood and his wife Sara, which contain many letters from Darrow and Mary Field and their associates. More Wood papers, and Sara's oral history, are available at the University of California at Berkeley, which also has the papers of Irving Stone, Hiram Johnson, Fremont and Cora Older, James Barry, Paul Scharrenberg, and Tom Mooney. Across the bay, at Stanford University, I made use of the Walter Bordwell and Meyer Lissner collections. UCLA holds the papers of LeCompte Davis, James Harlan Pope, and Dr. Perceval Gerson, as well as several oral histories from the period, most notably that of Oscar Lawler. Another Lawler oral history can be found at Claremont College.

The Idaho State Historical Society has most of the important papers from the Steunenberg case, including transcripts from the Bill Haywood and second Steve Adams trials and the Pinkerton reports to Governor Gooding. The College of Idaho has put selections of the George Crookham papers online, including the Steunenberg family correspondence describing the assassination.

In Hawaii, the folks at the Hawaii State Archives were most helpful and patient, as I plowed through the papers of Lawrence Judd, Victor Houston, and John Kelley, the Pinkerton investigative files, and the surviving trial transcripts from the Ala Moana case. The archivists at the Bishop Museum opened the Walter Dillingham papers to me.

The New York Public Library has the leading collection of Henry L. Mencken's letters, small selections on Katherine Leckie and Edgar Lee Masters, and court files from the Red Scare, including transcripts or excerpts from the Benjamin Gitlow and William B. Lloyd trials. The Lincoln Steffens and Charles Yale Harrison papers are at Columbia University. And Princeton University holds the ACLU, Scribner's, Julian Street, Louis Adamic, and Arthur Garfield Hays papers, and another Mencken collection. Alice Beal Parsons left her papers on the Person trial to Syracuse University. The papers of Hugo Munsterberg and of Sacco and Vanzetti are cared for by the excellent staff of the Boston Public Library. The records at the Franklin D. Roosevelt presidential library give a unique glimpse at the relationship between Darrow and FDR.

The McNamara papers are at the University of Cincinnati, and the E. W. Scripps collection is at Ohio University in Athens. The Toledo-Lucas County Public Library maintains the papers of Samuel Jones and Negley Cochran. The University of Colorado has an excellent collection on the Western Federation of Miners.

The University of Michigan has many important collections that I used, including the Alex Baskin, Frank Murphy, Cash Asher, Joseph Labadie, Ossian Sweet, Josephine Gomon, Moses Walker, and Walter Drew collections, and a copy of the Ossian Sweet trial transcript. The Labadie collection's acquisition of the notes of journalist Margherita Hamm, who covered the Haywood trial for *Wilshire's Magazine*, offers a fresh perspective to the Steunenberg case.

The courthouse still stands, and the courtroom is much as it was, in Dayton, Tennessee. In the basement is an exhibit where the famous table from Robinson's drug store is displayed. The John Neal and Sue Hicks papers at the University of Tennessee in Knoxville were helpful. The staff at the University of Texas, where the Edgar Lee Masters papers reside, were their usual expert, friendly selves.

Darrow's papers and cases are scattered around the country, but the travel and time it took to tap these collections allows me to assure readers that there are no manufactured conversations or novelistic assumptions in this book. I relied first on official court transcripts and, only when they were not available, on edited versions of Darrow's courtroom addresses, or on contemporary newspaper coverage. The correspondence, autobiographies, and memoirs of Darrow and his friends and associates supply the remaining quotations. In chronicling Darrow's childhood, I relied on both *Farmington* and *The Story of My Life*. One is a novel and the other an autobiography, but I am confident that Darrow would agree that the selections I chose are accurate.

I also received help, in person or via e-mail or regular mail, from scholars and librarians at Colby College, the University of Wyoming, the Smithsonian Institution, the U.S. Supreme Court, the Eastern Washington State Historical Society, the Tennessee State Library and Archives in Nashville, the University of Pennsylvania, the Western Reserve Historical Society library, the Ohio Historical Society, Radcliffe College, the Indiana Historical Society, the American Jewish Archives, the Trumbull County Public Library, Cornell University, the University of Rochester, New York University, the City University of New York, Dartmouth College, the University of Oklahoma, the Nebraska State Historical Society, the University of Missouri, Harvard University, the Minnesota Historical Society, Smith College, Northeastern University, the University of Iowa, Indiana University, Indiana State University, the University of Illinois, the Cook County Clerk of the Circuit Court, Boise State University, the University of Wisconsin-Milwaukee, Idaho State University, Brigham Young University, Emory University, the University of Denver, Berea College, Southern Illinois University, the Colorado Historical Society, the University of Colorado, Pittsburg State University, Penn State University, the Sherman Library, the Siouxland Heritage Museums, and the University of Virginia. To all these archivists, I offer immense thanks.

I owe thanks, as well, to those who gave me a platform, a paycheck, a reference, permission, sound advice, a kindness, good company on the road, or the well-timed dose of wine, including Marjorie Farrell, Caledonia Kearns, Craig Baker, Jill James, Marie Reilly, the Anspach clan, Brian and Ellen Donadio, Carlos Mejia, Greg Moore, Randall Tietjen, Geoffrey Cowan, Kenneth Ackerman, Adam Clymer, David Stannard, Paul Morella, Edward Larson, Jim Lighthizer, Steve Jacobs, George Mitrovich, Susan Page, Carl Leubsdorf, Peter Blodgett, Kathy Kupka, Tom Coakley, Bob, Tom and Pete Hughes, Dick Ryan, Pat Poole, Stan Penczak, Scott Sherman, Bob Selim, Steve Kurkjian, Gerard O'Neill, Jack Beatty, Walter Robinson, Matt Storin, Anne Kornblut, Bill Tranghese, Tod O'Connor, Ken Burns, Doris Kearns Goodwin, Stephanie Cutter, James Alexander, Sandy Johnson, John Solomon, Bill Buzenberg, Bill Hamilton, Marith Fisher, Norm Ornstein, Tom Oliphant, David Maraniss, John Donovan, Roy Black, Douglas Brinkley, Alan Dershowitz, Peter Carlson, John Harris, John Kerry, Terry Anderson, Mike Riddick, Drex and Ann Knight, Beth Frerking, Janet Schrader, Douglas Trant, Lawrence O'Donnell, Dee Dee Myers, Charlie Sennott, Phil Balboni, Ray Ring, Rob Schlesinger, Laura Longsworth, Ben Loeterman, Jonathan Eig, David Shribman, David Morehouse, Michael Kranish, Judy Pasternak, Steve Braun, Joel and Lisa Benenson, Anita Weinberg, Carl Cannon, David Von Drehle, Doyle McManus, Marty Nolan, Bill Walker, Sharon Williams, Alex Beam, Barry Rosenbaum, Mary McGarvey, Jonathan White, Alan Partin and, most especially, Peter, Jake and Nora Gosselin and the late Robin Toner.

NOTES

ABBREVIATIONS IN NOTES

AB—Alex Baskin papers, University of Michigan, Ann Arbor
ACLU—American Civil Liberties Union papers, Library of Congress, Washington, D.C.
ALW—Arthur and Lila Weinberg papers, Newberry Library, Chicago
BU—Leo Cherne papers, Boston University, Boston
BW—Brand Whitlock papers, Library of Congress
CD-CHI—Clarence Darrow papers, University of Chicago
CD-LOC—Clarence Darrow papers, Library of Congress
CD-UML—Clarence Darrow papers, University of Minnesota Law Library, Minneapolis
CDMFP-NL—Clarence Darrow and Mary Field Parton papers, Newberry Library
CESW-HL—C. E. S. and Sara Wood papers, Huntington Library, San Marino, CA
CESW-UC—C. E. S. and Sara Wood papers, University of California, Berkeley
ELM—Edgar Lee Masters papers, University of Texas, Austin
HDL—Henry Demarest Lloyd papers, Library of Congress
IHS—Idaho State Historical Society, Boise
JG—Josephine Gomon papers, University of Michigan
JK—John Kelley papers, Hawaii State Archives, Honolulu
KD—Karl Darrow papers, American Institute of Physics, College Park, Maryland
LAL—Los Angeles Law Library
MFP—Mary Field Parton papers, University of Oregon, Eugene
NAACP—NAACP papers, Library of Congress
OHL—Jessie Ohl Darrow scrapbook, Newberry Library
PP—Pinkerton Papers, Library of Congress
WD—Walter Drew papers, University of Michigan
WJB—William Jennings Bryan papers, Library of Congress

INTRODUCTION: JEFFERSON'S HEIR

1. *Chicago Tribune*, Jan. 21, 1893. Adjusted for inflation, $500,000 in 1893 would be worth $11 million today.

2. Edgar Lee Masters in the *Mirror*, May 16, 1907.

3. *Chicago Tribune*, Apr. 28, 1893.

4. President Woodrow Wilson would tell his contemporaries: "You may think Cleveland's administration was Democratic. It was not. Cleveland was a conservative Republican." *New York Times*, Nov. 27, 1894. *Plessy v. Ferguson* was decided in 1896. The income tax case was *Pollock v. Farmers' Loan & Trust Co.* (1895). Monopolies were protected in *United States v. E.C. Knight Co.* (1895), and in *Lochner v. New York* (1905) the court struck down an 1895 New York law that limited the workday to ten hours.

5. *Chicago Tribune*, Apr. 28, 1893; *Chicago Daily News*, Apr. 28, 1893; *Chicago Times*, Apr. 28, 1893; Matthew Josephson, *The Politicos* (New York: Harcourt, Brace & World, 1938).

6. *Chicago Times*, Feb. 16, 1892, Feb. 24, 1893; William T. Stead, *If Christ Came to Chicago* (Chicago: Laird, 1894).

7. Brand Whitlock to Octavia Roberts, Aug. 2, 1898, BW; Darrow to Older, July 26, 1911, ALW.

8. Darrow to Jane Addams, Sept. 11, 1901, ALW; Mary Field Parton diary, MFP.

9. Forrest quoted in Stead, *If Christ Came.*

10. *Chicago Times*, Dec. 14, 1894. The visiting socialist was John Burns, and his comparison of Chicago to hell was widely cited around the turn of the century.

11. Darrow to Henry Demarest Lloyd, Dec. 28, 1891, HDL.

12. *Chicago Tribune*, Apr. 28, 1893; *Chicago Daily News*, Apr. 28, 1893; *Chicago Times*, Apr. 28, 1893; Lincoln Steffens, "Attorney for the Damned," *Saturday Review*, Feb. 27, 1932.

13. Natalie Schretter, "I Remember Darrow," unpublished manuscript, Lilly Library, Indiana University; Francis Wilson, Stone interviews, CD-LOC.

14. Ruby Darrow, letters to Stone, CD-LOC; Steffens, "Attorney for the Damned."

15. William Allen White, *The Autobiography of William Allen White* (New York: Macmillan, 1946).

16. Ben Hecht, *Gaily, Gaily* (New York: Doubleday, 1963).

17. Darrow, "The Rights and Wrongs of Ireland," in *Verdicts Out of Court*, ed. Arthur and Lila Weinberg (Chicago: Quadrangle, 1963).

18. Darrow file, Louis Adamic papers, Princeton University.

19. C. E. S. Wood to Melvin Levy, Feb. 6, 1932, NAACP; Ruby Darrow, letter to Stone, CD-LOC; Herb Graffis to Elmer Gertz, Mar. 8, 1957, Elmer Gertz papers, Library of Congress; Lt. Com. L. Johnson to Stone, Aug. 26, 1940, Irving Stone papers, University of California, Berkeley; Arthur Garfield Hays, *City Lawyer* (New York: Simon & Schuster, 1942).

20. *Kansas City Star*, May 17, 1925.

21. Arthur Garfield Hays, *Trial by Prejudice* (New York: Covici, Friede, 1933).

22. Attorney General Thomas Stewart, in Scopes trial transcript; *Kansas City Star*, May 17, 1925; Arthur Garfield Hays, remembrance of Darrow, *Unity*, Darrow memorial issue, May 16, 1938.

23. Nathan Leopold, *Life Plus Ninety-nine Years* (New York: Doubleday, 1958).

24. Darrow to Mary Field Parton, July 4, 1913, CD-LOC; Mary Field Parton, journal, MFP.

25. Darrow remarks at sixty-first birthday banquet, Apr. 18, 1918; Darrow, "Is Life Worth Living?" Dec. 17, 1916, CD-LOC; W. W. Catlin to Wood, Aug. 5, 1907, Wood to Levy, Feb. 6, 1932, CESW-UC; S. J. Duncan-Clark, "Clarence Darrow's Fight Against the Death Penalty," *Success*, Dec. 1924.

26. Frederic Howe, *Confessions of a Reformer* (New York: Charles Scribner's Sons, 1925); Victor Yarros, *My Eleven Years with Clarence Darrow* (Girard, KS: Haldeman-Julius, 1950); Steffens, *The Autobiography of Lincoln Steffens* (New York: Harcourt, Brace, 1931); Clarence Darrow, *The Story of My Life* (New York: Charles Scribner's Sons, 1932).

27. Darrow, *The Story of My Life*; Victor Yarros, remembrance of Darrow, *Unity*, Darrow memorial issue, May 16, 1938; Gertrude Barnum, "Darrow, the Enigma," *The Ladies' Garment Worker*, Nov. 1912; Harold Mulks, Stone interviews, CD-LOC; Mary Bell Decker, "The Man Clarence Darrow," *University Review*, summer 1938; Darrow file, Louis Adamic papers, Princeton University; E. W. Scripps to Neg Cochran, Nov. 20, 1911, E. W. Scripps papers, Ohio University.

28. *The World*, Feb. 19, 1928; Mark Sullivan, *Our Times*, vol. 2 (New York: Charles Scribner's Sons, 1927).

29. C. Vann Woodward, "What the War Made Us," in Geoffrey Ward, *The Civil War* (New York: Knopf, 1990); Henry J. Abraham, *Justices, Presidents, and Senators* (New York: Rowman & Littlefield, 2007); Paul Johnson, *A History of the American People* (New York: HarperCollins, 1997); Frederick Turner, *The Frontier in American History* (New York: Henry Holt, 1920).

30. David Lilienthal, Darrow profile, *The Nation*, Apr. 20, 1927; John H. Holmes, remembrance of Darrow, Darrow memorial issue, *Unity*, May 16, 1938; Darrow, "Rights and Wrongs of Ireland"; *New York Sun*, Dec. 23, 1927.

31. H. L. Mencken, tribute to Darrow, *Vanity Fair*, Mar. 1927.

CHAPTER I: REBELLIONS

1. *The Eddy Family, Reunion at Providence to Celebrate the 250th Anniversary of the Landing of John and Samuel Eddy* (Boston: J. S. Cushing, 1881); *The New England Historical and Genealogical Register*, July 1854.

2. *Biographical History of Northeastern Ohio* (Chicago: Lewis Publishing, 1893).

3. In his autobiography, Darrow suggests that George Darrow was one of the founders of New London. This is not true. It was founded in 1646 by men from Massachusetts. Frances M. Caulkins, *History of New London* (New London, CT: H.D. Utley, 1895).

4. Revolutionary War records show that several of Darrow's ancestors, on both sides of his family, were Minutemen, KD; *History of New London*; Henry A. Baker, *History*

of Montville, Connecticut (Hartford, CT: Case, Lockwood & Brainard, 1896); Merton Edwin Krug, *History of Reedsburg and the Upper Baraboo Valley* (1929); Revolutionary War Pension Applications for Ammirus and Jedediah Darrow, National Archives and Records Administration; John C. Fitzpatrick, ed., *The Writings of George Washington from the Original Manuscript Sources*, http://etext.virginia.edu/washington/fitzpatrick/index .html.

5. Darrow pension applications, National Archives and Records Administration; A. Tiffany Norton, *History of Sullivan's Campaign Against the Iroquois* (Lima, NY: 1879); Fitzpatrick, *Writings*; *Public Papers of George Clinton, First Governor of New York* (Albany: State of New York, 1899); Daniel E. Wagner, *Col. Marinus Willett: The Hero of Mohawk Valley* (Utica, NY: Oneida Historical Society, 1891); *The New England Historical and Genealogical Register*, Oct. 1849, July 1854, Apr. 1868; *Record of Service of Connecticut Men in the War of the Revolution* (Hartford, CT: Adjutant-General's Office, 1889).

6. *Commemorative and Biographical Record of Columbia, Sauk and Adams Counties, Wisconsin* (Chicago: Ogle, 1901); Krug, *History of Reedsburg*. Sarah is listed as Sarah Melona on Ammirus's application for a Revolutionary War pension, but as Sarah Fisher in Krug and the *Commemorative and Biographical Record*, and as Sarah Fisher Malona and Sarah Malona Fisher in yet other sources. See Darrow collections at the Newberry Library and, for learned speculation on this and other matters, the online genealogy of the Darrow family compiled by Dean Hagen, one of George Darrow's descendants. It contains a long letter on family history, written in 1923, by Clarence's brother Everett.

7. Ammirus Darrow was known as Amarius, Amirus, and Ammiras, and his grandson as Ammirus and Amirus. For simplicity, I refer to the elder as Ammirus, and the younger as Amirus. Untitled reminiscence of Sarah Darrow, KD.

8. Grandfather Jedediah and several of his children settled in the Kinsman area as well. *Chicago Daily Chronicle*, Apr. 25, 1904; *Chicago Tribune*, Apr. 24, 1904; Darrow family records, KD; U.S. census, 1860; Clarence Darrow, *Story of My Life* and his short story "The Black Sheep," CD-LOC. The University of Michigan "Catalogue" for 1864 credits Amirus with a BA from Cleveland University but does not give the date; the Ohio school, however, operated for only two academic years, from 1851 to 1853. The alumni record of the University of Illinois, in 1913, lists Cleveland as the place of Mary Darrow's birth in 1852.

9. Freeman was found guilty, but Seward convinced the state supreme court to grant him a new trial. The prisoner died in jail in 1847, of tuberculosis, before he could be tried again. An autopsy showed a diseased brain. At the time of Darrow's birth, Seward was a leading candidate for the Republican nomination for president, which he lost to Abraham Lincoln. He served in Lincoln's wartime cabinet as secretary of state, survived an assassination attempt by the plotters who killed the president, and went on to negotiate the treaty in which the United States acquired Alaska from Russia. His argument in the Freeman case was included in Seward's *Works* and in Hall's book (both cited below), and in pamphlets and collections of oratory of the day. It is unlikely that Amirus and Clarence did not know of it. Seward, *The Works of William H. Seward* (New York: Redfield,1853); Benjamin Hall, *The Trial of William Freeman* (Auburn, NY: Derby, Miller, 1848).

10. In the years after Darrow's death, his son Paul spun a colorful but unlikely tale in which Amirus conveyed fugitive slaves under loads of hay in midnight wagon rides, with toddler Clarence at his side. The country lanes of the Western Reserve were indeed an important link in freedom's railroad across Lake Erie to Canada, but the Darrow name does not appear in the surviving records of the movement. Given the clandestine nature of the work, however, that is not determinative. Darrow and Paul also claimed that Amirus was a friend of the militant abolitionist John Brown. It is possible, as Brown's son John Jr. was then living in nearby West Andover, Ohio, and helped gather men and arms for his father's raid on Harpers Ferry. But there is also evidence that the Darrows exaggerated the relationship. In addition to embellishing Paul's dubious account of the midnight wagon rides, Irving Stone conveyed, uncritically, a family tale in which Brown tells the solemn Clarence, age five, that "the Negro has too few friends; you and I must never desert him." Brown was long dead when Darrow turned five in 1862, and critics pointed this out. Lilienthal, Darrow profile, *The Nation*, Apr. 20, 1927; Charlotte Kinney, "Clarence Darrow As He Is," *Psychology*, Aug. 1932; Darrow, *Farmington* (Chicago: A. C. McClurg & Co., 1904); Darrow, *Story of My Life*; Irving Stone notes on interview with Paul Darrow, CD-LOC; Wilbur H. Siebert papers on the Underground Railroad, Ohio Historical Society.

11. University of Michigan, "Catalogue," listing of "Students of Law," 1864.

12. It is not surprising that this champion of the damned was, in his adult years, a Chicago Cubs fan. Darrow, *Farmington* and *Story of My Life*; Darrow, "Response to Birthday Greetings" and "The Myth of the Soul" in Weinberg, *Verdicts*; Darrow family records, KD; *Akron Times-Press*, Mar. 15, 1938; *Cleveland Plain Dealer*, Apr. 18, 1937; Darrow to James Kennedy, Mar. 21, 1925, Ohio Historical Society; *Chicago Daily News*, May 20, 1925; Darrow, "Attorney for the Defense," *Esquire*, May 1936; Darrow closing address, Arthur Person trial, Apr. 24, 1920.

13. Darrow, *Farmington* and *Story of My Life*; Darrow, "Black Sheep"; *Akron Times-Press*, Mar. 15, 1938; Darrow to Julia Porter, Kinsman Library, Feb. 17, 1932; Jenny Darrow interview with Stone, CD-LOC; Darrow to Kennedy, Mar. 21, 1925; *Chicago Tribune*, Nov. 8, 1924; *Chicago Daily News*, May 20, 1925.

14. Darrow, *Farmington* and *Story of My Life*; Ohio Secretary of State, annual report, results of Oct. 9, 1883, election; Darrow family records, KD.

15. When asked, as an adult, why he didn't eat chickens, Darrow replied, "They could never make up their minds." Darrow, *Farmington* and *Story of My Life*; Darrow, "Black Sheep"; Ruby Darrow letters to Stone, CD-LOC; *Chicago Daily News*, May 20, 1925; Darrow testimony, Commission on Industrial Relations, 1915.

16. The family correspondence from the summer of Emily's death is in the Karl Darrow papers. Darrow, *Farmington* and *Story of My Life*; *Akron Times-Press*, Mar. 15, 1938; *Cleveland Plain Dealer*, Apr. 18, 1937; Darrow, Stone, and Weinberg erroneously give Darrow's age as fourteen when his mother died.

17. Ruby Darrow's story of her husband's request comes from a letter to Stone in his papers at the University of California, Berkeley: "He not only could not bear to live without me, but he could not bear to die without me! In confidence when he realized that he had to go, he begged me to devise some manner whereby I could go with him,

sweetly saying that if we could go together, then he wouldn't mind it much. I would have, but that I knew I had to remain to do everything to make his going as comfortable and painless as possible."

18. Darrow, *Farmington* and *Story of My Life*; *Cleveland Plain Dealer*, Apr. 18, 1937; *Boston Globe*, Mar. 17, 1927; *Akron Times-Press*, Mar. 15, 1938; *Kinsman Journal*, Sept. 11, 1936; Darrow to James Kennedy, Mar. 21, 1925, Ohio Historical Society; Robert Murphy to Elmer Gertz, Apr. 10, 1957, Elmer Gertz papers, Library of Congress.

19. University of Michigan, general catalog, 1902; *Ann Arbor Courier*, Dec. 14, 1877.

20. In one tale, Darrow said that he missed the bar exam because he and a man he met in the tavern went on an all-night bender. He passed the test, he said, after discovering the next morning that his drinking companion was the bar examiner. In his autobiography, Darrow erroneously says he was living in Ashtabula when he married Jessie Ohl. Stone relates a tale, told by Paul Darrow, alleging that Roberts was a ne'er-do-well who absconded with Darrow's law books. In fact, Roberts went on to become a respected judge. U.S. Census, 1880; *Cleveland Plain Dealer*, Jan. 27, 1935, Apr. 18, 1937; *Warren Chronicle*, Sept. 30, 1924; *Democratic Standard*, Mar. 12, 1885; *Kinsman Journal*, Sept. 11, 1936; *Boston Globe*, Mar. 17, 1927; Charles B. Galbreath, *History of Ohio* (Chicago: American Historical Society, 1925); Clyde Miller, *The Process of Persuasion* (New York: Crown, 1946); unidentified newspaper clipping, Kinsman, Ohio, Dec. 1879, ALW.

21. Darrow address to Society of Medical Jurisprudence, New York Academy of Medicine, Jan. 13, 1931; *Jefferson Gazette*, Sept. 2, 1881.

22. *Andover Citizen*, Apr. 22, 1884; *Democratic Standard*, June 4, 1886; *Painesville Democrat*, Aug. 21, 1886; *Cincinnati Enquirer*, Aug. 19, 1886; Darrow, *Story of My Life*; *Brockway v. Jewell*, 52 Ohio 187 (1894); *Chicago Tribune*, Sept. 3, 1900, Aug. 7, 1899.

23. *Ashtabula Standard*, Mar. 5, 1887; Darrow address to Society of Medical Jurisprudence, New York Academy of Medicine, Jan. 13, 1931.

CHAPTER 2: CHICAGO

1. According to a March 1938 account in a Rockford, Illinois, newspaper, "for a brief period before he moved to Chicago in 1887, [Darrow] practiced at Harvard, Ill." In a 1962 letter to Arthur Weinberg, lawyer Floyd Eckert recalled Darrow sitting in an empty office in Harvard, with no business to occupy his time, slowly feeding one stick at a time into a stove to keep warm. At least one of Darrow's Harvard cases lodged in people's memory. A hardware store owner, standing guard with a shotgun after two burglaries, shot and captured a youth who was trying to break into the store one night. Darrow defended the boy and won an acquittal by pleading that it was his first offense and that he had been led into crime by his companion. In an interview with Irving Stone, Jessie placed Darrow's time in Harvard before their marriage. Lincoln Steffens, "Chicago: Half Free and Fighting On," *McClure's*, Oct. 1903.

2. *Chicago Times*, Dec. 14, 1894; Donald L. Miller, City of the Century (New York: Simon & Schuster, 1996).

3. The Storey incident won considerable attention when Union loyalists on the police force declined to arrest Eddy, but it should be noted that, on another occasion, Eddy

defied a lynch mob and cut the noose from the neck of a "Rebel sympathizer" named Doolittle. The Eddy real estate case dragged on for more than a decade with various disputes about portions of the property. The bulk of the estate ultimately went to his daughter Clara, who, at her death, bequeathed what was left to her Darrow cousins. *Chicago Tribune*, Mar. 4, 1865, Mar. 16, 1866, Feb. 19, 1874, July 9, 1876, Sept. 21, 1878, Jan. 27, 1878, May 2, 1888, Jan. 21, 1893, Feb. 22, 1896; *Chicago Times*, May 2, 1888, Jan. 30, Dec. 14, 1894; Besse Louise Pierce, *As Others See Chicago* (Chicago: University of Chicago Press, 1933); Jeffrey Adler, *First in Violence, Deepest in Dirt* (Cambridge: Harvard University Press, 2006); Edward Price Bell, *Seventy Years Deep*, unpublished autobiography, Bell papers, Newberry Library; George Ade, *Single Blessedness and Other Observations* (Garden City, NY: Doubleday, 1922); Ida Tarbell, "How Chicago Is Finding Herself," *American Magazine*, Nov. 1908; see Karl Darrow to Darrow, Oct. 23, 1927, and Karl Darrow to Bowen, Dec. 4, 1932, KD; John J. Flinn and John E. Wilkie, *History of the Chicago Police* (Chicago: Chicago Police Book Fund, 1887); Stead, *If Christ Came*. Darrow bounced all over town in his early years, renting and buying property, selling to cinch a profit, and rooming in the intervals with his family at 905 Sawyer Avenue and at 3559 Vernon Avenue, 4219 Vincennes Avenue, and 1321 Michigan Avenue.

4. In his autobiography, Darrow said he arrived in Chicago in 1888, though correspondence and contemporary news accounts clearly place him there in 1887. Darrow to Lloyd, Jan. 4, 1888, HDL; *Inter Ocean*, Aug. 25, 1887; *Chicago Times*, Apr. 2, Oct. 7, 1888, Mar. 10, 1889; *Chicago Tribune*, Apr. 2, Sept. 3, Oct. 5, 10, 11, 20, 1888; untitled Rock Island, Illinois, newspaper clipping, Oct. 29, 1888, OHL; Schilling remarks from Darrow's sixty-first birthday dinner; Sissman interview with Stone, CD-LOC; Caro Lloyd, *Henry Demarest Lloyd* (New York: Putnam, 1912).

5. Paul Avrich, *The Haymarket Tragedy* (Princeton, NJ: Princeton University Press, 1984); Adolph Fischer to Lloyd and Salter, Nov. 4, 1887, HDL; *Chicago Tribune*, May 5, 1886; Philip Foner, *The Autobiographies of the Haymarket Martyrs* (New York: Humanities Press, 1969); Harry Barnard, *Eagle Forgotten* (Indianapolis: Bobbs-Merrill, 1938); Darrow, "Justice to the Anarchists," *Solidarity*, Dec. 24, 1887; *New York Times*, May 6, 1886.

6. W. P. Black to Lloyd, July 22, 1893, HDL.

7. Darrow was clear-eyed: he always believed that one of the defendants, Louis Lingg, had made the Haymarket bomb and furnished it to the bomb thrower. Lingg was convicted with the four other condemned anarchists but cheated the executioner by igniting a dynamite cartridge, clenched in his teeth, in his cell on the eve of the hangings. *Democratic Standard*, Sept. 2, 1887.

8. "We believe that capital punishment is unnecessary, barbarous and not in keeping with modern civilization; that it tends to cheapen the value placed on life, and to blunt the finer sensibilities of human nature," the group declared (*Chicago Herald*, Oct. 14, 1887). Though the author of the resolution is not named, it is reasonable to assume that Darrow wrote it, or played an important role in its adoption, as Jessie Ohl Darrow included the news of it in her scrapbook of his accomplishments. It is an early public expression of his opposition to capital punishment.

9. Darrow, "Justice to the Anarchist," *Solidarity*, Dec. 24, 1887.

10. *Chicago Times*, Feb. 20, 21, 1889; *Chicago Herald*, Feb. 21, Apr. 15, 1889; *Chicago Tribune,* Feb. 21, Apr. 15, 16, 1889; Darrow, *Story of My Life*; *Sunday Globe*, Apr. 21, 1889; Darrow to Lloyd, May 14 and May 20, 1889, HDL; Barnard, *Eagle Forgotten.*

11. Clarence Darrow oral history (interview with Agnes Wright Dennis), Illinois Historical Survey, 1918; Altgeld tribute, circa 1903, CD-LOC; Schretter, "I Remember Darrow"; Waldo Browne, *Altgeld of Illinois* (New York: Huebsch, 1924); Darrow, *Story of My Life*; Barnard, *Eagle Forgotten*; *New York Times*, June 20, 1888; *Chicago Times*, June 20, 1888, Apr. 2, 1889.

12. *Chicago Tribune*, May 2, June 21, 1889; *Chicago Daily News*, June 20, 1889; *Chicago Times,* June 21, 1889.

13. Carter Harrison Jr., *Stormy Years* (Indianapolis: Bobbs-Merrill, 1935).

14. Darrow's allies were back, "booming" him as an independent-minded candidate for Cook County attorney in 1891, but the corrupt county commissioners reached a back-room deal to name a more controllable candidate. *Chicago Tribune,* Sept. 1, Nov. 14, 1889, Jan. 3, 12, Mar. 21, 22, Apr. 17, 22, May 26, Aug. 24, Sept. 4, 16, 21, Oct. 12, 1890, Jan. 28, 29, Feb. 12, 14, 26, 1891; *Chicago Post,* Sept. 9, 18, 1890; *Chicago Herald,* Dec. 25, 1889; Nov. 2, 1890; *Chicago Times,* Dec. 25, 1889, Jan. 30, Feb. 1, Mar. 22, Apr. 23, May 6, 1890, Jan. 28, 29, Feb. 21, 25, 1891, Dec. 14, 1894; *Inter Ocean*, Oct. 24, 1890, Jan. 29, 1891; *Democratic Standard,* Sept. 2, 1887; undated newspaper clipping, OHL; W. B. Conkey, *Opinions of the Corporation Counsels and Assistants*, January 1872 to March 1897, published by the City Council of Chicago; Lloyd Wendt and Herman Kogan, *Lords of the Levee* (Indianapolis: Bobbs-Merrill, 1943); Richard Lindberg, *Chicago by Gaslight* (Chicago: Academy Chicago, 1996); Darrow, "Corruption," CD-LOC.

15. *Chicago Times,* Nov. 19, Dec. 10, 1890, and Jan. 19, 20, 22, 23, Feb. 6, Mar. 12, 1891; *Chicago Post*, Feb. 5, 1891; *Chicago Tribune,* Feb. 5, 6, 1891; *Chicago Herald,* Feb. 3, 4, 6, 7, 1891; Medill letter quoted in Thomas Pegram, *Partisans and Progressives* (Urbana: University of Illinois Press, 1992).

16. Paul Darrow and Wilson interviews with Stone, CD-LOC; Jane Addams to Marcet Haldeman-Julius, CD-LOC; *Chicago Times*, Aug. 10, 1890; *Chicago Tribune*, May 24, 1890; Oct. 20, 1891, May 30, Dec. 24, 1892; *Chicago Herald*, April 26, 1891.

17. Edgar Lee Masters, *Across Spoon River* (New York: Farrar & Rinehart, 1936); Darrow, "The State: Its Functions and Duties," *Echoes of the Sunset Club* (Chicago: Sunset Club, 1891). Darrow "spoke everywhere, promulgating the socialistic theories of Edward Bellamy, and the crude philosophy of Herbert Spencer, pleading against the conviction of the Anarchists, denying orthodox religion and advocating free trade, the eight hour day and the programme of Henry George," said the *Chicago Journal* on July 13, 1893. For examples of Darrow's radical views on women's rights, capital punishment, American foreign policy, and other issues during this period, see Sunset Club yearbooks and *Chicago Times*, Feb. 3, 1889; *Chicago Tribune*, May 29, 1889, Feb. 4, 28, Apr. 11, 1890, Oct. 14, Nov. 6, 1891, Dec. 30, 1892, Jan. 27, Feb. 23, 1893; *Chicago Evening Post*, Nov. 7, 1891; the clippings saved in the Jessie Ohl Darrow scrapbook, including the *Daily Evening Call*, Jan. 24, 1891, the *Rockford Register-Gazette,* Sept. 8, 1891, the *Rockford Morning Star*, Sept. 8, 1891, and an untitled Rockford newspaper, Aug. 6, 1889.

18. *Chicago Times,* Apr. 2, 3, 1891; *Chicago Tribune*, Mar. 20, Apr. 4, Apr. 10, Aug. 1, 1891.

19. Darrow oral history, 1918; Darrow, Altgeld memorial address, Apr. 20, 1902, CD-LOC.

20. Joseph Gary, "The Chicago Anarchists of 1886; The Crime, the Trial, and the Punishment," *Century Magazine*, Apr. 1893. Darrow to Lloyd, Apr. 28, 1893, HDL.

21. *Chicago Tribune*, Apr. 30, 1893; *Chicago Journal*, July 13, 1893.

22. Darrow to Lloyd, May 17, 1893, Alzina Stevens to Lloyd, May 30 and June 7, 1893, HDL; *Chicago Tribune*, May 16, 1893; Jessie Darrow interview with Stone, CD-LOC; Adolf Kraus, *Reminiscences and Comments* (Chicago: Rubovits, 1925); Harrison, *Stormy Years*; Miller, *City of the Century*.

23. Darrow oral history, 1918.

24. John P. Altgeld, June 26, 1893, "Reasons for Pardoning Fielden, Neebe and Schwab." The text of the governor's pardon message was reprinted in pamphlets at the time. It can be found at the Chicago Historical Society's site: http://www.chicagohs.org/hadc/books/b06/B06.htm.

25. Darrow, Altgeld tribute; *New York Times*, June 28, June 29, 1893; see also the *Chicago Tribune*, June 27, 1893, which said that Altgeld was "not merely an alien by birth, but an alien by temperament and sympathies" with "not a drop of true American blood."

26. H. L. Mencken, *American Mercury*, Oct. 1924.

27. Schilling to Lloyd, Aug. 1, 1893, HDL; Sunset Club yearbook, 1893.

28. *Chicago Times*, Sept. 17, 1893; *Chicago Record*, Feb. 18, 1897; Altgeld to Harrison, Sept. 13, 1893, Carter Harrison papers, Newberry Library.

CHAPTER 3: PRENDERGAST

1. Accounts of Harrison assassination and funeral coverage, *Chicago Tribune* and *Chicago Times*, Oct. 29 through Nov. 5, 1893.

2. *Chicago Herald*, Nov. 18, 1893.

3. Accounts of testimony, Prendergast trial, *Chicago Times* and other papers, November and December, 1893; *Chicago Times*, Oct. 29, 1893, June 28, 1894.

4. *Chicago Times*, Dec. 19, 1893; *New York Times*, Dec. 30, 1893; *Chicago Tribune*, May 6, 1894.

5. *Chicago Times*, Nov. 5, 1893.

6. *Chicago Daily News*, Feb. 14, 1894; Darrow, *Story of My Life*.

7. *Chicago Tribune*, Feb. 17, 20, 1894; *Chicago Times*, Feb. 18, 1894.

8. *Chicago Evening Post*, Feb. 20, 1894; *Chicago Daily News*, Feb. 24, 1894; *Chicago Times*, Feb. 25, 1894.

9. *Chicago Times*, Mar. 22, 1894; *Chicago Daily News*, Mar. 22, 1894; *Chicago Tribune*, Mar. 23, 1894; Trude to Todd, Mar. 2, 1894, Carter Harrison papers, Newberry Library; Brand Whitlock, *Forty Years of It* (New York: Appleton, 1914).

10. *Chicago Times*, Mar. 26, 27, 28, June 17, 1894; *Chicago Daily News*, Mar. 30, 1894; *New York Times*, May 22, 1894.

11. *Chicago Times*, June 15, 26, 27, 1894; *Chicago Daily News*, June 26, 1894.

12. *Chicago Daily News*, June 26, 1894.

13. *Chicago Times*, July 3, 4, 1894; transcript, Darrow closing argument, CD-LOC.

14. Stone begins his biography with fanciful scenes that place Darrow at the heart of the action of the Debs Rebellion in the first days of July, without any mention of the Prendergast trial, which in fact was consuming Darrow's time. Elsewhere, Stone mistakenly puts the formation of Darrow's law firm, the Harrison assassination, and the "Pendergast" trial in 1895, and erroneously states that the mayor was shot at City Hall. *Chicago Tribune*, July 13, 14, 1894; *Chicago Times*, July 13, 14, 1894; *Chicago Daily News*, July 13, 14, 1894.

15. Medill to Harrison, July 17, 1894, Carter Harrison papers, Newberry Library.

CHAPTER 4: POPULIST

1. *Chicago Times*, Apr. 24, 1894; Gompers quote in *New York World*, Feb. 1, 1894, quoted in Philip S. Foner, *History of the Labor Movement in the United States*, vol. 2 (New York: International, 1955).

2. Darrow, *Story of My Life*; Ray Ginger, *Altgeld's America* (New York: Funk & Wagnalls, 1958).

3. *New York Times*, Apr. 12, 1893, July 1, 1894; *Chicago Times*, Jan. 10, 1890, Dec. 10, 11, 1893, Apr. 23, June 2, 1894; *Inter Ocean*, July 2, 3, 1894; *New York Sun*, Oct. 11, 1885, and *Chicago Tribune*, Sept. 21, 1888, quoted in Almont Lindsey, *The Pullman Strike* (Chicago: University of Chicago Press, 1942); Richard Ely, "Pullman: A Social Study," *Harper's Magazine*, February 1885; U.S. Strike Commission, *Report on the Chicago Strike* (Washington, D.C.: GPO, 1895).

4. Cleveland veto message, Feb. 16, 1887. See Allan Nevins, *Grover Cleveland* (New York: Dodd, Mead, 1932).

5. Milchrist to Olney, June 30, 1894, Records of the Department of Justice, National Archives; Richard Olney to C. E. Perkins, Dec. 28, 1892, Olney papers, Library of Congress; see Matthew Josephson, *The Politicos* (New York: Harcout, Brace & World, 1938) and Gerald G. Eggert, *Richard Olney: Evolution of a Statesman* (State College, PA: Pennsylvania State University Press, 1974).

6. U.S. Strike Commission, *Report*; I used newspaper coverage of the strike between July 1 and July 13, 1894, from the *Chicago Times*, *Inter Ocean*, *Chicago Tribune*, *New York Times*, and *Chicago Daily News*; Pullman strike records in Records of the Department of Justice, National Archives, see especially Walker to Olney, July 2, 3, 6, 14, 20, 1894, and related correspondence in the *Appendix to the Annual Report of the Attorney General of the United States for the Year 1896* (Washington, 1896); McAlister Coleman, *Eugene Debs: A Man Unafraid* (New York: Greenberg, 1930).

7. With everything else he had to do in this chaotic summer, Darrow still made the time to take *Brockway v. Jewell* to the Ohio Supreme Court—and won. Eugene Debs to Caro Lloyd, Jan. 31, 1905, Florence Kelley to Henry Lloyd, July 18, 1894, HDL; Arthur

Garfield Hays, *Democracy Works* (New York: Random House, 1939); Masters, *Across Spoon River*; Jane Addams, "A Modern Lear," *Survey*, Nov. 2, 1912; Darrow, *Story of My Life*.

8. *Chicago Times*, Sept. 27, 1894; *Chicago Tribune*, Sept. 27, Dec. 15, 1894; *Milwaukee Sentinel*, Sept. 27, 1894; *Denver Post*, Dec. 19, 1894; *Inter Ocean*, Dec. 15, 1894; *New York Times*, Dec. 15, 1894.

9. *Chicago Tribune*, Jan. 13, 15, 17, 30, Feb. 7, 1895; *Chicago Times*, Jan. 13, 14, 15, 27, 29, 1895; *Inter Ocean*, May 31, 1894, Jan. 27, 30, Feb. 6, 7, 8, 18, 1895; *New York Times*, Jan. 17, 1895; *Denver Post*, Jan. 26, 1895; *Milwaukee Journal*, Feb. 13, 1895; Theodore Roosevelt to White, Nov. 30, 1908, Theodore Roosevelt papers, Library of Congress; Theodore Debs to L.W. Rogers, Jan. 12, 1944, Bernard Brommel and Eugene Debs papers, Newberry Library.

10. *Chicago Tribune*, Mar. 26, 27, May 28, 1895; *Chicago Times*, Mar. 26, 27, 1895; *New York Times*, Mar. 26, 27, May 28, 1895; Edwin Walker to Olney, Apr. 27, May 21, 1895; and U.S. attorney John C. Black to Judson Harmon, Feb. 28, 1896, U.S. Department of Justice records, National Archives.

11. Lindsey, *The Pullman Strike*; Barnard, *Eagle Forgotten*; Waldo R. Browne, *Altgeld of Illinois* (New York: B.W. Huebsch, 1924).

12. Barnard, *Eagle Forgotten*.

13. Richard Hofstadter, *The Age of Reform* (New York: Vintage, 1955); *Chicago Times*, Feb. 4, 1895; Willis J. Abbott, "The Chicago Populist Campaign," *The Arena*, Feb. 1895.

14. Keeping the other guys from stealing the election was an essential ingredient for victory in Chicago. Darrow defended one Democratic faction that turned off the lights, boarded up the windows, and built a wooden barricade across the door to a polling place so that the voters had to stand on tiptoe to hand their paper ballots to the armed poll workers inside. It was necessary, Darrow contended, in order to keep the ballot boxes from being carried off by the other side. But voters were advised to remove any rings before voting, lest they disappear into the dark with the ballot. *Chicago Tribune*, Aug. 8, Oct. 7, 20, 23, 31, 1894, Mar. 17, 1895; *Chicago Times*, Sept. 22, 30, Oct. 7, 20, 25, Nov. 4, 1894, Feb. 4, 1895; *Searchlight*, Oct. 25, 1894.

15. *Chicago Times*, Nov. 8, 1894; Darrow to Lloyd, Nov. 22, 1894, Apr. 23, 1896, Lloyd to Darrow, Nov. 23, 1894, Darrow to Caro Lloyd, Nov. 9, 1905, HDL.

16. Darrow, Altgeld memorial address, Apr. 20, 1902; *Chicago Tribune*, Feb. 23, Apr. 19, 24, 25, Nov. 14, 1895, Jan. 5, Sept. 16, 17, Nov. 10, 1896; *Chicago Record*, Dec. 25, 1895; *Chicago Times Herald*, Feb. 23, Mar. 16, Apr. 24, 28, June 3, 25, 1895; *New York Times*, June 7, 1895, July 1, 2, 4, 7, 8, 11, 26, 1896. Barnard, *Eagle Forgotten*; William Allen White, *Autobiography*; Edgar Lee Masters, *The New Star Chamber and Other Essays* (Chicago: Hammersmark, 1904).

17. In his autobiography, Darrow erroneously maligned Congressman Belknap as "a clerk in a railroad office who had never taken any interest in politics." *Chicago Tribune*, May 11, 12, July 23, 24, Aug. 31, Sept. 9, 10, Oct. 6, 13, 15, 29, Nov. 10, 1896; *New York Times*, Nov. 1, 1896, Jan. 24, 1897; Kelley to Lloyd, Oct. 1, 1896, R. H. Howe to Caro Lloyd and Lloyd to Howe, June 1911, Altgeld to Lloyd, Aug. 2, 1899, Lloyd to Fay, Mar. 10, 1898, HDL; Edgar Lee Masters to Carter Harrison, Mar. 21, 1938 ("He always hated

and envied Bryan"), ELM; Schretter, "I Remember Darrow"; Darrow testimony, 1900, United States Industrial Commission; Darrow, *The Story of My Life*; Darrow, Altgeld memorial address, Apr. 20, 1902; Barnard, *Eagle Forgotten.*

CHAPTER 5: FREE LOVE

1. Paul Darrow and Wilson interviews with Stone, CD-DOC; Darrow to Jessie, Jan. 8, 1896, CD-UML; Masters, *Across Spoon River*; Darrow to Lloyd, Jan. 2, 1895, ALW.

2. Harrison was a lifelong foe of Sullivan and for years gathered information on the Ogden Gas deal. He determined that one of the eleven controlling shares was divided into small pieces as "chicken feed" for unnamed persons who helped the scheme but did not rate a full cut. See "Notes on Ogden Gas Company," Carter Harrison papers, Newberry Library; *Chicago Tribune*, Feb. 26, 27, 28, Mar. 4, 6, 7, 9, 20, 21, 22, 26, Apr. 4, 1895, Jan. 16, 19, 20, 1897; *Chicago Times Herald*, Mar. 4, 5, 6, 7, 14, 21, 22, May 15, July 3, 1895; *New York Times*, May 1, 1897; Barnard, *Eagle Forgotten*; Harrison, *Stormy Years*; Carter Harrison, *Growing Up with Chicago* (Chicago: Seymour, 1944).

3. A typewritten transcript of the "My Dear Miss S" letter from Darrow to Starr, but not an original, is in Darrow's papers at the Library of Congress. I presume it is authentic and accurately transcribed. Need and greed drove Darrow's actions, but he may have been motivated, as well, by devotion to Altgeld. The economic hard times had wrecked the governor's finances and compelled him to take loans from an unprincipled banker. To meet the payments, Altgeld secretly borrowed money from the state treasury and from banks that were custodians of state funds. Altgeld did not profit from the gas deal as much as he might have. Needing cash, he sold his interest for some $35,000 to a downtown pawnbroker named Jacob Franks. When Ogden Gas was dealt, Franks's shares were worth $666,000. Harrison, *Stormy Years.*

4. The sequence of Darrow's articles, which ran through August and September in the *Chronicle*, places him in England, Venice, Switzerland, and, finally, Paris. But it seems that the order was scrambled, as he wrote from France about "coming out of London into Paris." Gertrude Barnum to Stone, Jan. 5, 1942, Irving Stone papers, University of California, Berkeley. *Chicago Record*, Sept. 18, 1895; Eliot White, letter to the editor, *Unity*, Darrow memorial issue, May 16, 1938.

5. *Chicago Tribune,* Nov. 24, 1895; Darrow, "Rights and Wrongs of Ireland."

6. Darrow to Jessie, Jan. 8, 1896, and undated financial statement, CD-UML; Paul and Jessie interviews with Stone, CD-LOC.

7. Mary Field, another of Darrow's lovers, would also leave Chicago to work for Dreiser. Leckie papers, New York Public Library; Chicago city directories; *Woman's Who's Who of America* (New York: American Commonwealth, 1914); *Chicago Tribune*, Mar. 9, 1897; Ruby Darrow to Helen Darrow, Nov. 30, 1941, KD; Darrow divorce records, Cook County Circuit Court; Darrow to Whitlock, Feb. 5, 1902, and others, BW; Darrow to Addams, Sept. 11, 1901, and Bradley interview, ALW; A. A. Dornfield, *Hello Sweetheart, Get Me Rewrite!* (Chicago: Chicago Academy, 1988); Margaret Haley, *Battleground* (Urbana: University of Illinois Press, 1982); Emma Goldman, *Living My Life* (New York: Penguin, 2006); Dorothy Dudley, *Forgotten Frontiers: Dreiser and the Land of the Free* (New York: Smith & Haas, 1932).

8. Bradley interview, ALW; Barnum to Stone, Jan. 5 and 9, 1942, Irving Stone papers, University of California, Berkeley; Schretter, "I Remember Darrow"; Ruby Darrow to Stone, CD-LOC; Mary Field Parton, journal, MFP.

9. Edgar Lee Masters, "My Youth in the Spoon River Country," manuscript, ELM; *Chicago Tribune*, Jan. 7, 1901, Feb. 6, Feb. 15, 1902; Rosa Perdue to Ely, Jan. 23, 1903, ALW; Ethel Colson, "A Home in the Tenements," *Junior Munsey Magazine*, 1901; Helen Todd file, U.S. Bureau of Investigation, National Archives; Ruby Darrow to Helen Darrow, KD; James Weber Linn, *Jane Addams* (New York: Appleton-Century, 1935); Mary Field Parton journal, MFP.

10. Ruby wrote a human-interest story about Darrow's nephew Karl, a "boy genius." He would grow up to be a famous American physicist. Ruby Darrow to Stone, CD-LOC.

11. Wood to George Field, Jan. 15, 1913, CESW-HL; Denslow Lewis, *The Gynecologic Consideration of the Sexual Act* (Chicago: Shepard, 1900).

12. James McParland, Pinkerton Detective Agency report, Mar. 5, 1907, IHS; Hutchins Hapgood, *The Spirit of Labor* (New York: Duffield, 1907) and *A Victorian in the Modern World* (New York: Harcourt, Brace, 1939); Mary Field to Sara, 1913, CESW-HL; *To-Morrow* magazine, various editions, 1907; Janice Ruth Wood, *The Struggle for Free Speech in the United States, 1872–1915* (New York: Routledge, 2008); Women's Legal History Biography Project, Stanford University; Sunset Club proceedings, Nov. 5, 1891.

13. Darrow, "Woman," *Bedford's Magazine*, July 1890. In "Some Reminiscences of a Pioneer Suffragette," *Chicago Tribune*, Dec. 5, 1909, Elizabeth Loomis recalled how "Clarence Darrow often attended our parlor debates about woman's suffrage." The Chicago papers of the late 1880s and 1890s contain ample references to Darrow's support of the cause (see, for example, *Chicago Tribune*, Feb. 3, May 29, 1889, Feb. 4, April 11, 1890, Oct. 14, Nov. 6, 1891; May 21, 23, June 6, 1905, and others in OHL).

14. Darrow, *A Persian Pearl* (East Aurora, NY: Roycroft Shop, 1899); White, *Autobiography*; Whitlock, *Forty Years of It*; Barnum, "Darrow, the Enigma"; see also Whitlock correspondence and diary notations, BW.

15. Darrow, *Resist Not Evil* (Chicago: Charles Kerr, 1902); *Chicago Tribune*, June 24, 25, Aug. 7, 1898; Darrow to Addams, Sept. 11, 1901, ALW.

16. The fellow-servant rule, according to *Black's Law Dictionary*, is "a common-law doctrine holding that an employer is not liable for an employee's injuries caused by a negligent coworker." The "Easy Lessons" series ran through the summer and fall of 1902 in the *Chicago American*. For sequence and subjects, see Willard D. Hunsberger, *Clarence Darrow: A Bibliography* (Metuchen, NJ: Scarecrow Press, 1981), and for analysis see Abe Ravitz, *Clarence Darrow and the American Literary Tradition* (Cleveland: Western Reserve University Press, 1962). Darrow was drawn into a sensational murder mystery when F. Wayland Brown, a private detective he knew, asked for his help. The pretty Marie Defenbach, twenty-four, an artist's model, had been conducting a torrid affair with Dr. August Unger, who was handsome, married—and broke. Together, they plotted to defraud several insurance companies by faking her death, substituting a vagrant's body, and having it cremated before anyone could raise questions. They hired Brown to help them with some logistical details. Then Defenbach died horribly, frothing at the mouth and twisting in agony—a few days after signing papers leaving her estate to Unger. The

doctor quickly had her body burned but, in his eagerness to collect on the insurance policies, provoked suspicion, and he and Brown were indicted for fraud. Unger had his own attorney and got the maximum jail time. (Since there was no body, the state could not prove murder.) But Darrow persuaded the judge that Brown had been duped. The court fined Brown and set him free. The cause of Marie's death remained unknown.

17. Virginia Glenn Crane, *The Oshkosh Woodworkers' Strike of 1898* (Oshkosh, WI: V. Crane, 1998); *Milwaukee Sentinel*, June 24, 1898; *Chicago Tribune*, June 24, 25, Aug. 7, and Dec. 23–31, 1898; Apr. 26, May 5, 6, 7, 10, 11, 12, 13, 14, 27, Aug. 8, 9, 1899, and Feb. 22, 1901; *Chicago Daily News*, Apr. 26, May 4, 8, 9, 10, 11, 13, 1899; Hapgood, *The Spirit of Labor.*

18. Darrow, Altgeld funeral address, Mar. 14, 1902, in *Story of My Life*; Jane Addams and Rev. Frank Crane of the People's Church also spoke at the Altgeld home on Friday. *New York Times*, Mar. 13, 15, 17, Apr. 4, 1902; *Chicago Tribune*, Mar. 12, 13, 14, 15, Apr. 21, 1902.

CHAPTER 6: LABOR'S LAWYER

1. Lloyd to his wife, Nov. 11, 1902, HDL; Anthracite Coal Strike Commission, *Report to the President on the Anthracite Coal Strike of May-October, 1902* (Washington, D.C.: GPO, 1903); Anthracite Coal Strike Commission (hereafter ACSC), transcript of hearings, Library of Congress; Rosamond Rhone, "Anthracite Coal Mines and Mining," *American Monthly Review of Reviews*, Nov. 1902; Donald Miller and Richard Sharpless, *The Kingdom of Coal* (Philadelphia: University of Pennsylvania Press, 1985); Robert J. Cornell, *The Anthracite Coal Strike of 1902* (Washington, D.C.: Catholic University Press, 1957).

2. ACSC hearings.

3. Darrow, "The Breaker Boy," in Weinberg, *Verdicts.*

4. Baer to Clark, July 1902, HDL; *New York Times*, Aug. 21, 1902; *Washington Post*, Jan. 10, 1903; *Chicago Tribune*, Jan. 10, 1903; ACSC, *Report to the President*; Cornell, *Anthracite Coal Strike.*

5. ACSC hearings; Roosevelt to Hanna, Sept. 27, 1902, Roosevelt to Lodge, Sept. 27, 1902, Roosevelt to Bacon, Oct. 5, 1902, Roosevelt to Morgan, Oct. 15, 1902, Roosevelt to Crane, Oct. 22, 1902, Lodge to Roosevelt, Sept. 27, 1902, Theodore Roosevelt papers, Library of Congress; *New York Times*, Sept. 26, Oct. 12, 1902; *Chicago Daily News*, Oct. 3, 4, 11, 1902; Roosevelt, *Theodore Roosevelt: An Autobiography* (New York: Macmillan, 1914).

6. ACSC hearings; Lloyd to his wife, Oct. 16, 20, 1902, Lloyd to Mitchell, Oct. 25, 1902, Mitchell to Lloyd, Oct. 25, 1902, Lloyd to Mitchell, Oct. 27, 1902, Weyl to Lloyd, Oct. 29, 1902, Mitchell to Lloyd, Oct. 30, 1902, Lloyd to his wife, Nov. 4, 1902, HDL.

7. ACSC hearings; *Chicago Daily News*, Nov. 17–26, 1902.

8. ACSC hearings; Lloyd to his wife, Nov. 14, 15, 18, 22, and 28, 1902, HDL; Mitchell to Wilson, Nov. 27, 1902, John Mitchell papers, Catholic University; *New York Times*, Nov. 22, 1902; *Washington Post*, Nov. 22, 1902; Hamlin Garland, *Companions on the Trail* (New York: Macmillan, 1931).

9. The wrenching human stories may have touched some journalists, but Darrow was still fighting a royalist press. The *New York Times* blamed the fathers of the mill girls, not the factory owners. The culprits were immigrant Irish parents, and "various lost tribes of Southeastern Europeans—Polacks, Hungarians, Bohemians, or what not—who have no civilization, no decency, nothing but covetousness, and who would with pleasure immolate their offspring on the shrine of the golden calf," the newspaper declared in a Dec. 17, 1902, editorial. ACSC hearings; *Washington Post*, Dec. 7, 16, 1902; *New York Times*, Dec. 16, 1902; *Chicago Daily News*, Dec. 9, 1902; *Wilkes-Barre Daily News*, Dec. 9, 10, 11, 16, 17, 18, 1902; Lloyd to his wife, Dec. 12 and 16, 1902, Lloyd to Brandeis, Dec. 16, 1902, HDL; E. Dana Durand, "The Anthracite Coal Strike and Its Settlement," *Political Science Quarterly*, Sept. 1903; Caro Lloyd, *Henry Demarest Lloyd* (New York: G. P. Putnam's Sons, 1912).

10. Darrow to Brandeis, Nov. 28, 1902, Brandeis to Darrow, Dec. 2, 12, and 13, 1902, Louis Brandeis papers, Library of Congress; Jones to Darrow, Dec. 11, 1902, Sam Jones papers, University of Toledo; Jones to Darrow, Feb. 13, 1903, CD-LOC; Lloyd to Brandeis, Jan. 29, 1903, HDL; ACSC hearings.

11. ACSC hearings.

12. Stone has Darrow speaking for three days; he actually spoke a day and a half. Similarly, Stone has Gray interrupting Darrow's declaration that the miners were outmatched by the corporations with an admiring murmur, "Except the lawyers!" The transcript shows that Gray, in fact, was teasing Darrow with the question "Except the lawyers?" ACSC hearings; *Philadelphia North American*, Jan. 16, Feb. 14, 1903; *Boston Globe*, Feb. 14, 1903; *Washington Post*, Feb. 14, 1903; *New York Times*, Feb. 14, 1903; *Chicago Daily News*, Feb. 12, 1903; unnamed newspaper clipping, Sept. 22, 1902, OHL; Lloyd to his wife, Jan. 13, 14, 16, 1903, HDL; Harriet Reid to Weinberg, May 11, 1958, ALW.

13. ACSC, *Report to the President*; *Washington Bee*, May 2, 1903; *Chicago Tribune*, Mar. 22, 1903; *New York Times*, Mar. 22, 1903; *Chicago Daily News*, Mar. 21, 1903; *Boston Globe*, Mar. 22, 1903; Robert Wiebe, "The Anthracite Strike of 1902: A Record of Confusion," *Mississippi Valley Historical Review*, Sept. 1961; Durand, "Anthracite Coal Strike"; Samuel Gompers, *Seventy Years of Life and Labor* (New York: Dutton, 1925); Darrow to Samuel Jones, Apr. 14, 1900, Sam Jones papers, University of Toledo.

14. Darrow letter to Cruice, quoted in unidentified newspaper clipping, OHL; Darrow to Mitchell, Jan. 23, 1903, John Mitchell papers, Catholic University; *Chicago Tribune*, Nov. 6, 1902; *Chicago Daily News*, Dec. 22, 1902, Feb. 1, 1903; Simons to Darrow, Nov. 8, 1902, HDL.

15. *Daily People*, Jan. 3, 1903; *Chicago Daily News*, Dec. 6, 1902; *Chicago Tribune*, Mar. 10, 1897, Mar. 21, 1901, Feb. 5, 1903; *Chicago Post*, Mar. 9, 10, 1897, Dec. 14, 1898; see Harrison, *Growing Up*.

16. Lloyd to his wife, Feb. 21 and 22, 1903, Abbot to Lloyd, Feb. 24, 1903, HDL; Gompers to Darrow, Mar. 5, 1903, Samuel Gompers papers, Library of Congress. The teamsters had refused to tote "scab" coal during a Midwest strike, and John Mitchell was in their debt. "He couldn't refuse when I asked him to tell Darrow to withdraw his name. Darrow couldn't refuse to do what Mitchell asked, and there you are," said Driscoll. "The votes that would have gone to Darrow went to Harrison."

17. Whitlock to Darrow, Feb. 11, 1903, CD-UML; *Chicago Daily News*, Jan. 31, Feb. 1, 3, 16, 18, 20, 23, 24, 1903; *Chicago Tribune*, Jan. 28, 30, Feb. 1, 3, 14, 15, 16, 20, 22, 23, 24, Apr. 5, 1903; *Daily People*, Jan. 3, 1903; *Chicago American*, Dec. 22, 1902; *Inter Ocean*, Feb. 3, 1903; *Los Angeles Times*, Feb. 15, 1903; untitled Washington, D.C., newspaper clipping, Mar. 12, 1903, OHL; Morgan to Lloyd, John Livingston papers, University of Denver.

18. The union accounts in the Mitchell papers at Catholic University confirm Darrow's $10,000 fee. *Chicago Tribune*, Apr. 2, 3, 4, 5, 8, 9, 1903, June 15, 1905; *Chicago Daily News*, Apr. 1, 2, 1903; *Washington Post*, May 22, 1904; *Rockford Herald*, Apr. 8, 1903; *Inter Ocean*, Apr. 8, 1903; *Rockford Morning Star*, undated clipping, CD-LOC; unidentified Chicago newspaper clippings, Apr. 3 and 4, 1903, OHL; E. Pomeroy to Mrs. H. D. Lloyd, June 22, 1904, HDL.

CHAPTER 7: RUBY, ED, AND CITIZEN HEARST

1. Ruby Darrow letters to Stone, and Stone interview notes, CD-LOC; Ruby letter to Jennie Moore, Nov. 25, 1911, CD-UML; *Chicago Tribune*, July 17, 19, Aug. 25, 1903.

2. Ruby letters to Stone, and Stone interview notes, CD-LOC; Darrow to Jessie, Sept. 8, 1903, and Mar. 10, 1904, CD-UML; Ruby Darrow letters to Helen Darrow, Helen Darrow letter to Jennie Darrow, and Karl Darrow diary, KD; McParland, report, Mar. 5, 1907; *Chicago Tribune*, July 17, 19, Aug. 25, 1903; Darrow letter to Ruby quoted in the *News-Review*, July 28, 2009.

3. Ruby letters to Stone, CD-LOC; Ruby letters to Helen and Jennie Darrow, and Helen to Jennie Darrow, KD; Ella Winter and Granville Hicks, eds., *The Letters of Lincoln Steffens* (New York: Harcourt, Brace, 1938).

4. Darrow to Whitlock, Nov. 17, 1902, BW.

5. *Chicago Tribune*, May 17, 1904; Masters to Harrison, Mar. 21, 1938, and Masters to Barnard, May 22, 1938, ALW; Masters, "My Youth in the Spoon River Country" manuscript and *Across Spoon River* manuscript and unfinished chapters, ELM; Masters, *Across Spoon River*; Ruby Darrow letters to Stone, CD-LOC.

6. Chicago Tribune, Mar. 16, 17, 1905, Jan. 7, 1912; *New York Times*, Oct. 24, 1903; Darrow to Mrs. Lloyd, Oct. 19, 1903, HDL; *Turner v. Williams*, 194 US 279; Sidney Fine, "Anarchism and the Assassination of McKinley," *American Historical Review*, July 1955; Masters, "My Youth in the Spoon River Country" manuscript and *Across Spoon River* manuscript and unfinished chapters, ELM; Masters, *Across Spoon River*.

7. Darrow's letter to the *Daily News* appears to have inspired a myth that he "fixed" the Iroquois Theatre probe. It was cited in a 1929 book by Lloyd Lewis and Henry Justin Smith (*Chicago: The History of Its Reputation* [New York: Harcourt, Brace and Co., 1929] and picked up by later writers as proof that Darrow had helped Harrison escape justice. Darrow's defense of the chief engineer of the capsized lake steamer *Eastland* in 1915—an accident that claimed more than eight hundred lives—shows that he was more than willing to take the unpopular side in such matters, but the available public record in the Iroquois case shows that Levy Mayer was the criminal defense lawyer, A. S. Trude represented Harrison, and Darrow, Masters & Wilson represented the families of vic-

tims who sued the theater owners. Anthony Hatch, whose book *Tinder Box* (Chicago: Academy Chicago Publishers, 2003) offers the most thorough account of the fire, found no evidence that Darrow played a nefarious role. And Masters and Harrison, two prolific memoirists who wrote about the Iroquois tragedy, and exchanged venomous gossip about Darrow, never mention his involvement in the episode. See Harrison, *Stormy Years*, and Masters, *Levy Mayer and the New Industrial Era* (New Haven, CT: Yale University Press, 1927); see also *Chicago Herald*, Jan. 27, 28, 1904; *Chicago Chronicle*, Jan. 30, 1904; *Chicago Tribune*, Nov. 24, Dec. 31, 1903, Jan. and Feb. 1904, and May 28, 1907; *New York Times*, Dec. 31, 1903, Jan. 1904; Chicago Fire Marshall, *Annual Report*, 1903.

8. The *American* was the inspiration for the play and motion picture *The Front Page.* Darrow also defended the newspaper when its two-thousand-pound electric sign, the biggest in the city, pulled free from its moorings and showered Mary Spiss, a woman on the sidewalk below, with chunks of masonry that broke her arm and thigh. The sign was illegal; the newspaper was found guilty of negligence, and she was awarded $8,000. *Chicago Tribune*, Aug. 5, 1896, Mar. 28, 1904; Lloyd to Bowles, Mar 17, 1897, HDL; *Hearst's Chicago American v. Mary E. Spiss*, 117 Ill. App. 436; George Murray, *The Madhouse on Madison Street* (Chicago: Follett, 1965); W. A. Swanberg, *Citizen Hearst* (New York: Scribner's, 1961).

9. The Oakley case was appealed, and she and the newspaper ultimately reached a settlement. Masters, *Across Spoon River*, and "My Youth" and "The Two Annie Oakleys," manuscripts, ELM; *Chicago Tribune*, Aug. 10, Oct. 2, 3, 29, Nov. 2, 16, 17, 27, 28, 30, Dec. 8, 1901; *Chicago Record Herald*, Dec. 4, 1901; *Chicago Daily News*, Dec. 7, 1901; the most colorful and complete coverage of Darrow's closing address was in the *Chicago American*, of course, of Dec. 4, 1901.

10. In the fall, Darrow wavered between the populist Tom Watson and the socialist Eugene Debs, who were on the ballot as minor-party candidates. Schilling to Charles Riefler, June 11 and 13, George Schilling papers, University of Chicago; Paul Darrow interview with Stone, CD-LOC; *Chicago Tribune*, Nov. 21, 1903, Mar. 28, June 15, July 9, Oct. 13, 28, Nov. 11, 1904; *Washington Post*, July 9, 1904; *New York Times*, June 21, July 4, 6, 8, 10, 1904; Ray Ginger, *Altgeld's America* (New York: Funk & Wagnalls, 1958); Champ Clark, *My Quarter Century of American Politics* (New York: Harper & Brothers, 1920); Ben Procter, *William Randolph Hearst: The Early Years* (New York: Oxford University Press, 1998); Alfred P. Dennis, "The Anomaly of Our National Convention," *Political Science Quarterly*, June 1905.

11. *New York Times*, Oct. 8, 1904, Sept. 13, 1905; *Chicago Tribune*, Apr. 24, Oct. 1, 1904, Oct. 14, 1905; Howells to Darrow, Nov. 20, 1903, Howells to Darrow, with rejection note, Jan. 21, 1904, CD-UML; Hamlin Garland, *Companions on the Trail* (New York: Macmillan, 1931); Darrow, *Farmington* and *An Eye for an Eye* (Girard, KS: Haleman-Julius, 1905).

12. Yerkes was backed by transit barons Peter Widener and William Elkins of Philadelphia. Stead died on the *Titanic*, and so did Widener's son George and grandson Harry. Stead, *If Christ Came*; Harrison, *Stormy Years* and *Growing Up*.

13. Altgeld wasn't looking for a fight with Yerkes, and offered to appoint a commission

to study the franchise matter. Yerkes sighed. It would only mean more palms to grease, he told the governor, and "we are taking care of too many now." Schilling to Dunne, Apr. 28, 1905, George Schilling papers, University of Chicago; Steffens, "Chicago: Half Free"; Stead, *If Christ Came*; Darrow, *Story of My Life*; Charles Merriam, *Chicago: A More Intimate View of Urban Politics* (New York: Macmillan, 1929); John Franch, *Robber Baron: The Life of Charles Tyson Yerkes* (Urbana: University of Illinois Press, 2006); Harrison, *Stormy Years* and *Growing Up*; *New York Times*, Dec. 12, 14, 1898.

14. Yerkes had, at various times, employed Darrow's former legal associates Goudy and Goodrich as lobbyists, but Darrow himself steered clear of the baron. Sunset Club proceedings, Jan. 17, 1901; Lloyd to Parsons, Mar. 17, 1897, HDL; Chester M. Destler, *Henry Demarest Lloyd and the Empire of Reform* (Philadelphia: University of Pennsylvania, 1963); Lincoln Steffens, "Enemies of the Republic," *McClure's*, Aug. 1904; Tarbell, "Chicago Is Finding Herself"; Ginger, *Altgeld's America*; Steffens, "Chicago: Half Free"; *Chicago Tribune*, Nov. 29, 1897, Dec. 2, 1898, Apr. 22–May 3, 1903; *New York Times*, July 4, 1897; *Chicago Daily News*, Apr. 23, 24, 1903.

15. The council ultimately approved twenty-year franchises that would ease the city toward municipal ownership. Darrow, "Mark Tapley Dunne," signed manuscript, CD-LOC; Henry Webster, "From Yerkes to Dunne," *American Illustrated Magazine*, Apr. 1906; Tarbell, "Chicago Is Finding Herself"; *New York Times*, May 4, 5, June 13, July 8, Oct. 29, Nov. 14, 1905, Mar. 13, Apr. 4, 5, 1906, Apr. 3, 19, 1907; *Chicago Tribune*, May 18, 19, June 8, June 30, Aug. 24, Sept. 2, 22, 23, 1905; Mar. 17, Apr. 2, 1907; Darrow to Dunne, June 19, 1905, CD-LOC; Darrow to Whitlock, Oct. 16, 1905, Apr. 8, 1907, BW; Austin W. Wright to C. E. S. Wood, Jan. 12, 1904, and May 23, 1907, CESW-HL; *Blair v. City of Chicago*, 201 U.S. 400; Steffens, *Autobiography*.

16. Darrow ultimately dropped the City company as a client, when asked to defend the firm against the lawsuits filed by those injured by its streetcars. Instead, in 1902 and 1905 Darrow's law firm carried lawsuits against the transit firm, involving the death and maiming of young boys run down by its cars, to the Illinois Supreme Court, winning one and losing the other. *Chicago Tribune*, Mar. 8, 10, 1896; Feb. 13, 1897; *New York Times*, June 27, 1897; see *Chicago City Railway Co. v. Tuohy*, 196 Ill. 410 and *Chicago City Railway Co. v. Jordan*, 215 Ill. 390, and Leeming note, Stone papers, CD-LOC; for International Harvester controversy, see footnote 4 in Chapter 12.

17. In Darrow's defense, it should be noted that others found the politics of the reform era as complicated. As Theodore Roosevelt told a friend: "I have had on occasions to fight bosses and rings and machines; and have had to get along as best I could with bosses and rings and machines when the conditions were different . . . I have seen reform movements that failed and reform movements that succeeded and have taken part in both, and have also taken part in opposing fool reform movements which it would be a misfortune to have succeed." See Roosevelt to Lorimer, May 12, 1906, Theodore Roosevelt papers, Library of Congress. In the otherwise excellent *Altgeld's America*, Ray Ginger mistakingly attributes the "Dear Miss S" episode to the jury-bribing case. Masters, *Across Spoon River*, "My Youth," and other unpublished manuscripts, ELM; *Chicago Tribune*, May 3, June 14, 18, 21, 27, 28, 29, July 25, Sept. 16, 1902, Nov. 24, 1903; Wright to Wood, Jan. 12, 1904, CESW-HL; Hapgood, *Spirit of Labor*.

18. Darrow's role in revealing Smith's dealings in the bank was beyond reproach; even Judge Kennesaw Mountain Landis, no fan of Darrow, praised his actions. "I do not think that I shall sit here and listen to any criticism of Mr. Darrow," said Landis, who was described as "trembling in anger" at the lawyers for Smith's cronies. "Mr. Darrow has done something in this case that few officers of a bank would undertake to do." Masters and Darrow tried for years to wring money from the bank's assets and, for leverage or in spite, opposed Smith's pleas for clemency. *Chicago Tribune*, Feb. 16, 17, 20, 1906, Apr. 7, 13, 16, 18, 20, 1907, Apr. 28, 1908, May 1, 16, June 2, 3, 13, 1909, July 13, 1910; *Chicago Daily News*, Feb. 16, 17, 19, 1906; *New York Times*, Feb. 16, 1906, Apr. 7, 1907; *Chicago Daily Journal*, Feb. 16, 1906; Darrow testimony, Commission of Industrial Relations, 1915; Masters, *Across Spoon River* and unpublished manuscripts, ELM; Hubbard, *The Philistine*, June–November 1906; Garland, *Companions on the Trail.*

CHAPTER 8: INDUSTRIAL WARFARE

1. Steunenberg family correspondence, Dec. 31, 1905, to Jan. 13, 1906, Frank Steunenberg family papers, Albertson College of Idaho, Caldwell, Idaho; Confession of Harry Orchard, PP.

2. William Hard, "The Western Federation of Miners," *Outlook*, May 19, 1906.

3. Lloyd, notebook, Darrow to Caro Lloyd, no date, HDL. The rosewater quote, by Honoré Mirabeau, a French revolutionary figure, is taken from Darrow, *Story of My Life*; Ray Stannard Baker, "The Reign of Lawlessness," *McClure's*, May 1904; Steffens to Laura Steffens, June 25, 1912, Lincoln Steffens papers, Columbia University.

4. James Hawley, "Steve Adams' Confession and the State's Case against Bill Haywood," *Idaho Yesterdays*, winter 1963/1964; Melvyn Dubofsky, "James H. Hawley and the Origins of the Haywood Case," *Pacific Northwest Quarterly*, Jan. 1967.

5. A. K. Steunenberg, quoted in Anthony Lukas, *Big Trouble* (New York: Simon & Schuster, 1997).

6. Abbot to Lloyd, Dec. 1899, HDL; U.S. House of Representatives, Committee on Military Affairs, *Coeur D'Alene Labor Troubles* (1900); William Gaboury, "From Statehouse to Bull Pen," *Pacific Northwest Quarterly*, Jan. 1967.

7. Theodore Roosevelt to Calvin Cobb, June 16, 1906, Theodore Roosevelt papers, Library of Congress; Baker, "Reign of Lawlessness"; AFL Circular, June 20, 1904, Samuel Gompers papers, Library of Congress; Philip S. Foner, *The Policies and Practices of the American Federation of Labor, 1900-1909* (New York: International, 1964).

8. Baker, "Reign of Lawlessness"; Darrow, *Story of My Life*; George Kibbe Turner, "The Actors and Victims in the Tragedies," *McClure's*, Sept. 1907; George Kibbe Turner, "Introductory Note to the Confession and Autobiography of Harry Orchard," *McClure's*, July 1907.

9. Philip S. Foner, *The Industrial Workers of the World, 1905-1917* (New York: International, 1965).

10. Pinkerton papers, HIS; Pinkerton papers, PP; Steunenberg correspondence, Frank Steunenberg family papers, Albertson College of Idaho, Caldwell, Idaho; *Idaho Daily*

Statesman, Dec. 31, 1905, Jan. 1–11, 1906; Luke Grant, "The Haywood Trial: A Review," *Outlook*, Aug. 24, 1907; *U.S. v. Barber Lumber Co.*, 194 *Federal Reporter*, 1912.

11. *Idaho Daily Statesman*, June 24, 1907.

12. McParland reports to Gooding, Orchard confession, Hassen to McParland, Apr. 2, 1908, Thiele memo, IHS; McParland reports, PP; Steunenberg correspondence, Frank Steunenberg family papers, Albertson College of Idaho, Caldwell, Idaho; *Idaho Daily Statesman*, Dec. 31, 1905, Jan. 1–5, 1906, June 14, 1907; Lukas, *Big Trouble*; Baker, "Reign of Lawlessness"; Debs, *Appeal to Reason*, Mar. 10, 1906; Darrow, *Story of My Life*.

13. Theodore Roosevelt to William H. Moody, Mar. 26, 1906, Theodore Roosevelt papers, Library of Congress; Darrow to Caro Lloyd, Dec. 8, 1910, HDL; Darrow to Mitchell, Mar. 13, 1906, and Mitchell to Darrow, Mar. 14, 1906, John Mitchell papers, Catholic University; Dubofsky, "Hawley and the Origins"; *Pettibone v. Nichols*, 203 U.S. 192 (1906); *Idaho Daily Statesman*, May 30, June 1, 1906.

14. McParland later told Gooding of a "rumor" that Adams and his uncle received $75,000—a titanic sum—to go over to the defense. The *Statesman* reported, citing no sources, that the defense had bribed Lillard through "the use of large amounts." McParland reports, HIS; McParland reports, PP; Stone, *Clarence Darrow for the Defense*.

15. Darrow was not operating alone. Richardson and Nugent accompanied him on his visits to Lillard and would have had to agree to the deal. Though the WFM received contributions from other organizations, it is difficult to see it raising $75,000—more than a million dollars by today's standards—for the Adams family. And, of course, the source must be considered. The Pinkertons spread cash around and presumed that the other side had its own "slush fund" to buy jurors, as detective Charles Siringo put it. McParland reports, HIS; McParland reports, PP; Charles Siringo, *A Cowboy Detective* (Chicago: Conkey, 1912).

16. *Idaho Daily Statesman*, *Daily Idaho Press*, and the Wallace, Idaho *Times*, Feb. 7–Mar. 8, 1907; McParland reports, IHS; McParland reports, PP; Darrow, *Story of My Life*; Arthur Weinberg, *Attorney for the Damned: Clarence Darrow in the Courtroom* (New York: Simon & Schuster, 1957).

17. McParland reports, HIS; McParland reports, PP. Adams took the news philosophically. He would have preferred to be acquitted, he told a deputy, but "it's better to hang the jury, than to hang the prisoner."

18. McParland reports, HIS; McParland reports, PP; *Idaho Daily Statesman*, July 7, 1907.

19. McParland reports, HIS; McParland reports, PP.

20. McParland reports, HIS; McParland reports, PP; Roosevelt to Attorney General Charles Bonaparte, Mar. 26, 1906, Roosevelt to Calvin Cobb, June 16, 20, 1906, Roosevelt to James Sherman, Oct. 8, 1906, Theodore Roosevelt papers, Library of Congress; *New York Times*, May 5, 1907; *Idaho Daily Statesman*, May 5, 1907; Lukas, *Big Trouble*.

21. Lukas, *Big Trouble*.

22. Roosevelt was lobbied by Gooding, Cobb, Borah, and others, including prominent journalists like William Allen White, to drop the case. "I cannot help feeling some

indignation at this desire of persons who profess to be friends . . . to have you . . . relieve Borah," Attorney General Bonaparte warned the president. "Most of the employees, both of my Department and that of the Interior, who have been engaged in the prosecution of land frauds in that region . . . are generally convinced of Borah's guilt." But Roosevelt contrived to pressure the leader of the investigation, U.S. attorney Norman Ruick, to resign, and Borah was then acquitted. McParland reports, HIS; McParland reports, PP; B. F. Cash to Bonaparte, Mar. 23, 1907, Bonaparte to Roosevelt, Mar. 29, 1907, Norman Ruick to Bonaparte, Mar. 29, 1907, Gooding to Roosevelt, Apr. 10, 15, 1907, Cobb to Gifford Pinchot, Apr. 13, 1907, Hawley to Roosevelt, Apr. 18, 1907, Borah to Roosevelt, Apr. 24, 1907, William A. White to Roosevelt, July 26, 1907, Theodore Roosevelt papers, Library of Congress; Bonaparte to Roosevelt, Aug. 1, 7, 10, 15, and Sept. 1 , 1907, Ruick to Treasury, Aug. 12, 1907, U.S. Department of Justice records, National Archive.

23. There was talk from one Idaho defense attorney, said Operative 21, about bribing the Haywood jurors. Such allegations made their way to the press and were repeated over the years, tarnishing Darrow's performance in Idaho. ("The newspaper grape vine is that Darrow bribed the Steunenberg jury," Edgar Lee Masters wrote, thirty years later.) But if an actual attempt was made to corrupt the jurors, it is likely that Operative 21 would have known about it, and that McParland would have exposed it.

24. *Mirror*, May 16, 1907; *New York Times*, May 17, 1907; *Boston Globe*, May 17, 1907; *Denver Post*, May 7, 1907.

CHAPTER 9: BIG BILL

1. The description of the Haywood trial is drawn from the trial transcript, available at the Idaho Historical Society, the *Idaho Daily Statesman*, *New York Times*, *Boston Globe*, *New York Sun*, and the Associated Press, May 9, 1907–July 29, 1907. See *Boston Globe*, June 3, 1906; Ethel Barrymore, *Memories: An Autobiography* (New York: Harper, 1955); William Haywood, *Bill Haywood's Book: The Autobiography of William D. Haywood* (New York: International, 1929).

2. Ruby Darrow to Stone, CD-LOC; Darrow to Whitlock, Apr. 8, 1907, BW; Darrow, *Story of My Life*; see *New York Sun*, May 9, 19 and June 3, 1907.

3. See *New York Times*, May 9, 16, 1907. The prosecution was incensed at Wilson's perfidy, and Cobb took revenge by informing Roosevelt, who was weighing candidates for a federal judgeship, that Wilson was given to "brutal and disreputable" drunken "sprees."

4. See November 1906 Darrow–Richardson exchange, CD-UML, and Darrow to the defendants, CD-LOC; *Harper's Weekly*, June 2, 1906. Richardson and John Murphy were the WFM's regular lawyers. Darrow brought in Peter Breen, a radical from Montana. Fred Miller of Spokane and young Leon Whitsell had represented the miners in the Coeur d'Alenes; John Nugent was a friend of Haywood from Idaho, and there were others with local insight or connections carried on the payroll.

5. *Idaho Daily Statesman*, June 2, 1907. The paper called the attack "neuralgia." In *Roughneck*, Haywood biographer Peter Carlson says physicians later identified it as a stomach ulcer.

6. McParland had tried to get Adams to write a narrative as well. "Orchard having written this biography it will simply be impossible for any counsel to shake his testimony," the detective told Gooding. But "Adams as we are all aware has a poor memory" and "will not make a first class witness." Like Orchard, Adams should write it all down and "read it over time and time again so that everything connected with this case and with his life will be freshly impressed and stamped upon his memory," the detective said. McParland reports, HIS; McParland reports, PP; Darrow, *Story of My Life*; Ruby to Stone, CD-LOC; Haywood, *Autobiography*.

7. See *New York Times*, June 6, 7, 9, 12, 1907.

8. Hawley remarks in "Arguments Presented in Favor of Commutation" at the Idaho pardon board hearing on Harry Orchard, Nov. 13, 1922; Pinkerton letter, Nov. 16, 1920, PP.

9. There was also testimony about an unsigned letter to Orchard that arrived in Caldwell after his arrest. He swore it was from Pettibone, assuring him that money was on the way. Yet the letter itself had been destroyed, and the Caldwell sheriff later denied, under oath, that it was Pettibone's handwriting. Hawley in "Arguments Presented"; *Denver Post*, June 17, 1907; *Idaho Daily Statesman*, June 22, 1907; *Boston Globe*, Dec. 28, 1907.

10. *Boston Globe*, June 15, 1907; *Idaho Daily Statesman*, June 22, 1907.

11. *Idaho Daily Statesman*, June 25, 1907; *New York Sun*, June 25, 1907; *New York Times*, June 25, 1907; *Chicago Record-Herald*, June 25, 1907; *Chicago Examiner*, June 25, 1907; *New York Daily Tribune*, June 25, 1907; Fremont Wood, *The Introductory Chapter to the History of the Trials of Moyer, Haywood, and Pettibone, and Harry Orchard* (Caldwell, ID: Caxton Printers, 1931).

12. *Boston Globe*, July 13, 1907; Haywood, *Autobiography*; *New York Times*, July 12, 1907; *Idaho Daily Statesman*, July 12, 1907; *Chicago Tribune*, July 12, 1907; *Chicago Daily News*, July 12, 1907.

13. *Chicago Tribune*, Aug. 3, 1907.

14. *Idaho Daily Statesman*, July 25, 1907; *Boston Globe*, July 25, 1907; *Idaho Evening Capital*, July 25, 1907; *New York Times*, July 25, 1907.

15. *New York Times*, July 26, 1907; *New York Sun*, July 26, 1907; *Los Angeles Times*, July 26, 1907; *Idaho Daily Statesman*, July 26, 1907; Haywood, *Autobiography*.

16. Jess Hawley, "Notes on Haywood," quoted in David Grover, *Debaters and Dynamiters* (Corvallis: Oregon State University, 1964).

17. Haywood, *Autobiography*; McParland reports, IHS; Statement of Anton Johannsen, CD-CHI.

18. Darrow, *Story of My Life*; Stone interview with Otto Peterson, clerk of court; Ruby Darrow to Stone, CD-LOC; *New York Herald*, July 29, 1907; *New York American*, July 29, 1907; *Philadelphia Evening Telegraph*, July 29, 1907; Haywood, *Autobiography*.

19. The journalist Mark Sullivan suggested that an old Scottish verdict—"not proven"—best described the outcome of the Haywood case. It remains an American mystery. There are surely assassins (John Wilkes Booth) who work within conspiracies. But it is possible that Darrow and Richardson had it right, and that Orchard, like most American assassins (Eugene Prendergast, Lee Oswald, James Earl Ray, Sirhan Sirhan, and many oth-

ers), bore some crazed grudge against Steunenberg and acted without specific direction, hoping to be hailed as a savior when the deed was done. Orchard was certainly not an efficient conspirator. He was broke, thieving, gambling, and clumsy, called attention to himself, and appears to have made no plan to escape or to hide the incriminating evidence contained in his luggage.

Haywood went on to a militant career with the Wobblies, grew even more radical, and died a revolutionary—yet no other Harry Orchard ever surfaced in his life, or that of Moyer. If there was a union conspiracy, it may have stopped at Orchard and Simpkins or reached only as far as Pettibone, the happy tinker of death. Yet anything short of Haywood and Moyer would have left the union leadership intact, and that was not what McParland, Hawley, and the others were aiming for.

C. P. Connolly of *Collier's* magazine listed a dozen "peculiar features" of the trial, suggesting that Judge Wood, his bailiffs, or the jurors were corrupted. In his own memoir, Oscar Davis wrote that "there was talk at Boise after Haywood had been set free that the jury had been bought. Whether there was any foundation for any such talk or not, I never knew." Both reporters, however, were Roosevelt and Borah partisans.

It took twenty years, but the prosecution did finally admit the weakness of its case. In 1927, Hawley spoke at the dedication of a statue of Steunenberg in Idaho. The "overwhelming confirmation of Orchard's testimony in regard to other crimes," he conceded, had lessened the convincing quality "of the small amount of corroborating proof connecting Haywood with the Steunenberg murder."

What did Darrow believe? We can't be sure. "Darrow clearly intimated to me that the Moyer people were guilty," Erskine Wood recalled. But it was probably just Darrow's "inordinate vanity" that caused him to say so. "I think he might say it, [even] if they were not," Wood said. Darrow rarely spoke about his trials when they were over. But years later, he almost blurted something to George Francis, a young lawyer who asked him about Idaho. "Haywood didn't kill Steunenberg. I'll tell you who did," he said, before catching himself and saying, "No, I won't either."

Stone interview with Francis and Hawley remarks, CD-LOC; Sullivan, *Our Times*; C. P. Connolly, "Pettibone and Sheriff Brown," *Collier's*, Jan. 25, 1908; Oscar Davis, *Released for Publication* (Boston: Houghton Mifflin, 1925); Roosevelt to Whitelaw Reid, July 29, 1907, Theodore Roosevelt papers, Library of Congress; Cobb to Alford Cooley, Oct. 3, 1907, quoted in Lukas, *Big Trouble*; Haywood, *Autobiography*.

CHAPTER 10: FRAILTIES

1. Darrow had to defend his remarks for years. He had never "urged cruelty or that the working man should be exempt from the law," he wrote journalist Mark Sullivan in 1930. What he said was "that regardless of how many wrongs they commit, or how many brutalities they are guilty of, their cause is just." Letter to Sullivan, quoted in *Our Times*; Darrow to Whitlock, Nov. 29, 1907, BW; Darrow to Debs, Oct. 1907, ALW; *Chicago Tribune*, July 29, 1907; *New York Sun*, July 27, 1907; *New York Times*, Aug. 7, 1907; *Idaho Daily Statesman*, Aug. 2, 1907.

2. Adams was tried one last time in the summer of 1908 for the 1902 murder of a mine manager in Telluride and found innocent. Darrow, *Story of My Life*; Ruby letters to Stone, CD-LOC; Adams trial transcript, CD-UML; Darrow to Wood, Dec. 26,

1907, CESW-HL; *Idaho Daily Statesman*, Oct. 11, Nov. 8–27, 1907; *Los Angeles Herald*, Nov. 14, 1907; *Chicago Tribune*, Oct. 5, 6, Nov. 14, 25, 1907; *San Francisco Call*, Oct. 20, 1907; *Washington Post*, Oct. 27, 1907; *Spokane Evening Chronicle*, Nov. 24, 1907; *New York Times*, Nov. 25, 1907, July 16, 1908.

3. *Idaho Daily Statesman*, Nov. 27–Dec. 31, 1907, Jan. 1–7, 1908; *Los Angeles Times*, Dec. 14, 27, 1907; *San Francisco Call*, Dec. 15, 29, 1907; *Salt Lake Herald*, Dec. 27, 1907, Jan. 5, 1908; *Boston Globe*, Dec. 28, 1907, Jan. 5, 1908; *Los Angeles Herald*, Dec. 29, 31, 1907; *Los Angeles Examiner*, Jan. 5, 1908; *New York Times*, Jan. 2, 5, Aug. 2, 4, 1908; *Chicago Tribune*, Jan. 21, Feb. 11, 1908; *McClure's*, June 1908; Noah D. Fabricant, MD, "When Clarence Darrow Had an Earache," *The Eye, Ear, Nose & Throat Monthly*, Dec. 1958; Jean Strouse, *Morgan* (New York: Random House, 1999) and Walter Lord, *The Good Years* (New York: Harper, 1960).

4. Masters, unpublished autobiography, ELM; Darrow to Edgar Lee Masters, Nov. 29, 1907, Masters to WFM, Jan. 4, 1908, Jan. 22, 1908, Jan. 28, 1908, and WFM to Masters, Jan. 6, 1908, Jan. 24, 1908, Masters to Carter Harrison, Mar. 21, 1938, ELM; Ruby Darrow letters to Stone, CD-LOC; Masters, *Across Spoon River*; Darrow, *Story of My Life*.

5. Masters, unpublished autobiography, ELM; Ruby letters to Stone, CD-LOC; Darrow to Brand Whitlock, Dec. 13, 1910, BW; Darrow to William Walling, July 14, 1910, NAACP; *Chicago Tribune*, Apr. 7, 1908.

6. *New York Sun*, May 30, 1909; *Chicago Tribune*, June 4, 1899; Mark Sullivan, *Our Times*; Stone notes, CD-LOC; Carole Merritt, *Something So Horrible: The Springfield Race Riot of 1908* (Springfield, IL: Abraham Lincoln Presidential Library Foundation, 2008); Ida Wells-Barnett, *Lynch Law in Georgia* (Chicago: Chicago Colored Citizens, 1899); Darrow, "The Problem of the Negro," transcription of remarks in the *International Socialist Review*, Nov. 1, 1901.

7. Darrow's talks on race earned him public censure. At one point in his Cooper Union speech he predicted that just as time and intermarriage had eroded the enmity among European immigrant groups, the problem of race relations "will undoubtedly some time far in the future be worked out by race amalgamation." Darrow "Advises Negroes to Marry Whites," read the headlines across the country, and for several days he was the target of anger and ridicule in white America. He caused another stir, and was booed and jeered, when he addressed fifty thousand union sympathizers in San Francisco on Labor Day in 1909—and urged them to move past racial prejudice and ease restrictions against Chinese and Japanese immigrants. *Evening American*, Aug. 19, 1908; *Chicago Tribune*, May 13, 17, 19, 20, 1910; Proceedings of the National Negro Conference, May 1910, NAAC; *New York Times*, May 13, 1910; Michael Kazin, *Barons of Labor* (Urbana: University of Illinois Press, 1987).

8. Darrow's failure in another case had long-lasting repercussions. In 1907, Fred Warren—the editor of the *Appeal to Reason*—had been incensed by the Haywood trial. No prominent capitalist would be kidnapped like the Federation leaders, Warren claimed—and to illustrate his point he offered $1,000 to anyone who would abduct William Taylor, a former Kentucky governor, and return him to the state for trial on an outstanding murder charge.

Federal prosecutors indicted Warren for misusing the mails, and Darrow was among the lawyers who defended the editor. "The government offered to take a fine of $25, in case of a plea of guilty," Darrow recalled. But Warren wanted "not an easy way out, but advertising notoriety for the paper and himself. I soon found out I was employed to sell newspapers . . . a disagreeable job." They lost the case; Warren blamed Darrow and began to collect and distribute derogatory information about him. Debs warned Darrow that "many of your former friends have lost confidence in you" because he had "gone over to the other side purely for money." When Darrow needed the support of the leading socialist journal, it would not be there. See U.S. Justice Department files, brief and correspondence on the Warren case, May 1909, National Archives, and also Debs to Darrow, Feb. 19, 1912, Warren to L. C. Boyle, Dec. 12, 1910, Eugene Debs collection, Indiana State University; Darrow to Caro Lloyd, Dec. 8, 1910, and Feb. 8, 1911, HDL. *Myeroff v. Tinslar*, 175 Ill. App. 29; Geoffrey Cowan, *The People v. Clarence Darrow* (New York: Times Books, 1993); *Chicago Tribune*, Nov. 3, 6, 12, 13, 1908, Sept. 25, Oct. 26, 1909, Feb. 10, 24, 25, 26, Mar. 4, May 9, 11, Aug. 4, 1910.

9. Edwin Maxey, "The Rudowitz Extradition Case," *The Green Bag: An Entertaining Magazine for Lawyers*, Vol. 21, 1909; Frederick Giffin, "The Rudowitz Extradition Case," *Journal of the Illinois State Historical Society*, Spring 1982; *New York Times*, Jan. 27, 1909; *Chicago Evening Post*, Dec. 6, 1908; *Chicago Daily News*, Dec. 5, 7, 1908, and Jan. 27, 1909; *Chicago Tribune*, Nov. 6, 14, 24–29, Dec. 1, 6, 10, 13, 24, 25, 27, 1908, and Jan. 4, 13, 14, 15, 27, Feb. 14, 15, June 17, 1909.

10. George Field was a man of old-fashioned values who saw moral decay everywhere, even in the celebration of Christmas. "Whipping, prayers, religion, dyspepsia part and parcel of memory," Mary recalled. "Bible soaked into us." When she got to college, "I knew nothing" about men, she said. She had been taught at home that "there was something nasty about sex." Mary Field Parton journal and oral histories, MFP; Sara Bard Field oral history, University of California, Berkeley; *Chicago Tribune*, Mar. 28, May 1, 7, 1909; Randolph Bourne to Prudence Winterrowd, quoted in Christine Stansell, *American Moderns* (New York: Macmillan, 2001); *Michigan Alumnus*, University of Michigan Alumni Association, 1913.

11. Darrow was asked to join the cause, looked into the shooting, and decided that Chief Shippy was telling the truth. But he didn't like the way that the newspapers and the police were whipping up fears about "anarchists" and worked to secure a platform for Emma Goldman when the police blocked her from speaking on Averbuch's behalf. The Averbuch incident is covered in Mary Field's taped oral histories and in Margaret Parton's unpublished biography of her mother, Mary Field, along with the letter to Graham Taylor, MFP; see also Sara Bard Field oral history, University of California, Berkeley. See also Walter Roth and Joe Kraus, *An Accidental Anarchist* (San Francisco: Rudi Publishing, 1998).

12. The ritual was repeated on another occasion when Darrow asked Mary to buy Mother Jones a warm winter coat. "Let me see how much I have on me," he said, hauling out a wad of bills. "Well, it is kind of messy, isn't it? But it will buy something." See Mary Field Parton oral histories and Margaret Parton unpublished biography of her mother, MFP.

13. Mary Field, taped oral histories, diaries, and letters and Margaret Parton, unpublished biography of her mother, MFP; Mary to Sara, correspondence, July 1909, June 1910, and August, 1910, CESW-HL; Sara Bard Field oral history, University of California, Berkeley; Darrow to Mary, Mar. 15, July 1910, CDMFP-NL; Karl Darrow diaries, KD; Henry Coit to Wood, June 14, 1910, CESW-UC; Darrow to Fremont Older, Sept. 21, 1910, ALW; *Chicago Tribune*, Jan. 4, Mar. 13, 14, 31, May 9, 1908, Sept. 11, Nov. 15, 1909, Sept. 4, 1910; Schretter, "I Remember Darrow"; Roger Bruns, *The Damndest Radical* (Urbana: University of Illinois Press, 2001).

CHAPTER II: LOS ANGELES

1. *People v. Caplan*, LAL; Robert Gottlieb and Irene Wolt, *Thinking Big* (New York: Putnam, 1977).

2. *People v. Caplan*, *People v. Schmidt*, LAL; *The Fireman's Grapevine*, Sept. and Nov. issues, 1960; *New York Times*, Oct. 3, 1910; E. W. Scripps, *I Protest* (Madison: University of Wisconsin Press, 1966); grand jury testimony of John Beckwith, William Mulholland, Harry Chandler, Olav Tvietmoe, Earl Rogers, Anton Johannsen, and Lindsay Jewell, WD.

3. The ironworkers' union considered Otis "the most unfair, unscrupulous and malignant enemy of organized labor in America." Theodore Roosevelt thought him a "scurrilous blackguard." See Roosevelt to Gompers, June 7, 1911, Theodore Roosevelt papers, Library of Congress; "General Otis, the Storm-Center of the Unpacific Coast" (no author listed by the magazine), *Current Literature*, Jan. 1912; *Los Angeles Times*, Oct. 1, 1933. The first-day headline in the *Times* got it wrong; the accepted number for lives lost in the bombing is twenty.

4. As part of the city's investigation, a committee of engineers, including its renowned water czar, William Mulholland, re-created the explosion. They took an identical charge of dynamite, placing it among barrels of ink, and set it off in an isolated shelter on city parkland. The bomb vaporized and ignited the ink, and spread it so far throughout the site that the engineers had to scurry to contain the subsequent fire. A "general ignition of combustibles, scattered about in the building," Mulholland said, was "hastened and rendered more universal instantly . . . by reason of the breaking of the gas pipes." *People v. Caplan*, *People v. Schmidt*, LAL.

5. The firm didn't routinely stock such powerful dynamite, but produced it as a special order, which the three men picked up from the company dock in Oakland with a motorboat. The load was so heavy that the boat listed precipitously, handled poorly, and made a lasting impression on those who saw it lurching across the bay. *People v. Caplan*, *People v. Schmidt*, LAL.

6. Burns was shrewd at manipulating the press, but those who worked with him on the McNamara case thought him a greedy and self-aggrandizing fraud. "Burns has misled and deceived his own clients," wrote Walter Drew, leader of the National Erectors Association, in a letter detailing the Burns agency's failures. "All that Burns accomplished was through one of the members of our association." It was a sentiment with which Oscar Lawler, a federal prosecutor in the case, agreed. Burns "never did and never will know any other purpose to serve than his own selfish ends," Lawler told Drew. *People v.*

Caplan, People v. Schmidt, LAL; AFL circular, Dec. 5, 1910, Samuel Gompers papers, Library of Congress; *Los Angeles Times*, Apr. 23, 24, 25, 1911, and *Boston Globe*, Apr. 23, 24, 25, 1911; "Statement of Anton Johannsen," CD-CHI; "General Otis,"*Current Literature*, Jan. 1912; Drew to Emery, Jan. 29, 1913, Lawler to Drew, Feb. 3, 1913, Drew to Burns, June 20, 1914, WD; J. B. McNamara to Robert McNamara, Sept. 12, 1931, and J. B. McNamara to Jock Rantz, Apr. 13, 1930, James and John McNamara papers, University of Cincinnati; Cowan, *The People v. Clarence Darrow*; Gottlieb and Wolt, *Thinking Big.*

7. In Chicago's recent garment workers' strike, labor's enforcers had made a practice of waylaying nonunion tailors and breaking their needle fingers. It was during that strike that Darrow forged what was to be a lifelong friendship with a young organizer, Sidney Hillman, soon to be founder and president of the Amalgamated Clothing Workers of America. Darrow to Lloyd, May 13, 1911, HDL; Darrow to Older, July 26, 1911, ALW; Howard to Porterfield, Apr. 27, 1911, E. W. Scripps to N. D. Cochran, Nov. 20, 1911, E. W. Scripps papers, Ohio University; Wilson to Stone, CD-LOC; trial transcript, *People v. Darrow*, LAL; Darrow to Paul, May 14, Aug. 11, and Oct. 27, 1911, and Ruby to Jennie Moore, Nov. 25, 1911, CD-UML; *Chicago Tribune*, Apr. 13, 1911; *Los Angeles Times*, Apr. 27, 1911; *Outlook*, Feb. 17, 1912.

8. The AFL records place Darrow's meeting with Gompers on May 1 in Kankakee, where Darrow was trying the Kankakee Manufacturing case. According to the Chicago newspapers, Gompers made the public announcement about Darrow the next morning, May 2. Stone, relying on Ruby's memory, says Gompers and Ed Nockels convinced Darrow at his apartment in Chicago the following weekend, after gradually wearing him down. "After many hours D came to me in the back, wearily, sadly taking my hand or arm and conducting me to a seat beside him, to break to me the news that he was asking me to break my pledge, made to him when we returned from Idaho, that if ever again he should be tempted, or urged, to go into another such terrific fight, I'd refuse to go along," she wrote. "He proceeded to explain that the men in the front room were saying that if he refused to take charge of the McNamara cases . . . that he would go down in history as a traitor to the great cause." Ruby said this took place on a Sunday, probably May 7. Union officials were indeed in lengthy consultation with Darrow at his apartment that day, but Gompers was not among them. See telegram from Frank Mulholland in Chicago to Gompers in Washington, May 7, 1911, Gompers to Tvietmoe, May 19, 1911, Gompers papers, Library of Congress; Darrow to Whitlock, Apr. 26, 1911, BW; "Gompers and Burns on Unionism and Dynamite," *McClure's*, Feb. 1912.

9. Los Angeles Cultural Heritage Commission report, 2007; *Los Angeles Express*, May 25, 1911; *Hamlin Garland's Diaries* (San Marino, CA: Huntington Library, 1968), entry of Mar. 19, 1911; Hugh Baillie, *High Tension* (New York: Harper, 1959); Ruby Darrow letters, LeCompte Davis papers, UCLA and CD-LOC; Darrow to Paul, July 25, 1911, CD-UML.

10. Sara Field, oral history, University of California, Berkeley; Sara Field to William Rose Benet, Nov. 30, 1949, Sara to Wood, mid-Oct. and Wood to Sara, Oct. 16, 1911, CESW-HL; Darrow to Wood, June 28, 1910, Louise Bryant to Wood, Jan. 19, 1915, CESW-UC; Stone, *Clarence Darrow for the Defense*; Robert Hamburger, *Two Rooms* (Lincoln: University of Nebraska Press, 1998).

11. *Los Angeles Times*, June 28, 29, July 6, 1911; Drew to Noel, Jan. 17, 1917, WD.

12. Transcript, *People v. Darrow*; *New York Times,* Sept. 12, Dec. 2, 1911; *Los Angeles Times*, Dec. 3, 1911, Jan. 31, 1912; William Hunt, *Front-Page Detective: William J. Burns and the Detective Profession 1880–1930* (Bowling Green, OH: Bowling Green University Popular Press, 1990); Darrow to Gompers, July 15, 1911, Darrow to Tvietmoe, summer 1911, Tvietmoe to Gompers, summer 1911, Samuel Gompers papers, Library of Congress.

13. William Kahrl, *Water and Power* (Berkeley: University of California Press, 1982). In March 1911 alone they filed a plan to subdivide 47,500 acres—the largest development in southern California.

14. Kahrl notes that the one-tenth interest in the San Fernando Mission Land Company that Huntington purchased for $15,000 in 1905 sold for $115,000 seven years later. The profits were far higher for those, like Otis and Chandler, who retained their property and purchased more for residential development in the boom years to come. Lissner to Julius Rosenwald, Oct. 12, 1911, Lissner to Hiram Johnson, Nov. 25, 1911, Meyer Lissner papers, Stanford University; Alexander Irvine, *Revolution in Los Angeles* (Los Angeles: Citizen Print Shop, 1912); Joseph Lippincott personnel file, U.S. Department of the Interior, National Personnel Records Center, St. Louis.

15. Otis to Taft, Oct. 12, 1911, Otis to Charles Hilles, Oct. 16, 1911, William Howard Taft papers, Library of Congress; Lawler to Wickersham, Sept. 21, 1911, J. E. Munson to Drew, Oct. 11, 1911, Lawler to Wickersham, Oct. 23, 1911, Lawler to Badorf, Mar. 5, 1913, Foster autobiography, list of union "deprivations," WD.

16. Taft may have had a personal interest in the case. After midnight on the sixteenth, just before the president's train crossed a railroad bridge near Santa Barbara, a watchman had frightened away unknown saboteurs as they prepared to set off thirty-nine sticks of dynamite. See Drew "deprivations" and correspondence, WD and Justice Department files, National Archives.

17. It wasn't just the jury. Darrow thought Bordwell was a biased judge. Bordwell had okayed Fredericks's use of the grand jury to intimidate the defense and Darrow had, unsuccessfully, tried to have the judge removed from the case. Indeed, Bordwell corresponded with Borah and Hawley in Idaho, and they covertly sent him the transcript of the Haywood case so he could study Darrow's techniques. See Bordwell to Borah and Hawley, summer 1911, Walter Bordwell papers, Stanford University; *Los Angeles Herald*, Nov. 22, 1911; *New York Times*, Oct. 14, 18, 1911; Anton Johannsen, "The Darrow Case," *The Carpenter*, Dec. 1912; Sara to Wood, fall 1911, Sara to Wood, Oct. 21, 26, 1911, Wood to Sara, Oct. 16, 1911, Sara to Albert Ehrgott, Oct. 14, 1911, CESW-HL; Catlin to Wood, June 3, 1911, CESW-UC.

18. Darrow, *Story of My Life*; transcript, *People v. Darrow*; *New York Times*, Dec. 3, 1911; see also Darrow to his brother-in-law, Howard Moore ("I wish it was over—it doesn't look good to me"), Oct. 6, 1911, CD-UML.

19. Steffens showed his eagerness when, while strolling on the beach in Santa Monica with Johannsen, he wished aloud that the union leader would be indicted. "I could get rich men who are interested in the social problems to finance the case," Steffens said. "The defense would be emotional insanity . . . all the sufferings and ill-being of Labor

during your lifetime could be introduced as testimony . . . the whole social system would be exposed." Johannsen "might get hung," Steffens conceded, "but it would make a hell of a good story." Anton Johannsen, "Statement," CD-CHI; Steffens, *Autobiography*; Steffens to Suggetts, July 3, 1911, Steffens to his father, Nov. 3, 1911, Lincoln Steffens papers, Columbia University.

20. Transcript, *People v. Darrow*; Scripps to Cochran, Nov. 20, 1911, Scripps to Ben Lindsey, Sept. 7, 1911, E. W. Scripps papers, Ohio University; Lincoln Steffens, "Explosion of the McNamara Cases," *New York Globe* (reprint of dispatches by Steffens); Drew to James Hunter, Nov. 25, 1911, Drew to Fredericks, Nov. 25, 1911, WD.

21. Transcript, *People v. Darrow*; *Los Angeles Tribune*, Nov. 23, 1911; *Los Angeles Herald*, Dec. 4, 1911; Steffens, "Explosion."

22. Franklin was not known to Darrow when he joined the defense, but the local U.S. attorney and others had vouched for him. Laborites given to conspiracy theories cited the suspicious number of Darrow's accusers who, like Franklin and Lockwood, had ties to the district attorney's office. Transcript, *People v. Darrow*; *Los Angeles Times*, Nov. 29, 1911, *New York Times*, Nov. 29, 1911.

23. Transcript, *People v. Darrow*; Fay Lewis to Irving Stone, Aug. 8, 1940, CD-LOC; J. B. McNamara to William Foster, Feb. 1, 1935, James and John McNamara papers, University of Cincinnati; Joseph Scott letter to C. J. Hyans, Sept. 6, 1950, California State Federation of Labor, Bancroft Library, University of California, Berkeley; fragments of second trial transcript, WD; *Los Angeles Record*, Nov. 29, 1911.

24. Sara Field oral history, University of California, Berkeley. A few liberal jurists endorsed Darrow's actions. "The unions . . . are to be congratulated on the wise and courageous action of Clarence S. Darrow," Louis Brandeis told the *Boston Globe*. "Unionism . . . would undoubtedly have suffered greatly from the prejudice created . . . by a continued contest which must have resulted in a verdict of guilty."

25. Emma Goldman called Darrow and Steffens "timid . . . infants" and concluded that "the collapse of the trial disclosed the appalling hollowness of radicalism . . . and the craven spirit of so many of those who presume to plead its cause." Maybe. But it should be noted that both Schmitt and Caplan were ultimately convicted and imprisoned on the evidence that Fredericks was prepared to present against James McNamara. Darrow probably saved his life. Emma Goldman, *Living My Life* (New York: Knopf, 1931); Job Harriman to Morris Hillquit, Dec. 19, 1911, Morris Hillquit papers, Wisconsin State Historical Society; Hutchins Hapgood, *A Victorian in the Modern World* (New York: Harcourt, Brace, 1939); *Los Angeles Times*, Dec. 2, 1911; *Los Angeles Herald*, Dec. 1, 1911; Irvine, *Revolution in Los Angeles*; Steffens, "Explosion."

26. A decade later, after his release from prison, John McNamara met Gompers at a union convention. "If you had told me in confidence you were guilty, I would not have betrayed you," Gompers told McNamara. Gompers refused to shake hands. "The last time I took your hand, you assured me of your innocence. After that, you betrayed yourself and labor." Lucy Robins Lang, *Tomorrow Is Beautiful* (New York: Macmillan, 1948); Bernard Mandel, *Samuel Gompers* (Yellow Springs, OH: Antioch Press, 1963).

27. Darrow told reporters on December 2: "I never told Samuel Gompers, or anybody else, that James B. McNamara was innocent." Indeed, Darrow said, it would have been

unethical for him to discuss the question of guilt or innocence with an outsider, even one who was paying the bills. Darrow to Gompers, telegram, Dec. 1, 1911, Samuel Gompers papers, Library of Congress; Steffens, "Explosion"; *Boston Globe*, Dec. 5, 1911; *Los Angeles Times*, Dec. 2, 1911; *Washington Star*, Dec. 2, 1911; *Washington Post*, Dec. 3, 1911; *Chicago Tribune*, Dec. 3, 1911; Sissman interview with Stone, CD-LOC; Sara Field oral history, University of California, Berkeley; Gompers statement, Samuel Gompers papers, Library of Congress.

28. *Los Angeles Times*, Dec. 6, 1911; *New York Times*, Dec. 6, 1911; *Los Angeles Herald*, Dec. 4, 1911; *U.S. v. Ryan* files, WD.

29. Johannsen fancied, at one point, that Darrow had initiated the plea negotiations "to save his own skin" after learning that Fredericks was on to the jury-bribing plot, several weeks before Franklin was arrested. See Wood to Sara, Apr. 12, 1912, CESW-HL; Lissner to Norman Hapgood, Mar. 22, 1912, Meyer Lissner papers, Stanford University; Lawler to A. G. Wickersham, Dec. 6, 1911, U.S. Department of Justice records, National Archives.

CHAPTER 12: GETHSEMANE

1. The scene is drawn by Mary Field's daughter Margaret Parton in an unpublished biography of her mother. ALW and MFP.

2. *Los Angeles Herald*, Dec. 4, 1911. James would die in prison, but John's sentence was reduced for good behavior, and he was released after serving a little more than nine years. Several thousand people crowded the street outside the courthouse to see the brothers hauled to jail. "You see?" James McNamara told Steffens. "You were wrong and I was right. The whole damn world believes in dynamite."

3. *Los Angeles Times*, Jan. 1, 1912.

4. Transcript, *People v. Darrow*; Darrow, *Story of My Life*; Ruby to Paul, Dec. 3, 1911, CD-UML. For Darrow on prison see letters to Paul, Jennie ("I am really convinced that it would do me good"), and Howard Moore, CD-UML; Lawler to Wickersham, Jan. 26, 1912, U.S. Department of Justice records, National Archives. To add to Darrow's woes, his old antagonist Elbridge Hanecy, now a counsel for a congressional panel probing corruption in Illinois, used the moment to exact vengeance. Hanecy called a witness who said that the International Harvester Company, via Darrow, had offered him $10,000 to drop a public-interest lawsuit. The committee dismissed the testimony as irrelevant, but the newspapers carried stories of the $10,000 "bribe." It dated back to Darrow's work for Hearst, whose editors in Chicago had been surprised when he suggested they call off their crusade against the Harvester firm, which had been dodging taxes. He had just lunched with the corporate counsel, Darrow told them, and the company was ready to make a huge payment to the public treasury. The journalists celebrated their victory. And then Darrow informed them that he hoped to take a fee from Harvester for brokering the deal. It had not occurred to the editors, who were paying Darrow to represent them, that he would accept money from the other side as well. Hanecy's witness was the leader of a taxpayer group allied with the newspaper. His complaint was investigated, and no action taken. See U.S. Congress, *Senate Select Committee to Investigate the Election of William Lorimer* report, which includes the transcript of the Dec. 9, 1911, hearing; *Chicago Tribune*, Dec.

10, 11, 31, 1911; *New York Times*, Dec. 15, 1911; George Murray, *The Madhouse on Madison Street*; Moses Koenigsberg, *King News* (Philadelphia: Frederick A. Stokes, 1941).

5. Transcript, *People v. Darrow*; Adela Rogers St. Johns, *Final Verdict* (New York: Doubleday, 1962); Baillie, *High Tension*; Alfred Cohn and Joe Chisholm, *Take the Witness* (New York: Frederick Stokes, 1934).

6. Darrow knew Rogers. A few years earlier they had been advocates for Anna Mayr, a wealthy California woman who, the press said, lived "a Bohemian existence and probably did not live congenially with her husband, who was of an entirely different type." Mayr had charged his wife with infidelity; Rogers represented her, and somehow Darrow ended up with the woman's expensive furniture, which her husband sued to recover.

7. Debs to Darrow, Feb. 19, 1912, Eugene Debs collection, Indiana State University; St. Johns, *Final Verdict*; Jerry Geisler, *Hollywood Lawyer* (New York: Simon & Schuster, 1960). Adela's biography of her father is the only voice that survives from the Rogers family. She admits it is subject to the vagaries of memory and emotion and contains errors. The sentiments it portrays, however, seem genuine.

8. Morrison to AFL colleagues, Dec. 2, 1911, Samuel Gompers papers, Library of Congress.

9. Darrow to Moore, Feb. 6, 1912, Darrow to Paul, Jan. and Feb. 1912, Ruby to Paul, Aug. 23, 1912, CD-UML; Catlin to Wood, Feb. 14, 1912, CESW-UC; Helen Darrow to Jennie Moore, Jan. 8, 1912, KD; Jennie Moore to Ruby, Feb. 1, 1912, Ruby to Ella Hoswell, Jan. 17, 1912, Leo Cherne papers, Boston University; Ruby letters to Stone, CD-LOC.

10. Gerson to Darrow, Jan. 17, 1918, Perceval Gerson papers, UCLA; Ruby letters to Stone, CD-LOC. "We understood too well his philosophy of life to care about his guilt," Reynold Blight, a friend from the Heart to Heart Club, told Irving Stone. "He was fighting for the underdog, who was being brutally abused by methods that were unjust and unfair; he felt he had to fight fire with fire."

11. Unpaid bills became a source of friction with Rogers—so that he would joke about it with the jury. "Do you believe that Darrow, a man who has financial peculiarities, would let go of $4,000?" Rogers would ask. "It is a physical, mental and moral impossibility. Witnesses testified that Darrow is the stingiest man in the world. And I believe it fully. I know whereof I speak."

12. Mitchell to Darrow, Feb. 12, 1912, Darrow to Mitchell, Feb. 20, 1912, John Mitchell papers, Catholic University.

13. Gompers was furious over a newspaper article in which Darrow was quoted saying that the AFL chief knew the McNamaras were guilty all along. When Darrow heard this, he wrote and wired Gompers, denying the story, but it made no difference. Darrow to Gompers, Feb. 1912, Gompers to Darrow, Mar. 16, 1912, Samuel Gompers papers, Library of Congress.

14. Stone, *Darrow for the Defense*; Ruby to Whitlock, Feb. 14, 1912, Mary to Whitlock, Jan. 24, 1912, BW.

15. *Los Angeles Examiner*, Jan. 30, 1912; *Chicago Tribune*, Jan. 30, 1912; *Los Angeles Times*, Jan. 30, 1912; *New York Times*, Jan. 31, 1912; Baillie, *High Tension*; Darrow to Everett,

telegram, Leo Cherne papers, Boston University; Darrow to Paul, Dec. 29, 1911, CD-UML; Darrow to Masters, Feb. 3, 1912, ELM.

16. Older to Darrow, Jan. 30, 1912, Barnum to Darrow, Jan. 31, 1912, Simon to Darrow, Feb. 1, 1912, Jones to Darrow, early 1912, Mary to Darrow, Jan. 29, 1912, Leo Cherne papers, Boston University; *Los Angeles Times*, Mar. 3, Apr. 27, 1912; Debs to Darrow, Feb. 19, 1912, Eugene Debs collection, Indiana State University; Darrow to Wood, Feb. 20 and 23, 1912, CESW-UC; Darrow to Wood, Mar. 1, 1912, CESW-HL; Ruby to Older, in Older to Masters, Feb. 2, 1912, Masters unpublished autobiography, ELM. Masters later griped that the "smell of Darrow on me" cost him a federal judgeship he craved in 1913.

17. Sullivan to Wood, Mar. 21, 1912, CESW-HL; Drew correspondence, Harrington statements, Foster autobiography, WD; Willard to Scripps, Jan. 26, 1912, E. W. Scripps papers, Ohio University; transcript, *People v. Darrow.*

18. Wood to Sara, Apr. 12, 1912, CESW-HL. There was nothing that Darrow could proffer to tie Gompers to the dynamite plots. No one probed the bombings for union connections more than Walter Drew, and, in the end, he absolved the AFL chief. "Are there any professional ethics in the detective business?" Drew wrote Detective William Burns. "Your continued remarks about Mr. Gompers and men 'higher up' etc. have, in the absence of any evidence whatsoever, become a boomerang and a source of embarrassment and injury . . . Had any evidence at any time been produced . . . our association would have followed it up."

19. Mary to Sara, May 1912, Wood to Sara, Apr. 12, 1912, Sara to Wood, Apr. 1912, CESW-HL; *Los Angeles Times*, May 17, 18, 1912; *Los Angeles Herald*, May 15, 1912; Foner, *Industrial Workers.*

20. Golding wrote Darrow asking for money in 1913. Darrow responded favorably and Golding wrote him back. "You must not consider that you are under obligation to me, because I stood for what was right and just," he said. But "had I fell into what they wished I would do, and taken a strong stand against you, I probably would not have any debts to worry me." Darrow left no record of what he gave Golding then, but he told his son Paul to send the juror $4,500 of their profits from the sale of the Greeley gas company in 1928. See Golding letter in CD-LOC and Darrow letter to Paul, Dec. 16, 1927, in CD-UML.

21. Except where noted, description of the trial comes from the transcript of *People v. Darrow* at the Los Angeles County Law Library and daily coverage of the trial in the *New York Times*, *Los Angeles Times*, *Los Angeles Herald*, and *Chicago Tribune*, supplemented by the *Los Angeles Examiner* and *Los Angeles Record.* St. Johns, *Final Verdict*; Drew to J. Badorf, June 5, 1912, WD.

22. It should be noted that the first time Harrington told the story of the $10,000 bankroll, to Oscar Lawler in February, he swore that the conversation took place in their offices in the Higgins Building. See Harrington statements, WD. Transcript, *People v. Darrow*; St. Johns, *Final Verdict*; Baillie, *High Tension*; Cowan, *The People v. Clarence Darrow*; Darrow to Paul, July 4, 1912, CD-UML.

23. Why was Darrow at the scene? In his autobiography, Darrow chose not to mention that he was there when Franklin was arrested, nor to explain why. The prosecutors did a good job tearing Hawley's explanation—that Darrow was needed for a political

consultation—apart at the trial. But their version—that Darrow was there to supervise Franklin—seems equally convenient, for Franklin had a dozen meetings with Lockwood, Bain, and others in which he attempted to bribe prospective jurors before he was arrested, and Darrow was not present at any of them. So why this day? Rogers contended that Darrow was lured into a trap by an anonymous caller. And Franklin had his own plausible version: that the defense had been tipped off by a source in the prosecution, spurring Darrow, too late, to rush out to stop the crime ("Bert, they are on to you!"). Transcript, *People v. Darrow*; *Los Angeles Examiner*, June 23, 1912; Mary to Wood, Aug. 6, 1912, CESW-HL. For a more extensive day-to-day portrayal of the trial, see Cowan, *The People v. Clarence Darrow*, and for an account that argues for Darrow's innocence, see Stone, *Clarence Darrow for the Defense*.

24. The account of the night of drinking and song with the labor leaders is from Mary Field Parton's journal, MFP; Johannsen, "Darrow Case."

25. "He needs friends," Steffens told Whitlock. "And when they are down and out and out and down and there's no one else, then it's up to us muckrakers to go and hold hands, isn't it?"

26. In a private letter from Reedy to Darrow, the publisher expressed similar sentiments: "You possibly took a long chance for your clients." Reedy to Darrow, Mar. 15, 1912; CD-LOC; *Mirror*, June 27, 1912.

27. Steffens testified that he ignored Darrow's order and tried without success to get the bribery case dismissed as part of the McNamara settlement. If so, his actions may have supplied the grounds for the subsequent suspicions of Johannsen, Lawler, and others that Darrow gave up the McNamaras to save himself. Steffens to Laura, June 25, 1912, Lincoln Steffens papers, Columbia University. Transcript, *People v. Darrow*; *New York Times*, July 19, 1912; *Los Angeles Record*, July 20, 1912.

28. When he testified before the grand jury, Tvietmoe denied that he had ever passed the $10,000 in cash back to Darrow, and said he still had $7,500 of it. There were other reasons why Tvietmoe needed money. According to Detective Burns, for example, Tvietmoe was in charge of funneling cash to Schmidt and Caplan, who were still on the run.

29. Transcript, *People v. Darrow*; *Los Angeles Times*, July 30, 1912.

30. It was a reach—that Darrow would stake so much on the unattested prospect that Frederick might feel charitable. If that was Darrow's overriding goal, he surely would have nailed it down by including the bribery case in the McNamara settlement. *Los Angeles Times*, July 30; Mary Field journal, MFP; Mary to Wood, Aug. 6, 1912, CESW-HL.

31. Transcript, *People v. Darrow*; *Los Angeles Times*, Aug. 14, 1912; *Los Angeles Examiner*, Aug. 15, 1912.

32. Transcript, *People v. Darrow*; Mary to Wood, Aug. 6, 1912, CESW-HL; *Los Angeles Examiner*, Aug. 15, 18, 1912; *Los Angeles Times*, Aug. 18, 1912; *Los Angeles Record*, Aug. 18, 1912, *New York Times*, Aug. 18, 1912.

CHAPTER 13: THE SECOND TRIAL

1. "Caesar had received his pound of flesh," said Johannsen, with a nice mix of metaphors. Sara to Wood, Mar. 9, 1913, Sullivan to Wood, Aug. 17, 1912, CESW-HL; Mary Field diary, Jan. 9, 1934, MFP.

2. *Los Angeles Times*, Feb. 14, 1913; Pettigrew to Darrow, Aug. 29, 1912, CD-LOC.

3. Anton Johannsen wrote to Darrow: "Our people seem to feel very kindly toward you and realize as best they can that you were up against the strong brace game, and while your judgment may have been poor in the selection of men such as Franklin and Harrington, they have nowhere questioned your integrity." Johannsen to Darrow, Oct. 17, 1912, CD-LOC; *Los Angeles Times*, Aug. 26, 27, 29, 1912; *Boston Globe*, Sept. 1, 1912; *San Francisco Daily News*, Sept. 2, 1912; *San Francisco Daily Morning Call*, Sept. 2, 1912; *San Francisco Chronicle*, Sept. 2, 1912; "If Man Had Opportunity," *Everyman*, Jan./Feb. 1915.

4. "Industrial Conspiracies," *Everyman*, Nov./Dec. 1913.

5. Sara to Wood, Sept. 7, 1912, CESW-HL.

6. Mary to Sara, no date, Oct. 1912, Mary to Sara, no date, Nov. 1912, CESW-HL; Lem Parton to Mary, no date, MFP; Ruby to Paul, Aug. 23, 1912, CD-UML.

7. Darrow to Mary, Oct. 22 and Nov. 12, 1912, CDMFP-NL.

8. Wood urged her to have an abortion, but she miscarried before making that decision. Ehrgott to Wood, Oct. 4, 1912, Ehrgott to Mary, Jan. 15, 1913, CESW-UC.

9. Older to Wood, June 21, 1912, Wood to Older, June 26 and June 27, 1912, CESW-HL; Steffens to Laura, July 20, 1912, Lincoln Steffens papers, Columbia University; Sara Field oral history, Berkeley.

10. Wood to Older, June 26, 1912, CESW-HL.

11. Wood to Older, June 27, 1912, CESW-HL.

12. Sara to Wood, Dec. 15, 1912, Mary to Sara, fall 1912, CESW-HL.

13. "I love a great masterful passion that sweeps over a man or a woman for the only beloved to the soul, and tears one up by his very roots like a great thunderstorm which leaves one's whole being cleansed and purified," Sara told Wood. But Darrow's "sort of oozy-woozy passion that is squeezed out like toothpaste on every attractive woman that appears—yea Gods how I hate it!" Sara to Wood, Dec. 15, 1912, CESW-HL.

14. *Bridgemen's Magazine*, fall 1912; Darrow to Mary, Nov. 28, 1912, CD-LOC.

15. Mary to Wood, undated, Nov. 1912, CESW-HL; Mary to Lem Parton, undated, Jan. 1913, Lem Parton to Mary, undated, Jan. 1913, MFP.

16. *Los Angeles Times*, Feb. 1, 1913.

17. Darrow to Paul, Jan. 9, 1913, CD-UML; Darrow, *Story of My Life*; *Los Angeles Times*, Feb. 5, 1913; *Los Angeles Record*, Feb. 5, 1913.

18. *Los Angeles Record*, Feb. 7, 1913; *Los Angeles Examiner*, Feb. 8, 1913.

19. Schilling to Darrow, Feb. 12, 1913, CD-LOC.

20. *Los Angeles Examiner*, Feb. 14, 1913.

21. Francis Peede interview with Stone, CD-LOC; Mary to Wood, Feb. 22, 1913, CESW-HL; Mary to Lem Parton, undated, Feb. 1913, MFP.

22. *Los Angeles Record*, Mar. 4, 1913.

23. *Los Angeles Examiner*, Mar. 5, 1913.

24. Darrow to Meyers, Feb. 24, 1913, CD-LOC; Wood to Sara, Feb. 24, 1913, CESW-HL. See also Darrow to Paul ("No one believes I will lose"), Feb. 15, 1913, CD-UML.

25. Transcript of Darrow's closing argument in his second bribery trial, CD-LOC.

26. *Los Angeles Examiner*, Mar. 6, 1913.

27. *Los Angeles Times*, Mar. 6, 1913.

28. Transcript of Darrow's closing argument, CD-LOC.

29. Johannsen, statement, CD-CHI.

30. Mary to Lem, undated, Mar. 1913, MFP.

31. *Los Angeles Times*, Mar. 8, 1913.

32. *New York Times,* Mar. 8, 1913; *Los Angeles Times*, Mar. 8, 9, 1913; Baillie, *High Tension.*

33. Yarros, *My Eleven Years.*

34. Transcript, *People v. Darrow*; Hapgood, *Spirit of Labor*; Wood to Sara, Aug. 30, 1912, CESW-HL; Baillie, *High Tension*; Darrow to Everett, early 1912, Leo Cherne papers, Boston University; Darrow to Paul, Jan. 13, 1912, CD-UML; *Los Angeles Times*, Feb. 28, 1915.

35. Even Darrow's version of that conversation was a non-denying denial: "If I had ever dreamed of any such thing it could not possibly have been." Transcript, *People v. Darrow*; Darrow, introduction to *The Autobiography of Mother Jones* by Mary Harris Jones (Chicago: Charles H. Kerr, 1925).

36. Wood to Sara, Mar. 11 and Mar. 13, 1913, CESW-HL.

37. Darrow to Paul, Mar. 8, 1913, CD-UML; Darrow to Wood, Apr. 17, 1913, CESW-HL. Darrow was broke, and had borrowed some $20,000 to conduct the second trial. Fred Gardner, a wealthy businessman from St. Louis, who would one day be elected governor of Missouri, heard of Darrow's troubles and sent him $1,000. Darrow wrote later of the "deep gulf" he faced "between blank despair and the illusion of hope" that Gardner's gesture helped him cross. But Gardner was not totally without motive. In a subsequent letter, he asked Darrow to say some nice things about him to union voters. See Darrow, *Story of My Life* and Gardner correspondence, CD-LOC.

38. Darrow to Wood, Apr. 17, 1913, CESW-HL; Darrow to Paul, Mar. 24, 1913, CD-UML; *Los Angeles Tribune*, Oct. 14, 1914.

39. *Chicago Tribune*, Apr. 4, 1913.

40. Sara to Wood, Apr. 4, 1913, CESW-HL.

CHAPTER 14: GRIEF AND RESURRECTION

1. The Olders forged ahead—prompting jokes in San Francisco about the "love colony"—but a persistent drought robbed their land of water and ultimately doomed the project. Cora Older to Wood, Sept. 14, 1913, and Cora to Wood, undated, 1914, CESW-HL; Ruby to Stone, CD-LOC.

2. Mary and Darrow remained faithful correspondents. "I have found out *beyond a doubt* that the one real supreme passion of Mary's life is Mr. D," Sara wrote Erskine in April

1913. "She still bows at that shrine of love and yet contemplates matrimony" to Lem. "If D. was half worthy of Mary he could make her happy without her being forced to another man for companionship and to escape the horror of a lonely old age," Sara added a week later. Mary would be content as "his intellectual food and his loving mistress" if Darrow was not "running after these disgustingly brainless women all the time."

3. Darrow to Paul, May 14, June 25, 1913, CD-UML; Darrow to Mary, July 4, 1913, July 10, 1913, Nov. 30, 1913, Mar. 1914, Mar. 29, 1915, CDMFP-NL; *Los Angeles Times*, Sept. 13, 1913; *New York Times*, Sept. 14, 1913; Mary to Wood, 1913, Mary to Sara, 1913, CESW-HL.

4. Darrow remarks at dinner of Lawyers Association of Illinois, May 10, 1913, CD-LOC; *Chicago Tribune*, May 11, 1913.

5. See *People v. Covitz*, 262 Ill. 514 (1914); *Chicago Tribune*, June 1, 29, 1913, Jan. 11, 1914; Darrow, Whitman fellowship remarks, CD-CHI; Darrow to Mabel Dodge Luhan, circa 1913–1914, ALW; Garland diary entry, May 19, 1913; Darrow to Paul, June 25, 1913, CD-UML. Ruby did not appreciate Sissman, who, she complained to Stone, had an accent that juries could not understand and spent too much time playing cards at his club. Sissman and Paul Darrow interviews with Stone, CD-LOC.

6. *Chicago Tribune*, Sept. 18, 20, 1914, Feb. 9, Mar. 4, May 16, 17, Nov. 17, 1915, Apr. 26, Dec. 17, 1916; *New York Times*, Dec. 4, 5, 9, 1914; *Chicago Herald*, Sept. 24, 1915; Darrow to Older, Jan. 2, 1914, ALW; Harold Mulks reminiscence, CD-LOC. The film is not to be confused with *A Martyr to His Cause*, another movie based on the McNamaras, which was made during the trial by the AFL to raise funds. Neither film has survived the years.

7. *Chicago Tribune*, June 5, 6, 1913, Mar. 14, 15, 1914; *Chicago Journal*, Mar. 15, 1914. Of eighty white women who killed their husbands in Chicago between 1875 and 1920, only seven were found guilty, and only two were sentenced to prison terms of more than one year. See Jeffrey S. Adler, " 'I Loved Joe But I Had to Shoot Him': Homicide by Women in Turn of the Century Chicago," *Journal of Criminal Law and Criminology*, Spring/Summer 2002.

8. Darrow scored a different kind of victory in front of the U.S. Supreme Court, where his argument on behalf of Charles Ramsay, a Colorado man who was challenging a disputed summons, was embraced by the justices.

9. The appeals court noted that seven defense witnesses had sworn to seeing Bond in Gary at the time of the murder, but demeaned them as "all colored." See *People v. Bond*, 281 Ill. 490 (1917). The *Boston Globe*, *New York Times*, *Washington Post*, and *Los Angeles Times* all carried lurid accounts of Leegson's murder. Bond died in jail a few years later. In a letter to Mary Field in the spring of 1915, Darrow said he had just received a $250 check from a philanthropist to pay for the appeal of "a colored man's case," so perhaps he received something for his efforts. See Darrow, *Story of My Life* and Yarros, *My Eleven Years*; Darrow Testimony, U.S. Commission on Industrial Relations, May 1915; Darrow to Field, Apr. 27, 1915, CDMFP-NL; *Chicago Tribune*, Oct. 7, 8,16, 22, 24, Dec. 1, 1913, Jan. 14, 15, 18, Feb. 1, May 11, July 8, 11, 14, 16, 18, 1914; *Washington Post*, Oct. 7, 8, 1913; *Boston Globe*, Oct. 7, 1913; *Los Angeles Times*, Oct. 7, 1913; *New York Times*, Oct. 6, 1913; Harold Mulks reminiscence, CD-LOC; Mary to Sara, June 9, 1914, CESW-HL.

10. Darrow worried that his presence might cause more violence; indeed, a riot would erupt when he spoke on industrial conditions in an appearance at Cooper Union in New York that spring. U.S. House Committee on Mines and Mining, "Conditions in the Copper Mines of Michigan," Feb. 1914; U.S. Dept. of Labor, "Strike in the Copper Mining District" (Washington, D.C.: GPO, 1914); Arthur Thurner, *Rebels on the Range* (Lake Linden, MI: John H. Forster Press, 1984); Steve Lehto, *Death's Door* (Troy, MI: Momentum Books, 2006); Steve Lehto, *Italian Hall: The Official Transcript of the Coroner's Inquest* (Troy, MI: Momentum Books, 2007); *Washington Post*, Dec. 26, 1913; *Chicago Tribune*, Dec. 27, 28, 29, 30, 31, 1913, Jan. 1, 2, 6, 9, Oct. 7, 1914; *Boston Globe*, Dec. 28, 1913, Jan. 1, 2, 3, 1914; *New York Times*, Dec. 28, 1913.

11. In the Triangle disaster of Mar. 1911, 146 garment workers were killed by the flames or when jumping from windows to escape the fire, after finding that the doors and exits had been locked by the factory owners. On Apr. 20, 1914, a few weeks after the collapse of the Michigan copper strike, the Colorado state militia, with the aid of machine guns, attacked and set fire to a colony of striking coal miners in Ludlow. At least twenty-one people died, including two women and eleven children, most of whom suffocated in a crude pit where they had taken shelter as the tent above them burned. Three union leaders who surrendered to the troops were summarily shot.

12. Darrow testimony, Commission on Industrial Relations, May 17 and 18, 1915. He wrote Mary Field: "Had a fine time telling the Commission about everything on earth."

13. Darrow, "The War in Europe," lecture before Society of Rationalism, Oct. 1914; Darrow had the speech printed as a pamphlet and gave versions of it several times in the months ahead, in Chicago and elsewhere. Darrow to Mary, July 4, 1913, CDMFP-NL.

14. Darrow to Wood, Jan. 4, 1914, Darrow to Mary, Oct. 31, 1913, Nov. 14, 1914, CDMFP-NL; Darrow to Gerson, June 29, 1915, Perceval Gerson papers, UCLA; Karl Darrow diary, KD; Schretter, "I Remember Darrow"; Ben Hecht, "Schopenhauer's Son" in *A Thousand and One Afternoons in Chicago* (Chicago: Covici-McGee, 1922); Yarros, *My Eleven Years*; Darrow, "Eulogy for John Howard Moore," CDMFP-NL; Darrow pamphlet, *Remarks of Clarence Darrow at Memorial Services to George Burman Foster and at the Funeral of John P. Altgeld* (Chicago: J. F. Higgins, 1919).

15. Erickson went on to serve ably in World War I and died in 1919, at the age of thirty-seven, of heart disease. George W. Hilton's painstaking study *Eastland: Legacy of the Titanic* (Stanford, CA: Stanford University Press, 1995), which includes commentary from several marine experts, shows the flaws in Darrow's theory, yet absolves Erickson of wrongdoing. See also F. W. Willard to Doubleday, Nov. 10, 1941, with attachment, Stone papers, Berkeley. The case is not mentioned in Darrow's autobiography. Stone's account, provided by Paul Darrow, is unreliable, with an apocryphal courtroom confrontation before a nonexistent jury. The trial was, technically, a proceeding before Judge Sessions to determine if the accused should be removed to face charges in Illinois. *Chicago Tribune*, July 25–Aug. 12, Sept. 22, 23, 24, 1915, Jan. 21–Feb. 19, 1916, July 21, 1935; *New York Times*, July 25–Aug. 12, 1915, Jan. 23, Feb. 19, 1916; *Kansas City Star*, May 17, 1925.

16. In 1917, Darrow wrote to Daniel Kiefer, an old friend who had criticized him for abandoning the Christian ideals of *Resist Not Evil*. "I did write a book advocating non-

resistance. Most of the things I said in that book I still believe. I hated war then and I do today," Darrow wrote. "My error then, as I see it now, was the belief that you could make a general rule of life that could cover every case." Darrow to Mary, Apr. 27, 1915, CDMFP-NL.

17. Darrow to Paul, Feb. 7, 1917, CD-UML.

18. *Chicago Tribune*, Aug. 25, Sept. 2, 6, 8, 11, Oct. 22, 23, Nov. 2, 18, 1917, Mar. 24, July 15, 1918; *New York Times*, Sept. 16, 1917; National Security League pamphlet, "Address by Clarence Darrow," Nov. 1, 1917; Darrow to Paul, Sept. 29, 1917, Hamlin Garland to Darrow, Dec. 21, 1917, CD-UML.

19. Johannsen to Sara, June 16, 1917, Wright to Wood, Feb. 8, 1921, Mary to Sara, undated, CESW-HL; Gerson to Darrow, Jan. 17, 1918, Perceval Gerson papers, UCLA; Darrow to Paul, July 17, 1918, Darrow to Jessie, July 20, 1918, CD-UML; *Chicago Daily Journal*, Oct. 21, 23, 25, 28, Nov. 4, 6, 8, 1918. The long excerpt is from an unattributed manuscript in the Mary Field Parton papers, which was identified by Margaret Parton as being Darrow's work. It mirrors the travels and observations Darrow relates in his censored newspaper reports and appears to be his writing but, like the "Miss S" letter, has an unverified provenance.

CHAPTER 15: RED SCARE

1. Many of Darrow's friends were also put under surveillance, including Lincoln Steffens, Anton Johannsen, Helen Todd, Mary and Lem Parton, former senator Richard Pettigrew, and architect Frank Lloyd Wright. On Darrow, see General and Special Staff, Military Intelligence Division report, May 7, 1920, Military Intelligence Division, U.S. War Department, National Archives. For other Wilson administration reports on Darrow, see documents dated Dec. 12, 1918, and May 26, 1919, U.S. Department of Justice records, National Archives; Darrow to Mary, Feb. 13, 1922, CDMFP-NL. David Kennedy, *Over There: The First World War and American Society* (New York: Oxford University Press, 2004).

2. Roger Baldwin statement, Mar. 18, 1960, ACLU; *Hearings Before the Special Committee Appointed Under the Authority of House Resolution No. 6 Concerning the Right of Victor L. Berger to Be Sworn as a Member of the 66th Congress* (Washington, D.C.: GPO, 1919); Ralph Izard memo, Jan. 8, 1918, from Federal Bureau of Investigation to Department of Justice, U.S. Department of Justice records, National Archives; *Chicago Tribune*, June 23, 1917; *New York Times*, July 7, 1917, Oct. 19, 1917; Kenneth Ackerman, *Young J. Edgar* (Cambridge, MA: Da Capo Press, 2007).

3. Debs would stay in jail until a new president—Republican Warren Harding—released him. He had turned down Darrow's offer to represent him at his original trial. Wilson to Darrow, Aug. 9, 1917, Palmer to Wilson, July 30 and Aug. 12, 1919, Darrow to Wilson, July 29, 1919, Wilson to Palmer, Aug. 1, 1919, Kent to Wilson, May 20, 1918, and Aug. 11, 1917, Woodrow Wilson papers, Library of Congress; Darrow to Mary, Jan. 29, 1918, CDMFP-NL.

4. Darrow to Wood, Aug. 26, 1919, CESW-HL.

5. Frank Lloyd Wright was almost as blunt. "The animosity of this false 'morality' has shocked and sickened me," he said, and he lashed out at a society which "meddles in

matters that can only be shown right or wrong by the hearts and consciences of those to whom they are sacred." Sara to Wood, Nov. 7, 1915, CESW-HL; Hecht, *Gaily Gaily*; *Chicago Tribune*, Nov. 5, 6, 7, 14, 1915, Feb. 29, May 16, July 7, 1916, Apr. 17, 21, May 3, 1918, Dec. 23, 1919; *Chicago Daily News*, Nov. 5, 6, 1915.

6. Masters also scorched Darrow in the poem "Louis Raguse," in a follow-up volume of Spoon River poems in 1924: "His ethical skin was thick / From handling and reaching for fees . . ." Masters, unpublished chapters of *Across Spoon River*, Reedy to Masters, Feb. 23, 1916, Masters to Tietjens, July 11, 26, 1921, Masters to Harrison, Mar. 21, 1938, ELM.

7. Masters, unpublished chapters of *Across Spoon River*, Reedy to Masters, Feb. 23, 1916, Masters to Darrow, Nov. 8, 1919, Darrow to Masters, Nov. 10, 1919, Masters to Tietjens, July 11, 26, 1921, Masters to Harrison, Mar. 21, 1938, ELM ; *New York Times*, Mar. 22, 1923; *Chicago Tribune*, Mar. 22, Apr. 15, July 15, Sept. 6, 1922, Apr. 14, Aug. 19, 1923. Literary critic Carl Van Doren thought that Masters owed an unacknowledged debt to Darrow's novel, *Farmington*. He ranked Darrow with Mark Twain and William Dean Howells as a pioneering critic of rural American life, and Masters as a follower. "Clarence Darrow in his elegiac *Farmington* had insisted that one village at least had been the seat of as much restless longing as of simple bliss," Van Doren wrote. "*Spoon River Anthology* in its different dialect did little more than to confirm these mordant, neglected testimonies."

8. Lem Parton to Wood, Apr. 29, 1918, Ehrgott to Sara, Nov. 21, 1918, and Dec. 6, 1918, Darrow to Sara, Nov. 16, 1918, CESW-HL; Darrow to Mary, Jan. 29, 1918, CDMFP-NL.

9. Darrow, "War Prisoners" speech, Nov. 9, 1919, CD-LOC; Paul Johnson, *Modern Times* (New York: Harper & Row, 1983).

10. *Bianchi v. State*, 169 Wis. 75; *New York Times*, Sept. 10, Nov. 25, 26,1917; *Washington Post*, Nov. 25, 1917; *Chicago Tribune*, Sept. 10, 1917.

11. The first neighbor to arrive was Franklin Roosevelt, the assistant secretary of the navy, who lived across the street with his wife, Eleanor, and five children. He had to step through splotches of blood and fragments of a body to get to the door. Ackerman, *Young J. Edgar.*

12. Ackerman, *Young J. Edgar*; Darrow to Cochran, Jan. 1, 1920, Negley Cochran papers, Toledo Public Library; Darrow to Mary, Thanksgiving Day, 1920, CDMFP-NL.

13. *People v. Gitlow* excerpts in *Gitlow v. New York*, 268 U.S. 652, 1925, New York Public Library; Arturo Giovannitti, "Communism on Trial," *Liberator*, Mar. 1920; Harold Josephson, "Political Justice during the Red Scare: The Trial of Benjamin Gitlow" in *American Political Trials*, ed. Michael Belknap (Westport, CT: Greenwood Press, 1994); Gitlow and Darrow, *The Red Ruby Address to the Jury* (New York: Communist Labor Party pamphlet, circa 1920); Benjamin Gitlow, *I Confess* (New York: E. P. Dutton, 1940); *New York Times*, Nov. 11, 15, 29, 1919, Jan. 22, 31, Feb. 4, 5, 6, 12, 1920; Darrow to Mary, Feb. 13, 1920, CDMFP-NL.

14. Liberals scored a major victory in the Gitlow case. The ACLU lawyers who handled the appeal took Darrow's argument on the constitutionality of the New York law to the U.S. Supreme Court, and though the court did not reverse Gitlow's conviction, the justices ruled, for the first time, that the First Amendment extended to the states.

15. Parson would write a novel about her experience, *The Trial of Helen McLeod*, in which Darrow appeared as a hero. *Rockford Daily Register-Gazette*, Jan. 2, 1920–Apr. 26, 1920.

16. *Address of Clarence Darrow in the Trial of Arthur Person* (Rockford, IL: Communist Labor Party of Illinois pamphlet, 1920); Apr. 24, 1920, CD-LOC; *Chicago Tribune*, Apr. 21, 22, 23, 25, 1920; *Chicago Daily News*, Jan. 8, 1920; Alice Beal Parson, *The Trial of Helen McLeod* (New York: Funk & Wagnalls, 1938); Parson to Stone, Oct. 4, 1939, Irving Stone papers, University of California, Berkeley; *Rockford Daily Register-Gazette*, Jan. 2, 1920–Apr. 26, 1920.

17. Lloyd was once arrested when cruising down State Street in his chauffeur-driven limousine decorated with the Red and American flags, offering free rides to those who would join the socialists.

18. Clarence Darrow, *Argument of Clarence Darrow in the Case of the Communist Labor Party* (Chicago: C. H. Kerr, 1920); *People v. William Bross Lloyd*, New York Public Library; *Chicago Tribune*, Oct. 26, Dec. 28, 1917, Feb. 22, 1919, Jan. 7, 16, 22, 27, Feb. 16, May 10, July 14, 24, 28, 29, 30, 31, Aug. 1, 3, 1920; *Chicago Daily News*, Jan. 6, 1919, Feb. 25, May 10, 1920; *New York Times*, Jan. 22, May 11, July 14, 1920; H. Austin Simons, "Guilty," *Liberator*, Aug. 1920.

19. Ackerman, *Young J. Edgar*; Johannsen to Wood, Mar. 10, 1919, CESW-HL.

CHAPTER 16: ALL THAT JAZZ

1. Illinois Association for Criminal Justice, "Tennes as a Vice Chief" in *The Illinois Crime Survey* (Chicago: Illinois Association for Criminal Justice, 1929); Darrow to Mary, Feb. 1, 1923, CDMFP-NL; Yarros, 192, *Independent*, vol. 119, Weekly Review 7.

2. If a judge "doesn't watch him in the early stages of a lawsuit," said Landis, "Darrow will ask some innocent question and get an answer in the record that will support some otherwise insupportable trick that he's going to pull on you later." Stanley F. Horn, oral history, Forest History Society, Santa Cruz, California, 1978; *Chicago Tribune*, Sept. 27, 1907, Aug. 27, 1911, Oct. 2, 3, 4, 5, 1916, Jan. 25, 1953; Masters to Harrison, Mar. 21, 1938, ELM.

3. *Chicago Tribune*, Nov. 28, 1914, Feb. 28, June 14, 1916, Jan. 18, 19, 20, 22, 24, June 1, 2, 5, 6, 8, 9, 10, 1917, Nov. 8, 1928; *New York Times*, Aug. 3, 1919; Robert Lombardo, "The Black Mafia: African-American organized crime in Chicago 1890-1960," *Crime, Law & Social Change* 38 (2002): 33–65.

4. For the cigar story see *New York Times*, Apr. 28, 1957. Darrow to Paul, Aug. 18, 1918, CD-UML; Darrow to Mary, Jan. 29, 1918, CDMFP-NL; *Chicago Tribune*, Oct. 15, 18, 24, 1916, Sept. 13, Oct. 15, 19, 21, 27, Nov. 13, 18, 22, Dec. 2, 3, 8, 24, 27, 1917, Jan. 1, 11, 13, 1918, May 17, 1922, Jan. 16, 19, 23, 27, 29, 1923; Ben Hecht, *A Child of the Century* (New York: Simon & Schuster, 1954); Charles Erbstein, *The Show-up: Stories Before the Bar* (Chicago: Covici, 1926).

5. According to Erbstein, at one point in the Healey trial, to relieve the tedium while the lawyers argued points of law, the judge gave the jurors a phonograph. One of Healey's codefendants, the mischievous Bill Skidmore, plunged the trial into chaos with a rumor that a record store owner had been "reached" and the jury was listening to the popular song "Please Don't Send My Darling Boy Away." On another occasion, says Erbstein,

the courtroom water cooler was filled with alcohol, and all the participants glowed with loquacious goodwill. See Erbstein, *The Show-up*.

6. Darrow to Paul, Oct. 10 and Dec. 9, 1917, June 28, 1920, CD-UML; Sissman interview with Stone, CD-LOC; Darrow to Mary, Nov. 16, 1921, CDMFP-NL.

7. The Kid outlived them all, and died at the age of one hundred in 1976, after a career during which, by his estimation, he made and spent $10 million. In one classic con, Weil told his victim that he had devised a way to tap the racing wire and delay the results just long enough to get a bet down on the winner. To seal the deal, the Kid escorted his prey to a phony betting parlor, built and manned by a coterie of con men. There, the victim "won" a $20 bet and became convinced that Weil was telling the truth. The next day, the mark returned with $12,000 and was told to place it on a chosen horse. He bet the horse to win and when it came in second demanded to know why. You didn't listen, Weil said—the bet was to place, not win. They agreed to try again the next day, but when the mark went looking for the Kid—and the betting parlor—they both had vanished. Weil's antics, and those of his colleagues, inspired the motion picture *The Sting*. Henry R. Chamberlin, "50-50, Fighting Chicago's Crime Trusts," 1916, CD-UML; J. R. Weil, with W. T. Brannon, *Con Man: A Master Swindler's Own Story* (Broadway Books, 2004); *Chicago Tribune*, Oct. 30, Nov. 21, Dec. 27, 1917, Jan. 19, Oct. 25, 26, Nov. 26, 28, Dec. 1, 1918, Feb. 8, 1924, Dec. 12, 1948, Feb. 27, 1976.

8. "Where did you get that stuff about my losing Simpson case?" Darrow asked Paul. "I won it," he boasted, and accurately predicted that Simpson would be freed from the asylum before long. Darrow to Paul, Oct. 4, 1919, CD-UML; Ruby letters and Sissman interviews with Stone, CD-LOC; *Chicago Tribune*, Dec. 20, 1920, Apr. 26, 27, May 19, Sept. 2, 9, 19, 20, 21, 23, 24, 25, 26, Oct. 3, Nov. 22, 24, 1919; July 15, 1921, Sept. 30. 1924, Feb. 27, 1925, Apr. 10, 11, 15, 16, 17, 18, 20, 1925; *New York Times*, July 2, Aug. 21, 1920, Apr. 9, 1925; *Chicago Herald Examiner*, Apr. 9, 1925; *Chicago Daily News*, Apr. 10, 1925; *Bloomington Sunday Bulletin*, Apr. 19, 1925. The McCormick divorce alone brought the firm $25,000, Sissman told Stone.

9. Darrow to Mary, June 10, 1921, CDMFP-NL; *New York Times*, Oct. 8, 1923; *Boston Globe*, Oct. 8, 1923; *Chicago Tribune*, Nov. 23, 25, 1917, Jan. 22, 1918, Feb. 17, 18, 20, June 12, 14, 1919, Apr. 13, Sept. 15, 1920, Jan. 25, Feb. 24, 1921, June 22, 1922, Oct. 8, 9, 11, 1923, Mar. 12, 1924, Mar. 6, July 10, 1927, Mar. 7, 1939; Florence Stauffer, "Darrow for the Defense," *Warsaw Times-Union*, Nov. 13, 1975.

10. Transcript of remarks at Darrow's sixty-first birthday dinner, CD-LOC.

11. *Chicago Daily News*, Feb. 4, 5, 6, 7, 9, 10, 11, 12, 16, May 6, 7, 8, 11, 13, 14, 18, 19, 20, 1920; *Chicago Tribune*, Feb. 11, 13, 16, Mar. 5, Apr. 2, May 11, 12, 22, 26, July 28, 31, 1920, June 14, 1921, Sept. 13, 1922, Feb. 16, 19, 26, 1923, June 27, 1928, Mar. 10, June 9, 1929, Nov. 13, 19, 1960.

12. Heitler was a whoremonger who was put to work by Al Capone and ended up murdered, his corpse incinerated, when he crossed the Outfit. *Chicago Tribune*, Oct. 6, 9, 27, Nov. 13, 1920, Feb. 16, 19, 25, Mar. 4, 6, 9, May 18, 1921, Apr. 27, Nov. 15, 17, 27, Dec. 2, 1923, Oct. 11, 1924; *San Juan Prospector*, May 9, 1914.

13. Darrow's support for the rumrunners fit with popular sentiment in Chicago. At one political banquet he lauded the anti-Prohibition stand of Anton Cermak, the president of

the Cook County board of commissioners, and could not finish his speech because, after stating, "I thank God bootleggers exist," he was drowned out by the audience, who stood on their chairs and cheered. *Chicago Tribune*, July 22, Aug. 24, Sept. 6, 7, 10, 1923, Jan. 13, 14, 18, 20, June 7, 1925, May 31, 1929.

14. Looney's story inspired a graphic novel, and a motion picture, *The Road to Perdition*. *Dispatch/Argus*, June 17, 1971, July 13, 2002; *Quad City Times*, July 2002; "John Looney Legend Tour," Rock Island Preservation Commission, 2008; *Chicago Tribune*, Feb. 23, 1909, Mar. 27, 1912, Oct. 7, 8, 11, 26, 27, 1922, Sept. 15, 1923, Nov. 13, 20, 29, 1924; *Los Angeles Times*, Oct. 26, 1912, Oct. 7, 1922, Nov. 14, 26, 1924; *New York Times*, Mar. 24, 1908, Mar. 28, 29, 1912.

15. Ruby Darrow note, June 21, 1920, CD-LOC; Ruby to Gerson, Jan. 21, 1922, Perceval Gerson papers, UCLA; Darrow to Older, Mar. 22, 1922, ALW; Darrow to Paul, June 28, 1920, July 19, 1921, CD-UML; Darrow to Mary, Nov. 16, 1921, June 17, 1922, Sept. 8, 1922, Feb. 1, 1923, Feb. 19, 1925, Aug. 25, 1928, CDMFP-NL; George Nathan, *The Intimate Notebooks of George Jean Nathan* (New York: Knopf, 1932); *Chicago Tribune*, Oct. 31, 1922, Dec. 6, 1922; Darrow, "The Ordeal of Prohibition," *American Mercury*, Aug. 1924.

16. *New York Times*, Jan. 30, 1923; *Chicago Tribune*, Jan. 30, Mar. 4, 1923, Apr. 11, 23, June 5, 9, 12, 13, 20, 30, July 11, 12, 13, 14, 1923; Darrow to Paul, July 19, 1921, and spring 1924, CD-UML; Darrow to Mary, Feb. 1, 1923, CDMFP-NL.

17. Thompson would return to office in 1927, but by then he and Lundin had fallen out. In one of the great stunts of Chicago politics, Thompson appeared on stage at a campaign rally with a caged rat he called "Fred." Wasn't it true, Thompson asked the rat, that it took Clarence Darrow and an all-star defense team to save him from the penitentiary? Hadn't he himself traveled all the way back from Honolulu to testify? "Wasn't I the best friend you ever had?"

The state and Darrow dueled on one more corruption case, in early 1924, when Thompson appointee Michael Faherty, who chaired the Board of Local Improvements, was charged with making an overpayment of $28,000 to a favored contractor. It was a simple case, and the jury settled it quickly, in Faherty's favor. The $28,000 overage was a legitimate bonus to spur the contractors to finish the job faster, Darrow had told the jurors.

CHAPTER 17: LOEB AND LEOPOLD

1. The press has promiscuously conferred the accolade. The McNamara, Haywood, and Scopes cases were all called crimes or trials of the century, as was the 1906 murder of architect Stanford White by millionaire Harry Thaw and a dozen sensational cases that followed, including the kidnapping of the Lindbergh baby, the Rosenberg spy case, the O. J. Simpson murder trial, etc. "In Re Nathan Leopold, Junior," psychiatric report of Dr. Karl M. Bowman and Dr. Charles Hulbert, 1925, Elmer Gertz papers, Library of Congress; report of Dr. James Whitney Hall, *Chicago Herald Examiner*, June 5, Aug. 11, 1924; *Erie Dispatch*, Mar. 10, 1926; *Life* editorial quoted in the *Literary Digest*, July 5, 1924; Paula Fass, "Making and Remaking an Event: The Leopold and Loeb Case in American Culture," *Journal of American History*, Dec. 1993. The public perception was that the victim and killers were all Jewish boys from the same community. Loeb's mother

was from a Catholic family, but he had been raised as a reform Jew, like Leopold. The Frankses were Jews who had left the faith and become Christian Scientists.

2. Trial transcript, *Illinois v. Nathan Leopold and Richard Loeb*, Elmer Gertz papers, Library of Congress; *Chicago Daily News*, May 31, June 2, 1924; *Chicago Tribune*, June 2, 1924.

3. *New York Times*, June 2, 1924. See undated letter, Ruby Darrow to Stone, CD-LOC. Ruby did not catch all their names. Accompanying Jacob Loeb were, probably, attorney Benjamin Bachrach and Nathan's brother Michael Leopold and maybe Nathan Leopold Sr., who was with the others for much of that weekend as they tried to organize a defense. Based on the overheated account from Ruby, who described the event in the third person ("Twas as quiet as the night before Christmas, when all through the house not a creature was stirring, not even a mouse—when suddenly out of a sound sleep the Darrows were startled by a frightening ringing of their front-door bell like a place afire or some other catastrophe"), Irving Stone re-created a scene, and dialogue, in which Loeb throws his arms around Darrow, begging him to "Save their lives! Get them a life sentence" and promising, "Money's no object. We'll pay you anything you ask." Stone and others place the nocturnal visit on June 2, but it was clearly June 1.

4. Darrow to Paul, June 25, 1924, CD-UML.

5. Darrow to Jessie, June 10, 1924, CD-UML. Years later, Darrow told a friend how, in one meeting with Leopold and Loeb, they had asked him if he could smuggle poison into the jail so that they might cheat the hangman. "I could," he told them, "but it's a little out of my line." George Whitehead interview with Stone, CD-LOC.

6. *Chicago Daily News*, June 11, 1924; *Chicago Herald Examiner*, July 23, 1924; *Chicago Tribune*, Dec. 23, 1903; Leopold, *Life Plus Ninety-nine Years*; Darrow, *Story of My Life*; Ruby letters to Stone, CD-LOC; *Illinois Crime Survey*; Leopold notes from "Compulsion" case, Elmer Gertz papers, Library of Congress; Leslie Fiedler, *The Collected Essays of Leslie Fiedler* (New York: Stein and Day, 1971); Harrison, *Growing Up*. Darrow told author John W. Gunn in 1925 that he had favored giving the case to Caverly because the judge was Catholic, according to a letter that Gunn's brother Harold wrote to Paul Douglas, Feb. 20, 1971.

7. Transcript, *Illinois v. Nathan Leopold and Richard Loeb*; *Chicago Daily News*, June 13, July 21, 22, 1924; *Chicago Tribune*, June 7, 13, July 22, 1924; *New York Times*, June 7, July 22, 1924; *Chicago Herald Examiner*, July 11, 12, 14, 15, 17, 18, 22, 1925; *Chicago Daily News*, June 4, 7, 1924.

8. Darrow to Paul, July 20 and Aug. 3, 1924, CD-UML.

9. Mary Field Parton diary and Lem to Mary, early summer 1924, MFP; Ruby Darrow letter to Stone, CD-LOC.

10. Transcript, *Illinois v. Nathan Leopold and Richard Loeb*; Yarros, *My Eleven Years*; *Chicago Daily News*, July 23, 24, 25, 1924; *Chicago Tribune*, July 24, 25, 27, 1924; *New York Times*, July 27, 1924. To placate Leopold, Darrow briefly cross-examined one witness who said he saw Loeb driving the death car on the day of the murder. Though Loeb ultimately admitted that he was the one in the backseat who struck Franks with the chisel, at first the two defendants blamed each other for the fatal act. "It's unimportant.

It's immaterial," Darrow told Leopold, who replied, "It's important to me . . . because this is the point on which Dick's story and mine differ, and I insist that you cross-examine. If you won't, I'm going to ask Judge Caverly to permit me to cross-examine." See Leopold notes for *Life Plus Ninety-nine Years,* in Elmer Gertz papers, Library of Congress.

11. Transcript, *Illinois v. Nathan Leopold and Richard Loeb*; *Chicago Herald Examiner,* July 28, 29, 1924; *Chicago Tribune,* July 28, 1924; Bowman-Hulbert, White, Healy, and Glueck reports, Elmer Gertz papers, Library of Congress; Leopold, *Life Plus Ninety-nine Years*; Leopold deposition, Elmer Gertz papers, Library of Congress; *New York Times,* Sept. 7, 1924; Leopold testimony to Illinois parole board, 1958, quoted in Gertz, *A Handful of Clients* (Chicago: Follett, 1965). In keeping with his cracker-barrel persona in court, Darrow used "skizzyphratic" and other nonsense words for "schizophrenic."

12. Transcript, *Illinois v. Nathan Leopold and Richard Loeb*; *Chicago Tribune,* July 31, Aug. 1, 1924; *Chicago Herald Examiner,* July 31, 1924. Pethick was the twenty-two-year-old delivery boy who had murdered Ella Coppersmith and her two-year-old son in 1915, then sexually abused her body. His name was also spelled, in the press, official records, and medical journals, as "Pethrick."

13. Transcript, *Illinois v. Nathan Leopold and Richard Loeb*; Leopold, *Life Plus Ninety-nine Years*; *New Statesman* commentary, published in *Living Age,* Nov. 1, 1924; William White to Darrow, July 24, 1924, Ruby to White, undated, William White papers, National Archives; *New York Times,* Jan, 13, 2008. In light of recent research into the causes of psychopathy, it should also be noted that Loeb had suffered a serious head injury in an automobile accident at the age of fifteen. The talk about sex had its limits. When it came time to discuss the defendants' sexual practices, Judge Caverly told the compliant newspapermen of the era: "This should not be published." And prosecutor Crowe displayed his naïveté (or perhaps it was his calculation) when, after one witness testified that gay sex was a not-so-unusual practice, he asked the psychiatrist: "Aren't you ashamed of yourself, doctor, to testify in that manner?"

"No. I should say not," the psychiatrist replied. "I have known of very nice children of very nice families who have gotten through with things of that sort."

14. Transcript, *Illinois v. Nathan Leopold and Richard Loeb*; *Chicago Herald Examiner,* Aug. 23, 1924. The text of Darrow's closing address has been pieced together from the surviving court transcripts. The first day's transcript can be found at the University of Minnesota Law Library Web site; the second and third days' in the Elmer Gertz collection at the Library of Congress. In his published version of the address, Darrow adjusted the number of guilty pleas from 350 to 450.

15. Transcript, *Illinois v. Nathan Leopold and Richard Loeb*; Loeb to Darrow, "Friday nite," CD-LOC; *Chicago Tribune,* Aug. 23, 1924; *Chicago Herald Examiner,* Aug. 23, 1924; *Chicago Daily News,* Aug. 23, 1924; *New York Times,* Aug. 23, 1924.

16. Transcript, *Illinois v. Nathan Leopold and Richard Loeb*; *Chicago Tribune,* Aug. 26, 27, 28, 1924; *Chicago Daily News,* Aug. 26, 28, 1924.

17. Transcript, *Illinois v. Nathan Leopold and Richard Loeb*; *Chicago Tribune,* Aug. 28, 29, 1924; *Chicago Daily News,* Aug. 28, 1924; *Washington Post,* Aug. 29, 1924; *New York Times,* Aug. 29, 1924.

18. *Chicago Daily News*, Sept. 10, 1924; *Chicago Tribune*, Sept. 11, 12, 1924; *New York Times*, Oct. 4, 1924; *Los Angeles Times*, Sept. 11, 1924; unnamed Omaha newspaper clipping, Jan. 5, 1925, CD-LOC; *University Review*, summer 1938; Leopold to Darrow, Sept. 10 or 11 (undated), Loeb to Darrow, Apr. 15, 1926, and Darrow to Leopold, Sept. 20, 1924, CD-LOC. A month later, from the hospital bed where he was treated for exhaustion, Caverly explained his reasoning. It was obvious that Darrow's arguments had an impact. The defense had left it on him. They had no grounds for appeal and "burned their bridges behind them," the judge told a reporter. "Why, Clarence Darrow . . . said himself: 'If you say those two boys must die, they will die.' " Burdened by that responsibility, "I think I did right," Caverly said. "There has never been a minor hanged on a plea of guilty . . . If I had hanged them, I would have been a great big fellow. I would have been praised on all sides. It would have been the path of least resistance. But my conscience told me what to do."

19. Charles Yale Harrison, *Clarence Darrow* (New York: Jonathan Cape & Harrison Smith, 1931); Stone, *Clarence Darrow for the Defense*; Ruby letters to Irving Stone, CD-LOC; *Chicago Tribune*, Jan. 9, 1925. Ruby was sore, and her anti-Semitism flared. "That these two happened to be Jewish families proves nothing whatever against their race," she told Stone, who was Jewish. But the episode had, she said, "added to the hateful stigma upon Jews as sharp dealers and dishonest people." There was a sad footnote to the case. When claiming that the wealth of the killers' families was distorting justice, Crowe taunted Darrow and asked why no tears were being shed for Bernard Grant, nineteen, who had been sentenced to death, along with Walter Krauser, twenty-one, for killing a policeman during a grocery store holdup. Surely a "boy" from a poor family deserved the aid that Babe and Dickie were getting. So Darrow joined the effort to win clemency for Grant and agreed to speak on his behalf to Illinois governor Len Small. The governor granted a reprieve, and things looked hopeful, until the mentally disturbed Krauser stabbed Grant to death with a shiv in the Cook County jail.

CHAPTER 18: THE MONKEY TRIAL

1. Darwin had published *On the Origin of Species* in 1859; his treatise persuaded scientists that life evolved from a common ancestry through a process known as natural selection. In 1871, the British naturalist followed up with *The Descent of Man*, which explicitly contended that human beings were animals descended from "a hairy, tailed quadruped." Herbert Spencer, a contemporary of Darwin, applied evolutionary theory to social progress; it was he who coined the phrase "survival of the fittest," which laissez-faire capitalists used to justify their success. Bryan seemed willing to accept Darwin's theory as it applied to animals, and to credit the findings of geologists that contradicted the biblical account of "days" of Creation. The Bible could "mean periods of indefinite lineage instead of twenty-four hour days," he told an ally. What Bryan resolutely opposed was what Darwin had to say about man. If human beings were not divine creations, Bryan said, man lost all his nobler attributes and aspirations.

2. Benjamin Kidd, a British writer, connected Darwinism and Nietzsche's writings to German aggression. James Leuba, an American educator, persuaded Bryan that the growing secularism in American schools threatened the nation's Christian character. See Scopes trial transcript for the text of Bryan's "Proposed Address," the great clos-

ing speech he had hoped to give, but was denied the chance, a copy of which was added as a courtesy to the record. See also Bryan's speech, "Is the Bible True?" Jan. 24, 1924, Nashville, Tennessee.

3. Debs to Darrow, June 4, 1925, Eugene Debs collection, Indiana State University; *Chicago Tribune*, July 4, 5, 1923; Bryan, "Proposed Address"; Bryan to Howard Kelly, June 22, 1925, WJB; for Bryan at the 1924 convention see Michael Kazin, *A Godly Hero* (New York: Borzoi, 2006) and Louis W. Koenig, *Bryan: A Political Biography of William Jennings Bryan* (New York: Putnam's, 1971).

4. Kenneth K. Bailey, "The Enactment of Tennessee's Antievolution Law," *Journal of Southern History,* Nov. 1950; Bryan to Samuel Untermyer, June 11, 1925, WJB; George Hunter, *A Civic Biology* (New York: American Book Co., 1914).

5. Darrow's sentiments about Kinsman were mixed. "Once in a while I go back to Trumbull County, but most all the names I used to know are chiseled on gravestones, so I do not get much of a kick out of it," he wrote to a fellow Ohioan, James Kennedy. "The last time I was there, I intended to spend a week. I got into Kinsman on the morning train and in an hour or two, thought I would want to spend two or three days. Along toward noon, I found there was an afternoon train out . . . But somehow I have a feeling for the old place and may possibly go back again this summer." See Darrow to Kennedy, Mar. 21, 1925, Ohio Historical Society.

6. *Kinsman Journal*, Oct. 3, 1924; *Warren Chronicle*, Oct. 1, 1924.

7. Darrow straddled the choice between Democratic senator John W. Davis and Progressive senator Robert La Follette in the 1924 election. Either one would be better than Calvin Coolidge, he said. Both lost.

8. Mary Field Parton diary, MFP; Darrow to Mary, Feb. 19, 1925, CDMFP-NL.

9. *Chattanooga Times*, May 4, 6, 1925; *Memphis Press* and Sue Hicks telegrams, May 14, 1925, Sue Hicks papers, University of Tennessee. Sue Hicks was named in honor of his mother, who died in childbirth. He is said to have served as an inspiration for a country song by Johnny Cash. ACLU papers, Library of Congress; John T. Scopes, *Center of the Storm* (New York: Holt, Rinehart and Winston, 1967); L. Sprague de Camp, *The Great Monkey Trial* (New York: Doubleday, 1968); Edward J. Larson, *Summer for the Gods* (Cambridge: Harvard, 1998); Ray Ginger, *Six Days or Forever* (Boston: Beacon, 1958).

10. John T. Scopes, *Center of the Storm*; *New York Times,* July 9, 1925; *Washington Post*, July 8, 1925; *Chicago Tribune*, July 8, 9, 1925; manuscript of a biography of Bryan, by his daughter Grace, WJB.

11. Mary Field Parton oral history, MFP; *Baltimore Evening Sun*, July 14, 1925; Scopes, *Center of the Storm.*

12. *Chicago Tribune*, May 17, 1925.

13. *New York Times*, June 7, 9, 10, 1925; *Chicago Tribune*, June 9, 1925; *New York Post*, June 11, 1925; George S. Thomas to Scopes, June 26, 1925, WJB; Mencken to "Garrison," July 6, 1925, Mencken papers, Princeton University; Scopes, *Center of the Storm*; American Civil Liberties Union, Executive Committee minutes, May 11 and 25, June 1 and 8, 1925, Bailey to Lippmann, June 12, 1925, ACLU; Bryan to W. B. Marr, June 11,

1925, WJB; *Chattanooga Times*, July 9, 1925; Mary Field Parton diaries, MFP; Mary to Sara, June 4, 1925, CESW-HL.

14. Dayton's cultural amenities were "Agri-cultural!" it boasted, and its resistance to change was represented in the promotional brochure *Why Dayton of All Places?* by the motto "Consistency Indeed a Jewel." Ignoring the satire, Dayton likened itself to Gopher Prairie, the hidebound setting of Sinclair Lewis's *Main Street*. "This is America—a town of a few thousand, in a region of fruit and corn and dairies and little groves," the pamphlet said. "Come on. Come to Main Street. Show us. Make the town—well—make it artistic. It's mighty pretty . . . Probably the lumber yard isn't as scrumptious as all these Greek temples. But go to it! Make us change!"

15. Mencken to "Garrison," July 6, 1925, Mencken papers, Princeton University; Mencken to Sara Haardt, May 27, 1925, quoted in Marion Elizabeth Rodgers, *Mencken and Sara: A Life in Letters* (New York: McGraw-Hill, 1987); Mencken to Masters, May 25, 1925, ELM.

16. *Chicago Tribune*, July 12, 1925.

17. "Light vs. Darkness," *Time* magazine, May 25, 1925; *Chicago Tribune*, May 26, 27, 1925; Ira Hicks to Herbert Hicks, June 5, 1925, and Ira Hicks to Sue Hicks, undated, Sue Hicks papers, University of Tennessee.

18. William Jennings Bryan to W. B. Marr, June 15, 1925, CD-LOC; Bryan to W. B. Riley, J. Frank Norris, and George M. Price, all on June 7, 1925, Untermyer to Bryan, June 25, 1925, Alfred McCann to Bryan, June 30, 1925, WJB; Sue Hicks to Ira Hicks and to Reese Hicks, both June 8, 1925, Ira Hicks to Sue Hicks, undated, Sue Hicks to Bryan, June 12, 1925, Hicks to John Raulston, July 1, 1925, Sue Hicks papers, University of Tennessee. In a June 13 letter Sue Hicks objected to Bryan's recruiting of Samuel Untermyer because "we somewhat doubt the advisability of having a Jew in the case for the reason that they reject part of the Bible."

19. Scopes, *Center of the Storm*; Sue Hicks to Bryan and Haggard to Bryan, June 23, 1925, and Bryan to Hicks, June 25, 1925, WJB; Jack Lait column in *Knoxville Sentinel*, July 10, 1925. Larson notes that a newsman traveling with Colby, Scopes, and Darrow described the trial as a murder case, not a rape; see Larson, *Summer for the Gods*.

20. Masters to Mencken, May 23, 1925, and Mencken to Masters, May 27, 1925, ELM; see also Mary Field Parton to Sara Field Wood, July 1925, CESW-HL. "It seems to me a beautiful climax to Darrow's life that he should transcend the particular . . . and defend Knowledge . . . as if it were his client," Mary wrote Sara. "Darrow will not be able to save Knowledge from the mob in Dayton . . . But the seeds will blow from those isolated mountains all over the land."

21. Schretter, "I Remember Darrow," Marcet Haldeman-Julius, *Clarence Darrow's Two Great Trials* (Girard, KS: Haldeman-Julius Co., 1927); Ruby Darrow letter to Stone, CD-LOC; Ruby to Helen Darrow, 1940, KD; Mary Bryan, "Bulletin No. 2," July 20, 1925, WJB. Bryan's wife Mary wrote a series of "bulletins" for her children, which were incorporated into an unpublished biography of Bryan written by his daughter, which can be found, along with some of the original bulletins, in the Bryan papers at the Library of Congress.

22. *Baltimore Evening Sun*, July 9, 14, 1925; Mencken to Haardt, July 9, 1925 in *Mencken and Sara*; L. Sprague de Camp, *The Great Monkey Trial.*

23. W. E. B. Du Bois, "Scopes," in the *Crisis*, Sept. 1925.

24. Trial transcript, *The State of Tennessee v. Scopes.* The trial transcript was published as *The World's Greatest Court Trial* (Cincinnati: National Book Co., 1925) and has been reprinted through the years. It can now be found on the Internet as well. *New York Times*, July 10, 11, 1925; *Washington Post*, July 11, 1925; *Los Angeles Times*, July 11, 1925; *Chicago Tribune*, July 9, 10, 11, 1925; Mary Bryan bulletin, WJB.

25. *Baltimore Evening Sun*, July 13, 1925; Will Rogers column, *Washington Post*, July 13, 1925.

26. Transcript, *The State of Tennessee v. Scopes*; Mencken to Haardt, July 14, 1925, in Rogers, *Mencken and Sara.*

27. Transcript, *The State of Tennessee v. Scopes*; *Baltimore Evening Sun*, July 14, 1925; *Los Angeles Times*, July 15, 1925; *New York Times*, July 14, 1925; *Chicago Tribune*, July 14, 1925; Masters to Monroe, July 16, 1925, ELM.

28. Transcript, *The State of Tennessee v. Scopes*; Curtis to Darrow, July 27, 1925, and excerpts from memoir, Winterton Curtis papers, University of Missouri.

29. Transcript, *The State of Tennessee v. Scopes.* "I reckon likely we never did get around to that evolution lesson. But the kids were good sports and wouldn't squeal on me in court," Scopes told Charles Potter. See Potter, "Ten Years After the Monkey Show I'm Going Back to Dayton," *Liberty Magazine,* Sept. 28, 1935.

30. Transcript, *The State of Tennessee v. Scopes*; John Scopes, "Reflections: Forty Years After," in *D-Days at Dayton*, ed. Jerry Tompkins (Baton Rouge: Louisiana State University Press, 1965); Mary Bryan, Bulletin No. 2, WJB; McGeehan *Herald Tribune* story reprinted in the *Los Angeles Times*, July 17, 1925.

31. Transcript, *The State of Tennessee v. Scopes*; *Baltimore Evening Sun*, July 17, 27, 1925; L. Sprague de Camp, *The Great Monkey Trial.*

32. Transcript, *The State of Tennessee v. Scopes*; *Chattanooga Times*, July 16, 1925; McGeehan in *Los Angeles Times*, July 17, 1925; Fay-Cooper Cole, "50 Years Ago: A Witness at the Scopes Trial," *Scientific American*, Jan. 1959; *Chicago Tribune*, July 18, 1925; Mary Bryan, Bulletin No. 2, WJB.

33. Mencken to Haardt, July 19, 1925, in Rogers, *Mencken and Sara.*

34. Mencken was not run out of town. Well before the townfolk gathered, Mencken had told Sara Haardt that he planned to leave on Saturday. Mencken to Harry Rickel, July 19, 1925, Henry Mencken papers, Princeton University; *Baltimore Evening Sun*, July 18, 1925.

35. Potter, "Ten Years After"; Eli Ginzberg, *Keeper of the Law: Louis Ginzberg* (Philadelphia: Jewish Publication Society, 1966).

36. *Chicago Tribune*, July 18, 1925.

37. Transcript, *The State of Tennessee v. Scopes*; Mary Bryan, Bulletin No. 3, WJB; Scopes, *Center of the Storm.*

38. Transcript, *The State of Tennessee v. Scopes.* At this point in their exchange, both Darrow and Bryan confused Bishop Ussher's date of creation with his date of the Flood. Darrow later misstated the age of Chinese civilization, but Bryan's lack of knowledge of ancient history cost him an opportunity to correct his adversary.

39. Transcript, *The State of Tennessee v. Scopes*; Scopes, *Center of the Storm*; Hays, *City Lawyer*; Hays, "The Strategy of the Scopes Defense," *The Nation*, Aug. 5, 1925.

40. Transcript, *The State of Tennessee v. Scopes*; Hays, *City Lawyer.*

41. Darrow to Mencken, Aug. 5, 1925, Mencken papers, New York Public Library; *Chattanooga News*, July 21, 1925; *New York Times*, July 21, 1925; Mary Bryan, Bulletin No. 3, WJB. The face-saving reason for not giving Bryan his shot at Darrow, which Bryan's loved ones clung to in the difficult days ahead, was that Dayton officials could not guarantee security. A gun-toting fundamentalist in the courtyard crowd had his hand on his weapon and was prepared to shoot Darrow, the Bryans were told. "Thus it will be seen," wrote Bryan's daughter Grace, "that my father relinquished his right to cross-examine the attorneys for the defense to prevent any tragedy."

42. Transcript, *The State of Tennessee v. Scopes*; Herbert Hicks to Ira Hicks, July 22, 1925, Sue Hicks papers, University of Tennessee; Russell Owen, *Current History Magazine*, Sept. 1925; *New York Times,* July 22, 1925.

43. Ruby Darrow to Stone, CD-LOC; *The Nation*, Aug. 5, 1925. Some time later, Darrow learned that a newspaper editor he knew, wanting to honor the Bryan of 1896, was going to raise money for a memorial. "Sentimental poppycock," Darrow told him. "It's the Monkey Trial Bryan those damn bells will ring for. And you'll pull the ropes . . . You're the last man in the world who should perpetuate such bigotry, such religious fanaticism." It was left to the fundamentalists to honor Bryan—at the site of his great humiliation. There is a single statue on the lawn of the Rhea County courthouse—it is of William Jennings Bryan.

CHAPTER 19: SWEET

1. Russell Owen, "The Significance of the Scopes Trial," *Current History*, Sept. 1925; Lincoln Steffens, "Attorney for the Damned"; *Vanity Fair*, Mar. 1927. Darrow stalks American literature in many guises. Sinclair Lewis created the Darrow-like lawyer Seneca Doane in *Babbitt* and long worked on an unfinished "labor novel" with a Darrowesque hero. In *Native Son*, Richard Wright patterned attorney Boris Max on Darrow, whom the author called "the quintessence of all that was good and great in an America that is no more." See Hazel Rowley, *Richard Wright* (New York: Henry Holt, 2001) and Robert Butler, "The Loeb and Leopold Case: A Neglected Source for Richard Wright's Native Son," *African American Review*, winter 2005. Theodore Dreiser told Darrow he was constantly in his thoughts as he wrote the trial section of *An American Tragedy*. Maureen Watkins reported on the Leopold and Loeb case for the *Chicago Tribune*, and the killers make a cameo appearance as clients of lawyer Billy Flynn in her 1926 play *Chicago*. The reference is explicit in the stage directions of the 1976 musical version ("Billy gets ready for his courtroom 'scene'—pulling his shirt out, roughing up his hair, exposing some down-home suspenders—his 'Clarence Darrow' look") as he sings "Give 'em the

old Razzle Dazzle." And Darrow is obviously Jonathan Wilk in the novel and motion picture *Compulsion*, based on the Franks murder, and Henry Drummond in the play and motion picture *Inherit the Wind*, which immortalized the Monkey Trial.

2. Wood diary, July 16, 1925, CESW-HL; Masters to Mencken, July 21, 1925, ELM; Whitlock diary, Aug. 14, 1925, BW; see also Matt Schmidt to Fremont Older, Aug. 31, 1925, Fremont Older papers, University of California, Berkeley.

3. Transcript, *The People of Michigan v. Ossian Sweet et al.*, University of Michigan. The Sweets bought the house from Ed Smith, a black man passing as white, and his white wife. "Only their close friends . . . seem to know that the Smiths are colored," Walter White reported. *Detroit News*, Sept. 10, Nov. 18, 19, 20, 1925; *Chicago Defender*, July 18, 1925; NAACP correspondence, especially White to Johnson, Sept. 16, 1925, and letter, undated, from Gladys Sweet, NAACP.

4. Transcript, *The People of Michigan v. Ossian Sweet et al.*

5. Transcript, *People of Michigan v. Ossian Sweet*; *Detroit Free Press*, Sept. 10, Nov. 21, 1925; *Detroit News*, Sept. 10, Nov. 18, 21, 1925; "Address of Arthur Garfield Hays," Jan. 3, 1926, NAACP; *Detroit Times*, May 5, 1926; Robert Toms, Otis Sweet, and Charles Mahoney, oral histories, AB; William Tuttle, *Race Riot: Chicago in the Red Summer of 1919* (New York: Atheneum, 1970). For further details of Dr. Sweet's background see Weinberg, *A Man's Home* (New York: McCall, 1971); Phyllis Vine, *One Man's Castle* (New York: HarperCollins, 2004); Kevin Boyle, *Arc of Justice* (New York: Henry Holt, 2004).

6. Transcript, *People of Michigan v. Ossian Sweet*; *Detroit Evening Times*, Oct. 16, 1925; Walter White, "The Burning of Jim McIlherron: An NAACP Investigation," *Crisis*, May 1918, and "The Work of a Mob," *Crisis*, Sept. 1918. White's bravery as an investigator for the NAACP is chronicled in his autobiography, *A Man Called White* (New York: Viking, 1948) and in Kenneth Janken, *White* (New York: New Press, 2003). See also James Weldon Johnson, "Lynching: America's National Disgrace," in *Current History*, Jan. 1924, in which the NAACP executive placed the number of lynchings in the four decades around the turn of the century at four thousand, and the following reports in the *Crisis*: "The Waco Horror," July 1916; "The Burning at Dyersburg," Feb. 1918; "Memphis, May 22, A.D., 1917," July 1917; and the NAACP publication "An American Lynching: Being the Burning at Stake of Henry Lowry at Nodena, Arkansas, January 26, 1921, as Told in American Newspapers" (New York: NAACP, 1921). The Sweet brothers were well aware of what happened at such events. There were claims by some defendants that shots were fired from the crowd on Garland Avenue, but no proof was ever offered at the trials. See White, *A Man Called White,* p. 74: "Instead of stones and bricks banging against the house, bullets pierced it."

7. Transcript, *People of Michigan v. Ossian Sweet*; *Detroit Free Press*, Nov. 19, 1925; Gladys Sweet to White, Oct. 1925, NAACP.

8. White, *A Man Called White*; Kenneth Janken, *White*. White became a good friend of Darrow's and named a son Walter Carl Darrow White. Correspondence with Detroit branch and NAACP headquarters, NAACP.

9. Darrow helped relieve the NAACP of the cost of his expenses in Detroit by making speeches. NAACP correspondence, records, and minutes. See especially "Memorandum

of Expenses in Case of Dr. Ossian H. Sweet et al.," Bagnall to Young, July 21, 1925, White to Johnson, Sept. 16, 1925, Johnson to Darrow, Oct. 7, 1925, Du Bois to Darrow, Oct. 7, 1925, White to Midgley, Oct. 22, 1925, Darrow to White, Oct. 22, 1925, and White to Seligmann, Oct. 22, 1925, NAACP; *New York Herald Tribune*, Aug. 5, 1925; Robert Toms oral history, AB. The story of Darrow's meeting with NAACP officials is told in the memoirs of White and Hays.

10. *Detroit News*, Oct. 16, 1925; *Detroit Free Press*, Oct. 16, 1925; David Lilienthal, "Has the Negro the Right of Self-Defense?" *Nation*, Dec. 23, 1925; White to Johnson, Sept. 17, 1925, and Walker to White, Oct. 27, 1925, NAACP; Josephine Gomon, unpublished biography of Frank Murphy, Josephine Gomon papers, University of Michigan; Otis Sweet oral history, AB.

11. *Detroit News*, Oct. 31, Nov. 1, 1925; *Detroit Free Press*, Oct. 31, Nov. 5, 1925; *Detroit Evening Times*, Oct. 31, 1925; Baker to White, Oct. 21, 1925, and White to Johnson (dated "Saturday night"), Oct. 31, 1925, Baker to White, Feb. 20, 1926, NAACP; Marcet Haldeman-Julius, "Clarence Darrow's Defense of a Negro," *Haldeman-Julius Monthly*, July 1926; Gomon diary, JG; Toms oral history, AB; Hays, *Let Freedom Ring* (New York: Liveright, 1928).

12. White was tireless, wrangling press credentials, lunching with the judge, orchestrating the performance of the black spectators, and winning reporters to the Negro cause with his perceptive commentary and helpful favors.

13. Transcript, *People of Michigan v. Ossian Sweet*; *Detroit News*, Nov. 11, 1925; *New York World*, Nov. 6, 1925; *Chicago Tribune*, Nov. 8, 1925; *Detroit Evening Times*, Nov. 6, 7, 10, 1925; White to Johnson, Nov. 13, 1925, NAACP; Cecil Rowlette and Mahoney oral histories, AB.

14. White to Johnson, Nov. 15, 1925, NAACP; Toms oral history, AB.

15. Ruby Darrow to Stone, CD-LOC. Actress and writer Anita Loos, in town for a production of her *Gentlemen Prefer Blondes*, came to see Darrow, as did Jeanne Eagels, who was in Detroit performing a role she had made famous on Broadway, the free spirit Sadie Thompson, in the touring production of *Rain*. A very young actress, Ruth Wilcox, came by, and the somewhat notorious former Ziegfeld girl Peggy Joyce.

16. *Detroit Free Press*, Nov. 9, Nov. 16, Nov. 18, 1925; *New York Times*, Nov. 9, 1925; Reinhold Niebuhr, *Leaves from the Notebook of a Tamed Cynic* (Louisville: Knox, 1990); Boyle, *Arc of Justice*.

17. Gomon diary, JG; Gomon was a remarkable person. She helped found the National Planned Parenthood League, worked as executive secretary to Mayor Frank Murphy, was named director of the Detroit Housing Commission, and served as an adviser to Murphy, Franklin Roosevelt, Henry Ford, and Walter Reuther.

18. The size of the mob was always in dispute. Negro witnesses placed it at over a thousand, and even the most conservative estimates established that more than enough people had gathered to endanger the Sweets. On the day after the shooting the *Detroit News*, relying on police and neighborhood sources, put its size at 150. Transcript, *People of Michigan v. Ossian Sweet*; *Detroit News*, Nov. 14, 16, 17, 1925; *Detroit Free Press*, Nov. 17, 18, 1925; Hays to NAACP, Oct. 19, 1925, White to Darrow, Oct. 20, 1925, and White to Hays, Oct. 21, 1925, NAACP.

19. Transcript, *People of Michigan v. Ossian Sweet*; *Detroit Free Press*, Nov. 19, 1925; *Detroit Evening Times*, Nov. 18, 19, 1925.

20. Transcript, *People of Michigan v. Ossian Sweet*; White to Johnson, Nov. 20, 1925, NAACP; Gomon diary, JG; Lilienthal, "Has the Negro the Right of Self-Defense?"

21. Transcript, *People of Michigan v. Ossian Sweet*; Gomon diary, JG; White to Johnson, Nov. 25, 1925, and press released dated Nov. 27, 1925, NAACP; *Detroit Free Press*, Nov. 25, 1925; Lilienthal, "Has the Negro the Right of Self-Defense?"; Toms oral history, AB.

22. *Detroit News*, Nov. 26, 27, 1925; *Detroit Evening Times*, Nov. 27, 1925; *Detroit Free Press*, Nov. 27, 28, 1925; Gomon diary, JG; NAACP press bulletin, Nov. 28, 1925, and White to Davis, Nov. 30, 1925, NAACP; Hays, *Let Freedom Ring*. The *Detroit Free Press* and others reported that the alternate charge the seven jurors favored was manslaughter; see oral history of Cecil Rowlette, AB.

23. White to Toms, Dec. 2, 1925, White to Davis, Nov. 30, 1925, Darrow to White, Dec. 3, 1925, Friedman to White, Dec. 4, 1925, and Hays to Johnson, Dec. 8, 1925, NAACP.

24. Mary Field Parton diary, MFP; *New York Herald Tribune*, Dec. 14, 1925; *New York World*, Dec. 14, 1925; *Amsterdam News*, Dec. 16, 1925; Darrow to White, Jan. 2, 1926, NAACP.

25. Gomon diary, JG.

26. White had thought about hiring Chawke in the fall but paled then, and now, at the lawyer's willingness to defend bootleggers and other reprobates. "Chawke has the reputation of getting any man free no matter how guilty," White reported to headquarters, "with none of the idealism of Darrow or Hays." But Darrow had no such qualms. "Can get Chawke. He is good and I think needed," he wired Hays.

27. Transcript, *People of Michigan v. Ossian Sweet*; Haldeman-Julius, "Clarence Darrow's Defense"; Asher to White, May 16, 1925, memorandum of meeting between Darrow, White, and Johnson on Feb. 2, 1926, NAACP; *Detroit Free Press*, Apr. 20, 21, 24, 25, 27, 28, May 1, 2, 6, 8, 1926; *Detroit News*, Apr. 21, 22, 27, 30, May 3, 5, 6, 7, 10, 1926; *Chicago Defender*, May 1, 8, 1926; Thomas Chawke and Mahoney oral history, AB.

28. Transcript, *People of Michigan v. Ossian Sweet*; Haldeman-Julius, "Clarence Darrow's Defense"; *Detroit Evening Times*, May 11, 1926; *Detroit Free Press*, May 12, 1926; James W. Johnson, "Detroit," *Crisis*, July 1926; Gomon diary, JG. The NAACP transcripts of the closing addresses are from the Burton Historical Library in Detroit, edited by Michigan law professor Bruce Frier and Patrick Hogan, available on University of Missouri professor Doug Linder's "Famous Trials" website http://www.law.umkc.edu/faculty/projects/ftrials/ftrials.htm.

29. *Detroit Free Press*, May 14, 1926; *Detroit Evening Times*, May 14, 1926; *Detroit News*, May 14, 1926; Gomon diary and unpublished chapter of Murphy biography, JG; Johnson, "Detroit"; Cash Asher, "Waiting for a Verdict with Clarence Darrow," *Crisis*, June/July 1937. The Asher account, written more than a decade later, contains errors.

30. "I dissent . . . from this legalization of racism," Murphy wrote in the Korematsu case. "Racial discrimination in any form and in any degree has no justifiable part whatever in our democratic way of life. It is unattractive in any setting, but it is utterly revolting among a free people who have embraced the principles set forth in the Constitution of the United

States. All residents of this nation are kin in some way by blood or culture to a foreign land. Yet they are primarily and necessarily a part of the new and distinct civilization of the United States. They must, accordingly, be treated at all times as the heirs of the American experiment, and as entitled to all the rights and freedoms guaranteed by the Constitution."

31. In 1943, racial tensions erupted in Detroit, and in the subsequent rioting thirty-four people died. In 1967, in one of the most destructive racial clashes in American history, another riot claimed the lives of forty-three people. The National Guard and U.S. Army were sent to restore order. Some two thousand buildings burned. Toms, Mahoney, Sweet oral histories, AB; Gomon diary, JG; White to Darrow, May 13, 1926, Darrow to Johnson, May 15, 1926, Johnson to Darrow, May 21, 1926, Darrow to Johnson, May 26, 1926, White, memorandum, Dec. 12, 1930, NAACP; *Detroit Free Press*, Mar. 21, 1960; Darrow to Sally Russell, 1926, "You are all right and dangerously lovable," quoted in Kevin Tierney, *Darrow: A Biography* (New York: Thomas Crowell, 1979).

32. For the posttrial fates of Ossian, Gladys, Iva, and Henry Sweet, see Boyle, *Arc of Justice*; Vine, *One Man's Castle*; Weinberg, *A Man's Home*.

CHAPTER 20: CRASHING

1. Rappelyea to Bailey, Aug. 7, 1925. "Now that the chuckling and giggling over the heckling of Bryan by Darrow has subsided, it is dawning upon the friends of evolution that science was rendered a wretched service by that exhibition," wrote Walter Lippmann, in the *New York World*. "The truth is that when Mr. Darrow in his anxiety to humiliate and ridicule Mr. Bryan resorted to sneering and scoffing at the Bible he convinced millions . . . that the contest at Dayton was for or against the Christian religion." *New York World*, July 28, 1925.

2. Bailey to Strong, Aug. 12, 1925, Bailey to Darrow, Sept. 2, 1925, Darrow to Bailey, Sept. 4, 1925, Hays to Nelles, Sept. 9, 1925, Nelles to Hays, Sept. 10, 1925, ACLU; Darrow argument before the Tennessee Supreme Court, transcript, CD-LOC.

3. Darrow to Whitlock, Nov. 28, 1926, BW; Ruby to Jennie Moore, Sept. 8, 1926, CD-UML; Ruby to Walter White, Sept. 7, 1926, NAACP; Mary diary, Dec. 9 and 10, 1926, MFP; Darrow to Mencken, Aug. 5, 1925, Henry Mencken papers, New York Public Library; Darrow to Oswald Garrison Villard, Oct. 2, 1925, Villard papers, Harvard University.

4. *New York Times*, Nov. 18, 1926, Jan. 16, 1927; Vanzetti to Donovan, Nov. 21 and Dec. 4, 1926, Jan. 1 and Mar. 21, 1927, Sacco and Vanzetti papers, Boston Public Library; Darrow to Older, June 30, 1927, Darrow to Steffens, Dec. 28, 1926, Lincoln Steffens papers, Columbia University; Older to Darrow, Dec. 23, 1926, ALW.

5. Darrow to Mary, July 15, 1927, CDMFP-NL; *Chicago Defender*, Aug. 6, 1927; W. H. Auden interview, *Paris Review*, no. 17, 1974.

6. Helen to Jennie, Aug. 24, 1927, KD.

7. Whitlock diary, Sept. 14 and 15, 1927, BW.

8. *Washington Post*, Dec. 9, 1927; *New York Times*, Dec. 9, 1927; *Chicago Tribune*, Dec. 8, 9, 1927; *Time*, Jan. 2, 27, 1928; Darrow debate with Stephen Wise, CD-CHI.

9. Mary Field diary, Nov. 4, 12, 1927, MFP.

10. *New York Sun*, Dec. 12, 23, 1927; *New York Times*, Nov. 12, Dec. 9, 10, 13, 14, 15, 16, 17, 20, 21, 22, 23, 24, 29, 1927, Feb. 20, 1928; *Atlanta Constitution*, July 1, 1928; Hays, *City Lawyer*; John Diggins, "The Italo-American Anti-Fascist Opposition," *Journal of American History*, Dec. 1967; *New York World*, Dec. 23, 24, 1927; *Brooklyn Eagle*, Dec. 18, 1927; *New York Telegram* Dec. 22, 1927; *New York Herald Tribune*, Dec. 26, 1927.

11. Darrow to Paul, June 5, 1927, CD-UML; *New York Times*, Dec. 29, 1927, Jan. 13, 1928, Mar. 13, 1929, July 25, 1942, Aug. 25, 1949; untitled Vermont newspaper clipping, Jan. 1928, CD-LOC.

12. Darrow also tried without success to smooth things over between Ossian Sweet and the NAACP as they bickered over the civil suit that was filed by Leon Breiner's widow. Walter White did not believe that the organization was obligated to defend Sweet in the litigation. But a defeat in the civil case "would discount the acquittal which we worked so hard to get," Darrow said. Besides, said Darrow, "I never like to leave a client in the lurch." They met with Sweet in Detroit. The doctor was haughty and seemed ungrateful. White concluded that Sweet was "a mental case, suffering from extreme ego and perfection complex," and even Darrow wondered "if Sweet is quite right." The case went to trial, and Sweet prevailed. See Darrow to White, Nov. 30, Dec. 3 and 18, 1930, White to Darrow, Feb. 3 and Dec. 12, 1930, and Sweet to Pickens, Dec. 20, 1930, NAACP. Darrow's ties to the organization remained strong. In 1930, he joined the NAACP, White, and other liberals to defeat the nomination of Judge John Parker to the Supreme Court seat vacated by Oliver Wendell Holmes, thus opening the way for Justice Benjamin Cardozo to take a seat on the court.

13. *New York Times*, May 13, 1928; Jonathan Kinser, "The Racketeer and the Reformer," graduate thesis, Youngstown State University, 2007.

14. "It has been my privilege at various times to introduce to Clarence young ladies whose loveliness has cost me on my part a pretty penny in silver desk frames," Nathan added. "And on every occasion, fifteen or so minutes after the prefatory amenities, the young lady has been discovered sitting as close to Clarence as two chairs would allow, and not only listening intently to every word he was saying but given every evidence . . . of being emotionally agitated to a very salubrious degree." Nathan, *Intimate Notebooks*. Ruby to Gerson, Sept. 25, 1928, Perceval Gerson papers, UCLA; Mary Field Parton diary, Apr. 4, Dec. 20, 1928, MFP; Darrow to Baldwin, May 19, 1929, ACLU; *New York Times*, Apr. 17, 18, 1929.

15. Darrow to Mary Darrow, July 7, 1929, CD-LOC; Curtis manuscript, Winterton Curtis papers, University of Missouri. For an account of Darrow's financial woes, see Darrow and Ruby to Paul, Sept. 23, 1916, Dec. 22, 1917, Jan. 8, 1918; on the sale of Greeley gas company in 1927 and 1928; on the stock market crash, Aug. 31, Sept. 27, Oct. 4, Oct. 29, 1929; and throughout the 1930s, CD-UML; also Darrow to White, Sept. 11, 1931, NAACP.

16. Whitlock diary, BW.

17. Darrow to White, Sept. 11, 1931, NAACP; Darrow to Mary, Oct. 1, 1930, CDMFP-NL; Mary Field Parton diary entries, Oct. 30, 1930, Jan. 18, 1931, MFP.

18. Jonathan Eig, in his book *Get Capone* (New York: Simon & Schuster, 2010), makes the case that Darrow's client White was the architect of the St. Valentine's Day Massacre.

Chicago Tribune, May 30, Sept. 22, Oct. 14, 16, 1926, July 17, Sept. 20, Oct. 1, 1930, Feb. 28, May 26, 1931; Rose Keefe, *The Man Who Got Away* (Nashville: Cumberland, 2005). Darrow to Stephenson, Nov. 2, 1928, and Darrow–Stephenson correspondence, CD-UML.

19. See 1931 correspondence between Walter White and Darrow, NAACP, especially White to Darrow, Apr. 10, Aug. 31, 1931, and White's reports to the NAACP board. See also White, "The Scottsboro Case," an Oct. 23, 1931, NAACP pamphlet; Dan T. Carter, *Scottsboro: A Tragedy of the American South* (Baton Rouge: Louisiana State University Press, 1969); Philip Dray, *At the Hands of Persons Unknown* (New York: Modern Library, 2002); *Chicago Tribune*, Apr. 10, 1933; *New York Times*, Dec. 28, 30, 1931, Jan. 190, 1932; Apr. 7, Jun. 23, 1933; *Pittsburgh Courier*, Jan. 23, 1932.

20. Darrow to Wood, Feb. 18, 1932, CESW-HL. The communists won new trials for the Scottsboro boys, and Samuel Leibowitz, a New York lawyer, agreed to represent the young men. Ruby Bates recanted her testimony, and Leibowitz raised serious questions about the absence of physical evidence—bruising, swelling, or sperm—that should have been present after a gang rape. When the jury still returned a guilty verdict, a most courageous Alabama jurist, Judge James Horton, tossed it out and ordered yet another trial. Years passed, trials were held, and the U.S. Supreme Court handed down two landmark rulings. But time and again, Alabama juries brought back guilty verdicts. After they had spent six years in jail, the state finally dropped charges against four of the young men. Others were eventually given parole or escaped. The last defendant did not leave jail until 1950.

21. Darrow had to explain his actions to Wood, Mary, and other friends, and to the liberal community in the essay "Scottsboro" in the *Crisis* of March 1932. See Darrow to Wood, Feb. 18, 1932, and Mary to Sara, Feb. 18, 1932, CESW-HL. On the showdown with the ILD, see Darrow to White, Dec. 31, 1931, March 10, 1932, and Roderick Beddow to White, Jan. 2, 1932, NAACP. Darrow's money woes are chronicled in Darrow to White, Sept. 11, 12, 1931, May 3, June 5, 1932, and White to Springarn, June 9, 1932, NAACP. Darrow paid the money back in $250 increments over the next two years. For accounts of the dispute between the communists and the NAACP see Hugh T. Murray, "The NAACP versus the Communist Party: The Scottsboro Rape Cases, 1931–1932," *Phylon*, vol. 28, 1967; Mark Solomon, *The Cry Was Unity: Communists and African Americans, 1917–1936* (Jackson: University Press of Mississippi, 1998); Hays, *Trial by Prejudice* (New York: Da Capo, 1970).

CHAPTER 21: CLOSING

1. Trial transcript, *Territory of Hawaii v. Grace Fortescue, et al.*, Hawaii State Archives; police statements and interviews, and Admiral Yates Stirling report to the secretary of the navy, Dec. 23, 1931, Victor Houston papers, Hawaii State Archives; Pinkerton report, " 'Ala Moana' Case," PP; Pinkerton interviews, Lawrence Judd papers, Hawaii State Archives; seaman Eddie Lord interview in Peter Van Slingerland, *Something Terrible Has Happened* (New York: Harper and Row, 1966).

2. Yates Stirling, *Sea Duty* (New York: G. P. Putnam's Sons, 1938); Admiral William Pratt, chief of naval operations, Dec. 21, 1931, Victor Houston papers, Hawaii State Archives; Pinkerton report, PP.

3. Transcript, *Territory of Hawaii v. Grace Fortescue, et al.*; see Thalia to Darrow, undated letter, Leo Cherne papers, Boston University; Alexander Robertson, "Memorandum: the Ala Moana Case," Houston papers; Pinkerton report, PP; Pinkerton interviews, Judd to secretary of the interior, Jan. 18, 1932, and Pinkerton to Judd, Oct. 3, 1922, Judd papers; Van Slingerland, *Something Terrible Has Happened*; David Stannard, *Honor Killing* (New York: Viking, 2005).

4. Transcript, *Territory of Hawaii v. Grace Fortescue, et al.*; Mills to Houston, Dec. 15, 1931, Houston papers; Judd to secretary of the interior, Jan. 18, 1932, Pinkerton to Judd, Oct. 3, 1932, Pinkerton interviews, Lawrence Judd papers; Pinkerton report, PP; *Honolulu Advertiser*, Jan. 9, 10, 1932; *New York Times*, Jan. 9–31, 1932; *Washington Star*, Jan. 10, 1932; Philip Kinsley *Chicago Tribune* story reprinted in *Honolulu Star-Bulletin*, Mar. 19, 1932; Dillingham to Warren, Jan. 29, 1932, Walter F. Dillingham papers, Bishop Museum, Hawaii.

5. *Time*, Apr. 18, 1932; NAACP to Adams, Jan. 15, 1932, NAACP; *Honolulu Advertiser*, Mar. 30, 1932.

6. Thalia liked Darrow and called him "Judge." She teased him about "that unstrained grape juice that made you sick." *New York Times*, Jan. 15, Feb. 25, 27, Mar. 2, 27, Apr. 2, 10, 1932; Dillingham to Louise, Jan. 19, 1932, Dillingham to Colby, Jan. 27, 1932, Dillingham to Warren, Jan. 29, Mar. 28, 1932, Walter F. Dillingham papers, Bishop Museum, Hawaii; Julien Ripley to Darrow, Mar. 3, 1932, Ripley to Darrow, memorandum on financial terms, and Leisure to Darrow with Ruby Darrow comments, Mar. 5, 1932, Leo Cherne papers, Boston University; Ruby to Darrow, Mar. 3, 1932, Leisure to Stone, Aug. 1, 1940, CD-LOC; Darrow to Barnes, Mar. 5, 12, 1932, ALW; *Chicago Bee*, Mar. 27, 1932; *Hawaii Hochi*, Mar. 29, 1932.

7. Darrow, "Conditions in the Hawaiian Islands," a talk on the Massie case to the Chicago Bar Association, June 4, 1932. Some of the newspapers counted Edward Goeas, a juror of Portuguese descent, as white, as I have. Others put him in the nonwhite category. Leisure to Stone, Aug. 1, 1940, CD-LOC.

8. Transcript, *Territory of Hawaii v. Grace Fortescue, et al.*; *New York Times*, Apr. 7, 1932; the account of the trial comes from the transcript, which has gaps, at the Hawaii State Archives and from newspaper coverage in the *Hawaii Hochi*, the *Honolulu Star-Bulletin*, the *Honolulu Advertiser*, *New York Times*, *Los Angeles Times*, and *Chicago Tribune*. Massie's account differed in minor ways from what Kelley alleged. According to Massie, Kahahawai sat on a chaise lounge, not a bed. Massie said he wore dark glasses as a disguise, but not a fake mustache.

9. Transcript, *Territory of Hawaii v. Grace Fortescue, et al.* Kelley never introduced the document as evidence, so we do not know what it contained. But Thalia later told Darrow that Tommie was cold, and physically abused her. If she informed Professor Kelly that Tommie was a cruel spouse, it would have confirmed for many in Hawaii the speculation that her injuries came at the hand of her husband. Van Slingerland, *Something Terrible Has Happened*; Kelly to Judd, Feb. 20, and Mar. 9, 1967, and Nov. 17, 1969, with Nov. 15, 1969, memo, Lawrence Judd papers, Hawaii State Archives.

10. Transcript, *Territory of Hawaii v. Grace Fortescue, et al.* Kelley had several rebuttal witnesses, including two psychiatrists from the mainland, who told the jury that Massie was surely sane at the time of the killing.

11. Transcript, *Territory of Hawaii v. Grace Fortescue, et al.* Darrow was grieving after hearing the news that his old friend Banks, the Chicago newspaperman, had been killed in a freak auto accident.

12. Dillingham's correspondence shows how Darrow cultivated the military and commercial leaders in Hawaii throughout the trial (see Dillingham to Lowell, May 6, 1932, "We met in the game room and the meeting lasted until midnight," Walter F. Dillingham papers, Bishop Museum, Hawaii). And the Dillingham, Houston, and Judd papers show how the initial outrage in Washington was tempered over time by the various strategic and commercial concerns. Van Slingerland says that President Hoover phoned Judd in Darrow's presence and ordered that the sentences be commuted. Judd's papers, however, contain his private and public notations insisting this never happened. Judd was in contact with Hoover's secretary of the interior, Ray Wilbur, throughout the drama, but the governor appears to have responded to congressional pressure, not White House interference. A copy of the Dillingham "Memorandum" is in the Lawrence Judd papers, Hawaii State Archives; *Los Angeles Times*, May 1, 1932; *Hawaii Hochi*, May 3, 1932; Judd memoir, Lawrence Judd papers, Hawaii State Archives; Leisure to Stone, Aug. 1, 1940, CD-LOC.

13. Wright to Darrow, May 7, 1932, BU; Darrow packed a three-day stay in San Francisco with errands and events on his way home. He gave three speeches in the Bay Area, visited with Fremont Older, saw J. B. McNamara at San Quentin, and traveled with Older to see William Randolph Hearst at San Simeon, presumably to ask for the publisher's help in winning McNamara his freedom. Older marveled at Darrow's drive and told a mutual friend that Darrow was physically frail, "flat broke through investments and . . . quite happy."

14. In addition to the comprehensive Pinkerton report, with its accompanying memos and transcripts of interviews, there are other investigative summaries in the Houston and Judd papers in the Hawaii State Archives, most of which raise doubts about Thalia's story. See Stirling's Dec. 23, 1931, report to the secretary of the navy; Professor Kelly's letter to Judd; Judd's May 17, 1932, report to the secretary of the interior; and the governor's discussions of why he refused to pardon the defendants (Judd to Caldwell, May 21, 1932, and Judd to secretary of the interior, May 19, 1932); a memorandum, "The Ala Moana Case," sent by Alexander Robertson, former chief justice of the Hawaii Supreme Court, to Representative Victor Houston; prosecutor Kelley's motion to nolle pros the original indictments; and an unpublished manuscript of Judd's memoir.

15. The letters of Tommie and Thalia to Darrow (BU), each maligning the other, are instructive. So are the records of Thalia's 1934 psychiatric examination by Dr. Walter White, contained in the St. Elizabeths Hospital file at the National Archives, and the naval personnel records for Tommie, in the military files at the archives. *Washington Post*, Oct. 15, 1933; *New York Times*, Feb. 24, 25, Apr. 7, 1934.

16. Darrow had recently cooperated with biographer Charles Harrison, whose book *Clarence Darrow* was published in 1931. Darrow, *Story of My Life*; Darrow to Barnes, Aug. 1, 1931, ALW; Perkins to Darrow, Oct. 10, Nov. 12, Dec. 10, 1931, internal Scribner's memorandum, Ruby to Scribner's, Dec. 1931, Scribner's archives, Princeton University.

17. *Time*, July 20, 1931; *New York Times*, Oct. 25, 30, 1931; Universal Pictures promotional copy, June 1932, CD-LOC; Nathan, *Intimate Notebooks*; *Chicago Tribune*, Apr. 24,

Oct. 20, Nov. 20, 21, 23, Dec. 5, 8, 14, 15, 17, 1932, Jan. 4, 6, 29, Feb. 8, 10, 19, Apr. 12, June 23, Dec. 5, 1933; *Chicago Herald Examiner*, Jan. 6, 1933; *People v. Varecha,* 353 Ill. 52; *Chicago American*, Apr. 11, 18, 1933; *Rockford Register-Republic*, Feb. 18, 1933; Darrow to Taylor, May 16, 1932 or 1933, John Livingston papers, University of Denver; McWilliams to Darrow, Nov. 10, 1935, Jan. 5, 1936, Dec. 27, 1936, and McWilliams, "Life History of Russell McWilliams," CD-LOC.

18. An administration review of the Darrow review board found much to agree with. Darrow speech, New York Academy of Medicine, Jan. 13, 1931; *Chicago Daily News*, Oct. 10, 1932; *Time*, Nov. 13, 1933; Masters to Roosevelt via Raymond Moley, May 21, 1934, Thompson to Roosevelt, June 13, 1934, Darrow to Roosevelt, Apr. 27, June 28, 1934, Darrow supplementary report, Franklin Delano Roosevelt Papers, FDR Library; Mencken to Masters, May 10, 24, June 9, 1934, ELM; Richburg to Darrow, May 29, 1934, M. H. McIntyre, on behalf of FDR, July 2, 1934, CD-LOC; Julian Street notes on conversation with Darrow, July 11, 1934, Julian Street papers, Princeton University; Ruby to J. B. McNamara, June 23, 1934, James and John McNamara papers, University of Cincinnati; Lowell Mason, "Darrow vs. Johnson," *North American Review*, Dec. 1934; *Washington Post*, June 10, 1934; *New York Times,* May 27, 1934; James MacGregor Burns, *Roosevelt: The Lion and the Fox* (New York: Harcourt, Brace, 1956), Hugh Johnson, *The Blue Eagle, from Egg to Earth* (New York: Doubleday, 1935); John Ohl, *Hugh S. Johnson and the New Deal* (DeKalb: Northern Illinois University Press, 1985).

19. Hays to Darrow, June 8, 1934, Ruby to Hays, June 16, 1934, Arthur Garfield Hays papers, Princeton University; *New York Times*, July 1, 2, 3, 4, Sept. 3, 1934; *Los Angeles Times*, July 3, 1934; *Washington Post,* July 3, 1934; "What I Think of Nazi Germany," symposium with Dr. Preston Bradley and Dr. Louis Mann at the Washington Boulevard Temple, Dec. 7, 1933, CD-LOC.

20. Julian Street, journal, July 11, 1934, Street papers, Princeton University; Helen to Jennie, July 18, 1934, KD; Mary Field diary, Jan. 18, 1934, MFP; ACLU to Darrow, July 25, 1934, Darrow to ACLU with Baldwin notation, July 30, 1934, ACLU.

21. Older to Lem Parton, Aug. 31, 1934, Fremont Older papers, University of California, Berkeley.

22. Ruby to J. B. McNamara, Oct. 1, Nov. 13, undated circa 1934 or 1935, James and John McNamara papers, University of Cincinnati.

23. Senate Finance Committee testimony, Mar. 20, 1935; *New York Times*, Mar. 21, 1935; *Chicago Tribune*, Mar. 21, 1935.

24. For church remarks see reprint of "Warren Ave. Congregational Church Sunday Evening Forum," Sept. 29, 1935, CD-LOC. Darrow said he was sad to get the news but that Loeb was probably "better off dead" (*New York Times*, Jan. 29, 1936), told an audience of University of Chicago students that Capone's conviction on tax charges was "a terribly wrong . . . outrageous deal" (*Time* magazine, Nov. 2, 1936), and told a United Press reporter that Bruno Hauptmann should get another trial because his conviction was "a farce" (*Rockford Morning Star*, March 29, 1936); *Chicago Daily News*, April 4, 1936; Paul Darrow to Fay Lewis, included in Lewis to Gerson, Feb. 2, 1938, Perceval Gerson papers, UCLA; Paul Darrow to Karl Darrow, Mar. 20, 1938, and Nov. 20, 1937, courtesy of William Lyon.

25. Lewis to Gerson, Feb. 2, 1938, Gerson papers; *Chicago Daily News*, March 5, 1938; *Akron Times Press*, Mar. 15, 1938. On Feb. 27, 1938, Mary Field Parton wrote to her sister Sara, "I have tragic word from Chicago; namely that Mr. Darrow has lost his mind, just walks up and down, up and down, mumbling and muttering. Paul, his son, writes that they have no hope of his recapturing his memory. Intimate friends are strangers. I personally think he has retreated from a world that was too inhuman and cruel for him to bear. Unlike you, he had no . . . refuge into which to escape: a world of beauty. He knew nothing of the solace of music. Science only confirmed his beliefs in the fixed pattern of homo-sapiens, his fundamental brutality, cruelty. Art was an unknown door. Nature alone comforted him. Of all the people I have met in a lifetime of meeting people I never knew a soul that shrank so before cruelty" (Mary to Sara, Feb. 27, 1938, CESW-HL). When she received word of his death, Mary wrote in her diary, "Good bye dear friend. We spoke the same language, the inarticulate language of the heart" (MFP). The Darrow obituaries are on March 14, 1938, in the Chicago newspapers. In Baltimore, Mencken hailed the "Gladiator of the Law" in the *Evening Sun*: "In his private life and philosophy he was singularly gentle and even sentimental, but when he enlisted for a cause he was a terror. It was to his credit that he was most often a terror to quacks and dolts, hypocrites and scoundrels."

26. *Chicago Tribune*, May 17, 1938; *Chicago Daily News*, May 16, 1938; *Chicago American*, Mar. 15, 1938; the *Chicago Herald Examiner* account of the scattering of Darrow's ashes is from *Unity* magazine, which published a memorial issue on May 16, 1938, that included tributes from James Weldon Johnson, Arthur Garfield Hays, Victor Yarros, and others, as well as Judge William Holly's funeral address.

A NOTE ON SOURCES

Irving Stone, the author of *Clarence Darrow for the Defense* (Garden City, NY: Doubleday, Doran, 1941), said that telling the story of Darrow's life was like writing about Paul Bunyan, John Henry, and other folk heroes. And he did so, magnificently. Stone used all his skills as a novelist and biographer, and the Darrow who emerges in his work is wry, compassionate, idealistic, folksy, and heroic. Written with the aid of Ruby and Paul Darrow, the book reinforced Darrow's iconic status, and looms above all subsequent titles.

But in working so soon after Darrow's death, Stone faced hurdles. Folks then were more reticent, and many of Darrow's friends and acquaintances were grieving. There were relatively few collections of important letters and documents open to researchers. And Ruby's cooperation came with a price. In her correspondence with Stone she spoke of the book as "their" project and pressured him to gloss over Darrow's flaws. "It would be regrettable if the biography should become a thorn for the rest of my life, something to be sensitive about instead of proud of," she told him. When Stone asked about Darrow's love affair with Mary Field Parton, for instance, Ruby replied: "She is the one you seem bent on injecting into your story. Please do not." Nor did Paul have an interest in challenging the myth.

Stone's work, then, was seriously flawed. To cite one lasting error, he begins his story with a great set piece of American biography: the vivid and detailed description, complete with dialogue, of Darrow resigning from the Chicago & North Western Railway in protest over the government's persecution of Eugene Debs and the American Railway Union. It places Darrow at the center of things in July 1894, confronting railroad president Marvin Hughitt, rushing back and forth between strife-torn Chicago and Governor Altgeld's office in Springfield, and conferring with Debs in prison. Stone cites the "Darrow family" as his source, and his account has been accepted and repeated by authors ever since. It makes for great reading, but it is fiction. Darrow left the railroad after the death of his patron, William Goudy, in May 1893, worked at City Hall and then went into private practice, and in 1894 was preoccupied by the Eugene Prendergast case—which Stone calls "Pendergast" and erroneously places in 1895. Darrow was certainly restless at the railroad and ultimately did represent Debs, and his departure marked the start of a brave and principled career—but he did not quit in protest in 1894. Stone made other errors, and left out Darrow's more unsavory clients and tactics. I have tried to correct the record in the text and footnotes.

The other great pillar of Darrow lore was set in place in 1954, when *Inherit the Wind* hit Broadway. The play, based on the Monkey Trial, became a sturdy favorite—to this day—of high school English classes, Broadway revivals, and community theater. Borrowing heavily from the trial transcript, the Jerome Lawrence and Robert E. Lee drama—and the 1960 motion picture starring Spencer Tracy—has at its climax the famous confrontation between Darrow and William Jennings Bryan. Lawrence and Lee wrote their play to sound a warning about McCarthyism and the suppression of free thought and expression. They acknowledged in their Playwrights' Note that "*Inherit the Wind* is not history . . . It is theatre." But the power of the imagery has lingered and cemented Darrow's status.

It is a challenging task for a biographer to escape the shadows cast by such totemic works, even more so if, as I do, he or she also sees Darrow as a heroic individual. Yet time passes. Men and women die. Their papers are left to university libraries; documents are rescued from attics or cellars. The opening of new collections of Darrow's correspondence in 2010 and 2011, including hundreds of previously unpublished letters to his friends and loved ones, and of other archives in recent years, gives today's historian advantages that Stone, no doubt, would appreciate. So call me a loving revisionist, one who believes that the story of Darrow's life is no less rich when grounded in the grays and contradictions of truth. Darrow's flaws, and his great fall in Los Angeles, make his subsequent struggles for freedom, civil rights, and liberty that much more admirable. I am fortunate to be the first to use these new resources in a biography of the Attorney for the Damned.

DARROW BIOGRAPHIES

Stone was not Darrow's first biographer: Charles Yale Harrison wrote the admiring *Clarence Darrow* (New York: Jonathan Cape & Harrison Smith, 1931) with some help from his subject. And of course there was Darrow's own *The Story of My Life* (New York: Charles Scribner's Sons, 1932). Darrow scholarship made a huge leap during the Cold War, when Arthur and Lila Weinberg, two feisty liberals from Chicago, published three landmark volumes. The first, *Attorney for the Damned* (New York: Simon & Schuster, 1957), was a book of Darrow's courtroom addresses. Next came *Verdicts Out of Court* (Chicago: Quadrangle Books, 1963), a gathering of excerpts from his speeches, writings, lectures, and debates. Then, in *Clarence Darrow: A Sentimental Rebel* (New York: G. P. Putnam's Sons, 1980), the Weinbergs gave their take on Darrow's life. Most notably, they persuaded Margaret Parton to let them publish selected excerpts from Darrow's letters to her mother, Mary Field Parton, and portions of Mary's diaries. Without this material, Kevin Tierney's *Darrow: A Biography* (New York: Thomas Y. Crowell, 1979) suffered in comparison but, especially because its author was a practicing attorney, it offered a unique perspective.

Several authors have examined Darrow's life in shorter forms, or from select angles. I found especially compelling insight in Ray Ginger's 1953 essay on Darrow in *The Antioch Review*; in unpublished works I found in the papers of Edgar Lee Masters at the University of Texas, and of Louis Adamic at Princeton University; and in Martin Maloney's chapter on Darrow in *A History and Criticism of American Public Address* (1960).

"Born into a society of independent men, he lived to see his country pass under the sway of vast impersonal bureaucracies. The process was brutal, and he was trapped in it," Ginger wrote. "But Darrow would not give up his battle for the rights of any individual, all individuals." Sadly, Ginger never completed a full-scale biography of Darrow, but *Altgeld's America* (New York: Funk & Wagnalls, 1958) captured Darrow's partnership with his great friend and mentor, John Peter Altgeld.

Abe Ravitz traced Darrow's philosophical journey in *Clarence Darrow and the American Literary Tradition* (Cleveland: The Press of Western Reserve University, 1962), as did John Livingston in *Clarence Darrow: The Mind of a Sentimental Rebel* (New York: Garland, 1988). Susan Jacoby's study *Freethinkers* (New York: Henry Holt, 2004) described Darrow's place in American secularism. Richard Jensen examined Darrow's oratory in *Clarence Darrow: The Creation of an American Myth* (Westport, CT: Greenwood Press, 1992). And Willard D. Hunsberger took on the arduous task of tracking Darrow's writings in *Clarence Darrow: A Bibliography* (Metuchen, NJ: Scarecrow Press, 1981).

Jack Marshall and Edward Larson offered a worthy sampling in *The Essential Writings of Clarence Darrow* (New York: Random House, 2007), as did S. T. Joshi in *Closing Arguments* (Athens, Ohio: Ohio University Press, 2005). More speeches by Darrow, and his contemporaries, can be found in *Echoes of the Sunset Club* (Chicago: Sunset Club, 1891) and the club yearbooks of the era. Many of Darrow's talks were printed as pamphlets during his life and are available, along with the text of or excerpts from his books, on the Internet or at the Library of Congress and other major libraries.

Darrow's *Story of My Life* and his biographical novel *Farmington* (Chicago: A. C. McClurg, 1904) are the primary sources for his childhood. Lincoln Steffens's *Autobiography* (New York: Harcourt, Brace & World, 1931) and Hamlin Garland's *Companions on the Trail* (New York: Macmillan, 1931) offer glimpses of Darrow in middle age, as does Hutchins Hapgood in *The Spirit of Labor* (New York: Duffield, 1907) and *A Victorian in the Modern World* (New York: Harcourt, Brace, 1934). The *Unity* memorial issue of May 16, 1938, is quite valuable, as is the newspaper and magazine journalism of Henry L. Mencken, David Lilienthal, and Marcet Haldeman-Julius.

DARROW'S CASES

Ray Ginger's *Six Days or Forever* (Boston: Beacon Press, 1958) and L. Sprague De Camp's *The Great Monkey Trial* (Garden City, NY: Doubleday, 1968) captured the circus in Dayton, as did Edward Larson in *Summer for the Gods* (New York: Basic Books, 1997) and John Scopes in *Center of the Storm* (New York: Holt, Rinehart & Winston, 1967). Jerry Tompkins edited the very useful *D-Days at Dayton* (Baton Rouge: Louisiana State University Press, 1965), and Leslie Allen did the same for *Bryan and Darrow at Dayton* (New York: Russell & Russell, 1925). The *New Yorker*, the *New Republic*, the *Spectator*, the *Literary Digest*, and the *Nation* offered lively coverage of the trial.

Given the impact of the Leopold and Loeb case on the American imagination, it is surprising that not until Hal Higdon wrote *The Crime of the Century* (New York, G. P. Putnam's Sons, 1974) did the trial receive an in-depth look. Before Higdon, readers had to settle for Meyer Levin's novel *Compulsion* (New York: Simon & Schuster, 1956). Nathan Leopold's *Life Plus 99 Years* (Garden City, NY: Doubleday, 1958) told the story of the crime and his rehabilitation. See also Simon Baatz's *For the Thrill of It* (New York: HarperCollins, 2008). *Liberty* magazine gave notable coverage to the trial in 1924.

In Geoffrey Cowan's *The People v. Clarence Darrow* (New York: Times Books, 1993) we get the finest account of the McNamara fiasco and Darrow's first bribery trial, and the first literary application of Sara and Erskine Wood's extensive archives, which also form the spine of Robert Hamburger's biography of Wood, *Two Rooms* (Lincoln, NE: University of Nebraska Press, 1998). See also *Bombs and Bribery* (Los Angeles: Dawson's Book Shop, 1969) by W. W. Robinson, Grace Stimson's *Rise of the Labor Movement in Los Angeles* (Los Angeles: University of California Press, 1955), and Luke Grant's account of the Los Angeles troubles in the U.S. Commission on Industrial Relations report *The National Erectors' Association and the International Association of Bridge and Structural Ironworkers* (Washington, D.C., 1915).

The story of General Otis and the *Los Angeles Times* is told in *Thinking Big* (New York: G. P. Putnam's Sons, 1977) by Robert Gottlieb and Irene Wolt.

On Earl Rogers, read Alfred Cohn and Joe Chisholm in *Take the Witness* (New York: Frederick A. Stokes Co., 1934), Adela Rogers St. John in *Final Verdict* (Garden City, NY: Doubleday, 1962), Jerry Giesler in *The Jerry Giesler Story* (New York: Simon & Schuster, 1960), *Once Upon a Time in Los Angeles* (Spokane, WA: Arthur H. Clark, 2001) by Michael Lance Trope, and Walton Bean's *Boss Ruef's San Francisco* (Berkeley and Los Angeles: University of California Press, 1968).

Gene Ceasar wrote of William Burns in *Incredible Detective* (Englewood Cliffs, NJ: Prentice-Hall, 1968). Alexander Irvine's *Revolution in Los Angeles* (Los Angeles: The Citizen Print Shop, 1911) offers a glimpse into socialist politics and Job Harriman's campaign for mayor. The invaluable book on the Owens Valley saga is *Water and Power* (Berkeley and Los Angeles: University of California Press, 1982) by William Kahrl. For the early history of organized labor in California see also Michael Kazin's *Barons of Labor* (Urbana, IL: University of Illinois Press, 1987).

Robert Munson Baker, in "Why the McNamaras Pleaded Guilty to the Bombing of the *Los Angeles Times*" (1949), and Richard Cole Searing with "The McNamara Case: Its Causes and Results" (1947) offered valuable insight in their master's dissertations for the University of California at Berkeley. See also the coverage by *Outlook, Collier's*, and *McClure's* magazines in 1911 and 1912, the *Survey* special issue in December 1911, and subsequent analyses in *Southern California Quarterly.*

Philip Foner, in the multivolume *History of the Labor Movement in the United States* (New York: International Publishers, Volumes II, III, IV, and V, 1955–1980), Louis Adamic in *Dynamite* (New York: Viking, 1931), and Graham Adams in *The Age of Industrial Violence* (New York: Columbia University Press, 1966) look at what drove the men and women of labor to violence.

Foner, Anthony Lukas in *Big Trouble* (New York: Simon & Schuster, 1997), and David Grover in *Debaters and Dynamiters* (Corvallis: Oregon State University Press, 1964) offer the best accounts of the Haywood and first Steve Adams trials. (Like Darrow's second bribery trial, the Adams retrials and the Pettibone trial have been neglected by historians.) See also Fremont Wood's *The Introductory Chapter to the History of the Trials of Moyer, Haywood and Pettibone* (Caldwell, ID: Caxton Printers, 1931) and Vernon Jensen's *Heritage of Conflict* (Ithaca, NY: Cornell University Press, 1950). Morris Friedman, who testified at the Haywood trial, detailed his experiences in *The Pinkerton Labor Spy* (New York: Wilshire Book Company, 1907), and James Horan profiles the detective agency in *The Pinkertons* (New York: Crown, 1968). See, as well, the William Borah and Bill Haywood biographies listed below and *The Rocky Mountain Revolution* (New

York: Henry Holt, 1956) by Stewart Holbrook. Francis X. Busch includes the Haywood case and the Leopold and Loeb trial in *Prisoners at the Bar* (Indianapolis: Bobbs-Merrill, 1952). Fine magazine coverage was provided by *Outlook*, *Current Literature*, *Collier's*, and *McClure's* and subsequent editions of *Idaho Yesterdays* and *Pacific Northwest Quarterly*.

Almont Lindsey's *The Pullman Strike* (Chicago: University of Chicago Press, 1942) and the *Report on the Chicago Strike* (1895) by the United States Strike Commission best tell the story of the Debs Rebellion. See also David Ray Papke's *The Pullman Case* (Lawrence: University Press of Kansas, 1999) and *The Pullman Strike and the Crisis of the 1890s* (Champaign, IL: University of Illinois Press, 1999), edited by Richard Schneirov, Shelton Stromquist, and Nick Salvatore. In telling the story of the fiendish Herman Mudgett in *The Devil in the White City* (New York: Crown, 2003), Erik Larson memorably paints Chicago during the days of the Prendergast case and the Pullman strike. Richard Ely's piece "Pullman: A Social Study" ran in *Harper's Monthly* in February 1885. See also Richard Morton's "A Victorian Tragedy: The Strange Deaths of Mayor Carter Harrison and Patrick Eugene Prendergast" in the *Journal of the Illinois State Historical Society*, Spring 2003, and Edward Burke on political homicide in Chicago in the *Journal of Criminal Law and Criminology* (Northwestern University, Spring–Summer 2002).

Two excellent accounts of the Sweet case are *Arc of Justice* (New York: Henry Holt, 2004) by Kevin Boyle and *One Man's Castle* (New York: Amistad, 2004) by Phyllis Vine. See also *A Man's Home, A Man's Castle* (New York: McCall Publishing Co., 1971) by Kenneth Weinberg. The Haldeman-Julius company published many of Darrow's writings, as well as valuable accounts of the Scopes and Sweet trials by Marcet Haldeman-Julius, which were collected as *Clarence Darrow's Two Great Trials* (Girard, KS: Haldeman-Julius Co., 1927). David Lilienthal's coverage of the first trial, together with a 1927 profile, is in the *Nation*. See also *Freedom's Sword* (New York: Routledge, 2005), the tale of the NAACP, by Julian Bond and Gilbert Jonas, and the biographies of Walter White, Judge Murphy, and James Johnson listed below. The *Crisis* offered heart-wrenching accounts of violence and hatred against African Americans in the time that Darrow was affiliated with the NAACP.

The Massie case has inspired several authors. The best accounts are *Honor Killing* (New York: Penguin, 2005) by David Stannard and Peter Van Slingerland's *Something Terrible Has Happened* (New York: Harper and Row, 1966). See also Theon Wright's *Rape in Paradise* (New York: Hawthorn Books, 1966) and Cobey Black's *Hawaii Scandal* (Honolulu: Island Heritage, 2002). Thalia's mother wrote a multipart series for *Liberty* magazine in the summer of 1932. George Leisure wrote of his participation in the *Virginia Law Review*.

The story of Darrow and the Red Scare is told in *Young J. Edgar* (New York: Carroll & Graf, 2007) by Kenneth Ackerman and in the autobiographical novel *The Trial of Helen McLeod* (New York: Funk & Wagnalls, 1938) by Alice Beal Parsons. Michael Belknap captures the tensions of the Gitlow and Debs trials, among others, in *American Political Trials* (Westport, CT: Greenwood Press, 1994).

Edmund Morris gives a lively description of Theodore Roosevelt's involvement in the anthracite coal strike in *Theodore Rex* (New York: Random House, 2001). The best overall account is by Robert Cornell in *The Anthracite Coal Strike of 1902* (Washington, D.C.: Catholic University, 1957). See also the *Report to the President on the Anthracite*

Coal Strike (1903) by the federal commission, Robert Janosov et al. in *The Great Strike: Perspectives on the 1902 Anthracite Coal Strike* (Easton, PA: Canal History and Technology Press, 2002), and *The Kingdom of Coal* (Philadelphia: University of Pennsylvania Press, 1985) by Donald Miller and Richard Sharpless. See, as well, the 1902 coverage by the *American Monthly Review of Reviews* and *Public Opinion* and Robert Wiebe's "The Anthracite Strike of 1902: A Record of Confusion" in the *Mississippi Valley Historical Review*, no. 48, 1961.

Arthur Schlesinger Jr. in *The Coming of the New Deal* (Cambridge, MA: Riverside Press, 1958) and James McGregor Burns in *Roosevelt: The Lion and the Fox* (New York: Harcourt, Brace and Co., 1956) give accounts of Darrow's clash with Hugh Johnson and Franklin Roosevelt over the NRA. See also Johnson's *The Blue Eagle* (Garden City, NY: Doubleday, 1935) and Lowell Mason's "Darrow v. Johnson," in the December 1934 edition of the *North American Review*.

Paul Avrich in *The Haymarket Tragedy* (Princeton: Princeton University Press, 1984) and James Green in *Death in the Haymarket* (New York: Pantheon, 2006) re-create that tragic episode. *The Oshkosh Woodworkers' Strike of 1898* is profiled by Virginia Glenn Crane in her 1998 self-published book on that topic. Steve Lehto in *Death's Door* (Troy, MI: Momentum Books, 2006) and Arthur Thurner in *Rebels on the Range* (Lake Linden, MI: John H. Forster Press, 1984) describe the Michigan copper strike and the Italian Hall tragedy.

In *Eastland: Legacy of the Titanic* (Stanford, CA: Stanford University Press, 1995), George W. Hilton offers an authoritative account of the tragic sinking. See also Jay Bonansinga's *The Sinking of the Eastland* (New York: Citadel Press, 2004). Anthony Hatch's *Tinder Box* (Chicago: Academy Chicago Publishers, 2003) tells the story of the Iroquois Theatre fire. Dan Carter's *Scottsboro* (Baton Rouge: Louisiana State University, 1969) traces that shameful saga.

Werner Troesken follows the history of the Chicago gas industry, in *Why Regulate Utilities?* (Ann Arbor: University of Michigan Press, 1996). The municipal ownership question was covered in April 1906 by Henry K. Webster in "From Yerkes to Dunne" for *American Illustrated Magazine*. Lincoln Steffens wrote about Chicago and other cities in several editions of *McClure's* magazine in 1903 and collected and published these pieces as *The Shame of the Cities* (New York: McClure, Philips & Co., 1904). See also John Fairlie in the May 1907 *Quarterly Journal of Economics*, and Ida Tarbell in the November and December 1908 issues of *American Magazine*.

CHICAGO AND THE TIMES

Donald Miller gives a panoramic view of Chicago's early history in *City of the Century* (New York: Simon & Schuster, 1996), and William Cronon outlines the city's economic rationale in *Nature's Metropolis* (New York: Norton, 1991). Lloyd Wendt and Herman Kogan tell the story of Hinky Dink Kenna and Bathhouse John Coughlin in *Lords of the Levee* (Chicago: Northwestern University Press, 2005), and of Mayor Bill Thompson in *Big Bill of Chicago* (Chicago: Northwestern University Press, 2005). Richard Lindberg gives glimpses of Chicago at the turn of the century in *Chicago by Gaslight* (Chicago: Academy Chicago, 2005). George Murray describes the Chicago newspaper world in *The Madhouse on Madison Street* (Chicago: Follett, 1965). Dale Kramer wrote on the *Chicago Renaissance* (New York: Appleton-Century, 1966). Karen Abbott described the *Sin in the Second City* (New York: Random House, 2007), as did Jeffrey Adler in *First in Violence, Deepest in Dirt: Homicide in Chicago* (Cambridge, MA: Harvard University Press, 2006).

Paul Green and Melvin Holli profile the city's mayoral history in *The Mayors: The Chicago Political Tradition* (Carbondale, IL: Southern Illinois University Press, 1995). Charles Merriam wrote *Chicago: A More Intimate View of Urban Politics* (New York: Macmillan, 1929). James Merriner follows *Grafters and Goo Goos: Corruption and Reform in Chicago* (Carbondale, IL: Southern Illinois University, 2004). Dick Simpson writes of *Rogues, Rebels and Rubber Stamps: The Politics of the Chicago City Council* (Boulder, CO: Westview Press, 2001).

Chicago's gangsters are ably chronicled in *The Wicked City* (New York: Da Capo Press, 1998) by Curt Johnson and R. Craig Sautter, and by Jonathan Eig in *Get Capone* (New York: Simon & Schuster, 2010) and Herbert Asbury's *The Gangs of Chicago* (New York: Knopf, 1940). Joseph Weil, the "Yellow Kid," tells his story with the help of W. T. Brannon in *Con Man* (New York: Broadway Books, 2004). See also the report of the Chicago City Council Committee on Crime (1915) and *The Illinois Crime Survey* (1929), a report by the Illinois Association for Criminal Justice, as well as Leigh Bienen and Brandon Rottinghaus on homicide in the *Journal of Criminal Law and Criminology,* vol. 92, nos. 3-4, 2002.

William Tuttle in *Race Riot* (Urbana, IL: University of Illinois Press, 1970) and Allan Spear in *Black Chicago* (Chicago: University of Chicago Press, 1967) describe the African American community in Darrow's era, as does *The Negro in Chicago*, the report of the Chicago Commission on Race Relations (1922).

Thomas Pegram examines the impact of *Partisans and Progressives* (Champaign, IL: University of Illinois Press, 1992) on Chicago and Illinois, and Richard Schneirov that of *Labor and Urban Politics* (Champaign, IL: University of Illinois Press, 1998). John Keiser describes Illinois in the years after the Civil War in *Building for the Centuries* (Urbana, IL: University of Illinois Press, 1977). See also the *History of the Illinois State Federation of Labor* (Chicago: University of Chicago Press, 1930) by Eugene Staley.

Harriet Taylor Upton takes up *The History of the Western Reserve* (Chicago: Lewis Publishing, 1910). Daniel Walker Howe paints the world of Amirus Darrow's youth in *What Hath God Wrought* (New York: Oxford, 2007) and H. W. Brands does the same for Clarence Darrow's era in *American Colossus* (New York: Doubleday, 2010) and *The Reckless Decade* (Chicago: University of Chicago, 1995). Matthew Josephson wrote delightful accounts of the Gilded Age in *The Robber Barons* (New York: Harcourt, Brace, 1934) and *The Politicos* (New York: Harcourt, Brace, 1938). See also *The Age of Excess* (New York: Macmillan, 1965) by Ray Ginger and Thomas Beer's *The Mauve Decade* (New York: Knopf, 1926). The impact of the industrial age is portrayed by Robert Wiebe in *The Search for Order, 1877–1920* (New York: Hill and Wang, 1967), Nell Irvin Painter in *Standing at Armageddon: The United States, 1877–1919* (New York: Norton, 1987), Alan Trachtenberg in *The Incorporation of America* (New York: Hill and Wang, 1982), and Thomas Schlereth in *Victorian America* (New York: HarperCollins, 1992).

Eric Goldman in *Rendezvous With Destiny* (New York: Vintage, 1956), Frederic Howe in *The Confessions of a Reformer* (New York: Scribner, 1925), John Chamberlain in

Farewell to Reform (New York: Liveright, 1932), and Richard Hofstadter in *The Age of Reform* (New York: Vintage, 1955) trace the populist and progressive roots of the reform impulse and modern liberalism. Charles Postel examines the origins of populism in *The Populist Vision* (New York: Oxford, 2007), and Robert Durden writes about the 1896 presidential campaign in *The Climax of Populism* (Lexington, KY: University of Kentucky, 1965). Michael McGerr examines the Progressive Movement in *A Fierce Discontent* (New York: Oxford, 2003). I enjoyed George Mowry's *The Era of Theodore Roosevelt* (New York: Harper & Row, 1958). See also C. Vann Woodward's biography *Tom Watson* (New York: Oxford, 1963) and Harvey Wish on Altgeld and the 1896 campaign in the *Mississippi Valley Historical Review*, March 1938.

Walter Lord profiles the period before World War I in *The Good Years* (New York: Harper, 1960). Lynn Dumenil's *The Modern Temper* (New York: Macmillan, 1995) is a scholarly look at the Roaring Twenties, and Frederick Lewis Allen has entertained millions with his popular account of the decade, *Only Yesterday* (New York: Harper & Row, 1931). Another lively chronicle of an era is *Our Times* (New York: Charles Scribner's Sons, 1926–1935) by Mark Sullivan, a multivolume set that covers the first twenty-five years of the twentieth century. David Kennedy captures the last decade of Darrow's life in *Freedom from Fear* (New York: Oxford, 1999). As always, I should acknowledge the influence of Paul Johnson's *Modern Times* (New York: Harper & Row, 1983).

AUTOBIOGRAPHIES AND BIOGRAPHIES

Lincoln Steffens's two-volume autobiography leads the pack of self-portraits from Darrow's friends and associates. Carter Harrison Jr. gave marvelous glimpses of Chicago in Darrow's era in the autobiographical *Stormy Years* (Indianapolis: Bobbs-Merrill, 1935) and *Growing Up With Chicago* (Chicago: R. F. Seymour, 1944), and Arthur Garfield Hays wrote several memoirs, including *City Lawyer* (New York: Simon & Schuster, 1942), *Trial by Prejudice* (New York: Da Capo Press, 1970), and *Let Freedom Ring* (New York: Boni & Liveright, 1928). Edgar Lee Masters lanced Darrow in *Across Spoon River* (New York: Farrar & Rinehart, 1936).

For a wider taste of the times, and glimpses of Darrow, see the published autobiographies, memoirs, or diaries of Willis Abbott, Jane Addams, Hugh Baillie, Ethel Barrymore, William Jennings Bryan, William Burns, Oscar King Davis, Charles Erbstein, Hamlin Garland, Benjamin Gitlow, Emma Goldman, Samuel Gompers, Bill Haywood, Ben Hecht, John Jardine, James Weldon Johnson, Mother Jones (edited by Mary Field Parton), Lawrence Judd, Moses Koenigsberg, Adolf Kraus, Lucy Robins Lang, Ortie McManigal, H. L. Mencken, George Jean Nathan, Fremont Older, Harry Orchard, Margaret Parton, Theodore Roosevelt, Margaret Sanger, E. W. Scripps, Charles Siringo, Melville Stone, Walter White, William Allen White, Brand Whitlock, Victor Yarros, and Stirling Yates.

See, as well, the published letters of Brand Whitlock, Theodore Roosevelt, Lincoln Steffens, Eugene Debs, H. L. Mencken, Hamlin Garland, Louis Brandeis, and Mother Jones.

Biographies of Darrow's friends and associates include Herbert Russell's *Edgar Lee Masters* (Champaign, IL: University of Illinois Press, 2001) and David Levering Lewis's *W. E. B. Du Bois* (New York: Macmillan, 2001), as well as *Samuel Gompers* (Yellow

Springs, OH: Antioch Press, 1963) by Bernard Mandel, *Altgeld of Illinois* (New York: B. W. Huebsch, 1924) by Waldo Browne, and Harry Barnard on Altgeld in *Eagle Forgotten* (Indianapolis: Bobbs-Merrill, 1938).

See also Craig Phelan's biography of John Mitchell, *Divided Loyalties* (Albany: State University of New York Press, 1994), Robert Crunden's book on Brand Whitlock, *A Hero in Spite of Himself* (New York: Knopf, 1969), Ray Ginger on Eugene Debs in *The Bending Cross* (New Brunswick, NJ: Rutgers University Press, 1949), Chester McArthur Destler's *Henry Demarest Lloyd and the Empire of Reform* (Philadelphia: University of Pennsylvania Press,1963), *Henry Demarest Lloyd* (New York: G. P. Putnam's Sons, 1912) by Caroline Lloyd, and *Lincoln Steffens* (New York: Simon & Schuster, 1974) by Justin Kaplan. Leroy Ashby writes on William Borah in *The Spearless Leader* (Urbana, IL: University of Illinois Press, 1972), as does Marian McKenna in *Borah* (Ann Arbor: University of Michigan Press, 1961).

W. A. Swanberg, in *Citizen Hearst* (New York: Charles Scribner's Sons, 1961), and David Nasaw, in *The Chief* (Boston: Houghton Mifflin, 2000), tell the story of William Randolph Hearst. Accounts of Bill Haywood's life are provided by Peter Carlson in *Roughneck: The Life and Times of Big Bill Haywood* (New York: W. W. Norton, 1983), Joseph Conlin in *Big Bill Haywood and the Radical Union Movement* (Syracuse: Syracuse University Press, 1969), and Melvyn Dubofsky in *Big Bill Haywood* (Manchester, UK: Manchester University Press, 1987). Jane Addams's story is told in *Citizen* (Chicago: University of Chicago Press, 2005) by Louise Knight, and in *American Heroine* (New York: Oxford, 1973) by Allen Davis.

See also Sidney Fine's *Frank Murphy* (Ann Arbor: University of Michigan Press, 1975–1984) and his biography of Walter Drew, *Without Blare of Trumpets* (Ann Arbor: University of Michigan Press, 1995); *The Damndest Radical* (Champaign, IL: University of Illinois Press, 1987), Roger Bruns's biography of Ben Reitman; John Franch's *Robber Baron* (Champaign, IL: University of Illinois Press, 2006), on the life of Charles Yerkes; *White* (New York: The New Press, 2003), Kenneth Janken's volume on Walter White; and *Mencken: The American Iconoclast* (New York: Oxford, 2005) by Marion Elizabeth Rodgers.

There are several good biographies of Bryan, including Louis Koenig's *Bryan: A Political Biography* (New York: Putnam, 1971), *A Godly Hero* by Michael Kazin (New York: Knopf, 2006), and Paolo Coletta's three-volume *William Jennings Bryan* (Lincoln: University of Nebraska Press, 1964–1969). Grover Cleveland's life and presidency are ably portrayed by Allan Nevins in *Grover Cleveland: A Study in Courage* (New York: Dodd, Mead, 1934).

Other volumes that I found valuable in capturing Darrow's times include *Morgan* (New York: HarperCollins, 2000) by Jean Strouse; *Ernest Hemingway* (New York: Charles Scribner's Sons, 1969) by Carlos Baker; *Lindbergh* (New York: G. P. Putnam's Sons, 1998) by A. Scott Berg; Ron Chernow's *Titan* (New York: Random House, 1998), about John D. Rockefeller; and *Andrew Carnegie* (New York: Penguin, 2006) by David Nasaw. Also of interest are *Triangle*, David Von Drehle's account of the tragic fire (New York: Grove Press, 2003); *American Eve* (New York: Riverhead, 2008), Paula Uruburu's biography of Evelyn Nesbit; Jacob Riis's *How the Other Half Lives* (New York: Charles Scribner's Sons, 1914); and Bruce Watson's *Sacco & Vanzetti* (New York: Viking, 2007).

I was schooled in law by Henry J. Abraham and relied on the lessons he taught me and his book *Freedom and the Court* (New York: Oxford, 1972). Any errors are mine, not his. The novels of Sinclair Lewis, Ernest Hemingway, F. Scott Fitzgerald, Theodore Dreiser, E. L. Doctorow, Booth Tarkington, Gore Vidal, and Upton Sinclair helped me paint the backdrop, as did, of course, the verse of Carl Sandburg.

WEB SITES

The Clarence Darrow Digital Collection of the University of Minnesota Law Library is the indispensable online resource. Almost as helpful are Douglas Linder's University of Missouri–Kansas City site *Famous Trials* and Northwestern University's *Homicide in Chicago* site.

The Web site of the Public Broadcasting System offers transcripts and exhibits from several documentaries about Darrow and his times, including fine *American Experience* productions on Chicago and the Scopes and Massie trials. The *American Heritage* site offers articles on Earl Rogers, the Sweet trials, and other subjects relevant to Darrow. Idaho Public Television has a top-notch site on the Haywood trial called *Assassination: Idaho's Trial of the Century.*

The online *Encyclopedia of Chicago*, maintained by the Chicago History Museum, the Newberry Library, and Northwestern University, was very helpful, as was Scott Newman's *Jazz Age Chicago* and two sites maintained by nonprofessional historians: *The Chicago History Journal* site of the indefatigable Sharon Williams, and the *Idaho Meanderings* site, maintained by John Richards, a descendant of Frank Steunenberg.

INDEX

PHOTOGRAPHY CREDITS

Chicago History Museum: page 11, top; page 12, top and bottom

Courtesy of Archives & Rare Books Library, University of Cincinnati: page 9, bottom

Courtesy of the Arthur and Lila Weinberg family: page 10, center

Courtesy of the Walter P. Reuther Library, Wayne State University: page 15, top left and top right

Idaho State Historical Society: page 7, top and bottom; page 8, top and bottom

Image courtesy of the Division of Special Collections and University Archives, University of Oregon Library System: page 5, top

Image used by permission of the Estate of Clarence Darrow; All Rights Reserved: page 2, top

Library of Congress Prints & Photographs Division: page 2, bottom; page 3, bottom; page 4; page 5, center; page 6, top and bottom; page 7, center; page 9, top; page 15, bottom; page 16

National Archives and Records Administration: page 11, bottom

Smithsonian Institution Archives: page 14

University of Minnesota Law Library: page 1; page 3, top; page 5, bottom; page 6, center; page 10, top and bottom

University of Tennessee Libraries, Knoxville, Special Collections: page 13, top, center, and bottom

ABOUT THE AUTHOR

John Aloysius Farrell is the author of the highly acclaimed *Tip O'Neill and the Democratic Century*, which was featured on the cover of the *New York Times Book Review*, received rave reviews from the *Wall Street Journal*, the *Atlantic Monthly*, and the *Boston Globe*, and was a *New York Times* "Notable Book" and a *Washington Post Book World* "Rave of the Year." He is a senior writer at the Center for Public Integrity in Washington, D.C. Previously, he was Washington bureau chief for the *Denver Post* and served as Washington editor and White House correspondent for the *Boston Globe.* He lives with his wife and two children in Washington.